AF269776

The Battle of the Frigidus River, AD 394

For Esther

The Battle of the Frigidus River, AD 394

Theodosius' Miracle

Nic Fields

Pen & Sword
MILITARY

First published in Great Britain in 2024 by
Pen & Sword Military
An imprint of Pen & Sword Books Limited
Yorkshire – Philadelphia

Copyright © Nic Fields 2024

ISBN 978 1 39909 625 6

The right of Nic Fields to be identified as
Author of this Work has been asserted by him in accordance
with the Copyright, Designs and Patents Act 1988.

A CIP catalogue record for this book is
available from the British Library

Typeset by Mac Style
Printed in the UK by CPI Group (UK) Ltd, Croydon, CR0 4YY.

Pen & Sword Books Limited incorporates the imprints of After
the Battle, Atlas, Archaeology, Aviation, Discovery, Family History,
Fiction, History, Maritime, Military, Military Classics, Politics,
Select, Transport, True Crime, Air World, Frontline Publishing, Leo
Cooper, Remember When, Seaforth Publishing, The Praetorian Press,
Wharncliffe Local History, Wharncliffe Transport, Wharncliffe True
Crime and White Owl.

For a complete list of Pen & Sword titles please contact

PEN & SWORD BOOKS LIMITED
47 Church Street, Barnsley, South Yorkshire, S70 2AS, England
E-mail: enquiries@pen-and-sword.co.uk
Website: www.pen-and-sword.co.uk
or
PEN AND SWORD BOOKS
1950 Lawrence Rd, Havertown, PA 19083, USA
E-mail: uspen-and-sword@casematepublishers.com
Website: www.penandswordbooks.com

Contents

List of Plates		vi
Maps		xix
Introduction		xxiii
Chronology		xxix
Abbreviations		xxxvi
Chapter 1	Crisis, what crisis?	1
Chapter 2	New World Order	13
Chapter 3	New Model Army	19
Chapter 4	Empire of the Cross	50
Chapter 5	Rank Usurpers	68
Chapter 6	Death in Vienna	82
Chapter 7	Civil War	88
Chapter 8	Erasing Eugenius	92
Chapter 9	Divine Wind	101
Chapter 10	The End and Beyond	122
Chapter 11	Pagan Resistance	131
Chapter 12	Through the Looking Glass	142
Chapter 13	Truth Triumphant	149
Chapter 14	Changing Nature of War	167
Chapter 15	Gothic Endings	182
Principal Literary Sources		193
Notes		206
Bibliography		288
Index		294

List of Plates

Colour

1. The eastern circuit of Thessaloniki. Valerianus' reinforced defences surrounding Thessaloniki had enabled the city to hold out against the invading Goths, who were not equipped with siege machines, until a relief army could reach it. The present course of the ramparts belongs to the reign of Theodosius and ran for some 8km (about half of which survives) with upwards of forty towers, almost all square and axially placed. The walls consist of the typical later Roman composite construction of rubble masonry alternating with bands of brick, sometimes with brick arches to provide extra strength. Their height, on average, ranged between 10m and 12m, and their thickness reached 5m. Like a C-shape, the walls cupped the city against the acropolis in the north. (© *Nic Fields*)

2. The famous red porphyry carving of the tetrarchs, which now adorns Basilica di San Marco in Venice (part of the booty carried to Europe by members of the Fourth Crusade who sacked Constantinopolis in April 1204). Dated to around 300, it neatly exemplifies the dramatic change in the type of men who now held the imperial office. Four co-rulers – to the left Diocletianus and Maximianus (*Augusti*); to the right Galerius and Constantius Chlorus (*Caesares*) – now watched each other's backs, in civil war and on the imperial frontiers. The embrace of the squat figures, one hand on another's shoulder in a friendly gesture while the other hand grasps an eagle-headed sword, was no doubt intended to convey a strong visual message about tetrarchic solidarity. What is equally striking is their practical military attire. Mentioned by Vegetius (1.20), note the ubiquitous pillbox headgear, *pileus pannonicus*, of rigid felt commonly worn by all ranks out of combat. (© *Nic Fields*)

3. What now serves as a car park for the Grand Bazaar, Istanbul, was once the Forum of Constantinus, an oval colonnaded portico. In the forum's centre Constantinus erected this column to celebrate the dedication of his city as the capital of the reunited empire on 11 May 330. On the column's summit there was a large capital, presumably Corinthian, upon which stood a statue of Constantinus, which once surveyed the world he ruled alone. The statue did not depict him as a humble Christian penitent, but exhibited

attributes of Sol Invictus, the Slayer of Darkness. An unapologetic exercise in exaggeration, the emperor was portrayed holding a sceptre in his right hand and a bronze orb containing a fragment of the True Cross on which Christ was crucified in his left. He wore a crown adorned with sunrays, which incorporated small pieces of the nails driven through Christ's hands and feet. This colossal portrait of the superhuman Constantinus illustrates the melding of traditional triumphal pagan imagery with Christian elements, demonstrating that the source of imperial authority is the ruler's relationship to the new Christian God. Grandeur and hype are always two sides of the same coin. Originally 50m tall, the column was constructed of cylindrical porphyry blocks, seven of which still stand, and goes by the local appellation of Çemberlitaş, the Hooped Column. (© *Nic Fields*)

4. East face of the Proconnesian marble plinth supporting the Obelisk of Karnak, Hippodrome, Istanbul. Erected in 390 by Constantinopolis' *praefectus urbi* Proculus to celebrate the victory of Theodosius I over the western usurper Magnus Maximus (Marc. Com. *Chron.* s.a. 390.3, *CIL* III.737). In this potent image of imperial power, Theodosius, the last ruler of a united Roman Empire, stands calm and majestic flanked by the adolescent cipher Valentinianus II (left rear), and his sons Arcadius (right) and Honorius (left), who would go on to rule the East and West respectively now that the empire was officially divided. The emperor is awarding a victory wreath to an unseen charioteer. Behind the imperial quartet stand Germanic *scholares* (Goths in the East, Franks in the West) of the *scholae palatinae*. Their long hair and torcs set them apart from the senators (holding *mappae*) standing either side of the *kathisma*, the imperial box. (© *Nic Fields*)

5. Gold *tremissis* struck during 393/394 in the Mediolanum (Milan) mint (*RIC* XI 29.1). The obverse depicts a bust of Flavius Eugenius facing right, pearl-diademed, draped and cuirassed. The inscription reads: D(*ominus*) N(*oster*) EVGENI-VS P(*ius*) F(*elix*) AVG(*ustus*). It is not known how much of this portrait was of the man himself and how much was the convention of representing emperors, but it is notable that Eugenius is depicted sporting a (philosopher's?) beard. The reverse bears Victory advancing left, holding a wreath in her right hand and a palm frond in her left. The inscription reads: VICTORIA AVGVSTORVM. The mintmark: M-D, Mediolanum. By spring 393 the breach between west and east was complete, and in April Arbogastes and Eugenius moved into Italy without resistance. (*Classical Numismatic Group, Inc. http://www.cngcoins.com/Wikimedia Commons/CC-BY-SA-2.5*)

6. Early fifth-century polychrome mosaic (Ravenna, Museo TAMO) from Domus di Via Dogana, Faenza. The scene shows the enigmatic Romano-Vandal *comes et magister utriusque militiae praesentalis* of the West, Flavius Stilicho (left foreground), with the western emperor Honorius (r. 395–423), 'heroically' enthroned and protected by two members of the *scholae palatinae*. Despite his father's origins, Stilicho was raised (and identified) as a Roman. He had become Theodosius' chief lieutenant during the waning years of his reign – he was present at the Frigidus alongside his future nemesis Alaric – and was married to his formidable niece Serena. The dynastic connection of Stilicho and the Theodosian house was further cemented by the marriage of his daughter Maria to Honorius (398), and when she died the emperor married her sister Thermantia (408). Stilicho (*cos.* I 400, *cos.* II 405) was to fall to a palace *coup d'état* and he himself was executed in Ravenna on the orders of Honorius (22 August 408). Stilicho was, in the fitting words of Edward Gibbon, 'the last of the Roman generals' (*D&F*, vol. 2, ch. 30, p.163). (© *Nic Fields*)

7. Pictogram titled *comes Italiae of Castra ad Fluvium Frigidum* depicted in the register known as the *Notitia Dignitatum* (*Occ.* XXIV.5, *tractus Italiae circa Alpes*). A Roman road, the Via Gemina, ran past the Castra linking Aquileia, one of the biggest cities in northern Italy, with Emona, short for Colonia Iulia Aemona (now Ljubljana), via the hilltop fort of Ad Pirum (now the hamlet of Hrušica) in between. Formerly a second-century guardhouse (a post station had stood here since the previous century), Ad Pirum was upgraded to a stronghold in the second half of the third century and incorporated into the *claustra Alpium Iuliarum* barrier system, thereby controlling the road by means of a double gateway. The stronghold was abandoned in the first three decades of the fifth century. By going directly over today's pass over the Hrušica Plateau (highest point 1,080m), where the Via Gemina reached its highest elevation (867m), the road avoided the morc difficult pass over the Nanos Plateau and so shortened the journey by one day. The route through the Vipava valley was the easiest way to reach Italy from the Adriatic and the Balkans, and the East thereafter. This is a facsimile edition on display in the Muzej Ajdovščina. (© *Nic Fields*)

8. The upper Vipava valley looking south-east from the eastern outskirts of Ajdovščina. Running from left to right are the abrupt cliffs of the Nanos (highest point Suhi Vrh, elevation 1,313m), a Slovenian karst plateau known as Ocra in antiquity; Strabo identifies it as 'the lowest part of the Alpes'. It was perhaps somewhere up there that Arbogastes fell upon his sword. Due to its abundance of accessible potable water – these limestone heights have a tendency to be arid – the plateau has been settled since prehistoric

times. The pass over the Nanos was once an important *via militaris* from Tergeste (Trieste, Italy) to Emona (Ljubljana, Slovenia), originally the site of two consecutive Roman camps. However, this route lost its importance when a speedier and shorter route connected Emona – founded as a colony sometime in the first decade of the first century – to Aquileia; the Via Gemina was built in the year 14 by *legio* XIII *Gemina* (*CIL* V.7989 = *AE* 2007, +00264). In spite of its constructors, the Via Gemina, the 'twin road', took its name from the fact that it departed from Aquileia along with the Via Postumia. The road followed the Vipava valley between the confluence of the River Vipava with the Isonzo/*Soča* at Pons Sonti (Gradisca d'Isonzo, Italy) and the modern town of Vipava, Slovenia. After the Via Gemina was built, a post station known as *mansio Fluvio Frigidio* stood on the site of the later *Castra ad Fluvium Frigidum*, today's Ajdovščina, Slovenia. (© *Nic Fields*)

9. The upper Vipava valley looking north-east from the confluence of the Hubelj and Vipava rivers towards the village of Col. Well-cultivated and fruitful, the narrow valley stretches roughly between the border with Italy to the west and the village of Podnanos to the east. Throughout its tangled history the valley has been an important corridor connecting northern Italy to central Europe as empires (Roman, Byzantine, Venetian, Ottoman, Napoleonic, Austro-Hungarian, etc., etc.) have tramped their armies and shifted the frontiers. Here you can come across villagers whose grandparents were born in Austria-Hungary, parents in the Greater Germanic Reich, themselves in Yugoslavia and their children in Slovenia. Today its main urban centre is the market town of Ajdovščina. Recent research suggests that the battle took place somewhere between Col and Sanabor, in the so-called gateway to Italy (a Roman milestone bearing a dedication to the emperor Iulianus was found in Col). When the armies of the east and west converged on the right bank of the Frigidus, Arbogastes forced Theodosius to approach from what is now known as the Postojna Gate with little room to deploy, let alone manoeuvre. He would thus fight a defensive battle, using all the possibilities offered by the features of the terrain. (© *Nic Fields*)

10. The tenth of the fourteen (or possibly sixteen) towers of *Castra ad Fluvium Frigidum*, eastern circuit, Ajdovščina. Now standing 14m to its crenulated crown, the original late Roman tower was only 9.6m in height as indicated by the lighter, more pinkish stone seen below the later mediaeval addition. The late Roman part has a diameter of 5.8m and walls 3m thick, thus reducing the interior diameter to 2.8m. The circuit wall is 3.84m wide at the foundations, above which there are usually two step-like stages. It is referred to as a *mutatio Castra*, a fortified relay station, in the *Itinerarium*

Burdigalense, a late Roman stronghold which constituted the centre of the *claustra Alpium Iuliarum*. Unlike a linear *limes*, this was an in-depth defensive system of interconnected barriers and fortifications stretching from the Gail valley (now Carinthia, Austria) to the Učka mountain range, north-western Croatia, which primarily secured the internal stability of the empire between northern Italy and Illyricum, the area where passage from the Balkan Peninsula into the Italian Peninsula was easiest. Though evidence suggests the circuit wall was started around the year 270, most of the construction was done after 284 under Diocletianus and Constantinus; it was demolished by Attila the Hun in 451. It was here that the late mediaeval market settlement of Ajdovščina developed at the confluence of the River Hubelj and the Lokavšček stream. (© *Nic Fields*)

11. The *frigidarium* of a small Roman bathhouse, *thermae*, with a deepened semicircular basin, Ajdovščina. Originally the bathhouse was adjoined to a residence and built around the year 300. In the second half of the fourth century the bathhouse became an independent narrow building with an annexe for the furnace. It also had an associated latrine and *palaestra* for exercising. Such private facilities had sophisticated underfloor heating and heating ducts built into the walls. The bathing process followed a set regime. The bather first entered the *frigidarium* and then proceeded through rooms of increasingly higher temperatures, thereafter retracing his steps to the *frigidarium*, where water splashed over the body served to close up the pores before the bather dressed and came out again into the open air. (© *Nic Fields*)

12. [Above] The confluence of the Hubelj River (right) and the Lokavšček stream (left), Ajdovščina. [Right] The confluence of the Hubelj (foreground) and Vipava rivers looking south-west. According to some authorities, the Frigidus, as the Romans knew it, should be the Hubelj, but it is a closer and much greater possibility that the 'cold river' is really the Vipava of our own day. In this land of limestone ridges, water and woods, the Hubelj wells up through numerous sinkholes in the subterranean karst at the foot of Navrše (elevation 857m) as well as originating from three main karst springs, some 3km north of Ajdovščina, and runs for only 5km before joining the Vipava to the south. Some observers would call the Hubelj a stream, but in times of heavy rainfall it becomes a lively, rumbling torrent of rising water. Potable to this day, the Hubelj would have provided fresh drinking water for the garrison and animals of *Castra ad Fluvium Frigidum*. (© *Nic Fields*)

13. The cold, crystal-clear waters of the Vipava, viewed from the footbridge below the village of Planina, looking upstream. Flowing through south-

west Slovenia and north-east Italy, the river is 49km in length, of which 45km is in Slovenia. Descending rapidly from high ground, this narrow river originates from nine large karst springs, besides countless smaller ones, beneath the western slopes of Nanos. Formerly called the Wippach and the Vipacco, the mountain-born Vipava is a left tributary of the River Isonzo/*Soša*, which flows generally from the north and into the Golfo di Trieste (Slovene: *Tržaski zaiv*) about 6km east of Aquileia. The temperature of the water at the springs is low and constant, indicating that the bulk of the water comes from the ice caves in the heart of Nanos and is deserving of its name 'cold'. (© *Nic Fields*)

14. Life-size 2-D display in the Muzej Ajdovščina depicting three of the major troop types that fought at the Frigidus: from left to right, an Alani horseman, a Goth warrior and a Gallo-Roman soldier. The Alani were seen as far more recent and exotic arrivals in the empire. They were one of the horse peoples of the Eurasian Steppe, probably of Iranian origin; Chinese sources suggest they originally lived close to the Aral Sea. Ammianus Marcellinus writes that the Alani 'live upon flesh and an abundance of milk, and dwell in wagons', adding that 'the young men grow up in the habit of riding from their earliest boyhood...and by various forms of training they are skilled warriors' (31.2.18, 20). The soldier historian almost certainly encountered Alani serving in the Roman army. The story of the Alani is a reminder of both the mobility and the flexibility of the marauding and migrating peoples of the time. (© *Nic Fields*)

15. Detail from the *Great Hunt* mosaic, Villa Romana del Casale, Piazza Armerina, Sicilia, showing two hunters. Their woollen tunics are decorated at the shoulders, cuffs and hems. They both wear military cloaks (*saga*) and broad waist-belts, and carry large round shields. The exquisite sporting polychrome mosaics of this Roman villa were being laid while the Goths were crossing the Danuvius into Roman territory. The identity of the owner of what is a lavish patrician residence is not known with any certainty. One theory is that it belonged to a member of the Roman senatorial elite who traded in exotic animals. The sheer size of the villa (more than sixty rooms on four levels) and the magnitude of the mosaics (3,500m^2) certainly suggest that the villa was the centre of the great estate of a high-level senatorial aristocrat. (*Robur.q/Wikimedia Commons/CC-BY-SA-3.0*)

Mono

1. Bronze bust (Thessaloniki, Archaeological Museum, inv. 4303) of Severus Alexander (r. 222–235), last of the Severan dynasty. Dominated by his mother Iulia Mamaea, the meek emperor had always been convinced

that the soldiers would remain loyal to him in the end, despite his lack of affinity for military life, but things did not turn out the way he had hoped. His assassination and the usurpation of Maximinus Thrax (r. 235–238) would lead to a half-century of anarchy in and around the empire. This situation was to dramatically transform when Diocletianus, adamant that the current version of the empire was no longer fit for purpose, introduced the tetrarchy. (© *Nic Fields*)

2. White marble head (Rome, Musei Capitolini, inv. MC0757) from a colossal seated enthroned statue of Constantinus I dating to 313/324, which originally occupied the west apse of the Basilica Nova – formerly the Basilica of Maxentius, which was remodelled and hastily renamed – on the Via Sacra, near the Forum Romanum. Only the head, which measures 260cm and weighs some 8 tonnes, hands and feet (each foot is over 2m long), remain of a colossus that once stood some 12m high. The body of the statue would have consisted of a brick core and wooden framework, possibly covered with gilded bronze. This is the best-known portrait of the emperor, with his gazing hooded eyes and hooked nose, and would have been more imposing when it was crowned with a bejewelled diadem. The statue's right hand, according to Eusebius, held 'a trophy of the Saviour's passion with the saving sign of the cross' (*Hist. eccl.* 9.9.11), possibly therefore in the form of a sceptre with the monogram XP affixed to it. By the time of his death in 337 the radical transformation of the empire was virtually completed. (© *Nic Fields*)

3. Miniature (Paris, Bibliothèque national de France, Codex Græcus 510, folio 440 recto) from the late ninth-century manuscript of the *Homilies* of the fourth-century church father and theologian Gregory Nazianzen. This tripartite painting illustrates a potpourri of the Pons Mulvius miracle. In the top register Constantinus dreams a vision of the cross. In the middle register, mounted on a white steed, he charges unaccompanied at Pons Mulvius and dispatches with his cavalry spear the fleeing 'pagan usurper' Maxentius. Constantinus' triumph is glorified by the cross shining in the skies above; the words ἐν τούτῳ νίκα ('By this, conquer!') are inscribed inside it. The consequences of this one moment are vast; so vast these words went on a great journey, travelling far beyond the scroll of Eusebius of Caesarea Palestinae where they were first written. Lastly, in the bottom register, we witness his mother Helena, a sincere Christian, discovering the True Cross. (*BnF Gallica Digital Library/Wikimedia Commons/Public Domain*)

4. Detail of miniature from the *Paris Gregory* (Paris, Bibliothèque nationale de France, Codex Græcus 510, folio 239 recto), a late ninth-century illuminated manuscript of the *Homilies* of Gregory Nazianzen. Gregory, depicted as the

bishop of Constantinopolis (r. 380–381), takes his leave of Theodosius I (r. 379–395). The emperor stands beside his bejewelled throne enclosed in a ciborium, attended by two palace guards. Both worthies' heads are nimbate. Gregory was one of the two Gregorys from the highlands of Kappadokia that had before been used only to breed horses and slaves. Escaping such rusticity, Gregory travelled to study in Athens where he met the future emperor Iulianus. He is supposed to have had the odes of Sappho erased by scrubbing the parchments on which they were preserved with pumice stone in favour of his own ecclesiastical sermons. His body lies buried in the Vatican, carried there secretly after the Latin sack of Constantinopolis in 1204. (*BnF Gallica Digital Library/Wikimedia Commons/CC-BY-SA-4.0*)

5. Full-length portrait marble statue (Geyre, Afrodisyas Müzesi) of the western emperor Flavius Valentinianus Iunior Augustus (r. 375–392), son of the hardy Pannonian general Valentinianus I (r. 364–375) and his second wife Iustina, a staunch Arian (Ambr. *Obit. Val.* 28, Philostorg. 10.7). On his father's sudden death, apparently from apoplexy while angrily haranguing a group of Germanic envoys, his generals acclaimed the 4-year-old Valentinianus *Augustus* on 22 November 375. The army was uneasy about the lack of military experience of Valentinianus' older half-brother, Flavius Gratianus, and so raised a boy who would not immediately aspire to military command. Gratianus, a cultured young man, was forced to compromise, so allowing Valentinianus to govern Italy, part of Illyricum and Africa. His untimely death has become one of history's murder mysteries. (*Brastite/Wikimedia Commons/Public Domain*)

6. Frieze slab decorating the pronaos, temple of Hadrianus (also dedicated to Artemis Ephesia and the *dēmos* of Ephesos), street of the Curetes, Ephesos. The relief (a copy of the marble original now on display in the Efes Müzesi, Selçuk) depicts Theodosius I, his father (also Theodosius), his first wife Aelia Flavia Flaccilla Augusta and their eldest son Arcadius in the company of a dozen pagan deities: Dea Roma, Selene (Moon), Helios (Sun), Apollo, Artemis, Androklos (the son of Kodros of Athens and founder of Ephesos) with his hunting dog, Herakles, Dionysos, Hermes, Aphrodite, Ares and Athena. This is certainly a bizarre way of commemorating the ultra-Christian emperor, and something that could hardly have been done after Theodosius' edict of 392 forbidding the practice of pagan cults. Even so, this illustrates the power the pagan gods continued to exercise after the triumph of Christianity. The temple was reconstructed by Theodosius to honour his father, but demolished not long after in 400. (© *Nic Fields*)

7. Icon (New York, Metropolitan Museum of Art, inv. MET, 1975.1.30) of Saint Ambrose by Giovanni di Paolo di Grazia (1403–82), egg tempera on

wood, gold ground. Theodosius, not without signs of irritation, appointed as one of his advisors the irrepressible Ambrose. It was probably under the bishop's influence that the campaign against paganism was eventually intensified, despite the emperor's initial tolerance of leading pagans. Was this a career-convenient conversion? Ambrose was a passionate opponent of Arianism; in 381 Theodosius convoked the Second Ecumenical Council at Constantinopolis, affirming the Nicene Creed. As a result Arianism ceased to play a politically important role in the empire. A prolific writer of letters, when we read these we cannot but feel that Ambrose is drawing us somewhere: it is as if he offers to sneak us, shackled as we are with our shaky gasp of spirituality, across the threshold of theology to reveal its true mysteries. In this he is our guide in letting us in on a splendid secret. (*Metropolitan Museum of Art/Wikimedia Commons/CC0 1.0*)

8. Chalcedony cameo (Firenze, Museo archeologico nazionale) full-length portrait of Flavius Eugenius (left) alongside a soldierly-looking figure, more than likely a representation of the *magister militum* Arbogastes. This would be a logical assumption as the story of Eugenius is in many ways that of Arbogastes. The role of emperor-maker seems to have been his passport to absolute power: elevate a puppet emperor, hostage to his ambitions. All went well until the levels of cordiality between the east and west seem, if anything, to have steeply declined. The final fall-out would result in the encounter on the banks of the Frigidus. (*Sailko/Wikimedia Commons/CC-BY-SA-3.0*)

9. One of the best known late antique ivories (c.395), generally known as the Stilicho Diptych (Monza, Museo e tesoro del duomo di Monza). On the left leaf is Serena, wife of Stilicho, niece and (according to Claudianus, who wrote extensively of the character and career of his patron) adopted daughter of Theodosius I. With her is their son, Eucherius. In her right hand she holds up a rose. On the right is Stilicho depicted in a military guise. His shield carries two imperial busts, believed to represent Arcadius and Honorius when both emperors were consuls (396, 402, or 407): the size of the boy on the diptych suits the 7-year-old Eucherius in 396. The original hinging indicates that the panels should be reversed. Some scholars argue that because the female figure lacks any specific imperial attribute (viz. either diadem or imperial *fibula*), she is not a member of the Theodosian dynasty and so no Stilicho, no Eucherius. Serena, however, was *neither* an imperial daughter *nor* an *Augusta*, which means any 'objection to identifying her as the Monza female fails' (Cameron 2016: 514). The diptych certainly captures the essence of Stilicho's power through marriage. (*Carlodell/Wikimedia Commons/CC-BY-SA-4.0*)

10. Gold medallion (Paris, Bibliothèque nationale de France, Département des Monnaies) depicting (definitely) Aelia Galla Placidia (392–450), struck in Ravenna in 425 and bearing the legend D(*omina*) N(*oster*) GALLA PLA-CIDIA P(*ia*) F(*elix*) AVG(*usta*). She was the daughter, sister, wife and mother of emperors. Many women are reduced to footnotes in history or are seen through the 'tragic heroine' lens. The daughter of the intolerant Theodosius I and half-sister of the ineffective Honorius, Galla Placidia was destined to lead an out-of-the-ordinary life. Married twice, first in 414 to the Gothic king Ataulf (she had been carried off in the sack of Rome), and second (against her will) in 417 to the Roman *generalissimo* Constantius, co-emperor of the West for just seven months in 421; he died from a bout of pleurisy. With Galla Placidia given the title *Augusta*, it was this marriage that catapulted her into power. As Honorius died childless, her infant son Valentinianus was the undisputed heir to the western throne; as regent she was to remain for a long time the most powerful figure in the West. Eventually, however, Galla Placidia had to yield this position to a new western *generalissimo*, a certain Flavius Aëtius. (*Clio20/Wikimedia Commons/CC-BY-SA-3.0*)

11. [Left] Low-cut relief (Linz, Schlossmuseum) depicting a legionary of the late third century. He appears to be wearing what is known as an Intercisa-type helmet, named after the find site, the Roman fortification of Intercisa (Dunaújváros, Hungary). Bipartite in construction, the two bowl halves were united by a longitudinal ridge running from front to back. Openings for the ears were formed by cut-outs both in the bowl and the cheek guards. Traces of silver on some examples imply that their iron bowls may originally have been covered with a thin silver sheathing. [Right] Modern re-enactor equipped as a legionary at the end of the third century. He wears *lorica hamata* and carries the *spatha*, the long double-edged sword that was the preferred sidearm of the later Roman soldier. Vegetius (2.18) states that in order to recognize their unit during battle, different emblems were emblazoned on the shields, together with the name of the soldier and the *cohors* or *centuria* to which he belonged. Ammianus Marcellinus (16.12.6) recounts an incident of which he was an eyewitness where the Alamanni, in fear of the Romans, suddenly recognized the blazons on their opponents' shields and, realizing that they had defeated these soldiers on a previous occasion, regained their courage. (*Left: Wolfgang Sauber/Wikimedia Commons/ CC-BY-SA-3.0; right: Matthias Kabel/Wikimedia Commons/CC-BY-SA-3.0*)

12. Part of the long narrative frieze panel on the southern façade above the left lateral archway of the Arch of Constantine, depicting the siege of the strongly fortified Verona. The triumphal arch spans the Via Triumphalis

in Rome. Erected in 315 for the tenth anniversary of Constantinus' rise to power, it was officially dedicated by the Senate and the Roman people to Caesar Flavius Constantinus Maximus, Pius Felix Augustus, to honour his victory over 'the tyrant and his factions', namely Maxentius, three years earlier. Constantinus' soldiers are spurred on by Victoria, the winged goddess of victory, above them as they attack the walls of Verona. (*FrDr/Wikimedia Commons/CC-BY-SA-4.0*)

13. Roman soldiers equipped with iron mail shirts with coifs, and carrying spears and large round shields as depicted in the miniature 'Ascanius and Trojan council' from the late antique *Vergilius Vaticanus* (Vatican, Biblioteca Apostolica, MS Cod. Vat. lat. 3225, folio 73 verso). An illuminated manuscript containing fragments of Virgil's *Aeneid* and *Georgics*, it was compiled in Rome around the year 400 and found in the monastery of Saint-Martin, Tours, during the second quarter of the ninth century. Infantry tactics were – and still are – dictated by the capabilities of the components of the foot soldier: man, weapons and equipment. (*Wikimedia Commons/Public Domain*)

14. A portion of bronze *lorica squamata* from Newstead-*Trimontium* (Edinburgh, National Museum of Scotland, inv. X.FRA 118.1), a site that has yielded no fewer than 346 scales to date. Each scale has four side-link holes and one lacing hole at the top. These overlapping scales would have been sewn to a flexible cloth or leather backing. This provided a balance of flexibility and protection. Scale armour could be made by virtually anyone, requiring patience rather than craftsmanship, and was very simple to repair. Though scale was inferior to mail, being neither as strong nor as flexible, it was similarly used throughout our period and proved particularly popular with horsemen and officers as this type of armour, especially if tinned, could be polished to a high sheen. Bronze *lorica squamata* replaced the more familiar steel *lorica segmentata* of the earlier legionaries, although iron ring mail was also worn. (© *Esther Carré*)

Maps

Map 1: The critical century xviii
Map 2: The tetrarchy xix
Map 3: Prefectures, dioceses and *provinciae* of the later Roman Empire xx
Map 4: *Claustra Alpium Iuliarum* xxi
Map 5: Battle of the Frigidus xxii

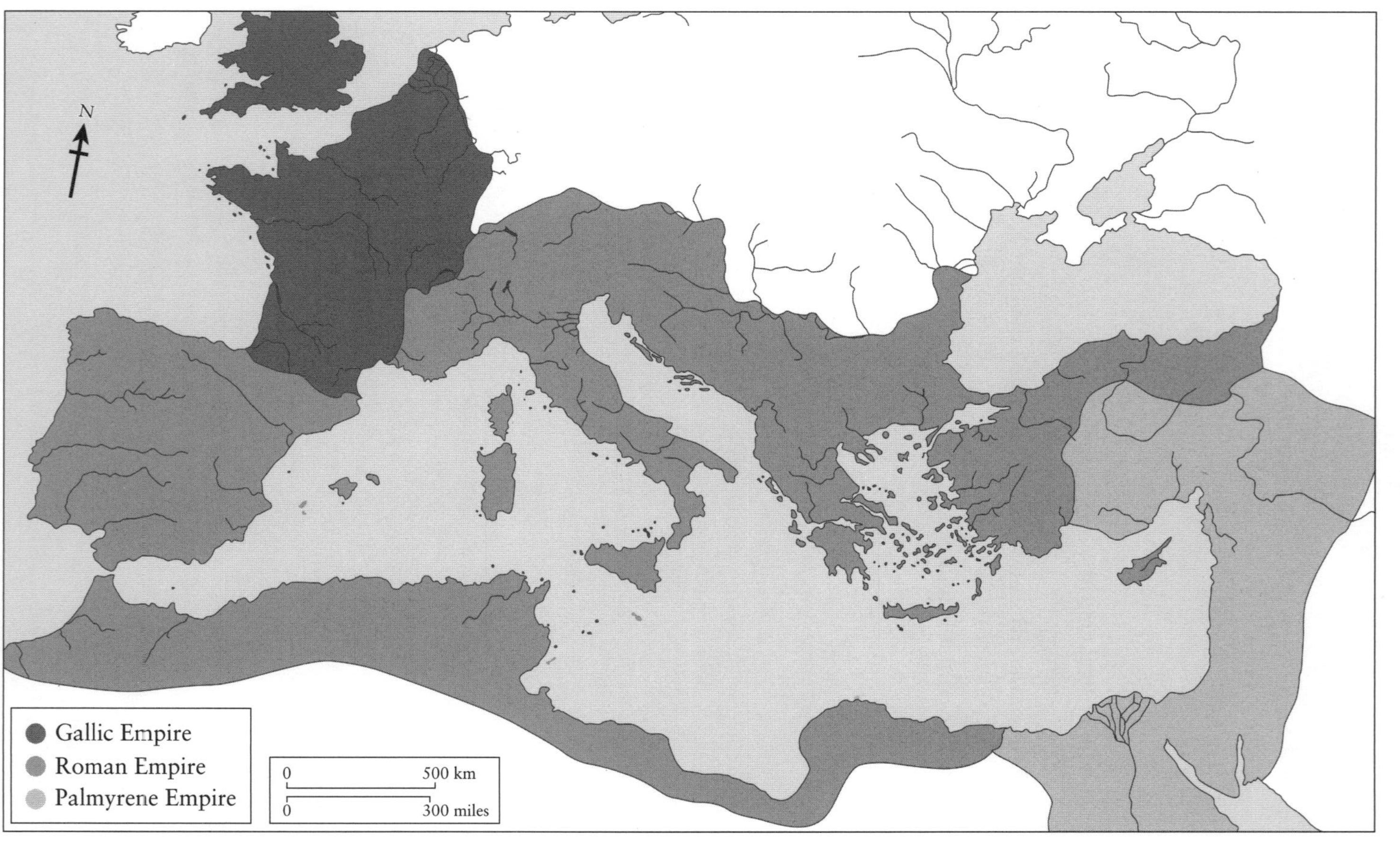

Map 1: The critical century.

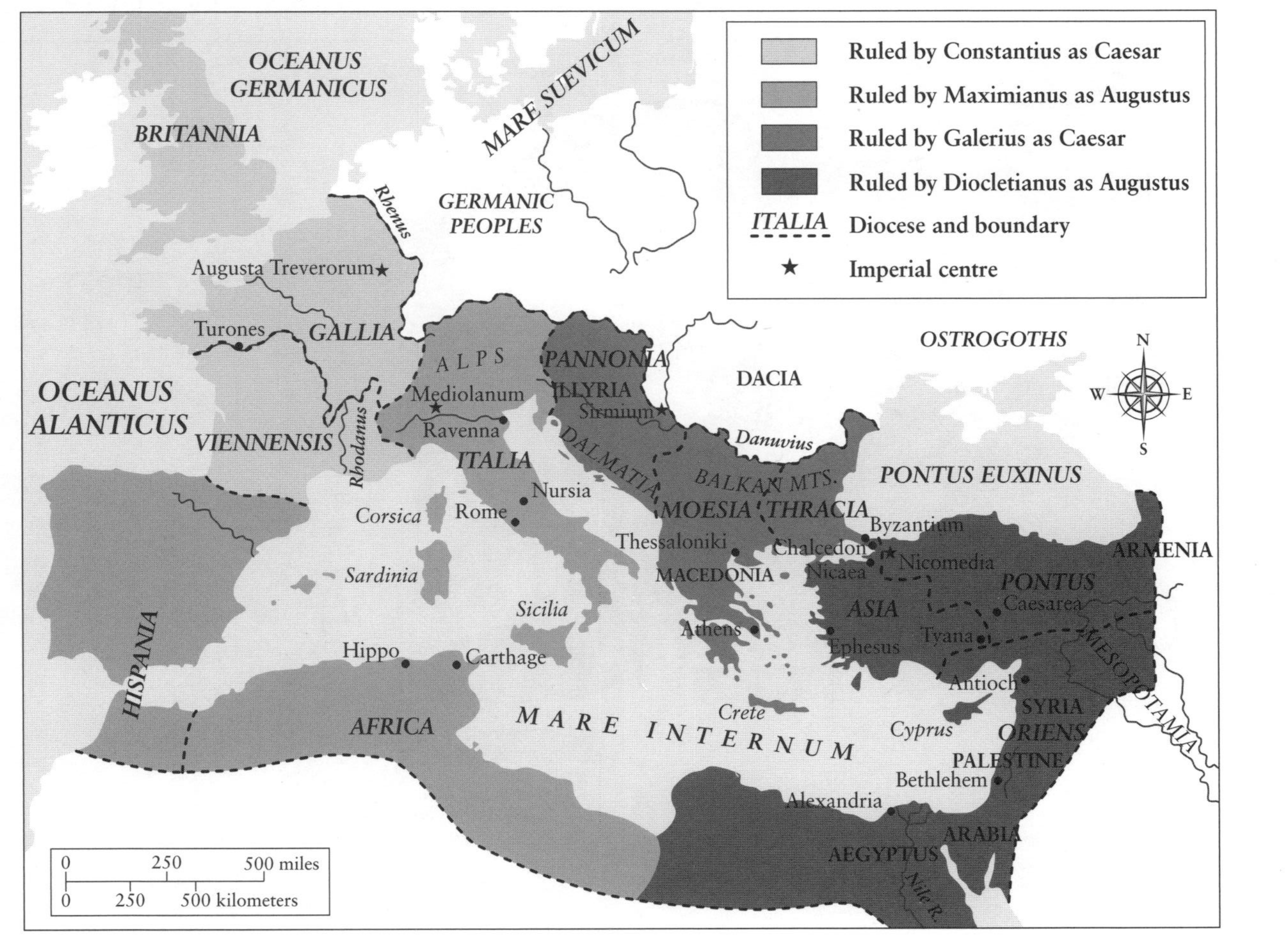

Map 2: The tetrarchy.

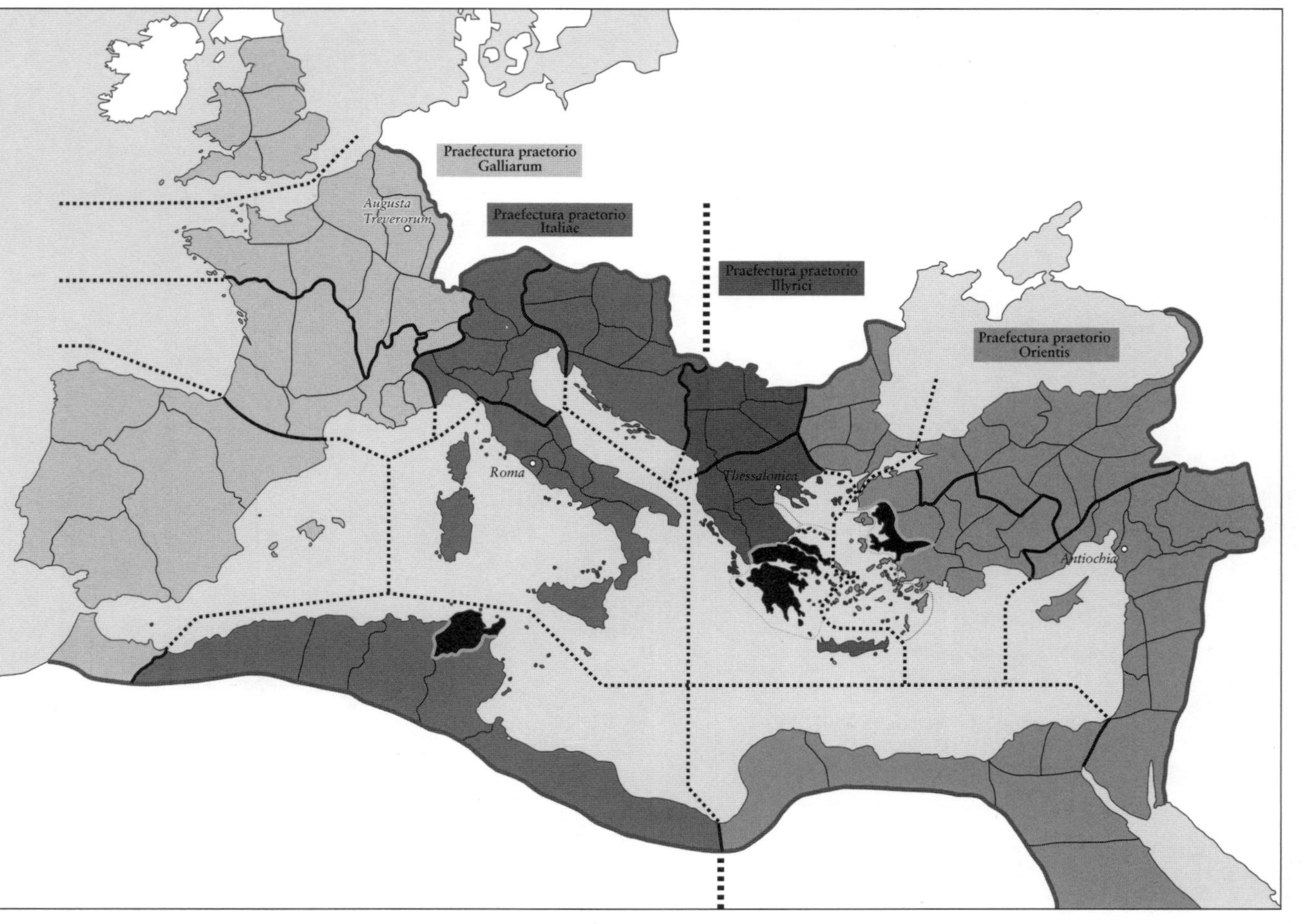

Map 3: Prefectures, dioceses and *provinciae* of the later Roman Empire.

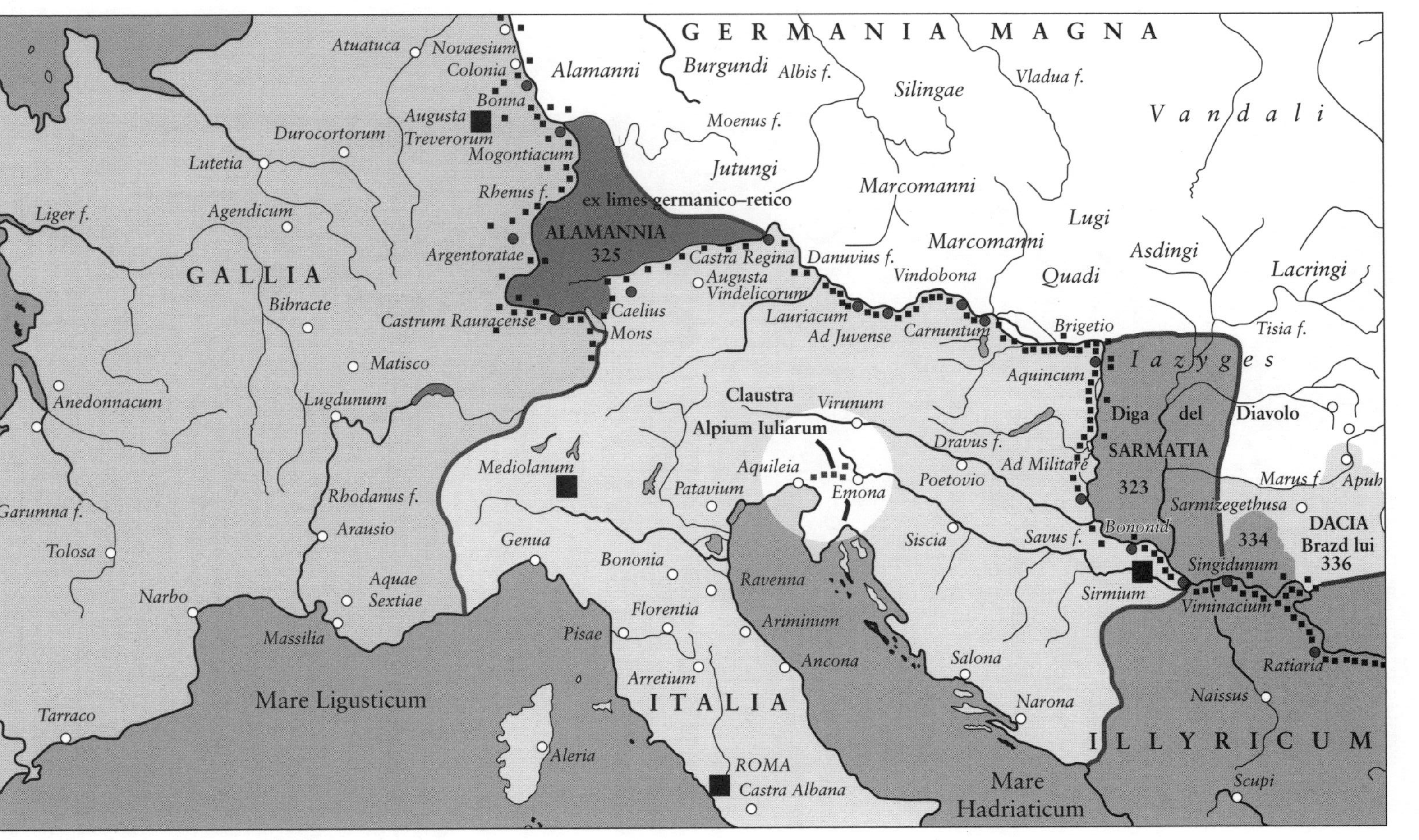

Map 4: *Claustra Alpium Iuliarum.*

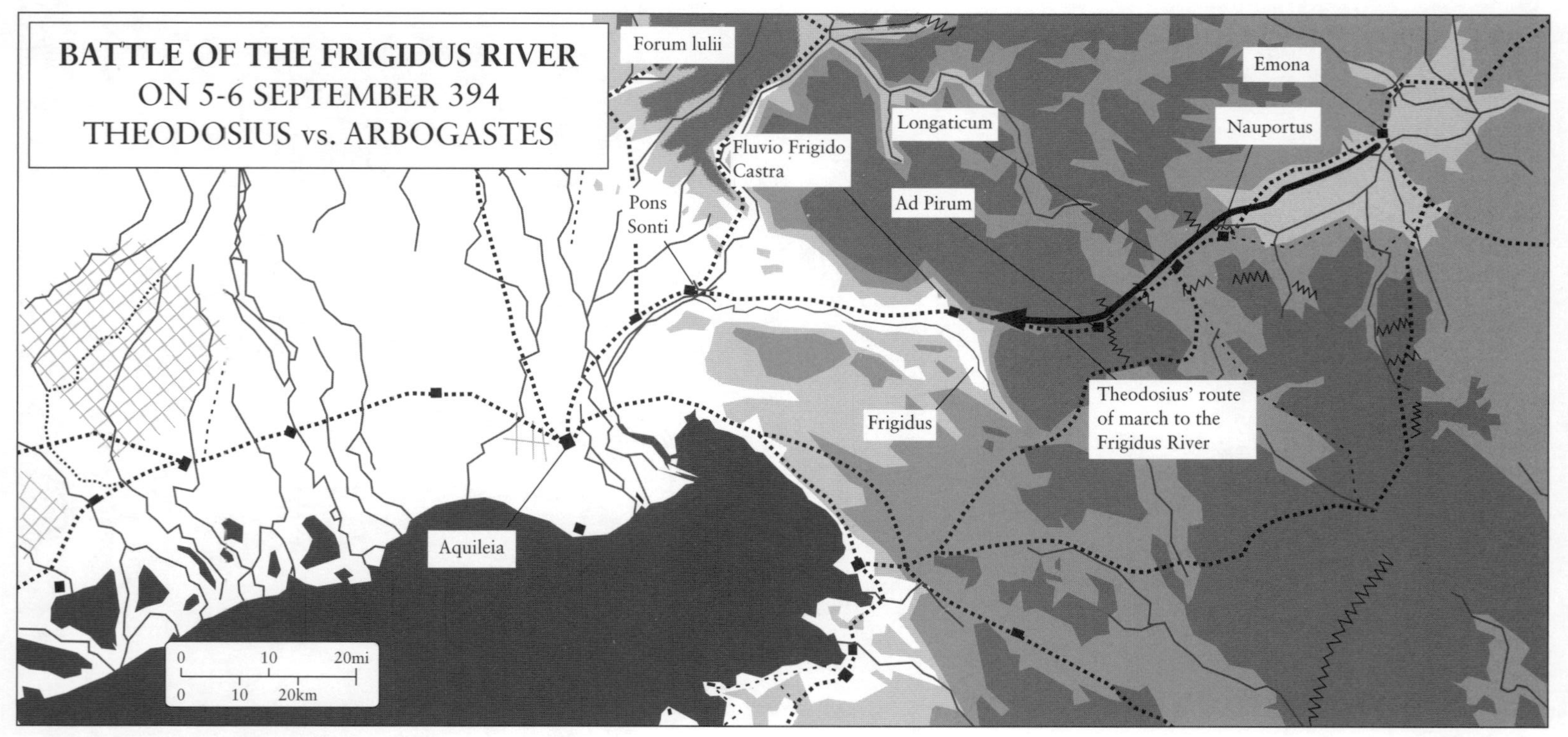

Map 5: Battle of the Frigidus.

Introduction

'If writers would adhere to the golden Rule for an Historian, viz. To write nothing which they did not know to be true, the Duke apprehends they would have nothing but little to tell.'

Arthur Wellesley, 1st Duke of Wellington

Battles are singular moments in history, productive of strange events. Much may depend upon a trifle, and the effects of a trifle may be victory and the effects of victory everlasting. The battle of the Frigidus River was such, for in a very real sense it symbolized the extinction of pagan liberty as opposed to a pagan revival. The Frigidus battle was fought on 5–6 September 394[1] between the eastern emperor Theodosius I (r. 379–395) and the western usurper Eugenius (r. 392–394), somewhere in the vicinity of what is now the fast-flowing Vipava River, which surges through south-west Slovenia.

There is a lot to unpack when it comes to the sorry events of early September 394. To begin with, the name Theodosius conjures up pictures of a grim-faced emperor issuing unforgiving decrees banning this, that and the other. Secondly, while Christian propaganda portrays the conflict between Theodosius and Eugenius as a pious war against paganism, the Frigidus being a victory (considered miraculous) over an attempted pagan revival (considered an anathema), the conflict itself originated with the weakness of the recently deceased western emperor Valentinianus II and the rise of warlord-like political-military figures. Spectacular as it was, Theodosius' victory at the Frigidus did not occur in a vacuum.

As for the battle itself, well, Christian tradition says that Theodosius leaped from his horse and fell upon his knees, fervently prayed to God and received a miracle, but tradition, Christian or otherwise, is always ready with such marvellous tales. In truth, did God answer Theodosius' fervent prayer by assisting him with a miracle or was this cooked up *vaticinium ex eventu* ('after the event') to make his complete victory seem all the more fantastical?

In one sense the two-day affair by the gentle banks of the Frigidus was a Christian fable waiting to happen, an invocation of the macabre elevated to the marvellous. For the Christian fathers it rightfully functioned as the second grand miraculous event of the century, the first of course being Constantinus' apparent celestial vision on the field of Pons Mulvius. For them these two battlefield 'miracles' serve as existential bookends for the fourth century. Battles, like history, can often be a matter of perspective.

The point is this: if you have even a passing interest in the history of the early Church, the fourth century is the foundation period. Still, when you directly answer propaganda – and sometimes you have to – you can get into a kind of unpleasant dance with the propagandists. It is much better to just fill up the space with the history. Usually the history is actually so much more interesting than the propaganda about it. However, a word of warning. The writing of history is forever plagued by the temptation of hindsight. Knowledge of the topic habitually becomes the starting-point of the quest for antecedents. Without doubt, the power of hindsight is a potent one, but the duty of a modern chronicler is – or should be – to demonstrate 'how it essentially was', as Leopold von Ranke (1795–1886), a noted German historian and a founder of modern source-based history, astutely put it.[2] If historians can be misled, tucked up safely *à la domicile* as they generally are, how much more difficult must it have been for the men on the battlefield to gain a distinct, comprehensive view of what they were fighting for and what they were actually achieving.

When ancient authors wrote about the past, they rarely had in mind what Ranke thought was the real aim of history; rather they mixed in generous dollops of myth and legend, gossip, hearsay, moralizing, ethnic stereotypes (much of it lazy stereotyping), political propaganda and plain wishful thinking; that is to say, the ways things should have been. So let us shelve for a moment the question of the religious misinformation regarding the divinely inspired Christian emperor and the alleged miracle at the Frigidus, and take a look at a much more recent wartime event that was quickly tinged with the vibrant colours of myth and legend, and is now encumbered with its own time-honoured tales.

It was the early afternoon of 23 February 1945, on the summit of Mount Suribachi (elev. 169m), Iwo Jima. Six battle-stained combatants of the United States Marine Corps raised the Stars and Stripes over the battle-blasted Japanese-held island. This was a brief moment in time captured in an iconic black and white photograph by Joe Rosenthal (1911–2006) of the Associated Press. Quickly released to the wider world, the photograph was widely assumed to signify that victory in the Pacific Theatre was imminent. In times of war people will believe anything. Yet at that instant, the horrific battle for Iwo Jima had been raging for five days and would relentlessly grind on for another thirty-one: the American command had allowed only five days for the taking of Iwo Jima by the Marines. Tragically, three of the six Marines captured in the photograph would perish in the apocalyptic combat on the tiny island where the Japanese were literally dug into its soft, grey volcanic ash. More to the point, the war in the Pacific was far from over and would not be so until September 1945.

Amphibious (and airborne) assaults are notoriously complex and difficult. Without doubt, they are the hardest joint operations to undertake and they are *always* a learning experience. In an amphibious operation, getting all the pieces and parts together in the proper sequences is a major challenge, and there is simply no substitute for combat experience. The Pacific island-hopping war was won by the combat-hardened Marine Corps, 'the most badass' of all the American armed services. As the brutal battle for Iwo Jima raged on, they were to prove this time and time again.

In point of fact, there were two American flags planted atop the extinct volcano of Mount Suribachi on 23 February of that year. The photograph that Rosenthal and the world saw was actually of the second flag-raising. This was when a larger replacement flag was raised by different Marines to those who had raised the first flag some ten minutes after the crest was captured; that is, around 1020 hours local time. A Marine photographer captured it. The first one was spontaneous; the second one was staged after a US commander considered the original flag was too small to be easily seen from a distance, particular to the north of Mount Suribachi where there was fighting going on.[3] Fluttering at the highest point of Iwo Jima, the totemic second flag was raised to boost the fighting spirit of the battle-weary Marines below and the supporting naval vessels offshore. A symbolic gesture, perhaps, but in war symbols can move armies. Yet that second photograph was extremely expensive for 2nd Battalion, 28th Marine Regiment: 3 officers and 112 men killed, plus 21 officers and 354 wounded during the assault on Mount Suribachi.

It is commonly said that a picture is worth a thousand words. Rosenthal's photograph of the *second* flag-raising quickly became one of most pervasive pictures in modern American history. It is a scene of powerful significance, and it is unsurprising that as a critical component of the official historical truth, this 'heroic' wartime image was to be reproduced in thousands of magazines, on millions of posters and on the first US stamp to depict living persons. Whereas the written word tends to work on the intellectual side of human nature, pictures operate at the visceral, emotional level. Compressed, intense and immediate, pictures are the ideal medium for evoking heroism and danger. The beleaguered men in the photograph were proclaimed heroes, and the three survivors were flown home to become reluctant public heroes.[4] The manipulation of history is hardly limited to the world of fiction, and the events on this seemingly insignificant Pacific island illustrate this process in a dramatic way. It is a battle we know as a historic parable.

Iwo Jima (19 February–26 March), which had resulted in such appalling carnage,[5] is historically associated with one of the largest and longest infantry battles of the war in the Pacific Theatre, and possibly ranks as the most intense battle of the Second World War. Just over a quarter of all the Congressional Medals of Honor awarded during the Second World War to US Marines were won there.[6] The conflict itself is now outside of living memory, which means it has been converted from contemporary history based on knowledge – that is to say, direct experience of the war – into documented and researched history; an event spoken of and written about at a popular level as well as a scholarly one. The first kind of history is informed by protagonists still alive to tell the story; namely first-hand history where we see in real time what the speaker saw. Of course, not all these voices are calm, even-handed or their testimony rooted in reality. The second kind of history we learn more from the archives, having lost these voices that are so important to posterity. This is inevitable. Yet much material has already been lost in the process, even though the Second World War is the most documented event of all time, and we are talking about not just words from eyewitness accounts of combatants and civilians long dead, but diaries, letters, films – some of them in colour – photographs and artefacts that exist.

Returning to the subject of photographs, some will serve as wordless historical essays, silently explaining the causes, or anticipating the effects, of the epochal events of history. Even if the camera never lies, it often fibs – serving to confirm a previously unarticulated belief or desire. And once it has, it sticks. In spite of that, that second photograph receded into myth, becoming in a sense a constant if ghostly image. Crucially, did those six flag-raising Marines on Mount Suribachi realize at the time that a myth was already being woven around them, a national legend that would outlive them all? I believe not.

This leads to a pointed and open-ended question: does any of the above really matter? In essence, this is a question about whether or not we want to believe in heroes: Odysseus, Achilles, Aeneas, Beowulf, Lagertha, Marco Polo and Jeanne d'Arc, to name just a few. Throughout recorded history, civilizations have embraced the epic adventures and struggles of their heroes. More often than not, the deeds of these men and women have transcended history and entered the realm of folklore, myth and legend. Some of these iconic personalities engaged in mortal combat with real or mythical foes. Beowulf exterminated the fearsome Grendel, Grendel's mother and the 'fire-dread dragon', suffering fatal wounds for his trouble. The wrathful Achilles avenged the death of his beloved Patroclus by slaying Hector, thus sealing the doom of Troy. The young warrior maiden Jeanne d'Arc lifted the siege of Orléans and turned the tide of the Hundred Years' War (1337–1453) before being betrayed by the Burgundians and burned by the English. Equally vigorous, independent and fiery-hearted was Lagertha (ON *Hlaðerðr*), a shadowy but possibly historical female figure. Unlike *La Pucelle d'Orléans*, however, the mythic *skjaldmær* ('shield-maiden') was a masterful killer, equally at home with swords and sex as weapons. Like most domineering women, Lagertha longed for domination and for devotion.

Such myth-stoking always adds to the fascination because the story that it does tell is frequently outrageous and often absurd. More commonly, these iconic mythical/historical figures undertook long and difficult voyages, in so doing overcoming both mortal and divine dangers. Odysseus survived a myriad of challenges on his ten-year return journey to Ithaca from the Trojan Wars. Marco Polo traversed the length of the Silk Road to the China of Kublai Khan and back, encouraging cultural and economic interchange between Europe and Asia. Aeneas, who survived the destruction of Troy, led his Aeneids to Italy to become the progenitors of the Romans. In these deeds, divine intervention was also a common theme: pre-Christian gods had intervened and aided Odysseus, Achilles, Aeneas, Beowulf and Lagertha in their battles, while later the Christian God had assisted Jeanne d'Arc and her heroic successors. Confounding heroes ask us questions. Heroes are dynamic, seductive people; otherwise they would not be heroes. It is not their task to pander to our preconceptions, parrot back our opinions and reassure us that we are right. Nor, for that matter, should they be always clear-cut white hats or black hats. Some were spotless, others were scoundrels. Some of them will appal us. Some we might quite like.

This brings us back to the manipulation by the US government and the news media of the iconic image of the second American flag being raised over Iwo Jima by embattled Marines. The image is sticky. Its herculean subject matter helps it to stay in the mind. Sticky images are powerful, and whatever may be the truth or feelings of the individuals involved, nations will compulsively create heroes when they need them, as with the men who raised the flag on Iwo Jima. It was a neat ruse really, but it was nothing new.

Sun Tzu famously said that 'all warfare is based on deception'.[7] We can add here that the public perception of war and its remembrance is equally based on deception. In the popular imagination the biblical David is linked with the Michelangelo's *David* (1501–04) white, naked, muscular, public body in the sunshine, his left hand holding a sling that is draped over his shoulder and runs down to his right hand. David is depicted *before* his battle with Goliath. Instead of being shown triumphant over a foe much larger than he, the classic portrayal,[8] David looks tense and ready for battle after he has made the decision to fight Goliath but before the battle has taken place. In a pious age, the Renaissance artist raised hymns to classical splendour inspired by the pagan Greeks and Romans.

Michelangelo was an artist of profound beauty who could create colossal unease. Think of the almost-breathing torso of *his* David. Yet the problem with the story of David and Goliath is that we have become too familiar with it. It does not mean that we know the biblical story too well, and more often than not we do not. As David went out to face Goliath, he was conspicuously carrying a staff. This was visibly a decoy weapon to divert the attention of his well-armed opponent from the vital components of his real weapon: the lethal ammunition of five stones 'in a shepherd's bag'.[9] This is understandable, since David did not have the ability to defeat this mighty warrior one on one.

The trick worked too. The overconfident Goliath evidently focused on the staff and jumped to the conclusion that David intended to fight him in a hand-to-hand encounter: '*Am* I a dog, that you come to me with sticks?'[10] This is the perceptual phenomenon known as 'inattentional blindness', a failure to recognize another visual object when sharply focused on something else that is also at the centre of the visual field. In this case, Goliath latched onto the staff but failed to see that David's 'sling was in his hand'.[11] David had identified Goliath's one weak point: although his entire body was well protected, his forehead was not. It was not David's carcass that became food for 'the birds of the air and the beasts of the field'[12] but Goliath's. An old maxim of war is to ask what your enemy most wants you to do, and try not to do it. This is what David did, and with good reason considering who he was up against that day.

We can set David and Goliath as two poles: David represents guile and Goliath represents force. Thinkers such as Jomini and Clausewitz, who kept their own formative experiences fighting in the Napoleonic Wars firmly in mind, enunciate strategic philosophies rooted in force. So, too, does God, who tends to place more stock in force than in guile. Guile, of course, is the hallmark of strategists such as Sun Tzu. Many strategists today view winning without fighting – in David's case without actually engaging hand-to-hand – as the cornerstone of Sun Tzu's overall military philosophy: 'For to win one hundred victories in one hundred battles is not the acme of skill. To subdue the enemy without fighting is the acme of skill.'[13]

In truth, what Sun Tzu is trying to avoid, if at all possible, is being forced into fighting a set-piece battle in which he might have an equal or greater chance of losing. Later in the same chapter Sun Tzu discusses force ratios and recommends the following: 'When five times his strength, attack him.'[14] In other words, Sun Tzu is certainly not hesitant about engaging in battle when he possesses a clearly superior advantage; what he is advocating is the rejection of offering the enemy a fair fight.

Indeed, the entire point of good generalship is to generate battles that are unfair to the enemy. So, in David's case, David is simply looking to avoid being forced into fighting hand-to-hand. Yet does it always work? What would David have done if the stone from his sling had missed or if Goliath's bronze helmet had been just slightly lower in front? These are arch speculation, of course. All the same, that advantage of surprise would have been lost, Goliath would have divined David's trick and the Israelite hero would have been at the utter mercy of the Philistine's overwhelming force.

Battles, like history, can often be a matter of perspective. It is up to us, not just the battles, to determine the perspective, as well as our history and our heroes.

Chronology

235 Murder of Severus Alexander; accession of Maximinus Thrax.

238 Gordianus I and Gordianus II proclaimed co-emperors in province of Africa.
Capellianus, *legatus Augusti pro praetore* of Numidia, defeats Gordiani.
Senate appoints Balbinus and Pupienus co-emperors in opposition to Maximinus.
Maximinus (and his son) murdered by his soldiers.
Gordianus III appointed co-emperor with Balbinus and Pupienus.
Balbinus and Pupienus murdered by *Cohortes praetoriae*; Gordianus III sole emperor.
Goths plunder Histria at mouth of Danuvius.

241 Šāpūr I king of Persia.

244 First campaign of Šāpūr; murder of Gordianus (11 February).
Iulius Philippus Arabs proclaimed emperor by army.

247 Philippus Arabs appoints his son Philippus co-emperor.

248 Philippus Arabs celebrates millennium of Rome.

249 Goths cross Danuvius.
Traianus Decius proclaimed emperor; Philippus Arabs killed in battle at Verona.

251 Traianus Decius appoints his son Herennius Etruscus co-emperor.
Traianus Decius and Herennius killed fighting Goths in battle of Abritus.
Hostilianus, son of Traianus Decius, appointed emperor by Senate; dies of plague.
Trebonianus Gallus proclaimed emperor by army.

252 Second campaign of Šāpūr; Sāsānian Persians invade Syria and sack Antioch.

253 Trebonianus Gallus murdered by his soldiers; Æmilianus proclaimed emperor.
Æmilianus abandoned and killed; Valerianus and Gallienus co-emperors.
Goths invade Balkans.

256 Third campaign of Šāpūr; destruction of Dura-Europos.
Franks cross lower Rhenus.

260 Fourth campaign of Šāpūr; defeat and capture of Valerianus.

Revolt of brothers Macrianus and Quietus.
Revolt of Postumus on Rhenus; establishment of Gallic empire.
261   Odaenathus seizes power in Roman east.
267   Assassination of Odaenathus; Zenobia assumes control in Syria.
Seaborne invasion by Heruli; sack of Athens.
268   Revolt of Aureolus.
Gallienus killed in *putsch*; Claudius II seizes power.
269   Alamanni invade northern Italy.
Goths invade Balkans; Claudius defeats them at Naissus.
Assassination of Postumus; accession of Victorinus in Gallic empire.
270   Death of Claudius from plague; his brother Quintillus seizes power.
Aurelianus proclaimed emperor in opposition to Quintillus; suicide of Quintillus.
Iuthungi invade Italian peninsula.
Zenobia annexes Arabia, Iudaea and Aegyptus.
271   Vandals invade Pannonia.
Zenobia invades Syria and Asia Minor.
Assassination of Victorinus; Tetricus proclaimed emperor of Gallic empire.
272   Death of Šāpūr.
Aegyptus recovered.
Aurelianus' first Palmyrene campaign; capture of Zenobia.
273   Aurelianus' second Palmyrene campaign; Palmyra razed.
274   Aurelianus' campaign against Tetricus; end of Gallic empire.
Triumph of Aurelianus.
275   Murder of Aurelianus; Senate appoints Tacitus emperor.
276   Murder of Tacitus; his brother Florianus appointed by army in western provinces.
Probus proclaimed emperor by army on Danuvius; Florianus killed.
282   Murder of Probus; Carus seizes power.
283   Death of Carus; his sons, Carinus and Numerianus, co-emperors.
284   Murder of Numerianus; accession of Diocletianus.
285   Victory of Diocletianus over Carinus near mouth of Margus.
286   Maximianus appointed co-emperor.
287   Carausius seizes Britannia.
293   Tetrarchy formed; Constantius Chlorus and Galerius *Caesares*.
Carausius' forces expelled from Gesoriacum Bononia (Boulogne-sur-Mer).
Carausius assassinated by Allectus.
296   Britannia recovered by Constantius Chlorus; major repairs to Hadrian's Wall.
Britannia becomes diocese of four provinces.
297   Picti first mentioned by name as raiding northern Britannia.

305   Diocletianus and Maximianus abdicate (1 May); Constantius and Galerius *Augusti*.

306   Death of Constantius; Constantinus proclaimed emperor, Eboracum (25 July).
Maxentius, son of Maximianus, seizes power in Italy.

307   Constantinus marries Fausta, daughter of Maximianus.

308   Valerius Licinianus Licinius appointed *Augustus* (11 November).

310   Constantinus takes up arms against Maximianus.
Maximianus found hung.
Šāpūr II king of Persia.

311   Death of Galerius.
Death of Diocletianus (3 December).

312   Constantinus' victory over Maxentius at Pons Mulvius (28 October).

313   Constantinus and Licinius meet; Christians of all sects accepted by Edict of Toleration.
Licinius marries Constantia, Constantinus' half-sister.
Maximinus Daia, nephew of Galerius, seizes Asia Minor from Licinius.
Licinius defeats Maximinus Daia near Adrianopolis (30 April).
Death of Maximinus Daia in Tarsus.

316   Constantinus and Licinius clash at Cibalae.

317   Constantinus and Licinius clash at Mardia; two *Augusti* patch up their alliance.

324   Constantinus defeats Licinius near Adrianopolis (3 July).
Constantinus defeats Licinius at Chrysopolis (18 September).
Constantia successfully pleads for her husband's life; Licinius surrenders.
Constantinus sole emperor; consecration of Constantinopolis (8 November).
Constantinus writes to Šāpūr II.

325   Constantinus has Licinius hung.
First Ecumenical Council, Nicaea I; formulation of Nicene Creed, Arius condemned.

326   Constantinus has his eldest son Flavius Iulius Crispus executed.
Constantinus has his wife Fausta put to death.
Licinius Iunior, son of Licinius and Constantia, killed.

328   Death of Helena, Constantinus' mother.

330   Dedication of Constantinopolis to Blessed Virgin Mary (11 May).

332   Constantinus appoints his son Constans as Caesar.

337   Death of Constantinus (22 May).
Constantius II, Constantinus II and Constans divide empire.
Murder by army of Iulius Constantius, half-brother of Constantinus; Iulianus escapes.

Constantius, Constantinus and Constans proclaimed *Augusti* by army (9 September).

340   Constantinus and Constans fall out; Constantinus killed while invading Italy.

Constantius exiles Iulianus.

341   Consecration of Ulfilas in Constantinopolis; translates Bible into Gothic.

343   Constans visits Britannia.

344   Indecisive engagement outside Singara.

350   Elevation of Magnus Magnentius (18 January); Constans ousted by army and murdered.

351   Iulianus' elder half-brother, Constantius Gallus, appointed Caesar (15 March).

Constantius and Magnentius clash at Mursa (28 September).

353   Constantius and Magnentius clash at Mons Seleucus in Gaul.

Suicide of Magnentius (11 August); Constantius sole emperor.

Constantius recovers Gaul and Britannia.

354   Fall and execution of Gallus.

Revolt of Silvanus (*magister peditum per Gallias*); murdered by his guards.

355   Constantius reluctantly appoints Iulianus Caesar (6 November); sent to Gaul.

357   Constantius visits Rome.

Iulianus defeats Alamanni at Argentorate.

359   Šāpūr II captures Amida on Tigris; Ammianus Marcellinus survives siege.

360   Šāpūr captures Singara and Bezabde.

Iulianus proclaimed emperor by soldiers at Lutetia.

Incursion of Picti and Scotti.

361   Iulianus advances against Constantius; Hispania and Italy go over to Iulianus.

Unexpected death of Constantius (3 November); Iulianus recognized as sole emperor.

363   Iulianus invades Persia; besieges Ctesiphon.

Death of Iulianus (26 June); army elects Iovianus emperor (27 June).

Iovianus concludes peaces with Šāpūr; fortresses of Nisibis and Singara ceded.

364   Iovianus found dead (17 February); Valentinianus I elected emperor (25 February).

Valentinianus appoints Valens co-emperor (28 March); Valens takes charge of east.

366   Rebellion of Prokopios, distant relative of Iulianus; quickly crushed by Valens.

367   Valentinianus falls seriously ill; Gratianus given title *Augustus* (24 August). *Barbarica conspiratio*.

368   Flavius Theodosius (the elder) sent to recover Britannia; Hadrian's Wall restored.

374   Ambrose appointed to bishopric of Mediolanum by public demand.

375   Death of Valentinianus (17 November).
Valentinianus II – still a child – proclaimed by army on Danuvius (22 November).
Huns cross Tanaïs (Don) river.

376   Huns invade territory of Goths; Teruingi permitted to cross Danuvius into the empire.

378   Destruction of eastern army at Adrianopolis (9 August); Valens killed.

379   Accession of Theodosius I (19 January).

381   Second Ecumenical Council, Constantinopolis I; reaffirmed Nicene Creed.
Death of Šāpūr II; accession of Ardašīr II.

382   Gratianus orders removal of Altar of Victory from Iulia Curia.
Goths permitted by treaty (3 October) to settle *en bloc* within empire.
Magnus Maximus checks incursion of Picti and Scotti.

383   Magnus Maximus hailed emperor by army in Britannia.
Gratianus treacherously murdered at Lugdunum (25 August).
Death of Ardašīr II; accession of Šāpūr III.

384   Flavius Stilicho marries Serena, niece of Theodosius.
Birth of Honorius (9 September).

385   Stilicho promoted *comes domesticorum*.
Hounding of Ambrose by Iustina and Valentinianus II.

386   Valentinianus passes decree for legal recognition of Arianism.

387   Magnus Maximus invades Italy; Valentinianus flees.
Peace with Sāsānian Persia.

388   Theodosius defeats Magnus Maximus at Poetovio.
Execution of Magnus Maximus outside Aquileia (28 August).
Death of Šāpūr III; accession of Bahrām IV.

390   Thessaloniki massacre; Theodosius does public penance.

391   Theodosius bans pagan worship.

392   Death of Valentinianus II (15 May).
Arbogastes raises Eugenius as emperor in west (22 August).

393   Theodosius declares Honorius emperor of west (23 January).

394   Battle of the Frigidus (5–6 September); Theodosius rules east and west.
Stilicho western *generalissimo* (*magister peditum praesentalis*).

395   Death of Theodosius (17 January); empire split east (Arcadius) and west (Honorius).

Arcadius marries Aelia Eudoxia, daughter of Flavius Bauto.

Augustine consecrated bishop of Hippo Regius.

396   Alaric tries to take Constantinopolis but repulsed; he enters Greece.

397   Revolt of Gildo (*magister militum per Africam*).

Alaric appointed *magister militum* in eastern Illyricum.

Death of Ambrose.

398   Honorius marries Maria, eldest daughter of Stilicho.

Gildo defeated by his estranged brother Mascezel; Gildo commits suicide.

Eutropius, chief palace eunuch, defeats Caucasian Huns invading Asia Minor.

399   Pannonia (Illyricum) returned to western jurisdiction; Alaric left 'unemployed'.

400   Aelia Eudoxia officially declared *Augusta* (9 January).

Short-lived *coup d'état* of Gaïnas in Constantinopolis.

Alaric's followers declare him *rex Gothorum*.

401   Birth of Theodosius II (10 April).

Invasion of Raetia and Noricum by Vandals and Alani; defeated by Stilicho.

Invasion of Italy by Alaric; Honorius narrowly escapes from Mediolanum.

402   Honorius transfers his imperial residence to Ravenna.

Stilicho checks Alaric at Pollentia (5 April), and defeats him at Verona (June).

404   Arcadius parades statues of *Augusta* Aelia Eudoxia alongside his own.

Death of Aelia Eudoxia.

405   Invasion of Italy by Goths under Radagaisus.

406   Stilicho defeats Radagaisus at Faesulae.

Vandals, Suevi and Alani cross Rhenus into Gaul.

Army in Britannia raises first Marcus and then Gratianus to the purple.

407   Army in Britannia ultimately raises Constantinus to the purple; crosses into Gaul.

Honorius is compelled to accept usurper Constantinus III as co-emperor.

Treaty between Stilicho and Alaric.

408   Death of Arcadius (1 May); accession of Theodosius II.

Death of Maria; Honorius marries Thermantia, her sister.

Olympius, *magister scrinii*, leads coup against Stilicho (13 August).

Fall of Stilicho and his execution with connivance of Honorius (22 August).

Alaric marches on Italy and blockades Rome.

Danuvian Huns under Uldin raid Thracia.

409   Serena executed in Rome.

Britannia revolts from Constantinus III; end of Roman rule in Britannia.

Vandals, Suevi and Alani enter Hispania.

Alaric again blockades Rome; raises Priscus Attalus as puppet emperor.
Alaric and Attalus besiege Honorius in Ravenna.

410   Alaric finally takes Rome; city pillaged for three days.
Alaric plans to cross to Africa; dies at Consentia, Bruttium.
Honorius tells Romano-Britons to look to their own defences.
Honorius appoints Flavius Constantius (future Constantius III) *magister peditum*.

411   Constantinus III defeated at Arelate by Constantius; he is captured and executed.

413   Theodosian walls of Constantinopolis built.

415   Constantius sends Goths to Hispania to fight Vandals.

417   Constantius marries Honorius' sister, Galla Placidia.

418   Constantius settles Goths in Aquitania Secunda.

421   Constantius becomes co-emperor as Constantius III, but dies soon after.

423   Honorius dies without issue.

425   Valentinianus III, son of Constantius, western emperor; Galla Placidia regent.

Abbreviations

AE	*L'Année épigraphique* (Paris, 1888–)	
AJA	*American Journal of Archaeology* (Princeton NJ, 1897–)	
Ambr.	Ambrose	
	Ep.	*Epistulae*
	Expo. in Ps.	*Expositio in Psalm* ('Exposition on the Psalms')
	Obit. Theod.	*De obitu Theodosii oratio*
	Obit. Val.	*De obitu Valentiniani Consolatio*
Amm. Marc.	Ammianus Marcellinus, *Rerum Gestarum*	
Anon. Vales.	*Anonymous Valesianus I, Origo Constantini*	
App.	Appianus	
	B civ.	*Bellum civilia*
	Hannib.	*Hannibalica*
	Illyr.	*Illyrike*
Archil.	Archilochos	
Arh. vest.	*Arheološki vestnik*	
Athan.	Athanasios	
	Ep.	*Epistulae*
	Fest. Ind.	*Index to the Festal Epistles*
	Hist. Ar.	*Historia Arianorum*
Aug.	Augustine of Hippo	
	Conf.	*Confessiones*
	Civ.	*De civitate Dei contra paganos*
	Expo. in Ps.	*Expositio in Psalm* ('Exposition on the Psalms')
Aur. Vict.	Sextus Aurelius Victor	
	Caes.	*De Caesaribus*
	Epit.	*Epitome de Caesaribus*
Bede	The Venerable Bede, *Historia ecclesiastica gentis Anglorum*	
BMC	*Coins of the Roman Empire in the British Museum, Vol. IV: Antonius Pius to Commodus*	
Caes.	Iulius Caesar	
	B civ.	*Bellum civile*
	B Gall.	*Bellum Gallicum*
Chron. min.	T. Mommsen, *Chronica minora* (Berlin, 1986/1898)	

Chrys.	Ioannes Chrysostomos	
	Galat.	*Commentary on Galatians*
	Hom.	*Homiliae*
Cic.	Cicero	
	Att.	*Epistulae ad Atticum*
CIG	A. Böckh, *Corpus Inscriptionum Græcorum* (Berlin, 1825–60)	
CIL	T. Mommsen et al., *Corpus Inscriptionum Latinarum* (Berlin, 1863–)	
C Ius.	*Codex Iustinianus*	
Claud.	Claudius Claudianus	
	B Gild.	*De Bello Gildonico*
	B Goth.	*De Bello Gothico*
	Cons. III	*Panegyricus de Tertio Consulatu Honorii Augusti*
	Cons. IV	*Panegyricus de Quarto Consulatu Honorii Augusti*
	Cons. VI	*Panegyricus de Sexto Consulatu Honorii Augusti*
	Cons. Stil. I	*De Consulatu Stilichonis Liber I*
	Cons. Stil. II	*De Consulatu Stilichonis Liber II*
	Fesc.	*Fescinnina de nuptiis Honorii Augusti*
	In Eutr.	*In Eutropium*
	In Ruf. I	*In Rufinum Liber I*
	In Ruf. II	*In Rufinum Liber II*
	Laus Ser.	*Laus Serenae*
	Nupt.	*Epithalamium de nuptiis Honorii Augusti*
cos.	*consul*	
cos. design.	*consul designatus*	
C Th.	T. Mommsen and P. Meyer, *Codex Theodosianus* (Berlin, 1905)	
D&F	E. Gibbon, *The History of the Decline and Fall of the Roman Empire*, 3 vols (London, 1890)	
Dig.	Iustinianus, *Digesta seu Pandectae*	
Dio	Cassius Dio	
Diod.	Diodorus Siculus	
DRB	Anonymous, *De rebus bellicis* ('On the Things of Wars')	
Eunap.	Eunapios	
	fr.	*Historiarum fragmenta*
	VS	*Vitae Sophistarum*
Euseb.	Eusebios	
	Hist. eccl.	*Historia ecclesiastica*
	Tric.	*Tricennial Orations*
	L Const.	*Laudes Constantini* ('In Praise of Constantinus')
	V Const.	*De vita beatissimi Imperatoris Constantini*
Eutr.	Eutropius, *Breviarium ab urbe condita*	

Evagr.	Evagrius, *Historia ecclesiastica*
Fest.	Sextus Festus, *Breviarium historiae Romanae*
FGrHist	F. Jacoby, *Die Fragmente der griechischen Historiker* (Berlin & Leiden 1923–58)
FIRA²	S. Riccobono et al., *Fontes Iuris Romani Anteiustiniani*, 3 vols (Firenze, 1940–03)
Frontin.	Frontinus, *Strategemata*
Gk.	Greek
Greg. Naz.	Gregory Nazianzen
	Or. *Orationes*
Greg. Nyss.	Gregory of Nyssa
	Fun. Pulch. *Funeral Oration for Pulcheria*
Greg. Tur.	Gregory of Tours, *Decem libri historiarum*[1]
Hdt.	Herodotos
Herod.	Herodian
Hom.	Homer
	Il. *Iliad*
	Od. *Odyssey*
Hor.	Horace
	Carm. *Carmina* ('Odes')
	Ep. *Epistulae*
	Sat. *Satires*
IG	*Inscriptiones Græcae* (Berlin, 1923–)
ILS	H. Dessau, *Inscriptiones Latinae Selectae* (Berlin, 1892–1916)
Iul.	Iulianus
	Caes. *Caesares*
	Ep. *Epistulae*
	Ep. ad Ath. *Epistula ad Athenienses* ('Letter to the Athenians')
	Misop. *Misopogon* ('Beard-hater')
	Or. *Orationes*
J Ant.	Ioannes Antiochensis
Jer.	Jerome
	Chron. *Chronicon*
	Ep. *Epistulae*
J Lyd.	Ioannes Lydos
	De mag. *De magistratibus rei publicae Romani*
	De mens. *De mensibus*
Jord.	Jordanes
	Get. *Getica = De origine actibusque Getarum*

	Rom.	*Romana = De summa temporum vel [= et] origine actibusque gentis Romanorum*
Joseph.	Flavius Josephus	
	AJ	*Antiquitates Iudaicae*
	B Iud.	*Bellum Iudaicum*
JRS	*Journal of Roman Studies* (Cambridge, 1910–)
Kedren.	Georgios Kedrenos, *Synopsis historiōn*
L	Latin
Lact.	Lactantius
	Div. Inst. VII	*Divinarum Institutionum libri VII*
	De mort. pers.	*De mortibus persecutorum*
Lib.	Libanios
	Ep.	*Epistulae*
	Or.	*Orationes*
Malal.	Iohannes Malalas, *Chronographia*
Maur.	Maurikios, *Stratēgikón*
ND occ.	O. Seeck, *Notitia Dignitatum in partibus Occidentis* (Berlin, 1876)
ND or.	O. Seeck, *Notitia Dignitatum in partibus Orientis* (Berlin, 1876)
NIV	New International Version
NKJV	New King James Version
Olympiod.	Olympiodoros of Thebes
ON	Old Norse
Or. Sib.	*Oracula Sibyllina*
Oros.	Orosius, *Historiarum adversus paganos libri VII*
Ov.	Ovid
	Fast.	*Fasti*
Pac.	Latinius Pacatus Drepanius, *Panegyricus ad Theodosium*
Pall.	Palladius Helenopolitanus, *Historia Lausica*
Pan. Lat.	*XII Panegyrici Latini*
Paulin.	Paulinus Mediolanensis, *Vita sancti Ambrosii*
P Col.	*Kölner Papyri* (Köln, 1976–)
PG	J-P. Migne, *Patrologiae cursus completus: Series græca*, 161 vols (Paris, 1857–66)
Philostorg.	Philostorgius, *Historia ecclesiastica*
PIR	*Prosopographia Imperii Romani*
PL	J-P. Migne, *Patrologiae cursus completus. Series Latina*, 217 vols (Paris, 1841–55)
Plin.	Pliny, *Historia naturalis*
PLRE I	A.H.M. Jones, J. Martindale and J. Morris, *Prosopography of the Later Roman Empire*, vol. I (Cambridge, 1971)

Plut.	Plutarch	
	Ages.	*Agesilaos*
	Ant.	*Marcus Antonius*
	Arat.	*Aratos*
	Mar.	*Caius Marius*
Polyb.	Polybios, *Historíai*	
P Oxy.	B.P. Grenfell, A.S. Hunt and H.I. Bell, *The Oxyrhynchus Papyri* (London, 1898–)	
Prokop.	Prokopios	
	De aedif.	*De aedificiis*
	Wars	*History of the Wars*
RA	Rufinus of Aquileia, *Historia ecclesiastica*	
RE	A. Pauly, G. Wissowa and W. Kroll, *Real-Encyclopädie d. klassichen Altertumswissenschaft* (Stuttgart, 1893–1972)	
RIC	*Roman Imperial Coinage*, vol. IX	
Rufin.	Rufinus of Aquileia, *Historia ecclesiastica*	
Rutil.	Rutilius Namatianus, *De reditu suo* ('Going Home')	
SEG	*Supplementum Epigraphicum Graecum* (1923–)	
SHA	Scriptores Historiae Augustae	
	Aurel.	*Divus Aurelianus*
	Claud.	*Divus Claudius*
	Sev. Alex.	*Severus Alexander*
	tyr. trig.	*tyranni triginta*
Sid. Apoll.	Sidonius Apollinaris	
	Carm.	*Carmina* ('Odes')
	Ep.	*Epistulae*
Sok.	Sokrates Scholastikos, *Historia ecclesiastica*	
Soz.	Sozomenos, *Historia ecclesiastica*	
Suet.	Suetonius	
	Aug.	*Divus Augustus*
	Caes.	*Divus Iulius*
	Calig.	*Caius Caligula*
	Vesp.	*Divus Vespasianus*
Sulp. Sev.	Sulpicius Severus	
	Chron.	*Chronica*
	V Mart.	*Vita Martini*
Symm.	Symmachus	
	Ep.	*Epistulae*
	Mem.	*Memorandum*
	Rel.	*Relationes*

Syn.	Synesios	
	De reg.	*De regno*
	Ep.	*Epistulae*
	Prov.	*Aegyptus sive de providentia*
Tac.	Tacitus	
	Ann.	*Annales*
	Germ.	*Germania*
	Hist.	*Historiae*
Themist.	Themistios, *Orationes*	
Theod.	Theodoret	
	Ep.	*Epistulae*
	Hist. eccl.	*Historia ecclesiastica*
Theoph.	Theophanes the Confessor, *Chronographia*	
Veg.	Vegetius, *Epitoma rei militaris*	
Vell.	Velleius Paterculus, *Historiae Romanae*	
Xen.	Xenophon	
	Anab.	*Anabasis* ('March up Country')
	Hell.	*Hellenika* ('History of My Times')
	Kyr.	*Kyroupaideia* ('Education of Kyros')
Zon.	Zonaras, *Epitome historiarum*	
Zos.	Zosimos, *Historia nova*	

Chapter One

Crisis, what crisis?

Severus Alexander (r. 222–235) was not a soldier himself, neither did he feel any particular affinity for a soldier's life nor the exiguity of a campaign tent, but his rule, 'as far as his subjects were concerned, was without fault or bloodshed.'[1] In fact, if we are to believe the Scriptores Historiae Augustae, Severus Alexander was one of those rare paragons of virtue.[2] Yet his assassination and replacement by a rags-to-riches, tough, no-nonsense career soldier from Thracia (or Moesia), Caius Iulius Verus Maximinus Thrax (r. 235–238),[3] was a stark reminder that in its current state the empire needed an emperor who knew and cared about the army. Whether or not he actually started life as a barefoot peasant, Maximinus was to be the first emperor to have risen through the ranks of the army to gain the imperial throne. As Herodian's evidence makes clear:

> He is reported to have come from a village where he was a shepherd boy once. As he grew to manhood, he was drafted into the army as a horseman because of his size and strength. Soon, with the help of a bit of luck, he progressed through all the ranks in the army and was given charge of legions and commands over provinces.[4]

Understandably, the soldiers themselves wanted to be led by men who would ensure victory and so practical military experience and ability became crucial criteria in the selection of emperors. Maximinus certainly fulfilled that role, for even as an emperor he actually fought in battle and dispatched single-handedly a number of the enemy; a virtually unprecedented action.[5] Certainly, Maximinus' attitude to his imperial obligations can be seen by the large pictures of his martial exploits, which he had displayed outside the Senate in Rome.[6]

Maximinus had added reason to proudly display his soldierly prowess, since he had ousted Severus Alexander by harping on his own military excellence in contrast to that feeble, effeminate coward. Alexander indeed chose to follow the advice of his dominant mother, Iulia Avita Mamaea, who was never far away from her son.[7] She made sure that her son did what she wanted,[8] and to that end she insisted that it was the responsibility of others to take risks for him; he must not get involved in battle.[9] The murder and proclamation at Mogontiacum (Mainz, Germany) in March 235 are highlighted by the late chroniclers as a dreadful turning-point: the accession of a man who had started as a common soldier. A full account is provided by Herodian, although he dispenses with many details:

> The soldiers decided to dispose of (Severus) Alexander and proclaim Maximinus as emperor and *Augustus*, as being their fellow soldier and tent-mate and appearing to be qualified for the present war by his experience and courage. Having assembled on the plain, fully armed as if for the usual training, when Maximinus approached to preside over them, they threw a purple imperial cloak on him and proclaimed him emperor – either he was unaware of what was being undertaken or he had planned it in secret. At first he refused and tore off the purple. But when they pressed him, threatening with drawn swords to kill him, he accepted the position, preferring to escape the immediate danger rather than a future one.[10]

Did the ordinary soldiers really take the initiative? Herodian did not know, but it appears that a certain Druid woman did. She had shouted out in her native tongue to Severus Alexander after telling to him to be on his way, 'And don't trust yourself to your soldiers!'[11]

Trust can be a peculiar thing: it is not always created from strict adherence to rules, but often built precariously. An equestrian outside the ruling clique, Maximinus had exploited the opportunities of the Severan army to gain numerous senior appointments. Having loosened the shackles of senatorial dominance, Maximinus also set the trend whereby succession by murder and civil war became the norm for the next half-century. As to Maximinus, as the first 'barbarian' emperor, he (naturally) has received a vicious press. Let us take, for instance, the testimony of Zosimos:

> Thus Maximinus was in firm control of the empire, although everyone regretted changing a moderate ruler for a cruel tyrant; for he came from an obscure family, and as soon as he took over the empire, those vices he naturally suffered from were made obvious by excessive power and he became unbearable to everyone. He not only insulted those in office but also behaved with utmost cruelty, favouring only sycophants, whose speciality it was to inform against un-ambitious men by accusing them of being debtors

to the imperial treasury. Finally, out of avarice he proceeded to the murder of men without trial, usurping public, and plundering private, property.[12]

Hardly surprisingly, to this particular imperial appointment the senatorial aristocracy could not agree and, after an eyeball-to-eyeball confrontation they managed to face the army down. According to senatorial political philosophy, nature has made only aristocrats fit to rule, enabling them to see further, deeper and higher than ordinary mortals. Accordingly, the subsequent run of emperors – the three Gordiani, Balbinus and Pupienus, Traianus Decius, Trebonianus Gallus, Valerianus and Gallienus – was one of 'gentlemen generals'. Yet the majority of them came to swift and disagreeable ends, while their military misfortunes would finally destroy the prestige of the Augustan system, leaving military rule as the only alternative. Maximinus, the Thracian soldier of obscure birth and exclusively military experience, unencumbered by any loyalty to the Senate, had set the uncomfortable trend whereby the army called the shots, putting forward their own commanders as new emperors. Now the idea of *commilitium*, fellow-soldier, had morphed into the almost total identification of the warrior emperor and his army.

Still, Maximinus' position was never secure, though he might have thought it was when he gave his son the title of Caesar and had his late wife deified. In the end the soldiers abandoned Maximinus outside Aquileia, partly because of his failure to pursue the unexpected siege successfully despite his previous victories, personal bravery and peculiar habits.[13] Herodian identifies *legio* II *Parthica* turning against Maximinus of its own accord because of the disastrous siege.[14] An emperor who consciously based his position largely on military power could find the soldiers capricious and perilous supporters. The soldiers of Maximinus threw his corpse along with that of his son into running water.[15]

Genesis

The interval from the dynasty of the Servi to Diocletianus begins and ends with strong government, separated by a period of political instability and military stress. Traditionally known as the 'period of anarchy' of the Roman Empire, this half-century saw at least fifteen 'legitimate' emperors recognized at Rome, and many more transient usurpers (a distinction that is not always easy to make), most of them generals proclaimed by armies asserting the priority of their own stretch of frontier.

This half-century was a wild era, which witnessed these numerous pretenders to the throne claiming power throughout the empire. What we are witnessing here, of course, is the centuries-long manifestation of Tacitus' observation that on the occasion of Nero's imperial exit the 'secret of empire was now revealed, that an emperor could be made elsewhere than at Rome'.[16] This was no mere Tacitean figure of speech, simply because imperial authority was ultimately based on control of the military. Thus, to retain power a player in the game of thrones had to gain an unshakable control over the legions, which were dotted along the fringes of the empire. Evidently, this in turn meant that the soldiers themselves could impose their own choice. Indeed, it turned out that even if an emperor gained recognition in Rome, this counted for nothing in the face of opposition from the armies out in the frontier provinces.

A good part of this was the consequence of the long process that anchored legions to the frontiers where they recruited, where the legionaries raised their families and retired. Marcus Aurelius was a devout stoic philosopher who once equated military operations across the Danuvius (Danube) River to a spider catching a fly,[17] forced by the logic of the military crisis of his day to be torn from his beloved scrolls and assume personal command so as to herd the Roman world amid sedition, pestilence, invasions and possible infidelity. This was to be blindingly true of his successors of the third century, and they would die if they lost the confidence of the army. Such was the brutal bargain of donning the purple: it offered hard edges, black-and-white certainties, one pedestal and one precipice. All things considered, an emperor sat on the highest seat in the empire, and proud men do not like looking up: in what was to become a familiar pattern, almost all met with violent deaths in civil strife or straightforward assassinations by their own soldiers and subordinates after short reigns.

Let us take the aforementioned Gallienus (r. 253–268); his fifteen-year reign was the longest in this age of violence when emperors perched precariously on their thrones. This was the cultured emperor who patronized Plotinus, the philosopher who made Neo-Platonism a rival to Christianity and in so doing the ancient and civilized pagan world reached its apogee in him. Gallienus was 35 years of age when his father Valerianus named him co-emperor in September 253 to rule in the west.[18] Seven years later his father disappeared into Persian captivity never to be seen again;[19] Gallienus was left to fend for himself as various interested parties attempted to seize power. With grit and luck he fought them off. The first was Ingenuus, the governor of Pannonia.[20] After his attempted takeover failed, Regalianus decided to have a go at it. He too paid for his failure with his life, as did the candidates who followed: Macrianus and Quietus, two brothers who led a rebellion in the eastern provinces but were eventually defeated. Gallienus' area of effective control, however, was confined to Italy, Dalmatia, Greece, western Illyricum and Africa, and though he managed to hold on to power for a further eight years, he was never able to reassert his authority over the whole empire. The problem of usurpation drained internal resources and undermined ambitions. Moreover, internal and external crises could become intertwined: the failure of the central authority to deal with invasions across the Rhenus (Rhine) River and the Euphrates would result in the establishment of separatist regimes in Gaul and the remarkable caravan city of Palmyra.

The Separatists

Of these two separatist regimes, the more serious threat to empire came from Marcus Cassianius Latinius Postumus (*cos.* 259),[21] a tough old soldier of humble origins, probably from the region of the lower Rhenus and possibly of Batavian origin.[22] Valerianus (r. 253–260) had left him in command of the army stationed on the Rhenus frontier,[23] and after a victory over the Germani he was elevated by his troops. A shrewd opportunist, Postumus managed to lop off parts of Gaul, Germania Superior, Germania Inferior, Britannia and Hispania (briefly).[24] For five years he successfully opposed the Germanic invaders of Gaul.[25] All the same, Gallienus sent Theodorus, Aureolus and Claudius against him, as well as campaigning in Gaul himself in 263.[26] The usurper, however, was only removed when he was lynched by his own soldiers at Mogontiacum. Postumus had marched against Laelianus, a rival who materialized at Mogontiacum. However, Laelianus' claim to power was a flash in a pan; having been in power for a brief five months, Postumus defeated and killed him. It was then that Postumus made a fatal mistake by denying his troops the opportunity to sack the city.[27] Clearly during this period of political uncertainty it was important to allow your men to enrich themselves through booty, plunder and the spoils of war if you wanted to retain their loyalty. Up to that point Postumus had been surprisingly successful. He had reigned at least for a decade, and along with his successors defended the autonomy of his illegitimate dominion, the splinter state the *magister memoriae* and historian Eutropius labelled *imperium Galliarum*,[28] for close to a decade and a half (260–274).

Likewise, 'Tadmor in the wilderness',[29] the oasis city known to the Greeks and Romans under the name of Palmyra, went its own way. Septimius Odaenathus, who was husband of the better-known Septimia Zenobia (*Znybyā Bat-Zabbai* in Aramaic), assumed control of the Roman east as the result of the yawning power vacuum following the disappearance of Valerianus in 260. Septimius Odaenathus sought an alliance with Šāpūr I, which was rejected and so, supplementing the Roman forces with his bowmen and *cataphractarii*,[30] he chased the Sāsānian Persians out of Syria and bounced them back across the Euphrates. For this deed he was awarded regal dignity by Gallienus and given Roman troops. In 262, he drove the Persians from the Roman provinces of Mesopotamia and

Osrhoëni, regaining Nisibis and Carrhae.[31] Flushed with victory, Odaenathus assumed the title 'king of kings'. Four years later, during his third campaign, he marched with his son to the gates of the Sāsānian capital of Ctesiphon (near modern-day Baghdad, Iraq). Then hearing of the Goths' invasion of Kappadokia, he turned around and marched rapidly to Herakleia Pontika, when en route he was murdered, together with his eldest son (by his former wife) Septimius Herodianus, at some point in early 267.[32] There is great divergence about the murderer and his motives,[33] one source even implicating Zenobia, stepmother of Herodianus, jealous for the position of her two sons by Odaenathus.[34] Guilty or not, she seized the regency on behalf of her eldest son, Septimius Vaballathus (*Wahb'alat* in Aramaic), then only 10 years old. The queen regent was ambitious.

Styling herself queen of Palmyra, she had Vaballathus adopt his father's titles of 'king of kings' and *corrector totius Orientis*, 'governor of the entire East'. Nevertheless, unlike Odaenathus, Zenobia was not content to remain a Roman client. In spring 272 a number of eastern provinces of the empire were annexed by Zenobia.[35] By expanding into the power vacuum of the east, her late husband, though loyally defending the empire against Persia, had in fact adroitly created for himself a position of independence in Palmyra. A later author, looking back in disdain on the recent past, may have moaned that 'the ruler of Palmyra thought himself our equal',[36] but in 261 Gallienus had belatedly appointed Odaenathus vice-regent of the east, declaring him *corrector totius Orientis*: he could do little else. Consequently, the Palmyrene prince held the supreme command of all the armed forces in the east with full authority over the provincial governors of the entire region from Asia Minor to Aegyptus. Unsurprisingly, therefore, Odaenathus awarded himself the self-adopted title of *dux Romanorum*.

Both of these separatists' regimes were to outlive Gallienus. When a given emperor's constitutional legitimacy and claim to sovereign authority was based solely on his control over the army there was little to prevent other commanders from attempting to claim legitimate authority by doing as he did and wresting control of the army's loyalty. In 268 Aureolus, Gallienus' gifted but capricious cavalry commander, who was stationed in Mediolanum (Milan, Italy) where he was supposed to be guarding Italy against Postumus, threw in his lot with the separatist regime. He was, however, defeated outside the city by Gallienus and besieged inside. While the siege was ongoing, Gallienus was struck down by the commander of the *equites Dalmatae*, Cecropius, as part of a conspiracy organized by a cabal of Illyrian senior officers.[37] However, Cecropius may have brought down Gallienus, but failed in his own tilt at the top job. As the famous political cliché asserts: 'He who wields the knife never wears the crown.'[38]

In the previous year, as already noted, Odaenathus' talented widow Zenobia had inherited his position of unprecedented power in the Roman east and waited for an opportunity to break completely with Rome and establish herself as an independent monarch. Zenobia was a true political animal, and in a male-dominated world like the empire, she bided her time. That moment came while Claudius II (r. 268–270), who had replaced Gallienus, and his cavalry commander Aurelianus were preoccupied with the Goths in the mountains of northern Thracia: she easily secured Arabia and Iudaea during the spring of 270. Then as the Iuthungi overran northern Italy and threatened the capital itself,[39] she overran much of Aegyptus during the autumn of the same year;[40] Tenagino Probus, the *dux Aegypti*, falling on his sword.[41] Next up for the taking was Syria, probably the most civilized of the Roman provinces, and a large chunk of Asia Minor, including Galatia, the following spring. Here was a queen who was celebrated at once for her talents, her warlike disposition and her refined taste, but her ambition was to cause her utter ruin.

With the death of Claudius, in all probability the victim of a contagious disease (the plague?), in September 270 his brother Marcus Aurelius Claudius Quintillus became his successor when the soldiers in Aquileia proclaimed him emperor, but the soldiers in Sirmium (Sremska Mitrovica, Serbia) had other ideas. They revolted and proclaimed Aurelianus (r. 270–275) emperor in the same month; Quintillus committed suicide in the traditional Roman way,[42] and so terminated his short-lived stint as emperor. As the rather fitting epigrammatic statement from the eleventh-century Byzantine chronicler Georgios Kedrenos proclaims: 'Quintillus, brother of Claudius, reigned six days. For when he understood that Aurelianus was about to assume the rule, he took his own life, having cut the vein of his hand with the help of a certain physician, until, after he had lost consciousness, he died.'[43]

Some things are just inevitable. It was expected that Aurelianus would be Claudius' successor. He had been involved in the *coup d'état* that had cost Gallienus his life. He had a reputation as a man of action and had played a leading role in Claudius' Gothic wars. Quintillus' downfall was only a matter of time.

Though at first conciliatory – the empire was currently facing the simultaneous invasions of the Asding Vandals on the middle Danuvius and the Iuthungi into the Padus valley – later Aurelianus felt obliged to reassert Roman authority in the east. After assembling a substantial expeditionary force in Asia Minor, he quickly vanquished the formidable horse army of Zenobia in two battles in the spring of 272. Septimius Zabdas, Zenobia's Syrian general,[44] had been unable to hold Antioch, and so made a stand at Immae (near Reyhanı, Türkiye), about 42km east of Antioch.[45] Here the famous Palmyrene *cataphractarii* apparently drove Aurelianus' cavalry from the field; in fact it was a ruse.[46] The emperor then clinched the battle during their absence and the remnants of the Palmyrene forces made a second stand at Emesa (Homs, Syria), only to be defeated again.[47]

The Palmyrenes soon found themselves beleaguered in Palmyra. The city fell to Aurelianus, despite Zenobia's efforts to involve Persia (summer 272). Zenobia was captured as she attempted to cross the Euphrates,[48] but as *Parthicus Maximus* (for the Parthian name seems to have been applied to any foe shooting arrows), the emperor spared her along with the city.[49] It was said that Zenobia 'was inured to hardship…being indeed the noblest of all the women of the East… and the most beautiful.'[50]

The following year, after successfully defeating the Carpi along the Danuvius,[51] the emperor was incensed when Palmyra had revolted and had slaughtered the Roman garrison he had installed there. He then executed a well-conducted foray that surprised the defenders, recaptured Palmyra and mercilessly razed it to the ground.[52] Being situated at a convenient distance from the Mediterranean Sea and the Persian Gulf, Palmyra had great advantages for caravan traffic. No more. From that time the City of Palms sank into quiet oblivion to become an unimportant provincial town on the outskirts of the Roman Empire: it was later fortified to serve as a frontier outpost by Iustinianus (r. 527–565). Zenobia, however, lived to grace Aurelianus' triumphal procession in Rome (autumn 274),[53] and ended her life as a fashionable Roman hostess with a pension and a villa at Tibur.[54] She is said to have married a Roman senator.[55] 'Her descendants still remain among the nobles of Rome.'[56]

Battle for the West

Independently but simultaneously, Rome's western neighbours were also changing. In response to both the aggression of newer peoples to the east and the opportunities of what seemed limitless reserves of booty in the Roman provinces, the earlier Germanic tribes had fused into tribal confederations. By the early third century three major groupings had emerged. The Suevic tribes of central Germania, with whom Caesar had first made contact and had been unnerved by their ferocity, had formed into the Alamanni; those of the lower Rhenus group into the Franks; and the sea peoples at the mouths of the Virsurgis (Weser) and Albis (Elbe) rivers into the Saxones.[57] Though still of loose internal unity, the scale of military expedition these tribal confederations could now mount was of an entirely new order, beyond what the existing Roman frontier defences had been designed to deal with.

Whether built in stone, timber or earth and turf, whether consisting of a military way or a line of a river, these fixed frontier lines (*limites*) separated those outside from those within, those becoming romanized from their still barbarous neighbours. Trade and contact persisted, but it had been geographically channelled through supervised customs and crossing-points. These physical barriers, therefore, had not been intended as impregnable fortifications or fighting platforms. On the contrary, they had been designed for surveillance and active, forward defence against anticipated raids or low-level incursions. As any fighting was intended to take place in the immediate zone beyond Roman territory, concentrated attacks could easily penetrate these defences.

During the late third century Roman defensive architecture as a whole was to change. As the empire descended into internal chaos, Rome lost its military reputation and capacity to maintain its frontiers. The empire, once the aggressor, found itself increasingly on the defensive. New defences, both military and urban, were built on an altogether massive scale. Curtains became thicker and higher than had previously been the norm, and increases in scales were accompanied by architectural innovations. Solid, forward-projecting towers usually sited less than 30m apart studded the new fortification circuits, thus providing stable firing platforms for light artillery. Gateways, of course, were potential weak points. They too became more heavily defended, often with flanking towers or towers on either side of a single, narrow entranceway. Usually a broad ditch or ditches surrounded the whole work. In consequence, Valerianus' defences around Thessaloniki had enabled the city to hold out against the Goths until a relief army could reach it. Similarly, the defences with which Gallienus had enclosed Verona had allowed it to escape the ravages of the Alamanni.

Clearly one very important factor for this change in defensive architecture was the shift in the nature and location of warfare. Whereas warfare had previously been conducted on or beyond the frontiers of the empire, in the third century, as we have already discussed, the theatre of war shifted to being largely within the provinces. For instance the cities in Gaul, when rebuilding and castrametation took place after the barbarian invasions of the middle decades of the century, their urban space typically contracted. This reduction in size is illustrated by Augustodunum (Autun, France), whose Augustan walls enclosing 200 hectares were now supplemented by an inner circuit covering just 10 hectares. The larger circuit continued to stand, but it probably had little defensive value. While in the Principate cities had not required circuits, they now started to acquire powerful as opposed to merely prestigious urban fortifications and to change their appearance into the walled city typical of late antiquity.

With the affairs of the east firmly under his iron grip, with the treasures of the east in his purse like Augustus, in the summer of 274 Aurelianus turned his attention west, specifically to the sub-empire of Gaul, which had been pursuing its independent course with some success for well over a decade now. The present ruler, Tetricus, believed that he could rule over his own Gallic empire just as Postumus had done before. Together with his young son of the same name he had managed to hold out for almost three years, but now it was all up for him,[58] although Aurelianus did spare the lives of father and son: they both featured alongside Zenobia as the star attraction in Aurelianus' magnificent extravaganza,[59] even going so far as re-confirming their senatorial status and granting the elder Tetricus a civil administrative post in Italy.[60] A few years later, Tetricus became the first emperor (or pretender) since Septimius Severus to die of natural causes (other than the plague).

The *imperium Galliarum* had been brutal, featuring coup upon military coup. Still, the political aberration of parallel rulers holding sway in different parts of the empire, which had persisted since the capture of Valerianus, was at an end. By all accounts, the spring of 275 witnessed concord being restored to the vast empire. Aurelianus had rightly earned his self-adopted title RESTITUTOR ORBIS, 'restorer of the world',[61] and everything seemed to suggest that the burly soldier emperor was in complete control of things.

In spite of everything, conceivably the most telling sign that the winds of change had begun to blow was Aurelianus' momentous decision to construct a formidable fortified ring around Rome (spring 271), the city wall that is still associated with his name to this day.[62] Though Aurelianus, by stupendous military exertions, had physically reunited the empire under his iron rule, it was still an empire battered and traumatized. For the first time since Hannibal rode up to Porta Collina the city of Rome itself had become vulnerable, a situation graphically illustrated by Aurelianus' greatest monumental achievement.

Aurelianus' fellow Illyrian hardman and successor Probus (r. 276–282), who extolled his memory and continued his policies, cleared Gaul, recently pacified but inadequately defended, of the Germanic invaders who took the opportunity to cross the upper Rhenus in force when Aurelianus was assassinated. In a double offensive Probus quickly turned the tide and expelled the invaders. He then carried the war across the Rhenus in a punitive expedition deep into Germania. Although the resulting peace treaty allowed the Alamanni to retain the territory they had seized in the Rhenus-Danuvius angle, it did attempt to disarm the tribes in the immediate frontier zone, as well as establishing a Roman military presence beyond the Rhenus and securing large numbers of hostages and recruits. Probus also completed Rome's new fortifications.

Rise of the Equestrians

The third century was above all a world dominated by armies. The emperors, created by these armies, were almost exclusively men of comparatively humble origin promoted on merit rather than social standing. In this martial climate, the senatorial aristocracy in Rome lost its pride of place. It no longer retained sole access to political power, still less control of it, but now emperors no longer resided in or were made at Rome. It was more practical for emperors raised in the field surrounded by their own troops, as most were, to appoint men from among their own kind, men like Aurelianus himself. Following the general rule of the day, his accession had been a military *coup d'état*, set in a military camp and marked by ceremonial acclamations hailing the new emperor as *imperator*.

From the late second century onwards the centre of power in the empire had become increasingly peripatetic, following the emperor as he spent even more time in the frontier zones. 'Rome', as the conceptual capital of the empire, thus became divorced from the physical city of seven hills, or, as Herodian properly puts it, 'Rome is where the emperor is.'[63] The emperor's presence on campaign often necessitated the elevation of his provincial headquarters into *de facto* regional 'capitals': that is, imperial centres in the frontier zones, often associated with regional branches of the imperial mint. This process would ultimately culminate in the foundation of Constantinopolis as a 'New Rome' on the Bosporus.

Herodian, in the above quote, was of course referring to Septimius Severus (r. 193–211). It was this warrior emperor, having fought his way to the imperial throne, who decided against a senatorial command of his three new legions (I-III *Parthica*), which were raised in 195 and each commanded by a *praefectus legionis*. As the third century progressed, the number of senior army positions held by men of senatorial rank gradually declined, and were possibly disappearing entirely from the time of Valerianus and Gallienus onwards.[64] Certainly senatorial legionary *legati* disappeared under Gallienus and their place was taken by equestrian *praefecti*. Though it is clear that there was never a formal ban and some senators did continue,[65] far more opportunities now lay open to equestrians, especially those who campaigned under the emperor himself. Unusually for an authoritarian regime, which tends to centre their promotion pattern on political loyalties and personal ties rather than competence, promotion was henceforth by merit and the high commands opened up to a far wider pool of talent.[66]

The equestrian officers who now dominated the army were in many respects career soldiers. The career of one such professional soldier is documented in a fragmentary inscription from Mauretania: he advanced from the rank of *decurio* in *ala Parthorum* to that of *centurio* in *legio* III *Augusta*, thereafter he became *centurio et protector* in *legio* IIII *Flavia* and then *primi pilaris protector*, both posts in the field army, and *primi pilus* II *protector* in the general staff of two *Augusti*, obviously Valerianus and Gallienus.[67] Fully professional and permanently serving, such men owed their advancement purely to their military record and the favour of the emperor. We shall return to this subject shortly.

Perverse as it may seem, it was usually these men who plotted to murder an emperor and nominated a usurper from their group. Several of the most successful emperors of the second half of the century came from a virtual junta of professional officers from the Danubian provinces (hence the loose term *Illyrici*, 'Illyrian'), men of obscure origins but undoubted military ability who worked their way up through the crisis years to the highest commands and then doggedly fought invaders and each other. In the third century limits of emperorship were often imposed by nothing more subtle than brute opposition to it.

The soldier emperors, like theatre actors, strutted and fretted their hour on stage. In such unscripted dramas, they could disappear as quickly as they appeared. Still, several of the most successful soldier emperors of the second half of the century came from this small group of Illyrian senior officers, a number of whom proved very able as well as supplying all the great soldier emperors including Aurelianus, Diocletianus and Constantinus. As Aurelius Victor grudgingly conceded, 'Although they were deficient in culture, they had nevertheless been sufficiently schooled by the hardships of the countryside and of military service to be the best men for the state.'[68] As mentioned earlier, Diocletianus, who may according to one source have been of servile origin,[69] is rightly regarded as the most successful of these *Illyrici* because, among other things, he managed to retain power for two decades, an achievement due in part to his willingness to share it with three co-emperors from similar backgrounds to himself, the so-called tetrarchs.

Chapter Two

New World Order

'Omnia mutantur, nihil interit/*everything changes, nothing perishes.*'
Publius Ovidius Naso, *Metamorphoses* 15.165

The first point to grasp is that, as in all walks of life, nothing ever stays the same: the role and power of the emperor at the turn of the fourth century, when Diocletianus held sway, had changed considerably since the time of the first emperor Augustus, but the second point to grasp is that, again as in all walks of life, sometimes change comes slowly and sometimes dramatically. The emperorship, and therefore every facet of life affected by it, changed dramatically and irrevocably because of Diocletianus' extraordinary career.

A grizzled veteran of Rome's forever wars, Diocles was elevated at Nicomedia on 20 November 284, allegedly accusing the rival candidate, the *praefectus praetorio* Aper, of having murdered his own son-in-law, the emperor Numerianus (r. 283–284). Diocles pointed his sword at the sun, swore a terrible oath that he was completely unconnected with the death of Numerianus – there were rumours that he and Aper had been in cahoots – and promptly cut down the bound *praefectus praetorio* on the spot in full view of the assembled soldiers, quoting from Virgil as he did so.[1] Any misgivings or suspicions were decisively smothered in the communion of this bloody sacrifice. Here was a man who was in full control of his world, or if not was quite ready to do what was required to bring it back under control.

Having reached the very apex of the greasy pole, Diocles then took the name Diocletianus.[2] In the contest to be leader of the Roman world, Diocletianus was now the man to beat. The following July he defeated Numerianus' older brother and co-emperor Carinus in a frantically fought battle near the mouth of the Margus (Great Morava) River in Moesia. Carinus had the advantage of a larger army, but Diocletianus had more loyal troops. After a close-run affair, Carinus lay dead and Diocletianus found himself the unchallenged ruler of the empire.[3]

The System

After a half-century crammed with critical foreign and civil wars, a measure of stability was created by Diocletianus, conceivably the greatest of the Illyrian soldier emperors, who gradually developed a system of power-sharing which became known as the tetrarchy. The genius of Diocletianus managed to reduce five decades of making do to a system. In its evolved form there were two senior emperors, each known as *Augustus*, who ruled the eastern and western provinces respectively, assisted by a junior colleague or *Caesar*. The authority of the two *Augusti* was equal and all laws and edicts were issued in their common name, but practically the empire had been divided into two separate administrative parts. In Diocletianus' view – and who are we to argue – he had overcome the dangerously separatist tendencies of regional military commanders by multiplying the number of imperial rulers, and what is more the empire had grown too large and too complex to be governed by one man. This idea was nothing new.

Marcus Aurelius (r. 161–180) had elevated Lucius Verus (r. 161–169), his brother by adoption, as co-emperor to share his power and preside over the war with Parthia (sadly, he turned out to be avaricious and bungling). Some 100 years later, Valerianus (r. 253–260) had divided the provinces on a geographical basis between himself and his son Gallienus (r. 253–268), to whom he allotted the western half of the empire. Yet Diocletianus' tetrarchic system went further. For not only was it designed to provide enough commanders to deal with several crises simultaneously, but by nominating the *Caesares* as successors to their senior colleagues it served to prevent civil war by providing for the ambitions of all men with armies. Marriage between the *Caesares* and the daughters of the *Augusti* cemented the tetrarchy. In time the two *Caesares* would became the new *Augusti* and appoint two new *Caesares* of their own. The Senate played no role in either the selection of emperors or the governance of the empire. To all intents and purposes, Diocletianus abandoned all republican traditions and undertook the reorganization of the civil and military administration.

Instigated by Diocletianus, the tendency to separate military and civilian careers was complete under Constantinus (r. 306–337). The two roles – which reported directly and independently to the emperor and not to each other – had been spilt for reasons of security. In Diocletianus' mind it made sense to keep the man who held the purse strings and the man who commanded the soldiers separate. The provincial governors (*praesides*), now stripped of military authority, had greater administrative responsibilities. Henceforth each province had both a civil governor (*praeses*) and a military commander (*dux*). This separation of military authority would thus make it more difficult for military commanders to revolt, since they would need to secure the support of the now separate civil authority. Likewise, the removal of civilian responsibilities would ease the promotion of competent men within the army, since the lack of a classical education would now no longer matter. The way was now open for the rise of men such as Flavius Stilicho, a parvenu and a *demibarbarus*, of whom much will be heard later.[4]

To further limit the possibility of military insurrection, Diocletianus also reorganized the running of the empire. His solution was to create three praetorian prefectures: Gallia, Italia and Oriens (in 347 there was a fourth with the addition of Illyricum).[5] Each *praefectura praetorio* was under a *praefectus praetorio*, of whom the *praefectus praetorio per Italiae* and the *praefectus praetorio per Orientis* were the highest-ranking officials in the empire and were sometimes referred to as *praesens*, attending the emperor himself. A dozen *dioceses*, or administrative units, each governed by an equestrian vice-*praefectus* or *vicarius* (pl. *vicarii*), represented one of the three *praefecti praetoria*. The latter had lost their military role and became heads of the civil administration within their prefectures: issuing edicts, which had the same force as those of the emperor, and supervised the governors and judges of the provinces, proposed their names and paid their salaries. He also had the general supervision of finances, coinage, manufactures, roads, courier service and grain supply. Needless to say, in spite of various restrictions, the power of a *praefectus* was very extensive. His office, like that of the other *illustres*, was large and well organized, with assistants, recorders, clerks, shorthand writers and mounted messengers. The *praefecti* acted as deputies to the two *Caesares*, who in turn were subordinate to the two *Augusti*.

Each *diocese* was divided into *provinciae* – each under a governor – which had been reduced in size and greatly enlarged in number. So, for example, the Diocese of Britanniae comprised four provinces: Maxima Caesariensis and Britannia Secunda in the east, Britannia Prima in the west, and to the north of all these, Flavia Caesariensis.[6] The diocesan capital was at Londinium. Provincial governors held various ranks, with titles such as *praeses*, *proconsule*, *consularis* and *corrector*. The metropolis of Rome and, latterly, Constantinopolis too, were not under the jurisdiction of any *praefectus praetorio*, but each had a *praefectus urbi*. The purpose of these divisions and of the consequent increase in the number of these and of other officials was to prevent any officer from becoming powerful enough to start an insurgency and interfere with the regular succession to imperial power.

The system sounds neat and tidy, but several dysfunctional developments soon appeared. The chains of transmission of power, resources and information between the centre and the periphery grew longer, clumsier and more attenuated. Few things grow as easily as state bureaucracies. The bureaucracy of what we call the later Roman Empire was hugely enlarged: three (later four) *praefecti praetoria*, a dozen *vicarii*, about 100 or so provincial governors, all with an obligatory cloud of minor functionaries, plus of course the separate and partly parallel structure of the military establishment.[7] The consequences soon became evident: the perennial problems of patronage, bribery and other forms of corruption.

Even lower down the imperial food chain there was a common practice among army officers to feather their nests by drawing the rations (*annonae*) for dead and missing men under their command.[8] The list of names was there, but the men were not. The gaps encouraged commanders to engage in habitual forms of cooking the books. This pernicious habit resulted in units remaining in reality under strength, even though on paper they had a full complement of men.[9] Synesios of Kyrene, the Alexandrian Neo-Platonist and – having changed directions – the bishop of Ptolemais (r. 410–413), records that Cerialis, *dux Libyarum*, pocketed the pay of his men by granting them prolonged leave from their units. One whose hands were not clean in money matters, Cerialis also exploited his province by moving his men from city to city, blackmailing their civilian populations into shifting the predatory soldiery elsewhere.[10] Having sacrificed to the golden calf, the profiteering provincial *dux* was obviously a favourite target of the bishop's busy pen, for he points out in one of his letters to his brother: 'I have with me soldiers of the *Balagritae*. Before Cerialis became commander they used to be mounted archers, but when he took command their horses were sold and they became just archers.'[11]

Clearly this rapacious *dux* viewed the people of his province, civilian and soldier alike, purely as profitable fodder, his covetous claws reaching out from his corrupt court to clutch it.

In spite of everything, top-heavy (and crooked) or not, by 293 the system was up and running. Diocletianus and his co-emperor Maximianus (r. 286–305, 306–308, 310), another Illyrian military strongman, were the highest-ranking executives.[12] Diocletianus reigned in the east, with Galerius as his *Caesar*; Diocletianus took Thracia, Aegyptus, Syria and Asia Minor, and assigned to Galerius the Danuvian provinces of Illyricum, Greece and Crete. Maximianus controlled the west with Constantius Chlorus as *Caesar*; Maximianus governed Italy and Africa; Constantius ruled Gaul, Hispania and, after 296, Britannia. This division was only for administrative purposes; the empire in reality consisted of two parts, of which the two *Augusti* were the supreme rulers.

The main purpose of the institution of the *Caesares* was to provide for the succession, and it was a part of the plan that when one of the *Augusti* died or resigned, his place should be filled by one of the *Caesares*, who at the time of their appointment were adopted by the *Augusti*. The arrangements were sealed by dynastic marriages and the adoption of Diocletianus' family name Valerius, and widely advertised on coins and in official panegyric. Naturally, all four claimed the right to be revered as gods' representatives on earth, Diocletianus himself adding the adjective *Iovius* ('dedicated to Iuppiter') to his name and adopting Persian pomp at the peak of his prestige.

While the architect's dominating personality was everywhere felt, the system held together. Then without precedent, but probably with that natural human longing for the peace of retirement, Diocletianus abdicated his position (1 May 305).[13] He felt that he had been in power long enough and there were ample safeguards to keep his new form of government in place. As the Spanish Jesuit and baroque philosopher Baltasar Gracián (1601–58) would bluntly warn his readers: 'Do not hang around to be a setting sun. The sensible person's maxim: abandon things before they abandon you. Know how to turn an ending into a triumph.... Someone sharp retires a racehorse at the right time, not waiting until everyone laughs when it falls in mid-race.'[14]

The maxims of Gracián give sound advice on how to flourish and thrive in the cutthroat world filled with cunning, duplicity and power struggles, a milieu that had been all too familiar to Diocletianus. So he sensibly retired, appropriately, to his fortified palace at Spalatum (Split, Croatia): according to the pagan authors he spent his days happily tending his vegetable patch.[15] However, the restless old Maximianus, aptly nicknamed *Herculius*, only surrendered the purple to his subordinate, Constantius Chlorus, with extreme reluctance. He would make a comeback, not just once but twice.

On the retirement of Diocletianus and Maximianus, Galerius and Constantius succeeded as *Augusti*, while Severus and Maximinus Daia, the nephew of Galerius, succeeded them as *Caesares*. However, by the following year there were four *Augusti* – Galerius, Severus (promoted to *Augustus* by Galerius), Maximianus and Maxentius – with two *Caesares* – Constantinus and Maximinus Daia – one with a pretty definite claim to the purple and the other bound not to be left out in the cold.

It was in late 306 when Maximianus took the title of *Augustus* again and aided his son, Maxentius (r. 306–312) and his rebellion in Italy.[16] The following year Maxentius (who, like Maximianus, was not recognized as a legitimate *Augustus*) and his father, faced with the prospect of defending Rome against two Roman armies – one led by Severus (r. 306–307) and the other by Galerius (r. 306–311) – reorganized the Aurelianic defences.[17] This was rapidly achieved by doubling their height, blocking several lesser entrances and strengthening a number of the remaining gateways and, according to Lactantius, 'began the digging of a ditch but did not complete it'.[18] Having overcome the dual threat to Rome, father and son quickly fell out, and in April 307 Maximianus attempted to depose his son in an assembly of soldiers in Rome. To his surprise, the soldiers remained loyal to his son.[19]

Meantime the growing procession of emperors was reduced by one. Severus, having been sent against Maxentius, was deserted by his soldiers, captured and slain,[20] still leaving five emperors or claimants: Galerius, Maxentius, Maximianus, Maximinus Daia and Constantinus.

Maximianus, after he had quarrelled with his son, betook himself to Augusta Treverorum (Trier, Germany), the court of Constantinus, who had succeeded his father Constantius Chlorus the previous year and was subsequently accepted by Galerius into the tetrarchy, *but* only as *Caesar*. Maximianus now made an alliance with Constantinus by giving his daughter Fausta in marriage.[21] He was to prove an uncomfortable relative.

Diocletianus' personal intercession at a conference in Carnuntum (near Petronell-Carnuntum, Austria) in Pannonia Prima on 11 November 308 prompted his old colleague to renounce his imperial claim again.[22] It appears that Maximianus' ambitions had been curbed, but the opposite was true. He retired to the residence of Constantinus at Augusta Treverorum, but scheming was part of his nature. The much-abused mother-in-law of fiction is not to be compared with this choice father-in-law of history. In July 310 Maximianus saw his chance to return to the throne. Constantinus was embroiled in a war on the Rhenus against the Franks, and the father-in-law made use of his son-in-law's absence to have himself proclaimed emperor in his stead. However, the old man had reckoned without his young host, for Constantinus soon made it clear he was not to be trifled with. He immediately took action against his errant father-in-law, who had gone to ground in Arelate (Arles, France). Before he could mount an effective defence of the city, Constantinus was already at the gates. Maximianus scuttled out of Arelate to Massilia (Marseille, France), where he was captured by Constantinus and stripped of his title for the third and last time. Whatever went on between the two – and the sources are vague and one-sided at this point: apparently, grateful for his son-in-law's leniency, Maximianus then plotted to throttle him in his sleep – by the end of the month Maximianus was found dangling from the end of a rope in one of the rooms of the imperial palace.[23]

Maximianus' overreach is a reminder, if ever one was necessary, of the flaws in the strongman model of history. Decades in office can cause a leader to succumb to megalomania and paranoia. The elimination of checks and balances, the centralization of power and the promotion of a cult of personality make it more likely that a leader will make a disastrous mistake. For all these reasons, which are still with us all these centuries on, strongman rule is an inherently flawed and dangerous model of government.

Chapter Three

New Model Army

'An army is a population that obeys.'
Honoré de Balzac, *Maxims et pensées de Napoléon* (Paris, 1838),
maxim no. 133

The Roman geopolitical objective was no longer adventurers of trans-frontier conquest but cis-frontier defence. The sweeping plans of Traianus, Septimius Severus and Iulianus, all gifted soldiers, were out of date as the imperial pulse of four centuries had died away. Model military operations, impressive sweeps and punitive raids deep into the enemy's heartland were a thing of the distant past. The later Roman army was no longer deeply steeped in the all-volunteer force-based expeditionary template which, after all, was ill-suited to territorial defence. The Principate army was designed to fight short, high-intensity wars. Without full conscription – not an option chosen by the emperors of the Principate who preferred a battle-tested professional-based army – it was too small and ill-suited to fight protracted wars of defence.

There is one point that must be made clear here. The Mesopotamian adventure of Iulianus, the last offensive undertaken for its own sake in the manner of his forbears, serves as a suitable metaphor for the later Roman Empire: it promised much, achieved little and was eventually abandoned. In reality, during the third-century crisis history was teetering on the edge. No one knew which way it would go. Maybe the empire would fall, but it did not. It absorbed the hit and survived, though it was not to enjoy the experience of conquest as it had done in the previous centuries of its imperial existence. Still, while Rome may no longer have been a full-spectrum superpower, it retained geopolitical tools and a willingness to take risks.

This brings us to an important issue. In the popular imagination Rome is frequently depicted at its height: the rise and apotheosis of Iulius Caesar, the triumph of Octavianus/Augustus and the passions and intrigues of those would suceed him. We see Rome of might: the Rome that conquered the Punic and Greek worlds, the Rome that allied itself with Herod the Great and appointed Pontius Pilate as *praefectus* of Iudaea. We do not see the declining empire of Septimius Severus. Later Rome can seem a rather untidy, messy subject; popular histories tend to dismiss it in sweeping statements about mass migration, decline and decay.

Family Crisis

On 4 February 211, having spent much of his reign fighting rivals or waging war against the likes of the Parthians and the Caledonii, Septimius Severus passed away in Eboracum (York, England). His dying words to his sons Caracalla and Geta were (allegedly): 'Be united, enrich the soldiers, and scorn all other men.'[1] Yet simmering behind the scenes was a vicious rivalry between the brothers. By December of that year, Caracalla had his younger brother assassinated – he was clutching his mother apparently[2] – and Geta was subsequently erased from the historical record. Despite Caracalla's apparent disregard for his father's reported words, they proved remarkably suitable for the crisis that was to unfold throughout that century. Severus highlighted the importance of the army, the primary source of the emperor's power, and everything else was trivial. Caracalla (r. 211–217) enjoyed playing soldier and liked to be seen dressed as a *miles* and using the hand mill to grind his daily grain ration into flour just as the *milites* did.[3] Still, just play-acting did not prevent the brother-killer and paranoid emperor being stabbed to death by a trooper from his own imperial guard as he stood behind a bush to urinate on the way to fight another forever war on the eastern front.[4] As previously discussed, this crucial dependence on the military led to the advent of the soldier emperor.

During this period of anarchy when legitimate succession meant little, the resulting internal instability had led to losses and defeats on all frontiers of the empire and further encouraged internal rebellions. Each emperor was required to campaign with little respite, since he could rarely afford to entrust the command of an army to a potential rival. When the emperor was required to campaign in one theatre of operations there was a great danger that other parts of the empire, feeling that their own difficulties were being neglected, would create a rival. It was Gallienus who developed the weapon with which his Illyrian successors fought off the Sāsānian Persians and the Germanic tribes alike.

This is what a contemporary calls the 'elite army': a mobile force not committed to frontier defence but stationed in northern Italy, the centre of the emperor's remaining authority. Made up of detachments, *vexillationes*, drawn from frontier units in Britannia and on the Rhenus and Danuvius rivers, this force operated independently and was perhaps the forerunner of the fourth-century *comitatenses*, what modern scholars call field armies. In fact, these *vexillationes* were units in their own right,[5] having their own recruitment and being filled up several times to reach necessary battle strength. There is evidence that a special system of recruitment and of recruit training was established that was independent from the mother units of the *vexillationes*. In 235, the popular and soon-to-be emperor Maximinus Thrax was commander of the recruit corps in which numerous recruits were trained to fill up the *vexillationes* and *legiones* currently operating on the Rhenus under Severus Alexander. In this position, according to the Scriptores Historiae Augustae, Maximinus formed *legio* IIII (*Italica*?) entirely out of fresh recruits.[6]

The Numbers Game

The *legio* had remained the backbone of the Roman army through the first two and a half centuries of the Principate. Its command structure, tactical organization and fighting methods – based on the offensive use of the *pilum*, *scutum* and *gladius* – had remained substantially unchanged. In addition, the total complement of *legiones* had remained remarkably stable, rising from twenty-five at the end of Augustus' reign to thirty-three by the end of the Severan era. With a roughly equivalent number of auxiliaries, the total numbers may have been in the region of 330,000 men at the beginning of the third century.[7]

Overall the later Roman army grew in size. The polemical Christian apologist Lactantius strongly implies that under Diocletianus its numbers increased fourfold, though this statement, obviously made to vilify the pagan emperor, should not be taken at face value.[8] Lactantius, for all his stylish Latin prose, seems to enjoy taunting and sneering at pagans, getting back at them for persecuting his Christian brethren. Other sources with less of an axe to grind do imply an increase of at least 33 per cent in the number of those serving with the army. An antiquary of the mid-sixth century, Ioannes Lydos gives a total for some point in Diocletianus' reign of 435,266 men in total, including 45,562 men of the navy.[9] This figure may be accurate, and probably refers to the end of Diocletianus' reign, since Ioannes worked in the office of the *praefectus praetorio* and could have had access to official records. We can compare this with a figure given by Zosimos. He claims that on the eve of the battle of Pons Mulvius, Constantinus had 90,000 infantry and 8,000 cavalry, and Maxentius, his brother-in-law and chief rival in the west, 170,000 infantry and 18,000 cavalry.[10] As A.H.M. Jones postulates, these figures should be taken as total army sizes and not field army sizes, thus giving a total strength of the early fourth-century western Roman army of 286,000.[11] The total increased to about 450,000 men under Constantinus as sole emperor, which presumably represents the manpower of the entire empire. When we arrive at our period of study, according to the statistics of the *Notitia Dignitatum*, the troops of the combined empire, east and west, numbered between 500,000 and 600,000, almost twice the size of the forces that had defended the empire two centuries earlier. This estimate ties in with the evidence of the sixth-century historian Agathias, who remarks that 'previously' the Roman army had 645,000 men, again this large figure probably referring to the manpower of the entire empire.[12]

Even so, not all of these troops were of a high calibre. In addition, while growing in numbers the *legiones* shrank in individual size – the post-Diocletianic *legiones* numbered 1,100 men, give or take – and were housed in smaller forts. *Betthorus*-El-Lejjun built for *legio* IIII *Martia* in Jordan was only 11 acres (4.45ha),[13] that is, less than one-fifth the size of a Principate legionary base such as *Isca Augusta*-Caerleon (50 acres/20.23ha) or *Deva Victrix*-Chester (56 acres/22.66ha).

All Change

As the institutions and the physical appearance of the empire changed, so did its army. The professional career army established by Augustus was to change radically under Diocletianus and Constantinus. The old *legiones* and auxiliary *cohortes* were now border troops (*limitanei*), greatly reduced in numbers. Field armies (*comitatenses*) now existed, consisting of cavalry detachments (*vexillationes palatinae*) and elite infantry units (*legiones palatinae, auxilia palatina*). The *comitatenses* were not involved in local policing and administration and so were not tied to one particular region or frontier. They formed central reserves against external threats and, perhaps more importantly, against political rivals from within the empire.

Consequently, as the *lorica segmentata* was no longer in use after the later third century, Roman soldiery, be they horse or foot, now donned scale (*lorica squamata*) or mail (*lorica hamata*) body armour.[14] Those legionary staples, the *pilum*, *scutum* and *gladius*, vanished in the third century too. Large oval and round shields, slightly concave in form and edged with rawhide, and an impressive number and variety of spears (*lancae*), short lead-weighted darts (*mattiobarbuli*,[15] known generally as *plumbatae*)[16] and javelins (*verrutae*) of various sorts had been in use since the early third century. The equipment of all regular troops, *legiones* and *auxilia*, was now comparable and all these troops could be deployed and employed in the same way.

Although weapons and armour were important, even more important were the men who could use them. In this matter the later Roman army implemented profound changes. The infantry now adopted a more defensive role on the battlefield, which is reflected in a tactical adaptation away from the 'volley and charge' shock tactics of the *legio antique*[17] towards a less flexible and more compact deployment that often remained stationary to receive the enemy attack while discharging a more sustained barrage of short-range missiles.

Vegetius, a contemporary high-ranking civilian bureaucrat, recommends that *plumbatae* be attached behind shields in groups of five and thrown in the first charge, or defensively, when employed by the third row of reserves.[18] Further information on their use in battle comes from the *De rebus bellicis*, which was possibly written circa 368/369 either to Valentinianus or his brother Valens. The anonymous author of this military treatise states that the *plumbata [et] tribolata*, as he calls it, was designed to be hurled by hand among the enemy at short range:

> It either lodges in him and kills him or, if it misses and falls to the ground without causing a wound, it pierces the foot of anyone who treads on it, because no matter in what direction it is turned it inflicts a wound by means of a prong projecting from its side.[19]

In other words, the weapon would also act as a caltrop, *tribulus*. As for its construction, our unknown author inventor has this to say:

> It is made from a length of wood fashioned like an arrow. A piece of iron is fastened accurately on to it to give it the general appearance of a hunting spear, except that the sleeve of this iron is somewhat longer. A short way above the sleeve prongs are fixed with lead, and project like caltrops (*tribuli*). At the other end of this javelin (*iaculum*) feathers are attached so as to lend it speed, as much space being left above these feathers as can be clasped by the fingers of him who wields it.[20]

The soldier emperor Maurikios (r. 582–602), in his *Stratēgikón*, strongly recommends that heavily-armed infantrymen should be trained 'in throwing the short javelin and the lead-pointed dart a long distance'.[21] Experimental reconstructions of this short-range missile have demonstrated that the weapon probably had a range of about 30m, increased to around 70m if thrown underarm,[22] which does suggest that *plumbatae* were thrown before charging. All the same, despite the obvious changes in weaponry, deployment for battle remained the traditional battleline of the Principate: close-order infantry massed in the centre, cavalry on the flanks and archers usually firing overhead from the rear. The Romans certainly deployed in this manner at Argentorate and Adrianopolis.[23] There will be more to say about these two battles later; but meanwhile this suffices.

From the late second century onwards, a straight two-edged sword with a long blade, the *spatha*, replaced the *gladius* and was used for slashing and thrusting in infantry combat. Likewise, the ring-suspension system had been replaced by the scabbard runner, and the sword was now carried on a wide leather baldric worn over the right shoulder. This arrangement brought the *spatha* to rest on the left hip rather than the right, as was the state of affairs with the *gladius*. The legionary helmet changed to the Weisenau-Niedermörmter type in the later second and early third century and also to the Niederbieber type, which was introduced in the later second century and represented the peak in the development of Roman helmets. The Weisenau-Niedermörmter type gave the maximum protection, but allowed only a small range of movement to the body. Soldiers had to be in an upright position in closed formation, which meant throwing the *pilum* or javelins became difficult and the sword had to be used downwards and directly forward. The Niederbieber type gave maximal protection too: only eyes, mouth and nose were uncovered, but the neck protection made it much easier to move the body. However, both types restricted the forward view.

Legions and auxiliaries, infantry and cavalry, used these types of helmet in the east and west until a total change in the late third century when it was replaced by the more open-faced *Spangenhelm* and the *Kammhelm* of the Deir el-Medineh and Intercisa types. The new types were influenced by Sāsānian Persian and Sarmatian models but were Roman constructions. The *Spangenhelm* was conical, the helmet bowl being composed of several plates of iron or bronze attached to an iron framework riveted to a headband. Hinged cheek pieces and a nasal guard were often provided, while a mail curtain might cover the neck.

As helmet bowls were now composite in construction with separate cheek pieces and neck guards or nasal guards, their production was much less complicated and more convenient for mass production in big state-run workshops, *fabricae*, which developed towards the end of the third century under the tetrarchy.[24] This fitted the pressing requirements of the empire, the relevant officials now more interested in the quantity turned out than the decorative quality that went before. It should be noted that previously the production and supply of armour and weapons was mostly regional and relatively small-scale. This was because communication and transport facilities did not make centralized supply easy, since techniques of production allowed only limited economies of scale. At the turn of the fourth century this was all to change when a more planned and centralized equipping of field armies needed to be facilitated with the establishment of large regional *fabricae* staffed by conscripted civilian workers.

The Right Stuff

As military historians we should never forget the details – the straps, the belts, the boot laces – no matter the period under study. All that and more is just as important as the arms and armour. A thirteenth-century German proverb, too well known, declares that 'the wise tells us that a nail keeps a shoe, a shoe a horse, a horse a man, a man a castle, that can fight.'[25] Severus Alexander is reported to have said: 'One need not fear a soldier, if he is properly clothed, fully armed, has a stout pair of boots, a full belly, and something in his money belt.'[26]

Whether or not the emperor actually said this and, as previously discussed, it was his not-to-be-feared soldiers that did for him in the end, the details are certainly correct as regards keeping the soldier fit for purpose.

The last will and testament of Valerius Aion, a *centurio* of the *equites promoti* of *legio* II *Traiana* based in Aegyptus in 320, gives a partial list of the basic equipment that soldiers might have carried with them. Besides shield, spear and sword, a soldier was expected to have an *alabandicum* (probably a type of woollen knee-length tunic with long sleeves), two hatchets, a cloak (*chlamys*), two haircloth sacks, a haircloth *thallium*(?), two saddlebags (one leather, one haircloth), a belt, a bronze table and a bronze measuring cup.[27] To this personal load can be added a blanket.[28]

Logistics is always a critical determinant of success in large-scale military operations, and the later Roman world was no different in this regard. In other words, the nature of logistics is constant, but the character of logistics is ever-changing. Nonetheless, in any period of history it takes an enormous amount of gear and rations to sustain military operations. To ensure that the army operated at maximum efficiency and so enable his soldiers to do their job, Constantius II decreed that 'Soldiers must receive from the state storehouses rations for twenty days, so that they may convey these supplies along with them to provide for their personal needs on campaigns',[29] and observed that:

> Study of past practice has revealed that our soldiers, during the time of a campaign, are accustomed to receive hardtack (*buccellatum*)[30] and bread, ordinary wine (*vinum*) and also sour wine (*acetum*),[31] and meat, both pork and mutton, as follows: hardtack for two days out of three, bread on the third day; ordinary wine on one day, sour wine on the other; pork for one day out of three, mutton on the other two days.[32]

Vegetius adds that '[s]hortages of grain, *acetum*, *vinum*, and salt should be prevented at all times.'[33] Undoubtedly a good commander did all he could to keep his army fed and watered, and the later Roman campaign ration was certainly more nutritious than that offered to an eighteenth-century scarlet-red-coated soldier of the British army. Bread or flour (450g), water, and butter or cheese (85g) formed his staple diet,[34] and if he wanted to supplement this meagre fare with meat or beer or whatever, then it could cost him again. The beer, incidentally, was of the watered, barely-alcoholic variety, brewed largely to make water safe and potable.[35] A timeless idea, for the *acetum* mixed with water, known as *posca*, imbibed by Roman soldiers served the same purpose. Its acidity not only meant it took longer to spoil, but it also killed harmful bacteria such as virulent strains of Escherichia coli (E. coli), a bonus when the only available water came from a dubious source. As well as purifying water, wounds could be washed clean with it, and the elder Pliny gives a long list of applications including its use as an eye salve and for the treatment of diarrhoea.[36] Obviously inadequate hygiene made diarrhoea a frequent comrade on campaign as soldiers no doubt often ate with their hands but they were not always able to observe the nicety of washing their hands before and after every meal.

It should be noted that in the Roman army meat was part of the daily diet, and even in his day Polybios observed that in Italy acorns were used to feed a large number of swine, which were slaughtered not only for private consumption but also to feed the army.[37] Whereas cattle fulfilled all kinds of practical functions, sheep provided wool, goats gave their milk, geese and chickens likewise their eggs, the only animal that had no other use than for the spit or the pot was the pig. Pork was succulent, sumptuous meat. Only the pig lives to be eaten. Indeed, the Romans ate every bit of the pig, apart from the bones and the eyes: the ears, the cheek, the jaw, snout and tongue were all considered delicacies. Just as the elder Pliny once wrote: 'No other animal produces so much material for cooking.'[38] All things considered, it does appear that the Roman soldier was fed better than or at least as well as many civilians of a similar social background.

The cereal that was used to make both the bread and the hardtack of the later Roman army was also sometimes turned into porridge, *puls*, although the following personal observation from Ammianus Marcellinus would have us believe that it was not a particularly popular dish:

> And the emperor [Iulianus], who had no dainties awaiting him, after the manner of princes, but a scant portion of porridge (*pultis portio parabatur exigua*) under the low poles of a humble tent – a meal which would have been scorned even by one who served as a common soldier.[39]

If true, then Iulianus, at the time Constantius' *Caesar* in the great prefecture of Gallia, which comprised Britannia, Gaul and Hispania, had spurned the luxuries of a pampered prince, and out went delicacies such as pheasant and sows' udders

– some examples of recipes for the latter with asafoetida and mulled wine can be found in the cookery book of Apicius – and in were soldiers' rations of *puls*, which in its purest form consisted solely of water and cereals. The dish, despite Ammianus' reservations – he was a well-heeled senior officer after all – was common in the army as it was very easy to make and filling too.

It appears that Iulianus, an eccentric to say the least, preferred to live simply, much like a soldier on campaign. When *Augustus* and while based in Antioch preparing his campaign against Persia, he contrasts the simple bed of straw (στιβάς) on which he slept and the luxury of the Antiochenes.[40] This is what Marcus Aurelius, a fellow philosopher emperor on campaign, called living 'the Greek lifestyle – the pallet and the skins'.[41] The Athenian soldier-of-fortune Xenophon provides us with a suitable soldierly sketch: 'It was a little before sunset and they [Chares' mercenaries] found the enemy at the fortification either bathing, or cooking, or kneading bread, or making their beds of straw (τοὺς δὲ στιβάδας ποιουμένους).'[42]

As previously stated, Caracalla enjoyed living the simple life of a soldier, and in doing so happily used the hand mill to grind his daily grain ration into flour just like the *milites*: 'He ate the bread that was available; with his own hand he would grind his personal ration of grain, make it into barley bread (μᾶζάν), bake it in the ashes, and eat it.'[43]

Quern stones were to be found among the equipment necessary for a military expeditionary force simply because they were, as Xenophon explains in the *Kyroupaideia*, 'the least heavy amongst implements used for grinding grain'.[44] This meant that the troops could carry unground grain and thus reduce the risk of spoilage, as well as allowing them to take advantage of grain collected on the march. Having roasted and milled his grain, a soldier then took the resulting meal and kneaded it up with a little water in order to produce a simple form of unleavened bread or damper. Made for the occasion, the fresh dough was probably twisted around a stick and then baked in the hot ashes of a campfire. Another form of unleavened bread was 'quick bread', *panis speusticus* (from the Greek word σπευστικός),[45] which was rolled into wafer-thin sheets and then baked quickly, probably on hot stone. When in camp the soldiers were offered two sorts of bread, presumably freshly-baked: the normal standard, *panis militaris castrenis*, and one of higher quality, *panis militaris mundos*, perhaps reserved for the officers.[46]

As a point of interest, Xenophon, who dined a lot on barley bread during his soldiering days with the Ten Thousand, says: 'If a person eats barley, he always eats the kneaded bread (μᾶζάν) with water.'[47] In other words, the bread is apparently considered too dry to eat as it is, and must be moistened with a liquid of some sort before swallowing to avoid choking on it.

The army's practice of allowing its soldiers to prepare their own bread had many advantages. Needless to say, food always figures in soldiers' minds. Worn with travel and fighting, campaigning soldiers have a propensity to be lean, ragged men with pinched faces, and of course there is a need to ingest sufficient calories to sustain a body engaged in manual labour. However, the preparation and consumption of food also gives a texture to the gruelling days on campaign, providing those little mental inducements that enable men to blunt the discomforts of the moments by looking forward to something as mundane as preparing unleavened bread, and gives a focus for the little communities gathered round a campfire.

Regrettably for our campaigning soldier, bread spoils in a relatively short time, tending to go mouldy after four to five days in a warm climate, or a week or so in colder weather. On the other hand, *buccellata* can keep for a month or two on campaign if properly prepared, are lighter than unground grain and required no cooking. Made from flour, water and sometimes salt,[48] hardtack had fed armies and navies from the beginning of recorded history and was the butt of many jokes. 'Twice-cooked' was so that it was hard but light and easily preserved, although if insufficiently baked or packed too soon after baking it was prone to turning mouldy. Baking cereal grains into a dense biscuit made for easy transport also reduced the risk of spoilage, although maggot and weevil larvae infestation was a different story. More importantly, it was relatively inexpensive and had a very long shelf life when cooked and stored correctly. The secret to making hardtack last so long was to draw out every last trace of moisture and, once in storage, keeping it bone dry.

Such care, sadly, was not always so. Prokopios scornfully relates how one government official, the *praefectus praetorio* John the Kappadokian, 'a man of worthless character', decided to save the public treasury in the following manner:

The bread which soldiers are destined to eat in camp must of necessity be put twice into the oven, and cooked so carefully as to last for a very long period and not spoil in a short time, and loaves cooked in this way necessarily weigh less; and for this reason, such bread [viz. hardtack] is distributed, the soldiers generally received as their portion one-fourth more than the usual weight [viz. of grain]. John, therefore, calculating how he might reduce the amount of firewood used and have less to pay the bakers in wages, and also how he might not lose the weight of bread, brought the still uncooked dough to the baths of Achilles,[49] in the basement of which the fire is kept burning, and bade his men set it down there. And when it seemed to be cooked in some fashion or other, he threw it into bags, put it on ships, and sent it off. And when the fleet arrived at Methone, the loaves disintegrated and returned again to flour; not wholesome flour, however, but rotten and becoming mouldy and already giving out a sort of oppressive odour.[50]

This reflects the central role of the *praefectus praetorio* in Constantinopolis in the financing of war in this period; a natural corollary of that official's responsibility for the collection and distribution of imperial revenues. The army of course was the largest consumer not only of the empire's human resources, but also of imperial revenues.[51] Still, the sorry outcome of all this governmental penny-pinching was to be appalling. Prokopios, who witnessed this tragedy, says on consuming the rotten hardtack the soldiers quickly became sick – the summer heat did not help either – and no fewer than 500 of them died.

If the soldiers were not being killed off by high-level state corruption, on campaign they would often crush the hard, dry biscuit and mix the resulting crumbs with water or sour wine to create a form of bread potage. The teeth (or lack thereof) of our forefathers would have been ill-equipped for chewing through what was essentially a tile made of soft rock.[52]

In the ancient Mediterranean world barley and wheat were the two main grains, and had been since time immemorial.[53] Oats (L *avena*) were viewed as a weed and thus considered fit only for animals, but given how well they grew in cold climates, they were popular among Celtic and Germanic peoples,[54] while rye (L *secale*), the closest relative of wheat (L *triticum*), was a 'northern' grain. Barley (L *hordeum*), unlike wheat, is normally husked and cannot be freed from its cover-gumes by ordinary threshing and is therefore roasted or parched prior to use. Unfortunately, this process destroys the gluten content of the grain – this determines the baking qualities of flour – thereby making it unsuitable for leavened bread. Barley, therefore, was usually eaten in the form of an unleavened 'kneaded thing' (Gk. μᾶζα) rather than leavened bread, and was generally known as 'fodder for slaves',[55] and considered far less nourishing than wheaten bread (Gk. ἄρτος), so much so that by the fourth century BC the preference for wheat (viz. spelt)[56] and the bread made from it, in affluent circles at least, had ousted barley from its prominent position in the Mediterranean diet. Wheat therefore became the staple cereal in the Mediterranean basin, and barley the cheaper but lowly alternative. In the Bible we read 'a *choinix* of wheat for a *denarius*, and three *choinikes* of barley for a *denarius*',[57] the measure of wheat being sufficient for a man for one day at a price equivalent to a labourer's daily wage. Though barley was generally considered suitable only as animal feed or as punishment rations for soldiers,[58] when on campaign, hungry soldiers could not be too picky. Bottled up outside Dyrrhachium by the Pompeians, Caesar's soldiers ran out of supplies and the wheat was not yet ripe. As a result, Caesar offered them alternative comestibles:

> They remember at Alésia they had endured great privation, still greater at Avaricum, and had come off victors over very important nations. When barley (*hordeum*) was offered them they did not refuse it, or vegetables; whereas meat, of which there was a very large supply from Epeiros, they held in high favour.[59]

Caesar highlights here the hardships of the military life.

An army, said Napoléon, or so we are reliably informed, marches on its stomach. There are no truer words in the annals of military affairs than these. Karl Maria von Clausewitz, who had served in the Prussian and Russian armies during the Napoleonic Wars, in particular playing a significant role in the 1813–15 campaign against Napoléon (or *Befreiungskriege* as the period is known in German historiography), and became the director of the Prussian *Kriegsakademie* in Berlin after Napoléon's final fall, wrote: 'Ability to endure privation is one of the soldier's finest qualities; without it an army cannot be filled with genuine military spirit. But privation must be temporary.'[60]

Clausewitz saw war, unlike his far more influential contemporary Antoine-Henri Jomini, as the realm of physical exertion, chance and danger, characterized by constant friction, which made even the simplest things difficult. To overcome logistical problems (in plain terms, supplying an army on campaign), Roman armies might on occasion hope to support themselves by foraging, harvesting or through confiscating the food stores of the local population.[61] Likewise, wood, either for cooking fires (the army's ration was issued unprepared) or for construction, was usually available, as was water. Even so, foraging among the local populace for food could yield only sparse returns, especially in areas too poor to have any kind of surplus, or emptied of their population and of everything edible and moveable.

For that reason the preferred Roman strategy was to prepare adequate logistical support for expeditions rather than rely on living off enemy or allied territory: thus Constantius, recognizing that he would have to confront the usurper Iulianus, ensured his control of Africa and its vital food supplies well in advance of his intended move westwards.[62] To this end he had 3 million bushels (109,106,160kg) of grain stockpiled in Raetia.[63] Similarly, Iulianus in Gaul arranged for grain to be shipped from Britannia to the armies on the Rhenus.[64] Armies took a lot of feeding. Even Iulianus' relatively small army at Argentorate three years earlier – 10,000 foot soldiers and 3,000 horsemen – would have required an iron mountain of supplies consisting of a minimum

30 tons (27,215.54kg) of grain, 13 tons (11,793.40kg) of fodder, and 30,000 gallons (136,382.7 litres) of water per day.[65] Then there was the baggage train to consider too. The campaigning season for *comitatenses* in Gaul, as elsewhere, was dictated by the availability of necessary supplies: grain for the soldiers, and fodder for their extensive baggage train. Time, logistics and mobility were vital to a Roman army's ability to successfully prosecute a campaign.

Post-Imperial Darkness

Here is the thing: history matters. Since she is not in the habit of repeating herself, Kleiō, our marmoreal muse of history, is no quick guide to the future. On the other hand, she and the stone ledger in which she inscribes as she tracks events in serene retrospect can be instructive all the same. As we currently debate slavery (and statues) and dispute the role of empire, we have become accustomed to constant sparring over the past. That said, until the modern era the march of time was delineated as a foreordained sequence of empires, a leaning that was only slightly amended by Hegel's notion of history as a continuous progress, gradually developing, changing and turning back, involving good changes and bad, but in general moving forward in a single mighty flow of human development. Because of the inevitability of empires moving from affluence to decadence easily, and then declining and decaying, Edward Gibbon being the perfect avatar of this mindset, even today the habit of imagining history as a succession of hegemonies is hard to shake.

At the moment of writing, for instance, in our post-democratic age there is much talk of the waning of the hegemonic status of the United States of America and the assumption of the mantle of world power by China, a revisionist autocracy. The belief among certain academic pundits and political actors is that the Americans are wavering on the point of introducing their successors and stepping off the stage of world history to shut out the world and retreat into splendid isolation behind the great moats provided by the Atlantic and the Pacific. If true, here history is indeed trying to remember an old song it heard once: Washington's wish to draw back as it did in 1918. Whether this portentous view of a new world order turns out to be justified, only time – and future historians – will tell.

Real world experiences, historians have noted, can offer important lessons for those willing to learn from the harsh realities of war. As I write, it seems that there is one question that is relevant: is this the moment of which Hegel spoke, the moment when the owl of Athena (he calls her Minerva) takes flight? As we well know, Athena is not only the virgin goddess of war but of wisdom too. The owl, a little owl (*Athene noctua*) to be precise, is her symbol. 'The owl of Minerva,' Hegel continues, 'takes its flight only when the shades of night are gathering', passing over the battlefields of history, providing wisdom but always looking back. It looks back because it is always easy and comforting to look at what we have, what we know, rather than at the unknown.[66]

Zosimos was not the only writer in late antiquity to look back and by doing so express reservations about the quality of the later Roman soldiery. Indeed, some scholars have assembled a litany of such complaints that cumulatively would seem to point inexorably towards only one conclusion. Yet the moralizing character of these complaints should give pause for thought, while careful consideration of individual instances often reveals problems with taking them at face value. Consider, for example, the following passage from Ammianus Marcellinus' account of the start of Iulianus' reign:

> These moral blemishes were accompanied by shameful defects in military discipline. Instead of their traditional chants the troops practised effeminate music hall songs. The soldier's bed was no longer a stone, as of old, but a yielding down mattress. Their cups were heavier than their swords, since they now thought it beneath them to drink from earthenware, and they expected to be housed in marble, although it is recorded in ancient history that a Spartan soldier was severely punished for daring to appear under a roof at all during a campaign. Moreover, the troops of this period were brutal and greedy in their behaviour towards their own people, and weak and cowardly in the face of the enemy.[67]

This description has been taken by some as a general indictment of the Roman army of the mid-fourth century. However, with greater attention to its context, it becomes apparent that Ammianus' strictures relate very specifically to the elite palace guard in Constantinopolis, the *scholae palatinae*. It goes without saying that similar care needs to be taken with other such complaints.

'Elite army'

In the half-century from the murder by mutinous soldiers of Alexander Severus to the temporary establishment of peace under Diocletianus, there was an 'elite army' permanently in the field. It was not always exactly the same army consisting of exactly the same units. Successive emperors commanded armies composed of *vexillationes* from various different *legiones*, *cohortes* and *alae* of the provincial garrisons, the choice of troops depending of course upon the location of the almost perpetual wars and availability of manpower. Although nothing new, these *vexillationes*, as opposed to whole legions, now become the standard combat formation. A good example for the career of a soldier serving in one of these armies of the tetrarchs is Aurelius Caius. He started his military life as *eques legionis*, then served as *lanciarius* in a *legio* and was promoted to several posts of *optio*. He served in an impressive number of provinces and fought several times in campaigns, once in Carpia, four times in Sarmatia, twice in Gothia and in the lands beyond the Rhenus and upper Danuvius.[68]

The legion-based army of the Principate was designed primarily for delivering powerful offensive strikes at specific fixed targets. In the military context of the third century, however, cavalry were fast becoming increasingly important in the defence of the empire and the struggle against rebels and usurpers. In both cases, mobility was essential.

To move an army from the Rhenus to Rome took eight weeks; to the Euphrates six months. Roman armies could no longer choose the time and place for their battles and mount a campaign with the advantage of time and planning on their side. The days of overt imperialism were over, a time when tribal aggression in any particular sector could be anticipated and neutralized outside Roman territory. Now the encounters were all too often sprung upon the emperor by barbarians or by fellow Romans, and often both simultaneously.

A Horse Army?

The precise nature of Gallienus' emphasis on cavalry, if it did in fact occur, and its relationship to a supposed change from a Roman 'strategy' of preclusive defence to defence-in-depth is much debated in scholarly circles.

Sometime around 255, when he was defending the Rhenus frontier and there was a desperate need for rapid movement, Gallienus created a horse army.[69] He almost certainly employed it as part of the expeditionary force hastily gathered together for the campaign against the Alamanni some three years later. This 'elite army' was quite small, Gallienus having assembled *vexillationes* from the static garrisons on the Rhenus, Britannia, Pannonia and Noricum, and brought *legio* II *Parthica* and the *Cohortes praetoriae* from Rome. From about 260 the horse army was stationed at Mediolanum under its single commander Aureolus, whose task, according to Zosimos, was to prevent the anticipated invasion by Postumus across the Alps from Gaul.[70] The threat from the breakaway Gallic empire was probably not Gallienus' sole concern, however. The much more pressing reason for occupying Mediolanum in considerable strength, with emphasis on mobility, was the threat posed by the Alamanni immediately to the north in Raetia.

Though little is known about Gallienus' horse army, it is likely that he seconded his troopers, undoubtedly horsemen of proven ability and skill, from existing units. It is known, for instance, that he extracted men from the mounted troops stationed in Dalmatia, the *equites Dalmatae*. Besides the regular *alae* and *cohortes equitatae* of the provincial garrisons, there were tribal contingents available as well, such as the Mauri from the fringes of Mauritania and the Osrhoëni recruited by Alexander Severus in Upper Mesopotamia, which the Romans knew as Assyria, and brought to the Rhenus frontier by Maximinus Thrax.[71] If they had enlisted for the statutory twenty-five years, they would have had a few years left to serve when Gallienus was seeking experienced horsemen.[72]

These horsemen were certainly brigaded together, but it is not known how they fought together on the battlefield. They seem to have employed different, specialized fighting techniques, the Mauri, nimble horsemen of legendary ferocity, being armed with javelins and the Osrhoëni, as befitting eastern horse archers, with the composite recurve bow, a powerful weapon whereby the wooden core is backed by sinews and bellied with horn. Individual units may have been employed for different purposes, but the cavalry had only one commander, and this unity of command implies unity of operation. We are probably not too far off the mark if we visualize these horsemen operating in the classic way: strike, retreat, pester rather than charge, probe for weaknesses and circumvent a frontal assault in preference for disruptive sallies against flank and rear.

The unity of command also facilitated potential usurpations, since the commander of the horse army had an excellent power base at his immediate disposal. As the most influential and hence the most dangerous subject in the embattled empire, Aureolus could not resist the temptation to rebel against Gallienus, but he did not succeed to the throne; he merely cleared the path to it for Claudius II (generally known as Claudius Gothicus) before being murdered himself.

The question of the survival of the horse army itself and whether Gallienus is really the innovator behind the fourth-century *comitatenses* is undoubtedly unanswerable given the lack of contemporaneous evidence. The eleventh-century Byzantine chronicler, Georgios Kedrenos, states quite firmly that the emperor was the founder of the first cavalry army, emphasizing that 'the Roman army having previously been largely infantry'.[73] Not all research-minded scholars would agree with his judgement. R.S.O. Tomlin, for instance, points out the independent cavalry forces that won victories for Traianus and Septimius Severus.[74] The Byzantine writers had the benefit of hindsight and were accustomed to the use of cavalry armies from the time of Constantinus onwards, therefore it seems natural that any army composed purely of horsemen, which was moreover not part of any provincial garrison but answerable via its commander to the emperor alone, would seem to be a direct forerunner of the later cavalry armies.

Louis de Blois points out that the cavalry were no longer stationed at Mediolanum after about 285.[75] By this time the Gallic empire had been quashed and Gaul was again back in the fold of the empire, and de Blois takes the view that Gallienus' horse army was not unlike the *vexillationes* employed in other wars, brought together temporarily for a specific purpose and disbanded when that purpose had been fulfilled. This view is shared by Arther Ferrill, who thinks that Gallienus had no permanent policy in mind.[76]

Pat Southern and Karen Dixon, on the other hand, raise a minor point that possibly contradicts this thesis and, in part, goes some way to rehabilitate the opinions of older scholars. Numismatic evidence demonstrates that the title given to Gallienus' horse army was simply *equites*, rather than *ala* or the less permanent *vexillatio*. This use of the non-specific title possibly signifies that the horse army was not intended to function after the fashion of the provincial *alae*, but at the same time it was not intended to function as another *vexillatio*.[77] An inscription, dating to the year after Gallienus' murder, preserves this distinction, whatever it may mean, by listing *vexillationes adque equites* side by side.[78] Yet, given the current state of evidence, it is not possible to refute or endorse the theory that Gallienus' horse army was intended to form the first permanent horse army, the precursor of the *comitatenses*.

Gallienus originally developed the horse army not from any comprehensive plan but in answer to his need for mobility on the Rhenus, and then adapted the use of this mobile force to the multiple desperate situations facing him in the ensuing years. Legend claimed there had been thirty usurpers during his comparatively long reign, so the permanent survival of the horse army could have been almost accidental at first, then regularized by custom afterwards. Southern and Dixon suggest that its disappearance from Mediolanum is a possible indication that after 285 the horse army was permanently in the field with the ruling emperor, employed in a similar fashion to the later *comitatenses*.[79]

The *equites Dalmatae* were an elite cavalry force who played an important part in the murder of Gallienus,[80] and later fought successfully under Claudius II.[81] It may have been used by Claudius against the Alamanni, who invaded Italy through Raetia just after Gallienus' death. After initial defeats, Claudius appointed Aurelianus 'commander-in-chief of the cavalry',[82] vacated by Claudius himself, who was to serve with distinction fighting against the Goths. Aurelianus had already achieved high military rank under Gallienus, but helped organize the plot that destroyed him. By now Aurelianus' ruthless nature and relentless emphasis on military discipline had given rise to the nickname *manu ad ferrum*, 'Hand-on-Hilt'.[83] There is no proof that his command embraced Gallienus' horse army, but it is at least likely that the remnants of it formed the rump of Aurelianus' horse army. There were certainly Dalmatian and Mauritanian cavalry units in his horse army, just as there were in that of Gallienus. When Claudius despatched Aurelianus to tackle the Gothic incursion of 269, his sizeable command certainly included the Dalmatian cavalry, which he used to great effect.[84] The Dalmatian horsemen seem to have been recruited under Gallienus to strengthen his field army in 260. Likewise Aurelianus, as emperor, used not only the Dalmatians that had distinguished themselves under his leadership in the Gothic wars, but also Mauri horsemen to defeat the formidable Palmyrene *cataphractarii* at Immae in 272.[85] This light-but-lethal equestrian force had flexibility of employment in many climes and places.

Aurelianus reigned for five years and two months. However, for an emperor of the third century, danger was always lurking just around the corner. As that well-worn aphorism goes, you should keep your friends close and your enemies closer, but what happens if you try to adopt this commonsense approach and you discover that you have far too many foes to hug them all close? Worse still, what happens when you discover that your so-called friends turn out to be your actual enemies?

Late in 275 Aurelianus, who was marching eastward through Thracia to wage war on the Sāsānian Persians, was assassinated 'between Herakleia and Byzantium'[86] by a group of his senior officers who had allegedly been misled by the emperor's secretary into believing themselves marked for execution:[87] and so disappeared from history an emperor who had done everything to halt the decline of the empire. Like Gallienus before him, Aurelianus realized that the empire could only be protected if the static concepts of frontier defence were abandoned. With the deployment of field armies – Aurelianus clearly placed his confidence in the horse army developed by Gallienus – there was now a conscious shift towards strategic mobility. Perhaps the most telling sign that the winds of change had begun to blow was the emperor's decision to provide Rome with fortification walls. On the other hand, Diocletianus, uneasy with Gallienus' system – he thought with good cause that it favoured favouritism – dispersed or at least greatly reduced the horse army by sending its units to the frontiers to support the legions.

Later Articulation

The later Roman army was articulated into several troop types, a gradation that came to replace the traditional division into legionaries and auxiliaries. At the core of the empire were the household troops, the *scholae palatinae*, crack troops raised by Constantinus – having disbanded the *Cohortes praetoriae* after his victory at Pons Mulvius,[88] they now functioned as a new bodyguard under the direct command of the emperor – and the other palatine units closely attached to the person of the emperor.[89] By the end of the fourth century, the *Notitia Dignitatum* records seven eastern and five western *scholae*.[90]

Next came the *praesentalis* field army, that is 'in the presence' of the emperor, and after them the regional field armies and the frontier garrisons. The field armies were known as *comitatenses*, literally 'companions'. The units on the frontiers were called *limitanei*, 'borderers' or *riparienses*, 'river bank troops'. These soldiers defended fortified strongpoints along the *limes* and patrolled the borders. Units of *limitanei* could be called upon and transferred to the field armies – becoming *pseudocomitatenses*, 'false *comitatenses*' – thus indicating that they must still have been considered capable of playing some battlefield role, even if only as reserves. This surely makes untenable the highly speculative argument that the *limitanei* were part-time peasant soldiers, who could not be expected to be of much use in time of war. The deterioration in the quality of the *limitanei* was, therefore, a very slow process.[91]

It is an open question whether the formal division between the *limitanei* and the units of the field armies, the *comitatenses*, was created under Diocletianus or Constantinus.[92] We should suppose an evolutionary process gradually developing during the third century. In a papyrus, which reports the composition of the army Diocletianus took to Aegyptus in 295, is listed a body of cavalry, alongside ordinary cavalry, as *comites*.[93] An inscription from Troesmis records a soldier of *legio* XI *Claudia* who was a *lectus in sacro comitatu lanciarius*.[94] The *lanciarii* were veterans selected from the legions and formed into a specialized force within the legion. They occupied an honoured position in the field army (*comitatus*) of Constantinus. By association, therefore, the presence of a *lanciarius in sacro comitatu* in Diocletianus' entourage lends some support to the theory that he had a field army, albeit small by later standards. Another inscription records the building of a temple by the *praepositus* of a Dalmatian horse unit, which is also styled collectively *comitatus*.[95]

The Brigetio Tablet,[96] from the Roman fort of Brigetio on the Danuvius,[97] bearing the Latin text of an imperial rescript of 9 June 311 implies that legions (*legiones*) and cavalry detachments (*vexillationes*) have a superior status, while cavalry *alae* and infantry *cohortes*, not specifically mentioned, have a lesser standing. A law of 17 June 325, belonging to Constantinus, is more detailed, and distinguishes between three classes of troops: first the *comitatenses*, then the *ripenses* and finally the *alares et cohortales*.[98] The division between the field troops, *comitatenses*, and the frontier troops, *riparienses*, *alae* and *cohortes*, was now complete. H.M.D. Parker rightly states that 'the work of Constantinus in separating the field army permanently from the frontier army is not an innovation, but the culmination of a natural process in the history of the Roman Imperial army.'[99] In that case, it is not important whether it was Diocletianus or Constantinus who was responsible for the final break, for it was bound to happen sooner or later. The usefulness of maintaining a standing field army, additional to frontier troops, gradually established itself as the constant wars with other Roman armies and with the barbarians became endemic on all fronts.

Comitatenses

The origin of the *comitatenses* lay in successive emperors' desire for protection against internal rivals rather than in the threat of external enemies. Initially there was one *comitatus*, which served as the imperial entourage, then during the tetrarchy one for each emperor. By the fourth century regional field armies had appeared to supplement the *praesentalis* forces. Thus in 350 there were three field armies, one *comitatus* each in the east, in Illyricum, and in Gallia. By the time of the *Notitia Dignitatum* further *comitatenses* had appeared in Hispania, Africa, Britannia and western Illyricum, while a second eastern field army had been created in Thracia to supplement that of Illyricum; eastern Illyricum, contrary to established tradition, was currently part of the eastern empire.

The *comitatenses* were formed partly by withdrawing some detachments from the old legions based on the frontier and partly by raising new units. Units descended from the old legions could still be identified by their numerical name, such as *Quinta Macedonica* listed under the command of the *magister militum per Orientem*,[100] which surely ranks as the longest-lived of all *legiones* as it was still to be found in Iustinianus' army.[101] The tactical units of a field army were *legiones* or *auxilia*: the former varied between 1,000 and 1,200 strong, and the latter varied between 600 and 700 strong,[102] and picked cavalry *vexillationes* around 600 strong. However, none of the units would have been at full strength. Even at the best of times, sickness, death, desertion and recruitment difficulties would deplete the ranks, and these were not the best of times.

Many *auxilia* operated in pairs. A word of caution is needed here: although the *comitatenses* were the striking forces of the Roman army, east and west, mobility should not be exaggerated; the speed of a *comitatus* was never faster than that of a marching infantryman; that is, around 20km (12 miles) per day.[103]

Constantius Chlorus or Maximianus probably raised the first *auxilia*: the *Cornuti*, 'horned ones', who are apparently depicted on the middle frieze of the Arch of Constantine, and the *Brachiati*, 'armlet-wearers'.[104] At the battle of Argentoratum on the left bank of the Rhenus in August 357, where Iulianus overwhelmed the whole army of the Alamanni,[105] while the pre-battle *barritus* of the *auxilia* pair *Cornuti* and *Brachiati* was of Germanic origin,[106] their steady shield-to-shield discipline that finally decided the battle was as distinctly Roman as any tactics of Scipio or Caesar. There is good reason to suppose that the formidable *auxilia* were raised and recruited from the Franks and the Alamanni along the Rhenus, whether volunteers or prisoners-of-war, or the young men of the *laeti* settlements of submissive barbarians of Germanic origin forcibly resettled on *agri deserti* in Gaul by Diocletianus and Constantinus. It is significant that the *auxilia* were given titles that distinguished them from the old-style *auxiliary cohortes*, a distinction they preserved throughout their later history.

Many individual units were titled *seniores* or *iuniores* (e.g. *Ioviani seniores* and *Ioviani iuniores*). One possible answer to the *seniores–iuniores* designation is that it reflects their origins as detachments derived from the same parent unit. Another possibility is that it came about because of the division of Iulianus' Persian invasion army, along with the empire, between the fraternal emperors Valentinianus I and Valens at Naissus in Thracia in the summer of 364.[107] If this was the case, then it is quite likely that those units going west with Valentinianus were called *seniores*, while those staying with Valens were called *iuniores*. The following year Valentinianus placed all of the *auxilia* in a new elite category of troops called *palatini*.[108] They were now *auxilia palatina*. He conferred this status on only a few of his *legiones*. The *auxilia palatina* were the most honoured of all the troops and were to serve in what was known as a *praesentalis* army.

The *praesentalis* army always moved with the emperor. Thus the *auxilia* pair *Celtae* and *Petulantes* based in Gaul under Caesar Iulianus campaigned in Illyricum in 361 (he was now Augustus Iulianus)[109] and in Mesopotamia in 363.[110] For campaign purposes larger armies were created by reinforcing regional field armies with the *praesentales* armies. In 363 Iulianus combined the eastern and western *praesentales* armies with the eastern field army and some eastern border troops to create a force of 83,000,[111] which made it the largest campaigning army ever raised by the empire for a foreign war. By the time of the *Notitia Dignitatum*, units of *comitatenses* and *palatini* became mixed in some regional field armies, although the latter continued to have higher status.

One final but important point. Although from the third century cavalry began to play a larger role within the Roman army as a whole, both tactically and numerically infantry forces were always at its core. The *Notitia Dignitatum* suggests that the late fourth-century army as a whole had approximately twice as many infantry units as cavalry. Since horse units were smaller than foot units, this shows the numerical domination by infantry. Recorded numbers for expeditions also support the numerical dominance of infantry. Iulianus at Argentorate led approximately 10,000 foot soldiers and 3,000 horsemen,[112] and at the end of the fourth century infantry remained tactically the most important branch of the Roman army, with cavalry in a supporting role, securing flanks, disrupting enemy formations and exploiting successes. This dominance of infantry and its centrality to success in pitched battles would continue well into the sixth century,[113] with the military handbooks of the period devoting substantial content to the training and manoeuvring of infantry.[114]

Limitanei

The less prestigious *limitanei* contained a greater variety of units than a *comitatus* as a result of their long period of evolution, that is, descendants of the old legions and auxiliaries. These were *legiones* and *cohortes* for the infantry, and *alae* and *equites* for the cavalry, the later being elite mounted units distinct from the former. It is difficult to estimate unit sizes, although it does appear that the practice of using detachments led to the reduction in size of the old legions. For example, it is probable that *legio Secunda Britannica*, recorded in the *Notitia Dignitatum*, was derived from a detachment of *legio* II *Augusta*.[115]

Often based in forts and watchtowers, the *limitanei* carried out military duties ranging from internal security, the policing of roads, defence against banditry and raiding, as well as support for officials such as tax collectors and magistrates. Deployed in small detachments, they were used to oppose small-scale enemy threats, and could be added to a *comitatus* operating in the area. Units attached to a *comitatus* for a long period (as we have already noted) assumed the grade of *pseudocomitatenses*. This title is first recorded in 365, and was applied, it would seem, to the units evacuated from the regions ceded by Iovianus (r. 363–364) to the Sāsānian Persians, which were incorporated in the eastern *comitatus*.[116] Even so, the practice occurred earlier, for Iulianus' expedition against Persia in 363 included two border *legiones*, I and II *Armeniaca*. Formerly based at Bezabde in 360 when it was lost to the Persians,[117] following their transfer to the field army the two units were still under the command of the *magister militum per Orientem* as *legiones pseudocomitatenses* some three decades later.[118]

In a polemic passage, the pagan historian Zosimos contrasts the military policies of Diocletianus and Constantinus:

Through Diocletianus' wisdom all the frontier areas of the Roman Empire had been protected in the way described above with settlements and strongholds and towers, and all the soldiers were based here. The barbarians therefore could not break in, as forces with the ability to repulse invasions would encounter them everywhere. Constantinus put an end to this security by withdrawing most of the troops from the frontiers and stationing them in cities that did not need protection, thereby depriving of protection those who were suffering from the barbarians and afflicting peaceful cities with the plague of soldiers.[119]

Owing to Zosimos' abhorrence of Christianity in any shape or form, he took a considerable delight in pointing to defects in government and the army under the Christian emperors. The above statement – an oft-quoted point of reference for commentators to draw attention to these turbulent times – is neither true for Diocletianus nor for Constantinus. Constantinus withdrew troops from the frontiers primarily for the civil wars. After the tetrarchy was established in 293, each of the two *Augusti* and two *Caesares* had his own field army. At the same time the frontier garrisons were strengthened, the density of the line of fortifications along the frontiers increased, and garrisons were established at important points in the rear of the frontier zones. Indeed, the archaeological evidence shows Constantinus to have been energetic on this front too.[120]

In sum, the *limitanei* were professional and well-trained army units, and would remain so well into the sixth century, and these were garrisoned in the frontier zones. It was forbidden by law for the soldiers 'who get their arms and supplies from the state' to work in the fields or to herd animals even as late as 458.[121]

Command and Control

As previously mentioned, the evolution of a separate military hierarchy led to the development of a professional officer class. By the second half of the third century this allowed men of low social origin to progress further than they could under the Principate. Diocletianus, born, at best, son of a freedman, and Galerius, who had been a herdsman, benefited from these changes, eventually becoming emperors. Less spectacular was the contemporary career of Valerius Thiumpus, who served in *legio* XI *Claudia*, then as a *lanciarius* in the *comitatenses* before becoming a *protector* and going on to command *legio* II *Herculia*.[122] Other officers of extra-imperial origin also did well.

Let us take the career of Gaïnas. He was a trans-Danuvius Goth from the Black Sea region,[123] who started at the bottom, a *pedes*, advancing to *comes rei militaris* by 394, when he commanded the Goths at the Frigidus.[124] The following year he returned to the east and murdered Flavius Rufinus, the *praefectus praetorio per Orientis*.[125] In 399 he stood accused of collusion with the Gothic chieftain Tribigild,[126] but was made commander against him and his rebellion.[127] Gaïnas' ambitions knew no limits, for in the same year he immersed himself in the acrimonious world of politicking in Arcadius' court. Having left the cut and thrust of the army, Gaïnas initially thrived in the cloak-and-dagger milieu of court. The outcome was the dismissal and execution of the eunuch Eutropius, Rufinus' successor as chief advisor to Arcadius, who was also Stilicho's enemy. Having achieved the rank of *magister utriusque militiae*,[128] to protect his position Gaïnas then set about exiling his opponents in an attempt to mirror the success of Stilicho in the West.[129] Still really an outsider in the institutionalized and cannibalistic world of the court, a world less of great forces clashing than of the constant collision of satanically ambitious men, the following year Gaïnas overreached himself by attempting a *coup d'état* at Constantinopolis.[130] When it failed he attempted to evacuate his soldiers, but even then the Constantinopolitans, who were predisposed to feel bitter about Goths and Arian Christians, managed to trap and butcher some 7,000 armed Goths, apparently one-fifth of Gaïnas' force.[131] In response Gaïnas tried to cross into Asia Minor, but he was defeated by Fravitta, a pagan Goth,[132] who prevented his army crossing the Hellespont, for which he was rewarded with the consulship for 401.[133] For the first time Gaïnas saw war at its worst among defeated troops and with a handful of followers, he managed to reach the Danuvius, but was eventually killed by the Huns.[134] 'Uldes [viz. Uldin],[135] the Hun leader, sent his head to the emperor Arcadius for which he was rewarded, and thereupon made peace with the Romans', so writes Zosimos.[136]

Constantinus, having deprived the *praefecti praetoriae* of their military functions – they were now the supreme civil magistrates under the emperor – appointed two new commanders, the *magister peditum* (infantry) and the *magister equitum* (cavalry), to command his enlarged field armies. Constantinus, after all, was by profession a general, and so it seemed logical enough for him to appoint the two *magistri* to command under him. The principle of collegiality was a longstanding Roman tradition, and initially the two *magistri* probably had equal power and influence to provide a counterbalance to each other. Furthermore, a great benefit of this dual arrangement for Constantinus was that it effectively barred any one officer, except for the emperor himself, from commanding the entire *comitatus*.

However, in the course of the fourth century, the rigid separation of the infantry and the cavalry commands fell into abeyance: it seems there were at least two *magister equitum* under Valentinianus I.[137] Besides, in the various contingencies the armies had to face, it was found necessary for the *magistri*, and for various lesser commanders as well, to have at their disposal units of both infantry and cavalry. The result was that the titles *magister peditum* and *magister equitum* lost their literal meaning; although their continued official existence is attested by the *Notitia Dignitatum*, they seem, in practice, to have been replaced by other titles. Thus there are variants such as *magister equitum et peditum, magister utriusque militiae* or the simple *magister militum*.

The senior of these officers who were in the presence of the emperor added *praesentalis* to their titles. Eventually, in contrast to the decentralization in the east, in the west the *magister peditum praesentalis* gained the ascendancy over all other officers. Certainly Stilicho enjoyed unrivalled power while in this office, and was occasionally addressed as the *magister utriusque militiae* – Master of Both Services – the most senior of Roman commanders after the emperor. In the *Notitia Dignitatum*, the western *magister peditum praesentalis* had command of all the troops, whether they were cavalry or infantry, and of the *laeti* and of the navy as well, giving him supremacy over the whole western military establishment.[138]

Next in seniority came the *comes* (pl. *comites*), literally 'companion', though the title itself was not specifically military in nature, nor did the possession of it imply that the owner held a specific post. However, if he was appointed to a specific post his official title became *comes et…* ('count and…'). So smaller field forces that had been detached from a *comitatus* usually came under the command of a *comes rei militaris*. The *Notitia Dignitatum*, for instance, lists the *comes Britanniarum* as commanding six cavalry and three infantry units of the diocesan *comitatus*.[139] So some of these officers had a great deal of experience, like the Bithynian Sebastianus who had first served as a border troop officer, *dux Aegypti*, serving around 356 to 358.[140] He was then attached to the *comitatus* as a *comes rei militaris* in Mesopotamia in 363, serving as the joint commander of Iulianus' Tigris force,[141] before moving with Valentinianus I to fight in Gaul, still holding the rank of *comes*, in 368.[142] He was still in the west in 375, fighting in Pannonia,[143] and so beloved of his troops, Sebastianus was almost elevated on Valentinianus' death.[144] Three years later he lost his post in a court intrigue, but was soon summoned by the eastern emperor Valens to act as *magister peditum* in the Gothic war.[145] Two months later he was to be killed in action at Adrianopolis.[146]

A *dux* (pl. *duces*), literally 'leader', was a professional soldier who had charge of a substantial body of soldiers and a certain initiative of action and in previous practice would normally have been a senator. *Duces* could command frontier regions, such as the *dux ripae Mesopotamiae* at Doura Europos, the Roman outpost on the Euphrates, although similar officials in Africa and Europe were still under the authority of the provincial governor. Other *duces* led small field armies, such as Aurelius Augustianus who commanded a force including a pair of *vexillationes* from *legio* II *Parthica* and *legio* III *Augusta* in Macedonia under Gallienus.[147] Following the reforms of the tetrarchy, the *dux* was a senior officer with military duties covering a designated sector of one of the frontiers of the empire, namely with a command spread over several provinces. The *dux Raetiae*, for instance, had to defend the upper Danuvius, while the *dux Valeriae* defended the middle bend of the same river. As such he was primarily responsible for the protection of the sector of frontier assigned to him, and as part of this task he was to ensure that fortifications were built where necessary and the existing ones were kept in good repair.[148] The *dux* also had charge of recruiting locally and assigning men to units under his command.[149] Constantinus insisted that *duces* should inspect all recruits who had already been approved, and weed out those who were unsuitable.[150] They were responsible to the *magister militum* of their region. Until the reign of Valentinianus I, the *dux* was normally of equestrian rank. However, Valentinianus always favoured military men and accordingly elevated the *duces* to the senatorial order.[151]

Governors had had *protectores*, who seem to have been simply senior bodyguards, since earlier in the third century, but it was Gallienus who gave the title to middle-ranking equestrians such as praetorian tribunes or legionary prefects who were marked out for higher command; later on, centurions were also appointed. In the fourth century the *protectores* became highly prestigious and were coupled with the *domestici*,[152] and their commander was one of the most important military officers in the empire.[153] As a matter of fact, from the reign of Constantinus, if not Diocletianus, the *protectores et domestici* became a kind of staff college in which junior officers prepared for more senior commands and were organized into *scholae* under the command of the *comites domesticorum*.[154] These consisted of ten divisions of fifty men each, commanded by *decemprimi*, of the rank *clarissimus*, and these were under the supervision of a *primicerius*[155] of the grade *spectabilis*. In order to gain experience, some of them could be sent to join the staffs of various field commanders. Ammianus Marcellinus reports he was one of the ten *protectores et domestici* serving on the staff of Ursicinus, *magister equitum per Gallias*.[156] Precise duties for *protectores et domestici* are hard to define, although individuals could perform a range of diverse functions such as rounding up deserters, planning and supervising exports from the empire. It is known, for instance, that from the early third century, if not before, exports of weapons, armour, iron, horses, money, grain, salt and anything else that might benefit an enemy were forbidden by law, but how effective could such a ban be in the conditions of the later Roman Empire?

Army officers were known as tribunes (*tribuni*) or prefects (*praefecti*). As stated above, the *protectores et domestici* provided a pool of officers from which the emperors chose the tribunes and prefects of the army. *Protectores* so promoted were eligible, if they proved themselves, for appointment as *duces*: in practice, of course, the emperor could appoint whom he pleased to any level of command. Tribune (*tribunus*) was the commonest title, and was often used loosely for all commanding officers. It was strictly accurate for the officers of the *scholae* and the *vexillationes*, *auxilia* and the *legiones* of the *comitatenses* and *palatini*, and also of the *cohortes* of the *limitanei*. His deputy was known as a *vicarius*.[157] Tribunes could also be in charge of manufactories of arms, *fabricae*[158] and of the imperial stables.[159] Prefect (*praefectus*) was the correct title of commanders of *legiones* (or their detachments),[160] *vexillationes*, *alae*, *numeri* and fleets in the *limitanei*.[161]

Recruitment and Conscription

Under the Principate soldiering was seen as a relatively attractive and safe career, and this permitted the empire to replenish its forces through voluntary recruitment rather than conscription; although the *dilectus* or enforced levy was a legal possibility, it was rarely used as serving as a soldier was viewed as a career choice and a life. By contrast in the later empire, although some men joined the army voluntarily – one was the future emperor Marcianus[162] – Roman citizens became less willing to serve.[163] The empire had a professional army and a bureaucracy to match. It therefore had a division between soldiers and civilians, unlike across the frontiers where every able-bodied free man was a warrior: to bear arms, of course, was an aspect of being male and free, not a profession.

The bulk of Roman recruits, therefore, were undoubtedly conscripts of one type or another who had never been in combat before. Sons of soldiers and veterans were obliged to serve if physically fit,[164] although they were given the privilege of holding a slightly higher rank on enlistment than other recruits.[165] This rule already existed in 313 and was probably instituted by Diocletianus.[166] How rigorously this was enforced is unknown. Martin, whose father was a veteran, tried to avoid service, but eventually served in a *scholares alas* for a number of years during the reign of Constantius II; apparently his father willingly enrolled him to purge his son of Christianity.[167] The future saint soldiered in Gaul under Caesar Iulianus,[168] but left military service at some point prior to 361 when he became a disciple of Saint Hilarius, the *Malleus Arianorum* ('Hammer of the Arians').

There was certainly resistance to their enforced enrolment, and within six months of the above privilege being granted a further law threatening soldiers and veterans who were not complying with the regulations had to be passed. These threats were repeated by Gratianus, Valentinianus II and Theodosius in 380.[169] A few years earlier another decree by the same three emperors had attempted to close the excuse of physical weakness by stating that such soldiers' and veterans' sons who would not qualify for the field army could be enlisted into the frontier troops.[170] The main source of recruitment was, however, the regular conscription initiated under Diocletianus in which, as Ammianus Marcellinus records, a tax (*aurem tironicum*) was sometimes substituted instead of levying men from a province.[171] However, earlier he had noted the popularity of paying the *aurem tironicum* with dismay, alleging that it was a major contribution to Rome's military decline.[172] Valens regularized a recruit's value at 30 *solidi* (gold coins) plus a further 6 *solidi* for his equipment, remarking that prior to his regulations 'outrageous prices had been demanded' in lieu of recruits.[173]

Recruits were examined before enrolment. The age limits, according to a law of 326 dealing with sons of veterans, were 20 to 25 years.[174] Later laws place the lower limit at 18 years of age and extend the upper limit to 35 years for sons of veterans who had eluded their call-up hitherto.[175] Apart from physical fitness, the other specific requirement that we know of was height, where the old minimum of the Roman measurement of 5 Roman ft 10 in (5ft 7.5in/1.71m) was reduced in 367 to 5 Roman ft 7 in (5ft 4.66in/1.64m),[176] these lower physical standards being applied to recruits to the *limitanei* rather than the *comitatenses*.[177]

A conscripted army is much more liable to desertion than a voluntary one, and this was certainly the case with the later Roman army at every point in a soldier's career. Desertion began as soon as the conscripts were led away to join the army;[178] in the *Vita Pachomius* we read of how recruits marched off to join the field army were held under lock and key at night to prevent desertion.[179] Indeed, desertion appears in fact to have been common: the extent of the problem is perhaps revealed by Gratianus' and Theodosius' decision in 380 to pardon deserters who returned to the army.[180] Again the extent of the problem is perhaps shown by the increasing severity of the laws dealing with punishments for the harbouring of deserters. Gratianus, Valentinianus II and Theodosius provided in 379 for the burning alive of farm overseers (*actores*) who harboured deserters as well as the confiscation of the estate where the deserter was found.[181] All provincials were empowered to seize deserters,[182] and rewards for revealing their whereabouts were great, including a grant of freedom for any slave informants.[183]

Having reached their units, recruits were entered on the records and took the military oath, the *sacramentum*. Being entered on the records was a legal requirement:

> An individual starts to have the right to make a will from the time when he has been entered on the records; before that time he does not have the right. Accordingly, men who are not yet on the records, even though they are selected as recruits and travel at public expense, they are not yet soldiers (*nondum miles sunt*). To be classified as soldiers, they must be entered on the records.[184]

They were also tattooed to facilitate recognition in case they deserted. Another law, dated to 398, affirms that: '*Stigmata*, that is, a public mark, must be made on the arms of *fabricenses* [viz. workers in *fabricae*] in the manner of recruits, so that in this way they may be recognised if they hide.'[185]

Something previously done only to slaves, criminals and prisoners of war,[186] the physical act of tattooing recruits is first mentioned by Vegetius.[187] However, in the *Acta Maximiliani* there is not only reference made to the soldier's lead identity disc, *signaculum*, but to some form of mark that was applied to the hand too.

The *Acta Maximiliani* is the story of a Christian conscientious objector, Maximilianus (274–295), who was summoned before Cassius Dion,[188] the *pro consule* of Africa, in the forum of Theveste (Tébessa, Algeria) in Numidia. He stood accused of refusing a summons to serve in the army. According to the official record of the public examination of Maximilianus, he was accompanied to the court of the *pro consule* by his father, Fabius Victor. Maximilianus' testimony has been transmitted to us in the *Acta*:

> The *pro consule* Dion said: 'What is your name?' Maximilianus replied: 'But why do you wish to know my name? I cannot serve because I am a Christian.' The *pro consule* Dion said: 'Get him ready.' While he was being made ready, Maximilianus replied: 'I cannot serve, I cannot commit a sin. I am a Christian.' 'Let him be measured,' said the *pro consule* Dion. After he was measured, the *officium* said: 'He is five [Roman] foot, ten.'[189] Dion said to the *officium*: 'Let him be marked (*signetur*, viz. tattooed).' Still resisting, Maximilianus replied: 'I will not do it! I cannot serve!'[190]

Maximilianus' father was a Christian too and was currently employed as a *temonarius*,[191] an agent who collected the *temo*, or tax levied for outfitting of recruits. Though obviously closely associated with the army, Fabius Victor neither bore arms nor shed blood, though this does not preclude the notion that he may have been a veteran. If this was the case, then the son was legally obliged to follow his father into the army. The possibility that Fabius Victor had formerly served as a soldier might explain why he was obliged to present his son for enlistment. After all, a veteran's duty was to present his able-bodied son for military service.

Maximilianus, although pressed by the *pro consule* to submit himself to the official procedure leading to induction into the army, mulishly stood firm. At one point he angrily declared, as a Christian, '*non licet mihi plumbum collo portare*',[192] a vigorous rejection of wearing a *signaculum*, which was carried in a leather or cloth pouch attached to a leather cord and worn around the recruit's neck. Let them cut off his head ('*caput mihi praecide*'),[193] he cried defiantly; he was not going to serve in the *militia Caesaris*, and so it came to be. Maximilianus was condemned to death, leading to his immediate beheading by the sword (*decollatio*).

Death was not then the legal punishment for those who refused the draft;[194] the *pro consule* justified the death penalty as a warning to others.[195] It appears that the *pro consule* believed that this young man had the support of the local Christian community.[196] Fabius Victor himself refused the appeal of the *pro consule* to try to persuade his son to compromise.[197] After his execution his body was obtained from the authorities and taken to Carthage for burial beside the tomb of Cyprianus, the bishop of Carthage (r. 248–258) who had suffered martyrdom there thirty-seven years earlier.[198] Soon matters were in hand for Maximilianus' canonization for suffering martyrdom as a *miles Christi*.[199]

It is assumed that by Vegetius' time the wearing of a *signaculum*, as was the practice at least until the reign of Diocletianus, had been totally replaced by the tattoo.[200] A quote from Aëtius of Amida (Diyarbakir, Türkiye), a Greek physician and complier of a vast medical treatise, implies that by the turn of the sixth century, 'tattoos (στίγματα)...on the hands of soldiers' were a common practice.[201] Interestingly, Vegetius refers to the tattooed recruit as a *signatus*,[202] his deliberate choice of word referring back to the wearing of the *signaculum*.

According to a law of 372, those with better physique were enrolled in the *comitatenses* and the inferior specimens in the *limitanei*.[203] By a law of Constantinus a son of a cavalry veteran had the option of being enrolled in a cavalry unit if he provided a horse of his own, and if he brought with him two horses or a horse and a slave, started with the lowest non-commissioned grade, that of *circitor*.[204] From the year in which he took the oath and was posted to his unit a recruit obtained, provided he did not desert, exemption from his poll tax (*capitatio*). There is, however, abundant evidence to show that military service had become unpopular among the Romans. Valentinianus I, a notoriously fierce man noted for his helmet-hurling rage, introduced a series of draconian laws to deal with the perennial problem of self-mutilation, in which men resorted to cutting off their own fingers or thumbs in order to avoid enlistment.[205] By the following year, patience having been obviously lost, another law was introduced by which all those who had mutilated themselves to avoid the draft were to be burned to death.[206]

These draconian laws against self-mutilation were clearly unenforceable because in 381 Gratianus, Valentinianus II and Theodosius, no doubt helped by the shortage of manpower caused by the disaster at Adrianopolis, decided that supplying two mutilated recruits would be the equivalent of producing one whole-bodied recruit and that self-mutilators should be specially tattooed to mark out their shame.[207] Ammianus Marcellinus says that this practice of mutilation was alien to the warlike Gauls, but prevalent in Italy.[208] In extreme situations like Radagaisus' invasion of Italy slaves were offered their freedom and 2 *solidi* if they volunteered for military service.[209] Slaves were normally ineligible for service, as were various other disreputable kinds of workers, for example brothel-keepers, cooks and bread-makers.[210] The imperial plea for more recruits did not stop with just slaves. One more edict of Honorius and Arcadius, likewise issued in April 406, proclaimed that 'freeborn persons...who take up arms under the auspices of the country shall know that they will receive 10 *solidi* each from our imperial treasury when affairs have been adjusted.'[211] Citizens of the later empire were clearly not too willing to die for their emperors.

From Diocletianus onwards, the divisions in the Roman army had become tribal from being functional, and the non-citizen became the more privileged soldier as the old recruiting grounds diminished.[212] Indeed, once recruited many soldiers had long careers. In the mid-fourth century Flavius Memorius spent twenty-eight years in the *Ioviani* as well as fourteen years in other positions for a total of forty-two years of military service, retiring gracefully as *comes Mauretaniae Tingitanae*.[213] The new field army units of the early fourth century, the *scholae*, *auxilia palatina* and cavalry *vexillationes* (except those like the *equites promoti* derived from *legiones*) had a new rank series above *miles* or *eques*.

The next ranks, in ascending order, were *semissalis*, *biarchus*,[214] *circitor*[215] and *centenarius*.[216] Above *centenarius* were a series of junior officer ranks, *ducenarius*,[217] *senator*[218] and *primicerius*,[219] the highest-ranking junior officer. The largest collection of later Roman soldiers' funerary epitaphs comes from the military necropolis of Iulia Concordia (Concordia Sagittaria, Italy),[220] on the Via Annia constructed in 131 BC by the praetor Titus Annius Rufus. Among some thirty junior officers and *milites* are a *biarchus* of twenty years' service, a *centenarius* of 22, two *ducenarii* 20 and 23 respectively, and two *senatores* aged 40 and 60.[221] There is also a *campidoctor*, drill instructor, of the *Batavi seniores*, who died after thirty-five years' service at the age of 60.[222] The epitaphs date from the late fourth and early fifth centuries and belong to members of *auxilia palatina* units such as *Heruli*, *Batavi*, *Mattiaci* and *Brachiati*, and *legiones palatinae* units such as *Ioviani*.[223] During this period the city had a considerable military presence.

Chapter Four

Empire of the Cross

'Let us imagine that the king of France decided to convert to Protestantism, the religion of a small minority of his subjects. Fired with pious zeal against "idolatry", he would have destroyed or allowed to fall into ruin all the most venerated sanctuaries of the kingdom, the abbey at Saint-Denis, Reims cathedral, the crown of thorns, the Sainte-Chapelle. That still only gives a faint idea of the frenzy that took hold of the Roman emperors in the fourth century.'
Ferdinand Lot, quoted in Braudel 2001: 354–5

In the centre of the oval Forum of Constantinus stood a towering column of porphyry, made up of cylindrical blocks (seven still stand and go by the local appellation of *Çemberlitaş*, the Hooped Column) and standing 50m tall.[1] It was erected by the emperor to celebrate the dedication of his new city as the capital of the empire on 11 May 330. On the column's summit there was a large capital, presumably Corinthian, upon which stood a statue of Flavius Valerius Constantinus, which once surveyed the world he now ruled alone. The statue did not depict him as a humble Christian penitent, but sporting certain attributes of Sol Invictus: Constantinus Chlorus, his father, had followed the cult of Sol Invictus, the supreme sun god of the emperor Aurelianus.[2]

An unapologetic exercise in gross exaggeration, the emperor-god was portrayed holding a sceptre in his right hand and a bronze orb containing a fragment of the True Cross on which Jesus Christ was crucified in his left hand. He wore a crown adorned with sunrays, which incorporated small pieces of the nails driven through Christ's hands and feet. The orb, of course, signified that the entire world was obedient to him. This colossal portrait of the superhuman Constantinus illustrates the melding of traditional triumphal pagan imagery with Christian elements, demonstrating that the source of imperial authority is the ruler's relationship to the new Christian God. Grandeur and hype are always two sides of the same coin.

The colossus survived until 1106 when it was blown off its porphyry perch in a powerful storm, killing several passers-by in the process.[3] It was not restored but replaced by Manuel I Komnenos (r. 1143–80) with a gilded cross. Underneath this colossal elevation, according to later sixth-century writers, it was said that Constantinus had deposited a curious collection of Christian relics: the hatchet of Noah, the stone from which Moses made the water flow, the crosses of the two common criminals who were crucified with Jesus Christ at Golgotha, the alabaster jar of Mary Magdalene and the dozen baskets of the miraculous loaves.[4] Also deposited, according to the same writers, was the Palladium of Troy, the city's traditional talisman, a wooden cult image (Gk. ξόανον/xóanon) of Pallas Athena that had been brought to the future site of Rome by Aeneas the exiled Trojan.[5] Old and new religions, Roman polytheism and Christian monotheism, or so it was believed, were thus entombed together.[6]

On 7 March 321 Constantinus, in his capacity as Pontifex Maximus, issued a civil decree declaring DIES SOLIS – the day of the Sun ('Sunday') – as an official day of rest:

All judges and city people and the craftsmen shall rest upon the venerable day of the Sun (*venerbili die solis*). Country people, however, may freely attend to the cultivation of the fields, because it frequently happens that no other days are better adapted for planting the grain in furrows or the vines in trenches. So that the advantage given by heavenly providence may not be the occasion of a short time perish.[7]

As we look at Constantinus' Sunday law, the first of two,[8] there is no reference to the God of the Christians, to the Lord Jesus Christ, or to congregational gatherings. In other words, Constantinus' Sunday was not the 'Lord's Day'. It would be Eusebius (†339), bishop of Caesarea Palestinae and Constantinus' self-proclaimed panegyrist, who would add a Christian meaning to the Sunday laws. In around 330 the bishop wrote a commentary on Psalm 92, a Psalm for the Sabbath-day. In it he proposed that the seventh-day Sabbath of the Bible was changed to Sunday, being a more suitable day as it is *kyriōtera*, 'more linked with the Lord', that is to say, the day of the Resurrection.[9] In his biography of Constantinus Eusebius even tells a tall tale in which it was the emperor himself who made Sunday the Lord's Day:

He [Constantinus] ordained, too, that one day should be regarded as a special occasion for prayer: I mean that which is truly the first and chief day of all, the day of our Lord and Saviour.... Accordingly, he enjoined on all the subjects of the Roman empire to observe the Lord's Day, as a day of rest...[10]

If it were not a blatant lie, it might have passed as a poignant example of unfounded faith. Sure enough, Eusebius set a precedent that would be followed by future ecclesiastical historians who, in their turn, tried to attach a Christian spin to the 321 Sunday laws.[11]

Even if there is no Christian meaning in these laws, we should not be unmindful of the fact that Christianity did no more than take over, and adapt to its own use, a symbolism already endowed with a deeply rooted prestige and importance. In this way the Christian empire appropriated a surprising amount from pagan imperial ideology, a circumstance explicable by the manner in which Constantinus came to announce his public support for Christianity. Indeed, pagan and Christian expectations were the same: piety brought god-given rewards in terms of imperial security and stability.[12] Rome's imperial destiny received a Christian gloss: God had ordained the establishment of the Roman Empire in order to facilitate the spread of the Gospel.[13] A question might fairly be asked at this point. How did it all begin?

The list of contributing factors is long, but akin to the Apostles, we can limit them to just twelve.

First: in his violent rise to supremacy Constantinus took advantage of the disintegration of Diocletianus' power-sharing quartet of *Augusti* and *Caesares*. The tetrarchic system was a political experiment born in blood and bolted together to stem the crisis of the third century with all its squalid horror. It barely outlasted its architect. On the death of Constantius I Chlorus his father, who had named him as his successor,[14] Constantinus was promptly proclaimed *Augustus* by the soldiers at Eboracum on 25 July 306.[15] Constantinus was 33 years of age.

This was a direct challenge to the process diligently built by Diocletianus. This was a throwback to the bad old days when emperors were liable to be slain and replaced by their own senior officers in a moment of failure or lack of vigilance. Indeed, other usurpations and appointments meant that at one time there were no fewer than six *Augusti* holding sway in different parts of the empire instead of the intended two. The tetrarchy had become unworkable because the leading players, now reduced to four with the deaths of Maximianus (310) and Galerius (311) – Maxentius, Valerius Licinianus Licinius (in 308 appointed *Augustus* by Galerius), Maximinus Daia and of course Constantius himself – each looked after their own interests above everything else. They kept a weather eye on one another, for every *Augustus* wanted a corner to himself and, having his corner, wanted that of somebody else or feared that somebody else wanted his.

The surviving Latin panegyrics, like that strange collection of gossipy imperial biographies, the Scriptores Historiae Augustae, emphasize common loyalty, unity and concord: 'Four rulers of the world they were indeed, brave, wise, kind, generous, respectful to the Senate, friends of the People, moderate, revered, devoted, pious.'[16] Such heavy-handed propaganda betrays the fragility of the new arrangement: the rule of four had rested on nothing more solid than consent. So, despite all Diocletianus' directorial genius and grim determination, the weakness of collegiate rule was that it ignored all logic of heredity and ambitions, of strong armies to have their own strongman as emperor. It only initiated in short order a new phase of the very kind of civil war it had been designed to prevent.

Second: viewed from the fortress of Eboracum, ruling the whole empire was a destiny that seemed attainable to Constantinus. Besides, he had reached the conclusion that none of the other *Augusti* were up to the job and so realized it was up to him to right this wrong. On the other hand, despite being in a strong position in far-flung Britannia, to the rest of the empire he was just another rebel: Constantinus had to fight his path to real power from this remote northern cantonment. Supported by his army, and also by Erocus, *rex* of the Alamanni,[17] he sent his portrait to Galerius, *Augustus* of the east, claiming the title of *Augustus* of the west. The eastern emperor refused to grant this but, much against his will, allowed him to have the title of *Caesar*.[18] Constantinus did not insist on his right to the greater title but bided his time, and in the interim contented himself with the lesser, as his coins of this period show.

Although it was not apparent at the time, his ambition was to prove extremely destructive. As he boasted in a long address to the inhabitants of the province of Palestine in 324:

> I myself, then, was the instrument whose services He chose, and esteemed suited for the accomplishment of his will. Accordingly, beginning at the remote Britannic ocean, and the regions where, according to the law of nature, the sun sinks beneath the horizon, through the aid of divine power I banished and utterly removed every form of evil which prevailed, in the hope that the human race, enlightened through my instrumentality, might be recalled to a due observance of the holy laws of God, and at the same time our most blessed faith might prosper under the guidance of his almighty hand.[19]

Correspondingly, in a letter to Šāpūr II of Persia (r. 310–381), Constantinus proclaimed that, 'with God's power as ally', he had come to bring peace and prosperity to 'the whole world'.[20] He was, of course, referring to the series of civil wars that he fought to fulfil his ambition. For it would take him six years of conflict to consolidate his position in the west, and a further dozen years before he could claim to be the sole emperor; the first time the empire had seen this in four decades. So the Roman world, reorganized under four rulers by Diocletianus, was reassembled by Constantinus. However, the geographical logic of the two-centred empire was clear.

Third: on 28 October 312 – the sixth anniversary of Maxentius' seizure of power – Constantinus defeated Maxentius, his brother-in-law and chief rival in the west, just outside Rome at Pons Mulvius, the bridge that carried the Via Flaminia across the Tiber.[21] Maxentius' head was impaled on a spike and carried through Rome. By a twist of fate (or was it?), the same year that Constantinus had been elected *Augustus* by his father's soldiers, at Rome Maxentius was proclaimed *Augustus* by the *Cohortes praetoriae*.[22]

Identification of turning-points is an understandable temptation for historians, and acceptable provided that the qualifications for each particular date are not forgotten. Pons Mulvius may have initiated the empire's transformation from polytheism to Christianity, but 1,700 years after the battle scholars continue to hotly debate the life and impact of the Roman emperor who converted to Christianity and founded a new imperial capital. It was on the eve of this crucial encounter that Constantinus, who had been raised as a pagan polytheist, is reputed to have had a vision of the True Cross in the sky arising from the light of the sun, carrying the evocative message 'By this sign you will be the victor'. Predictably, Pons Mulvius would become one of the most famous (and controversial) battles in Roman history, but that is mainly because of Constantinus' apparent pronouncement afterwards that he owed his victory to the Almighty God of the Christians.[23]

There are three contemporary versions of this remarkable story. Some weeks prior to the battle, according to Eusebius the emperor saw a sign in the sky at midday, a cross of light superimposed on the sun. He took this as a sign of victory from the Christian God whose symbol was the cross, testifying that he saw the words, written in stars around said cross, *in hoc signo victor eris* in the Latin of the emperor. English translation: 'By this sign you will be the victor.' Alternatively, ἐν τούτῳ νίκα in the Greek of Eusebius. English translation: 'By this, conquer!' The night before the battle, or so the story continues, Christ appeared to him in a dream and instructed him to reproduce the heavenly symbol and use it for protection against the attacks of his enemies. He apparently did so with the desired results. For when the emperor awoke (the story continues), he commanded the construction of the *labarum* (Gk. λάβαρον); a military standard that Eusebius insists featured the CHI-RHO monogram (XP), the first two Greek letters of Christ's name superimposed (viz. Χριστός).[24] The story would be difficult to believe, Eusebius tells us, except that Constantinus himself swore oaths on the verity of the tale and, he adds, permitted his biographer to view the *labarum* with his own eyes.[25]

According to the more credible version, that offered by the man Constantinus had hired as tutor to his eldest son and heir, Caesar Crispus,[26] the Latin rhetor and Christian convert Lactantius, the night before the battle Constantinus dreamed that he was advised 'to mark the heavenly sign of God on the shields of his soldiers' as a divine talisman. On awaking the next morning he put his faith to the test when he ordered his men to paint the CHI-RHO monogram on their shields. 'Armed with this sign, the army took up its weapons',[27] and was victorious. There was no vision of the Cross.

This seems to be the sole display of any personal Christianity by Constantinus in Lactantius' pamphlet, composed in 315 or thereabouts, for although the author goes on to cite the decree by Constantinus and Licinius that lifted the persecutions on Christians and gave them freedom to worship, it seems to be an equating of all religions. It must also be taken into account that nowhere in *De mortibus persecutorum* does Lactantius actually claim that Constantinus was a Christian, or does he claim that the emperor was converted as a result of his dream, even though he may have been inclined to believe such a thing was plausible. Rather, his portrayal of Constantinus in his pamphlet is as a *sympathizer* of Christianity, but nevertheless an unwitting agent of the Christian God and recipient of his assistance: God elevated Constantinus in order to end the persecution of his worshippers and depose the persecutors, and offered divine protection in battle in return for token representation on the soldiers' shields.

Though *De mortibus persecutorum* was written relatively soon after Constantinus' victory over Maxentius, Lactantius is not the earliest source for this historical event. A panegyric delivered at Augustus Treverorum in August 313 describes extensively not only Pons Mulvius, but Constantinus' progress from the Alps to Rome.[28] In his narrative of the events leading up to the famous battle the anonymous panegyrist mentions neither dreams nor visions; rather, he refers vaguely to 'divine inspiration' in connection to the entire campaign.[29] More explicitly, the panegyrist states that Constantinus ventured over the Alps seeking 'no doubtful victory, but one divinely promised'.[30] This version is certainly similar to Eusebius' first version of events in his *Historia ecclesiastica*, which was written around 313, where he says Constantinus procured the assistance of 'God who is in heaven, and His Word, even Jesus Christ the Saviour of all' prior to invading the Italian peninsula.[31] Also, the panegyrist of 313, describing the aftermath of Pons Mulvius, says: 'After the Tiber had swallowed the impious, the same Tiber also snatched up their leader [Maxentius] himself in its whirlpool and devoured him.'[32] Again, this ties in nicely with Eusebius' biblical parallel when he likens the engulfing of Maxentius' fleeing pagan troops in the Tiber to the fate of the pharaoh's chariots at the crossing of the Red Sea.[33]

As we can gather from the short résumé above, the battle itself was obviously the subject of much invention – and uncertainty – as shown by the divergent sources. Either the bridge, which carried the Via Flaminia across the Tiber, was broken in his rear when Maxentius left Rome to confront Constantinus.[34] Once defeated, as Lactantius records: '[T]he army of Maxentius was seized with terror, and he himself fled in haste to the bridge which had been broken down; pressed by the mass of fugitives, he was hurled into the river.'[35]

Or, alternatively, Maxentius was trapped on his retreat by the narrowness of the stone bridge and drowned while trying to swim the river on his horse.[36] Or, alternatively, Maxentius was thrown from his horse and drowned while hastening to cross a bridge of boats a little above the slighted Pons Mulvius,[37] a scene flamboyantly depicted on the Arch of Constantine. This was the triumphal arch erected near the Colosseum in 315 to honour Constantinus' victory over his rival 'by the inspiration of the divinity' (INSTINCTV DIVINITATIS), a curious phrase deliberately chosen for its ambiguity so as to please both pagans and Christians. There is no mention of Christ or of the Cross. The well-made bridge of boats thus became the means of his destruction offered initially by Eusebius, and the version of events followed by Aurelius Victor and Zosimos too: Maxentius was defeated by his own *insidia*, trap, which had been set for Constantinus when *he* was meant to cross the Pons Mulvius.[38]

Certainly Constantinus' victory against overwhelming odds required special explanation: miracles in Christian sources,[39] Maxentius' insanity in the panegyrist.[40] Yet Eusebius, in his first version dealing with the battle, fails to mention a vision, dream or any similar miraculous experience at Pons Mulvius and, as stated above, is content to liken Constantinus' victory to the Israelites crossing the Red Sea. When Eusebius finally recorded Constantinus' vision of the Cross almost two decades after the event, he said that 'the victorious emperor himself long afterwards declared it to the writer of this history.'[41] If Constantinus only told Eusebius long afterwards, then why would Lactantius have written a version of the event two decades earlier?

Fourth: victorious in the west, Constantinus now came to a grudging agreement with the eastern *Augustus* and last remaining Diocletianus tetrarch, Licinius, who Iulianus would later dismiss as a 'miserable old man'.[42] In February 313 an *entente* only patchily *cordiale* was drawn up in Mediolanum, one of the empire's imperial centres, where Constantinus' half-sister Flavia Iulia Constantia was wed to Licinius as a sign of good faith.[43] Also on this occasion the two emperors formulated a common religious policy. One of the conditions of the Edict of Toleration, as it was called, meant that Christianity was given the status of a recognized religion.[44] As a result, being a Christian was no longer a punishable crime and Christians were now allowed to openly practise their religion. This edict was *not*, it should be noted, the work of Constantinus alone, *nor* did it make Christianity the sole and official religion of the state.[45] It was not until later in the century that paganism was overtly persecuted, and not until the end of the century, under Theodosius I, that it became the sole acceptable state faith. This is a subject to which we shall return at a later time. Suffice to say at this point that what Constantinus (and Licinius) did by this edict was to make Christianity an acceptable religion.

During Licinius' absence in Mediolanum, Maximinus Daia swung into action after being proclaimed *Augustus* by his soldiers: his uncle Galerius, sadly aware that with Constantinus, Maximinus and Maxentius all having claimed the title in the recent past it was in danger of becoming seriously devalued, had refused point-blank, offering him instead the meaningless lesser title *filius Augusti*, 'son of the *Augustus*', essentially just an alternative title for *Caesar*. Maximinus Daia left Syria and dashed westward, passed Bithynia, crossed the Bosporus and took Byzantium and Herakleia Propontis, cities belonging to Licinius. Taking a small force and summoning reinforcements to join him en route, Licinius headed eastward at a cracking pace. He planned to meet his enemy on the field of battle, even though his army numbered no more than 30,000 while Maximinus had some 70,000 troops. On 30 April 313 the decisive confrontation took place, not far from Adrianopolis in Thracia, and despite the odds and the fact that his army was footsore, Licinius emerged victorious. Maximinus fled the battlefield wrapped in a cloak taken from a slave. That summer, he met his end in Tarsus.[46]

Licinius and Constantinus were too ruthless and too obsessed with their own success for any hope of coexistence to last long. Licinius himself remained a staunch pagan, and relations between him and Constantinus gradually deteriorated until verbal conflicts became physical. First, they fell out over the appointment of a *Caesar* in Italy, and they fought two battles by which Constantinus gained control of the Illyrian and Balkan provinces (316–317). Next they carried on a cold war over religion, with Constantinus expanding support for Christianity and Licinius affirming his loyalty to paganism. The former removed the pagan gods from his coins and allowed the use of Christian motifs thereupon, while the latter emphasized his relationship with Iuppiter and kept Christian motifs off his coinage. It should be noted, however, that Constantinus' propaganda and his *post eventum* glorification in Christian sources at the expense of and through the demonization of Licinius grossly misrepresent the latter's complicated and evolving policies with regard to Christians, which never seem to have involved outright persecution.

When Constantinus, inadvertently or otherwise, pushed into Licinius' domain to punish some Sauromatae who were wreaking havoc in Thracia and Licinius allowed the martyrdom of some Christians, the cold war turned hot. In 323

Constantinus marched eastward, and in two tough but decisive battles (24 July at Adrianopolis and 18 September at Chrysopolis) the following year annihilated his last rival.[47] In the apocalyptic climate of victory, the official line was that Constantinus and Christianity had triumphed over Licinius and paganism.[48] That sealed Licinius' fate. Initially, yielding to the pleas of Constantia, Constantinus spared the life of his brother-in-law, but some months later he ordered his execution, thereby breaking his solemn oath.[49] Before too long Licinius Iunior,[50] too, fell victim to Constantinus' anger or suspicions.[51] This was Constantinus at his worst. Thereafter, Constantinus ruled as sole emperor until his death, the first time the empire had witnessed this in four decades.

Fifth: when first Nicomedia, Diocletianus' main residence, and thereafter Byzantium, as it was then known, was chosen as an eastern imperial centre (the term 'capital' is rather misleading); strangely enough, 'ancestral' Troy had been mulled over at one point.[52] This relocation led to the gradual but inevitable separation of west and east that followed: the iron law of ruling the later Roman Empire dictated that at least two people should be wearing purple – one in each half of the empire – if for no other reason than to hold potential usurpers in check. The three legitimate sons and heirs of Constantinus were to painfully rediscover the basic lesson of Diocletianus' political experiment.

Sixth: with the foundation of the *new Rome* on the site of the ancient city of Byzantium to shield the new weakness of the old Rome, however much he appreciated what he was doing, Constantinus was in actuality establishing one of the principal factors through which the empire would survive in at least some, albeit shrunken, form. By the following century, Roman history would be withdrawn from its native land and acclimatized to the Bosporus at the furthest extremity of the continent of Europe.

One thing is sure. A quick glance at a map would have demonstrated the matchless qualities of the site Constantinus chose in terms of the simultaneous supervision of the empire's two vital riverine frontiers, the two that consistently gave it the most headaches; that is to say, the Rhenus-Danuvius line in the north and the Euphrates in the east. What is more, the great advantage of Byzantium was its defensibility, being built on a hilly promontory and surrounded on three sides by water with fast-flowing currents, making it difficult to attack from the sea. On the landward side to the west a relatively short stretch of fortifications could be erected.

The building project began on 4 November 326 when Constantinus, on foot and with spear in hand, personally traced out the limits of his new city.[53] With typical lack of modesty, Constantinus named the city 'after his own name',[54] Constantinopolis (Gk. Κωνσταντινούπολις, L *Constantinopolis*), '*polis* of Constantinus'.[55] So it was to remain for more than a millenium.

When former farmer Cain built up the walls of his city, it was a defence mechanism against those who might now come seeking to kill him. Equally so for the empire: defence was to be the new keynote. It was during the tumultuous third century that Rome had to face predators simultaneously on three of its frontiers: to repeat, the existing city of Byzantium, where Europe and Asia met, looked both ways, towards the Rhenus and the Danuvius, and to the Euphrates. The focal role of Constantinopolis can hardly be exaggerated. In the west, the function of political hub had shifted from Rome, the ancient and traditional metropolis, to Mediolanum, a working imperial centre close to the northern frontiers and main communications routes, and then, as we shall discover, to the Adriatic city of Ravenna, all but an island protected on its landward side by marshes, a ceremonial refuge perilously distant from the armies and the centres of real power. The latter defines the dramatic change in status of the western emperor from active ruler to cloistered figurehead.

Seventh: although Constantinus embraced and supported Christianity, Constantinus' commitment was Augustinian: 'baptise me – but not now'.[56] In fact, he put off being baptized until his deathbed,[57] though even that had been in question:

Those who say that [Constantinus] was baptised in Nicomedia at the time of his death by Eusebius of Nicomedia, the Arian, lie. For they say that he delayed the baptism through the hope he would be baptised in the Jordan. For what, indeed, was impeding him, campaigning against Galerius in the east and advancing toward Persia again a second time, from going off and being baptised in the Jordan? Furthermore, slandering him as a bastard, too, is utter malice. For his lineage was royal even prior to Diocletianus. In fact, his father Constantius was son of the daughter of Claudius (II Gothicus) the sovereign, and from Helena, his first wife, he had Constantinus, as has been said.[58]

Then again, there was much about Constantinus that offended:

The royal garb he [Constantinus] adorned with gems, and his head, at all times, with a diadem…. He was a mocker rather than a flatterer. From this he was called after Trachala in the folktale, for ten years a most excellent man, for the following twelve a brigand, for the last, on account of his unrestrained prodigality, a ward irresponsible for his own actions.[59]

Merely wearing one's sleeves a tad too long, as the young Iulius Caesar had done, had been enough to raise eyebrows and suspicions in the Senate.[60] Constantinus favoured such a profusion of jewels and silks that even his hagiographer Eusebius was forced to defend him:

> He smiles at his vesture, embroidered with gold and flowers, and at the imperial purple and diadem itself, when he sees the multitude gaze in wonder, like children at a bugbear, or the splendid spectacle. Himself superior to such feelings, he clothes his soul with the knowledge of God, that vesture, the broidery of which is temperance, righteousness, piety, and all other virtues; a vesture such as truly becomes a sovereign.[61]

Dutifully putting on a show for the common herd he may have been, but Constantinus, like Alexander the Great, was not one for self-effacement.

There have always been multiple competing versions of Constantinus' legacy, falling along different axes as to his morality, his sincerity, his competence, and then there is the question of his faith. Constantinus was a pagan. Constantinus may have once been a pagan. Constantinus talked and acted like a pagan. Was Constantinus actually a Christian at all? It helps to divide his adult life into two periods. The era with Constantinus as the slightly wild-looking man of imperial destiny will remain untouched, a wonder of a troubled age. By the time he became the sole ruler of the Roman world there was a sense of some cranky outmoded usurper, striding the imperial corridors in his gem-encrusted diadem, feared for his ideas, his brutish mannerisms and his questionable actions.

Let us take just two conflicting views from more recent times to better illustrate the point. Jacob Burckhardt's Constantinus is a scheming secularist, a politician who manipulates all parties in a quest to secure his own power.[62] Alternatively, Otto Seeck's Constantinus is a straight war hero whose ambiguities were the product of his own naïve inconsistency.[63] Which of these two views is true is interesting as an academic debate, but both raise the same question concerning the nature of his conversion after he had witnessed a cross in the sky: was it a personal spiritual awakening, or a political ploy to prop up support for the empire in a period of crisis?

To a degree the matter of the rise of Christianity and Constantinus' conversion is an academic one since we will never know fully this controversial ruler's mind. Nor will we ever know why he cast in his lot with a sect that represented only a small percentage of the empire's population. One thing is certain, however. It was not uncommon to postpone baptism until late in life.[64] Already a century earlier, Tertullian's writings clearly indicated that baptism was viewed by many as an initiation rite, a magical sacrament that obliterated from a person all past sins, but not future ones.[65] In fact, it made future sins even more difficult to erase. This made for a very real dilemma for a Christian emperor who knew that in the coming years his official duties would include taking part in battle, ordering executions and overseeing justly a predominantly pagan population and governmental system. It has been proposed that it is this above all that led Constantinus to delay his own baptism for twenty-five years.[66] Needless to say, the catechumens, who were waiting for baptism, were not allowed to share in or even view the celebration of the sacrament, or to take full part in the worship of the Christian community.

This much then is known, but not much more. The faith of Constantinus does seem troublingly ambiguous. Two years before Pons Mulvius Constantinus had a prior celestial vision, that of Apollo in the guise of the supreme sun god, Sol Invictus, the Slayer of Darkness, and so sharing in the divine light and divine power of his protective deity. Constantinus was not raised a Christian. When he had to respond to yet another Frankish raid across the Rhenus, he sought guidance from his father's preferred god, the gifted Apollo. He had a vision of light. So, in 310, an anonymous panegyrist suggested that Constantinus saw Apollo in the guise of Sol Invictus who had become his divine protector.[67] It is argued, therefore, that it is this occurrence that was *later* reinterpreted by the emperor as a vision of Christ following a dream-vision on the night before Pons Mulvius. Coins of the emperor depicting him as the companion of Sol Invictus were minted as late as 323/324, some eight years after the battle.[68] Statuettes of Sol Invictus, carried by standard-bearers, appear in three places in frieze slabs on the Arch of Constantinus, which was constructed just three years after the battle. Likewise, there two carved medallions on each end of the monument. One depicts Apollo (or Sol Invictus), and the other Diana in honour of the Moon.

In actual fact it was Eusebius, a diehard Christian apologist, who *later* contended that the emperor had a vision and a dream in which he saw Christ, *not* Apollo,[69] as did Paul on the road to Damascus: 'About noon, O King [Herod Agrippa] as I was on the road, I saw a light from heaven, brighter than the sun, blazing around me and my companions.'[70]

A voice calls out and addresses Paul personally by his Hebrew name, Saul. When Paul asks to whom the voice belongs, the reply is, 'I am Jesus.' All those accompanying him are affected by the experience, either seeing the light but not hearing the voice, or vice versa.[71]

Whatever it was that happened to Constantinus before Pons Mulvius, there is no doubt that Constantinus showed conspicuous favour to the Christians, then a vocal if small sect among many others, and continued to wear the symbol of Christ against every hostile power he faced.

In the final analysis, although it is difficult to gauge the extent to which he had genuinely embraced Christianity beforehand, for Constantinus Christianity was not just a passing fancy. Perhaps we should bear in mind the words of

Raymond van Dam, who warns us that 'before Constantine was a Christian emperor, he was a typical emperor'.[72] In a similar vein Voltaire has this to say:

> I admit that the emperor Constantine was a scoundrel. I do not deny that he was a parricide who had smothered his wife [Fausta] in a bath, butchered his son [Crispus], murdered his father-in-law [Maximianus], his brother-in-law [Licinius], and his nephew [Licinius Iunior]. I agree that he was a man bloated with pride and plunged in pleasure. He was a detestable tyrant like his children, *transeat* [i.e. 'so be it']. But he had commonsense. One does not become an emperor, one does not subjugate all one's rivals, without having reasoned clearly.[73]

As his nephew Iulianus would mockingly say, Constantinus was a tyrant with the mind of a banker.[74] Constantinus may have been an inscrutable political operator, but one thing is certain: he was an opportunist all his life; there is no getting round this.

Constantinus' conversion is perhaps instructive here. Having had himself baptized on his deathbed, Constantinus left the Church triumphant but divided. Amusingly, when news of his death reached Rome, the Senate, in accordance with old tradition, declared Constantinus a god.

Eighth: with the foundation of 'The New Rome which is Constantinopolis',[75] Christianity was acknowledged as the root of the new empire. However, when Constantinus made his historic alliance between the state and the Christian church he had hoped, among other things, that this new, energetic and disciplined religion would rigidly buttress his unified empire with a unified faith. Constantinus, feeling sure of himself, accordingly demanded the adoption of a creed throughout the empire. He was to be frustrated and disappointed, so much so that he was soon deposing and banishing bishops who would not abide by *his* rulings. Thus when a number of churches in Africa objected to the patronage of the Roman state – the Donatists who challenged the legitimacy of those clergy who had not stood up to persecution in the third century – Constantinus played an active part in their suppression. He even re-imposed a brief persecution, with the support of the mainstream Church, in the regions where Donatists had support.

Whatever Constantinus' true motives regarding the creed, one thing is certain: he decided, after gaining complete control of the empire in 324, that the Christian religion should take the most favoured status in the empire. Moreover, his deathbed baptism left little doubt about how Constantinus wanted to be perceived: as the first Christian Roman emperor.

Ninth: by Constantinus' death the radical transformation of the Roman world was virtually complete. The most conspicuous signs of change to men of the time (depending on their viewpoint) were security of frontiers; a mighty, bejewelled emperor ruling the world from his new and splendid capital in the east, over-empowered and unaccountable; the new religion of Lord Jesus Christ, visible everywhere in the building of churches and the influential figures of bishops, zipping about their clerical affairs like court officials;[76] the thriving country estates and villas of the local magnates; the fat jobs in the civil service, the proliferating new titles, uniforms and dignities; a locust-like army of bureaucrats with their endless headcounts and tax reckonings; the tightening of servitude on the poor man and the peasant. The gap between Christianity's ruling principle, namely the life of the spirit and of the afterworld was superior to the here and now, and material life on earth is the great pitfall of Christendom.

Returning to those self-important bishops and their new public role, in particular in the service of Constantinus' son Constantius II (r. 337–361), Ammianus Marcellinus writes:

The plain and simple religion of the Christians was bedevilled by Constantius with old wives' fancies. Instead of trying to settle matters he raised complicated issues which led to much dissension, and as this spread more widely he fed it with verbal argument. Public transport hurried throngs of bishops hither and thither to attend what they call synods, and by his attempts to impose conformity Constantius only succeeded in hamstringing the post service.[77]

Now Ammianus, a pagan soldier, was relatively nonchalant about religious matters, capable of being equally scathing about pagans and Christians alike. Nevertheless, seeing the first stages of this development and watching the new imperial churches under construction, many pagan subjects of Constantinus himself must have shared Ammianus' exasperation.

Moreover, in many areas of the empire, the bishops and their officials had become the official civil service or local government on behalf of the Roman bureaucracy. In other words, the bishops and their officials collected taxes, distributed alms and supervised local legal cases and land disputes. Increasingly, they also assumed responsibilities for civic developments, such as the maintenance of roads and other public works.

The bishops had taken the place of the time-honoured Roman magistrates and emulated the proudest perfumed princes in their fine linen, glittering jewels and expensive garments, tiptoeing through puddles, as the cranky ascetic Eusebius Hieronymus Sophronius – thankfully known as Jerome (†420) – put it, who thought 'of them more like bridegrooms than as clergy'.[78] A more scathing observation of Jerome, Christian scholar and future saint comes when he outlines the history of the Church that he planned to write but never did:

> How and through whom, from the coming of the Saviour to our day – that is, from the apostles to the dregs of our time – the Church of Christ was born and matured, waxed in persecutions, was crowned with martyrdoms, and, after the coming of Christian emperors, became greater indeed in power and riches but meaner in virtues.[79]

Take, for instance, the aforementioned Synesios: as bishop of Ptolemais he helped to maintain law and order during the yearly incursion of neighbouring tribes.

Tenth: though Constantinus advocated Christianity for others without committing himself to baptism and the public participation in church life that his baptism would have allowed, nobody would question his sincerity and the Christians certainly began to regard him as one of them. The Roman Catholic Church came to have a much more positive view of the emperor, viewing him as a hero for ending the era of persecution and championing the faith. The Orthodox Church went even further, for he is hailed as the second founder of Christendom, and referred in their liturgy as the Equal-to-the-Apostles (Gk. *ισαπόστολος/isapóstolos*), or sometimes the Thirteenth Apostle.[80] Such veneration, be it Roman Catholic or Orthodox, is not by virtue of any religious authority, but because Constantinus was instrumental in the dissemination of Christ's teachings to the universal Roman Empire.[81] Whatever the reason or reasons may have been, and many ingenious hypotheses have been advanced, the prosaic fact remains that Constantinus took the step. Moreover, Christian or not, it does not matter, for this change, which affected the entire course of history, was not due to a dramatic attack of piety on the part of Constantinus but was driven by the direct material interests of the imperial system he represented. In other words, it was part of his consolidation of a strong dynastic regime militarily, economically, fiscally and administratively.

Clearly the two churches were not put off by the emperor's behaviour; even though he had his eldest (probably illegitimate) son poisoned and executed his wife. This is a strange family tale. In March 326 Flavius Iulius Crispus, Constantinus' son from his first liaison, with Minervina (Constantinus either took her as a concubine or married her in 303),[82] was executed for reasons that have never come to light. Indeed, the cause of Crispus' death was unknown to contemporaries, being deliberately concealed,[83] but was connected with that of Fausta shortly after. Jerome simply says 'Constantinus killed his wife Fausta.'[84] One fuller version of the story (based on the accounts of Zosimos and Zonaras) is that Fausta was having an illicit relationship with Crispus and when he broke it off she accused him of adultery in front of Constantinus, knowing full well that the emperor had recently issued a law criminalizing adultery.[85] A minor variant indicates that Fausta was adulterous with someone else.[86]

On the other hand, it is equally possible that Fausta insisted on her stepson's execution in order to clear the way for her own sons, unsurprisingly perhaps. Fausta herself would also meet a sticky end; she was apparently done away with in an overheated bathhouse.[87] Helena, Constantinus' mother, succeeded in convincing her son that Crispus had been falsely accused.[88] It is said that the emperor turned to pagan priests who were friends of his, such as the renowned Neo-Platonist philosopher Sopateros of Apameia, for the purification of his soul, but they refused, considering the act committed by Constantinus as unforgivable.[89] Still, suffering *damnatio memoriae* ('condemnation of one's memory'), the names of Crispus and Fausta were erased from inscriptions,[90] and references to their lives were eradicated from the literary record. Eusebius, for instance, edited out any praise of Crispus from later copies of *Historia ecclesiastica*, and his *De vita beatissimi Imperatoris Constantini* contains no mention of Fausta or Crispus at all.

Eleventh: if Constantinus can be blamed for anything, it is failure to make any clear arrangements for his succession. The purpose of any military autocracy is to ensure its self-preservation, power, prestige and continued existence, and that of the Constantini was no exception. From 306 to 324 Constantinus certainly fought remorselessly to reinstate dynastic succession, and as sole emperor he obviously had a plan initially. Seen as Constantinus' heir and successor, Crispus had been appointed, alongside his younger half-brother Constantinus and his first cousin Licinius Iunior, *Caesar* at Serdica (Sofia, Bulgaria) on 1 March 317,[91] but only Crispus assumed actual duties. Moreover, he had shared the consulship with his father on three occasions (*cos.* I 318, *cos.* II 321, *cos.* III 324). He was also entitled *princeps iuventutis*, 'prince of youth'. As *Caesar*, he was sent to administer the troublesome prefecture of Gallia, where in 320 he defeated the Franks,[92] and in 323 the Alamanni. The following year he successfully commanded the fleet for his father in the civil war against Licinius. In the subsequent battle of the Hellespont, Crispus' 200 ships managed to decisively defeat the enemy fleet, which was at least double in number.[93] In 326 he was to be sent back to Gaul, but was killed at Pola, Histria (Pula, Croatia), by 'cold poison'.[94] Before his life came to a sudden end – surely analogous to that found on the pages of a Greek tragedy – Constantinus had kept Crispus constantly by his side. Surviving sources are unanimous in declaring him a loving, trusting and protective father to his first son. Constantinus had even entrusted the boy's education to Lactantius, among the most influential Christian teachers of his day.

Twelfth: dysfunctional family issues aside, and his personal life could be gently called complicated, the sincerity of Constantinus was one that ran off in several opposite directions: he left, on his death, a rich heritage and too many male heirs.

In the power struggle that ensued, the three legitimate sons, with their too-similar names, were to emerge winners and divide the empire between them: Constantinus II, the prefectures of Britannia, Gallia and Hispania; Constans, those of Italy, Illyricum and Africa; Constantius II, Asia Minor, Syria and Aegyptus and so inheriting the war with Šāpūr II.[95] It is generally thought that the Great King was attempting to take advantage of what he perceived to be a period of confusion and, therefore, an opportunity after Constantinus' death to redress the balance that had tilted in Rome's favour as a result of a peace treaty agreed upon back in 298 or 299. Each of the brothers enjoyed the advantages of a separate *comitatus*, field army, and so it was with the empire and its forces were fragmented.

In biblical terms the land of Nod is not a state of unconsciousness but the place where Cain was condemned to live after he had killed his younger brother, Abel.[96] The story of fraternal frictions and jealousies is one of the founding myths that have informed the Abrahamic religions and our understanding of the hatred that can accompany brotherly love. We already made mention of the murder of Geta by his brother Caracalla, but Rome itself begins with Romulus fortifying the Palatine, 'the scene of his own upbringing'.[97] It was also rather bloody. The story is well known: Romulus and his twin brother Remus quarrelled over which hill on which to build, and the latter was brutally cut down as he contemptuously leaped over his brother's rising walls (a vivid and compelling image still), thus making an almost biblical scenario of the kind of brotherly love in which the winner takes all. Admittedly the stuff of fable demands that every hero must possess a flaw, but this was an unusual twist to the type of folklore that is quite frequent for founding heroes in many societies worldwide, who invariably start their outstanding careers as foundlings. Abandoned at birth and miraculously saved from a watery death (reminiscent of Moses), the divinely begotten twins (reminiscent of Castor and Pollux) were believed to have been suckled by a she-wolf and raised by the wife of a simple shepherd (reminiscent of Paris or Kyros). At any rate, such brotherly love-turned-hatred speaks of something impassioned and primal, a powerful force that is immune to reason, which certainly corresponds to the bloody kind of fraternal interaction when the three Constantini brothers came to fall out.

Their very names were suggestive of family solidarity, so much so that the three brothers were very alike and equally ambitious, but one of them would end up with the whole empire. Family loyalty was hardly the dominant motif of the dynasty of the Constantini: legitimacy was up for grabs, resulting in a complicated sequence of rivalries, treachery, fratricide, rebellions and civil wars. The blood of Constantinus would all run out in the twenty-six years following his death.

Sibling rivalry is often described in evolutionary terms as the competition for scarce resources, most notably in primates for parental attention. This competition tends to dissipate as they develop beyond maternal dependence, but one reason humans are frequently an exception to the rule is family inheritance. The competition to gain the lion's share of accumulated parental spoils – in Constantinus' case a vast, wealthy empire – can bring together acquisitive instincts in the most destructive manner.

Chapter Five

Rank Usurpers

'Sire, c'est là une question de date/*That, Sire, is a question of dates.*'
Talleyrand[1]

On 17 November 375 Valentinianus I unexpectedly dropped dead at Brigetio (Szőny, Hungary) in Pannonia Valeria.[2] Flavius Merobaudes, who was of Frankish origin and currently *magister peditum per Gallias* commanding the troops on the Rhenus frontier,[3] decided to consolidate his position of power by legal and extra-legal means. Within a few days of Valentinianus' death, he was instrumental in the elevation of the dead emperor's younger son to the title Valentinianus II. The move was carried out on the Danuvius frontier in the camp at Aquincum (Budapest, Hungary) in Pannonia Valeria,[4] where Valentinianus I had been campaigning against the Quadi and Sauromatae, and where he had been joined by his wife Iustina and younger son. Merobaudes feared that if the troops were not quickly presented with an emperor from the family of Valentinianus, they were going to acclaim the *comes rei militaris* Sebastianus, Merobaudes' rival,[5] for Gratianus, the oldest son who had been appointed *Augustus* by his father in 367,[6] was far away in Augusta Treverorum.

This shift represented a combination of allegiance to the family of Valentinianus and of self-interest on Merobaudes' part, for he obviously anticipated being able to exert considerable influence over the 5-year-old Valentinianus II and his mother Iustina in governing the slice of the west that would be allotted to them by the senior emperor Gratianus. This example of emperor-making was well calculated to avert usurpation by a commander who was not a member of the imperial family and the resultant possibility of civil war, and in this light it was accepted in good faith by Gratianus and by his uncle Valens (r. 364–378) in Constantinopolis. Still, the elevation by a general of a boy emperor who would be unable to command an army was a pattern that would be repeated more than once in the decades to come.[7] As a non-member of the imperial family, Merobaudes was to enjoy considerable influence under the rule of Gratianus, even holding the consulship twice (377, 383).[8] He finally came to grief at the hands of a usurping general who did not shrink from the role of emperor.[9] That man was Magnus Maximus.

Turning-Point

Flavius Eugenius, a Nicene Christian, was either a former teacher of grammar[10] or of rhetoric,[11] who had risen in his civil service career to become *magister scrinii*, chief secretary to the emperor, at Vienna (Vienne, France).[12] In that functionary role he had made the acquaintance of Flavius Arbogastes,[13] *magister militum in praesenti*, that is, commander of the armies in attendance on the emperor. More importantly, Arbogastes was currently *de facto* ruler of the west, a position he had in fact held since Theodosius left Mediolanum on 15 April 391. Arbogastes, more than likely a pagan,[14] was the nephew of another distinguished Frank, Flavius Richomeres, who held the position of *comes et magister utriusque militum*. It was Richomeres who had first introduced Eugenius to his nephew.[15]

Serving at the time as Gratianus' *comes domesticorum*, commander of the *protectores et domestici* and member of the emperor's *consistorium*, Richomeres had fought (and survived the ensuing carnage) on the plains outside the great walled city of Adrianopolis (Edirne, Türkiye) in Thracia. The previous year he had been sent east by Gratianus to help against the Goths.[16] Apparently, he had tried to persuade Valens to wait on Gratianus for support, planning to negotiate with the Goths gathered at Adrianopolis, but the opening of hostilities prevented him doing so.[17] Having survived that fateful day, Richomeres was to be suitably rewarded by Theodosius; elevated to the rank of *magister militum per Orientem*,[18] awarded the consulship of 384,[19] while another fat promotion, that to *comes et magister utriusque militum*, came his way in 388.[20] In the same year he was to play an important part in the campaign against the western usurper Magnus Maximus.[21] He was given the important task of commanding Theodosius' cavalry during the crucial campaign against that other western usurper Eugenius – whose army of course was commanded by his nephew Arbogastes – but passed away before the final showdown between Theodosius and Eugenius by the River Frigidus.[22] Fond of literature and rhetoric, Richomeres was a pagan who was intimate with the literary giants of the day, men such as Libanios, Symmachus and Augustine.

Black Day

The date was 9 August 378. This turned out to be a military debacle that drove home the lesson that Roman infantry were no longer masters of the battlefield after being swept away in an infantry battle by an army of Goths, Alani[23] and Huns,[24] the latter two peoples seen as far more recent and exotic arrivals on the fringes of Roman territory. In the chilling phrase of Theodosius' court orator Themistios, in one blistering hot August afternoon 'an entire army vanished like a shadow.'[25] A greater Cannae, the contemporary soldier Ammianus Marcellinus saw Adrianopolis as a turning-point, both in the history of the empire and in the history of warfare.[26] He was not alone in his gloomy judgement. Ambrose, bishop of Mediolanum (r. 374–397) and eventually, of course, a saint, called the battle 'the end of all humanity, the end of the world'.[27] 'The Roman legions were surrounded by the Goths, and slaughtered to the last man,' wrote Jerome one year after the catastrophe, a rhetorical exaggeration.[28] For his erstwhile friend, Rufinus of Aquileia, was writing a generation later, 'this battle was the beginning of evil for the empire, then and thereafter.'[29] The forces of *barbaricum* had destroyed a Roman army for the first time since the ignominious military mess resulting from the folly of Varus marching his three legions too far into the arboreal wilderness of Germania more than three and a half centuries previously. Though the *clades Variana* wiped out two decades of military effort east of the Rhenus and cost Rome Germania, this time it was not an isolated incident: it was a turning-point.[30] The Goths would sack Rome thirty-two years later.

There is an ancient Chinese proverb that says 'A general who is stupid and courageous is a calamity.'[31] In other words, soldiers will ask more of their general than a show of mere bravery. Certainly then, physical courage must be joined by intelligence. There is a quote from the reveries on the art of war of Maurice de Saxe (1696–1750) regarding the necessary qualities of generalship:

> Of all the accomplishments, therefore, that are required for the composition of this exalted character, courage is the first; without which I make no account of the others, because they will be rendered useless. The second is genius, which must be strong and fertile in expedients. The third is health.[32]

In an era of small armies and controllable wars, Maurice de Saxe was far from a pampered laced-and-brocaded nincompoop. He was a formidable fighting general of great physical and moral courage and ability,[33] who excelled at his deadly serious work. Young Maurice first went to war when he was just 12 years old and commanded his own regiment at age 17 in 1713. A bastard child of an infamously profligate monarch, it was to be a long journey, managing his military and social career – he had almost as many enemies at his back as on the battlefield[34] – getting mentioned in royal dispatches, and distinguishing himself in each post.[35] In 1743 his merits were rewarded by promotion to *maréchal de France*. Finally his career was crowned when, in 1747, Louis XV (r. 1715–74) revived the office of *maréchal général des camps et armées du roi*, previously held by the great Turenne (1611–75), who led the armies of Louis XIV between 1660 and 1675, to bestow the prestigious baton on de Saxe. He was never defeated in battle.

Much as in all walks of life, leadership at the top can be good, bad and indifferent. Perhaps the point to be made here is about the very human nature of generalship. Personally speaking, I am fascinated by the hard-to-define difference between the successful and unsuccessful general, the great captain and the failed commander of opinion. By all accounts the eastern emperor Valens has been lumped into the second category, although nobody said he was not brave.

The bare historical facts on record of this military debacle are the following. On the day he was killed Valens had marched, in oppressive heat and dust, some 13km from Adrianopolis to attack the Goths. With 5,000 horsemen and 10,000 infantry,[36] he outnumbered the 10,000 foot warriors which his scouts said were defending a wagon laager atop a low ridge,[37] a figure that his eastern army could handle without Gratianus' assistance, although his imminent arrival had been announced by messenger. All that said, however, Valens' contemporary Ammianus Marcellinus dismisses this as an underestimation without giving an alternative figure.[38] Generally speaking, recent research has revealed a lot of things about the culture and the nature of barbarians. First, there tended not to be very many of them.[39] More importantly, their tribal or ethnic or national identity tended to be very fluid, and in times of war or migration that identity became even more open to fluctuation. This fluid identity, and the relatively small numbers identified with a particular identity at a particular time, has consequences. It has been shown that when on the move, our late antique barbarians behaved very much like mobile armies and it is now very hard to maintain the traditional view that along with every barbarian warrior there were four non-combatants in tow.[40]

All these observations have been developed with special reference to the Goths, despite the fact that a number of our Roman sources actually do describe late fourth- and early fifth-century Gothic movements as the migration of a large people, elderly, women and children included.[41] Think of it this way: Valens may well have underestimated his opponent's strength and so was tempted to engage the Goths then and there, but defeat was not on Valens' mind on 9 August 378. The emperor had already defeated them on the Danuvius nine years earlier, so defeat at the hands of the Goths was unthinkable and not even considered. Valens was confident – perhaps too confident – of victory. Then, as now, defeats often stemmed from overconfidence.

If these numbers seem small, it is important to remember that by this period there were few if any larger armies. Still, a Gothic wagon laager was not some hastily arranged affair. Ammianus Marcellinus, our main authority here, says the laager at Adrianopolis was formed so perfectly as though 'turned by a lathe'.[42] Claudius Claudianus, a contemporary poet, describes one in which the Goths dug a 'double moat, planted stakes two deep…and set the wagons rigged with ox-hide all round like a wall'.[43] A touch of poetic licence perhaps, but a wagon laager was no flimsy affair.

With the Gothic horsemen currently absent foraging, time was pressing for Fritigern, the chief Gothic leader that day. Cleverly playing for time, he fired the summer-dry grass on the plain below and despatched an embassy to Valens. This was briskly dismissed and, as it was departing, a skirmish broke out between the Gothic front-line sentinels and the Roman archers. The emperor now attacked and at the outset had the battle well in hand. With the infantry holding the centre, the cavalry on his right wing advanced towards the laager and engaged. We should not assume that the Goths fought from behind their laager, for it was their usual practice to engage their enemy in the open and fall back on their laager only when things were not going to plan. Besides, their preferred tactic was to charge into hand-to-hand combat brandishing spear, sword and shield. A massive Roman charge almost reached the Gothic laager, but was thrown back. A hand-to-hand fight followed as missiles rained down on both sides.

The Romans had been exposed to hot sun for several hours, and by now were thoroughly exhausted. Unexpectedly, some 5,000 Gothic horsemen returned and 'dashed out as a thunderbolt does near high mountains, and threw into confusion all those whom they could find in the way of their swift onslaught, and quickly slew them'.[44] Attacked boldly on the right wing, Valens' weary army was checked and the right wing horsemen were quickly sent off in a disorderly rout, leaving the still-engaged infantry trapped between the Gothic horse and foot. The latter made a charge and speedily overwhelmed the horsemen who had just managed to deploy on the Roman left wing. Outflanked and hemmed in on all sides, the infantry eventually broke, scattering like rabbits before the Gothic onslaught. Valens tried to stem the tide and shore up the rear with two units of *auxilia palatina*, but to no avail. All was lost, and so too was the emperor.[45]

A New Broom

So that was the short version, but of course there were reverberations. News travelled extremely slowly in the ancient world, the speed of communication being no faster than a man on a horse. Furthermore, given the colossal size of the empire, factors of distance and time determined how closely central government could control information. The supply of inadequate information about the bloody events outside Adrianopolis and the loss of the eastern emperor would have set the whole empire buzzing with rumours, and rumours can quickly become the sweet breath of truth before turning sour. As Gregory Nazianzen apocalyptically wrote: 'The cities are devastated, myriads of people are killed, the earth is soaked with blood, and a foreign people (λαὸς ἀλλόγλωσσος) are running through the land as if it were theirs.'[46] With all this uncertainty, the situation was almost hopeless, or so it seemed.

One thing was certain, however. The catastrophic outcome of the battle was to see Flavius Theodosius brought out of virtual retirement – he had prudently withdrawn to his family estates in north-western Hispania following the fall and execution of his father in mysterious circumstances[47] – and appointed by Gratianus, the western (and now sole) senior emperor, to the rank of *magister militum* to drive out the Goths. The following year – 19 January 379 – he was acclaimed *Augustus* of the east, to which was added the eastern half of the prefecture of Illyricum – the dioceses of Dacia and Macedonia – which had formerly belonged to Gratianus' domain.[48] This was done at the frontier city of Sirmium in Pannonia Secunda after a period of campaigning, one source emphasizing that he was 'chosen ruler…by the vote of all the soldiers'.[49] On becoming emperor, the Goths topped Theodosius' to-do list.

Later Roman convention called for acclaiming the emperor as 'conqueror of all barbarians' (*victor omnium barbarorum*),[50] but in fact the new eastern emperor had inherited a desperate military situation, one that would dominate the rest of his life. Though a capable and experienced officer,[51] Theodosius was unsuccessful in his bid to expel the Goths from the empire. They became what a twenty-first-century strategist would identify as 'a permanent potential security risk'. There have always been two ways of dealing with a problem of this nature. The first is to try to induce the alien populace to assimilate and thus join it to the body of the nation. The other more frequently applied though often counterproductive approach is the subjugation of the alien elements. Theodosius chose the latter option to deal with the Goths.

Facing a prolonged conflict that the empire had no capacity to win in any meaningful sense, on 3 October 382 Theodosius, making a virtue of necessity, assigned the incomers suitable lands to cultivate in the diocese of Thracia by treaty, *foedus*. In effect, Theodosius signed a peace deal with an enemy he had tried to bludgeon but botched.[52] It was not a victor's peace laden with its maximalist demands. The problem was that Roman success had always relied on military strength, and now at this critical juncture the army no longer had the manpower and discipline to maintain that strength. Without both, Theodosius and Gratianus were forced into accommodations with the Goths – barely a third of the force embarrassed at Adrianopolis had survived and their morale was shot – which over time would bring about the disappearance of the *comitatenses* in the west and their replacement with *foederati*, military-obligated barbarian settlers.

Apparently, Arbogastes had earlier been expelled from his homeland,[53] and subsequently had joined the imperial service of Gratianus.[54] As an efficient and loyal commander, he made rapid advancement thanks to the influence of Flavius Bauto, Gratianus' *magister militum*, who possibly shared ties of kinship.[55] So much so, in fact, that in 380 the western emperor sent Arbogastes, then *comes rei militaris* (literally 'count of military affairs'), along with Bauto to aid a struggling Theodosius against the Goths and their leader Fritigern after they had pillaged and plundered the unlucky rural areas of Macedonia and Thessaly that year and the year before.[56] The western *comitatus*, commanded by Bauto and Arbogastes, and that from Theodosius in the east, successfully levered Fritigern and his Goths out of Macedonia, out of Illyricum altogether and back to Thracia where their devastating raids had begun. The Goths quarrelled among themselves about their next move. One of their chieftains, Athanarich, deserted to Theodosius. Fritigern died suddenly; there has never been a hint that it was anything other than a natural death. However, with a plethora of troubles knocking at his door, Gratianus was forced to recall Bauto and Arbogastes, which left Theodosius without the means to resolve the Gothic problem by arms. For that reason the eastern emperor had to seek a diplomatic solution with the Goths, which ultimately established the aforementioned treaty of 382.

Pyramid of Political Power

In the spring of the following year Magnus Maximus (Macsen Wledig[57] of Welsh oral poetry), *comes Britanniarum* (though some argue he was only *dux Britanniarum*),[58] was hailed emperor by the field army in Britannia.[59] The affair developed as a military usurpation in the traditional Roman manner with Maximus speedily crossing over to the prefecture of Gallia, determined to strike the first blow, and as such he marked himself out as entirely different from Postumus. Thus began what the French would call his *fuite en avant*, his 'flight forward'.

As discussed previously, emperors were often challenged and all too often overthrown by usurpers, but these were almost invariably the emperor's own officers, most typically those who had been successful in a major campaign. Successful campaigning resulted in close bonds between commander and troops, which the commander could, and often did, try to exploit to his own advantage. This he did by attempting to mount a *putsch*, which would be carried out by a loyal faction within the army.[60] During the third century, incumbent emperors could be challenged from anywhere in the empire. In the fourth century, such challenges came mainly from the west. In the third century, challenges had a good chance of success. In the fourth century, it was usual for them to fail, the notable exception being Iulianus, for reasons we shall come to later.

From the tetrarchy to the Theodosian dynasty Britannia proved to be a diocese with a particular penchant for this sort of thing. One reason for this was its remoteness from imperial centres of patronage, especially when emperors were not residing in Augusta Treverorum. Moreover, no legitimate emperor would visit Britannia again after Constans had done back in early 343.[61] In the long run this proved to be a recipe for discontent. Ambitious men who had grand designs on imperial power usually found the troops in Britannia willing to throw their weight behind their candidature. So the island produced a rich crop of usurpers, forming a bastion for the usurpations of Carausius (286), Allectus (293), Constantinus I (306), Magnus Maximus (383) and Constantinus III (407), who was the last of the series proclaimed by the army in Britannia.[62] Indeed, Jerome refers to Britannia specifically as a 'province rich in usurpers'.[63] Subsequently, with the backing of loyal soldiers drawn from Britannia and never to return, Magnus Maximus (r. 383–388) ousted Gratianus after his forces deserted him en masse.[64]

There is still no clear reason why Gratianus' support crumbled so quickly, although it is reported that some of his Roman soldiers had become disaffected through his evident favouritism towards a body of Alani *foederati*. In order to court their friendship, it appears he had granted the Alani warriors provisions and donatives greater than those given to Roman soldiers, even appearing in public wearing Alanic attire.[65] Gratianus was the eldest son of the great Valentinianus, and although still young he had been senior emperor in the west for eight years, during which time he had campaigned extensively and successfully against the external enemies of the empire. Indeed, he had been sole emperor in the brief period after Adrianopolis before he appointed Theodosius as his colleague, and had been the principal agent in holding the empire together in the face of the Gothic victory. He was certainly no untried boy emperor.

On the other hand, we do have the testimony of the contemporary Ammianus Marcellinus. Despite some early promise in living up to 'the reputation of his family and the glorious deeds of his forebears',[66] by his early twenties Gratianus had descended into a military lethargy that encouraged opposition to his rule. It is possible that many veteran officers yearned for a return to the strong, thoroughgoing military regime of his father, Valentinianus I. Rightly styled the 'frontier emperor', Valentinianus had moved his headquarters from Lutetia (Paris) to rule from Augusta Treverorum close to the Rhenus, and his aggressive campaigns and great fortification programmes along that troublesome frontier and later along the Danuvius even crossing into barbarian territory.[67] When Maximus made his bid for the western throne, whatever the reason, from that point on the resistance left Gratianus. After a brief skirmish near Lutetia, all was up for Gratianus.[68] Horrified to see that his own army had melted away with shameless speed, Gratianus fled southward only to be outrun by a cavalry commander called Andragathius who had been sent hotfoot by Maximus after the fugitive emperor. Gratianus was delivered up for execution at Lugdunum (Lyon, France) on 25 August 383.[69] His body was left unburied.[70] He was only 24 years old.

Magnus Maximus, a defeated ruler, could be portrayed as a usurper who had seized power illegitimately,[71] but as he had been a fervent orthodox persecutor of insidious heresy,[72] some Christian writers could express this more mildly: 'he was created emperor by the army almost against his will.'[73] Maximus himself told Martin, the saintly bishop of Turones (formerly Caesarodunum, now Tours, France), that 'he had not taken the imperial power of his own accord but had defended with armed force the necessity of rule imposed on him by the soldiers in accordance with the divine will.'[74] The Venerable Bede, who was writing – in what was then the Anglian kingdom of Northumbria – long after the Romans had abandoned Britannia to its fate,[75] saw Maximus in a comparable light:

> At this moment, an energetic and upright man named Maximus, one worthy of the title of *Augustus* had he not risen to the rank of usurper by breaking his oath of allegiance, was elected emperor by the army in Britannia almost against his will, and crossed to Gaul. There he treacherously murdered the emperor Gratianus, who had been terrified by the sudden incursion and was intending to cross into Italy.[76]

It is highly likely that Orosius was Bede's literary source here. Conversely, for the orthodox ecclesiastical historians, it was for his treachery in murdering Gratianus alone that Theodosius took justified revenge on Maximus.[77] Still, being defeated by another Christian emperor of unimpeachable orthodoxy meant there had to be a sound reason. According to Orosius, though a lesser warrior, Theodosius excelled Maximus in faith alone.[78]

By contrast the later Greek writers were sure that Magnus Maximus was motivated by resentment that he had not achieved higher rank; perhaps, as a former officer of Theodosius' father, to whom he claimed to be related,[79] he had hoped to be *magister militum* rather than only *comes Britanniarum*. Modern historians suspect that he may have been encouraged to depose Gratianus by Theodosius. Indeed, there were reasons why joint rule by Theodosius and Maximus might have been a well-balanced long-term arrangement. After all, Maximus also hailed from Hispania,[80] and had successfully served with Theodosius' father in Britannia. Africa, Hispania, Gallia and Britannia happily acknowledged Maximus, while even the volatile Alexandrians shouted for the western *Augustus*.

As *de facto* senior *Augustus* in the west (there were uneasy diplomatic relations with Gratianus' younger half-brother, Valentinianus II), Magnus Maximus established his imperial headquarters at Augusta Treverorum, the great imperial centre of Valentinianus I 'on the half-barbarian banks of the Rhenus'.[81] By and large, having deftly dismantled Gratianus' realm, Maximus' *coup d'état* was bloodless. The courtiers and clique of Gratianus were allowed to go into comfortable retirement, and were quickly replaced by picked men of the new order. For so-called heretics, however, it was to be a different matter. Maximus personally took a leading part in the trial of heretics (viz. nonconforming Christians),[82] and would have used troops to hunt them down if not dissuaded. His use of the death penalty caused concern even among his fellow Nicene Christians.[83] As a devout Christian, Maximus has gone down in history as the first Christian emperor to put a heretic to death:

> 'The theory of persecution,' wrote Edward Gibbon, 'was established by Theodosius, whose justice and piety have been applauded by the saints; but the practice of it, in the fullest extent, was (AD 385) reserved for his rival and colleague, Maximus, the first among Christian princes who shed the blood of his Christian subjects, on account of their religious opinions.'[84]

Coping with his own difficulties closer to home, Theodosius initially sought to avoid a civil war with Magnus Maximus. Indeed, it is suggested that Theodosius recognized Maximus quickly after Gratianus' murder, as did Valentinianus.[85] Unlike the third century, when extreme bloodshed was often avoided thanks to the last-minute exit of one of the principal players, the fourth century, on the other hand, saw some of the bloodiest civil war battles in Roman history. In the furnace of civil war battles, the uncertain but often fatal prospects for the close supporters of the defeated faction made for long struggles: terrible pitiless grinding affairs that degenerated into a conflict of extermination. Fought to the finish, these civil wars were not about domination or overawing the enemy, but achieving a clear decisive victory. Most were decided by one or more pitched battles. The armies involved in these actions were some of the largest ever put into the field, for victory went more often to numbers and determination than tactical subtlety. Battles were often confused, long-drawn-out slogging matches, many soldiers simply clinging to the basic instinct for survival as the two sides ground away at each other to the bitter end. In Theodosius' childhood, Constantius II (r. 337–361) had defeated the western usurper Flavius Magnus Magnentius (r. 350–353) in three major battles over an agonizing period of three years.

The second of these was a real bloodletting for both sides, one the empire could ill avoid. This was on the broad, open plain north-west of Mursa (Osijek,

Croatia) in Pannonia Secunda, not far from the Dravus (Drava) River, a tributary of the Danuvius, on 28 September 351. According to Zonaras, once the dust had settled some 54,000 men had fallen that day,[86] the most destructive battle of the century. As Jerome (he would have been 3 or 4 years old at the time of the battle) tersely put it, 'the might of Rome perished'.[87] The terrain was advantageous to Constantius because of his large force of cavalry. A further advantage was brought to Constantius in the defection of the *schola armaturaram* of Magnus Magnentius with its commanding officer, the *tribunus* Silvanus.[88] Even so, by all accounts, it was a pyrrhic victory for the emperor, with almost half his army wiped out.[89]

Two years later Magnus Magnentius was to suffer another defeat in the passes of the Alpes Cottiae.[90] After this rout, his third, the issue of the war had already been decided, Magnentius having run his last lap. Nevertheless, Magnentius still had troops available and apparently they were willing to fight; the civil war was only ended by his suicide at Lugdunum,[91] and that of his brother Magnus Decentius, who he had made *Caesar*.[92] Augustine (354–430), the venerable bishop of Hippo Regius (Annaba, Algeria), and later sainted, may approve of war on certain occasions. After all war, like other social and political evils, is a punishment for original sin, but he firmly rejects that of the internecine nature and demands 'what fury of foreign peoples, what barbarian cruelty, can be compared with the harm done by civil wars?'[93]

For the time being political survival meant dealing with the enemy. So it was, in the words of Zosimos, 'Theodosius thereupon recognized Maximus as emperor and considered him worthy of sharing his statues and imperial title, but secretly prepared for war and outwitted him by every kind of flattery and favour.'[94] In the interim, Theodosius compromised. He arranged with Maximus that Valentinianus should rule Italy, Africa and the western half of the prefecture of Illyricum; the young emperor would serve as a suitable buffer between them, a reasonable accommodation with Maximus on the basis of what can be perceived as a balance of interests.[95] As a result, for four years Maximus presided over a violent reign, tightly controlling Britannia, Gaul and Hispania.

This was a very ominous situation, and like most ominous situations, it presented itself as a solution but was not. For Magnus Maximus regarded the youth as little more than a proxy for Theodosius; he was the centre of power, but was virtually powerless. With a worldview akin to the Athenian soldier historian Thucydides, 'the strong do what they can and the weak suffer what they must',[96] Maximus decided to claw back some more of the geopolitical space that belonged to the western half of the empire. He, in other words, had designs on Italy, and the Arianism of Valentinianus afforded the champion of orthodoxy a laudable pretext for action. So with Valentinianus' headlong flight to Thessaloniki, along with his mother Iustina and most of the 'heretical' court, in the autumn of 387 Maximus became master of Italy.[97] After all, Valentinianus – unlike Gratianus, who was declared *Augustus* at the age of 8 and trained vigorously as a soldier as soon as he could mount a horse and swing a sword – had received little or no military apprenticeship. On the contrary, the prince was weak, having been swaddled from reality and protected in a plush pocket of privilege from the moment he was born. He had been a purely titular *Augustus* till Gratianus' death in 383, when at the age of 12 he suddenly acquired a court of his own at Mediolanum. Still too young to be a player, Valentinianus II was to remain a puppet of his mother, ministers and eunuchs, the classic child emperor.

Sea Change

One of the most influential of these 'puppeteers' was Bauto. After Gratianus' death, the Frankish *magister militum* was back in Italy in the service of Valentinianus, defending the Alpine passes against a threatened attack by Magnus Maximus.[98] However, despite Bauto organizing the military defence of Italy,[99] Maximus quickly took the prefecture as Theodosius looked on with impotence and resignation, or so it may have appeared to Maximus. He took good note. Having thus consolidated the west, the western usurper could engage in dialogue and diplomacy on his terms. Theodosius promptly demanded that Valentinianus be restored to the rank of emperor. Maximus ignored the request.

Theodosius, however, was a far tougher challenge; not only politically, but also a military challenge that Magnus Maximus was unable to overcome. True, Theodosius had not stopped Maximus in the first instance, but he had at least limited the damage: he had forestalled an initial expansion into Italy, and while Valentinianus was still in play bolstered his authority of his court at Mediolanum. Of course, Theodosius clearly recognized that he had to prepare for an eventual civil war with Maximus. It may have been too awful to contemplate, but legitimacy was the issue at stake. All wars end in either victory for one side or in a negotiated settlement. For Theodosius, however, the option of the latter was out of the question: he could not admit the right of Maximus to legitimately call himself *Augustus* in the west since it would render his own position in the east open to challenge.

Political victory could only be secured by removing the usurper, and for Theodosius that meant by victory on the field of battle. This he would win, but it would be a victory that came with a huge bill attached. Magnus Maximus was eventually defeated by Theodosius' eastern army at Poetovio (Ptuj, Slovenia), Pannonia Prima, in 388. It was a major battle, stubbornly contested: 'The enemy…fought with the desperation of gladiators. They did not yield an inch, but stood their ground and fell.'[100] Theodosius followed hard on the fugitive's track. Maximus with the reckless courage of the desperate fell upon his pursuers, but was driven back into Aquileia and forced to surrender. Maximus was beheaded outside Aquileia on 28 July 388, not quite five years after the slaying of Gratianus.[101] His severed head then went on a grisly tour of the provinces. Theodosius was merciful to Maximus' supporters, save his infant son and his Moorish bodyguard.[102] Arbogastes was employed to hunt down the usurper's son, Flavius Victor, who the Frank finally tracked down and strangled at Augusta Treverorum in the autumn of the same year.[103]

Magnus Maximus having fallen, Theodosius reinstated Valentinianus II, now sole *Augustus* in the west. Still, while posing as the saviour of Valentinianus, he was rightly less than confident of the unfortunate young emperor's capacity to rule. The panegyric of Pacatus Drepanius, delivered in July 389 before Theodosius and the Senate in Rome, contrives to say almost nothing about Valentinianus, while opening proclaiming that the future rulers of the Roman world would be the two (even younger) sons of Theodosius.[104]

In practice, therefore, Theodosius quietly marginalized the youth, making sure that a number of major offices were held by men of his own, many of whom he had brought with him from the east. There were 'westerners' who could be trusted, or so it seemed at the time. So it came about that Valentinianus was left in charge of Bauto. From this point on, he seems to have virtually ruled Valentinianus' ever-diminishing slice of the western empire on the boy's behalf. His military authority as *magister militum* enabled him to assume a position of influence well beyond his public duties. He soon gained a degree of independence from and authority over the young emperor, so much so that Ambrose, no doubt with some justification, accused the Frank of 'pulling the strings' behind the throne.[105] Bauto's influence stemmed from his military position as evidenced by his use of fellow Franks in the war against Magnus Maximus.[106]

From his position of virtual control over Valentinianus' court, Bauto pursued his own political agenda, becoming *consul* in 385. After the death of Bauto and the overthrow of Magnus Maximus,[107] Arbogastes exploited his own popularity with the troops to secure the position of *magister militum*,[108] having previously consolidated his reputation in the campaign against Maximus.[109] Arbogastes, like Bauto before him, dominated Valentinianus, and despite the independent commands of the *magister militum* Flavius Rumoridus in Italy[110] and the Mauri noble Gildo in Africa,[111] Arbogastes soon established himself as the unrivalled military power in the west. This was the real basis of his political power, which allowed him to give the key positions in the military hierarchy to his 'Frankish accomplices' and his 'sworn followers',[112] and he used his relations with the Franks to bring auxiliaries into the empire.[113] Arbogastes began also to establish some control over civil power,[114] all of which he achieved as the special appointee of the absent Theodosius.

In the short term Theodosius was planning to administer Italy, Illyricum and Africa from Constantinopolis himself and confine Valentinianus to the prefecture of Gallia, under the military thumb of the *magister militum* (as he hoped) Arbogastes. In the long term he was hoping to supersede this lone survivor of the previous dynasty with one of his own sons when a suitable opportunity arose. However, hope can turn out to be a fool's ally. In the cutthroat world of politicking, those who are full of certainty are usually wrong. The capacity to listen, to observe, to weigh up evidence and to change your mind is one of the most important qualities in any leader. Of all the different kind of fools, the most dangerous kind is the clever fool.

For Arbogastes soon proved to be more than a mere watchdog for Valentinianus since he came to completely control the boy emperor and his mincing court; so much so that he swept out of the way anyone who opposed him, though it is probable that many of the individuals he removed were corrupt. In the labyrinthine court politics that centred on personal animosities, treachery and opportunism, Arbogastes, it seems, would not brook anyone other than himself taking advantage of the situation. On one occasion he reportedly drew his sword on Harmonius, one of the emperor's intimate councillors accused of bribery. Arbogastes chased him throughout the chambers of the palace until finally he caught up with his victim, seeking protection under the emperor's robe, and promptly ran him through.[115]

Chapter Six

Death in Vienna

'Woe to you, O land, when your king is *a child/And your princes feast in the morning!'*

Ecclesiastes 10:16 NKJV

With regard to the battle of the Frigidus, what is important is not what was going to happen on those fateful two days, but how it happened. In a sense, the characters of this depressing drama are playthings and puppets, jerked around cruelly by fate for reasons that remain obscure to them. One character, on the other hand, at least knew who was pulling the strings.

Accidents do happen

For this adolescent man who posed as an emperor, a terrible dilemma had arisen. After enduring years of being ignored by Gratianus, deposed by Magnus Maximus, sold short by Theodosius and dominated by his mother Iustina, being ordered about by one of his own supposed subordinates seems to have been the last straw for the young emperor. So, restive in his gilded cage, in the spring of 392 Valentinianus gave his overbearing protector his marching orders. Such princes have to be reassured, flattered, humoured and encouraged.

That was not Arbogastes' approach. For military strongmen like him, power was for getting things others cannot have; if others ask for something you do not wish to give, respond with violence. For Valentinianus, on the other hand, it was all about respect. Arbogastes retorted that because he had not been appointed by Valentinianus, he could not be dismissed by him. He then proceeded to rip up his letter of dismissal and, roaring with exquisite rage, stormed out with a drawn sword. Valentinianus was beginning to realize that his Frankish minder was not a man to be trifled with. Alarmed, he implored Theodosius for aid, but the eastern emperor vacillated.[1] A letter was despatched by Valentinianus urging Ambrose to come to him with all speed to administer the sacrament of baptism: clearly he thought his life was threatened. The outcome was Arbogastes placing the boy emperor under virtual house arrest. The chronicler Sulpicius Alexander writes 'the emperor Valentinianus was shut in the palace in Vienna and reduced almost to the status of a private citizen.'[2] For the remainder of his short life he was to be nothing more than a hostage of Arbogastes.

Whether or not Arbogastes orchestrated the untimely end of Valentinianus, soon after his confinement in the imperial palace in Vienna, on 15 May 392 the emperor's body was found swinging from the end of a rope in his apartments. According to one version of events, the emperor had seen fit to commit suicide. The other more widespread version was that the emperor was murdered by Arbogastes. Even if it was suicide – which is not impossible – the accusation of murder was inevitable. The versions of his liquidation vary, most commonly that he was strangled, suffocated or stabbed inside or outside the palace by Arbogastes or his agents:[3] this obviously became the official version[4] and Sokrates Scholastikos even implicates Eugenius.[5]

Other sources are noncommittal.[6] Indeed, our closest source to the death, Rufinus of Aquileia, confesses that nobody is sure exactly what happened in Vienna on that fateful day, nor is there any way of verifying the conflicting rumours.[7] Augustine, who may or may not have had information independent of Rufinus, reflects the same perplexity.[8] We can do no better than agree with Edward Gibbon that 'The variations, and the ignorance of contemporary writers, prove that it was secret.'[9] It is Orosius who first makes the claim that Valentinianus was done away with through the treachery of Arbogastes, who then strung him up on a length of rope to make it appear that the young man had hung himself.[10] This heinous crime is picked up by Zosimos, whereby Arbogastes approached the unsuspecting emperor and 'struck him a mortal blow and killed him'.[11] On the other hand, Zonaras says 'Valentinianus, seized with fear, betook himself from life by hanging.'[12] However, the crucial testimony is that of Ambrose. The body of Valentinianus was sent by Arbogastes to Mediolanum for a suitable imperial interment: Ambrose pronounced a funeral oration that could be taken to suggest foul play, but later considered him a suicide.[13]

So, depending on which literary source one wishes to believe, Arbogastes may or may not have been guilty of murdering Valentinianus. Certainly it is easy to point the finger at Arbogastes, but there is one salient issue we need to consider before we do so: the time lapse. A good interval of three months elapses before Arbogastes takes the next logical step, irrevocable but not yet necessarily belligerent, of elevating Eugenius to the position of *Augustus* in the west (22 August 392). Brian Croke robustly argues that the period between the death of Valentinianus and the promotion of Eugenius was sufficient for him to appear innocent, implying that if Arbogastes had plotted an assassination, he would have installed a replacement for Valentinianus almost immediately.[14] In other words, Arbogastes had not formulated any particular plan to replace one unwanted ruler with one that was more malleable.

In view of that, if Arbogastes had murdered Valentinianus, it does seem more likely that Theodosius would have viewed this as an overt act of usurpation and reacted more rapidly than he eventually did. In the meantime, Theodosius had apparently maintained silence despite a number of friendly overtures from Arbogastes, but continued with his energetic anti-pagan legislation. During the summer, Theodosius removed from office in Rome the *praefectus praetorio per Italiae* Virius Nicomachus Flavianus, a prominent pagan and close associate of Arbogastes, and the following month saw the fall of another prominent pagan, Flavius Eutolmius Tatianus, the *praefectus praetorio per Orientis* at Constantinopolis, together with his son Proculus (or Proklos), who was *praefectus urbi* in the same city.[15] Such concentration of power in the hands of father and son caused the envy (and the dread) of powerful men. Both were arrested and the father later exiled to his native province of Lykia, while his son was beheaded in the Hippodrome.[16] During the course of the summer, Arbogastes must have realized that he was a likely Theodosian target and that he would have to take more energetic steps to secure his current position. He needed a new emperor. It was at that moment that the Frank decided to revolt.

A Useful Idiot?

Arbogastes, clearly taking a different approach to that taken previously by Magnus Maximus, put forth Eugenius as the imperial candidate for the western throne.[17] After this piece of unauthorized emperor-making, one of the first acts by Arbogastes was to cross the Rhenus *limes* in 393 to exact revenge against his own Ripuarian Franks (L *Ripuarii*) and their chieftains Sunno and Marcomeres who had plundered the regions north of the Rhenus while the west was still under the rule of Valentinianus. In launching this punitive campaign 'in the full blast of winter',[18] which was met with little opposition, Arbogastes was successful in restoring Colonia Claudia Ara Agrippinensium (Köln, Germany), re-establishing it as the first city of Germania Secunda, which, at this time, was the last time the Roman army would occupy the right bank of the Rhenus.[19] In addition, Arbogastes was able to conclude a peace treaty with the Ripuarian Franks, so providing the western army with able-bodied Frankish (and much-needed) recruits.

His ambition was great: the choice of Eugenius, over proclaiming himself, offered to Arbogastes three strong advantages. First Eugenius, a Roman, was more suitable than Arbogastes, a Frank, as an emperor. Second, the Senate would have been more likely to have supported the affable and respectable Eugenius than the non-Roman military strongman Arbogastes since men of his race, however great their *de facto* power in the imperial administration, were not acceptable as emperors. Third, and more importantly, being a courtier and devoid of military experience, the civilian Eugenius would not endanger Arbogastes' military authority. In office but not in power, Eugenius fitted Arbogastes to a tee. By the spring of 393, Eugenius was recognized in Italy as well as in Gaul. Even so, Theodosius refused to acknowledge Eugenius. To do so would undermine Theodosius' position since Gratianus, Valentinianus' half-brother, had appointed him.

So this action was a direct challenge to Theodosius. In addition there was the issue of Valentinianus' untimely death, which had never been resolved to his satisfaction and, of course, to that of Galla, his second wife who just happened to be the sister of the deceased.[20] The occasionally erratic and hostile chronicle of Zosimos writing a little over a century later portrays Theodosius (he gets a particular kicking here) easily seduced by the charms of Galla, who had first entranced the emperor, only just a widower, and whose bride-price had been the previous civil war on Magnus Maximus:

As Theodosius listened to her he became captivated by the sight of the girl's beauty and showed in his eyes the striking effect she had on him. He deferred a decision, although he gave them reason to hope, until, his desire for the girl being increasingly excited, he went to Iustina to ask for her daughter in marriage.... She said she would not give her to him unless he undertook war against Maximus to avenge Gratianus' death, and restored his father's kingdom to Valentinianus.[21]

Zosimos is clearly promoting the idea that the principal reason behind Theodosius going to war with Maximus was the fact that Iustina dangled the prospect of marriage to her fine-looking daughter. Theodosius did indeed marry the seemingly beautiful Galla,[22] thereby cementing dynastic ties between the eastern and western halves of the empire, but he would never award her the title *Augusta*. Still, there is no reason to doubt that he was not strongly attracted to her, or that Iustina deployed her daughter dexterously in this political role.

After all, Iustina was a skilful survivor, her first husband having been Flavius Magnus Magnentius,[23] an army officer of maternal Frankish descent, a *laetus*,[24] who had declared himself *Augustus* at Augustodunum (Autun, France) in the early hours of 18 January 350. The so-called 'after-dinner emperor',[25] he had himself proclaimed during a dinner party to celebrate the birthday of the son of Marcellinus, Magnentius' most loyal ally. As tends to happen on such occasions, all partygoers drank heavily and talked a lot; Magnentius apparently left the festive get-together to relieve himself and returned dressed in imperial purple. The loud drinking revellers immediately proclaimed him emperor. True or not, by the end of the month the usurper had overthrown and killed Constans.[26] Magnentius' assassins had dragged the deeply unpopular western emperor – he was arrogant, greedy and impulsive, and a predatory homosexual too[27] – from the church in which he had sought refuge and killed him.[28] As one Byzantine commentator contemptuously put it: 'Constans, having taken his ease in revelries and drunken carousals and unnatural erotic dalliances, gambled the whole empire without a care, dancing away the majesty of the realm.'[29]

As a result, much like his father before him, Constantius II found himself the official sole ruler of the empire, although with the predicament of a usurper at large in the west.

However, effect should not be confused with cause.[30] Theodosius' first wife, Aelia Flavia Flaccilla Augusta,[31] had died in 386 and his dynastic ambition may have been a motive for remarriage; the marriage would cement his dynastic alliance to Valentinianus II and enable Theodosius to control the newly-installed boy emperor in the west. Yet this marriage was a commitment to the war against Magnus Maximus and not its reason.

Contra Zosimos, we could retort that Theodosius seemed to be playing the long game rather skilfully. According to Claudius Claudianus, the pagan poet who wielded his pen in the Christian court of Honorius, two of the most prominent usurpers were Magnus Maximus, who was responsible for the death of Gratianus, and Flavius Eugenius, whose *magister militum in praesenti* may or may not have murdered Valentinianus II:

> Two tyrants burst upon the western climes,
> Their savage bosoms stored with various crimes;
> Fierce Britannia was to one the native earth:
> The other owed to Germania his birth,
> A banished, servile wretch: both soiled with guilt:
> Alike their hands a master's blood had spilt.[32]

As for Eugenius, once in power he apparently purged his administration of Theodosian appointees. He reinstalled Virius Nicomachus Flavianus as *praefectus praetorio per Italiae*, and installed his son, Nicomachus Flavianus, as *praefectus urbis Romae* and Numerius Proiectus as *praefectus annonae*.[33] Nonetheless, Eugenius is found proclaiming the legitimacy of his regime by implication in continuing to recognize the imperial authority in the east, deliberately recording the titles of Theodosius and his elder son Arcadius in public as *Augusti*. There was, however, no joint rule of the empire. The west had for the present once again slipped from Theodosius' grasp: Valentinianus II, after all, had been no

The eastern circuit of Thessaloniki. Valerianus' reinforced defences surrounding Thessaloniki had enabled the city to hold out against the invading Goths, who were not equipped with siege machines, until a relief army could reach it. The walls consist of the typical later Roman composite construction of rubble masonry alternating with bands of brick, sometimes with brick arches to provide extra strength. Their height, on average, ranged between 10m and 12m, and their thickness reached 5m. (© *Nic Fields*)

The famous red porphyry carving of the tetrarchs, which now adorns Basilica di San Marco in Venice (part of the booty carried to Europe by members of the Fourth Crusade who sacked Constantinopolis in April 1204). Dated to around 300, it neatly exemplifies the dramatic change in the type of men who now held the imperial office. (© *Nic Fields*)

What now serves as a car park for the Grand Bazaar, Istanbul, was once the Forum of Constantinus, an oval colonnaded portico. In the forum's centre Constantinus erected this column to celebrate the dedication of his city as the capital of the reunited empire on 11 May 330. (© *Nic Fields*)

East face of the Proconnesian marble plinth supporting the Obelisk of Karnak, Hippodrome, Istanbul. Erected in 390 by Constantinopolis' *praefectus urbi* Proculus to celebrate the victory of Theodosius I over the western usurper Magnus Maximus (Marc. Com. *Chron.* s.a. 390.3, *CIL* III.737). (© *Nic Fields*)

Gold *tremissis* struck during 393/394 in the Mediolanum (Milan) mint (*RIC* XI 29.1). The obverse depicts a bust of Flavius Eugenius facing right, pearl-diademed, draped and cuirassed. The inscription reads: D(*ominus*) N(*oster*) EVGENI-VS P(*ius*) F(*elix*) AVG(*ustus*). (*Classical Numismatic Group, Inc. http://www.cngcoins.com/Wikimedia Commons/CC-BY-SA-2.5*)

Early fifth-century polychrome mosaic (Ravenna, Museo TAMO) from Domus di Via Dogana, Faenza. The scene shows the enigmatic Romano-Vandal *comes et magister utriusque militiae praesentalis* of the West, Flavius Stilicho (left foreground), with the western emperor Honorius (r. 395–423), 'heroically' enthroned and protected by two members of the *scholae palatinae*. (© *Nic Fields*)

Pictogram titled *comes Italiae of Castra ad Fluvium Frigidum* depicted in the register known as the *Notitia Dignitatum* (*Occ.* XXIV.5, *tractus Italiae circa Alpes*). A Roman road, the Via Gemina, ran past the Castra linking Aquileia, one of the biggest cities in northern Italy, with Emona, short for Colonia Iulia Aemona (now Ljubljana), via the hilltop fort of Ad Pirum (now the hamlet of Hrušica) in between. (© *Nic Fields*)

The upper Vipava valley looking south-east from the eastern outskirts of Ajdovščina. Running from left to right are the abrupt cliffs of the Nanos (highest point Suhi Vrh, elevation 1,313m), a Slovenian karst plateau known as Ocra in antiquity; Strabo identifies it as 'the lowest part of the Alps'. (© *Nic Fields*)

The upper Vipava valley looking north-east from the confluence of the Hubelj and Vipava rivers towards the village of Col. Well-cultivated and fruitful, the narrow valley stretches roughly between the border with Italy to the west and the village of Podnanos to the east. Throughout its tangled history the valley has been an important corridor connecting northern Italy to central Europe as empires (Roman, Byzantine, Venetian, Ottoman, Napoleonic, Austro-Hungarian, etc., etc.) have tramped their armies and shifted the frontiers. (© *Nic Fields*)

The tenth of the fourteen (or possibly sixteen) towers of *Castra ad Fluvium Frigidum*, eastern circuit, Ajdovščina. Now standing 14m to its crenulated crown, the original late Roman tower was only 9.6m in height as indicated by the lighter, more pinkish stone seen below the later mediaeval addition. The late Roman part has a diameter of 5.8m and walls 3m thick, thus reducing the interior diameter to 2.8m. The circuit wall is 3.84m wide at the foundations, above which there are usually two step-like stages. (© *Nic Fields*)

The *frigidarium* of a small Roman bathhouse, *thermae*, with a deepened semicircular basin, Ajdovščina. Originally the bathhouse was adjoined to a residence and built around the year 300. (© *Nic Fields*)

[Above] The confluence of the Hubelj River (right) and the Lokavšček stream (left), Ajdovščina. [Right] The confluence of the Hubelj (foreground) and Vipava rivers looking south-west. (© *Nic Fields*)

The cold, crystal-clear waters of the Vipava, viewed from the footbridge below the village of Planina, looking upstream. Flowing through south-west Slovenia and north-east Italy, the river is 49km in length, of which 45km is in Slovenia. (© *Nic Fields*)

Life-size 2-D display in the Muzej Ajdovščina depicting three of the major troop types that fought at the Frigidus: from left to right, an Alani horseman, a Goth warrior and a Gallo-Roman soldier. (© *Nic Fields*)

Detail from the *Great Hunt* mosaic, Villa Romana del Casale, Piazza Armerina, Sicilia, showing two hunters. Their woollen tunics are decorated at the shoulders, cuffs and hems. They both wear military cloaks (*saga*) and broad waist-belts, and carry large round shields. (*Robur.q/Wikimedia Commons/CC-BY-SA-3.0*)

more than cipher for Theodosius. It was effectively in the hands of three men: Arbogastes himself, Eugenius and Virius Nicomachus Flavianus.

The temporary loss of Gaul to a usurper might be sustained, but no emperor sitting in Constantinopolis could tolerate an enemy in control of Italy, which was still the strategic heartland of the west, the key to control of the western Mediterranean, the granaries of Africa and the vital communication routes through Illyricum to the east. As was the situation with Magnus Maximus previously, Eugenius was in a position to threaten Theodosius' own security in the east. The omens of war now seemed to be lining up like the horsemen of the apocalypse.

When a delegation of western envoys arrived in Constantinopolis to request that Eugenius be acknowledged as the legitimate *Augustus* in the west, Theodosius was noncommittal, even if he received them with splendid gifts and vague promises.[34] Politically, the embassy was obviously unsuccessful as the east and west recognized different consuls: in 393, Theodosius and Abundantius in the east, Theodosius and Eugenius in the west; in 394, Arcadius and Honorius in the east, the Virius Nichomachus Flavianus (without colleague) in the west. Whether Theodosius had already decided on an offensive against Eugenius at this point is unclear. In the end, however, after declaring his son Honorius, then 8 years old, as the legitimate *Augustus* of the west on 23 January 393, Theodosius finally resolved to invade the west.[35]

Chapter Seven

Civil War

'ARBOGAST, Count of the Franks, who had the world in his hands, and dropped it.'

'EUGENIUS, the pretender Emperor, the last of the last of the pagans.'
R.A. Lafferty, *The Fall of Rome*, p.2[1]

In almost all usurpations the legitimate emperor and his rival recruited large contingents of allied barbarians. Hired for the duration, as experienced warriors they would be far more effective than citizens hastily raised through conscription. Magnus Magnentius, for instance, had hired Franks and Saxones for his fight against Constantius II, who in turn had hired Goths.[2] Similarly, Magnus Maximus is said to have boasted that 'so many thousands of *barbari* fight for me and receive rations (*annonae*) from me.'[3]

These Things Take Time

According to Philostorgius, Theodosius spent the entire winter preparing for the campaign against Eugenius before he set out for the invasion of Italy.[4] When the eastern emperor had faced Magnus Maximus back in 388,[5] and due to his success then with an army based on a Roman regular core heavily supported by 'an assemblage of many fierce nations',[6] that is to say Goths, Huns, Alani, Armenians, Iberians and Isaurians,[7] it is likely that Theodosius would have gone with a similar force in 394. Similarly, we suspect, the preparations for this western campaign were along the same lines as those for the campaign against Maximus, the details of which are revealed by Pacatus: '[Y]ou carried out the war with such careful planning and so many calculations that you seemed to be preparing to meet some Perseus (of Macedon) or Pyrrhos (of Epeiros) or even Hannibal himself.'[8]

To that end, along with the emperor himself and his *magistri* Timasios and Stilicho (Richomeres having died shortly before), several non-Roman officers are recorded commanding *foederati* – Saul (rank unknown), Bacurios (*dux* or *magister militum*), Gaïnas (*comes rei militaris*) and Alaric (rank unknown).[9]

Meanwhile in the West

Arbogastes also had significant numbers of non-Roman soldiers in his army. His campaigning beyond the Rhenus and around Colonia Claudia Ara Agrippinensium would have brought Franks into his army. As Orosius makes clear:

> [Arbogastes] himself a barbarian, seeking to control the empire, outstanding in courage, judgement, valour, boldness and power, assembled from all sides innumerable unconquered forces, either from the garrisons of the Romans or auxiliaries of barbarians, relying on, in one case, his power, and in the other, his kinship.[10]

As well as his fellow Franks, transrhenane barbarians would have included Alamanni and Burgundi too; the former had been in all likelihood clients of Magnus Maximus.[11] The migrations forced by the Huns may have brought Suevi and Vandals to the Rhenus and the upper Danuvius as well as perhaps a limited number of Goths, Alani and Huns that were left over from Gratianus' army or the defeat of Magnus Maximus.[12] These allied forces on top of contingents from the various pockets of *laeti* and *dediticii* dotted across the west would have provided much of the striking power for the Roman nucleus of Arbogastes' army.[13] However, the migrations would also have increased the need for strong frontier garrisons along the Rhenus and the upper Danuvius, forcing Arbogastes to leave more men behind in Gaul than he would have originally wanted.

However, aside from the possibility of up to 20,000 Goths serving under the terms of the 382 *foedus* further swaying the numerical advantage to Theodosius, there is little evidence to illuminate the size of the barbarian contingents at the Frigidus. In the past, the Romans sought to employ as many auxiliaries and allies in battle as they did regulars and while it is not out of the question that this policy continued, trying to find and control perhaps 40,000 to 50,000 barbarians[14] would have been a difficult task for either Arbogastes or Theodosius. It is more likely that both commanders recruited or extracted as many barbarians as they could find or expect to reward, though Arbogastes was able to command considerable loyalty from his army.[15]

Who Fought at the Frigidus?

Because of the religious nature of our sources, little specific is known about the actual composition of the armies that Theodosius and Arbogastes brought to the Frigidus. The *Notitia Dignitatum*, despite its anomalies and discrepancies, can be used to give a rough outline of the regular forces available to both sides.[16] The western army included perhaps up to 113,000 troops of the *comitatenses*[17] supported by 135,000 troops of the *limitanei*.[18] However, the logistical problems of defending the Rhenus and the upper Danuvius and the Theodosian allegiance of the *magister militum per Africam* Gildo, who had up to 15,000 men under his command,[19] would have severely reduced the total of 248,000 western troops available to Arbogastes to confront Theodosius. The ambiguous allegiance of the forces in Illyricum in the *Notitia Dignitatum* could also see western numbers bolstered by forces that were actually available to the east,[20] while it is not certain whether Arbogastes was able to take command of any forces in Italy following his move into the peninsula. If any of these forces escaped, it is more than likely that they, along with the Illyrian field army, would have joined up with the advancing Theodosius. In total, the eastern emperor had access to perhaps 104,000 troops of the *comitatenses*[21] plus another 248,000 troops of the *limitanei*.[22]

The *Notitia Dignitatum* must be used with great caution. Fundamentally the document sets out the situation as it was supposed to be, which of course is not necessarily how it actually was at any given time. Like law codes, it is prescriptive, not descriptive; this makes it dangerous to take its figures on trust unless they can be corroborated by other sources.

Since the *Notitia Dignitatum* only recorded permanent *palatini*, *comitatenses* and *limitanei* units, any numbers extrapolated for east and west do not include any barbarian troops. The vast majority of the sources give very little information on the composition of the barbarian auxiliaries with the ecclesiastical historians being particularly unhelpful.[23] Those sources that do elaborate on barbarian origins and numbers are also open to scrutiny: for example, Orosius' claim of more than 10,000 Gothic casualties[24] could be seen to be exaggerating the obstacles overcome by Theodosius, while historians such as Jordanes who claim that there were 20,000 Goths at the Frigidus,[25] Zosimos, who mentions a contingent of Alani led by Saul[26] and Ioannes Antiochensis, who claimed that 'many of the Huns of Thracia with their *phylarchoi*'[27] were present were all writing at least a century after the battle with differing politico-religious agendas. The contemporary poet Claudianus provides a long list of barbarians serving at the Frigidus: Arabs, Armenians, Orientals from the Euphrates, the Halys and the Orontes, and Colchi, Iberians, Medes from the Mare Caspium, Parthians from the Niphates, Sakae and Indians as well as Goths and Alani.[28] However, he too is subject to criticism for being biased towards the Theodosian cause and his romantic notions that Roman influence penetrated far beyond the existing frontiers.

All this said, with both Theodosius and Arbogastes possibly having similar resources of Roman regulars and similar frontier responsibilities reducing how many men they could bring with them, it is possible that their armies were similar in size. Even with the direct and indirect information that can be gleaned regarding the armies of the Frigidus, the circumstantial nature of it makes it very difficult to be anything other than speculative. Andrej Štekar believes that possibly 10,000 to 15,000 men made up Eugenius' army, whereas that of Theodosius contained around 15,000 to 20,000.[29] The soldier emperor Maurikios considered a force of 15,000 to 20,000 sufficient for campaigning purposes,[30] and what we know about the size of later Roman armies, from the standpoint of numbers, these figures are certainly within the realm of credibility. Depending on which sources they believe, anyone may choose to quarrel with these figures. Yet nobody will ever know an exact count based on the available evidence.

Chapter Eight

Erasing Eugenius

'Extincto Eugenio/*Eugenius was exterminated*'
Paulinus Mediolanensis, *Vita sancti Ambrosii* §31

Led by Theodosius himself and, according to Zosimos, 'taking his younger son, Honorius, with him',[1] the eastern army set out towards the west from Constantinopolis in May 394. Destination: Pannonia.

While his eastern army gathered and was organized, Theodosius had apparently found enough time to pray and fast: 'He was prepared for war not so much with the aid of arms and missiles but of fasts and prayers.'[2] In a brief moment of sycophancy, Ambrose compared Theodosius with Moses, Joshua, Samuel and of course David.[3] A master communicator, Ambrose understood the power of biblical allegory and often took the opportunity to sprinkle a few biblical verses into his letters. Still, the emperor of the east did not rely on a simple shepherd's sling; he marched at the head of a formidable army. It appears that the emperor set a steady, almost brutal pace in an effort to prepare his soldiers for worse hardships to come: for the battle itself. Their rapid advance through Illyricum to the Alpes Iulii went unopposed, and Theodosius and his staff must have had suspicions about what lay ahead when they discovered that the eastern ends of the mountain passes had been left undefended. Arbogastes had, based on his previous experiences fighting against the usurper Magnus Maximus in Gaul, decided that the best strategy was to keep his forces united to defend Italy itself, and to that end he went so far as to leave the Alpine passes unguarded. Arbogastes' army consisted mainly of his fellow Franks and Romano-Gauls, plus his own Gothic *foederati*.

Arbogastes mustered his army near Mediolanum. Instead of overstretching his forces and employing them foolishly by splitting them up into penny packets, he kept his army as a cohesive entity so as to effectively make Theodosius' entry into Italy costly. Simple awareness of geographical realities make it clear that Theodosius expected to face Arbogastes somewhere in Pannonia, whose terrain and location made it a convenient meeting-place for armies, so much so that many civil wars had been fought there over the previous two centuries. Yet, thanks to Arbogastes' strategy of maintaining a single, relatively cohesive force, the eastern army passed through the Alpes Iulii without any hitch and descended towards the valley of the River Frigidus. It was in this narrow, mountainous locality that Theodosius came upon the western army's encampment within the *claustra Alpium Iuliarum* barrier system, the *tractus*, in the opening days of September. Arbogastes had seen to it that the choice of the site of the coming battle would be his, and the style of combat as well.

An iron maxim of war is to imagine what your enemy most wants you to do and not do it. By opting to keep his army together and force battle at a place of his choosing and on his terms, Arbogastes demonstrated particular ingenuity in his selection of the valley on the northern bank of the Frigidus. Perhaps no element of warfare has been of greater importance to the conduct of battle than terrain, the ground that constitutes the tactical or strategic box within which armies have to fight. One does not have to be a master of tactics to be aware that, in warfare, terrain features, whether they are woods, rivers or heights, exercise a powerful influence on the conduct of operations and that the possession, in this particular case, of a restrictive piece of ground can be of inestimable value to one side (viz. Arbogastes' army), operating greatly to the detriment of the opposition (viz. Theodosius' army). Napoléon famously looked for 'lucky' generals on whom good fortune smiled. He spoke of the *coup d'œil* – 'stroke of the eye' – as the 'gift of being able to see at a glance the possibilities offered by the terrain'.[4] With Theodosius looking to compel a confrontation, Arbogastes had so far been scrupulous in not playing the eastern emperor's game. According to the advice of his contemporary Vegetius: 'For good generals do not attack in open battle where the danger is mutual, but do it always from a hidden position, so as to kill or at least terrorise the enemy while their own men are unharmed as far as possible.'[5]

Vegetius was writing in the aftermath of Adrianopolis. What he is arguing here, therefore, is that while engaging in pitched battle was potentially decisive, the risk of suffering catastrophic defeat necessitated astute commanders to also consider less direct methods of attack. Arbogastes' location for what he saw as an unavoidable battle was chosen so as to force the eastern army to mount its attack upon his position from a karst plateau. Known today as the Hrušica Plateau (elev. 1,080m) and situated in the south-eastern sub-Alpine region of Slovenia, it was the location of a Roman fort called Ad Pirum, while up and over it ran the Via Gemina.

Waiting for Theodosius

We come soon to the main battle, but before we do we should always bear in mind that the clash by the Frigidus took place between two Roman strongholds, namely Castra ad Fluvium Frigidum (Ajdovščina) and Ad Pirum (Hrušica), two of a series of interconnecting Roman fortifications that defended the hilly and mountainous eastern approaches to the Italian peninsula. The Romans had been erecting military camps, barriers, ramparts, watchtowers and forts in this region since Octavianus (the future Augustus) campaigned here in 35 BC,[6] though the complete pacification of Illyria would not be achieved until the year AD 9. As Sextus Festus, *magister memoriae* to Valens, notes: 'Under Iulius Octavian Caesar Augustus a road was made through the Alpes Iulii; when all the Alpini had been conquered, the provinces of the Norici were added.'[7]

This road would have been the Via Gemina. Among the first strongholds were Castra ad Fluvium Frigidum and Ad Pirum, as well as that of Nauportus (Vrhnika),[8] which defended a port at the nearby river that in earlier times had received waterborne cargoes.[9] The distance between Castra ad Fluvium Frigidum and Ad Pirum was 15km (9 miles), a comfortable day's march for a Roman soldier.[10]

The construction of the *claustra Alpium Iuliarum* system developed gradually from the late third century until the second half of the fourth century; after the fifth century the fortifications fell into disrepair. Basically a defence system erected in three lines, the forts were supplemented by wooden palisades, signal posts, watchtowers and hilltop fortified settlements, which beetled over muscular contours. Taking advantage of the diverse terrain, barrier walls were incorporated between steep limestone ridges and precipitous mountain faces. The barrier walls, for example, at Ad Pirum were almost 2km in length, and enclosed the valleys north and south of the pass, while the main Roman road ran through the fort itself. The latter was roughly oval in shape with a circumference of more than 600m, with a circuit at a height of 6 to 8m and a thickness of some 2.7m, studded with towers 10m in height. Well adapted to the mountainous topography, this in-depth defensive system of an already arduous passage across the rough, trackless terrain of the Alpes Iulii was principally a fortified military zone on the border of northern Italy and the provinces to the east, where traffic was funnelled along controlled routes.[11]

Since it was ideally suited for defence, it is deeply ironic that the *claustra Alpium Iuliarum* barrier system demonstrated its worth in the wars between emperors and usurpers and not against barbarian invasions from the east. So it was that in 352 Constantius II won his second victory over his western rival Flavius Magnus Magnentius – who had passed this way the previous spring[12] – by taking and holding Ad Pirum. In 388 the same fort played a crucial role in the two battles between Theodosius and Magnus Maximus. As there was not, and is not, any other practical route for an army to come into the Italian peninsula from the east, the fort would once again serve this purpose on 5 and 6 September 394.

Although there are no surviving eyewitness accounts of the battle, the picture portrayed by the sources seems to suggest that Arbogastes simply waited for Theodosius to emerge from the narrow pass at the southern end of what is now called the Postojna Gate (Slovene: *Postojnska vrata*) – the northern end being the Hrušica Plateau – and deploy his forces. However, it is unlikely that a seasoned veteran like Arbogastes would have missed an opportunity to prepare the battlefield to his liking and to harass the Theodosian column-of-march as it wormed its way down the pass. There is evidence that the western *magister militum* made good use of field fortifications such as ditches and palisades similar to an overnight camp.[13] There is also some suggestion that Arbogastes mistook Theodosius' movements on the Hrušica Plateau as attempts to outflank his position and removed some of his fortified positions in the Alpine passes.[14]

On the other hand, this could just have been Arbogastes continuing to keep his forces together with these outlying fortified positions perhaps acting more as forward observation points. Furthermore, Arbogastes seems to have retained control of enough of the Alpine passes to funnel Theodosius towards the Frigidus and occupy the high points overlooking his route of descent.[15] Naturally, for Arbogastes' strategy to be successful he would have to anticipate Theodosius' movements, and so it was to be.

War has always involved the mind, defined by Clausewitz as 'an act of force to compel our enemy to do our will.'[16] Similarly, the French specialist in naval strategy Hervé Coutau-Bégarie reminds us that strategy is 'a dialectic of intelligence in a conflict environment',[17] wherein each side tries to anticipate the reactions of the other in order to gain the advantage. As Clausewitz himself would admit, war takes place in a haze: 'War is the realm of uncertainty; three-quarters of the factors on which action in war is based are wrapped in a fog (*nebel*) of greater or lesser certainty. A sensitive and discriminating judgement is called for; a skilled intelligence to scent out the truth.'[18]

We see that most of the knowledge of the enemy is uncertain; importantly, just as much of the knowledge about one's own force and disposition. Moreover, even the degree of uncertainty is uncertain. It is *mehr oder weniger* ('more or less'). This German phrase is one of the most common ones that Clausewitz employs, a trick to indicate that he is always hedging his bets. Admittedly, war is more than dialectic of will and intelligence as organization and technologies also matter, and did so in late antiquity even if arms and the mode of combat have undergone a complete change during these centuries.

As we return to Arbogastes and the opening stages of the battle of the Frigidus, the steep descent from the Hrušica Plateau to the river valley below compelled Theodosius to squeeze his army through the narrow pass of the Postojna Gate. As was intended, this gave him no time or space for the full deployment of his forces or to fully scout the disposition of the opposing forces. To all intents and purposes, it was an intentionally arranged killing ground draped between the Frigidus and a backdrop of mountain ranges, the ideal staging ground for a battle of annihilation. In the acute analysis of Edward Gibbon:

> He (Theodosius) descended from the hills, and beheld, with some astonishment, the formidable camp of the Gauls and Germans [viz. Gallo-Romans and Franks] that covered with arms and tents the open country, which extends to the walls of Aquileia, and the banks of the Frigidus, or Cold River. This narrow theatre of the war, circumscribed by the Alps [viz. Alpes Iulii] and the Hadriatic (Sea), did not allow much room for the operation of military skill.[19]

Being denied by immutable facts of geography, in theory Theodosius had two options open to him. The first, of course, was to refuse to be drawn onto the terrain where Arbogastes wanted to fight. The other was less palatable to Theodosius, which was to opt for tactical inflexibility; that is to say, a more direct, blunt-force approach against a formidable defensive position. Two options there may have been; however, the crushing reality for Theodosius was option two: to barrel ahead with a full-on attack. By divining the tactical qualities of the battlefield, Arbogastes had made the geographical features of his theatre of war his greatest ally. In short, he had adopted a strategy of trading space for strength, and in so doing making the defence dominant and complicating Theodosius' offensive posture. As Clausewitz would much later put it, 'it is easier to hold ground than take it'; in other words, 'defence is the *stronger form of waging war*.'[20] On Arbogastes' terms, the battle of the Frigidus was about to begin.

Gothic Surge

For Theodosius this was a frustrating state of affairs. He had come westward for a fight. He had a clear strategy based on rapid forward movement. He was prepared for a decisive showdown on the open plains of Pannonia, but here he was bottled up in the lower reaches of the Alpes Iulii.

The general narrative is that the eastern emperor launched the Goths under the young Alaric in what can be described as a human-wave attack against Arbogastes' battleline. With the Goths simply going forward despite the consequences, this was perhaps, said argument continues, an attempt to follow the traditional Roman policy of intentional wastage towards his *foederati*, letting them bear the brunt of the fighting. In the words of Zosimos: 'Preferring to use barbarian legions against the enemy and to risk them first, Theodosius ordered

Gaïnas to advance with his men, followed by the other barbarian commanders with their cavalry, mounted archers and infantry.'[21]

Levelling such an accusation against Theodosius comes easily to the pagan Zosimos, who was no fan of the Nicene emperor. Yet even so, Orosius, a fellow Nicene Christian, makes a similar claim when he says: '[T]he ten thousand Goths, who, it is said, were sent ahead by Theodosius and destroyed to a man by Arbogastes; for the loss of these was certainly a gain and their defeat a victory.'[22]

If the emperor was relying on using overwhelming numbers with little consideration for losses by tossing into action waves of Gothic attackers against Abrogastes' position, Theodosius may have foreseen that the battle with the westerners would be a brutal physical encounter. If this was indeed the case, and the Goths were therefore viewed as distinct shock troops, then we have to assume that he organized the make-up of his eastern army accordingly with barbarians as opposed to Roman soldiers, fated to absorb the majority of casualties. Later on Alaric was certain to use to his political advantage the disquiet among his followers caused by the Gothic losses at the Frigidus and the rumour that Theodosius held an utter disregard for mounting losses and they had intentionally been used as 'cannon fodder'.[23]

Was Theodosius just throwing in 'meat' on the first day of the battle by the Frigidus? As a practical matter, even if Rome had a long history of using *foederati* to achieve its military goals, it would have been extremely chancy for Theodosius to have risked such an ulterior motive when he was facing a skilled opponent who posed a legitimate threat to his reign. On the one hand, Theodosius almost certainly believed that an all-out Gothic assault looked to destroy all ahead of it. On the other hand, due to his careful preparations it is entirely feasible that Arbogastes forced battle before the eastern army was fully deployed, leading to the heavy casualties suffered by Theodosius' vanguard, which just happened to comprise Goths led by the still relatively unknown Alaric.

As already mentioned, Orosius reckons Gothic casualties being as many as 10,000 out of a total force of 20,000.[24] Whether or not these figures are correct – and they are most likely an exaggeration – it is highly plausible that come the day's end Alaric's forces were half gone, for a 50 per cent casualty rate (including the injured and the missing) is plausible in what appears to have been a bloody head-to-head battle. By the same token, whether or not it was pre-planned, and we should perhaps not view this as a slaughter of the Goths, Theodosius' *foederati* did bear the brunt of the heavy fighting at the Frigidus. Alaric's men made two full-bore assaults against the densely-packed Gallo-Roman infantry in the centre of Arbogastes' battleline only to be slammed back by a feisty defence. The fighting must have been hectic and bitter, just as the courage of the Goths was impressive, but all was in vain as the strength of Arbogastes' position failed the offensive. Theodosius was likely forced to continue fighting even as his *foederati* suffered horrendous casualties, including his Iberian commander Bacurios;[25] such was his need to escape the confined space of the Postojna Gate, especially as Arbogastes still controlled many of the passes and heights surrounding his current precarious position.

Though they fought spear to spear and shield to shield for a long time, thus far the encounter had prospered for the westerners. I think it may safely be said that Arbogastes had never heard of the Chinese military genius Sun Tzu, let alone have read his work on strategy, but the Frankish *generalissimo* would have certainly agreed with the following principle:

1. Generally, he who occupies the field of battle first and awaits his enemy is at ease; he who comes later to the scene and rushes into the fight is weary.
2. And therefore those skilled in war bring the enemy to the field of battle and are not brought there by him.[26]

Controlling others rather than being controlled by others was one of Sun Tzu's fundamental tenets, and many of his tactical measures are devoted to appropriately manipulating the enemy. As Sun Tzu had encouraged almost a thousand years earlier, Arbogastes arrived first at the place of battle, gained the initiative and waited. By so doing, he was to shape the coming conflict by bringing Theodosius to the battlefield of his choice. So far, so good for Arbogastes.

The night before the battle Theodoret claims that Theodosius was visited by two heavenly riders in white raiment on white horses: John the Evangelist and Philip the Apostle. They bade him to take courage. A common soldier, continues Theodoret, had the same dream.[27] For what they were about to face, both the emperor and the common soldier needed all the courage they could muster, and much more besides.

Judgement Day

The western lines had buckled and groaned, but did not break: Theodosius' main axis of attack had been firmly rebuffed and had come to a shattered standstill. So stymied, the battered and mauled eastern army was forced to withdraw. This was the moment of supreme crisis for the eastern army. Exhausted, haggard and reeling, its surviving soldiers spent a nervous night mulling over the disappointment of the day. Morale is the most vital factor for soldiers. It is not just how they feel about their prospects relative to the enemy – who had fought bravely, cold-bloodedly and decisively – it is also about the experiences they have had recently and how they are anticipating the future. Now rather brutally thinned out by the day's events, for the easterners huddled around their camp fires the future did not look too bright.

Meanwhile, the emperor himself almost certainly fretted that perhaps God had forsaken him. Seeing the battering his army had taken both in terms of casualties and morale and knowing that the likelihood of a repeat performance the next day would bring about the physical and mental collapse of his forces, his reign and perhaps even his efforts to impose Nicene orthodoxy on the empire, Theodosius seemingly had no cards left to play. The emperor therefore looked to prayer for salvation.

As day dimmed into the long hours of darkness, for Theodosius this was going to be the moment of truth. Often, when someone expects to fail, the expectation becomes self-fulfilling. In the western camp, on the other hand, it was a night for jubilant carousing. As Zosimos reports:

> When night came and the armies separated, Eugenius was so pleased with his success that he rewarded his bravest soldiers and allowed his men to eat, in the belief that there could be no more fighting after such a defeat. Just before dawn, however, the emperor Theodosius made a full-scale attack. Eugenius' troops, who were either resting or occupied with their meal, were killed before they knew what hit them.[28]

Still, in his pagan bias, as we can see, Zosimos has absolutely no room for God's miracle – more of which anon – as he has Eugenius' men caught off guard by a postprandial predawn assault upon their camp. In Orosius' Christian account, on the other hand, God's miracle has yet to be. The ever vigilant Arbogastes was neither resting on his laurels nor was he feasting: he was already planning to press home his hard-won advantage on the following day. Using his control of many Alpine passes, on the night of 5 September, Arbogastes sent a detachment of his army under *comes* Arbitio around the Theodosian position to blockade them in the Postojna Gate.[29] Perhaps sensing the disenchantment rife in the eastern camp, Arbogastes may have hoped to end the conflict without further bloodshed; a not unreasonable hope as many of the men in both armies had fought side by side as recently as six years earlier when Theodosius had drafted western units to bolster the Roman portion of the eastern army.

However, it was not to be. Arbogastes was to suffer the consequences of the illegitimacy of his elevation of Eugenius. Upon making contact with Theodosian troops, Arbitio played the traitor's part when he and his men signified their willingness to defect for financial remuneration. While giving Theodosius respite from being surrounded and reducing Arbogastes' army, this did not change the tactical situation. The importance of this desertion lay more in its timing rather than the numerical swing as it was interpreted as an answer to Theodosius' prayers. God was with his faithful followers on the Frigidus and this gave the eastern army the much-needed motivation to fight again the following day, and that was not the end of God's apparent designs, for he was not done with Theodosius and his followers just yet. To quote the idiosyncratic words of R.A. Lafferty, 'They had lost the battle at sundown. But victory was waiting for them in the morning.'[30]

Chapter Nine

Divine Wind

'How often have I said to you that when you have eliminated the impossible,
whatever remains, however improbable, must be the truth?'
As Holmes asks Watson in *The Sign of Four*

As we saw, the first day of battle had fallen heavily on the Theodosian vanguard, which was composed of the *foederati*, Alaric and the Goths, half of whom, whatever their true numbers, were left for dead upon the field. It seemed as if the west was going to triumph over the east. Prior to the battle, Eugenius and Arbogastes had apparently placed a statue of Iuppiter wielding a thunderbolt of solid gold on the peaks of the Alpes Iulii – presumably to hurl their thunderbolts at the Christians if they dared to cross into Italy – and had ordered images of Iuppiter's powerful son and helpmate Hercules Invictus to be applied to the battle banners of the western army.[1] The day's end saw Eugenius' camp celebrating its success. Battle is about achieving victory. In this simple framing, you are either winning or you are not. Things were not looking good for Theodosius; the tactical endgame looked clear. He needed nothing short of a miracle to dodge a devastating defeat. Miracles happen, but you do not predict them.

The Power of Prayer

Theodosius got his miracle in the heat of the second day of battle. They say desperate times call for desperate measures. An impetuous wind suddenly sprang up and carried air down the mountainside, slamming into the rear of his men, giving them added momentum while blinding the opposition and wrestling the weapons from their grasp.

A sermon preached by Ioannes Chrysostomos, bishop of Constantinopolis for six stormy years (r. 397–403, †407) in the Church of the Holy Apostles, on the anniversary of Theodosius' death, probably 17 January 399, happens to refer to this 'miraculous' wind and, mentioned earlier, the emperor's prayer:

When the two armies were drawn up facing each other, and clouds of
spears were hurled, and his own troops were being turned back by the

violent onslaught of the enemy, Theodosius leapt from his horse, threw his shield on the ground, and fell to his knees calling for help from heaven, transforming the site of the battle into a church, fighting with tears and prayers, not arrows and javelins and spears. At this a sudden wind arose, and the spears of the enemy were blown back on those who had thrown them. Seeing this, the enemy, who till then had been breathing fury and slaughter, changed tack, acclaiming Theodosius as their emperor.[2]

So, according to Chrysostomos, it was Theodosius alone, through fervent prayer, who won the battle, though it could be argued that any regard for accuracy was not allowed to interfere with the imagination of our preaching prelate.

The End Comes

Imperial prayer or not, in short order the tide of the battle was turned. This was a moment celebrated by the new court poet Claudianus in his inaugural panegyric for Honorius' third consulship, recited at Mediolanum in early January 396:

> Thanks to thine influence the wind of the frozen North
> Overwhelmed the enemy's line with his mountain storms,
> Hurled back their weapons upon the throwers
> And with the violence of his tempest drove back their spears.[3]

Claudianus, despite being 'a most obstinate pagan',[4] does not fail to mention the Frigidus miracle. On the other hand, he does so by praising the god Aeolus (Gk. *Αἴολος*), the Keeper of the Winds,[5] who 'frees the armed tempests from his cave' to aid Honorius' pious father Theodosius.[6] After all, the eulogist was a broad-minded pagan and not a dyed-in-the-wool Christian.

Twenty years later Augustine, in an account of the battle, echoes the same episode in prose, citing Claudianus' hexameters but naturally omitting to mention Aeolus.[7] Augustine's disciple Orosius, writing after 417, also omitted the same couplet and, on top of it, even censored Claudianus' name.[8] Aeolus or no Aeolus, following a terrible struggle, the resistance of the western army was well and truly shattered, going down to defeat. What had started out as a pending disaster for one side turned out to be the disorderly rout of the other. At the battle of the Frigidus, not far from where Magnus Maximus had been executed, the western army of Eugenius was utterly defeated.

In the immediate aftermath, Eugenius was surrendered by his own soldiers and brought before the eastern emperor in shackles. His pleas for mercy went unheeded and he was beheaded; the severed head of the erstwhile learned professor was paraded around the victor's camp.[9] Having no reason to expect clemency from Theodosius, Arbogastes fled into the nearby mountains and two days later fell upon his sword like king Saul on Mount Gilboa and so perished.[10] So fell the last of the antagonists of Theodosius. As for the defeated soldiers of Eugenius, Zosimos, certainly no fan of the emperor, does stress that Theodosius wisely granted them a general amnesty.[11] This of course was the common practice of the time, troops being then a very valuable commodity.

Roman Holiday

Zosimos' claim that Theodosius visited Rome immediately after his victory at the Frigidus has received much scholarly debate. The emperor certainly visited the ancient capital after Maximus' defeat sometime in June 389.[12] Many have taken Zosimos as misdating this visit, not mentioned under 389. Zosimos may, however, be right, and Theodosius may have visited Rome twice: (i) the details here are not simply a doublet of 389; (ii) Theodosius' harangue to the Senate fits 394 well, especially his withdrawal of state subsidies for pagan cults; (iii) Theodoret does refer to a visit after 388/390;[13] (iv) epigraphic evidence suggests that Theodosius addressed the Senate in 394,[14] but this may refer to a deputation of senators to Mediolanum; (v) Ioannes Antiochensis mentions a triumph in Rome in 394,[15] and if this was so then surely Theodosius must have been present; (vi) Zosimos refers again to this visit,[16] where his source is probably Olympiodorus.

Apart from the grave uncertainties and obscurities of many of the aforementioned sources, three points may be noted. First, Theodosius appointed an acting *praefectus urbis Romae*, Fabius Pasiphilus, after the Frigidus, who was still in office on the emperor's death. If he had come to Rome, he would have appointed a new regular prefect. Second, there was hardly any time between the battle and his death the following January to visit Rome, given his slowness in travelling at the best of times, let alone then when he was already gravely ill from the hydropsy that was to kill him. Third, it would suit the pagan prejudices of Zosimos to change a humiliating procession of senators to Mediolanum to beg Theodosius' pardon into a journey of the emperor to harangue the pagan Senate in Rome.[17]

Controlling the Narrative

A miracle was performed, a pious emperor victorious, God had spoken. A pagan-loving usurper was discomfited. The apparent absurdities – or more to the point, the acceptance of them – of Theodosius' miracle can wait for later.

Let us first focus on what the Christians thought of it all, for unlike Robert Graves' imagined Marathon for the Persians,[18] the Frigidus was not going to be something one avoided discussing too much. Quite the opposite, in fact.

Nothing is more important to an accurate retelling of history than good method. What we believe happened, how it happened and why it happened all derive from good method. The problem is that if you cannot recognize poor methods, you are more likely to read something and believe it. This can lead to an incomplete telling of the past and the propagation of myths. The better way is to read something, analyze it, and then decide whether or not to believe it.

When we turn to the Frigidus we immediately note that Christian chroniclers, viewing the usurpation and battle through the lens of pagan-Christian conflict, understandably interpreted the final day as a divine judgement on the pagans. The contemporary church historian, Rufinus of Aquileia, has this to say:

> It may perhaps be hard for the pagans to believe what happened; for it was discovered that, after the prayer that the emperor [Theodosius] poured out to God, such a fierce wind arose as to turn the weapons of the enemy back on those who hurled them. When the wind persisted with great force and every missile launched by the enemy was foiled, their spirit gave way; or rather it was shattered by divine power.[19]

There is truth in this statement and much fiction too. This was certainly an unforeseen climatic event or – if the Christian story is totally to be believed – a God-given miracle in the form of an extraordinary tempest. As Rufinus himself claims, his account of the miraculous wind came from 'officers who were present'.[20] Naturally, this was soon interpreted as divine intervention on behalf of the pious Theodosius. Hence Orosius, on the second day of the battle, just as the two armies were about to get to grips with each other, has this to say:

> Immediately a great and indescribable whirlwind blew into the faces of the enemy. The darts of our men, which were shot and carried through the air and were borne through the great void further than any man could throw, were almost never allowed to fall before striking a mark. And furthermore, the unceasing whirlwind struck the faces and breasts of the enemy, now heavily dashing their shields together and taking their breath when it pressed them closely together; and now tearing their shields violently away, it left them unprotected, and now holding their shields together, it drove them back; the weapons also which they themselves had hurled strongly were caught by the backward force of the wind and, when driven back, transfixed the unfortunate throwers themselves.[21]

Such, then, is the story that lay behind the defeat of the pagan foe. The victory and its explanation were, of course, subjects of heated dispute among pagans and Christians, with sharp disagreement and a considerable amount of noise. This is not surprising.

To explain this difference of opinion, you have to wade into the weeds of the politics of the day. There, we come upon the busy bishop of Mediolanum, who though a servant of the Lord had an extraordinary influence on imperial politics and for him there was no other narrative.

Ambrose would eagerly exploit Eugenius' ostensible concessions to pagans for his own *political* advantage and then advertised his *religious* opposition in part to proclaim his fidelity to the victor, Theodosius. While Ambrose was always energetic in promoting his particular brand of Christianity – building churches and discovering relics to underpin their sanctity – this was all very personal for him too. Before departing for the front to play their part in the coming confrontation with Theodosius, Arbogastes and Virius Nicomachus Flavianus had made a menacing promise to the good bishop, saying that 'they would turn the basilica of Mediolanum into a stable, and enlist the clergy into the army' when Eugenius returned victorious.[22] Fortunately for Ambrose, such a victory was not to be: both men ended up committing suicide after their defeat at the Frigidus.

Ambrose was to write to Theodosius immediately after he had received the news of the emperor's victory sometime in September, so not long after the battle itself. In this letter he says:

Thanks to the Lord our God who has responded to your faith and piety. He has refashioned an ancient type of holiness, letting us see in our time what we marvel at as we read the Scriptures, namely the mighty presence of divine help in battle, so that mountain heights have not slowed up the course of your coming, nor did enemy arms prove any obstacle.[23]

Apart from the divine help on a biblical scale and a speedy transit westward across the Alpes Iulii, there is no suggestion in the bishop's epistle of a miraculous wind.

In a follow-up letter to Theodosius, perhaps written no later than November of the same year, Ambrose again mentions the emperor's victory:

It is said that your victory was granted in the manner of the ancients, with ancient portents (*vetustis miraculis*) like those of the blessed Moses; the blessed Joshua son of Nun, of Samuel, and of David. It was granted not by man's foresight but by the outpouring of heavenly grace (*caelestis gratiae effusione*).[24]

Once again Ambrose attributes the emperor's victory to divine help, citing the customary biblical examples. There is no mention of any miracle, wind or otherwise, although the reference to exemplary biblical warrior Joshua may suggest such when we think about the collapse of the walls of Jericho or the hailstorm that fell on the Amorites when they were ready to engage the Israelites in battle, the day the sun stood still.[25]

We first get a glimpse of Theodosius' miracle some five months after the welcome victory. The occasion was a solemn one. On 25 February 395, in the Basilica Portiana, Mediolanum, the bishop was venerating the memory of the same emperor, who had passed away forty days earlier on 17 January,[26] a little more than four months after his 'miraculous' victory. An accomplished orator, he transported the congregation gathered that day back to the recent battle, in which many of whom undoubtedly took part. Ambrose spoke thus:

> When because of the problems of the terrain and the hindrance of the camp followers, the army was falling into battle line too slowly, and through delay in joining battle the enemy's horsemen were seen to be charging, the emperor leapt down from his horse and, advancing alone before the line, cried out, 'Where is the God of Theodosius?' He was saying this as one already close to Christ. For who possibly could say this except one who knew himself to be united with Christ? By this cry he put heart into everyone, by his example he moved everyone to arms, a man undeniably advanced in years, but mighty because of his faith.[27]

Incidentally, this may be the ultimate source for the detail of Theodosius leaping off his horse in the aforementioned sermon of Ioannes Chrysostomos. It does not appear in Rufinus – he has the emperor climb up on a rock so that he is in full view of both armies[28] – and so it is also missing from all those who used him as a source. Anyway, once again Ambrose makes no direct mention of a miraculous wind, though he does apparently touch upon it a few sentences later when he reminds soldiers who were at the battle that, like the prophet Elisha in Samaria,[29] Theodosius' faith blinded his foes: 'You have surely heard, you soldiers who were surrounded, that wherever there is perfidy (*ubi perfidia*), there is also blindness. So the army of unbelievers (*exercitus infidelium*) deserved to be struck blind (*ibi caecitas*).'[30]

Nonetheless, Ambrose did make a direct reference to the divine wind of the Frigidus a month later. This was in a sermon he preached on Psalm 36: 'An oracle is within my heart/concerning the sinfulness of the wicked:/There is no fear of God before his eyes.... See how the evildoers lie fallen –/down, not able to rise.'[31]

Thus David notes that those who reject God find themselves overtaken by sin. What is more, they assume that what they do will never be punished, or never even found out. Sin being addictive, those who turn from God find themselves forever pursing depravity. The psalm ends with David envisaging these enemies of God as already defeated, so utterly overcome that they never regroup.

For Ambrose Psalm 36 is an attractive Trojan horse to help him convey the righteousness of Theodosius' triumph over Eugenius. For in his sermon the bishop vividly calls to mind the way a sudden wind at the Frigidus turned imminent defeat into glorious victory:

> For spears often rebound on those who have thrown them. This happened in the recent war, when faithless and sacrilegious men (*infideles et sacrilegi*) attacked a man trusting in the Lord, and tried to snatch his throne away from him, making dire threats of persecuting the churches of the Lord, so that suddenly a wind arose which tore their shields from the hands of the faithless and turned all their spears and missiles back on the army of the sinner. Brought low by their own weapons, they gave ground to the attacking winds even before their adversaries reached them. Yet these wounds to their bodies were no more severe than those to their spirits, for they lost heart when they found God was fighting against them.[32]

Here we must imagine Ambrose pausing at one point, letting the silence gather, and then sharing his feelings. Anyway, this particular passage has been universally and almost certainly correctly understood as a direct reference to the 'miracle' on the Frigidus just six months after the battle, and the 'miraculous' wind is perhaps based on eyewitness accounts. And so Theodosius' miracle took shape.

The Will of God

Never shaken in his faith that he had a firm grip on the only truth that mattered to his audience, Ambrose worked hardest at making his version of the events on the Frigidus as attractive as possible. So it is small wonder that Ambrose turns out to be the standard-bearer for the belief that Theodosius was a true instrument of God. In this respect, it was one small step to regard the battle of the Frigidus as an event wherein pagan turncoats and their *exercitus infidelium* were triumphed over by a blessed and pious emperor and his faithful followers.[33]

In what was an extremely religious age, Abraham Lincoln was clearly a pious man with an honest soul who strongly believed in the will of God shaping great events. For that reason, he would often ruminate on the Almighty's intentions *vis-à-vis* the survival of the American republic. In September 1862, following the Union defeat at the Second Battle of Bull Run (28–30 August 1862), the president grappled with the working of God's will in the war currently tearing the republic apart. In a private memo for himself he leaves no doubt whatever that God would finally choose one contestant over another:

> The will of God prevails. In great contests each party claims to act in accordance with the will of God. Both *may* be, and one *must* be, wrong. God cannot be *for* and *against* the same thing at the same time. In the present civil war it is quite possible that God's purpose is something different from the purpose of either party – and yet the human instrumentalities, working as they do, are of the best adaptation to effect His purpose. I am almost ready to say that this is probably true – that God wills this contest, and wills that it shall not end yet. By his mere great power, on the minds of the now contestants, He could have either *saved* or *destroyed* the Union without a human contest. Yet the contest began. And, having begun, He could give the final victory to either side any day. Yet the contest proceeds.[34]

In the contest by the banks of the Frigidus the independent will of God had evidently chosen Theodosius. In God's judgement Eugenius was no longer a Nicene Christian like his virtuous opponent, but something simpler and more manageable: a defector. The upstart usurper was tainted with guilt by association, making common cause with those steadfast pagans Arbogastes and Virius Nicomachus Flavianus. Still, if 'paganism' was a twisty, slippery word, it is worth noting who was using it, for subsequent ecclesiastical historians, if they cared to mention Eugenius' faith, settle for a simple but searing 'insincere'.[35] Pause for a moment to admire the cynical cleverness of the slur. No one can conclusively disprove it.

There was plenty more of this stuff. Ambrose, and those that followed in his hallowed footsteps – Rufinus, who wrote (in Latin) in 402/403; and Sokrates Scholastikos, Theodoret and Sozomenos, who wrote (in Greek) one after the other in the 440s – clearly wanted to focus on how God had assisted Theodosius' victory over 'the barbarian bandit' and the 'unworthy usurper'.[36] This was a familiar theme, for the panegyrists of Constantinus had condemned Maxentius and his troops as 'impious' on the grounds that the power of the 'legitimate' emperor had come from God.[37] Not only that, for the term *tyrannus*, 'usurper', had taken on 'the additional connotation of a persecutor of Christians' and – on top of that – as a person who was 'by no means sincere in his profession of Christianity'.[38] This was unquestionably false.

Eugenius himself was certainly a Christian, and so were a good many members of his court as well as many of his soldiers. As for implying that Theodosius' entire army was Christian, that is undoubtedly false too. Many of the rank and file in the eastern *comitatus* were *foederati*, at this date predominately 'heretic' Arians or even pagans.[39] On top of that, many of Theodosius' senior officers were still pagans. As mentioned before, until his sudden death shortly before the campaign, the man picked to command the cavalry was Richomeres, a staunch pagan. It would be many decades before the Romans would field an army that consisted entirely of Nicene Christians.

The Ambrosian narrative on Theodosius' victory over his rival has been heavily worked over to give it an ecclesiastical flavour. Invoking the panegyric theology of Nicene victory, Nicene orthodoxy being his *idée fixe*, always on his mind if not on his tongue, Ambrose zeros in on the argument that Theodosius' faith not only blinded his foes but, more importantly, enabled him to triumph over paganism too.[40] For the bishop the battle was nothing other than the conflict between a Nicene emperor and a pro-pagan usurper. The miracle, in other words, was patiently midwifed by Ambrose and his fan club, the first of these hagiographers being his secretary, the deacon Paulinus Mediolanensis, who was quick to consolidate the bishop's reputation through a biography written soon after his death in 397. As with so many incidents, the miracle grew with the telling.

The Twilight Zone

It is a truism that religion and politics could not be separated in ancient Rome. Today, by contrast, conformity is more often demanded to political rather than theological orthodoxy, the supposed tyranny of traditional organized religion having been drained out of politics. As a result, there is a tendency to yield to the crisp but cautious rhetoric of academic safeguarding, which is part of the legacy of the Age of Reason, with its propensity to undervalue spiritual empathy and endeavours to emancipate western thought from the iron grip of religious dogma.[41] There is a feeling, once the layers of academic rhetoric are peeled back, that anyone would think our new post-modern world does not like miracles, God-given or otherwise, and I would rather accept the traditional accounts over verdicts handed down from the great house of Anglophone academe. The conclusions of cold, factual research seem like striking the air with one's fist or catching a rainbow in one's fingers, and who can seize that? Of course, if you are not on board with this idea, the following paragraph may not be for you.

My clear-eyed, tidy take? In our nuclear age of ultra-complicated technology, when the tides of time and taste, not to mention political power, are against it, it is easy (I think) to lose the sense of astounding power of the supernatural that people in the ancient world witnessed routinely and make sport of such zeal. Perhaps it is more apposite not to dismiss everything as ridiculous or unbelievable when their concerns were far removed from ours. The soldiers on the field of the Frigidus, therefore, were wholly men of their time, that is the fourth century, in which what we dismiss as the supernatural was taken for granted by everybody, Christian and pagan alike.

All that being said, we should never dismiss out of hand the simple fact that even today soldiers are some of the most superstitious folk imaginable, along with mariners and miners and others in hazardous professions that assume a high and sometimes deadly risk to life. After all, our modern skulls house a Stone Age mind and the most ancient things remain in the ceremonies of life and death, ritual performances from pre-civilized times. Additionally, we share our skull space with our sentiments: the subconscious can easily envisage that the real world has room for superstitions, even for God's miraculous interventions, when assaulted by the hideous truth of war. However, it must be said, our sentiments can arouse ancient emotions more primitive than Christianity.

Let us take a look at a fitting example of such soldierly behaviour from the later Roman world. Bestowing the title of *Caesar* upon each of his sons, Carinus and Numerianus, Carus (r. 282–283) led his troops against Persia with Numerianus, the younger of the two. The Sāsānian king, Bahrām II (r. 274–293), was considered weak, therefore factions within his court were vying for power. When Persian ambassadors came to the Roman camp they found Carus seated on the ground enjoying the same rations as his soldiers. Carus curtly told them that unless Bahrām acknowledged Rome as his master, Carus' army would render Persia as bare of trees as the emperor's own bald head. True to his threat, Carus took Ctesiphon and then penetrated beyond the Tigris,[42] where he died suddenly and mysteriously, allegedly struck by lightning while he lay sick in his camp bed. The Roman army was traditionally superstitious, and an ancient prophecy stated that the Tigris was to be the eastern frontier of the empire; hence Roman conquest was to go no further. Filled with superstition, the army of careworn professional soldiers pressured the young Numerianus, now emperor, to march out of Persia with victory almost within their grasp.[43]

In our run-of-the-mill daily lives, we exist in a cacophony of beliefs; in this a sharp line is drawn between the secular and the sacred. So religion is of roughly as much interest to us as the mysterious § symbol on our keyboard: it exists, you ignore it and everything is fine. Certainly, occasionally we may talk about our God and think of ourselves while we tick the Christian box as our cultural identity without having any religious belief. In that sense, we feel culturally Christian, so deeply imbued with its myths, canvases, hymns and parables. We turn to soldiers. Deep down it is the soldiers who experience combat that have never changed. Equally, war has not changed, but the tools, methods and perceptions of war have.

Of course, it goes without saying that human society is continuously shaped by social, political and technological developments. Still, change the uniforms they wore, change the weapons they wielded, change the burdens they carried, change the food they ate, change the means of transportation and change the topography, but the issues of combat soldiering and the campaigning life they live corresponds with what went before, no matter the epoch. Generally they are concerned with the problems of finding food, shelter, a dry bed, alcohol (the never-failing token of a soldier's life), and women, and of course with staying alive. Who can deny this?

Soldiering brings out many things in a man, but above all it makes him measurelessly down to earth. 'But how come you so bare?' the peacenik Erasmus once asked the warmongering soldier. 'Why,' he replied, 'whatsoever I got from pay, plunder, sacrilege, rapine and theft was spent in wine, whores and gaming.'[44] Erasmus was the marvel of Europe with his scholarship and his study of antiquity but, on the other hand, it was still a cruel and crude age, and states could not stop their subjects privateering or enlisting in foreign armies. Such matters seem timeless, and indeed they are. As the mercenary-cum-versifier Archilochos,[45] using the sticky and earthy wit typical of a soldier at war, sang: 'how wealth that was built up by much hard work/all drains away into a harlot's gut.'[46] Though exaggerated for effect, this merely colours common knowledge. We get the distinct impression that Archilochos was the sort of old sweat who drinks to get drunk, and goes straight from upright and thirsty to horizontal and silent: no unseemly shouting or brawling, no 'who dare meddle with me' taproom heroics. He probably had not developed the capacity for small talk, or could never see the point of it.

Thanatophobia

In choosing to study the ancient world the student pretty much ends up in a world of approximations, one where perception, judgement and even facts are in suspension and could shift at a moment's notice. Still, in the real world, even the ancient one, the student needs to study people, not pure hardware, and all soldiers harbour a common fear: that of death. Literary embellishments notwithstanding, did not Horace himself claim, in a sly reference to his undistinguished military career, to have shamefully thrown away his shield in a panic to facilitate his escape from the horrors of the field of Philippi where Romans had chosen to kill each other?[47] Conscious of daily hardship and threats, combatants who under desperate circumstances have every reason to fear for their lives find there is a universal 'brotherhood of arms' that transcends geography and history. This may seem a little trite to non-combatants – experts of the armchair variety particularly – but, as Polybios once wrote, it is impossible for a man lacking in the experiences of warlike operations to write about war itself.[48]

War is a terrible and impassioned drama regulated, it is true, by four or five general rules. For that rough edge of battle, combat is the most important drama in a soldier's life. It occupies only a short time. Nonetheless, these vivid moments acquire an extraordinary importance, since it is within the arena of the bloody battlefield that he witnesses the greatest violence in war. For him it is a wildly unstable physical and emotional environment: a world of boredom and bewilderment, the quotidian tedium that makes up the greater part of the ordinary soldier's experience, punctuated by moments of depression and delirium, of triumph and terror, of anger and angst, of courage and cowardice.

Combat veterans learn early on that fear is contagious and that a man who gives in to it is a man out of control, a man befuddled and confused and a danger to everyone around him, but especially to himself. To survive in combat, you have to be cool and calculating and clearheaded, but most of all, as a veteran believes, you have to have an infinite faith in the idea that you are going to survive the battle and make it home. This calls to mind the doomed Confederate attack on the last day of Gettysburg. As the butternut-brown-clad infantrymen gathered in the woods of Seminary Ridge, a furry creature scampered into the distance, and one of them is believed to have said in his slow southern drawl: 'Run, ol' hay-uh! If ah was an ol' hay-uh, ah'd run too.'[49] This was a hopeless charge that killed or injured more than half the aggressors.[50] It was not all valour.

The slow retreat became a panic-stricken rout. Already men were breaking away, running wild and witless here and there, flinging away their weapons to facilitate their swift career, crying out in fear and flying. It is a truism that he who thinks only how to flee counts every foeman twice. Colonel Charles Ardant du Picq, a brilliant young French officer whose writings concentrated on the behaviour of the individual under the stress of combat and, in particular, emphasized the vital importance of the morale and discipline of soldiers (he was soon to be killed in action during the opening stages of the Franco-Prussian War), once wrote the following: 'Man's heart is as changeable as fortune. Man shrinks back, apprehends danger in any effort in which he does not foresee success. There are some isolated characters of iron temper, who resist the tendency; but they are carried away by the great majority.'[51]

This was written by a fighter who knew what it was to be scared stiff. There is that old cliché: a coward dies a thousand deaths, but a brave man only one. That is wrong, as du Picq understood rightly enough. No man is once and for always a cringing coward, nor once and for always a courageous champion. On the contrary, a man will act cowardly and at other times act with courage, each in different measures and each with varying consistency. It was exactly the same for Archilochos all those centuries before, just as it was for countless combatants before and after him. For our soldier poet the heart ($\theta\upsilon\mu\acute{o}\varsigma$) was that part of the man where rage and courage, fear and desire stalk:

> O heart, my heart, seething with unmanageable woes, rise up (?) and defend yourself, setting your breast against the enemy in their ambush, and standing firm hard by the foe. When victorious do not exult openly, but when defeated do not fall down lamenting at home, but rejoice in joyful times and grieve in bad ones in moderation. Know what pattern controls mankind.[52]

In reality, you can call upon heart for courage, but the result may not be what you want.

The suppressing of one's instinct for safety is not easy, particularly at moments when your stomach turns over and will not go back into its place. Some men, remembers Polybios, another who knew battle first-hand, are brave in single combat but simply fall to pieces when formed up in ordered ranks and are 'sharing the risks with their comrades'.[53] Pre-battle jitters do not just afflict the ordinary soldier either. The Akhaian leader Aratos of Sikyon (271–213 BC), again according to Polybios, was noted for his distinct lack of manly courage when it came to actual battle.[54] In particular, he would suffer from cramps in the bowels, palpitations of the heart and a sudden loss in colour prior to combat, or so says Plutarch.[55]

Archilochos, Polybios and du Picq all perfectly understood that bravery and boldness were not everything. All men were brave and all men were cowards, depending on the circumstances. As anyone who has been to war knows, it is the great leveller. It shows a man as he really is, not as he would like to be, nor as he would like others to think he is. It shows him stripped, with his greatness mixed with pathetic fears and weaknesses.[56] As combat veterans know all too well, if you were not scared, something was wrong.

The present author has digressed from the subject. Soldiers have very little influence over the great events they witness. All they habitually see of a battle, apart from their fellow soldiers and the enemy assault, is their immediate superiors. They may kill, witness killing and lose their comrades, but that is all they actually know of the battle. This should come as no surprise, for a soldier can only be in one part of the battle at a time. As Rifleman Benjamin Harris recollects of his experience at the battle of Roliça (17 August 1808): 'I do not pretend to give a description of this or any other battle I have been present at.

All I can do is to tell the things which happened immediately around me, and that, I think, is as much as a private soldier can be expected to do.'[57]

A completely honest and fair assessment. Soldiers see little that could be classed as heroic, and no one who could be described as a hero. Also out of battle there is the frightful load of his equipment, the pinch of a sodden boot, the gnawing bite of hunger, and of course the small quotidian joys of comradeship.

War naturally generates a sense of unity, of pride, of identity and of excitement, but war also generates a human cost, and such costs are measured in death, wounds and profound personal suffering. The fear of war's price tag is the soldier's universal lot. So how does a soldier, beset by the danger of death, dread of wounds and the greatly increased risk of succumbing to disease which membership of an army has entailed for most of military history, sustain his will to combat?

Rituals are comforting; they bring order into a world in which soldiers have little control. Rituals help deal with mental stress arising from the apparent randomness of death and injury in battle. Rituals, usually personal and done in an unemotional manner, are prescribed behaviours in which there is no empirical connection between the means (e.g. tapping the helmet three times before engaging in a firefight) and the desired end (e.g. surviving incoming rounds from beyond the perimeter wire). Because there is no connection between the two, rituals are not rational and sometimes they are actually irrational. Besides, an individual soldier's superstition is not a sort of magical panacea during the noises and strains of a combat situation, neither is it an off-the-shelf one-size-fits-all sort of protection. The bottom line in combat is fear: the feeling of fear is there to protect; a soldier's barometer.

Acts of God(s)

Time and again combatants have concluded that natural phenomena, such as the sudden change in the direction of the wind that caused the conflagration of the wooden defence wall at Masada or the great storms that severely mauled *la Armada Felicisma*, were acts of God. So, as an afterthought, soldiers on the second day of the battle of the Frigidus perhaps interpreted a chance local meteorological phenomenon as a supernatural intervention, and this was a phenomenon that, unlike a 'Vision of the Cross' in the sky or the 'Angels of Mons', for instance, could only blow in favour of one army: Theodosius on his knees uttered a prayer and the tide of battle was turned in his army's favour.[58]

It should be borne in mind that a soldier's existence fed an instinct that humanity had forgotten millennia earlier: that life is ruled by a daily struggle to find food and water and to be protected from the elements. Campaigns must, of course, be fought in all kinds of weather, fair or foul, and except for the soldiers' timeless complaints of frigid cold, beating rains and harsh sun, most conditions pass without mention, but in the thick of battle, any unexpected – and decisive – meteorological phenomenon assumes a special significance. The more dramatic and unexpected the circumstances of tempest or torrent, the more unquestionably some god or gods had intervened on behalf of one side against the other. Was not weather the weapon of choice when David called upon God for deliverance from the hands of his enemies,[59] and again when the Amorites fled from Joshua's army?[60] Theodosius was to appeal to the same God who had saved the Israelites.

One word more and we must leave this subject. Soldiers do not fight out of patriotism, but out of loyalty to their comrades, the people they would never have met if it had not been for the uniform. Patriotism, a common resort of the apologist, is a bit esoteric for most, if not all soldiers; too large-scale to see. For some reason, in the minds of many civilians the love of one's country can turn suddenly into a willingness to die for it, as in Horace's '*Dulce et decorum est pro patria mori.*'[61] Yet the soldiers' autonomous unit is their fatherland and their home (viz. the regiment is the soldier's 'tribe', the battalion his 'village', the company his 'street', the platoon/troop his 'house', the section/squad his 'room'). It is here that they belong, fostering that self-respect and need for the respect of his mates and his pride in being one of them; what is called morale or *esprit de corps*. He marches, fights, eats and sleeps beside them, and comes to know them as well as he has known his childhood brothers. Every serious study of individual motivation among combat soldiers confirms that the key to a man's behaviour in war's stern service is his feeling of mutual dependence and obligations towards these immediate comrades; the only men on earth whose opinions matter to him. Again we turn to the personal reminiscences of Rifleman Benjamin Harris:

> The field of death and slaughter, the march, the bivouac, and the retreat, are not bad places in which to judge men.... I enjoyed life more whilst on active service that I have ever done since, and I look back upon my time spent in the fields of the (Iberian) Peninsula as the only part worthy of remembrance.[62]

Soldiers belong to a small, self-contained unique world, live by the same rules and share the same mentality. Indeed, a single-minded adherence to an ethical code at the top of which are courage, loyalty, honour and love – unselfish qualities uncontaminated by the political hyperbola designed to warm up the young for war – is one of the elements that turns feeble citizens into formidable soldiers.

When all is said and done, the conventional notion of 'Queen/King and Country' turns out to be little more than a quaint and empty slogan suitable for flag-waving civilians, from whose mental world soldiers have long since separated. This kind of humbug does not survive the actual experience of battle. It is replaced by simpler concerns, which seem to remain constant throughout history because they have brought genuine comfort and a sense of security to men who are often frightened, often cold and wet, often confused, often in discomfort and often deadly bored. Soldiers do not care for abstract notions; they do not keep off the rain. They do not care for the quarrels of princes or politicians; you cannot toast a claim of sovereignty on the end of a blade on a chilly, damp night. As for the rights and wrongs of their war, or any war, such debates will not stop a swinging sword or a zinging bullet. Flag-waving civilians and brass bands were last seen sending off the Falklands Task Force, but traditions are not killed by facts, and the tradition of flag-waving and brass bands, along with that of tub-thumping politicos, lingers on to put a gloss of romance over everything.

End Times

The apocalypse of course is always preceded by all sorts of events that are never supposed to come to pass. The moon turns red and the sun goes black and it rains torrents of blood.[63] Theodosius' miracle at the Frigidus could be on that list, if one were to believe in the miraculous of course. In fact, it is all about bridging fantasy and reality. For his battlefield 'miracle' was actually a katabatic wind known as the Bora, an ice-cold, often dry, northerly to north-easterly wind, which blows, sometimes in severe gusts, down from the *Altopiano carsico*, the Italian name for the Karst plateau in neighbouring Slovenia, on the eastern shoreline of the Adriatic Sea.[64] When a polar high-pressure area hovers above the interior plateau's snow-covered mountains, it blows the hardest, carrying high-density air from a higher elevation down the steep barren maritime mountains under the force of gravity, reaching hurricane speeds. Its initial temperature is so low that it arrives at the lowlands as a frigid wind, notwithstanding the warming caused by its sudden drop.

Well known in the region, the wind itself is known by various renderings of the name of the mythological Greek deity Βορέας, the North Wind,[65] such as *bura* in Croatian, *burja* in Slovene, буран in Bulgarian and βοράς in Modern Greek. The most commonly used *Bora* is probably from the Ottoman Turkish.

Of course, weather is not the same thing as climate: one happens over days, the other decades, but climate impacts weather. That is to say, climate change does not cause hurricanes, but it cause hurricanes to be more deadly and more destructive. The Bora is still a recurring meteorological feature of the Vipava valley; so much so that its boreal fury, which will ferociously rip through everything in its way, influences the layout and architecture of settlements in the region. Narrow streets bordered by robust buildings with heavy stone roofs predominate in many towns in the path of the Bora and ropes and chains are stretched along footpaths should people get caught outside. In Slovenia, the most affected area is usually the upper Vipava valley, stretching from Ajdovščina to Podnanos, where the speed of the wind can exceed 180km/h and even 200km/h. This was the very location of the dramatic events of 5–6 September 394: 'Local historians assure us that the outcome of a battle fought up on the Karst in A.D. 394 was so affected by a bora – they call it the Battle of the Bora – that it led directly to the end of the Roman Empire.'[66]

Perhaps a tad too much on the nose, but there you go. Yet as a précis on the battle, it surely rings truer than this rather trivializing announcement:

> The miraculous wind is the high point of most surviving accounts of the Frigidus. Sudden storms during the first weeks of September are indeed common in this area. But they are normally accompanied by torrential rain (not mentioned in these texts), which might have been expected to inconvenience both sides equally. A storm consisting solely of a wind that affected only one side is neither probable in itself nor in keeping with local conditions. And a storm that literally blew spears back on those who had thrown them is sheer fantasy.[67]

Really? Rain or no rain, anyone who has experienced first-hand a wind of 200km/h or more would surely see the final resounding statement as unmoored from facts.

Thunderstruck

Some scholars may well rubbish the idea of a 'divine wind', but let us take a look at a couple of examples of similar dramatic meteorological events from the annals of Roman history. Our first example of weather magic happened back in 113 BC when the Roman Republic was facing the threat of the Cimbri and the Teutones, two migratory peoples looking for greener pastures far from their homeland in what is now the Jutland peninsula. Rome had always been obsessed with tribal invasions, and the *consul* Cnaeus Papirius Carbo was sent to deal with the situation at the head of some 30,000 troops. Hearing rumours of the military might of the Republic, even if they were strangers to Rome, the two tribes accepted Carbo's proposal to pull back from the Italian peninsula. He then offered guides to escort them, but it was a ruse.

Not content with a peaceful resolution, Carbo wanted the triumph with which he hoped a victory would crown him. He was counting on a surprise attack, surprise being one of the enduring principles of war. The guides were instructed to lead the tribes towards Noreia (precise location unknown), where the *consul* would set an ambush. It did not turn out that way. For some bizarre reason, the Cimbri managed to discover the plot and turn the tables on the Romans. The ambushers became the ambushed. The Cimbri smashed full force into the Roman column of march, swinging and slashing and cutting and chopping their way among the surprised Romans, sealing their fate. Under this unexpected onslaught the Romans crumbled within minutes. The surprise was complete and the victory absolute.

The Roman army no longer existed, its former presence confirmed by scattered survivors seeking safety while bloodied and battered bodies dotted the landscape. It is reported that only about 6,000 Romans managed to escape, the triumph-seeking Carbo among them. In less time than a written account of it takes to read, the Cimbri had made short work of the Roman army. So it was that the perfidious Carbo was denied the triumph he so earnestly desired. On this matter Appianus pulls no punches when he says:

> He (Carbo) suffered for his perfidy, and lost a large part of his army. He would probably have perished with his whole force had not darkness and a tremendous thunderstorm fallen upon them while the fight was in progress, separating the combatants and putting an end to the battle by sheer terror from heaven.[68]

Like many supposedly superior fighting forces since, from the Americans and their allies in Afghanistan to the Russians trundling towards Kyiv, the Romans were vulnerable when tricked, ambushed, and trapped. Fortuitously for the surviving Romans, torrential rain stopped play. Iulius Obsequens, diligently recording his prodigies for that year, briefly recounts that 'After crossing the Alps, the Cimbri and Teutones cruelly slaughtered the Romans and their allies.'[69] Carbo was indicted for losing his army, but escaped conviction by committing suicide.

Our second example of weather magic belongs to the reign of Marcus Aurelius. It must be remembered here that the emperor loved literature, had refined tastes, and was no mean writer himself, being the author of the Stoic reflections entitled *Things to Oneself* (Τὰ εἰς ἑαυτόν), popularly known as *Meditations*. By way of complete contrast, the Column of Marcus Aurelius in Rome depicts murderous untidy episodes (unlike the neat and tidy warfare of its predecessor, Trajan's Column) across the Danuvius. Of particular interest is the carved relief depicting the emperor's soldiers victorious under the outstretched wings of a non-canonical bearded deity responsible for the event known as the 'Rain Miracle',[70] which probably occurred in the summer of 174.[71] A Roman army had been cut off in the territory of the Quadi and was suffering from heat and thirst. With parched throats gasping for water and too fatigued to put up a fight, pleas to the gods were voiced to the heavens. Suddenly an ominous dark mass of clouds gathered above and swept towards the field of conflict. Thankfully for the legionaries, there was a violent thunderstorm and they were drenched in rain (potable) water, while the Quadi were struck by lightning.[72]

Various people claimed the credit, including the Christians. The ante-Nicene Church Father Tertullian of Carthage (155–220), whose parents were pagans and had given him a good education, relates the legend of 'the shower obtained through the prayers of Christians who happened to be in the army'.[73] Apparently, according to the later source of Eusebius, they just happened to be serving in *legio* XII *Fulminata* (meaning 'thunderstruck' or 'bearer of lightning' and its emblem was a thunderbolt).[74] We do know from an inscription that *legio* XII *Fulminata* did serve in a victory under Marcus Aurelius.[75] However, Eusebius' story of the legion gaining its name as a result of the 'Rain Miracle' is quite clearly wrong, for the legion had been known by this name at least since the time of Octavianus as other inscriptions unmistakably indicate.[76]

Cassius Dio, a contemporary of Tertullian and our main literary source for the event, never mentions any Christians at the battle. Indeed, he believes that an Egyptian magus named Harnouphis had done the job by procuring the rain from 'Mercury, the god of the air (Hermes Aerios)'.[77] This provoked the indignation of his eleventh-century epitomizer Xiphilinos, who inserted a rival version, to prove the point made by Tertullian; that is to say, it was the prayers of Christian soldiers in the aforementioned legion that had saved the day for the Roman army. Despite the obvious Christian propaganda, we do know that Harnouphis was a real Egyptian priest who did travel with Marcus Aurelius during the emperor's Marcomannic campaign as an altar bearing his name as 'the sacred scribe of Aegyptus' was found at Aquileia.[78]

In fact, the 'Rain Miracle' is an example of an extremely well-attested pagan miracle, far better attested than any Christian miracle. Eusebius is in fact reporting what the Christian apologist Apollinaris wrote (now lost) some eight years after the event, and the same story was echoed by Tertullian a quarter of a century later. Tertullian claims to have learned of the story from a letter written by Marcus Aurelius himself.[79] The letter is a fake. So it turns out that the myth of the miracle of the Christian legion was founded on a forgery. Our sole reference by any contemporary of the emperor to any Christian serving in the army is actually from Tertullian himself. Here our Christian apologist reports the moment a soldier was discovered to be a Christian; he was promptly discharged and incarcerated.[80] Oddly enough, Tertullian goes on to say that no Christian should ever serve in the army.[81]

Despite seemingly contradicting himself, Tertullian does have a point concerning Christians not serving in the army. From a theological perspective no syncretism between the gods of the army and the Christian God was possible. First, the Christians could not worship idols. Second, a strict moral code highlighted the incompatibility of the soldier's oath, *sacramentum*, and the sacraments, also *sacramentum*, the army of the emperor and the army of Christ, even to the point of forbidding the spilling of blood. After all, worship was an integral part of army life, ensuring, as it did, allegiance and discipline. Thus the life of soldiers was organized around a series of sacrifices in which commemoration of important imperial anniversaries was prominent. Likewise, images of the current emperor or emperors were placed between the standards so that they shared the fierce loyalty attracted by the eagles. The major persecutions in the third century were triggered by imperial demands to sacrifice for the safety of the empire.

Beyond the realms of Roman history we do have a curious parallel from the Old Norse world. It concerns the semi-legendary battle of Hjörungavágr, a sea fight fought in 986 on the landward side of the island of Höð (Hareidlandet in Møre og Romsdal, Norway). The scenario is almost identical to the Frigidus: the battle has two phases, the loser of the first, *jarl* Hákon Sigurðarson of Lade (ON *Hlaðir*), seeks supernatural intervention by offering 'his own seven-year-old son',[82] and a violent storm turns the battle decisively in the second phase against his opponents, a Danish invasion fleet led by the Jomsvíkings, the famed members of a bachelor brigand community that feared no man and dared all. Having returned to his ships he urged his men to renew the fight:

And right soon the weather began to thicken in the north and clouds covered the sky and the daylight waned. Next came flashes of lightning and thunder, and with them a violent shower. The Jomsvíkings had to fight facing the storm, and the squall was so heavy they could hardly stand up against it; men had cast off their clothes earlier because of the heat, and now it was cold.[83]

A full-on pagan, Hákon Sigurðarson gains a convincing victory and thus remained the de facto ruler of Norway until his untimely death in 995.

Let us return to the miracle on the Frigidus. Today, when death on the battlefield is often inflicted from a distance (or even displayed on social media video), it is sometimes forgotten (although rarely by infantrymen, who regularly go into 'the meat grinder') that in the ancient world death was dealt by one's adversary closely and personally so that pain, suffering, fear and gore were readily apparent to the slayer. Of course the Christian chroniclers were not interested in this, being content to concede and sanction the belief that the 'pagan' army of Eugenius was powerless before the might of God. As such it was pitted not against a human enemy but against the power of God, which could not be combated as He would manage the battle through to its inevitable conclusion. In the rhetoric of these ecclesiastical propagandists, the God that abetted the 'Christian' army of Theodosius was the same God who wanted Nicene orthodoxy to be the sole religion of the state. The miracle on the Frigidus forged a new popular mythology for the 'true believers'. The *oddness* of that!

Truth be told, God – Nicene or otherwise – did not assault Eugenius' soldiers. These human victims were merely in the way of something much larger than themselves. The real enemy was the gap between the power of nature and the power of human beings. The terrible two-day battle had been a near-run thing for Theodosius, a costly but complete victory, with the forces of nature having proved stronger than the tactical acumen of Arbogastes.

There are two reasons for everything: the good reason and the real reason. In the case of the battle of the Frigidus, the good reason was the idea that the wind that blew on the second day was indeed a God-sent miracle for those soldiers who had survived that ferocious encounter near the crystal cold waters of the Frigidus, having witnessed, during the messy stabbing-punching-biting lethal brawl, with stark clarity the brutal realities of the sword. The real reason, of course, was the fact that the key passage of the battle came from a genuine unicorn event: the weather magic known as the Bora.

Chapter Ten

The End and Beyond

'Romanus orbis ruit/*The Roman world is falling*'
Jerome, *Epistulae* 60.16

The Frigidus was Theodosius' 'miraculous' victory, but he had suffered heavy losses in gaining it. Yet even so, the prefectures of the west quickly submitted to the eastern emperor. He was now, although he can hardly have known it, the last emperor to rule over a united Roman Empire, east and west alike, an empire as great in extent as that left by Augustus. Yet he only ruled over it for little more than four months, passing away in January of the following year aged only 48. After him would come a sequence of rulers continually haunted by the twin spectres of unity and universalism but whose ability to achieve them was continually frustrated by strategic considerations and limited resources.

The Final Curtain

Over the winter Theodosius had fallen seriously ill with the vascular disease of hydropsy. Ever since his critical illness of the winter of 379/380 he had not enjoyed perfect health, and now his attendants and court were seriously alarmed. Almost overnight the political atmosphere abruptly changed from the pride and relaxation of victory to the tense apprehension of an imminent change of emperor. If Theodosius died there was nobody of remotely comparable power and authority to replace him. Arcadius and Honorius, although both legally *Augusti*, were both too young and inexperienced to rule in their own right. The two most powerful figures in the background were, in the east, the *praefectus praetorio per Orientis*, the Gaul Flavius Rufinus (who, as *magister officiorum* in 392, had shared the consulship with Arcadius, a singular honour),[1] and in the west Flavius Stilicho, who by July 393 had reached the military rank of *comes et magister utriusque militiae*.[2]

The previous year, at the time of the expedition against Eugenius, Stilicho, then a *magister militum* (probably of Thracia), had gone westward with Theodosius[3] and remained there after the emperor's death in the capacity of senior military commander, *magister utriusque militum praesentalis*.[4] He also twice held the consulship (400, 405), and was styled patricius, *patrician*, a title that had been revived by Constantinus I.[5] It was not an office *per se*, i.e. with particular duties and rights, but a high-status personal designation or dignity. It was held for life and its possessor took precedence over all officials except consuls in office. The combination of supreme military rank together with the title of *patricius* would come to mark the dominant politico-military figure in the west.

In contrast to the east (where there were five holders of such offices, and the senior figure below the emperor was the civilian *praefectus praetorio*), in the west there were only two commanders of such rank and one was always, in practice, the senior figure.[6] Stilicho's family links with Theodosius left no-one in any doubt that it was he, and not Timasios,[7] his military colleague in command of the expedition against Eugenius and Arbogastes, who was that figure.[8] Subordinate only to Theodosius himself in military matters, Stilicho was given command of all the remaining forces in the west after the Frigidus. This concentration of eastern and western forces in the hands of one man was never achieved again. In effect, Stilicho was carefully being moved into the same position occupied by Arbogastes; something much more than merely a senior military commander, a *generalissimo*, to use the title coined by J.M. O'Flynn.[9] Like Arbogastes (and unlike Magnus Maximus) he would not aspire to the purple himself since his Vandal paternity made him *demibarbarus*, as his detractors commonly called him.[10] Additionally, he was bound to the Theodosian dynasty by marriage, and his legitimate ambitions depended on that.

In 383 Theodosius had made his eldest son Arcadius joint emperor with himself, although Arcadius was then just 6 years old. The following year Honorius was born and he was honoured in the same way in 394. The following year, on 17 January, Theodosius died.[11] However, before he did, we are told, he appointed Stilicho sole guardian (*parens*) of both his imperial sons: Honorius, who was 10 and had inherited the western half of the empire, capital Mediolanum, and Arcadius, who was about 18 years old and had inherited the eastern half of the empire, capital Constantinopolis. The tradition was well-established, and by making them joint emperors Theodosius was only doing what Constantinus I had done many decades before, but Constantinus' sons were adults and had at least some of the knowhow needed to rule their domains, although, as we have seen, they abused that by fratricidal squabbling. Moreover, the split between the two halves of the empire was now permanent; that is to say, the East and the West.

Arcadius and Honorius, on the other hand, were not of the right calibre for the job and, to be honest, were pathetic heirs to their father's and their grandfather's memory. So it was inevitable that another would hold the real power. Unfortunately there were no witnesses to this deathbed scene.[12] Ambrose, however, publicly avowed its enactment and authority:

> Theodosius is more glorious in this also, that he did not make a will in accordance with public law; he had nothing further to determine as regards his sons, to whom he had given everything, except to place them under the protection of a close relative, who was present.[13]

Most others in the court at Mediolanum agreed with the bishop, although the latter, always the astute politician, was probably recognizing Stilicho's supreme position in the West rather than any legitimacy in Stilicho's claim.

If the machinery for the transfer of power was placed in Stilicho's hands, the plausibility and the implications of his claim are questionable, but the fact that in making it he received the support of so prominent a figure as Ambrose lent it an air of respectability. If Achilles, for his untarnished fame, had the blind but golden-mouthed bard Homer, then Stilicho had the eulogizing court poet Claudianus. It was he, effectively Stilicho's own permanent propagandist, who later paraded Theodosius' solemn bequest in vivid tones at many places in his narratives and panegyrics, even suggesting – extraordinarily – that the dying Theodosius dismissed all his attendants except Stilicho.[14] However, at a later date the same propagandist hints about the restriction of Stilicho's claims to a guardianship of Honorius alone,[15] which probably explains why Stilicho did not make public the so-called claim that the dying Theodosius had secretly asked him to oversee *both* his sons.

Ambrose organized and showcased Theodosius' lying in state in the Basilica Portiana, Mediolanum. Ambrose delivered a panegyric titled *De Obitu Theodosii* before Stilicho and Honorius in which Ambrose praised the suppression of paganism by Theodosius. It differed radically from the form of Roman imperial funerals for the previous four centuries. It was, instead, an uncompromising Judeo-Christian apotheosis, delivered pointedly forty days after the emperor's death. His body was finally taken to Constantinopolis, where it was solemnly interred on 8 November 395 in the imperial funerary chapel in the great Church of the Holy Apostles (long since disappeared), where he lay in peace until the sack of the metropolis in April 1204.

Theodosius' army rapidly dissolved after his death. True, Stilicho commanded – for the present – the main field armies of East and West, but it soon became clear that these two *comitatenses*, who had so recently been slaughtering one another, were not going to cooperate harmoniously, and that large numbers of them were in such a poor state of discipline that their obedience might not be relied on in a new campaign. Zosimos states that after Theodosius' death,

Stilicho kept for himself the best troops and sent the inferior ones to the East.[16] Initially Stilicho hoped, on the basis of his guardianship and combined army command, to exercise authority over both halves of the empire just as Theodosius had done, and as he clearly believed was his legal and moral right. Yet from the outset it was obvious that this was a very distant goal indeed with the intrigues of the eastern court rivals Flavius Rufinus and Eutropius – and what was to follow, the rebellion of Gildo[17] – and the Gothic *foederati* raiding as far as Constantinopolis itself.

From the outset it was clear that Arcadius had got the better end of the stick. In the conflicts with the Goths the emperors of the East hardly had to surrender any territory and there had been no major organizational changes in that half of the empire either. The central government in Constantinopolis and the provincial and local authorities were not significantly altered. The West, which had never reached the high level of development enjoyed by the East, lacked the urban network that made effective government possible. Besides, the crisis of the third century had left deep scars, and the civil wars of the following century, ugly affairs measured in blood and treasure, had further exacerbated the resulting social and economic problems. There were differences in the military too. The West was dependent on Germanic recruits from outside the empire, which meant that the West no longer had a professional army in the traditional Roman sense, while in the East the strength and discipline of the army could be maintained by drafting good men from the Balkans, Anatolia and Armenia; that is to say, from within the empire.

Commanding from the Palace

Neither Arcadius nor Honorius ever showed any sign of fitness to rule; they were youths without an inkling of military experience and their reigns were to be marked by a series of disasters. Theodosius had not been blessed in his male offspring: Eunapios of Sardis, like Zosimos an aggressive pagan, says that they were rulers in name only.[18]

Arcadius, an arrogant, inept man who suffered from an acute want of leadership and decision-making, was served by a number of advisers who were both far more clever and cunning than he. The *praefectus praetorio per Orientis* Flavius Rufinus, and Eutropius, the first eunuch to become a *consul* in the empire,[19] each had the emperor in their power for some time. In addition, he also suffered from the intrigues of his wife Aelia Eudoxia, who was his superior in every way. Little wonder, therefore, Arcadius was politely urged by Synesios of Kyrene that 'he should regularly associate with soldiers and not stay in his chamber, for it showed that goodwill, the one solid safeguard of kingship, was strengthened by this daily contact.'[20] This sound advice fell on death ears.

Meanwhile, his younger sibling Honorius was pious and gentle, but incompetent and mulishly obstinate. He too depended on advisers who set his policies. The most influential of these was of course Stilicho, de facto ruler of the West by virtue of his undisputed military command and who had a strong *de jure* presumption as son-in-law of the late emperor, with the consequent customary *parentela* status towards both of Theodosius' sons.[21] In other words, Stilicho's power rested on a combination of military power and a special moral prestige derived from his relationship by marriage to the Theodosian dynasty and from the wishes of Theodosius as expressed at the close of his life. However, his wider claims over the eastern throne were not recognized at all in Constantinopolis, where Arcadius was currently under the influence of Flavius Rufinus, who indeed had as good a claim as Stilicho to be Arcadius' guardian.[22] Tellingly, despite his unrivalled military position and favoured relationship with the imperial family, Stilicho had no power base in the East.

It might seem that the easiest way for Stilicho to consolidate his power, at least in the West, would have been to take the characteristic step of making himself *Augustus*. Indeed, it was alleged immediately after his death by his opponents and by several writers of the fifth century and later that he was not only going to betray the empire to the barbarians but had been plotting to grab the throne too, *affectation regni*, and make his son Eucherius emperor of the East in place of the infant Theodosius II.[23] The next western *generalissimo*, Flavius Constantius, did just that to become the third of his name. It was not necessary, at that time, to eliminate the incumbent *Augustus* in order to don the purple, and it is commonly supposed that Stilicho's *demibarbarus* origins made him hesitate to take this step himself.

Confronting and understanding the mental models and world views of people from other times and places and cultures is challenging work. Yet the barbarian nature of Stilicho is dubious, and to label him a 'Vandal' is wide of the mark. The Vandal influences on his upbringing were minimal. After all, his Vandal father had been an officer in a Roman equestrian unit and presumably he (or his father) had already undergone the challenging process of 'becoming Roman', while Stilicho's mother was Roman.[24] Stilicho himself would have been brought up at court and in the camp, employed his own panegyrist, married the niece of one emperor and married off his daughter to another. To be clear, Stilicho's world view was thoroughly shaped by Roman culture, standards and society. To label him *demibarbarus* is bizarre.[25] Undoubtedly he was unpopular, but so were most Roman politicos and functionaries. A.H.M. Jones rightly observes that Stilicho and his successors in the fifth century actually chose not to become emperors, wanting instead to remain close to the army, which was the real source of power.[26] Theodosius had been a very active soldier, although in the quarter-century since his death his inactive sons had contributed much to turning the *Augustus* into a beautiful but practically useless icon. Indeed, after 395 it was unusual for an emperor to take to the field himself, and ambitious men in the West no longer aspired to become emperor.

Already, in 392, Arbogastes had preferred to raise a non-military figure to the throne rather than take the honour for himself. The emperor still occupied the most honorific and ceremonial-bound position in the state, but his power was a mere shadow of what was once denoted by the freighted term *imperium*. While people prostrated themselves before him, someone else behind the scenes manipulated the machinery. Bauto and Arbogastes had stumbled upon a realization of this new order of things; Stilicho had grasped it fully by 395, and his whole career was built around it.

A Violent Religion?

The Bible explicitly mentions the Almighty as 'the Lord of Hosts' (*Adonai Tzva'ot*).[27] Christianity was predominantly seen as a religion of war, led by a God of Battles with a range of fighting prototypes in the Old Testament such as Joshua and David. Even before the conversion of Constantinus it is clear that Christians served in the armies, presumably roughly in proportion to their numbers in the general (or rural) population: a military martyr like Marcellus was a *centurio ordinarius* in *legio* II *Traiana* and so had probably served for several years before something prompted him to force his religious beliefs on the attention of his superiors;[28] many serving Christians felt no need to imitate such attention-seekers.[29]

After Constantinus' conversion worship was regularized, with time off for services and chaplains attached to individual units.[30] However, the pacific tendency in Christianity with which we are more familiar was also evident in antiquity. After all, Martin of Turones was handed over, contrary to his religious inclinations, by his father, an ex-*tribunus*, in response to an edict requiring the sons of veterans to enlist.[31] Although in theory religious convictions might offer an escape from enlistment,[32] even that representative of western asceticism, Augustine of Hippo, found it necessary to argue in favour of military service as a defence of general peace and security, developing the deeply ontological notion of the 'just war': 'No one must ever question the justness of a war waged on God's command...God commands war to expel, crush or subdue the pride of mortals. Enduring war exercises the patience of His saints, humbles them and helps them to accept His fatherly correction.'[33]

Augustine's conception of the just war derives from the idea that there is order in the world that can be disturbed by an act of aggression. In this early Christian model, a just war re-establishes the order of Providence. However, this image of Christian writers portraying the unlikely events and natural phenomena of the battle, which gave victory to a seemingly defeated Theodosius as proof of Christianity's superiority is just that: an image.

The Fall-Out

On the other hand, what cannot be questioned is the certainty that the political importance of the Frigidus was irreversible. It was fivefold.

First, there was the final albeit brief unification of the Roman Empire under Theodosius before the final collapse of the western part some fifty-two years later, which witnessed a king and not an emperor sitting in Ravenna, the then western imperial residence, and the ultimate irreparable division of the empire after Theodosius' death.

Second, it heralded the desertion of Alaric, a Goth who apparently belonged to the ruling house of the *Balthi* dynasty, or so says Jordanes,[34] although there is no real evidence that Alaric belonged to any long-established ruling house. Alaric was angered because Theodosius in reorganizing the army had excluded him from the command of Roman troops. Barbarian leaders were just as sensitive to issues of status, rank and honour as Roman senators. Alaric also believed, not without cause, that Theodosius had exploited the Goths in the recent bloodletting at the Frigidus. This belief led him to take his followers to the Balkan Peninsula and spread rapine and outrage through Roman territory, capturing and laying waste cities such as Athens, Corinth and Argos.

Third, it allowed the rise of Stilicho, the son of a Vandal in Roman pay who served Valens, who rose to high rank and married a Roman noblewoman.[35] Stilicho began his military career in the elite corps of *protectores et domestici*,[36] where only young Romans of good birth and barbarian nobles could serve.[37] Like his father before him, who was to attain the rank of *tribunus*, the son was to rise rapidly through the cavalry commands. However, he later displayed considerable political as well as military skills, to a degree still rare among so-called barbarian commanders. He was promoted to *comes stabuli sacri* in charge of the supply of remounts for the army, then to *comes domesticorum*,[38] this latter post being that of commander or one of the senior officers of the *scholae palatinae*, the inner core palace security unit acting as the personal bodyguard of the emperor. Most importantly, he was awarded the singular distinction of marriage to Theodosius' niece Serena in 384.[39]

She was the emperor's adoptive daughter and so Stilicho became his son-in-law, or so says Stilicho's creative panegyrist Claudianus.[40] Such a marriage was the clearest signal that henceforth Stilicho was elevated above other court and military officers to the very right-hand of Theodosius' throne.[41] The younger Honorius was entrusted to Serena, and she accompanied him to the West in the winter of 394/395.[42] The dynastic connection of Stilicho and the Theodosian dynasty was further cemented by the marriage of his eldest daughter Maria (aged about 12 in early 398) to Honorius,[43] and when she died childless the emperor married her sister Thermantia.[44] Thus Stilicho was nephew by marriage to Theodosius, father-in-law to Honorius and, he hoped, grandfather to the future *Augustus*.

Stilicho and Alaric would meet again, but on different sides of the red field of strife. Before this showdown between these two 'warlords' Alaric was to have a chequered career as an imperial general (397–400 in eastern service; 405–408 in western service),[45] but during the times he found himself stranded outside imperial service, Alaric maintained a firm authority over the Goths as leader of his people but not as king (*rex*, as inferred in the literary sources) in the monarchical sense, simply because the institution of monarchical authority was lacking.

Fourth, it saw the eventual disintegration of the western Roman army, whose field armies, the *comitatenses*, experienced massive casualties and suffered heavily from attrition throughout this period, as reflected in the *Notitia Dignitatum*.[46] The damage was still being repaired a decade later when the upper Danuvius and the Rhenus frontiers came under severe pressure. Then there was the question of the loyalty of the western army, which seems hardly surprising given that they were now serving under a man they had been facing across the battlefield only a year earlier: Stilicho's position as head of the (defeated) western army was probably further complicated by memories of the particular ferocity of the two-day bloodletting on the Frigidus. So lack of discipline and concerns about disloyalty among his soldiers seem the most likely explanation for Stilicho's failure to bring Alaric to heel during the military campaigns of 395 and 397.

In brief, losing at Adrianopolis, the Romans had lost more than they could well afford to lose. At the Frigidus, on the other hand, they lost what they could not afford at all.

Fifth, affairs were tense between East and West, with various attempts to weaken each other. Accordingly, relations between the two began to become truly dire, so dire in fact that this must be seen as a major factor in the debilitation of the weaker partner, the West. Flavius Rufinus, having forced Stilicho to return to the West in 395, soon fell from power and was assassinated by Gaïnas in November of the same year.[47] This was almost certainly at the instigation of

Stilicho. The death of his hated rival did not deliver the East to Stilicho, for the eunuch Eutropius took over Rufinus' post as chief advisor to Arcadius and so became the most powerful figure in Constantinopolis.

Aware of Stilicho's intent to gain influence over the eastern court, Eutropius was rightly suspicious of his western rival. Following his failure to bring Alaric to heel in 397, Eutropius seized the opportunity to have Stilicho declared a public enemy, *hostis publico*, by the Senate of Constantinopolis. At the same time Alaric himself secured that major wish for a senior command when he was appointed *magister militum per Illyricum* by the government of Arcadius. This was especially troublesome for Stilicho, for not only were the provinces of eastern Illyricum themselves a matter of dispute between East and West, but also Alaric's appointment not only provided him pay and provisions for his followers but also gave him legal access to the five *fabricae* manufacturing arms there to equip them.[48] Unsurprisingly, Alaric could now boast without exaggeration that Thracia forged him spears, swords and helmets.[49] Obviously this was a step that caused consternation in the West, and Stilicho is likely to have had a hand in hurrying the despised courtier Eutropius to his final reward two years later.

For the next decade the two parts of the empire were in a state of latent and at times open warfare. The mercenary armies of the period had mostly served the empire before greed or hunger led them to turn on it, and in the following century Sidonius Apollinaris was to write to Maiorianus (r. 457–461), the last competent emperor of the West ever produced: 'Every band has at some time caused Rome to tremble.'[50] Alaric regarded Stilicho as a rival warlord and was not willing to see him control both parts of the empire unless there was a substantial *quid pro quo* for himself and his Goths. Alaric may have been an opportunist, but above all he wanted an official seat at the top table. Stilicho's style, on the other hand, was always to be the power behind the throne, not a member on a council of equals.

Chapter Eleven

Pagan Resistance

'*During the reign of Imperator Augustus Flavius Claudius Iulianus the worship
of the gods was restored, and the temple reconstructed and consecrated.*'
Inscription[1] found in Ma'ayan Barukh, Israel

In its relatively short life, the reign of Eugenius represented the last opportunity for the pagans. For the political flipside of all this turmoil allowed the senatorial class to oppose the complete Christianization of the empire. Though himself a Christian, Eugenius adopted a policy of religious toleration, but with a bias in favour of Roman polytheism; during his brief reign, the cherished Altar of Victory, *ara Victoriae*, was again restored to the Curia.[2] The age-old symbol of Roman religion and might, the altar had been removed in 382 on the orders of Gratianus, who had been prodded by the pope, Damasus I (r. 366–384), and Ambrose, bishop of Mediolanum. Claiming to represent a Christian majority in the Senate, they prevailed upon the emperor to refuse to receive a deputation headed by the pagan Symmachus.[3]

This is the back story. The cult of the goddess Victory was not native to Italy; *Victoria* was merely the Greek Νίκη under a Roman name.[4] A statue of Victory found at Tarentum – probably the work of a Greek artist, it had been abandoned by Pyrrhos of Epeiros and taken as spoil by the Romans in 272 BC – had been placed on an altar in the Curia Iulia by Augustus following his decisive victory over Marcus Antonius and Kleopatra VII at Actium almost five centuries earlier.[5] Though this was to be the most famous of Roman statues of Victory, it was not so much to commemorate that naval victory as to epitomize the eternal triumph of the Spirit of Rome over all its adversaries.

The mood of the time, if correctly reflected in the literature of the day, leans unmistakably towards expansion on the grounds of mission, destiny and divine will. For example, the elder Pliny on the role of Italy and the Latin language: 'A land chosen by divine providence to unify empires so disparate and races so manifold; to bring to a common concord so rough, discordant voices; to give culture to mankind; to become, in short, the world's homeland.'[6]

An altruistic view, to say the least. 'The Gods favour us,' says Tacitus more tersely,[7] while Horace broadcasts:

> Because you consider yourself lesser than the gods, you hold power:
> Derive every beginning from this, and to this each ending:
> Neglected gods gave many misfortunes
> to mournful Hesperia.[8]

Horace's words contained the simple, central message of the Roman official religion, which had been so amply borne out by the metropolis' unique and glorious history. A Greek quip, relayed by Cicero, might best describe the credible opinion at the everyday level: 'No matter that they hate us, as long as they fear us.'[9] This, of course, was the unsentimental pragmatism of a man of affairs.

The *ara Victoriae* was a potent visual symbol of the empire, to which senators had regularly burned incense and made libations before their proceedings, colourfully stirred up by Ambrose in his emotionally engaging description of Christian senators with eyes streaming from the smoke and choking on cinders.[10] Then again, Ambrose, a rhetor of uncommon skill, was certainly one to grasp the tight connection between storytelling and politics.

Over the course of the fourth century the statue itself had become a political football. There is no indication that Christians had any objection to the statue until it had been removed on the orders of Constantius II, probably during his state visit to Rome in 357,[11] forty-four years after the Edict of Toleration signed in Mediolanum. Much earlier in his reign, Constantius, who happened to be an avowed Arian[12] and an Anomoean Arrian into the bargain, had made a law forbidding 'the madness of sacrifices'.[13] By this act the emperor had reversed roles. During the reign of Traianus Decius, for instance, a pledge of loyalty in the form of a sacrifice was demanded from Christians and putative Christians. Anyone who refused was killed; whoever obeyed received a certificate that was authorized and signed by a qualified official. Some of these certified avowals written on papyrus have emerged from underneath the sands of Egypt. Here is an example:

> Aurelia Leulis from the village Euhemeria in the district Themiste to those appointed to see to the sacrifices. I have always continued to sacrifice and pay respect to the gods. Together with my underage children Palempis and T[illegible]eris I have now made libations and blood sacrifices in your presence, in accordance with the statute, and I have eaten from the sacrificial meat. I give you therefore this certificate and request you to undersign it (then follow signatures and the date of issuance of the certificate).[14]

To the most committed of Christians this act of the Egyptian Aurelia Leulis was, of course, an abomination.

In any case, the altar itself was then restored, probably by Constantinus' cousin Iulianus, whose name is a byword for apostasy. The Christian emperors Iovianus and Valentinianus I left it unmolested, the latter emperor famously doing his best to be neutral in matters of religion.[15] His religious policy was one of toleration towards paganism and non-interference in the affairs of the Church. The statement for which he is remembered, spoken to a group of Arian ecclesiastics, sums up his position: 'I am a layman and should not interfere in such matters [viz. details of Faith]. Let the priests, whose concern these things are, assemble where they please.'[16]

Valentinianus, after all, had other work. First and foremost a soldier, he was more concerned with stabilizing the troublesome western frontiers than dealing with equally troublesome priests. In a way, there was a kind of genius to the perpetual dissatisfaction of Ambrose regarding all things pagan; not so much a tyranny of expectations as a theocracy of expectations, a Nicene of expectations.

Pagan Prince across the Water

Paganism, in truth, was to have one last imperial champion, and it was certainly not Eugenius. Although his name is not as well known as it once was, he was commonly known in the Christian world as *Apostata*, the Apostate. Flavius Claudius Iulianus (r. 361–363) had already given proof of his ability as a leader of men at Argentorate (Strasbourg, France), his first major battle, a surprising victory giving him the initiative over the Alamanni, which he exploited in a campaign of reprisal against their homeland. After the battle Iulianus crossed the Rhenus to attack the Alamanni. The following year, he returned to complete the task that the onset of winter had forced him to leave undone.[17] The year 359 saw further action against the Alamanni, among others, inflicting considerable damage by the use of speed and surprise. An eccentric scholar, his tactics, as befits someone devoted to Roman history, are strongly reminiscent of Iulius Caesar on the same ground four centuries earlier. Yet it was as the gifted philosopher – he had once quoted Plato while he learned to drill ('If an ox can carry a knapsack, then so can I') – rather than the formidable man of action that the emperor set his energetic mind to overturn Christianity. In this he was to fail spectacularly. Even so, his story makes for fascinating reading.

Iulianus wanted to return to a wistful pagan past, an aeon before the knowledge of sin when the gods and their votaries danced, drank and copulated without rule or reason, or so iconography and archaeology inform us. This picture of paganism is more a constructed pick-and-mix memorabilia. A re-imaging of the times of yore, the emperor's desires may have been little more than a ghostly link to what he perceived as a more glorious past, but spiritually he was seeking revenge for past sins. For Iulianus was the last surviving member of the dysfunctional house of the Constantii following five decades of bloody inter-family feuds, fratricidal struggles, treachery and illicit sex, and he had been marked by events in his early childhood. The memory of the liquidation of at least eight male relatives by the army following the death of Constantinus and the elevation of his three sons, which he and his half-brother Constantinus Gallus, who was his senior by some years, narrowly escaped – the former was considered too young to be any real threat (Iulianus was born in 331) and the latter was thought to be terminally ill – haunted him for the rest of his life.[18]

The fact that his Christian cousins Constantinus II, Constantius II and Constans had stood by and allowed the carnage to take place had a lasting influence on the development of Iulianus' political world view. Hardly surprising, perhaps, when you consider that virtually the whole collateral line of Constantius Chlorus' children by Flavia Maximiana Theodora, his first wife and eldest daughter of Maximianus,[19] was wiped out during a so-called 'rebellion' at Constantinopolis. This resulted from a rumour that Constantinus had been poisoned by his half-brothers, one of whom was Iulius Constantius, Iulianus' father.[20] This must have been before the proclamation by the army of Constantinus' three sons on 9 September 337.[21] Even so, all the males who could have posed a credible challenge to the throne had been liquidated. With all potential rivals removed, the three brothers now had the empire to themselves.

As with other triumvirates, soon there were only two. As the oldest of the three brothers, Constantinus II enjoyed the greatest respect. He also acted as regent for Constans, who as a teenager was considered too young to be able to discharge all the duties of ruling on his own. Two and a half years later Constantinus took his supervisory role quite literally and began to eye up Constans' territory. Exercising his perceived rights of primogeniture, Constantinus was killed in an ambush near Aquileia at Alsa attempting to add his brother's portion to his in March 340,[22] and Constans became the sole emperor in the west. Once again, the empire found itself split in two. Ten years later Constans was to be liquidated and three usurpers appeared: Magnus Magnentius in Gaul, Nepotianus at Rome and Veteranio at Mursa in Pannonia. The last two were quickly disposed of: Nepotianus was killed less than a month after his elevation to the supreme rank, and Veteranio was defeated and deposed by Constantius after ten months. As we have previously discussed, the contest with Magnentius, who had appointed his brother Decentius to the position of *Caesar*, lasted for three years; Constantius defeated the western usurper at Mursa and drove him into Gaul, where Magnentius was again defeated and took his own life.

Power of Nostalgia

These brutal family relationships are more than a passing interest: they cast a long shadow over the short and violent span of Iulianus' life. For it was against this dark background of personal trauma that Iulianus began to erect the intellectual scaffolding of his pagan universe. Seldom far from his scrolls and philosophic discussions, Iulianus left behind him a massive compilation of writings hostile to 'the Galileans',[23] as he contemptuously called the Christians (he also called their churches 'charnel-houses' on account of the relics), and on philosophical questions too. For the loquacious heterodox emperor it was easy to parody parochial beliefs of Christians, as his short satirical fantasy *Symposium* or *Kronia* (L *Saturnalia*), generally known as *Caesares*, shows.

Perhaps written for the occasion of the Saturnalia of 362,[24] during the winter which the emperor spent in Antioch,[25] in this biting vignette Iulianus portrays Constantinus as a sensualist in every sense. At one point Constantinus is asked to pick a god; the emperor runs first to Licentiousness (Gk. *Τρυφή*) who takes him to meet Incontinence (Gk. *Ἀσωτία*), with whom he finds Jesus of Nazareth who cries out:

> He that is a seducer, he that is a murderer, he that is sacrilegious and infamous, let him approach without fear! For with this water will I wash him and will straightaway make him clean again. And though he should be guilty of those same sins a second time, let him but smite his breast and beat his head and I will make him clean again.[26]

Constantinus comes across much like the uncle who says and does dodgy things, but gets invited to the family get-together anyway: what is the worst thing that could have happened? Such sarcastic scorn is readily taken up by Voltaire, who with his customary wit writes: 'This is how he [Constantinus] reasoned: baptism purifies everything; I can therefore kill my wife, my son and all my relations; after which I shall have myself baptised and I shall go to heaven; and in fact that is just what he did.'[27]

Are we really to believe like Voltaire that Constantinus was such a despicable opportunist? Iulianus believed so. Indeed, there is truth in the caricature of his uncle, for the *Caesares* is less a satire than a sneer, and unmistakably the author's target is religious hypocrisy. An apotheosis can arise in an epiphany or in an act of prostration, and it can also happen through poetry and painting, or even through pantomime.

Witty, spiky and lively a read, today's equivalent of a staged version of the *Caesares* would be the theatrical entertainment the Anglophone world knows as the pantomime. With its clownish caricatures, corny gags, slapstick comedy, saucy innuendo and a degree of gender-bending, pantomimes offer light relief, distraction and a chance to poke fun at the powerful. No one is safe from the booing and hissing. All are lampooned and ridiculed, often with satirical intent. In this respect, pantomime is a popular art form that speaks of and for the people in all their folly and vivacity. It is silly and rude. Surely, if the *Caesares* was re-imagined as a Christmas pantomime today, Constantinus would not be cast as the pantomime villain, all but inviting the audience to boo and hiss, but as the hilarious fool. How do you kill a god, if not by killing? One method is through maliciously lampooning the past.

As so often, though, nothing is as simple as it appears. Iulianus may have perfected his tools of influence – satire, parody, mockery – but the utter futility of his attempts, indeed their sheer eccentricity, is a good indication of the inroads Christianity had made within the space of four decades. This was all the more complex due to the nature of Iulianus' personality. His own hubristic belief in his own genius blinded him to this bitter truth, and if it had not been for his untimely death in the sands of Mesopotamia the political forces unleashed by his anti-Christian edicts would have eventually consumed him. It was as if his brief life was like a Greek classical tragedy, the end foretold from the start: Iulianus stops being an emperor and starts being the tragic hero who conjures up his own nemesis.

Towards the end of 347 the adolescent Iulianus had been free to study. As you would have thought, he was a diligent student, first at Constantinopolis, and then at Pergamum and Ephesus and at both these Greek centres of learning he made contact with pagan philosophers and mystics. However, he had spent the preceding six years removed from the imperial court and in exile in the wastelands of Macellum in Kappadokia. This exclusion from public life (which probably saved his life) had the same effect as on the emperor Claudius: he acquired a passionate interest in the past, in classical literature, Roman religion and Roman tradition. As emperor one of his more well-known edicts attacked those Christian teachers who, while praising classical literature in their classes, openly denied the existence of the pagan gods. By not allowing them to teach, he was depriving them of their best audience and potential converts:

> But I give them this choice: either not to teach what they do not think admirable, or, if they wish to teach, let them first really persuade their pupils that neither Homer nor Hesiod nor any of these writers whom they expound and have declared to be guilty of impiety, folly, and error in regard to the gods, is such they declare. For since they make a livelihood and receive pay from the works of those writers, they thereby confess that

they are most shamefully greedy of gain, and that, for the sake of a few *drachmae*, they would put up with anything.[28]

In other words, a Christian teacher who despised the pagan gods could never correctly explain to his pupils the works of Homer, Hesiod, Demosthenes, Herodotos, Thucydides, Isokrates and Lysias (Iulianus lists them all). There is the poetry and passion of what we want, and the blood and grind of how we get it. Here we should call to mind a quote attributed to Otto von Bismarck, whereby he said 'politics is the art of the possible, the attainable – art of the next best'.[29] By the same token purity can be a dangerous thing in politics. The world is full of impurities. Compromise is not a dirty word; compromises are often needed to make policies work, for politics is an unpredictable, nebulous game of manners. Predictably, as it turned out, the tactless Iulianus sung in vain. No matter how many fans Iulianus had in the empire (and, let us be honest, there were quite a number), like all the emperor's religious measures, this educational law did not survive past his brief reign. Nostalgia is a pleasing emotion, but it is also a simplifying one.

Iulianus had created a world full of haters, real or imagined, and they wanted him to be a black and white villain, one who was acting in his perceived self-interest or for revenge, but Iulianus had no malevolent scheme. Brimming with missionary zeal, he wanted to turn the clock back, but he just did not want to believe it was impossible to do so. All the same, it was the single event for which the educationalist emperor (in itself a novelty) became notorious. It is said that politics can be as exhilarating as war and just as perilous, but the truth is that in war you can only be killed once. Indefatigable commentator after commentator ever since has spluttered his disapproval, drawing deeply on the well of indignant metaphors and adjectives. 'How did it come into your head, to deprive Christians of words, you silliest and greediest of mortals?' Gregory Nazianzen exploded with rage.[30] Locked in a damaging, dead-end and antagonistic deadlock, back and forth they went, in tiny bursts and towering speeches, the emperor and his enemies shifting endlessly and seamlessly between vitriol and virtue. For both sides outrage was a weapon, not simply an indulgence. That said, the responses from the Christian fathers were so rehearsed and so optimized for a polarizing landing that the issue seemed to say more about their rigid vision of Christianity, a cold credo that wanted to subjugate life to the demands of a monotheistic religion – in their eyes – that never should be questioned.

It was all one ecosystem, one that was constantly disguising its uniformity with cries of censorship and cancellation. The Nicene Christian powers-that-be, the Gregorys of this world, wanted the emperors to play by the rules of the church-political complex: a few anti-pagan decrees here, a few religious convictions here, and the applecart left unmolested. Then there was the safeguarding of state baubles to feed their ambition. When it came to Iulianus, however, there was a certain dark inevitability about the whole thing, although it is easy to exaggerate with hindsight.

The Christian fathers might have ridden their usual angry anti-pagan hobbyhorse to death (not to put it more strongly), but even Ammianus Marcellinus, a pagan admirer of the emperor, scornfully called it a 'harsh act' that should be buried in 'lasting oblivion'.[31] Perhaps he was bewildered about why the emperor staked so much political capital on sinking the sway of Christian teachers. It is as if the soldier scholar was asking the philosopher emperor why he was selecting that as the hill on which he wanted to die.

Superbly spiteful the smug emperor may have been. Yet this was no minor moment of madness. Iulianus' law was very Iulianus and a masterstroke too, for he had marginalized Christianity to the point where it could have withered and died within a generation or two. The choice of the parent was stark: either conform or commit your son to being an uneducated outcast. 'We are shot with shafts feathered from our own wing,' writes Theodoret. The irony is, of course, that the good bishop was citing Aischylos, one of the greatest of Athenian playwrights.[32] According to the classically educated bishop, the emperor planned 'a war on Christianity after the fighting with the Persians was over'.[33] It was as if Theodoret was inhaling fear and exhaling anger. Not that the relatively new Christian state was vulnerable to a pagan revival. Quite the opposite, in fact. It was the pagans who were vulnerable to the cunning misinformation that sought to overturn everything that did not fit into the mandatory polemic of the Christian apologists.

Even so, Iulianus did not conceal his hostility towards Christianity. Another of his anti-Christian gambits was to order the recall of all ecclesiastics who had been exiled by his predecessor, his cousin Constantius. They were, he cheerfully said, free to observe their own beliefs without opposition. In one sense, the one he was happy to broadcast, this was an act of tolerance, but in another it was a formidable means of sowing discontent in the ranks of the Christians. This was clear to contemporaries. As Iulianus' admirer Ammianus Marcellinus noted:

> On this he took a firm stand to the end that as this freedom increased their dissension, he might afterwards have no fear of a united populace, knowing as he did from experience that no wild beasts are such enemies to mankind as are most Christians in their deadly hatred of one another.[34]

The results were not quite what Iulianus expected. On the whole, Christians drew together in the face of a common peril. For instance, on 21 February

362, banished Nicene bishop of Alexandria, Athanasios I, entered the city in triumph. It was not long before he was making his eloquent voice heard again.

Some five decades before, on the eve of the battle of Pons Mulvius, Iulianus' uncle had seemingly embraced Christianity – in its Arian form – and had in so doing started a development that would make this religion – in its Nicene form – at the end of the century the official state religion. From the time he ascended the throne in late 361 the nephew tried to stop this development and, if possible, to reverse it. He remained firm in his opinion, and death soon found him. At the time, of course, no one could know that Iulianus' untimely death would end this attempt prematurely.

Galilean Revenge?

It is absurd that so much can rest on something so tiny and trivial. One spear strikes wide and another smacks the target, and on these fates entire projects and professions are made and broken. The hands of the three Fates (or those of a traitor)[35] were again busy when Iulianus was struck in the right side by a spear during a brief skirmish in Mesopotamia and so met a shabby end.[36] The morning following his death, 27 June 363, the generals gathered to consider the question of who should be Iulianus' successor. They looked at various candidates, but divergence of opinion between eastern and western generals made a quick decision impossible. For time it seemed as if Iulianus' *praefectus praetorio per Orientis*, Saturninius Secundus Salutius, would be an acceptable candidate for all concerned. Though the obvious choice, Secundus Salutius did not want the job (he declined for reasons of old age and ill-health),[37] even though it meant continuing Iulianus' mission. Secundus Salutius did not share the late emperor's parochial attitudes or specific beliefs.[38]

While the discussions were still in progress, a number of soldiers in the camp proclaimed Flavius Iovianus emperor. For lack of a better alternative – Iovianus was currently a *primicerius domesticorum* – the generals made no protest. Understandable when we consider the army's dire predicament: Ammianus Marcellinus saw this affair and comments on the lack of water and food, while Zosimos, noting the lack of water too, points out the difficulty of the terrain.[39] A Nicene Christian, at least nominally, and a gourmand of spotty education, Iovianus was nothing like Iulianus; not in his military qualities and certainly not in the originality of his ideas.[40] Our on-the-spot eyewitness Ammianus Marcellinus asserts that initial support for Iovianus as emperor was quite limited.[41] Nonetheless, Iovianus was to perform one major act in his brief reign: he surrendered a slice of the empire to the Sāsānian Persians. Such was the desperate and disorientated condition of the empire that Iulianus' premature exit was seen as an uneasy moment, replete with both hope and danger. For the pagans the heroic Iulianus' success was squandered by the cowardly Iovianus, whereas for Christians Iovianus' piety had rescued the Romans from Iulianus' folly. Whichever side you chose to pick, the last pagan emperor had made the eastern expedition in vain.

Myriad Gods

Paganism was diverse and tolerant of this diversity; Iulianus' ideological hard religious policy turned out to be a grand delusion. As the banished Alexandrian bishop Athanasios mused to his weeping flock, this emperor was 'but a cloud which will speedily be dispersed'.[42] He was right.

We may now leave Iulianus dead in the desert and return to Eugenius and his commonsense policy of open-mindedness regarding religious pluralism. As well as the second restoration of the *ara Victoriae*, private funds were also provided to senators for the restoration of many pagan ceremonies, temples and sacrifices,[43] and prominent pagans were given high offices such as the reappointment of Virius Nicomachus Flavianus as *praefectus praetorio per Italiae*. This was the positive attitude, Christian and pagan, strophe and antistrophe in the same chorus. When Symmachus pleaded in the Senate when the pagan altar was about to be removed in 382, he came across as the voice of reason: 'There cannot be only one way to so great a secret.'[44] The sentiment was sincere, at least, but utterly fanciful. Many pagans must have wished Christianity had never entered the world. However, now no one can have imagined that it would simply disappear and certainly realized there was no battle pagans could hope to win. Most, like Symmachus, simply wanted coexistence, to be allowed to maintain the traditional public cults. Still, when Symmachus presented his petition, Ambrose immediately lodged his objections. The cerebral battle had begun.

Though an uncompromising pagan warrior, Symmachus was widely known to be a moderate who enjoyed good relations with prominent Christians. He was, like his chief antagonist Ambrose,[45] despite their opposing positions, a product of classical education, still based on the standard authors – in Latin, Cicero, Sallust, Livy, Horace and Virgil – and both could express themselves with unusual eloquence (not to be equated with passion) and nostalgic charm. Here is the thing, though. Once through his education, a man shared the cultural assumptions of all those who, whether they came from Britannia, Gaul, Italy or Africa, or whether they were pagan or Christian,[46] had studied the same poets and philosophers and had modelled their prose on the same great orators. In other words, the exact origin of the man did not really matter, because the education experience was designed not only to equip a man to obtain and hold public office, but to produce a shared mindset too. The elite ecosystem was a monolith. Throughout his professional life Symmachus continued to preach what is today a deeply unfashionable gospel of compromise and coexistence, which so often is essential to successful statesmanship because it is the only way of meeting a situation without violent upheaval. As he poignantly points out in his memorial, addressed in the name of the Senate nominally to the three emperors Valentinianus II, Theodosius and Arcadius, although really to the first of these alone, the western emperor:

> It is right to believe that that which all men worship is The One. We gaze up at the same stars; the sky covers us all; the same universe encompasses us. What does it matter what practical system we adopt in our search for the truth? The heart of so great a mystery cannot be reached by following one road only.[47]

Few nobler words have been spoken in the cause for the right to seek 'The One' in his or her own way. Indeed, Symmachus liked to see the possibility of everything: no God; lots of gods. Yet as he himself apparently once said in a throwaway remark, 'Good blood tells and never fails to recognize itself.' It is not surprising that he and Ambrose were, and always remained, close personal friends.[48]

For many modern commentators, the intellectual confrontation between Symmachus and Ambrose is the bona fide battle between paganism and Christianity. Yet the most basic question of all that we need to ask ourselves is whether Iulianus' pagan policy really was a pre-Constantian reprise? No, nothing akin to it: not history repeated, not even as farce; just a philosophical pastiche, as preposterously presumptuous as the wilful young emperor who proposed it in the first place. Christianity would be the one great survivor of the eventual collapse of the western empire. This was the religion that had risen from very small and shaky beginnings over the previous centuries to become, under Theodosius, the official ideology of the empire. Iulianus' work perished with him. So it was the Symmachi were to become one of the leading families in a now Christian Rome. Symmachus, who was accorded the honour of the consulate in 391 – an extraordinary honour for a civilian who had not held court office and had supported Magnus Maximus (the consulate was in the later empire still the most prestigious function for any Roman citizen, including the emperor) – would die a pagan, but his grandson, great-grandson and great-great-grandson all became consuls (446, 485 and 522 respectively), the grandson (if not the son) having abandoned the family paganism in order to further the family fortunes. The world of politics, right up to and including the present time, has ever been one of muddy compromise and rugged imperfection.

Chapter Twelve

Through the Looking Glass

'As those present wept, he [Iulianus] said that it was beneath their dignity to mourn for an emperor who was favoured by heaven and the stars.'
Fik Meijer, *Emperors Don't Die in Bed* (London, 2004), p.133

When the news of Iulianus' death broke, the sophist Libanius of Antioch, one of the emperor's closest friends and a self-professed pagan, lamented:

Gone is the glory of the good: the company of the wicked and licentious is uplifted. Laws, the suppressor of evil, are either laid low or soon to be so, and if they remain, they will remain as ineffectual ciphers. The human race has experienced the fate of cities whose walls are laid low. Their defence is gone, and all that the rightful owners possess passes to the stronger, who fall upon them looting and murdering, and ravishing their captive wives and children. Now the broad path, the great doors lie wide open for the doers of evil to attack the just. The walls are down.[1]

At the same time, Gregory Nazianzen, a former fellow student from Iulianus' time in Athens – for a brief moment the representatives of the pagan and Christian heirs to the classical heritage had met at the cradle of the classical world – could not but trumpet the death of the pagan emperor, who was '[T]he dragon, the apostate, the great mind, the Assyrian, the public and private enemy of all in common, him that has spoken and mediated much unrighteousness against Heaven.'[2]

The two stood as far apart politically as it would be possible for two men to stand when they represented two different views of a world of which only one could survive. Small wonder, therefore, that Iulianus could provoke such violent extremes of admiration and hostility, both during his life and after it.

Such an outpouring of grief or relief, depending on the ideology of the beholder, was all very personal. At the political level, however, the death of Iulianus abruptly brought about the end of the house of the Constantii (and therefore any obvious candidature for the succession). Throughout the troubles of the third century the uncertainty of the succession was the root of the conflict and invited usurpers to further mischief in their own selfish quest for the throne. Then again, Iulianus' premature demise not only blighted any obvious candidature for the succession, but also reopened the religious question. On 16 September 363 a decree was posted in Alexandria that 'only the Highest God and Christ were to be honoured, and that the people were to meet together in the churches for worship'.[3]

Servant of God?

With his usual flair for elegant irony, Edward Gibbon put it best when he wondered why the Romans, who were so tolerant of every religion, would take after such a moral and just people as the Christians with such ferocity. After all, the paganism of the Roman state was willing to be all things to all men. Being polytheistic, it was multiple and versatile. It was very far from exclusive. Nor was it generally intolerant. True, it had developed intolerance to the Christians, because the Christians, since they owed loyalty to a higher master, seemed to be denying the sufficient minimum loyalty to the emperor and the nation. As a child of the eighteenth-century Enlightenment Gibbon was not fond of revealed religion, but he was also no hater. He viewed his task as a historian of early Christianity as a dispassionate, scientific one: to see things as they are, rather than as the pious would want them to be. In that sense, Gibbon casts a less than favourable light on the legalization of Christianity in Rome. Like Voltaire (who Gibbon knew and admired), what seemed to him the hypocrisy of the Christian ideal as opposed to natural human functioning was his particular dislike, and it is this problem that runs through his highly engaging and magnificent *magnum opus*. For Gibbon it was Constantinus' adoption of Christianity that assisted a process of decline by finally abandoning earlier Roman mores and values, so leaving Rome open to more virile conquerors.

So was it sincere piety and personal faith that prompted Constantinus' actions? Or was it something more prosaic? It all depends on how one chooses to weigh the evidence. To some he saw the advance of the Christian faith as essential to Rome's glorious future and himself as the key player in God's cosmic plan. To others he was a wily politician whose main agenda was to reunite and strengthen a fragmented and failing empire, who embraced a faith offering practical advantages in a period of crisis. Yet to others his alleged conversion was not a religious epiphany but another example of the shift of emphasis from the troubled western part of the empire to the more prosperous, albeit more theological eastern part. Then there are those who see only Constantinus' cold and terrible lust for naked power, a reference to the stories of the emperor's murder of his then wife Fausta and his bastard son Crispus, to name only a few.

Zosimos, for instance, states that Constantinus' inability to find 'pagan' forms of absolution led him to Christianity, which promises forgiveness for every sort of wickedness.[4] We must remember, however, that Zosimos was a big fan of the emperor Iulianus and an avid enemy of Constantinus on account of his religion.

Militant Christianity

Constantinus' actions had thereby raised a relatively small and non-influential Christian community to a dominant position in the state, and following three decrees of Theodosius forbidding pagan sacrifice and pagan cult, Christianity would become the empire's only official religion in November 392, more of which anon.

A pious man and strenuous adherent to the Nicene Creed, which defined the relationship of God the Son to God the Father, namely the Father and the Son to be of *one substance*,[5] Theodosius is perhaps best remembered as a champion of Nicene orthodoxy and for his confrontations with Ambrose, whose career was devoted to bringing emperors under the authority of bishops: he would claim emperors were *in*, not *above*, the Christian church. During the waning years of his life Theodosius became the first Roman emperor to turn full circle on the issue of universal religious tolerance. After centuries of Christian persecution[6] and then another three-quarters of a century whereby Christians and pagans coexisted more or less peacefully, Theodosius began the active persecution and steady elimination of all non-Christian sects and their sanctuaries. He also intervened actively in church organization and theology. Indeed, his three edicts not only decreed the total union between state and church, but also proclaimed Orthodox Christianity (i.e. the faith as proclaimed in 325 at Nicaea I, the first of the seven recognized Ecumenical Councils of the church) as the only proper worship due to God, who is of one essence mysteriously manifest in three hypostases consisting of the Father, the Logos or Son and the Holy Spirit, each an equal aspect of the same single God. From now on, only those who followed the Nicene Creed, namely the Trinity of the 'three-in-one' God were acceptable as bishops.

Although the Creed is still used today as the cornerstone of mainstream Christian belief, at the time it was anything but a solution to the squabbles, chief of which was the argument about whether Jesus and God were of 'one substance' (the Nicene view) or whether Jesus was a later creation of God and so in a sense secondary to the latter (the view of the Arians). The word orthodox comes from the Greek ὀρθός (*orthós*, correct) and δόξα (*dóxa*, opinion) and implies a purity of doctrinal teaching inherited from Christ and the Holy Catholic and Apostolic Church; that is, the Early Church devoid of all manner of disunity, as founded by Christ and handed by Him to the care of the Twelve Apostles. The controversy between the various sects over the single or double nature of Christ need not be detailed here.[7] Suffice to say the Christological controversy affected not only clerics and educated laymen, but the common people as well, as may be concluded from an amusing anecdote told by Gregory of Nyssa (Nevşehir, Türkiye) in Kappadokia:

> If you ask about your change, the shopkeeper philosophises to you about the Begotten and the Unbegotten; if you enquire the price of a loaf, the reply is 'The Father is greater and the Son inferior', and if you say 'Is the bath ready?' the attendant affirms that the Son is of nothing.[8]

Of its three main branches, the Nicene, which has remained, for example, the orthodox in the Roman Catholic Church,[9] held the two natures, human and divine, to be 'without division or separation'; it was supported by Rome and frequently by Constantinopolis and was able, at intervals, to fraternize with the Nestorians, who also believed in the two natures, 'conjoined but separate' (in reality, no Persian bishop had actually attended Nicaea I).[10] However, neither of these two faiths could for one moment tolerate the Alexandrian and Syrian Monophysites, who believed in one divine nature only as opposed to the doctrine of two natures, and were repudiated by the pope in Rome and the patriarch in Constantinopolis as well as the Persian Nestorians.

Rather than the inspiration of the Holy Spirit, it does all seem to be a sort of unholy fudge that meant different things to different people, so much so that these doctrinal disputes were often accompanied by violence. Such conflicts were only made worse when the Trinity, a mystery that must simply be believed without being understood, was decreed the only option by Theodosius. We can perhaps understand how easy it was for Muhammad to blow the whistle on the whole confusing game with the simple, uncompromising assertion that God Is One. As Napoléon mused on the South Atlantic island of Saint Helena:

> The Qur'an is not only religious; it is political and civil. It contains all the ways of governing. The Christian religion only preaches morality. Yet the Christian religion is a greater revolution than the other, which is but a manifestation of it. The Christian religion is the reaction of the Greeks to the Romans, of spirit against force.[11]

During his campaign in the heat and dust of the 'Land of the Bible', it is said Napoléon carried with him a New Testament along with the Qur'an, under the characteristic title *Politiques*. Yet it was at Saint Helena, in bitter banishment '*cloué sur ce roc*',[12] that the modern Prometheus had the best opportunity to reflect on the vanity of earthly things.[13]

His mind, as it always was, a swirl of thoughts and ideas, in this abyss of misery and wretchedness that Napoléon decided to dictate his *Mémoires* to *généraux* de Montholon, Gourgaud and Bertrand. His erudite conversations were also recorded by another participator in the imperial captivity, his chamberlain Emmanuel de Las Cases in the vastly popular *Mémorial de Sainte-Hélène*. This was publicized as an 'oral history' of Napoléon's spoken reminiscences, but was in truth a far less trustworthy record than that penned by Gaspard Gourgaud. Napoléon had always felt compelled to tinker with history to put his own spin on it and no less so with these various memoirs, which were to justify himself in the eyes of his contemporaries and of future generations. At one point Napoléon complained to Charles Tristan de Montholon of having no chaplain. Pope Pius VII (r. 1800–23) petitioned the Prince Regent of England to grant the emperor's wish, and the young Abbé Agne Vignali was despatched to that far distant island in the midst of the ocean to serve as his chaplain as well as his physician. Napoléon confirmed to de Montholon his belief in God and read aloud the Old Testament, the Gospels and the Acts of the Apostles, stating:

> The Bible is no mere book, but a Living Creature, with a power that conquers all that opposes it…Alexander, Caesar, Charlemagne and myself founded empires. But on what did we rest the creations of our genius? Upon force. Jesus Christ alone founded his empire upon love: and all at this hour, millions of men would die for him.[14]

He is different things to different people and, much like Iulianus, was the focus of 'unremitting hatred,/And unconquerable love'.[15] Yet even so, when it comes to the greatest military talent and the geographical sweep of military conquests, Napoléon remains the alpha and omega of military geniuses.[16] Many have observed his techniques but not mastered them.

It is a deeply unfashionable idea. What the academics call the 'great man theory' of history seems terminally *passé*, the intellectual equivalent of a forgotten statue of a fighting general on horseback. As an individual with outsized talents in military matters, Napoléon may have turned the wheel of French history but his victories were gained, of course, with the help of innumerable lower-level actors. Among them all the most important may have been the French infantrymen fighting with their Charleville muskets and bayonets. Much as I share the scepticism of Leo Tolstoy, a combat veteran who was famously anti-war, about the individual's impact on history, these sweeping victories were accomplished with the irrepressible confidence of a commander convinced that the stage was his own. These days, it is *de rigueur* to believe that our world is shaped and crafted not by individuals, heroic or otherwise, but by deep, underlying forces. Put another way, there is an ineluctable tide of history that this man or that woman might ride for a while, but which is bound to surge ahead regardless. For better or worse, leadership does matter, and we should take seriously the notion that individuals in wartime deeply matter to the outcome of every conflict. Ukraine's Volodymyr Zelenskiy appropriately reminds us of our most recent example.

Then again, and this is what concerns us here, whether or not Napoléon was a true Christian is another matter entirely.[17] On his deathbed he submitted to the rites of the Roman Catholic Church,[18] yet he passed away amid dreams and visions of war and glory. His dying words were apparently '*La France, l'armée, tête d'armée, Joséphine....*'; if true, a somewhat suitable summing up of his life.

We now turn from one man who still splits opinion to another. The historian and Catholic apologist Hilaire Belloc once observed that a nontrinitarian Arian world '[W]ould have rendered the new religion something like Mohammedanism or perhaps, seeing the nature of Greek and Roman society, something like an Oriental Calvinism.'[19]

The doctrine and the rationalistic inclinations of Arianism, if it had blossomed, denied the full Godhead of Christ. Christ was, in effect, the prophet of God, but he was not God. Actually, there were various shades of Arian, mostly believing in broad terms that the Father and the Son were not the same but *similar* (think Unitarianism). Iulianus did not have any sympathy for the orthodox dogma of Holy Trinity that had been accepted at the Council of Nicaea in 325: 'You are quite right to believe that he whom one holds to be a god can by no means be inserted into a woman's womb',[20] the emperor confided in a letter to Photinos, Arian bishop of Sirmium. Iulianus deemed Christianity, in contrast to ancient Judaism, an arrogant modernism and full of inconsistencies at that. How was it possible, for instance, that the Nicene Christians preached monotheism, but at the same time proclaimed that there were three gods, the Father, the Son and the Holy Spirit? Such questioning led in turn to the Islamic rejection of the Trinity, the Eucharist and the Holy Mass.[21] Even today the most conspicuously fundamentalist Muslims will reproach modern Christians for having *three* gods,[22] but that is another story which is beyond the scope of this book.

And Then There Was One

Still, one does wonder what would have happened if Iulianus had reigned as long as his uncle. Moreover, the greater part of his time in power was spent in preparing for war; first a civil war against his cousin Constantius and then a campaign against Persia. After Iulianus' Germanic soldiers had raised him on a shield and proclaimed him *Augustus* in the spring of 360,[23] Constantius, the incumbent *Augustus*, refused to accept the declaration of Lutetia. It looked as if the struggle for the throne would end in bloodshed. Constantius left Mesopotamia, where he had tried to appease the aggression of the Sāsānian Persians, and moved westward at the head of his army, while Iulianus marched from Gaul to meet him. His soldiers, though well seasoned and truly devoted, were in numbers no match for the eastern army of his cousin, but Constantius, while marching through Cilicia to oppose the western usurper's advance, caught a fever and died near Tarsus on 3 November 361 after designating Iulianus as his successor. Iulianus, now in his thirtieth year, thus succeeded peacefully to the throne and made a triumphal entry into Constantinopolis on 11 December.

The first thing Iulianus did was to clean out the court. The crowds of parasites and eunuchs were given their marching orders. Cooks and barbers, chamberlains and the rest were sent packing; so too was the secret police, many of whose officials paid for their tyranny with their lives. For the first and last time in the later empire the emperor became an approachable head of state and not some oriental demi-god. Thus the Arian bishops who had surrounded Constantius were replaced by Neo-Platonist scholars.[24]

Iulianus also began to prepare for a Persian expedition. It was time for a new, albeit old school, imperial adventure, and his cousin's cautious, defensive strategy regarding Persia was quickly abandoned. There was little point in this invasion as in that of Crassus and all those in between, but as a second Alexander the Great,[25] Iulianus intended to defeat the enemy on his own soil. In the beginning he was rather successful but, as we have seen already, a cavalry spear put an end to his life and his aspirations. His death of course also meant the end of his anti-Christian measures.

From a modern perspective it may seem that the accession of the orthodox Christian emperor Theodosius in 379 and the laws he issued to suppress the pagan cults marked the final stage of the advance of Christianity that had begun after the conversion of Constantinus in 312, but to Theodosius' contemporaries this was not so clear. Paganism was not dead yet, and it did not seem impossible that a new Iulianus would ascend to the throne. Semantics aside, even though Theodosius' ban was neither complete nor universally applied, was the pagan cause definitely discredited when Eugenius was defeated in September 394? However, it would be wrong of us to see Eugenius planting himself at the head of the standards of the pagans so that he could make war on Christianity as represented by Theodosius. Eugenius, like Iulianus, may have sported a (pointed philosopher's?) beard, but he certainly was no second Iulianus.

Chapter Thirteen

Truth Triumphant

'Si Dieu n'existait pas, il faudrait l'inventer/*If God did not exist, it would be necessary to invent him*'

Voltaire, *Épître à l'Auteur du Livre des Trois Imposteurs*

(10 November 1770)

In general, history should not be studied exclusively for its own sake – yes, it can be intriguing, fascinating, entertaining even – but because it holds wisdom for the present too, and sometimes it presents analogies that help us think through the challenges of our own day. If it is worthwhile remembering the past – for comparison – we should spend less time discussing whether history is relevant and more time focusing on whether it is resonant. Life imitates life. History can be repetitive. All the same, history does not exist merely as a compendium of examples to be applied to the future; delving through the centuries of history and stripping events of their historical context renders them meaningless anyway.

History casts no light on the future. On the contrary, it furnishes us with patterns, though these are not identical ones but repetitions of basic configurations of human interactions, such as jealousy and competitive behaviour between rivals, short-sightedness and narrow interests, the distrust of any rising power, and so on. Yes, we can learn from history, but history itself does not offer pat lessons. Historians do, some wisely, some less so, and the great contribution of the wise ones is their ability to provide context in chaos, and by doing so organize our ignorance of the past. History occurs when historians write about it. Bottom line: though it can often be vexing, we must not forget the lessons of the past.

The Greatest Myth

At the centre of our historical narrative lies one man: the grim and authoritarian Theodosius. He, unlike Constantinus, was a Nicene Christian before he became emperor, and he had never followed any other doctrine, never weighed the pros and cons of rival gods. In his world of black and white, there was to be no grey (always a sacred place where people can meet) of any other religions or beliefs. After assuming the purple he remained a faithful Son of the Holy

Church, and in matters of religion he saw entirely through its eyes. He never wavered in his conviction that this creed was not only the true faith, but the integrating force that would bind the entire Roman world together. Anyone who stood in his way was to be dispensed with. They were not of the one and only true faith. As a consequence he allowed the church a political influence that no previous emperor had done, and Ambrose was duly appreciative: 'A pious emperor, a merciful emperor, a faithful emperor, concerning whom the Scripture has spoken.... What is more illustrious than the faith of an emperor whom sovereignty does not exalt, pride does not elevate, but piety bows down?'[1]

Ambrose's world view was about how one should determine the truth. For him the vital question was twofold: from where are you getting the truth, and what is your relationship with the truth? For Ambrose, one's foundational relationship with the truth was determined by faith, its definition that you cannot quarrel with it or question it. The leap between the yearning for one single theory that explains everything and true faith is not that great. On the other hand, theory and practice are usually far apart; their separation is as universal as old men speaking of the good old days.

In 380, after only one year in office, Theodosius had been quite prepared to use the full force of the state to force Gregory Nazianzen and orthodoxy on the people of Constantinopolis (under Valens, Arianism had reigned supreme).[2] He knew nothing of the conditions in the east, but he had a clear aim in mind: that of imposing orthodox unity on all his subjects. At the start of the following year he opened his campaign against heterodoxy by an edict that proclaimed the orthodoxy of the Nicene faith alone, and forbade 'heretics' of any colour to assemble.[3] In the west, Ambrose of course was to provide him with a perfect partner, both in methods and ideas.

Having chosen the right side of history, Theodosius has, of course, gone into the collective memory as 'the Great'. Given his place in history as an outwardly pious emperor, this was the title by which he was to be revered, principally in gratitude for his establishment of *Unam Sanctam Catholicam Apostolicam Ecclesiam*. An intensely religious emperor,[4] despite his earlier tolerance of leading pagans, he was certainly the bane of heterodox 'heretics'. The uncompromising orthodoxy that characterized his imperial programme included those three successive edicts proscribing pagan worship in every form,[5] whether in public or private, bringing to an end, among other changes, a millenium of that strongest link with the pre-Christian world, the Olympic Games. That was followed at Olympia almost immediately by the conversion of one of the more suitable buildings into a Christian church, and it is unthinkable that the Games, disdained as Hellenic 'idolatry', were permitted to coexist with a Christian community and Christian worship. The chilling atmosphere is unmistakable, and of course Ambrose exults in this extirpation, which he ranks among Theodosius' great achievements: 'Theodosius who, after the example of Jacob, supplanted perfidious tyrants and hid the idols of the gentiles (*abscondit simulacra gentilium*) [viz. the pagans]; who in his faith wiped out all worship of graven images and trampled down their ceremonies.'[6]

As Edward Gibbon remarks, all this was the more ironical in view of the complacent ease with which, very soon, the bishops adopted and renamed local gods as saints, shrines as reliquaries and rustic festivals as feast days without too much painful soul-searching.[7]

However that may be, it should be said that not all prelates were so indiscriminate *vis-à-vis* the Christian subversion of the old and affirmation of the new. In the renowned fourth-century *Vita Martini* by Sulpicius Severus, the first miracle that the saint performs after becoming bishop of Turones involves the discrediting of a false cult; the people venerated a local tomb, believing its occupant to be a martyr, but Martin summoned up the dead man's spirit and made him confess that he was only an executed robber.[8]

While festivals and ceremonies acquired a new Christian colour, those pagan temples not repurposed as sites of Christian worship began to fall into disrepair. These once bustling and brilliant buildings were now, as Jerome writes, 'covered with soot and cobwebs, and the people hurry past the ruined shrines and pour out to visit the martyrs' graves'.[9] What Jerome fails to mention of course is that these decaying walls, empty grand structures and deserted porticoes of these polytheistic leftovers were the product of the outright vandalism of Christians too: did not Augustine, a dominant figure in mainstream Christian thought, himself exult over the destruction of pagan altars, shrines and temples?[10] Better known for his philosophical and theological musings, Augustine (now revered as a saint) once declared to a congregation in Carthage 'that all superstition of pagans and heathens should be annihilated is what God wants, God commands, God proclaims!'[11]

The Graeco-Syrian teacher of rhetoric Libanios describes to Theodosius the destruction of temples (including the famous temple of Zeus at Apameia)[12] in 385 by Christian mobs in Syria:

> These people hasten to attack the temples with sticks and stones and bars of iron, and in some cases, disdaining these, with hands and feet. Then utter desolation follows, with the stripping of roofs, the demolition of walls, the tearing down of statues, and the overthrow of altars, and the priest must either keep quiet or die.[13]

This is punchy, pungent and potent, and it is all true. While it is true that pagan mobs committed sporadic acts of violence against Christians, these cannot justly be compared to Christian violence. The partially approved thuggery of Christian zealots involved the wholesale destruction of classical cultural heritage – statues, shrines, altars, temples and even libraries – whereas the former arose as a response to the threat to classical civilization that Christianity represented. Before it preserved, the Church destroyed.

The greatest myth of Christianity is that it was a force for civilization that drove out pagan brutality. This brings us to the matter of the book-burnings, always an obligation for pie-eyed fanatics and their like. Book-burning (or banning) has a long and dark history and the reasons for the ritual destruction of books by fire have fluctuated over time, but fall roughly into three broad categories: religion, obscenity and political control. In 213 BC, for example, Qín Shǐ Huáng, 'The First Emperor of Qín' (r. 221–210 BC), apparently buried 460 Confucian scholars alive and burned all the philosophy texts in his kingdom so he could control how history would remember his reign (in 2013 his distant successor Xí Jìnpíng banned the meme comparing the tubby Winnie the Pooh and the trim Tigger to him and Barack Obama respectively). During the Peasants' Revolt of 1381 in Cambridge, rebellious townspeople sacked university buildings and burned legal documents and charters in Market Square, shouting: 'Away with the learning of clerks, away with it!' The first known official list of books forbidden in Christianity was issued around 492 by Pope Gelasius I (r. 492–496).[14] Some eighty years earlier, in 409, the emperors Honorius and Theodosius II ordered that astrologers burn their scrolls on pain of expulsion.[15]

The 'heretical' *Adversus Christianos* of the Neo-Platonist philosopher Porphyrios of Tyre (†305), which was condemned and banned on the orders of Constantinus,[16] was burned by order of Theodosius II in 435 and again in 448.[17] An intellectual alternative to Christianity, Neo-Platonism was a more spiritualized late antique version of some of the ideas of Plato. Otherwise it was an eclectic movement, which borrowed from other scholastic world views. Some combined this with Epicureanism, others with forms of Agnosticism. Porphyrios himself is well known as a fierce critic of Christianity: his world view was focused very much on the here and now, like Epicurus of Samos in his philosophy. With it came a distinctly religious and superstitious tinge, especially through the practice of theurgy, a technique of calling the gods by magical or occult means; the ultimate aim of Neo-Platonism was the union of the soul with God. Everyday magic and miracles was simply a lower rung of the ladder leading the adept to this mystical union. Like Christianity, Neo-Platonism emphasized asceticism and self-restraint.

Before the Frigidus, Theodosius had already tilted the Christian playing field in his favour and progressively extended his grip over the eradication of paganism. A half-century or so later, however, paganism was still active enough, even at that late date, to prompt Theodosius II and Valentinianus III to also consign Porphyrios' works to the flames. Even Stilicho, normally tolerant of pagans and who had stopped the destruction of temples and had the statue of *ara Victoriae* returned to the Senate,[18] had changed his attitude. In around 407, in his anxiety to win the favour of the Christian aristocracy, he ordered all temples confiscated and cult objects destroyed,[19] and on top of it he had apparently felt it necessary to burn the Sibylline Books (L *Libri Sibyllini*),[20] a collection of oracular utterances (L *Oracula Sibyllina*) set out in Greek hexameters and considered the most sacred documents of paganism. Apparently the *generalissimo* believed that the books were being employed to undermine his legitimacy and leave his authority in tatters. The pagan soldier Ammianus Marcellinus, a witness of at least one of these events, has this to say this about book-burnings:

> Innumerable books and whole heaps of documents, which had been rooted out from various houses, were piled up and burnt under the eyes of the judges. They were treated as forbidden texts to allay the indignation caused by the executions, though most of them were treatises on various liberal arts and jurisprudence.[21]

Indeed, although Christians ostensibly burned books pertaining to magic, divination and Christian heresy,[22] works of philosophy were sometimes fair game and so lumped in this all-encompassing category. A common belief among early Christians was that pagan works of art, literature and philosophy and so on harboured spells and charms and so were demonic.

The roots of Christianity were not Hellenic but Judaic. It had inherited the jealous, militant monotheism of Exodus, as well as the pre-eminent Judaic concern with the Law. All other gods were evil demons, if they existed at all. Once and only once had the Divine assumed human form, in the supreme mystery of Christ's incarnation. Again Augustine, who thundered: 'All pagans were under the power of demons. Temples were built to demons, altars were set up to demons, priests ordained for the service of demons, sacrifices offered to demons, and ecstatic ravers were brought in as prophets for demons.'[23]

Thus Augustine's approach, much like that of the Bible,[24] to the gods of the pagans is not as simple as mere scoffing and consigning them to the realm of fantasy. In reality, the belief here is that the world we inhabit is a perilous place, crammed full of malevolent supernatural beings, which sometimes manifest themselves in the form of fake gods. Paganism was thus seen as a diabolical disease. It was natural, then, that good Christians like Augustine would want to eradicate it. Such acts ably demolish the resilient popular myths that Christianity triumphed solely through peaceful means and that Christianity preserved more than it destroyed. As Tertullian arrogantly demanded, 'What indeed has Athens to do with Jerusalem?'[25] Perhaps an exaggeration on the part of the Christian apologists from Carthage – he does tend to shock you with the sheer force of his invective – but the expression does capture the essence of a Christianity grounded in a faith (Jerusalem) that transcends philosophical inquiry (Athens).

It was, to any pagan listening to Tertullian, a curious choice of words. Paganism of the Roman state was willing to be all things to all men. To repeat, being polytheistic, it was multiple and versatile. It was very far from exclusive. Nor was it generally intolerant. True, it had become intolerant towards the Christians because they seemed to be denying the sufficient minimum of loyalty to the emperor and the state. Like the Jews, they were monotheistic and unfavourably disposed towards the pagan majority of the 50 to 80 million people in the *imperium Romanum*. This was of course at a time when the Christians were a small and exceptional minority – perhaps 10 per cent of the population at this point – that often faced animosity and ridicule. Yet even when Constantinus converted to Christianity, with his gradual but bold conversion of the state to the same faith, the Christians were *still* a minority; the estimated percentage of Christians in the beginning of Constantinus' reign is 20 per cent. However, by the end of the fourth century, even though they still remained a minority, they had grown in numbers and were now fashioning a Christian empire. Christianity as the state religion would not have happened without Constantinus, but it is wrong to say that it happened only because of him.

Conflict of Interests

Christianity started as a minority Jewish sect, and gradually came to take over the Roman Empire. This is the familiar story of late antiquity, often called the Christianization of Rome. Ever since Eusebius of Caesarea Palestinae founded Church history during the reign of Constantinus, the big picture painted by ecclesiastical historians – with an obviously self-serving slant – was a narrative of God's providential transformation of the world. Augustus' empire grew precisely to make possible the spread of Christianity. Rome came to power as part of God's long-range plans for the governance of the world, and so Constantinus saw that vision of a cross in the sky with the motto ἐν τούτῳ νίκα and the rest is history.

One of the fundamental contrasts between pagan cult and Christianity was the passage from oral culture of myth and conjecture to one based firmly on written texts. In the first Christian communities, there had already been a significant break with contemporary habits of reading: Christians used the codex, or book, for their scriptural texts, whereas pagans still vastly preferred the roll. The Christian codex was made of papyrus, not parchment. It made it compact and better suited to people on the move, and it was an easier form in which to refer to and fro between texts. In a sense, the Christian revolution lies at the beginning of the history of the modern book.

While pagan priests and magistrates competed in their *philotomia*, Christians looked upon this as pure vainglory. While civic cults of the empire paid honour to the presiding manifest divinities of the town, the Christian 'city' lay in the Kingdom of Heaven and their 'assembly' was the gathering of people of God throughout the world. The cults and myths gave the pagans a focus for their civic patriotism, yet Christians obeyed one law, the same from city to city. Indeed, a person whose loyalties were less engaged by the hometown, or enlarged by travel beyond it, could respond to this idea of a universal assembly. At their festivals, the elite pagan families made distributions to the civic authorities, members of their own ruling class. Christians brought their funds to those in need, men and women, citizen and non-citizen. Christian charity differed in motive from pagan philanthropy: it earned merit in heaven and sustained that dear to God, the poor. Indeed, Christianity appealed to the poor because it promised a better life after people died. Little wonder, then, that the poor were attracted to a faith that taught that all people were equal. The idea of 'doing unto others as you would wish them to do unto you' was not alien to pagan ethics, but there was no precedent for the further Christian advice 'to love one's enemies'.

No Compromise

Ambrose was to stigmatize the Arians for 'leaving the Apostle to follow Aristotle':[26] the pious Theodosius was to ruthlessly impose Nicene orthodoxy. The actions of these two, prelate and potentate, would result in a much narrower and less accommodating militant Christian identity. This was one that meant there was no more room for those orthodox Christians, as in the case of Eugenius, who could still envision a world filled with other gods. The earlier emperors had been comparatively tolerant of rival Christian doctrines and their refusal to criminalize heresy outright had often been a matter of practical politics, but it had been tolerance nonetheless. The policies of Theodosius brought it to an end. It was a far cry from Constantinus' emphatic rejection of coercion when he first adopted Christianity: 'No one should injure another in the name of a faith he himself has accepted from conviction. He, who is quickest to understand the truth, let him try as he may to convince his neighbour. But if this is not possible, he must desist.'[27]

It was shortly after his victory at the battle of Pons Mulvius in October 312 that Constantinus, together with his eastern colleague and stepbrother Licinius, issued a directive to provincial governors about religious tolerance.

Its key statement was that the emperors would grant freedom of worship to all religions 'to the end that whatever divinity there be on the heavenly seat may be favourably disposed and propitious towards us and all those placed under our authority'.[28]

The truth of all this serves as a potent reminder of the threat that biblical monotheism has posed and continues to pose to European civilization, though we should not go so far as Edward Gibbon did when he came to identify the key factors in the decline and fall of Rome and cite the Christians as one of the prime instigators, their zealotry, he thought, ultimately responsible for creating citizens contemptuous of their public duty. Undoubtedly Rome would have fallen, as it did, even if Christianity had not found adherents within its frontiers: other and deeper causes, social, political and military, were at work, sapping the foundations of vitality and strength. As the prominent poet and popular philosopher Ralph Waldo Emerson (1803–82) once held, a thing cannot be crushed by a blow from without until ready to perish from decay within.

A quick aside on that: the universe in Gibbon's day seemed to rest in the safe and intelligible certainties of Newtonian mechanics, Euclidian geometry and Aristotelian logic. All three have now been overturned and we are gloriously at sea again.

Hindsight bias is a concept that refers to an exaggeration, in hindsight, of what foresight could have predicted. Yet hindsight is not equal to foresight. So it is that blessed with the luxury of hindsight, the historian can easily see that Adrianopolis in 378 was a far greater disaster than the sack of Rome in 410, yet it occasioned none of the existential hand-wringing brought about by the metropolis' fall. After all, Valens, the near-paranoid emperor who owed his throne entirely to his elder brother, the ferocious and warlike Valentinianus I, and was destined to perish on the field at Adrianopolis, was a Christian, but he had opted to support an unorthodox version of the religion and had come down hard on those who stuck to the Nicene Creed. So, as far as that sect was concerned, he was a 'beer-swilling' heretic who simply got what was coming to him.[29] All his defeat meant was that God did not just want the empire to be Christian, He wanted it to be Nicene Christian.[30]

Yet a more serious matter was the mortal dangers bubbling beneath the surface. Adrianopolis was a major battlefield disaster and a significant blow to Roman prestige, but a defeat that was largely the result of Valens' indecisiveness – at one moment he wanted to attack, perhaps for vain motives, and at the next to negotiate a bloodless victory – and tactical misfortune rather than the army's inefficiency. After all, the trust that existed between the two brothers provided both political accord between them and the much-needed teamwork in protecting the empire. With the rank of *Augustus*, Valens was content to play the part of *Caesar*: the older brother gave the orders; the younger one obeyed. However, after Valentinianus died unexpectedly in 375, Valens was left without his fraternal mentor. He had received neither a classical nor a military education. As a military leader he was an amateur who lacked the innate talent that Iulianus had possessed. A classical education undoubtedly played a part in Iulianus' surprisingly successful career as a young commander, while there is more substance to Eunapios' criticism of Valens' lack of education as a factor in his defeat at Adrianopolis than a cynical modern commentator might suppose:[31] a well-educated person might not have succumbed to the pressures that led Valens to a rapid engagement, or might have considered the possibility that only part of the Gothic host was visible on the plain. In the words of Libanios, Valens engaged 'with more ardour than skill'.[32] Valentinianus' nepotism had cost the empire dear.

To be sure, it is a gross mistake to suppose, as many have done, that because the Roman army was defeated that day this army was tactically of low quality. Lacking his brother's aggressive zeal and his detailed understanding of matters military, Valens was outclassed by a cooler Fritigern, a man of stubborn ability and much military talent. Furthermore, Valens' fears, bred by his own incompetence, were the source of the fatal errors of judgement that brought about his defeat and death. In contrast, his army, surrounded as at Cannae, kept their discipline and fought on for many hours and even then about a third of them managed to break out of the encirclement and escape in reasonable order.[33] In the conditions of that collapse it was remarkable that so many of the army managed to escape, largely due to their determination, which prolonged the fight until dusk, but the Roman losses that day were so great that, after this, the strategic balance was permanently changed. Theodosius' manpower shortage was now so critical that he could not realistically hope to regain the position before 378.

On the other hand, the death of Valens may have been good for Nicene orthodoxy, but Adrianopolis shattered the eastern army. Militaries just do not bounce back that quickly from such a devastating loss. The severe shortage was of men (above all foot soldiers), not officers, and this led to the employment of barbarian armies, and ultimately to Alaric and all that. In Genesis the Israelite God had promised Abram he would spare even so a sinful city as Sodom if as few as ten innocent inhabitants could be found within its walls.[34] Why, then, did He not spare Rome, a Christian city, home to the shrines to Saints Peter and Paul? Still, as Augustine initially responded (put simply) to his African congregation: 'It could have been worse: it could have been better, perhaps, but it could have been worse.'

Seven years after the sack the pagan poet Rutilius Namatianus posthumously assailed Stilicho for consigning the Sibylline Books to the flames.[35] He also declared Stilicho a traitor and condemned him for his anti-pagan policies. What is more, he reiterated firmly once again that it was because of the Romans' desertion of their traditional gods that disaster had overtaken them, and he derided the Christian God for failing to save the city.[36] There were those with a longing for the old gods who liked to hint that they would rise again and save the empire. They did not. Now Augustine was a cleric of unusual eloquence, energy and commitment. Three years after the sack he set himself the task of writing a comprehensive work that would not only reply to pagan sniping about the sack of Rome and the invidious spread of Christianity, but also brilliantly clarify the faith to intelligent and thoughtful pagans. The result was the *De civitate Dei contra paganos*. Written towards the end of his life, it would take him more than a dozen years to complete it.[37] Rather than adopt a position of defence, Augustine stays on the offensive for all twenty-two books. Performing verbal gymnastics, Augustine astutely argues that the Christian God should not be blamed for Rome's fall, but Christians themselves for allowing paganism to flourish in the metropolis. That, and not the end of state support for the old rites, is what led God to chastise the Romans through the agency of Alaric's Goths. *De civitate Dei* is a masterwork – written in clear, simple, forceful Latin prose – a cornerstone of the new civilization rising on the foundations of old pagan Rome, and rightly holds a gilded position in European ecclesiastical literary history.

Christian Triumphalism

In the view of Catherine Nixey the stock picture of Rome's conversion to Christianity remains, even two centuries after Edward Gibbon, glossed by Christian triumphalism. History, in her view, has given the Church an easy ride. Polytheistic Rome tends to get painted as cruel, capricious and castigatory; it is thought to be 'a chilly, nihilistic world'.[38] Christianity, conversely, is painted as valiant, principled, compassionate, all-encompassing and optimistic. What concerned Gibbon was the clash between faith and reasons. For Nixey, these clashes are physical ones. 'But it is undeniable that there have been,' she writes, 'and there still are…those who use monotheism and its weapons to terrible ends.'[39]

It was never quiet in the menagerie of theologians. Their views clashed. All tricks were allowed, as long as they discredited those who thought differently and gained an audience for certain ideas. An important theme in the writings of Ambrose and Augustine is the idea of the one true religion, but one ecclesiastic's orthodoxy is another ecclesiastic's heterodoxy. It has been said that the English cleric and theologian John Wesley (1703–91) founded Methodism in order to make people feel guilty about absolutely everything. True or not, he certainly was no stranger to the immense, omnivorous *œuvres* of the Enlightenment luminaries, who crusaded under the motto *écrasez l'infâme*,[40] and had little good to say about them. The literary hero Voltaire was a 'consummate coxcomb!' while William Robertson, a Christian divine, deserved censure for writing history 'with so little Christianity in it' and instead attributing events not to God but to fortune or chance.[41] Intriguingly, regarding the learned and lively Edward Gibbon, whose vast, swaggering monument of a *magnum opus* admittedly did not appear in final form until 1788, Wesley remains mute.[42]

Barbarian Armies?

As in the sanguinary civil war against Magnus Maximus, commander of the *comitatenses* in Britannia and an earlier usurper who came to grief on a battlefield far from said diocese,[43] Theodosius' forces for the current civil war against Eugenius were mainly barbarian.[44] More tellingly, the crucial Frigidus battle can be viewed as part of a trend towards using increasing percentages of imported barbarian soldiery, especially in the western half of the empire. Unfortunately, this development has led to the popular claim that the impact of so-called barbarization of the later Roman army resulted in the weakening of the empire itself, particulary so in the western half of the empire after it metamorphosed into the West following the death of Theodosius and the division (now permanent) between his two sons.[45]

True, some civilian contemporaries, such as the Neo-Platonist bishop Synesios who had much to say on the subject, moaned about the number of barbarians in the army.[46] Likewise Zosimos would later rattle on about Theodosius' alleged barbarization of the army and it was one of his major themes.[47] True again, the military crisis of the time, coupled with the loss of professional manpower the later Roman army could not replace, led to severe conscription,[48] never the best of solutions in any age. Considering how widely accepted this idea is, it is surprising that no soldier, such as Ammianus Marcellinus or Prokopios, suggests that this 'barbarization' affected the army's performance.[49] Even the theoretical military writer Vegetius, apart from his tirades regarding the deterioration of military discipline,[50] never suggests that the decline of the army was due to its recruitment of barbarians.

The *Epitoma rei militaris* of Publius (or Flavius) Vegetius Renatus is a unique example of a general military treatise in Latin. Its author was a *vir illustris* and *comes*, a high-ranking civilian bureaucrat with a sense of history, who also wrote the equine veterinary treatise *Digesta artis mulomedicinae*. The core of his proposals in the *Epitoma* is a return to the traditional methods of recruitment, training and deployment, rather than a dependence on barbarian *foederati.* This was the *antiqua disciplina* of an earlier age that, in his view, had fully prepared soldiers for war. Its reintroduction, he argues, would restore the army of his day to its supposed former glory. The other concern, of course, was that poorly-trained soldiers fight poorly.

However, let us not forget that once joining the Roman army, these barbarians (outsiders) served under Roman officers and received formal military training. Generally speaking, untrained men are not dependable in battle and, as recent events in eastern Europe have evidently demonstrated, it can prove to be poor policy to base military operations on such uncertain elements. As Vegetius makes clear, 'Few men are born naturally brave; hard work and good training makes many so.'[51] It is for this reason that the basic aim of any military training is the creation of *esprit de corps*, a soldier's confidence and pride in his unit. Personal bravery of a single individual does not decide the issue on the actual day of the battle[52] but the bravery of the unit as a whole, and this rests on the good opinion and the confidence that each individual places in the unit of which he is a member. Formal military training of course is a means to an end and the real measure of any soldier is his experience of battle, the central act of war. Training transforms a raw recruit into a trained soldier, but battle (if he survives the 'baptism of fire' both mentally and physically) finally elevates him to veteran status.

Also, these barbarians at most times were an infiltration rather than an invasion, and as previously discussed they were becoming prominent at all levels of Roman society. There was a constant flow seeking military service or to be settled within the empire. Once they joined the army, they seem to have been loyal to it. Instances of barbarian treachery were few and far between.[53]

Silvanus, a career soldier of Frankish origin – disloyalty can be contagious, particularly when a state is embroiled in civil war, but his father Bonitus had stayed loyal to Constantinus in the civil war against Licinius – was stationed at Colonia Claudia Ara Agrippinensium as *magister peditum per Gallias* tasked with quelling lawlessness in the prefecture of Gallia.[54] After being falsely accused of treason (true, he had formerly served Magnus Magnentius before deserting the latter for Constantius shortly before the incredibly bloody battle of Mursa),[55] he considered seeking sanctuary across the Rhenus. In early August 355 he was finally compelled to proclaim himself *Caesar* to protect himself against plotters who had trumped up evidence that he did indeed harbour imperial aspirations. Twenty-eight days later he was stabbed to death on 7 September at Colonia Claudia Ara Agrippinensium by some of his own soldiers who had been bribed by another commander, Ursicinus.[56] Ammianus Marcellinus, whose early life is closely connected with the career of Ursicinus to whom he was strongly attached, portrays Silvanus, the twenty-eight-day emperor, as a tragic individual, a man of military *virtus*, loyal to Roman *imperium*, ensnared by mendacious conspirators.[57] He concludes his narrative of the fall of Silvanus, a man he knew personally, with this damning condemnation of a certain cabal of his fellow Roman officers: 'So fell by this manner of death a general of no slight merits, who through fear due to the slanders in which he was ensnared during his absence by a clique of his enemies, in order to save his life had resorted to the uttermost measures of defence.'[58]

Equally, no Roman source mentions that barbarian recruits, having sworn an oath of loyalty to the emperor, were prone to desert the army. As one Frankish veteran buried at Aquincum (Budapest, Hungary), Pannonia Inferior, described himself in Latin,[59] *Francus ego civis Romanus miles in armis*, 'I am a Frank, a Roman citizen and a soldier in the army.'[60]

By the terms of the peace treaty of 382, the Goths were awarded lands within the empire on condition that they promise peace with the empire and readiness to perform military service on request. The Christian panegyrist Pacatus Drepanius may extol Theodosius for imposing orderly behaviour on the Goths (along with the Huns and Alani) in his army, who now 'followed standards which they had once opposed',[61] but there was an innovation. The Goths were not distributed throughout the empire as *coloni*, individual settlers who were subject to tax, rent and military conscription, nor were they subject to Roman administration; they were acknowledged as an allied people with their own territory, laws and culture. Their military obligations to the empire were not to supply recruits who would be integrated into the Roman army structure, but to fight *en masse* as *foederati* when required as a national contingent. Theoretically they were to serve under a Roman *dux*, but in reality they followed their own native leaders.[62] Unlike previous immigrants – it should be remembered that the practice of taking barbarians into military service was not invented by the later Roman emperors – their tribal structure and identity remained intact. That they were not given the right of *conubium*, the right to intermarry with Roman citizens, further set these Goths apart and stood in the way of assimilation. Though nominally subject to the empire they were, in effect, a foreign nation in arms established on Roman territory. As Prokopios was later to state, the Romans called the Goths *foederati* because they had been bound to the empire by a *foedus* and had 'come into the Roman political system not in the condition of slaves, since they had not been conquered by the Romans, but on the basis of complete equality'.[63]

This was a hazardous state of affairs, for which Theodosius has been much blamed, both in antiquity[64] and in recent times, perhaps unfairly.[65] Iulianus may have declared once that the empire should not rely on foreign troops for its defence,[66] but the loss of experienced manpower at Adrianopolis and

Theodosius' ensuing embroilment in civil war meant that in the eastern army reliance on barbarian troops increased (after the Frigidus, the same would go for the western army).

Hindsight is easy. Yet the use of such troops caused anxiety in some contemporary circles, an anxiety that can be seen in the aforementioned panegyric to Theodosius in which Pacatus Drepanius labours the point that the emperor's new troops did have Roman commanders after all.[67] So it does seem that Theodosius had little choice in the matter,[68] and his policy of peaceful accommodation with the Goths did, at the very least, obtain some respite for the embattled Romans. All in all, the eastern emperor clearly knew what he was doing. There is a strain of special pleading in Themistios' New Year's address of 1 January 383:

> Which then is better: to fill Thracia with corpses or with farmers? To fill it with graves or with people? To travel through wildernesses or cultivated lands? To count those who have perished, or those who are ploughing? … I hear from those returning from there, that they are remaking the iron from their swords and breastplates into hoes and sickles, and that those who formerly loved Ares now worship Demeter and Dionysios.[69]

The pragmatic Theodosius would not have taken this literally for he would not have expected the Goths to become law-abiding citizens, but he certainly expected them to hang on to 'their swords and breastplates' with the hope they would serve him not only when he had need of them but also as a bulwark against external threats.[70] In reality, it was against the internal kind that Theodosius' Goths were to prove their worth. Theodosius' expedition against Magnus Maximus in 388 was notable for the unprecedented size of its barbarian contingents.[71] Revealing too is Jordanes' description of Theodosius as 'a lover of peace and the Gothic race'.[72]

The emperor himself may have been a fan of Goths – it is more likely he was a fan of their highly portable martial skills – but hostility and prejudice against them there certainly were. This was exemplified by the orations of the bishop of Ptolemais, Synesios, who thought the policy of Theodosius was a grave mistake, made not out of weakness but his extreme clemency to a defeated foe, but the Goths do not understand clemency. They should never have been granted land; they should instead be forced to work the land for the Romans as the Spartans once did with the Messenians.[73] The anti-Gothic sentiment of Synesios was widely echoed among many Greek cities, reflecting not just perennial Greek contempt for all non-Greeks, but also long memories of the very destructive Gothic sack of so many cities in the third century and shorter ones of the Gothic depredations with fire and sword after Adrianopolis. Formerly enemies from without, the Goths were now enemies within.

One Spring Day in Thessaloniki

One of those Greek cities was Thessaloniki, today one of the few cities in Europe that can boast a continuous history as an important urban centre for more than 2,300 years. Founded in 316 BC by Kassandros of Macedon, husband of the half-sister of Alexander the Great, under the Christian emperors Thessaloniki (L *Thessalonica*) was the second city of the empire after Constantinopolis and would remain so right up to 1453 when it fell to the Ottoman Turks. By simply looking at a map of the later Roman Empire we can appreciate its strategic position. First, it lies in the long quiff of northern Greece, with the militarily important Danuvian provinces to the north. Second, it is about halfway between Constantinopolis and the Adriatic seaboard, linked to both by the Via Egnatia. Third, it lies between the Aegean Sea and the Danuvian cities such as Singidunum (Belgrade, Serbia) in Illyricum and so was accessible to the heartland of central Europe via road and river. Not only that, it had a splendid deep water harbour and substantial fortification walls. This axial position in the heart of the empire was to play a crucial part in the city's turbulent and splendid history, and it was here that Theodosius had directed his operations against the Goths.[74] Thessaloniki was, and still is, a nervy city.

Thessaloniki was adorned with all the grand trappings of an imperial city: forum, baths, palace, long expansive porticoes, theatre and hippodrome. Concerning the latter structure, the most destructive acts of civilian unrest were the occasional bouts of urban rioting associated with the circus factions, some of whose conflicts were virtual battles, as was to take place in Thessaloniki. In April 390, Butheric,[75] a favoured Goth who currently served as *magister militum per Illyricum* and was based in the city, had a popular charioteer imprisoned for a homosexual offence; he had attempted to rape a cupbearer or a male servant in a hostelry,[76] though some modern commentators say Butheric himself was the victim.[77] Christian attitudes to homosexual sex were more extreme than those of its parent religion of Judaism. The Church's view on the matter was founded in the scripture: 'Do not lie with a man as one would with a woman; that is detestable.'[78] Eventually, the Church's condemnation of any type of non-procreative sexual intercourse brought about the outlawing of homosexuality and an edict of Theodosius that very year threatened with public burning the forcing or selling of males into prostitution.[79] Behind this edict lay not a disgust of prostitution, but the fact that the body of a man would be used in homosexual intercourse in the same way as that of a woman, and that was unacceptable, for as our arch-Christian convert Augustine would later make clear, 'the body of a man is as superior to that of a woman as the soul is to the body.'[80] In our time, of course, this sort of thing sounds too much like the sort of self-certification that old school misogynists issue, when every open-minded male takes the opposite view. There again, Augustine, a future saint, was definitely not of our time.

To return to the age of Theodosius, chariot-racing fans were fanatical, and violence would appear to be a natural consequence of such fanaticism. Those of Thessaloniki demanded the release of the charioteer and, as Butheric bluntly refused, a riot ensued. This resulted in the unruly mob lynching him and at least one Roman official. The city's reaction to the upheaval of the Gothic incursions of the previous decades resonates all too well with life in the twenty-first century, when migration, immigration, terrorism, refugee crises and fear of the 'alien other' are widespread.

The reaction of Theodosius was to have dreadful repercussions. For the emperor, at the time resident in Mediolanum, briefly allowed his temper to get the better of him and before he could regain control of the situation he ordered the Goths of the garrison to quell the disturbance. It did not end well. That hardly needs saying. The Goths herded the citizens of the city into the hippodrome, its largest edifice, and butchered them in revenge, leaving some 7,000 men, women and children dead.[81] Theodoret of Kyrrhos (Nebi Huri, Syria), admittedly neither a witness nor a contemporary of the massacre, reports:

> The anger of the emperor rose to the highest pitch, and he gratified his vindictive desire for vengeance by unsheathing the sword most unjustly and tyrannically against all, slaying the innocent and guilty alike. It is said seven thousand perished without any forms of law, and without even having judicial sentence passed upon them; but that, like ears of wheat in the time of harvest, they were alike cut down.[82]

In the ensuing chaos and panic, many people could have been trampled underfoot.[83] Whatever the true numbers, no Roman city had experienced anything like this in living memory: it was something only brutal conquerors did to captured enemy cities, and it put the emperor's Gothic soldiery in exactly that light, as a foreign occupation force.

The Bishop and the Emperor

Such, then, was the Thessaloniki massacre. The moral shock throughout the empire was, if anything, accentuated by the carefully cultivated court image of Theodosius as a merciful and humane ruler.[84] The bishop of Mediolanum, Ambrose, was whipped in conniption.

The upshot: Ambrose excommunicated Theodosius. Taking full advantage of the guilt-ridden emperor, in a letter written immediately after the massacre (without actually describing it), the bishop told the emperor to imitate David in his repentance as he had imitated him in guilt.[85] Ambrose, in piety, had declared himself independent of all authority save that of God, an important point in the light of later events. Stunned, Theodosius accepted full responsibility and went on a month-long period of penance during which time he sought to appease the church (and Ambrose) by enacting a number of steps designed to sweep all traces of paganism from the empire:

> And straightaway, when the sovereign had commanded that this [law] be written and had confirmed it with his own hand, Ambrose released the bond and allowed him to enter the church. And when he had entered, having fallen flat upon the floor, he cried with a shout, 'My soul is joined to the floor. Revive me according to your word, Lord' [Psalms 119:25]. And with his hands he began to tear the hairs from his head, to smite his face, to drench the earth with tears, and to importune God until the hour of communion. Then, when he had arisen and approached the chancel, wishing to enter, he was hindered by Ambrose, who declared to him, 'Know, sovereign, that the things within are accessible to priests alone, but to all others inaccessible and not to be touched. Indeed now, depart and share the space with the others. For a purple robe normally makes sovereigns, not priests.' And when he heard this, he responded, 'I have not done this through presumption, but I have learned this was the norm in Constantinopolis. I owe thanks to you, too, for this remedy.' Virtue of such a kind and quantity did the archpriest and sovereign radiate! And the sovereign, when he had returned to Constantinopolis and a festival was taking place, after he had borne the gifts to the holy table, straightaway departed. And when Nektarios, the patriarch at the time, asked the reason, he said, 'I have been adequately instructed about the difference between a sovereign and a priest. For I know Ambrose alone is deservedly called "Bishop".'[86]

Our Byzantine chronicler, Georgios Kedrenos, has undoubtedly added some colour and detail here, yet he had obviously read his Ambrose. According to Ambrose's own testimony, the pious bishop only readmitted the penitent emperor to the Eucharist in time for the Nativity mass, 390, another year almost gone, when Theodosius had endured an *eight*-month penance. As Ambrose reported five years later (no doubt with some exaggeration), Theodosius 'threw on the

ground all the imperial attire he was wearing, wept publicly in the church...
and prayed for pardon with groans and tears'.[87] Seeing *Dominus Noster Pius
Felix Augustus* humiliate himself in front of a mere cleric must have shocked
many pagans. Theodosius had deferred in spectacular fashion to the power of
the Church.

Words did (and still) matter. They were all you had as an ecclesiastic. They
were your only weapon of choice. An astute bishop such as Ambrose could wage
a verbal confrontation and broker a valuable covenant with words. He could
stir up or he could subdue. The emperor could terrify people into compliance
with the sword, but a bishop of the church could govern his eternal destiny.
The words of Ambrose make us think how power can be exerted without really
exerting itself.

Though Ambrose had ranged his considerable power against Theodosius, the
situation would often get out of hand. Now seemingly empowered with state and
Church sanction, emboldened Christian mobs, bands of black-hooded monks
armed with cudgels prominent among them, opted to flex their monotheistic
credentials and double down on pagan survivals in the empire. This they did
by taking to the streets all across the empire to lynch influential pagans and lay
waste their temples. Hatred is the ugliest of emotions.

Case in point: the orgy of sectarian violence culminated in 391 with the
bishop of Alexandria, Theophilos (r. 385–412), who egged on his own posse
against the pagan and all his sinful doings. The agitator succeeded handsomely,
for his followers seized the opportunity to strip the great Serapeion, the famous
temple of the Hellenistic Egyptian god Serapis,[88] of its sacred treasures, burning
thousands of scrolls housed within and finally razing it to the ground. Along with
the anti-pagan legislation, the senseless destruction of the Serapeion, described
by Ammianus Marcellinus as 'next to the Capitol, which is the symbol of the
eternity of immemorial Rome, the most magnificent building in the whole
world',[89] provoked high feelings. The Serapeion was given the appearance of
a battlefield in one short day, and upon its ruins the bishop erected a church.[90]

Alexandria was often a city out of control, since its bishops financed an
enormous clerical establishment, including hundreds of monks in the nearby
desert who could be brought into the city and mobilized when needed. Emperors
did not keep enough troops in Aegyptus to confront what was a potent
combination of power, corruption and patronage. Besides, it was far easier to
come to an accommodation with the preferred leader of the Alexandrian Church.
Of course the bishop of Alexandria was exceptional in absolute terms, but in
most of the empire's cities the local bishop was a leading property owner and
patron as well as a person of good education. As such, they were often trusted
to represent their cities.

Chapter Fourteen

Changing Nature of War

'πάντα χωρεῖ καὶ οὐδὲν μένει/*Everything changes and nothing stands still*'
Herakleitos of Ephesos apud Plato *Kratylos* 401d

Conventionally in the West, when reflecting upon decline and collapse and recovery we tend to call to mind just three things: the collapse of the Roman Empire, the so-called 'barbarian successor' kingdoms and the eventual rebirth of Europe in what is habitually called the Renaissance. Of course, conventional thinking here is rather myopic. As we have seen, the tale of the 'decline and fall' of Rome is only a small part of a much larger story. A much broader view of history shows that failure and renewal of civilization is the rule. This was true from the very beginning in Bronze Age Mesopotamia, where temple states rose and collapsed rapidly. To name two examples among many, the Third Dynasty of Ur, something of a high point for early civilization, enjoyed slightly more than 100 years of relative stability and then collapsed, only to be replaced eventually by the First Dynasty of Babylonia. The Egyptian Old Kingdom, which lasted some six centuries, must have seemed indestructible in comparison, but it too disintegrated. At the time of writing, the international economic and political order is in crisis, and may be in terminal decline as we enter the age of populism and post-truth.[1]

Nothing lasts forever. Empires rise and fall, the world gets a little older, and so it was that by the turn of the seventh century, Europe looked very different. Trade was almost non-existent, taking with it the economy and the basis of civilized life, and almost no major urban centres were left, those cities that survived having shrunk to villages. Education and literacy was virtually extinct, and the arts and sciences were all but forgotten. All in all, a basic siege mentality gripped Europe. In outlining the peoples of the world for his contemporaries, the Baghdadi Alī al-Masʿūdī (†957), the peripatetic polymath sometimes referred to as the 'Herodotos of the Arabs', described Europeans as having 'large bodies, gross natures, harsh manners, and dull interests...and those who live farthest north are particularly stupid, gross and brutish'.[2] So, in the mind of our intellectual Arab, people living in Europe were almost a different race of people. Their dress was different, their manners primitive, their culture ridiculous and their language unintelligible. As libertarian savages – people so uncivilized and uneducated that they are simply not able to govern themselves – their fate, politically speaking, was doomed. Rome's absence on the Western European stage brought with it tremendous change and none of it seemed very positive.

War begins with Sumer

We do not know on what day or where the first two men engaged in single combat. Nor do we know the first time man expanded the realm of single combat whereby two bodies of men decided to fight to the death or on what battlefield this was done. Innovations, if armies fighting armies can be categorized as one, are in their purest form when first crafted. They are bare, organic, utilitarian versions of what they will become. Yet if you thought war was a relatively recent innovation, you would be wrong. Believe it not, war was very much a part of the daily life in Bronze Age Mesopotamia. Nearly every civilization and ruler of the time believed in expansionism, which they officially justified by declaring they were commanded by the gods to conquer their near neighbours. This was the way of life: conquering and avoiding being conquered.

The decline and eventual disintegration of the western half of the Roman Empire brought to a close a three-millennium period of almost constant progress in the fruition of human progress. The Fertile Crescent, the rich agricultural zone stretching from Egypt to Iran, was where farming, writing and the wheel first emerged. It also saw the evolution of the art of war, an evolution that was set in train with the clashing armies of southern Mesopotamia, or Early Dynastic Sumer, in the third millennium BC and went on to produce every major social, economic, political and military structure required to wage a war in a modern sense and on a modern scale.[3] Additionally, this period produced the prototype of almost every weapon the world would witness until the paradigm-shattering advent of industrialized warfare that commenced with those four years of stygian gloom and bloody destruction of that most terrible of all wars, the First World War. By the close of the late antique period, man had brought into being and largely developed his most recent social invention: the practice of war on a large scale.

Whatever else war may be, as an anthropological entity its evolution can be counted among the earliest of man's social inventions. Not only that, the speed of its development was remarkable until the end of the Roman Empire in the West, there being a perpetual interaction of tactics, technology and human creativity that occurs in war. This development then slowed considerably and, for a period of almost 1,300 years, actually reversed itself in a number of important aspects. Because the rate of military evolution since the Industrial Revolution has been so rapid, it is more than tempting to assume that this development continued at an equal pace after the end of the Roman war machine, but in truth the collapse of the western Roman world brought with it a severe retrogression in almost all areas of human endeavour in Europe, including the art of war. This reverse was not righted until around the mid-nineteenth century when three technological advancements made 'automatic' firearms possible: the percussion cap, unitary cartridges and breech-loading. These inventions made it possible to load and fire a gun with rapidity and consistency. Think the rapid-firing Gatling gun.[4]

Collapse Reloaded

The slowdown in military development was a functional collapse of the larger social, economic and political framework of the Roman world upon which it rested. This collapse was also accompanied by a replacement of the common language of Western Europe by a hodgepodge of tribal tongues, many of which had no written forms. The impact on the transfer of knowledge from culture to culture was tremendous. Destroyed was the common language of art, literature, politics, law, engineering and commerce. The sweeping aside of a common currency, accounting methods and weights and measures and the loss of manufacturing and agricultural technologies restricted the continuous flow of informational transfer and storage central to maintaining the empire. Basic technologies – roads, postal services, record-keeping, water supply and building construction – gradually decayed and eventually ceased altogether. Within two centuries the knowledge required to rebuild these imperial tools was also lost. Under these conditions, it is not surprising that the military arts were also lost.

With its frontiers crumbling like undermined dykes, the West was overrun by a series of tribal migrations composed of peoples who were far less sophisticated and less capable of sustaining a culture of a higher order. The imperial social structure, the prime mover in marshalling and directing resources on a grand scale, was itself removed and replaced by a mosaic of rival tribal chiefdoms, each controlling relatively small chunks of the defunct western half of the empire. This fragmentation led eventually to feudalism, the breakdown of the social fabric into land baronies, none of which was capable of mustering the social resources on a scale that could provide the edifice for the continued development of war or any other aspect of human social activity.

An important result was the general depression of human knowledge of all kinds, and Europe plunged into an intellectual trough in which technical progress was at a lower ebb than any other time in the previous 3,000 years. Literacy, for example, fell close to a level found before the Achaemenid Persian Empire. As a point of interest, Charlemagne was distinguished among his peers because he could write his name; however, there is no evidence that he could read at all.

The standard of living sank to almost Bronze Age depth. Standards of human health and longevity also dropped to Bronze Age levels. The ability of man to understand his immediate environment and to contribute to the knowledge declined, in the main, drastically.

As Napoléon rightly pointed out, 'Education and history are enemies of religion.'[5] By the tenth century, this ability was further restricted by the rise of the Roman Catholic Church as a temporal power, with the result that a heavy cloak of religious orthodoxy backed by the feudal sword prevented further technical and intellectual development. Undeniably, the Church of Rome, which today remains essentially an ultra-conservative political organization, has stood against progress in science, in politics and in education. It was not, for example, until the fourteenth century that medical men dissected bodies, a practice forbidden by the Church under penalty of death. Mental illness, regarded by both the Greeks and Romans as a disease of the brain, came to be seen as resulting from sin or demonic possession, retrogression to the views held by the Hebrews of the second millennium BC. While some of the knowledge of the Greek and Roman worlds survived in texts copied by monastic scholars, there was little in the way of social or economic structures that could aid in transferring this knowledge into practice.

A Long Waning

In almost all respects, the conduct of war after the fourth century did not return to a level of sophistication demonstrated by the Romans until well into the nineteenth century.

The size of armies, for instance, did not reach Roman levels until the introduction of the *levée en masse* in August 1793 (the second year of the Republic) during the French Revolutionary Wars (1792–1802). The *levée en masse* heralded the age of national participation in warfare and displaced the restricted forms of warfare, most notably the *Kabinettkriege* that affected Europe during the period of absolute monarchies from the 1648 Peace of Westphalia to the 1789 French Revolution. This was a time when armies of highly-trained professional soldiers fought without the general participation of the population.[6] These were the days of the king's shilling. The cost of armies coupled with the fact that they were financed by the king meant they were small. These armies trained hard, fought hard and, being tools of the state, were almost universally despised by the people they protected.

By comparison, it has been estimated that in the course of fifteen years (1800–15) Napoléon, first as *Premier consul de la République* and then as *l'empereur des Français*, raised about 2 million conscripts in France alone, about 7 per cent of the total population. Napoléon burst a lot of bubbles when he came on the campaigning scene in 1796. Granted many pre-existing notions had already been shattered by Revolutionary France's 'shocking' ideas of warfare, that is to say, mass conscription but with a twist: a cause to fight for. Napoléon wielded this instrument of 'the motivated nation in arms' ferociously, rampaging across Europe until other states adopted his methods, if not the empowerment of their citizenry, to survive his onslaught. Importantly, the *levée en masse* meant casualties could be replaced annually as a new class of young men came of age.[7] The extreme example of this practice is of course *la Grande Armée* of 1812, which numbered about 600,000 men, even if only about half of them were French conscripts. Still, one thing did not change, and that was the matter of uniforms. These remained colourful, but designed for comic opera rather than for the rigours of the battlefield, and were worn in every climate from the coldest to the hottest. Likewise, just as the soldier wore the same uniform in every climate, so he was given the same starchy food.

Similarly, the standards of health, training and combat proficiency remained much lower than those of the Roman Empire until at least the Napoleonic Wars (1803–15). The logistic ability to support a large army over long distances did not exceed that of the Romans until railroads were employed as a major tool during the protracted American Civil War (1861–65),[8] although it should be noted that the Kingdom of Prussia had successfully transported the 12,000 men, along with their horses and guns, of its VI *Armee-Korps* on two railway lines from Breslau (Wrocław, Poland) to Kraków in 1846. Likewise, during the revolution of 1848 the railroads allowed the Prussian army to swiftly deploy mobile reaction forces of a few battalions to actual or potential trouble spots. Equally, the technique of railway transport would play a vital part in the Austro-Prussian War of 1866. Almost 200,000 men were sent to the frontiers by railway, and the lessons learned stood Prussia in good stead in 1870. The railroads offered new strategic opportunities. Troops could be transported six times as fast as the armies of Napoléon had marched.

Tactical flexibility remained easily behind both Achaemenid Persian and Roman armies until the era of Napoléon. Tactics as a practical art declined, and the predominance of cavalry relegated artillery and infantry to such secondary roles that most battles showed the tactical proficiency of little more than armed scuffles in the dust. The great hosts of the deeply Christian mediaeval world, for instance, tenuously welded together by ties of kingship and obligation, were formidable only by reason of their size and because of the very variable military skills of their individual members. Crowd-like throughout their existence, they were tactically quite unarticulated. Until the Crimean War (1853–56), western armies, notwithstanding the fact that they were now nuclear professional armies, could hardly find each other to give battle. Cartography, which had reached such proficient heights under the Romans, virtually disappeared.[9]

A Gunpowder Revolution?

The technology of war slumped to very low levels, as did most other military organizational skills. The killing power of most weapons was reduced far below that of Assyrian, Hellenistic and Roman armies. This fact is often overlooked because the advent of gunpowder weapons in the early fourteenth century seems to have been a military revolution of major proportions. Yet the killing power of gunpowder did not, in a practical sense, begin to equal that of earlier muscle-powered weapons until well into the eighteenth century. To give a single illustration about which rather more is known than usual: the Basilika of Mehmet II *Fatih* (r. 1444–46, 1451–81) deployed during his siege of Constantinopolis. This truly was a leviathan of a weapon. Its length of barrel was estimated to be 40 spans, and the circumference of the barrel 4 spans at the rear, 12 at the mouth, and it was capable of firing a stone ball weighing 540kg over a distance of 1.6km on a relatively shallow arc.[10] However, mainly because of immobility, slow cleaning and reloading, long cooling and difficulty of aiming this gargantuan gun, the Basilika could only be fired three times a day.

By comparison, Roman *ballistae*, twin-armed torsion stone-throwing machines, employed by *legio* X *Fretensis* during the siege of Jerusalem,[11] were most feared weapons: 'the stones that were cast were of the weight of one *tálanton* (26.2kg/57.76lb), and were carried two *stadia* and further (c.400m).'[12] The rate of fire of these machines was not impressive either. A *ballista* could fire one shot every two minutes and was capable of mincing anything in its path. The Jewish rebels began keeping a weather eye out for incoming missiles and shouting 'Baby on the way!' as a warning.[13] Observing this, the Roman artillerists, who had probably been carving their ammunition from the local light-coloured limestone, began to paint the projectiles in a darker hue. This made them far less visible as they approached out of the sky and once again increased the rebels' losses to artillery fire.[14] Similarly, Roman *scorpiones*, twin-armed torsion bolt-firing machines, could fire three to four 'three-span' (c.69cm) iron-tipped missiles (L *spicula*)[15] each minute up to 400m.[16] Clearly these machines significantly outranged any other missile weapon and fired a heavy bolt with greater force. During the earlier siege of Jotapata, the eyewitness Josephus describes the lethality of these machines, saying that the force of the *scorpio* 'was such that a single projectile ran through a row of men'.[17] Another eyewitness of a siege, this time Prokopios, reports that a lone Ostrogothic archer was shot by a bolt from a machine mounted on a tower, the missile passing through his cuirass and body and pinning him firmly to the tree he was standing next to.[18]

Such machines mark the introduction into warfare of the first weapons with a destructive power far greater than that attainable by human physical means alone. This advance had three immediate effects on warfare. First, it gave Hellenistic and Roman armies a distinct advantage over their enemies, as they were, with one or two exceptions, the only militaries able to build and use these weapons. Second, no defensive personal equipment – helmet, body armour or shield – could withstand a *scorpio* bolt or a *ballista* stone. Third, in one sense warfare became impersonal for the first time, as any soldier could be struck down at any time by a projectile without even seeing where it had come from.

A Napoleonic *canon de 8 Gribeauval*, with an effective range of 725m, fired a solid iron ball – roundshot – that weighed 8 *livre* (3.92kg/8.64lb) at an average rate of two and a half rounds per minute; thus a battery of six cannon could loose off a total of fifteen shots in the space of sixty seconds. The guns of *la Grande Armée*, at the time, were the most efficient and mobile artillery in Europe.[19] Notwithstanding, even the torsion-powered artillery of the *Diádochoi*, the rival generals and friends of Alexander the Great who fought for control of the empire after his death in 323 BC, had greater reach and accuracy, discharging heavier shot over longer distances at greater rates of fire.[20] A further very important consideration is that we are dealing with a period much before the introduction of smokeless powder and Alexander's artillery did not suffer from being speedily shrouded in the heavy fog of gun smoke that obscured vision and stung the eyes having fired off a few shots.[21]

Hot Lead and Cold Steel

The lethal effect of small arms manifested a similar decline when compared with the missile weapons of antiquity. The British muzzle-loading .753-calibre smoothbore flintlock Land Pattern Musket (and its later variants), better known as the Brown Bess,[22] had a maximum firing range of 1,200 yards (1,097m) at 60° elevation, the Prussian *Infanteriegewehr Modell 1801*, the *Nothardt-Gewehr*, reached 975m at 40° elevation.[23] However, these maximum firing ranges differ significantly from the effective range of a smoothbore musket; that is to say from the firing range that actually has any effect in combat and at which there is a relevant hit probability. Firing two rounds a minute, although this could vary depending on the skill of each soldier, the smoothbore musket used almost universally by infantry during the Napoleonic Wars was only marginally accurate at 50m, while its killing power dropped off to almost zero beyond 100m (109 yards), hence the need for concentrated infantry formations operating in the open and delivering well-drilled volleys of fire at a single target. In addition, it was common for musket fire to be high and so pass over the heads of the intended target. Soldiers were constantly being admonished by their sergeants to fire low.

There were innumerable variables concerning the Brown Bess, such as temperature, humidity, elevation above sea level, variances in the quality of the gunpowder, failure of the flint to spark, uniformity of the solid lead spherical ball itself, the size of the ball versus the size of the interior of the barrel,[24] etc., etc., not to mention the soldier himself, who in the heat of action could be expected at times to do all sorts of weird things: he could keep on loading and reloading his musket without having the sense to fire it at the enemy, or he could leave his ramrod in the barrel and fire it still therein. As Lieutenant Colonel George Hanger (1751–1824), 4th Baron Coleraine, was to explain to the then Secretary of State for War and the Colonies, Robert Stewart (1769–1822), Viscount Castlereagh, concerning the accuracy of contemporary musketry:

> A soldier's musket, if not exceedingly badly bored, and *very crooked, as many are*, will strike the figure of a man at 80 yards, it may even at 100 yards; but a soldier *must be very unfortunate indeed* who shall be wounded by a *common musket* at 150 yards, PROVIDED HIS ANTAGONIST AIMS AT HIM; and as to firing at a man at 200 yards with a common musket, you may just as well fire at the moon, and have the same hopes of hitting your object. I do maintain, and I will prove, whenever called on, that NO MAN WAS EVER KILLED AT TWO HUNDRED YARDS by a common soldier's musket, BY THE PERSON WHO AIMED AT HIM.[25]

If you do not know who George Hanger is, it matters not. He was considered one of the finest marksmen in all of Europe. Additionally, he certainly knew what he was talking about, having seen serious action during the American War of Independence (1775–83), first serving as a staff captain with a *Jäger* rifle company from Hesse-Kassel, true marksmen to a man,[26] and then in the south with the youthful, red-haired Lieutenant Colonel Banastre Tarleton (1754–1833), one of the finest cavalry leaders of the war.[27]

At the very best the 'common musket' was a diabolically inaccurate weapon. It approximately matched the Roman legionary's *pilum* in killing range but was far less likely to kill. It is said that the infantry of Friedrich II der Große opened fire at 300 yards but this, it was admitted, was simply to frighten the enemy, there being no possibility of an effective fire at that range. At the battle of Mollwitz (10 April 1741) Friedrich's 21,600 soldiers faced 15,800 Austrians. Despite their victory, the Prussians suffered 4,850 casualties to the Austrians'

4,550. Friedrich's instructions to his officers that day explain why the casualties were high and roughly equivalent on both sides:

> [B]attalions must attack when they are within twenty paces, or better still, within ten paces (at the commander's discretion), and give the enemy a strong volley in the face. Immediately thereafter they should plunge the bayonet into the enemy's ribs, at the same time shouting at him to throw away his weapon and surrender.[28]

This was brutal. When the cavalry forming his right wing was beaten, Friedrich was persuaded to quit the field, but the battle, his first since his accession to the Prussian throne, was won for him by the combination of discipline and rapid volleys of his infantry. Even so, at the battle of Chotusitz (17 May 1742), the same infantry fired 260 rounds for every Austrian killed.[29] The figure is consistent with eighteenth-century and early nineteenth-century pitched battles.

A popular soldier's short ditty of the period about the musket shots of the Brown Bess and its French counterpart, the .69 (17.5mm) calibre *Fusil Charleville Modèle 1777*,[30] neatly sums up the inaccuracy common to smoothbore muskets: 'One went high/and one went low,/and where in Hell/did the other one go?' While there was no telling what direction a musket shot would take, such lack of accuracy was the overriding trait of gunpowder weapons during most of their history.[31] All the same, for up to 150 years soldiers shot into each other at close range with smoothbore muskets. Yet research proves pretty conclusively that the number of occasions when formed bodies of infantry actually crossed bayonets in open-country fighting were few and far between, and musketry was usually sufficient for one of the combatant sides either to fall back or even break and run long before the two antagonists came to sufficiently close quarters to use their bayonets.

With this fact borne well in mind then, we should say that the *pilum* was inferior to the musket in one important detail: it was exhausted by a single discharge, so leaving the legionary standing naked of missiles. Even so, this discharge was remarkably effective. Modern experiments have shown that a *pilum*, thrown from a distance of 5m, could pierce 30mm of pine wood or 20mm of plywood.[32] The maximum range of the *pilum* was some 30m, but its effective range was something like half that.[33] Unsurprisingly, throwing a *pilum* at close range improved both accuracy and penetrative power.

In our period of study the *pilum* had already been replaced by the *plumbata*. The advantage, of course, lay in the fact that the legionary could carry five *plumbatae* as opposed to one or two *pila*, thereby subjecting the enemy to a greater barrage of missiles before engaging in hand-to-hand combat. Ammianus

Marcellinus has left a vivid picture of the battle of Argentorate in which the air seemed to be full of volleys of missiles.[34] Moreover, due to their smaller size and lighter weight, *plumbatae* possessed a greater effective range. Still, a *plumbata*, with its limited killing potential, was more of a nuisance weapon. As Vegetius acknowledges, *plumbatae* 'wound the enemy and his horses before they can get not merely to close quarters, but even within the range of javelins'.[35] A *pilum* penetrated shields and bodies with little difficulty. Furthermore, a *pilum* could be used in hand-to-hand combat.[36]

The Weapon of David

We know that David killed Goliath with a sling. Yet the sling is an ancient long-range weapon known even to Neolithic peoples around the Mediterranean basin where examples of slingshot embedded in human skulls have been discovered, though it is possible that it was invented in the Upper Palaeolithic at a time when new technologies such as the spear-thrower and the bow and arrow were emerging as weapons of the hunt. The earliest known surviving slings from the biblical world were discovered in the tomb of Tutankhamen, who died around 1325 BC. A pair of finely plaited slings was found with other royal weapons.

Since the time of David, if not before, the sling had been popular with highland herdsmen to protect their charges from carnivorous predators since ammunition was readily to hand in hill country (ideally round stones or pebbles), and thence it came to be used in battle. The sling had always been the weapon of choice of the herder, who relied on its range and accuracy to keep predators at bay. David himself, as the youngest son of Jesse the Bethlehemite, had tended his father's sheep.[37] However, life as a herder was hard and the living meagre, so it was not unusual for hardy herders to come down from their hills to offer their services as mercenaries: their proficiency in long-range skirmishing made them a valuable component of state armies.

Slingers normally served as a complement to archers, the sling not only out-ranging the bow but a slinger was also capable of carrying a larger supply of ammunition than an archer. Slingshots were not only sun-dried clay balls, ground-stone balls or pebbles, but in later periods also of lead, acorn or almond-shaped, and usually weighing some 20g to 30g, but occasionally up to 55g. Like the bow, proficiency with the sling could only be achieved by constant practice. The Greek military writer Onasandros makes it clear that it was essential for slingers to have enough elbowroom to use their weapons effectively, as they needed 'to execute the whirling of their slings'.[38] This whirling action obviously built up speed before one end of the sling was released, projecting the slingshot, and modern experiments with slings have demonstrated that they can have an effective range of 200m or thereabouts, whereas the Roman standard for a proficient military slinger was the ability to strike targets with lead shot at 100m.[39] However, unlike the arrow a slingshot could not be seen in flight and so could not be avoided. Indeed, in the right hands, the sling was a most deadly weapon. A fast-moving slingshot did not need to penetrate body armour or a helmet to be horrifically effective.[40]

According to Aulus Cornelius Celsus, a Roman encyclopaedist and possibly a practising physician, a blow from a slingshot on a helmet could be enough to give the wearer concussion, if not a fatal internal injury,[41] which brings us back to the biblical battle between David and Goliath. The Philistine champion Goliath of Gath was an enormous, well-equipped and seasoned warrior. David convinced Saul to let him challenge Goliath on behalf of the Israelites. Equipped with just a sling, five suitable smooth stones snatched from a nearby arid streambed, a sword and his staff, David takes out the bronze-clad Goliath with one well-aimed shot to the forehead.[42] The light and nimble fighter defeats the heavy and slow one. As Vegetius himself points out, slingshots 'inflict a wound that is still lethal, and the enemy dies from the blow of the stone without loss of blood'.[43] The slinger could therefore be far more dangerous to armoured targets than an archer.

The sling, as deadly as it was simple, was made of inelastic material such as woven reeds, rush, flax, hemp or wool (flax and hemp resisted rotting, but wool was softer and free of splinters). Braiding the material resisted stretching and so produced an accurate sling. The sling itself comprised a small cradle to house the slingshot (usually just a widening or strengthening of the material in the centre of the loop), and two braided cords, one of which was secured to the throwing hand (the retention cord) and the other held, simultaneously, between the thumb and forefinger of the same hand (the release cord). The slingshot was seated in the cradle. It was then cast, after a single whirl either horizontally (around the head) or vertically (parallel to the ground), the slingshot being fired at the moment that the second cord was released, its range being related to the angle of discharge, the length of the whirling cords and the amount of kinetic energy imparted by the slinger. The sling was rather easy to make, but not easy to use and few of us truly appreciate David's prowess in the art of throwing a slingshot. Forget the difference in size between the two opponents: it is the weapons that matter, and David was the one with the clear advantage.

Paying the Butcher's Bill

The principal offensive weapon of the Assyrian infantry was the bow (*qaštu*) used by men in groups, or individually when covered by a companion who defended the archer with a body shield. The iron-tipped reed arrows fired by the powerful composite recurve bow of the Assyrian could let fly, from 175m, a hail of effective missiles that would whisper down on the enemy.[44] Since an Assyrian quiver could contain up to fifty arrows, the firepower before or during a charge, or from massed standing archers, was formidable. Furthermore, the ancient bow had a rate of fire four to five times that of the smoothbore musket of the early eighteenth century. The Brown Bess carried by Wellington's infantrymen at Waterloo was not markedly different from that used by their grandfathers under Marlborough at Blenheim, and its various patterns were still to be found on the battlefields of the Crimea. Indeed, no firearm approached the rate of fire of the bow until the introduction of the M-1862 Dreyse needle-gun,[45] a Prussian bolt-action, breech-loading rifle with a rate of fire of six rounds per minute.[46]

Hardly surprising, then, that the lethality of weapons in the period from the fall of Rome to the Franco-Prussian War of 1870 actually declined. This helps to explain to a large degree the very high numbers of battle casualties suffered by ancient armies compared with those suffered by later armies. In the Peninsular War (1808–14), the British army lost 8,889 to enemy fire, a figure that pales in significance when compared to the 24,930 men lost to camp disease, a worse scourge to soldiers than all the bullets, shot and shell the enemy could hurl. However, in the midst of a carnival of death, this does not match up to manpower losses incurred by the Roman defeats at Trasimene and Cannae during the Hannibalic War (218–202 BC), which cost Rome some 15,000 and 50,000 men respectively,[47] each in a single one-day battle. Even if such innovations as the needle-gun helped to make infantry more lethal on the battlefield, so making massed formation and manoeuvre prohibitively difficult, such casualty levels were not to be reached until the First World War hugely ramped up the butcher's bill. This was when the Rubicon was crossed and the savage, indiscriminate efficiency of modern weaponry heralded a bloodletting that hideously reflected the modern industrial world in miniature.

At the end of the first four months of this war, the armies in Europe had experienced what may have been the greatest military bloodletting in history. Between August and December 1914, 116,000 German and 189,000 Austro-Hungarian soldiers were killed, but this fell short of the 16,200 soldiers of the British Expeditionary Force and 30,000 Belgians killed alongside 300,000 French soldiers in the same four-month span. It is hard for most to come to terms with the horrors of the Western Front, but consider, for instance, the British losing 57,470 men, of which 19,420 were fatal, in a single summer's morning on the Somme when the Allies made a wrenchingly futile attempt to break the ordeal of static frigid trench warfare two years later. Admittedly, with its extraordinarily difficult tactical problems the maelstrom of fire and filth that blood-and-mud caked soldiers were cast into, 'the "animal horror" of trench warfare',[48] was an incomparable form of fighting: even the struggle for Normandy between 6 June and 31 August 1944 cost the British only 83,825 men, of which 16,138 were fatal, over the entire period.[49] Battles between ancient armies may not have lasted as long as modern battles,[50] but their casualty rates were horrendous in both absolute and relative (as a percentage of force deployed) terms. Also it is wise to remember two things. First, that all the slaughter was accomplished at very close range, predominantly in hand-to-hand combat – man against man – the stronger being sure of his victory. Second, war at that time was all about metal and mettle.

Still, we should not get hung up on the figures. Think instead of war as a human institution that reached a very high level in its evolution long before the introduction of technologically advanced weaponry. True, the crucial aspect of contemporary technological warfare is the essential invisibility of one side to another. Post-1900 warfare, certainly since the rapid development of long-range rifles and armament in the latter part of the nineteenth century, and of course even more so with aerial bombardment and now the use in the battlespace of telecommunications, sensors and armed drones, is death at a distance, to kill and be killed by people you cannot see and do not know. Yet, when we view war from a long historical perspective, *le longue durée*, there is little that humankind has added to it that was not already evident by the fourth century.

The Universal Soldier

Of course there is no such being as the universal soldier. The soldier is shaped far more by the mores of the society that bears him than by the experience of soldiering itself. In a brutal and unenlightened age, the soldier will be brutal and unenlightened; in a superstitious culture, he will be equally superstitious. All the same, as alluded to previously, the soldiering life is one of those professions that sets a man rather emphatically apart from the attitudes of the mass of his contemporaries on certain narrow aspects of life; and for all that he is a creature of his time, he has more in common with soldiers of other epochs and nations than his own civilian brothers in his reactions to certain situations. Equally, most are soldiers for a number of tangled motives and there is no single, simple answer to the question 'What makes a soldier?' This becomes plainly evident when we consider that the term 'soldier' encompasses a whole host of men. There have always been soldiers, and the motives why men become soldiers are many and mixed: the desire to escape personal stagnation, plain boredom, the simple hunger for riches or craving for adventure. Then there were also those few with deeply ingrained principles.

Wellington may have harshly described his common soldiers as 'the scum of the earth',[51] but his Waterloo counterpart Napoléon called them 'the soul of the army'.[52] Hardly surprising when you consider that the conquering emperor, with a genius for bold gestures, waged war with the legs of his line infantrymen or *fantassins*. Even today, despite the deadly marvels of the high-tech battlefield, there still exists that most traditional soldier life form, that mire-hampered, hot and cold suffering hoofing-hiking-humping-hunting infantryman of universal history, the mainstay of battle, who withstands the brunt of the enemy's attack and strives to advance to take possession of his ground. It is this graft, boiler-room stuff that gives generals the platform to prevail. 'Soldiers generally win battles; generals get credit for them.'[53]

Hard truth: grunt, ground-pounder, squaddie, pongo, stubble-hopper, clodhopper, footslogger, call him what you will, the infantryman has been around since armies have been around, habitually up to his knees in soupy mud and getting shot at. Consider that although technology and tactics may change, basic human nature does not. Look at the average, run-of-the-mill soldier of today compared with the average, run-of-the-mill infantry soldier of, say, the Napoleonic Wars. Sure, today's infantry soldiers are better trained, better fed and much better equipped – and now include infantrywomen in their ranks – but they are still just mud-caked and dirt-grimed individuals plodding through a pre-modern quagmire harbouring the same hopes, emotions and vulnerabilities, and still regarding their combat leaders with a complex mixture of distrust, fear, loathing and grudging respect.[54]

Anyone who knows something about warfare at first hand understands the private's dislike of an ornamental and pompous officer, the arrogance of authority as authority, the relief at finding a decent officer who was probably a manual worker in Civvie Street but in combat a solid fellow you could count on. Take, for instance, Plutarch on Caius Marius, who had 'won the affection of the soldiers by showing he could live as hard as they did and endure as much'. The biographer continues:

And what a Roman soldier likes most to see is his general eating his rations of common bread with the rest, or sleeping on a simple bed of straw (στιβάς), or joining in the work of digging a trench or raising a palisade. The commanders whom I admire are not so much those who distribute honours and riches as those who take a share in their hardships and their dangers; they have more affection for those who are willing to join in their work than those who indulge them in going easy.[55]

Marius' worth and authority had been tested in the furnace of war. From his continuous experience he knew soldiers and he knew how to get the best out of them. This is a sentiment that is timeless, for in the lyrical words of the seventh-century BC soldier poet Archilochos: 'I don't care for a general who is tall and takes long strides, proud of his/curls and partly shaven. No, for me let him be short and bandy-legged to/look at round the shins, but stand firm on his feet, and full of heart.'[56]

Archilochos looked for virtues that could cover the fighting soldier, the filthy and ragged campaigner 'suffering from lice',[57] regardless of his rank. As opposed to his decorative appearance (swaggering gait and hairstyle), the combat leader should have traits that are actually useful on the battlefield (standing firm).[58] Anyhow, the final verdict of the muse of history, Kleiō: 'They were only wretched footsloggers.'[59]

Combat is the realm of our universal soldiers, the dispassionate art of taking and holding the battlefield through victory over opposing forces by force of arms. They therefore bear the particular burden of executing combat with the distinct possibility of staring into the eyes of the foe. It is common for combatants at the start of a life-or-death struggle to feel the urge to bolt: self-preservation, nerves, stress or second thoughts. After all, fear affects unconditionally: mind, body and spirit. It becomes a soldier's shadow. Realizing this, it has become one of the commander's greatest challenges to set his soldiers' minds at rest prior to a major battle. If fear, panic and irresolution are removed, the soldiers can be used to their full potential and their fearlessness increase the despair of their opponents.

How can this be done? Traditionally, the commander may explain logically why they should win in a speech to his men. The pre-battle address by a commander to his men is certainly a common theme in our ancient sources. More importantly, their emotions are soothed with religious ceremonies aimed at attracting all the available supernatural forces to one's assistance. This might include sacrificing and the interpretation of omens, prayer, calling upon the gods for protection and promises in the event of victory, recognition of signs of the gods' favour and so forth. And then there are battlefield miracles.

Chapter Fifteen

Gothic Endings

*'Alaric, the Gothic King,/Whose knee I sat on as a child,/Yesterday took Rome.
Took me./ His men stole, raped, set fires, no worse,/My Goth nurse says, than
Romans, when/They laid waste her kin.'*

Galla Placidia[1]

The Goths have loomed large right through our narrative, be it as individual captains or as the nameless masses that made up the *foederati* faithfully serving the empire. It is fitting, therefore, that we end our story with their story. While our Graeco-Roman sources imagined the Goths as scarcely individuated hordes whose destiny was to be savagely victorious at Adrianopolis or thrown to the slaughter at the Frigidus, it must be remembered they did have souls and personalities.

Origins

The Goths were Germanic peoples of Scandinavian origin according to the Romano-Gothic historian Jordanes,[2] writing from his home in Constantinopolis. True or not, and virtually everyone would now discard the idea of a prior origin in Scandinavia,[3] by the end of the second century the Goths possessed large tracts of the Eurasian steppe north of the Euxine (Black Sea), what Graeco-Roman authors habitually called 'Scythia'. Like the other communities in this region making the most effective use of their surroundings, the Goths were semi-sedentary, their subsistence strategies including agriculture, pastoralism, hunting and fishing, as well as loafing, quarrelling and refusing to worry about the menace of Hunnic aggression. Long contact with the nomadic peoples of the western steppes stimulated the development of horse-riding among the Goths and their associates. Deep in the territory once belonging to the Sarmatian Roxolani, it was from these people that the Goths learned the use of shock – as opposed to skirmishing – cavalry. What is certain is that by the middle of the third century these Goths were the most formidable military power beyond the lower Danuvius frontier.

The first certain indication of the presence of a rising military power north of the Danuvius came in 238, when an army of Goths broke across the river

Bronze bust (Thessaloniki, Archaeological Museum, inv. 4303) of Severus Alexander (r. 222–235), last of the Severan dynasty. (© *Nic Fields*)

White marble head (Rome, Musei Capitolini, inv. MC0757) from a colossal seated enthroned statue of Constantinus dating to 313/324, which originally occupied the west apse of the Basilica Nova on the Via Sacra, near the Forum Romanum. Only the head, which measures 260cm and weighs some 8 tonnes, hands and feet (each foot is over 2m long), remain of a colossus that once stood some 12m high. (© *Nic Fields*)

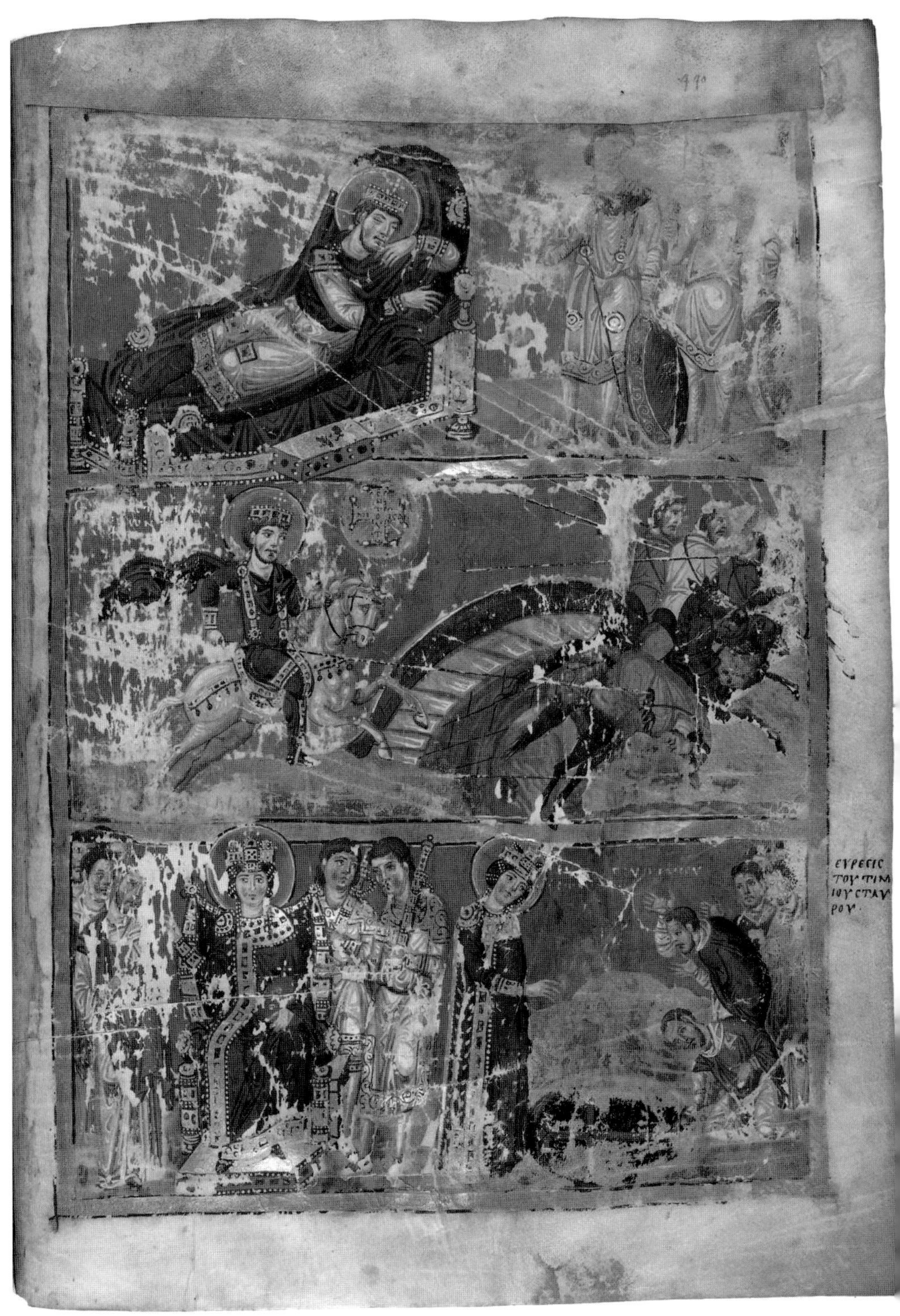

Miniature (Paris, Bibliothèque national de France, Codex Græcus 510, folio 440 recto) from the late ninth-century manuscript of the *Homilies* of the fourth-century church father and theologian Gregory Nazianzen. This tripartite painting illustrates a potpourri of the Pons Mulvius miracle. (*BnF Gallica Digital Library/Wikimedia Commons/Public Domain*)

Detail of miniature from the *Paris Gregory* (Paris, Bibliothèque nationale de France, Codex Græcus 510, folio 239 recto), a late ninth-century illuminated manuscript of the *Homilies* of Gregory Nazianzen. Gregory, depicted as the bishop of Constantinopolis (r. 380–381), takes his leave of Theodosius I (r. 379–395). The emperor stands beside his bejewelled throne enclosed in a ciborium, attended by two palace guards. (*BnF Gallica Digital Library/Wikimedia Commons/CC-BY-SA-4.0*)

Full-length portrait marble statue (Geyre, Afrodisyas Müzesi) of the western emperor Flavius Valentinianus Iunior Augustus (r. 375–392), son of the hardy Pannonian general Valentinianus I (r. 364–375) and his second wife Iustina, a staunch Arian (Ambr. *Obit. Val.* 28, Philostorg. 10.7). (*Brastite/Wikimedia Commons/ Public Domain*)

Frieze slab decorating the pronaos, temple of Hadrianus (also dedicated to Artemis Ephesia and the *dēmos* of Ephesos), street of the Curetes, Ephesos. The relief depicts Theodosius I, his father (also Theodosius), his first wife Aelia Flavia Flaccilla Augusta and their eldest son Arcadius in the company of a dozen pagan deities. (© *Nic Fields*)

Icon (New York, Metropolitan Museum of Art, inv. MET, 1975.1.30) of Saint Ambrose by Giovanni di Paolo di Grazia (1403–82), egg tempera on wood, gold ground. (*Metropolitan Museum of Art/Wikimedia Commons/CC0 1.0*)

Chalcedony cameo (Firenze, Museo archeologico nazionale) full-length portrait of Flavius Eugenius (left) alongside a soldierly-looking figure, more than likely a representation of the *magister militum* Arbogastes. (*Sailko/ Wikimedia Commons/CC-BY-SA-3.0*)

One of the best known late antique ivories (c.395), generally known as the Stilicho Diptych (Monza, Museo e tesoro del duomo di Monza). On the left leaf is Serena, wife of Stilicho, niece and (according to Claudianus, who wrote extensively of the character and career of his patron) adopted daughter of Theodosius I. With her is their son, Eucherius. In her right hand she holds up a rose. On the right is Stilicho depicted in a military guise. His shield carries two imperial busts, believed to represent Arcadius and Honorius when both emperors were consuls (396, 402, or 407). (*Carlodell/Wikimedia Commons/CC-BY-SA-4.0*)

Gold medallion (Paris, Bibliothèque nationale de France, Département des Monnaies) depicting (definitely) Aelia Galla Placidia (392–450), struck in Ravenna in 425 and bearing the legend D(*omina*) N(*oster*) GALLA PLA-CIDIA P(*ia*) F(*elix*) AVG(*usta*). She was the daughter, sister, wife and mother of emperors. (*Clio20/Wikimedia Commons/CC-BY-SA-3.0*)

[Left] Low-cut relief (Linz, Schlossmuseum) depicting a legionary of the late third century. He appears to be wearing an Intercisa-type helmet. Bipartite in construction, the two bowl halves were united by a longitudinal ridge running from front to back. Openings for the ears were formed by cut-outs both in the bowl and the cheek guards. Traces of silver on some examples imply that their iron bowls may originally have been covered with a thin silver sheathing. [Right] Modern re-enactor equipped as a legionary at the end of the third century. He wears *lorica hamata* and carries the *spatha*, the long double-edged sword that was the preferred sidearm of the later Roman soldier. (*Left: Wolfgang Sauber/Wikimedia Commons/ CC-BY-SA-3.0; right: Matthias Kabel/Wikimedia Commons/CC-BY-SA-3.0*)

Part of the long narrative frieze panel on the southern façade above the left lateral archway of the Arch of Constantine, depicting the siege of the strongly fortified Verona. The triumphal arch spans the Via Triumphalis in Rome. (*FrDr/Wikimedia Commons/CC-BY-SA-4.0*)

Roman soldiers equipped with iron mail shirts with coifs, and carrying spears and large round shields as depicted in the miniature 'Ascanius and Trojan council' from the late antique *Vergilius Vaticanus* (Vatican, Biblioteca Apostolica, MS Cod. Vat. lat. 3225, folio 73 verso). (*Wikimedia Commons/Public Domain*)

A portion of bronze *lorica squamata* from Newstead-*Trimontium* (Edinburgh, National Museum of Scotland, inv. X.FRA 118.1). Each scale has four side-link holes and one lacing hole at the top. These overlapping scales would have been sewn to a flexible cloth or leather backing. This provided a balance of flexibility and protection. (© *Esther Carré*)

close to its mouth and pillaged the province of Moesia Inferior. They extracted payment from the Roman government before they withdrew and returned prisoners, though it is possible that they had been receiving monetary subsidies before this. Soon afterwards, Goths appear in the Roman armies led against the Sāsānian Persians by Gordianus III,[4] perhaps under the terms of a formal treaty struck in 238. The payment of subsidies was stopped in the afterglow of Roman successes on the Danuvius frontier in the following decade, which was to simply provoke a massive invasion by the Goths and others.

On this occasion the barbarian leader was the Gothic chieftain Kniva, one of the most astute and able of Germanic war leaders, entering Thracia and Greece following a dramatic victory over Traianus Decius in early June 251 on marshy ground some 15km north-west of Abritus (Razgrad, Bulgaria),[5] one of the largest urban centres in Moesia Inferior. This was a terrain on which Kniva's tactical expertise could have full play, for his confederation of Goths and Scythians won a comprehensive victory. The Roman emperor lost his life, along with his older son and heir: 'On foreign soil, among disordered troops, he drowned in the waters of a swamp, so that his corpse could not be found. His son, in fact, was killed in the war. He lived fifty years.'[6]

The diehard Christian Lactantius, as we would expect, is more damning in his reportage of this Roman battlefield disaster:

He (Traianus Decius) was suddenly surrounded by the barbarians, and slain, together with the greater part of his army; nor could he be honoured with the rites of sépulture, but, stripped and naked, he lay to be devoured by wild beasts and birds, a fit end for the enemy of God.[7]

The shattered remains of his army were extricated with difficulty and only after payments had been made to the victors. Thereafter the Goths launched seaborne raids along the coast of the Euxine, penetrated the Aegean Sea, even reaching Cyprus (268–269), and on land the Heruli, a Germanic people associated with the Goths, brought fire and sword to Greece as far south as Athens (267). The invaders were finally evicted by Claudius II Gothicus and his successor, Aurelianus, though the latter emperor did allow them to settle north of the Danuvius in what had previously been the Roman province of Dacia (271).

Across the Danuvius

The land south of the Danuvius was not there for the taking, but required one of two options: confrontation or negotiation with the Romans. Around the year 370, their kingdoms suddenly overrun by the hard-riding Huns,[8] the Goths chose the second option by seeking the right to settle within the Roman Empire by promising to serve in its armies.

Valens, preoccupied with Sāsānian Persia over the kingdom of Armenia,[9] agreed but strove to ensure that the Goths should disarm before they were admitted as settlers in Thracia.[10] At this juncture the Goths were a whole people on the move, refugees in truth, rather than an organized army of invasion. As for their numbers, the figure of 200,000 given by Eunapios is much exaggerated;[11] Ammianus Marcellinus says expressly that all efforts to count the Goths failed and merely adapts a quotation from Virgil, likening the refugees to the grains of sand that were swept over the Libyan Desert by Zephyros, the West Wind.[12]

The operation, however, was bungled. Food ran short. The local imperial officials in the Danuvius region shamelessly exploited the starving Goths, selling them even rancid dog meat at the rate of one man per dog.[13] Foreign in tongue, alien in outlook and comparatively few in number, the Goths were inevitably perceived, and perceived themselves, as outsiders. As a result, and to paraphrase Benjamin Franklin, they had to hang together lest they be hanged separately.[14] After all, for the Goths freedom was not some lofty ideal to bandy about in civil circles, it was imperative for their survival. So they rose in revolt and Valens was obliged to take command of the situation himself. As already referred to, Valens, along with two-thirds of the eastern *comitatus* lay dead on the field of Adrianopolis (9 August 378). Despite the loss of so much irreplaceable combat value, the Goths, lacking both the skill and resources to storm fortifications, failed to overrun the empire. Theodosius, Valens' successor, recruited Goths to resist the newcomers. Unable to completely subdue the Goths a treaty was made with them in 382, according to which they were allowed to settle south of the lower Danuvius as a confederate people under their own chieftains, *foederati*, in return for military service *with* the Roman army.

Two Sides of the Same Coin

Long before the arrival of the Huns, according to Jordanes, the Goths were already divided into two peoples: the Ostrogoths and the Visigoths.[15] During our period of study, 'Ostrogoths' were still well to the north of the Danuvius and would not appear south of it in the Balkans until the second half of the fifth century. It is incorrect of us, therefore, to call those Goths who crossed the Danuvius the 'Visigoths', and they are not known as such until Cassiodorus used the term when referring to their crushing defeat by Clovis at Vouillé in 507. According to Herwig Wolfram, Cassiodorus created this east-west appreciation of the Goths.[16] After all, even when the context was clear, the Romans simply called both nations Goths or barbarians, *Gothi* or *barbari*. At the time the Huns menaced the Goths, however, there were actually six or more Gothic tribes – the so-called 'Visigoths', for instance, were divided into two main militarily efficient supra-tribal groupings, the *Teruingi* and the *Greuthungi* – and it was this event that created the division of the Goths into two peoples. The contemporary historian Ammianus Marcellus, among others, makes it clear that only certain elements of both the *Teruingi* and the *Greuthungi* crossed into Roman territory, leaving others still settled north of the Danuvius.[17]

It is now generally accepted that the self-identification of the people who are now known as the Visigoths (and would have thought of themselves as just being Goths) was the product of the chaotic years that followed the battle of Adrianopolis. So, those Goths – along with other individuals and groups from a variety of cultural, genetic and linguistic backgrounds – who entered the Roman Empire and eventually established a kingdom in southern Gaul became the Visigoths,[18] while those who remained behind became subjects of the Huns and were designated the Ostrogoths.[19] The latter would eventually establish a kingdom in Italy.

Whatever we choose to call them, there is a risk, when looking at these peoples from the perspective of the empire (or of sources written within the empire), of misinterpreting their ambitions and misunderstanding the dynamics at play. In particular, the entire rationale for their activities can be reduced to violent rivalry with Rome; however, their interactions with the empire were driven not simply by hostile or covetous intentions towards Roman territory but also by internal concerns. With no central organization or administration, Germanic societies set considerable store by martial ability and raiding the empire could reflect efforts by Germanic leaders to establish themselves as warlords. Indeed, leadership of the tribes, clans and war bands was very personal.

Enter Alaric and Company

With the passing away of Theodosius and the succeeding division of the empire – though to consider this division as absolute from this date is in fact an oversimplification – the Goths had taken the opportunity to relinquish their treaty with the empire. Six years later Alaric, who exercised the leadership of what, effectively, was a mercenary army except that they had their families in tow and Alaric was not really a mercenary for hire as such,[20] decided to move southwards, crossing Ad Pirum into Italy on 18 November 401 just before the pass was blocked by snow.[21] Claudianus would have us believe that it was Alaric's wife and her yearning for Roman bijoux that urged the Gothic warlord southward.[22] Poetic licence or not, Claudianus' benefactor and Alaric's one-time comrade-in-arms, Stilicho, prosecuted two defeats, the first at Pollentia

(Pollenzo, Italy) on Easter Day 402,[23] and the second near Verona sometime in the following June.[24] Alaric, who as Edward Gibbon said only 'escaped by the swiftness of his horse',[25] was forced to withdraw from Italy in considerable disarray, and many of his men deserted and joined Stilicho, including senior figures (Sarus, Ulfilas) along with their personal retinues.[26]

In late 405 or early 406 a new crisis struck. The Goth Radagaisus, a former associate of Alaric, launched a major attack on Italy, having crossed the Danuvius with an army which Zosimos claims numbered as many as 400,000.[27] Using Huns under the command of Uldin,[28] and Alani and Goths under Sarus,[29] the struggle to contain the invaders took up Stilicho's attention for a good part of a year. Matters improved when Radagaisus divided his army into three – probably to ease supply problems – and attempted to besiege Florentia (Florence, Italy) with his main force. He was driven back to Faesulae (Fiesole, Italy) by Stilicho where the Hun horsemen prevented his foraging.[30] Under pressure of famine, Radagaisus attempted to make a break, the day ending a satisfyingly thorough victory for the *generalissimo* before the gates of Faesulae on 8 August 406. Radagaisus was captured and executed,[31] while large numbers of his followers were enrolled in the western army as *foederati*, and those of lower status, according to Orosius, sold off in droves like cattle for an *aureus* a head. It was a great triumph and Stilicho made much of it.[32]

In the following year Alaric, still in the north-eastern Balkans where he was attempting to secure a permanent territory, was appointed *magister militum* by Honorius as part of a western effort to annex the peninsula. The planned campaign was mothballed, and relations between Alaric and Honorius soured, and Alaric invaded Italy again to secure payment for his contracted services. The finale of all these comings and goings was to lead to Alaric's three-day Roman holiday.

Honorius was now to make what many modern commentators believe was a monumental miscalculation: Stilicho was to fall to a well-orchestrated palace revolution and he himself was beheaded (22 August 408).[33] Honorius' principal commander had been condemned for 'his crimes against the state', whereby he quietly surrendered and 'submitted his neck to the sword'.[34] Heracleianus, Stilicho's nemesis, was rewarded with the office of *comes Africae*. Cruel, avaricious and drunken, two years later he was to hold Africa for Honorius during Priscus Attalus' brief reign in Rome (more of which anon),[35] and held back Rome's grain supply in an attempt to starve out Alaric's Goths.[36]

There is the human capacity for cruelty, a lust even, and Honorius was to terminate his marriage to Stilicho's daughter Thermantia, packing her off to her mother in Rome. On top of that, Honorius had Stilicho's son Eucherius, who had sought refuge in Rome,[37] murdered.[38] A case can be made that if

Honorius died childless – he may well have been sterile or impotent[39] – there was no successor to the western throne, and Eucherius might easily have been selected. His mother was Serena, niece of Theodosius, and Stilicho had been contemplating a marriage for his son with Galla Placidia, daughter of the same Theodosius.[40] Eucherius would have been the obvious successor to Honorius; by 408 he must have been around 21 years of age and recently had been elevated to the rank of *tribunus et notarius*.[41]

Always a shrewd manager, this was probably Stilicho's plan B in the case of Honorius' death or failure to produce children. It also had the added benefit of eliminating any potential rival to the power of Stilicho's family who might be created through the marriage of any other party to Galla Placidia.[42] After all, his marriage ties with the Theodosian dynasty gave him a far more powerful position than Arbogastes before him had enjoyed. Furthermore, Stilicho had the examples of the fate Valentinianus II before Honorius (and the one attempting to be his keeper) to learn from. Stilicho certainly lasted much longer in this role than Arbogastes, though in the end he was to suffer a cataclysmic fall on the orders of the same young emperor he had striven to manage.

Being a *generalissimo* on the front lines of power and policy was no easy task. Stilicho of course understood that the preservation of his privileged position was not only subject to the whims of his patron, it was also contingent on his mastery of the complexities of the *arcana imperii* and on his practical wisdom, or prudence in the Aristotelian sense. His political (and physical) survival also hinged on a grubbier set of skills: how to navigate the treacherous shoals of court politics, and skirt the snake pits of deadly plotting and backstabbing. Still, even the most brilliant of men forget to be mindful of the power of Fortuna, and of the nigh impossibility of accurately predicting certain developments.

By this act, Honorius had rid himself of a *generalissimo* he suspected, but was left without any strong allies to take his place. The cloistered incompetent court at Ravenna immediately descended into an orgy of palace intrigue, just when the death of Stilicho inspired Alaric to resume raising havoc in Italy. In fact, the execution of Stilicho was followed by a flood tide of disasters. One dreadful and immediate result of this act was a xenophobic backlash in which the wives and children of *foederati* were liquidated throughout Italy. The stupidity of this despicable act is supposed to have swollen the ranks of Alaric's followers, with the outraged *foederati* who had been in the dead *generalissimo's* entourage flocking to join him, eager to make war on Rome. Indeed, it is said by Zosimos that slightly more than 30,000 Germanic *foederati* went over *en masse* to Alaric.[43] These Germanic allies clearly saw their commitment as having been to Stilicho, the commander in the field, rather than to the emperor in Ravenna, who now had blood on his hands. In a sense these men were merely acting in the capacity of hired mercenaries. Besides, the mercenary army of Alaric that had taken shape after the death of Theodosius was made up of elements of not just the *Teruingi* and *Greuthungi*, but also from several other ethnic groups from both north and south of the Danuvius. Furthermore, this confederacy would subsequently pick up and drop off components of itself in the course of its movements through Illyricum, Italy and Gaul between the years 405 and 415. Certainly the question remains: were Alaric's Goths a mercenary army or a nation on the move seeking a home?[44]

Roma Aeterna

Within two years Alaric would sack Rome with them. Meanwhile, Honorius and his advisors who had overthrown Stilicho would skulk in Ravenna marooned in the marshes at the ends of the earth.[45] Before that tragedy unfolded, however, Alaric made a second invasion of Italy in 408: he seems to have come down the Via Aemilia to Ariminum (save the strange detour to Cremona) and then down the Via Flaminia to Rome, although his rebuff at Narnia[46] probably forced him to approach Rome along the Via Salaria. Though outside the gates of Rome,[47] in truth the invasion was to end in failure like the first, but this time Alaric constrained the Senate in Rome to pay him a hefty endowment. Alaric's demand for 4,000 pounds of gold was not much beyond the average annual income a Roman senator earned from his leases alone.[48] Nonetheless, although the senators were lavish with themselves, there was much hand-wringing among them, one even grousing 'This is not peace; it is a pact of slavery.'[49]

Payments of tribute by the Romans could be presented as acts of imperial magnanimity, but requests that the Romans should pay tribute often foundered precisely because paying tribute made the empire look subservient or even weak. That was not the Roman way; instead, it was the barbarians who should beg for terms. Still, Stilicho persuaded the reluctant and outraged Senate to pay Alaric off anyway.[50] It was this act of appeasement that was the turning-point in Stilicho's career, weakening Honorius' trust in his *generalissimo*, while for his detractors it was the final proof of his treason. He was accused of using Rome's wealth to incite barbarians against the empire.[51] Being found a traitor is never attractive.

At the time of Stilicho's execution, Alaric still had not received the payment agreed to by the Senate, and it was clear that the agreement would not be honoured. Wasting no time on anger, Alaric blockaded Rome once more (late 409) to force Honorius, safe behind the walls and surrounding marshes of Ravenna, to give his followers land and annual payments of gold and grain.[52] When negotiations broke down and Honorius refused his demands because of the promise of aid from Gaul,[53] and from the Huns who currently resided in Thracia,[54] Alaric set up a transient emperor, Priscus Attalus, the current *praefectus urbis Romae* (the official intermediary between Senate and emperor).[55] Upon his elevation by Alaric, Attalus promptly made him *magister utriusque militiae*.[56] As the second blockade tightened its grip around Rome, Serena was falsely accused by the Senate of conspiring with the Goths. She was throttled to death when Galla Placidia gave her consent.[57] Perhaps the real reason was out of fear that Serena, her former guardian, would avenge her husband's and son's murders.

Alaric may not have been classically educated, but he was anything but politically naïve. In the face of continued intransigence Alaric marched on Rome for a third time and broke in at Porta Salaria under the cover of darkness (24 August 410).[58] The Goths plundered the city for three days, but did comparatively little collateral damage.[59] Alaric once more withdrew, this time heading south. He planned to cross to Africa, but while endeavouring to do this he, 'suddenly overtaken by an early death, departed from human affairs'.[60]

Today, of course, Alaric and his peripatetic Goths are largely remembered for capturing the eternal metropolis, spending three days looting, pillaging and plundering, but this was not apocalyptic urbicide, a fifth-century Stalingrad or Mariupol pounded into rubble and then ripped apart by street-to-street fighting. As opposed to turning Rome into a smouldering cauldron, the physical damage and the long-term effects of the Gothic sack of Rome were trifling and certainly not as destructive as the Vandal sack forty-five years later. On the other hand, the psychological effects of the blow were immense: it was the first time the metropolis had fallen to an invader since the Gaulish sack some eight centuries earlier. This signal failure amounted to persuasive proof that the Christian God was not up to the task of protecting the new Christian empire. 'By the standards of the day,' writes Harold A. Drake, 'Alaric's victory amounted to a complete and utter failure of the Christian God to do his job.'[61] Even though the *Urbs Romana* had long since ceased to be the capital of the empire, it remained its symbolic heart,[62] and this was a disaster that was almost incomprehensible to most citizens of the empire. After all, the great, beautiful and historic metropolis was believed to be inviolate.

According to the Christian Palladius Helenopolitanus, Alaric's capture of Rome was 'long ago foretold in prophecy',[63] by which he probably meant the Sibylline oracle that Rome would become a ruin (Ῥώμη ῥύμη),[64] already reported by Lactantius.[65] Still, Jerome, who was in his monastic cell in Bethlehem at the time, half a world away, took it as hard as anyone else. Alaric's earlier activities had already filled him with fatalistic gloom and forebodings, and now, three years after the sack of the city, he recalls the arrival of the news: 'It is the end of the world! Words fail me; sobs prevent me from speaking. That city which had taken the world was itself taken!'[66]

Equally shocked, the Romano-Briton theologian (and heretic: he admitted neither Original sin nor Original fall) Pelagius (†420), who was actually in Rome at the time, used language that echoed the biblical vision of Armageddon to convey the horror of the moment: 'It happened only recently, and you heard it yourself. Rome, the mistress of the world, shivered, crushed with fear, at the sound of the blaring trumpets and the howling of the Goths.'[67]

Others made the argument that it was human sin that caused the scourge of the barbarians, and that the wise man should put his trust in heaven and not value earthly goods, as in an anonymous contemporary poem:

This man groans for his lost silver and gold,
another is racked by the thought of his stolen goods
and of his jewellery now divided amongst Gothic brides.
This man mourns for his stolen flock, burnt houses, and drunk wine,
and for his wretched children and ill-omened servants.
But the wise man, the servant of Christ, loses none of these things,
which he despises; he has already placed his treasure in Heaven.[68]

To be sure, the end of the world as they knew it seemed to be at hand.

The callow Honorius was momentarily aghast. Having never set foot on the battlefield, he led an oddly domestic lifestyle in the remote but easily defensible marsh-locked Ravenna. His incompetence as a ruler is ideally illustrated, according to a scathing but bizarre anecdote of Prokopios, by his reactions on being told that Rome had perished. This imperial incompetent exclaimed in perplexity that it had just taken food from his hands. Matters were quickly explained to him and he sighed with relief: his enormous pet rooster, which was named *Roma*, was still in the very best of health.[69] Sadly, there is little positive that can be said about his reign. He came to the throne as a pampered child and always remained a pampered child. He had to look on while Rome was ravaged and territories were taken, and he was threatened by numerous pretenders to the throne. Even so, Honorius managed to stay in power for three decades. There were far better emperors who had done a lot worse.

Still, behind its massive city walls, Rome remained a vigorous and lively place. There has been a tendency to assume that after Alaric's success the *urbs aeterna* was semi-ruinous, dreary and beggarly. There is no justification for this cynical view. Apart from some material damage, the actual result of the 'sack of Rome' was a great loss of prestige and shock. The very presence of its strong defences meant that a civilized and prosperous life could go on. For Prokopios sixth-century Rome, although signs of depopulation and decay were already visible, remained 'the grandest and most noteworthy of all cities under the sun'.[70] Despite the palpable embellishment of a tourist, the name of old Rome still had power, and in Constantinopolis, the New Rome, the emperor Iustinianus longed to re-establish single control over the old empire and its capital, so much so that the restoration of the universal Roman Empire animated his every move. This obviously included the recovery of the western lands occupied by the various Germanic nations. The talented general Belisarius sailed to Africa in 533 with a force of 18,000 troops, and within a year secured the submission of the Vandals, and two years later he began what would become a two-decade-long war against the Ostrogoths in Italy. Eventually Iustinianus' armies under the command of the eunuch general Narses completed the subjugation of the Italian peninsula. A coastal slice of Hispania was also re-conquered, and for a short while the Mediterranean almost became a Roman lake again.

Gothic Precipitations

On the sudden death of Alaric, probably from malaria, his cousin and brother-in-law Ataulf assumed the leadership of the wandering army.[71]

Early in the year 412 Ataulf left the Italian peninsula and went to Gaul, carrying off Galla Placidia, the half-sister of Honorius. After bringing about the demise of the new usurper Iovinus, who had started an insurrection in 411 and found many adherents, he made overtures to the emperor, but as he refused to give up Placidia, nothing came of them. According to Orosius, he wished to support Rome with barbarian arms.[72] When negotiations with Honorius failed to bring rewards, Ataulf showed both his anger and his desire to be associated with the empire by marrying Placidia, who had been a captive since 410.

Vigorous measures by Honorius' latest *generalissimo*, Constantius, made Ataulf's situation in Gaul precarious; he therefore proceeded to Hispania early in the following year, probably intending to found a kingdom in the province of Tarraconensis, which had not been occupied by the previous Germanic invaders, the Vandals and the Suevi.[73] Ataulf was, however, assassinated at Barcino (Barcelona, Spain); seven days later the same fate befell Sigeric,[74] his successor, and Vallia became king. Debarred from food supplies by the Romans and foiled in an attempt to cross to Africa, Vallia came to terms in 416, agreeing, in return for large supplies of grain, to restore Placidia and to make war upon the Vandals and Suevi. On the first day of the following year Constantius married Placidia.[75] Subsequently – perhaps in 418, perhaps in 419 – a new treaty brought the Goths back to Aquitaine Secunda, which extended from the Liger (Loire) River to the Garunna (Garonne) River, where they finally settled as *foederati*. Thus began the Visigothic kingdom in Gaul.[76]

At War

Finally, the Goths at war. Those Goths who crossed the Danuvius did not take to the horse anything like their eastern cousins, namely those who became the Ostrogoths.[77] Chieftains and their companions, *comitatus*, might fight mounted, but the bulk of a Gothic army was made up of archers and spearmen, the latter, as with other Germanic warriors, fighting in a dense mass, and the former, according to Vegetius, being in great number.[78] Like other Germanic bowmen the overwhelming majority would be armed with self or compound bows, the former being a plain bow in one piece and the latter built up by uniting two or more staves of similar material.

The account of the sanguinary battle at ad Salices, Moesia, in the summer of 377 by Ammianus Marcellinus probably provides the best description of how the Goths fought, by and large: '[A]fter attacking each other from a distance with javelins and other missiles, they came together menacingly for hand-to-hand conflict; the shields were fixed side to side [viz. locked] in the form of a tortoiseshell (*in testudinum formam*), and they stood foot to foot.'[79]

So battle opened with arrows, javelins and the like, and then the foot warriors attacked. The basic mêlée weapon was the spear, by far the most common weapon found in Germanic graves in general, while swords were less common.[80] Spears, of course, were simple to produce and an effective weapon when wielded by foot warriors fighting in close formation. Shields were the most common type of defensive equipment, complementing the spear, body armour being the privilege of the few. Still, as Ammianus Marcellinus says of the aftermath of Adrianopolis, the Goths 'plundered the dead bodies and armed themselves in Roman equipment'.[81]

Generally speaking the Germanic peoples remained largely illiterate until well into the migration period. Not until the mid-fourth century is there any clear record of an attempt to commit a Germanic language to written form and the attempt when made seems almost herculean. The sole surviving Gothic words relating to warfare are preserved in extant fragments (*Codex Argenteus*)[82] of the Gothic Bible.[83] This was allegedly composed by the Arian bishop and missionary Ulfilas (Wulfila), the Goth of Kappadokian Greek descent who is also credited with devising the Gothic alphabet for that specific purpose.[84] Here can be found the word *sarwa* for armour, *wēpn* for weapon, *brunjō* for mail coat, *skildus* for shield, *hilms* for helmet, *mēki* for sword and *fōdr* for scabbard. The subdivision of a host (viz. army), *harjis*, was the band, *hansa*, both undoubtedly of shifting size.[85] Believe it or not, Ulfilas is said to have omitted the two books of Kings from his translation of the Bible so as to avoid stoking the aggressive disposition of a war-loving people.[86]

Principal Literary Sources

'You know well that if anyone extinguished our literature, we are put on a level with the barbarians.'

Libanius to Caesar Iulianus in *Epistulae* 369.9

As an investigator one is always reluctant to lament the paucity of the available evidence. However, the central problem for the study of the late antique world is the dearth of source material, both in terms of quantity and quality. Unlike the Principate, for instance, with its cornucopia of contradictory sources, investigators of the later Roman period are somewhat in a cleft stick: they are not only forced to rely on ecclesiastical historians of dubious veracity when it comes to secular affairs, but are unable to contrast evidence and check information. Adoptions of arguments *e silentio* is a logical fallacy, ignoring as it does the historical empirical practice *testis unus, testis nullus*.

Still, it is always unwise to assume that today's history is better than yesterday's. In reality, despite the meagre and often obscure material, there are real gems to be had, particularly the voluminous letters of Symmachus, Ambrose and Jerome; history unfiltered, if you will, not refracted through a chronicler's imagination. There are one or two Greek anti-Christian histories (Eunapios, Zosimos) too, although no western Latin examples have come to light. Unlike one group of scholars who see all the sources as so unreliable that we might just as well pack up our historical kitbags and all go home, we will brush aside the defeatism and take a brief overview of these so-called questionable sources for this period, but before we do a brief word on the language of the late antique world.

Today, just like art and sport and music, language is one of the few things found in every culture on the planet. As for the language of the late antique world, much of the secular and religious literature was the empire composed in the two dominant languages, Greek and Latin: much like today, the spoken word can be political, since language and politics walk in lockstep. The natural ethnic frontier (if we are to go by language, the only acceptably measurable standard) existed as a linguistic border that divided the Latinized province of Tripolitania from Greek-speaking Libya and Aegyptus in the south, and the Romanized dioceses of Pannonia and Dacia from Hellenized Greece. Territories to the west of this arbitrary line spoke and wrote in Latin, and those to the east,

Greek. An advanced knowledge of Greek became rare in the western part of the empire. In the eastern part a familiarity of Latin was still indispensable in the fields of administration, law, military affairs and business. Still, attachment to Hellenic culture was steadfast: 'Although I was an Arcadian of Messene, my father did not give me a Greek education, but sent me here [to Rome] to learn jurisprudence,' says a youth disgustedly in Philostratos' novel based on the life of Apollonios of Tyana (which, to us, is simply an ancient romance),[1] written for Iulia Domna, wife of Septimius Severus.

A word of caution is needed, however. If Latin had no serious rival in the west, in the fields and in the streets other local languages still proved tenacious. Oscan, the language of the central Italian highlands, was still being scribbled on the walls of Pompeii in 79, the year of its destruction. Irenaeus (†202), the Greek-speaking bishop of Lugdunum (Lyon, France) in the late one-seventies, writes that he was glad to have learned some Gaulish back home in Galatia because it stood him in good stead with the local inhabitants of his new diocese. In his most famous work, *Adversus haereses*, the later saint writes: 'You will not expect from me, as a resident among the Keltae, and accustomed for the most part to use a barbarous dialect, any display of rhetoric.'[2] What we should imagine, therefore, is Latinized urban centres with an indigenous peasantry all around.

Ambrose (Saint), c.339–397: born Aurelius Ambrosius into an elite Roman household at Augusta Treverorum (Trier, Germany), Gallia Belgica. In Rome he studied law, rhetoric and literature (he quotes with ease Virgil and Thales, Pythagoras and Plato, Aristotle, Homer and Euripides, as well as the Greek fathers). After serving as the *consularis* or governor of the important province of Aemilia-Liguria (roughly Piedmont and part of Lombardy), he was unexpectedly made the bishop of Mediolanum (Milan) in 374 by popular acclamation. A few messy details – he had never been baptized and had never held clerical office – were resolved in double-quick time. As bishop, he took a firm position against Arianism (the Arian cry on the Nature of Christ, *there was a time when the Son was not*)[3] and attempted to mediate between Theodosius and the western usurper Magnus Maximus. His works include sermons, hymns (of which only four are certainly his compositions) and ninety-one extant epistles.

Ambrose is a saint and one of the four Latin doctors of the Church, but he was also very much a late Roman of his class, thoroughly trained in all the rhetorical arts and capable of twisting the truth. So it was that Ambrose was able to justify the speed of his transit from baptism to episcopacy in the course of a week. He was a natural at orating, his secular career having armed him with the skills to manipulate councils to support his views, and the experience to stand up to emperors. Accordingly, as a prelate, Ambrose became a most powerful influence on Gratianus, on Valentinianus II, and on the orthodox Theodosius himself. There is no doubting whatsoever that Ambrose was a great church politician, and he worked his connections with the very highest in the empire, but he was also deeply devout.

Ammianus Marcellinus, c.330–c.391: born at Antioch (Antakya, Türkiye), a Greek-speaking pagan soldier – he was an officer in the elite *protectores et domestici* – who wrote history of the years 96–378, of which books 14–31 survive covering the period 353–378, the seventeenth year of the reign of Constantius II, to the battle of Adrianopolis. Written in Latin and soberly told, he revives the grand style of the bitterly truthful Tacitus, the 'most unmilitary of historians', in writing a multivolume account of the recent past. On publication his *œuvre* received a favourable review from a fellow eminent Antiochene, Libanios: 'I hear that Rome herself has crowned your work, and that her verdict is, that you have surpassed some and equalled others.'[4]

A candid writer, Ammianus Marcellinus gives first-hand accounts of later Roman warfare – he saw active service – as well as observations, albeit with an eagerness to employ phrases and sentences taken from earlier classical authors, on many of the peoples he encountered during his peripatetic military career. In this regard, he is clearly following the ancient ethnographic tradition that stressed the inherent moral superiority of Greeks and Romans over their neighbours.

With his sharp eye for the bizarre, Ammianus Marcellinus saw the world, and especially human beings, in lurid terms, as is shown in his famous judgement on Valentinianus I, where he remarks that the emperor 'had two savage man-eating she-bears called Gold-dust and Innocence, to which he was so devoted that he had their cages placed near his bedroom'.[5] Ammianus' work is not flawless; we should make allowance for retrospective embellishments and anachronistic perspectives. Even so, *Res Gestae* is by far the most important historical work of the fourth century and, compared to some writers, remarkably free from religious or personal bias, save for his partiality to Iulianus (for instance he paints a rather rosy picture of his hero's actions in Gaul). Certainly, unusually for a pagan, he refers quite openly to Christians and Christianity, sometimes favourably, more often not. Moreover, he does speak of Christian rites, ceremonies and officials in a way that shows a lack of familiarity with them.[6]

All in all, *Res Gestae* is never a quiet or dull *œuvre*. As Edward Gibbon rightly said of Ammianus Marcellinus: 'It is not without the most sincere regret that I must now take leave of an accurate and faithful guide, who has composed the history of his own times without indulging the prejudices and passions which usually affect the mind of a contemporary.'[7]

When Ammianus Marcellinus died is quite uncertain. The latest allusion in his *Res Gestae* is to the consulship of Neotherius in 391.[8] In the same year the Serapeion at Alexandria was burned, but the historian refers to the temple as if it were still standing;[9] other indications are his references to Probus and Theodosius.[10]

Augustine (Saint), 354–430: Aurelius Augustinus was born in Tagaste (Souk Ahras, Algeria), the son of a pagan Roman citizen named Patricius (he converted in 371 on his deathbed) and his Christian wife Monica (later Saint Monica). Augustine was bishop of Hippo Regius (Annaba, Algeria), and one of the most prolific Latin authors in terms of surviving works (a vast sprawling library of treatises, sermons and letters). He is probably most familiar as the author of the *Confessiones* (397–400), a personal account of the upheavals of his youth and the stages of his disorderly quest for wisdom, and *De civitate Dei contra paganos* (412–426), which he wrote in order to restore the confidence of his fellow Christians following Alaric's sack of Rome.

Augustine's contemporaries were suspicious of him because of his hedonistic lifestyle as a youth in Carthage,[11] his brilliant career as a rhetor and his status as a former follower of Manichaeism, which was Persian in origin and dualist in outlook.[12] One of the purposes of the *Confessiones*, which Augustine began when he was 43 years old and one year after occupying the See of Hippo, was to defend himself against this kind of criticism by explaining how he had become a changed man through Christ (baptized in 387 by Ambrose; ordained four years later) and demonstrating that his beliefs were truly Christian.

Augustine regarded himself not so much as an innovator but a summator. He was less a reformer of the Church than the defender of the Church's true faith. His self-chosen crusade was to save Nicene orthodoxy from what he regarded as the disruptions of heresy and the calumnies of the pagans. In that respect he wrote in clear, simple, forceful Latin prose; the reader is impressed above all by a feeling of his humility in addition to his great dignity and restraint, but he has different virtues, and a different attitude to virtue itself. Augustine is not a fighting general or politicking statesman: he is a saint. His aim is to get to Heaven, and help the reader to come along as well. The Catholic Church was to bestow upon Saint Augustine his aptest title, that of *doctor gratiae*.

Claudianus, †404: Claudius Claudianus is widely recognized as the last pagan poet of the classical tradition. Although a native speaker of Alexandrian Greek (he came from Aegyptus), Claudianus is one of the best Latin poetry stylists of the late antique world: Latin literature did not end with Seneca and Juvenal in the early second century. He was associated with the court of Honorius at

Mediolanum, and particularly with Stilicho; his works include propagandistic praise poems for the deeds of his benefactor, Stilicho. Claudianus' relationship with Stilicho and the series of works the poet composed under the patronage of said *generalissimo* provides a constant image of the way in which Stilicho's regime wished Honorius to be presented.

Claudianus' poems therefore offer an unusually large corpus of evidence regarding a single emperor in the form of the three panegyrics he wrote for Honorius' consulships, as well as numerous other poems – such as those for his wedding, those on the military campaigns against the Goths and Gildo, and the three-book panegyric – reams of sympathy and regard – for Stilicho's consulship in 400.

Both Augustine and Orosius invoke him as a hostile pagan witness testifying to God's support in battle for Theodosius: Augustine calls him 'alien from the name of Christ', while Orosius describes him as 'a distinguished poet but a most obstinate pagan'.[13] Still, all his poems were written for Christian patrons and performed before an overwhelmingly Christian audience at the court in Mediolanum and (later) Ravenna – a very private world of which the *demibarbarus* Stilicho was a full member – though he wrote only one overtly Christian work, *De Salvatore*.

***Codex Theodosianus*:** a collection of imperial legislation put together in Constantinopolis by a group of legal commissioners during the reign of Theodosius II. It was issued by the said emperor in 438. A vital source for the history of the period, it contains all the imperial legislation from the reign of Constantinus I onwards. Arranged thematically, according to subject and in chronological order within the subject headings, there are 16 books containing more than 2,500 statutes in all. They begin in 311, and build on two earlier collections made under Diocletianus, the *Codex Gregorianus* and the *Codex Hermogenianus*. Book VII is devoted to legislation affecting the army.

However, the *Codex Theodosianus* is not complete, many statues were shortened and it contains many repetitions. Moreover, the compilers themselves were using sources already centuries old. The greatest value of the *Codex Theodosianus* lies in its provision of firm dates.

Herodian (Herodianos): probably of Greek origin, perhaps from Antioch, Herodian was a subordinate official in Rome early in the third century and probably an imperial freedman. He wrote a *History of the Empire after Marcus Aurelius* in eight books from the death of Marcus Aurelius to the beginning of the reign of Gordian III (180–238). Moralizing and rhetorical, his work is often unreliable. For our purposes, however, his value increases with his contemporary knowledge.

Iulianus, †363: Flavius Claudius Iulianus, better known as Julian the Apostate, has handed down to posterity more written works than any other Roman emperor. His letters especially are an invaluable source of information. These texts, written in Iulianus' mother tongue of Greek (but, to quote Ammianus Marcellinus, 'he knew Latin well enough to be able to discourse in it'), are complemented by coins, laws and inscriptions on stone.

John of Antioch (Ioannes Antiochensis): believed by some scholars to be two chroniclers living in the seventh (may have been a monk and might possibly have been the Monophysite bishop of Antioch from 639 to 649) and tenth centuries respectively, but who drew from a wide range of earlier sources, pagan and Christian. His/their *Historia chronike* is a universal history encompassing the period from Adam to the overthrow of the emperor Flavius Phokas (r. 602–610), but it unfortunately survives only in fragments. A work of considerable quality and value, he/they tended to follow the classicizing historians and generally omitted church history and religious issues. In this instance, Theodosius' prayer is not given credit for the victory; rather the emperor's surprise attack on his enemies turns the tide in a war caused, according to him/them, by the anger of Arbogastes. He/they depicts these events as a power struggle won by the rightful ruler.

Jordanes, †583: a Goth, by his own affirmation, living in Constantinopolis, which he casually calls the *urbs*,[14] who wrote a Latin history of his people. He wrote for a Gothic audience. As such he glorifies the deeds of his people at the expense of others. The *Getica*, completed in 551, drew heavily on the completely lost work of Cassiodorus,[15] an early sixth-century Italo-Roman senator and historian who served the Gothic kings of Italy. He lived close enough to the conventional 'end of Rome', but the Constantinopolitan perspective of Jordanes overshadows his Gothic theme: although a self-confessed Goth,[16] Jordanes was a thoroughgoing Byzantine in outlook. Tellingly, Jordanes shows himself to be a loyal and admiring subject of Iustinianus, whose wars for the suppression of the Goths in Italy and Hispania he reports on numerous occasions with unqualified approval.[17]

Generally speaking, Jordanes is poorly regarded both as a historian and stylist. Indeed, Arnaldo Momigliano goes so far as to call the Gothic notary 'a clumsy man who could hardly keep his Latin together'.[18] Still, beggars cannot be choosers, and to borrow the words of Otto Maenchen-Helfen, 'we must be grateful to the stammering, confused, and barely literate Jordanes.'[19]

Notitia Dignitatum: a collection of administrative information, which includes a list of civil and military officials, listed by title or rank, and of military units and their forts in both the east and the west. The *Notitia Dignitatum* is divided into chapters, each one devoted to a high official or army commander, with a schematic picture of his duties and a detailed list of his subordinates and other responsibilities. For instance, a *comes* commanding a *comitatus* is thus represented by the shield devices of his units listed by unit type and seniority, while a *dux* is represented by a picture of his frontier sector and a list of garrison units with their stations.

The exact date and purpose of the *Notitia Dignitatum* are still matters for scholarly dispute. The eastern half most likely dates to Theodosius' campaign against Eugenius in 394, yet the western copy was several times edited and amended after this watershed date. This probably reflects the supremacy of Flavius Stilicho when the western military establishment was being brought under his personal control.[20] Several indirect copies survive, made in the fifteenth and sixteenth centuries from a unique Carolingian copy, the *Codex Spirensis*, preserved at Speyer but long since disappeared. Both eastern and western chapters contain a great deal that is earlier than 395 when the empire was divided in this way. The western chapters include a unique feature, a breakdown by army of all field units. These points suggest that our copy of the *Notitia Dignitatum* might have come from the files of the *magister militum praesentalis*. The lists that survive in the *Notitia Dignitatum* are full of chronological problems: thus the garrison of Hadrian's Wall seems to have survived intact from the early third century, whereas the garrisons along the Rhenus cannot be earlier than around 368. The last datable western military unit is the newly-raised *Placidi Valentiniaci Felices*; a clear reference to Flavius Placidus Valentinianus III, who was born on 2 July 419 and elevated to the western throne in 425.[21]

At the end of the day the most important fact to remember is that such a document would need constant revision. Moreover, although the *Notitia Dignitatum* can be said to generally represent the army of the late fourth century, the complete text is composed of elements of different dates and therefore is not representative of the whole empire at one time. Nonetheless, used with wise caution the document is invaluable, simply because there is nothing to match it for the study of the later Roman army.

Orosius: probably born at Bracara Augusta (Braga, Portugal), Paulus Orosius was a Christian presbyter with a good knowledge of both pagan and Christian cultures. Written in the years 417–418 at the encouragement of Augustine of Hippo, the *Historiarum adversus paganos libri VII* also incorporated elements of the latter's pagan-Christian narrative; that is, to compare pagan past with Christian present. In so doing, Orosius judges the doings of non-Christians by a Christian standard, rewriting other peoples' past along lines they would not have chosen themselves.

The work itself is the longest surviving summary of the whole range of ancient Roman history, covering more than eleven centuries from before the foundation of Rome – following Livy by placing the foundation in the year 751 BC as opposed to the Varronian chronology's 753 BC – up until Orosius' own time. Another important aspect of his work, which is the first world history by a Christian, is the importance he placed on geography in his role as a historian.

Philostorgius, 368–c.433: born of a humble Arian family in Borissus, Kappadokia and came to Constantinopolis to complete his studies. He was an Anomoean (or *heteroousian*, as he preferred to be called, as opposed to a believer in the doctrines of *homöousios* or *homoiousios*) Church historian and his *Historia ecclesiastica* commences with the outbreak of the contest between Arius and Alexander, the bishop of Alexandria, which he regarded as the beginning of the Arian schism. Some Arians, such as Philostorgius, regarded the Son in every respect dissimilar (Gk. ἀνόμοιος/*anhomoios*) to the Father. His work, likely written circa 430 during his exile from Constantinopolis, has unavoidable gaps. What survives of Philostorgius is based on excerpts by Photios I, learned writer and patriarch of Constantinopolis (r. 858–867, 877–886, †893), and on passages in the anonymous *Vita Constantini* and *Artemii passio* (the latter commonly attributed to Ioannes Damascenes). Given his own experiences – he was persecuted as an Arian by the orthodox Theodosius – it is understandable why Philostorgius was hostile towards the emperor. Unlike the other Christian eastern ecclesiastical historians, he does not attribute Theodosius' victory to divine intervention but to treason; he diminishes Theodosius' success still further by emphasizing its human cost.

Prokopios, c.500–after 562: was a highly-educated Greek speaker from Caesarea Palestinae (near Zikhron Jaakov, Israel) and, by universal agreement, considered the last of the great historians in the classical Greek tradition. Prokopios and many others – but probably not the emperor Iustinianus himself – were at home in both Greek and Latin, but increasingly Greek had become the common language of Constantinopolis. Those who had mastered Latin such as the administrator Ioannes Lydos (c.490–c.565) could feel aggrieved that its use was declining even in the prefectural office.[22]

In 527 he was appointed *assessor* or legal secretary to the *magister militum* Belisarius during his Persian, Vandalic and Gothic wars. Prokopios was thus actually present at many of the incidents he recounted and took an active part in these wars. He may have been that Prokopios who became *praefectus praetorio* of Constantinopolis in 562, but the date of his death is unknown. He wrote, in Greek, *History of the Wars*, *De aedificiis* (*On the Buildings*) and *Anékdota* (*Secret History*), which – though wildly entertaining – verges on the pornographically absurd.

It is his *Wars* that are of pre-eminent importance with their detailed account of campaigning during the first twenty-five years of Iustinianus' reign, but caution must also be exercised, for the two fundamental features of the *Wars* that make them so useful to the military historian are double-edged. The first feature, their very focus on warfare, derives from their genre as classicizing history, but Prokopios' aspiration to emulate Herodotos and Thucydides also means that his descriptions of battles and sieges can occasionally owe more to centuries-old generic stereotypes. The second feature, their claim to derive substantially from personal autopsy, derives from Prokopios' privileged position as secretary to Belisarius, but his very proximity to Iustinianus' top *magister militum* sometimes made it difficult for him to maintain an unbiased perspective on events. Having said all that, however, the *Wars*, although postdating our period of study, do contain valuable information on the nature of late antique warfare.

Rufinus of Aquileia, c.345–412: was born at Iulia Concordia (Concordia Sagittaria, Italy), near Aquileia. He was a monk, historian and theologian. He is best known as a translator of Greek patristic works, especially the work of the third-century Alexandrian theologian Origen of Caesarea (Origenes Adamantius) – the most finely-tuned mind of Christianity's earliest teachers and the first to employ the forms of Greek scholarship in Christian literature – into Latin at a time when knowledge of Greek was declining in the West. After study at Rome, where he met Jerome (who, along with Origen, had mastered Hebrew), Rufinus entered into a sort of informal monastic community in Aquileia. Jerome (Eusebius Sophronius Hieronymus), translator and monastic leader, often visited the monastery and the two became close friends.

Jerome (c.347–420), the Christian scholar who translated the Bible into Latin,[23] was a cheerless man possessing a loveless soul: he held an unusual number of men in contempt, including Ambrose, and wrote a great many letters asking for the forgiveness of those he had offended and attacking those who would not forgive him. The two of them would eventually fall out over the teachings of Origen, whose amiable heresy destroyed him; he had suggested Jesus was subordinate to God, and had thought Lucifer himself might have been saved had he been able to repent. Jerome named Rufinus *Tyrannius*,[24] obviously utilizing Acts 19:9 in a pejorative sense, and would continue to denounce and ridicule his former friend even after he was dead.

Rufinus' *Historia ecclesiastica* is a continuation of the *Historia ecclesiastica* of Eusebius of Caesarea Maritima, who had long been regarded as the father of Church History as well as the spokesman for the Constantian regime. Rufinus would establish a monastery of his own by the Mount of Olives.

Scriptores Historiae Augustae: a compilation of imperial biographies from Hadrianus to Carinus (117–285) that purports to be the work of six different authors writing under Diocletianus and Constantinus. Actually it is the labour of a single author, writing in the late fourth century and, for obscure reasons, deciding to conceal his true identity behind six invented pseudonyms. An outlandish *œuvre*, with its prurient content it comes across as more scandal sheet than historical record. Whichever way you look at it – and it does contain more of invention than matter of fact – the Scriptores Historiae Augustae is a tale of vice and folly.

A fitting example is the story of one Firmus, a usurper against Aurelianus based in Aegyptus. No coins of his are known, and it appears to have been a favourite device of these biographers to embellish the importance of pretenders by asserting that they issued coins (cf. SHA *Firmus* 2.1). In actual fact, Firmus' life is so embellished that it includes details of him riding a hippopotamus and an ostrich (ibid. 6.2), swimming with crocodiles (ibid. 6.1) and eating so much meat that he consumed an ostrich a day (ibid. 4.2). The revolt is attested by Zosimos (1.61.1), though without mention of his name, and this particular 'Firmus' probably never existed. Despite its narrative trickery, the SHA is an essential source, in particular for the often shadowy world of the third century.[25] It remains the subject of scholarly controversy, both as to its date (e.g. Syme c.395, Cameron c.375/380) and its purpose.

Sidonius Apollinaris, c.430–c.488: Gallo-Roman aristocrat, poet and historians' *bête noire*, (Caius) Sollius (Modestus) Apollinaris Sidonius was born at Lugdunum (Lyon, France), bishop of Arverna (Clermont-Ferrand, France) in 469. Sidonius wrote panegyrics and other poems, and nine books of letters: the most accomplished man of letters in fifth-century Gaul proved deaf to two requests that he should turn his hand to history. In this refusal, he differed from other skilled authors only in that his decision is known to us. He considered historical writing to be most inappropriate for members of the clergy.[26]

Sidonius was a younger contemporary of Attila (r. 434–453), king of the Huns, and Gaiseric (r. 428–477), king of the Vandals. The campaigns of Flavius Aëtius took place in his boyhood; he was around 20 years old when the Huns were defeated on the Catalaunian Plains. Four years later he witnessed the extinction of the house of Theodosius with the assassination of Valentinianus III and the Vandals plundered Rome. He was still alive when Romulus Augustulus laid down his diadem and went off into comfortable exile. He was a son-in-law of one emperor, rebelled against another, happily played *tabula* with a Visigothic king and became a prisoner of that monarch's successor. Sidonius, bishop and saint, enjoyed an outlook over two contrasting worlds: the old Roman civilization in its decay and the early mediaeval society in its beginnings.

Sidonius' father, whose name is unknown, had been *praefectus praetorio per Gallias* under Valentinianus III, and as such the young Sidonius went through the usual courses in grammar, literature, rhetoric, philosophy (with its satellites of arithmetic, geometry, astronomy and music) and law. His prospects, already bright, were soon greatly enhanced when he married Papianilla, daughter of Avitus, who was to be proclaimed emperor in July 455.

On the first of January in the following year the new emperor assumed the consulship, and Sidonius delivered to an applauding throng a long panegyric in verse (*Carmina* 7), but his elation was to be short-lived. With the fall of Avitus, Sidonius took an active part in the subsequent insurrection of the Gallo-Romans. Providentially, Maiorianus, the new emperor who was an admirer of Sidonius' work, granted him a pardon. When the emperor visited Lugdunum late in the year 458, Sidonius took the opportunity to deliver a panegyric in his honour (*Carmina* 5).

Sokrates Scholastikos, c.380–after 439: born at Constantinopolis, he was an orthodox Christian who adhered to the canons of Nicaea I; scholars only differ on whether or not he was a member of the Orthodox Church or of the Novatian sect. He was a historian of the Christian Church. His *Historia ecclesiastica* covers the history of the Early Church during the years 305 to 439. He effusively praised Theodosius and emphasizes the emperor's divine favour, as manifested by the miraculous wind that came in answer to his prayer.

Sozomenos, c.400–450: Salamenes Hermias Sozomenos was born at Bethelia (Beit Lahia), a small town near Gaza, into a wealthy Christian family. He was a historian of the Christian Church, a work he wrote in Constantinopolis after Sokrates Scholastikos but before 448. Once again, Theodosius' prayers and miraculous wind are proof positive of the true faith of the orthodox emperor. His attitude to usurpers is clear; because it is not the function of human foreknowledge to understand God's thought, no-one has the right to meddle in the imperial succession. Usurpers are therefore contrary to God's designs. In

Constantinopolis he practised as a lawyer well-trained in rhetoric and dedicated his work to Theodosius' grandson, Theodosius II. Sozomenos was an admirer of Ambrose, was aware of Ambrose's views, and was considered the most polemic of the ecclesiastical historians in his opposition to paganism. This is a stance that has suggested to some that his audience still included some pagans.

Symmachus, c.340–c.402: Quintus Aurelius Avianius Symmachus, Roman senator, *praefectus urbis Romae* 364–365, *consul ordinaries* 391, leading pagan and orator. Fragments of his speeches survive, as well as ten books of letters. Some Chalcedonian and East Syriac Christians regard him as a 'full' saint.

Themistios, c.317–388: born in Paphlagonia (northern Türkiye), he was a pagan philosopher and rhetorician who wrote orations, mainly official addresses, of which thirty-four survive, and paraphrases of Aristotle. He served Christian emperors apparently without difficulty, and was actually out of favour during the reign of the pagan Iulianus. He was the tutor of the young Arcadius.

Theodoret, 393–466: Theodoretos was born at Antioch (Antakya, Türkiye). He was an influential theologian of the Antiochene School,[27] biblical commentator and bishop of Kyrrhos (423–449, 451–457) in northern Syria. A voluminous writer, Theodoret wrote numerous works, including *Historia ecclesiastica* to 428, and thirty ascetic biographies of his *Historia Religiosa*. He was one of the leading Christian controversialists of his day, and was deposed by the infamous 'Robber Council' of 449, only to be reinstated by the Fourth Ecumenical Council convened at Chalcedon in 451. Theodoret wrote in Greek, although his native tongue may have been Syriac and the majority of the rural population of his diocese were non-Greek-speakers.

Zonaras, fl. twelfth century: at the apex of his public career, Ioannes Zonaras was the Grand Commander of the Palace Watch (*Megas Drouggarios tēs Biglas*) and First Secretary of the Chancery (*Prōtoasēkritēs*), perhaps during the reign of Alexios Komnenos (1081–1118), though Zonaras' public career could fall in the reign of Alexios' successors John (1118–43) or, less likely, in the reign of Manuel Komnenos (1143–80). Withdrawing from public life, he retreated to the monastery of Ayía Glykeria on the island of Hagia Glykeria (İncir Ada, Türkiye), where he completed his *Epitome historiarum*. This recounts the events from the creation of the world through to the death of Alexios Komnenos in 1118; about 6,619 years by Byzantine reckoning. Composed in the first half of the twelfth century, the work is the most substantial extant historical work written in Greek between Cassius Dio's eighty-book history of Rome of the early third century and the fall of Constantinopolis. It comprises three substantial volumes.

Zosimos: tentatively identified with a sophist of Ascalon (Ashkelon, Israel) or Gaza, an early sixth-century *comes* and advocate of the imperial treasury. Renowned for his militant paganism – paganism still flickered in Constantinopolis, basically a post-pagan hangover that still coursed through late antique life[28] – he wrote in Greek an unfinished *Historia nova* covering the period from Augustus to 410, the year Alaric captured Rome. The climax of his history, Zosimos viewed the events of 410 as the definitive collapse of the Roman Empire. Consequently, his two major themes are the decline of paganism and the 'barbarisation' of the empire; he portrayed Christian emperors, notably Constantinus and Theodosius, as bearing a heavy responsibility for the fall of the empire.

Though virulently anti-Theodosian – he portrays Theodosius as a lazy, sensual, careless ruler who wanted to avoid the exertions of war if possible, and needed some powerful stimulus to spur him into action – the history of Zosimos contributes much detail.[29] He had access to earlier sources, such as the lost polemical history by the fourth-century pagan sophist Eunapios of Sardis (b. 346), who wrote a history embracing the events from 270 to 404, a continuation of the *Chronikē Historia* (now lost) of Dexippos (†273). Zosimos himself gives the clue to the identity of another major source, Olympiodoros, who wrote a detailed history covering 407 to 425.[30] Since these two historians' works survive now only in fragments, it is fortunate to have Zosimos' summary of them. However, he is more than a century removed from the events leading to the Frigidus and prone to make mistakes. In particular, though his narrative is chronological, his sense of chronology is not reliable. Likewise, much of his anti-Christian abuse was a commonplace of the contemporary pagan tradition.[31]

By no stretch of the imagination can Zosimos be called a great historian. Nonetheless, along with Ammianus Marcellinus, Zosimos is the only source we have that provides anything like a complete history of our period of study, though his coverage of fourth-century western affairs is thin. For all his faults, however, Zosimos is arguably the first historian to substantially write about the decline and fall of Rome.[32]

Notes

Introduction

1. The date: Sok. 5.26. All dates are AD unless otherwise stated.
2. Leopold von Ranke, *Sämtliche Werke* 33–34 (Leipzig, 1874), p.vii.
3. The first flag measured 54in by 28in. It was raised on an abandoned 20ft section of water pipe repurposed as a flagpole. Caught by a stiff breeze and despite being small, the flag could be seen from the ships out at sea. On the ships, whistles, horns and bells rang out in celebration. The second flag was twice as large. Rosenthal's photograph won the 1945 Pulitzer Prize for Photography, the only photograph to date to win the prize in the same year it was taken.
4. The six Marines: Sergeant Michael Strank (KIA); Corporal Harlon Block (KIA); Private First Class Ira Hamilton Hayes; Private First Class Harold Keller; Private First Class Harold H. Shultz; Private First Class Franklin Sousley (KIA). There were, however, incorrect identifications in the official release of the names: Block was identified as Sergeant Henry O. 'Hank' Hansen until January 1947; Sousley was identified as Pharmacist's Mate Second Class John Bradley, USN until June 2016; Shultz was identified as Sousley until June 2016; and Keller was identified as Private First Class Rene Arthur Gagnon until October 2019.
5. Although most of the 21,060-strong Japanese garrison were draftees, they refused to surrender, fighting tenaciously until only 216 remained to be taken prisoner. The 70,000 US Marines thrown into the battle suffered 27,071 casualties, of which 6,102 were fatal.
6. The Medal of Honor is the highest military decoration awarded by the United States government. Twenty-two medals were presented to Marines (eleven posthumously), and five presented to sailors, four of whom were hospital corpsmen (two posthumously) attached to Marine infantry units: twenty-two Medals of Honor was 28 per cent of the eighty-two awarded to Marines in the Second World War. Source: 'Medal of Honor recipients', *Medal of Honor Statistics* (United States Army Center of Military History, Fort Lesley J. McNair, Washington DC).
7. Sun Tzu, *Art of War* 1.17 Griffith.
8. E.g. Donatello's *Davide* carved from marble, or Titian's *Davide e Golia* oil painting (c.1542–44).
9. 1 Samuel 17:40 NKJV.
10. Ibid. v. 43.
11. Ibid. v. 40.
12. Ibid. v. 44.
13. Sun Tzu, *Art of War* 3.3 Griffith.
14. Ibid. 3.15 Griffith.

Abbreviations

1. Gregory was not responsible for the familiar title *Historia Francorum, History of the Franks*, whose earliest occurrence is in manuscripts of late Carolingian date. The simple rendering of *Decem libri historiarum* is *Historiae, Histories*.

Chapter One

1. Herod. 6.9.8.
2. SHA *Sev. Alex.* 27.5–10, 30.1–3, cf. *Maximini Duo* 7.3.
3. The nickname Thrax, 'the Thracian', is not recorded until the fourth century ([Aur. Vict.] *Epit.* 25.1).
4. Herod. 6.8.1. Jordanes promotes a strange tale whereby Maximinus is the son of 'a Goth named Micca and…an Alani woman named Ababa', who 'after rustic life came from the pastures into military service' (*Get.* §83). As well as the distant ancestry and parent, Jordanes trots through Maximinus' *cursus honorum*, accession to the emperorship 'by vote of the army, without a decree of the Senate', three-year reign culminating in a violent death (*Get.* §88). Sandwiched between these sober facts is seemingly slapstick. Fresh from his pastures, the 8ft boor stumbles upon Septimius Severus holding military games and asks in his native tongue to join in; he wrestles sixteen camp servants to the ground without pausing for breath, runs tirelessly beside the emperor's trotting horse, converses with Severus and wrestles with seven very strong recruits as continuously and victoriously as before. These amusing details, including Maximinus' supposed barbarian parentage, stem from the controversial Scriptores Historiae Augustae (*Maximini Duo* 1–4). All the same, Jordanes is making a moral here: the 'Goth-Alani' Maximinus Thrax was an excellent Roman soldier, but turned out to be a shocking Roman emperor. Maximinus is an object lesson why 'barbarians' should not occupy the imperial throne.
5. Herod. 7.2.6–7.
6. Ibid. 7.2.8.
7. Before his adoption by Elagabalus (r. 218–222) and elevation to *Caesar* (June 221), Marcus Aurelius Severus Alexander (*PIR* A 1610) had been called Bassianus Alexianus. His father was Gessius Marcianus (*PIR²* G 171). His mother Iulia Avita Mamaea (*PIR²* I 649) was a niece of Elagabalus' mother. He was hailed *imperator* by the *cohortes praetoriae* (13 March 222), and the following day recognized by the Senate as *Augustus*.
8. Take, for instance, when son went against mother by marrying Cnaea Seia Herennia Sallustia Orba Barbia Orbiana (*PIR²* S 252), and then awarding her the title *Augusta*, he thereby incurred Mamaea's wrath. Orbiana was banished and her father killed.
9. Herod. 6.5.9. According to Eusebius (*Hist. eccl.* 6.21.2–4) and Orosius (7.18.6) Iulia Avita Mamaea was a Christian for, in Antioch, having summoned Origen of Caesarea, she was instructed in the mystery according to Christ.
10. Herod. 6.8.5–6.
11. SHA *Sev. Alex.* 60.6.
12. Zos. 1.13.3.
13. For one, Maximinus Thrax is said to have been addicted to industrial inebriation; namely he filled his 8.5 Roman feet (2.5m) frame (SHA *Maximini Duo* 6.6, cf. Herod. 6.8.1, 7.1.2) with a daily dose of 'a Capitoline *amphora* of wine' (SHA *Maximini Duo* 4.1). The *amphora* was a unit of liquid measure containing about 26.2 litres or 35 regular bottles of wine; a vessel of standard size was kept on the Capitoline as an exemplar.

One question: did this heavy-drinking hardman soon-to-be emperor tipple his wine neat 'in the Scythian fashion' or, as decorum dictated, mixed with water? The proportion of water to wine noted by ancient authors is 3:1, 5:3 and, at its strongest, 3:2.

14. Herod. 8.5.8. Evidence for the legion at Aquileia is provided by a *milites* who died and is commemorated on an inscription (*ILS* 2361) dating from this time. One of his own creations, II *Parthica* had been the favourite legion of Septimius Severus.

15. SHA *Maximini Duo* 28.5.

16. Tac. *Hist.* 1.4.1.

17. Marcus Aurelius *Meditations* 10:10.

18. The sixth-century Syrian chronicler Ioannes reports that Gallienus was around 50 years old at the time of his death.

19. In a rock-cut relief from Naqš-e Rustam, Valerianus is portrayed standing up, his hands are held by Šāpur I, a reference to the fact that he was taken prisoner, an ignominy that had never previously befallen a Roman emperor. To reinforce the insult, Šāpur is said to have used the captive emperor as a human mounting block. Lactantius (*De mort. pers.* 5.6) records the lurid story that after Valerianus died in miserable servitude he was flayed and his skin, dyed crimson, was stuffed with straw and put on public display to impress Roman ambassadors.

20. Aur. Vict. *Caes.* 33.2.

21. *CIL* II.4943 for Postumus' full name and title.

22. His imperial coinage honours such deities as Hercules Mausanus and Hercules Deusonienis, who were very popular among the Batavi. Tacitus says that the Germani 'tell that Hercules, too, once visited their country, and he is first amongst the heroes whose praises they chant when they are about to go into battle' (*Germ.* 3.1).

23. SHA *trig. tyr.* 3.9–11, Aur. Vict. *Caes.* 33.7, Zon. 12.24, Zos. 1.38.2. In the Scriptores Historiae Augustae Postumus is listed among the *Triginta Tyranni*, 'Thirty Tyrants'. In the words of Edward Gibbon: 'To illustrate the obscure monuments of the life and death of each individual would prove a laborious task, alike barren of instruction and of amusement' (*D&F*, vol. 1, ch. 10, p.213).

24. *ILS* 564–5.

25. SHA *tyr. trig.* 3.6, 5.4, Aur. Vict. *Caes.* 33.7, Eutr. 9.9.1, Oros. 7.22.10, *ILS* 561–2, *CIL* II.4919.

26. SHA *Gallieni Duo* 4.4, 7.1, *tyr. trig.* 3.5, 6.1, Zon. 12.24.

27. Aur. Vict. *Caes.* 33.8, Eutr. 9.9.1, Oros. 7.22.10, contra SHA *tyr. trig.* 3.7, 5.1.

28. Referring to the elevation of Victorinus – who was ably aided by his mother Victoria – following the assassination of Postumus by his mutinous soldiers, Eutropius uses the phrase *Victorinus postea Galliarum accepit imperium*, 'Victorinus took command of the Gallic provinces' (9.9).

29. 1 Kings 9:18 NKJV, 2 Chronicles 8:4 NKJV, cf. Ezekiel 47:19. The Semitic name *Tadmor* is connected with the *tamar*, 'palm tree': Josephus (*AJ* 8.6.2 §154) calls it Ταδάμορα/*Tadmora*.

30. Palmyra had for long patrolled and policed the eastward caravan routes on which its prosperity depended. This was a pertinent preparation for military power. In other respects, also the Semitic, semi-Hellenized Palmyra was well-qualified to fill the role of Roman sword-bearer in the east. The Sāsānian army relied extensively on noble cavalry, the *clibanarii* ('oven-men', cf. Gk. *klibānos*, 'baking oven'). These were horsemen, as their

name suggests, fully encased in metal scale armour and mounted on horses protected by housings of leather or thick felt. The Palmyrene army also deployed heavy armoured cavalry, the *cataphractarii*. By comparison, however, the Palmyrene *cataphractus* was a fully-armoured man aboard a horse that was also usually armoured, but not necessarily so. Both Sāsānian and Palmyrene horsemen, however, were armed with a heavy spear some 3.65m in length and held two-handed without a shield. The *contus* (Gk. *kontós*) was a weapon for shock action, being driven home with the full thrust of the body behind it. The greater weight of men, horse and equipment meant that their charge was considered to be more powerful than that of conventional cavalry.

31. Zos. 1.39.1–2.
32. Ibid. 1.39.2.
33. SHA *tyr. trig.* 15.5, 17.1, Zon. 12.24, J Ant. fr. 152.
34. SHA *tyr. trig.* 17.2.
35. Zos. 1.39.2.
36. *Pan. Lat.* 8.10.
37. SHA *Gallieni Duo* 14.4, 7–9, Aur. Vict. *Caes.* 33.17–18, Zos. 1.40.1–3, Zon. 12.25, cf. J Ant. fr. 152: Gallienus 'was cut down by the cavalry commander of the *Dalmatae*. This was Heracleianus, who, after he had collaborated with Claudius, through one of the most daring [men], at mealtime slaughtered Gallienus.'
38. Michael Heseltine: quoted in *New Society*, 14 February 1986.
39. Dexippos *FGrHist* IIA 460 F7, SHA *Aurel.* 21.1–3.
40. Zos. 1.44.1.
41. *PRLE* I, p.740.
42. SHA *Aurel.* 37.5–7, Zos. 1.47. Official propaganda claimed on his deathbed Claudius had designated Aurelianus as his successor (Euseb. *Hist. eccl.* 7.28.4, Zon. 12.26). Aurelianus, perhaps in 272, formally placed his *dies imperii* on the day of Claudius' death (sometime in September 270), thereby dismissing Quintillus as a mere usurper.
43. Kedren. p.454.11–22.
44. *PLRE* I, p.990, SHA *Claud.* 11.1, *Aurel.* 25.2–3, Zos. 1.44.1, 51.1. His gentile name is known from a Greek-Aramaic inscription from Palmyra (*IGR* 3.1030).
45. Fest. 24, SHA *Aurel.* 25.1–3.
46. Zos. 1.50.3–4.
47. SHA *Aurel.* 25.1–3, Zos. 1.52.3–53.3.
48. Zos. 1.55.2, SHA *Aurel.* 28.1–3, *tyr. trig.* 30.3, 23, cf. Eutr. 9.13.2.
49. Zos. 1.56.2–3, SHA *Aurel.* 30.3.
50. SHA *trig. tyr.* 15.6–8.
51. Aur. Vict. *Caes.* 39.43, [Aur. Vict.] *Epit.* 39, SHA *Aurel.* 30.4.
52. Zos. 1.61.1.
53. SHA *trig. tyr.* 30.27.
54. SHA *Aurel.* 33.2, *trig. tyr.* 30.24–7, cf. Zos. 1.59: 'Aurelianus marched towards Europe, taking Zenobia, her son, and everyone who took part in their revolt. It is said, however, that Zenobia died either from disease or by refusing to eat, and that all the others, save her son, were drowned on the crossing from Chalcedon to Byzantium.' Perhaps Zosimos is trying to associate Zenobia with that other magnificent eastern queen, Kleopatra VII.
55. Synkellos I 721.740, Zon. 12.27.
56. SHA *trig. tyr.* 27.2.

57. The Welsh and Irish terms for 'the English' remains to this day 'Saxons' (Welsh *Saeson*, Old Irish *Saxan*). Gildas (†570), like other writers in Latin, termed the Germanic settlers in Britannia *Saxones* in his polemic sub-Roman history of Britain, *De Excidio et Conquestu Britanniae* (II.23). It is thus something of a puzzle why Pope Gregory I (r. 590–604) termed them 'English', a usage that prevailed. It is said, when noticing fair-haired slaves for sale in an Italian marketplace, he was told they were Angles (OE *Ængle*, L *Angli*). 'Not Angles, but angels' was said to be his reply. Whether this tale is true or not, what is known is that in 597 the pope dispatched a Roman mission of forty monks headed by Augustine (of Canterbury), the prior to the Benedictine monastery of Saint Andrew in Rome, to convert these pagan 'angels with dirty faces' to Roman Christianity. Although the inhabitants of lowland Britain at that time were in fact made up of many rival kingdoms, including *Seaxan*, *Iutæ* and *Ængle*, Gregory considered them as one nation, only ever referring to them as *Angli*. The story of the conversion of the *Angli* is recorded by Beada, or the Venerable Bede (†735), a scholarly monk of the Northumbrian monastery of Jarrow, in his *Historia ecclesiastica gentis Anglorum* (1.23–7). Bede himself of course fully understood the relationship between the Germanic invaders and the various English people of his own day: 'They came from three very powerful nations of the *Germani*; that is, from the *Saxones*, *Angli* and *Iutæ*' (1.15, cf. 5.9, Prokop. *Wars* 8.20.7). In representing the *gens Anglorum* as a composite people drawn from the three distinct Germanic nations Bede was reflecting the common opinion of his time.

58. SHA *Aurel.* 32.3, *tyr. trig.* 24.2–3, Aur. Vict. *Caes.* 35.3–5, Eutr. 9.13.1, Zos. 1.61.2, Zon. 12.27.

59. Fest. 24, Eutr. 9.13.2.

60. Aur. Vict. *Caes.* 35.5 [Aur. Vict.] *Epit.* 35.7, SHA *Aurel.* 39.1.

61. For example, a silvered *antoninianus* from the Serdica mint (*RIC* V.1 #290), the obverse IMP(*erator*) AVRELIANVS AVG(*ustus*), radiate and cuirassed bust right, the reverse RESTITVTOR ORBIS, Orbis Terrarum, draped, standing right, presenting wreath to Aurelianus, standing left, holding sceptre, suppliant captive between them. The *antoninianus* was a rather miserable denomination that had been introduced in 215 by Caracalla as a double-*denarius* silver coin, yet by the mid-third century it had become so severely debased that it amounted to a mere copper coin containing less than 5 per cent silver.

62. Zos. 1.49.2, Aur. Vict. *Caes.* 35.7, [Aur. Vict.] *Epit.* 36.6, Eutr. 9.15.1, SHA *Aurel.* 39.2, Malal. 12.30.

63. Herod. 1.6.5, cf. 2.10.9.

64. Aur. Vict. *Caes.* 33.33–4.

65. For example, the last consular *legatus propraetore* is attested in 270 in Moesia Inferior (*CIL* III.14460), while a consular is found at Lambaesis in around 280 as governor of Numidia (*CIL* VIII.2729).

66. E.g. *ILS* 2742, two senior centurions appointed as *legati*.

67. *AE* 1954, 135.

68. Aur. Vict. *Caes.* 39.26. Rising from humble origins, the historian Sextus Aurelius Victor served as governor of Pannonia Secunda under Iulianus and in 389 was appointed *praefectus urbis Romae* by Theodosius.

69. Eutr. 9.22.

Chapter Two

1. *'Aeneae magni dextra cadis'*, SHA *Carus, Carinus et Numerianus* 13.3. The line, which translates as 'you fell by the hand of the great Aeneas', is taken from *Aeneid* 10.830.
2. It is Lactantius (*De mort. pers.* 9, cf. Aur. Vic. *Caes.* 39.1) who tells us Diocletianus' pre-imperial name was Diocles.
3. According to the epitomizer of Aurelius Victor, 'He [Carinus] was tortured to death chiefly by the hand of his *tribunus*, whose wife he was said to have violated' (*Epit.* 38.8).
4. Incidentally, true Flavii were rare, whereas it was usual for an imperial servant to use the dynastic title 'Flavius', to which he was entitled, and his last name only. Given the numbers of barbarians brought into the Roman army by the Constantii, it is understandable that they should adopt the *gentilicium* of their *patronus*. Hence the proliferation of the *praenomen* Flavius in late antiquity, e.g. Richomeres, Bauto, Arbogastes, Theodosius (father and son), Eugenius, Stilicho, Rufinus, etc., etc.
5. After Constantinus' death the praetorian prefectures were as follows: *praefectura praetorio Galliarum* = diocese of Britannia, Gaul, Viennensis, Hispania; *praefectura praetorio Italiae* = diocese of Italia, Africa, Pannonia, Dacia, Macedonia; *praefectura praetorio Orientis* = diocese of Thracia, Asia, Pontus, Oriens. The creation of *praefectura praetorio Illyrici* = diocese of Pannonia, Dacia, Macedonia. In 379 the diocese of Pannonia was removed (and renamed diocese of Illyricum) from the *praefectura praetorio Illyrici* and incorporated in the *praefectura praetorio Italiae*.
6. Another province, Valentia, is known but may be one of the former provinces renamed.
7. *Vide* Lactantius (*De mort. pers.* 7.4), who is bitterly hostile to Diocletianus and all his works, the reorganization of the empire and its bloated bureaucracy included.
8. Lib. *Or.* 47.31.
9. Themist. 10.136b.
10. Syn. *Ep.* 130.2, dated to 405.
11. Ibid. 132.5, dated to 405, cf. 104.2, dated to 401.
12. Maximianus added the adjective *Herculius* to his name, which reflected how he assisted Diocletianus on an earthly plane just as Hercules assisted Iuppiter on a cosmic one (*Pan. Lat.* 4 (10).11.6).
13. Lact. *De mort. pers.* 20.4, *Pan. Lat.* 7 (6).15.16, Eutr. 9.27.
14. Baltasar Gracián, *Oráculo manual y arte de prudencia* (Huesca, 1647), *máxima* no. 110.
15. Lactantius (*De mort. pers.* 42.3), on the other hand, who wished to give Diocletianus a suitably nasty end as a wicked enemy of God, has him slowly sink into madness and starving himself to death.
16. Eutr. 10.2, Zos. 2.10.
17. The walls of Rome represent at once both the most emblematic and the most enduring of Aurelianic monuments. Indeed, nothing else so eloquently demonstrates that, by Aurelianus' day, the empire was now on the back foot. The circuit itself was a massive obstacle, 19km of brick-faced concrete nearly 3.7m thick and 8m high (rising to more than 15m after the reorganization of Maxentius), with 381 enfilading towers and 18 gateways. *Vide* Fields 2008: 23–47.
18. Lact. *De mort. pers.* 27.
19. Eutr. 10.3, Sok. 1.2, Zos. 2.11.
20. *Anon. Vales.* 4 §10, Eutr. 10.2, Aur. Vict. *Caes.* 40.7, Zos. 2. 10.

21. Flavia Maxima Fausta, younger daughter of Maximianus (Iul. *Or.* 1.9C, 2.51C, Eutr. 10.3, Zon. 12.33, 13.1, Lact. *De mort. pers.* 27.1, 30.2), by his Syrian wife Eutropia. She was born in Rome (Iul. *Or.* 1.5C), probably around 298. This would mean she was aged about 9 when married to Constantinus, but note that she did not bear her first child until 317. She was married in Gaul in 307 (Lact. *De mort. pers.* 27.1). The story that she revealed her father's plot to murder her husband is doubtful (ibid. 30.2–3, Eutr. 10.3, Zos. 2.11). It seems that only Constantius II and Constans were her sons (Iul. *Or.* 2.51C, *ILS* 723 725 730), while Constantinus II may have been the son of a concubine (*ILS* 710).

22. Euseb. *Hist. eccl.* 8.13.14, Lact. *De mort. pers.* 20.3, 29.1–3, Aur. Vict. *Caes.* 40.8, Eutr. 10.4.1.

23. Lact. *De mort. pers.* 30.1, Euseb. *V Const.* 1.47, Eutr. 10.3.2, Aur. Vict. *Caes.* 40.21, cf. Sok; 1.2 and Zos 2.11, who both confuse the death of Maximianus in 310 with that of Maximinus Daia at Tarsus in 313.

Chapter Three

1. Dio 77.15.2.
2. Herod. 4.4.3.
3. Ibid. 4.7.4–7, 12.2.
4. Dio 79.5.4.
5. *C Ius.* VII.64.9, X.55.3.
6. SHA *Maximini Duo* 5.5. The only certain reference to *legio* IIII *Italica* is to be found in *ND or.* VII.54. *Vide* Mann 1999: 228.
7. Augustus (or Octavianus as he was then known) had some sixty legions under his command shortly after Actium, far more than he needed or indeed could afford. In his *Res Gestae* (15.3) he boasts of having set up some 120,000 discharged soldiers in veteran colonies, which amounts to 24 legions or thereabouts. According to Tacitus (*Ann.* 4.5.2–5, cf. Dio 55.23.2) there were 25 legions in service in AD 23–8 on the Rhenus, 4 in Syria, 3 in Hispania, 2 each in Africa, Aegyptus, Pannonia, Moesia and Dalmatia – around 125,000 citizen soldiers, with probably an equal number of auxiliaries; three legions (XVII, XVIII and XVIIII) had been wiped out with Publius Quinctilius Varus (*cos.* 13 BC) in the four-day running fight known to posterity as Saltus Teutoburgiensis (AD 9) and were never replaced or their (unlucky) numbers reused (Vell. 2.119, Tac. *Ann.* 1.43.2, Dio 56.20.5). No new legions had been raised in the latter part of Augustus' reign, and it is generally agreed that there were twenty-eight as far back as 15 BC, when the brothers Drusus and Tiberius (Livia's sons and Augustus' stepsons) campaigned north of the Alps. Two new legions were raised by Caligula, one by Galba and three more under Nero, Vitellius or Vespasianus. The four were disbanded by Vespasianus after the rebellion of Civilis and replaced by two re-formed units. Thus the total now stood at twenty-nine, increased to thirty by Domitianus in AD 83 by the creation of *legio* I *Minervia pia fidelis*. One legion, V *Alaudae*, was lost probably by AD 92, so that when Traianus raised *legio* XXX *Ulpia* for the Dacian wars, as its number implies, there were thirty legions. However, Traianus also raised II *Traiana* and this probably replaced XXI *Rapax*, which had disappeared earlier. An inscription (*ILS* 2288) from Rome, datable to the start of the reign of Marcus Aurelius, lists twenty-eight legions in a west-to-east-to-west order (i.e. Britannia to Hispania) with *legiones* VIII *Hispana*

and XXII *Deiotariana* missing. The first may have been lost on the Danuvius or in Kappadokia in 161 and the last in the final messianic Jewish revolt of Shimon Bar-Kokhba in 132–135. In 165 Marcus Aurelius raised two new legions in Italy, thereby putting the total number back up to thirty. These two *legiones*, II *Italica* and III *Italica*, stationed in Noricum and Raetia respectively (Dio 55.24.4), have been added at the end of the inscription. Thus, for more than a century and a half between twenty-five and thirty legions were judged sufficient for the security of the emperor and his empire.

8. Lact. *De mort. pers.* 7.
9. J Lyd. *De mens.* 1.27.
10. Zos. 2.15.1–2.
11. Jones 1964: 679.
12. Agathias *Historiae* 5.13.7.
13. *Legio* IIII *Martia* was under the command of the *dux Arabiae* (*ND or.* XXXVII.9).
14. Vegetius' problematic and certainly rhetorical comment that from the reign of Gratianus (375–383) Roman infantry neglected armour and helmets has until recently been accepted (Veg. 1.20). Vegetius' precise meaning is disputed, but the archaeological, monumental and historical evidence points to the infantry's continued use of helmets and scale or mail body armour. On scale, *vide* Sid. Apoll. *Carm.* 7.242, 15.13. On mail, *vide* Amm. Marc. 16.10.8, Sid. Apoll. *Carm.* 2.143, 321–2, *Ep.* 3.3.5. Finally, the *Notitia Dignitatum* records numbers of *fabricae* producing *scutaria et armorum*, the latter probably referring to armour rather than weapons (*ND or.* XI.18–35, *occ.* IX.15–36).
15. *Mattiobarbulus*, as referred to by Vegetius (1.17, 2.15) is presumed to be a scribal error for *martiobarbus*, meaning 'little barb of Mars'. The barb obviously refers to a barbed head, and Mars was the god of war (and agriculture). These darts had iron, lead-weighted heads, which averaged 10–20cm in length, with a wooded fletched shaft of about the same length. *Vide* Thomas Völling, '*Plumbata-Mattiobarbulus-Marzobandoulon? Bemerkungen zu einem Waffen-fund aus Olympia'. Archäologischer Anzeiger* (1991), pp.287–98.
16. Veg. 3.14.
17. Ibid. 2.4–18.
18. Ibid. 1.17, 2.15, 16, 3.14.
19. *RB* 10.1 Thompson.
20. Ibid. 2–3.
21. Maur. 12B.2, cf. 4, 5. The author, it is clear, was a veteran campaigner who had commanded troops on at least two fronts.
22. Southern-Dixon 2000: 115.
23. The reign of Maurikios, in the words of George Ostrogorsky, 'marks an important step forward in the transformation of the worn out late Roman Empire into the new and vigorous organisation of the medieval Byzantine Empire' (*History of the Byzantine State*, trans. Joan Hussey [New Brunswick, NJ, 1969], p.80). Maurikios' most important accomplishment was probably his reform of the Roman army. For this he was eminently well prepared, bringing with him a wealth of personal experience gained in the Balkan Peninsula against the Avars and the Slavs, and on the eastern frontiers against the Sāsānian Persians. He was a very practical man and knew what was needed. Much if not most of the weaponry and tactics that had developed since the debacle of Adrianopolis was retained or improved.

24. The *Notitia Dignitatum* records the presence of twenty *fabricae* in the western half of the empire (*ND occ.* IX 14–36, *occ.* IX.17–35) and fifteen in the eastern half (*ND or.* XI). Evidently they are generally located where the majority of the army was stationed, viz. along the Rhenus and the Danuvius, and throughout the provinces of the eastern frontier. *Vide* James 1988: 263–71.

25. In Middle High German: *Diz lagent uns die wilen, ein nagel behalt ein îlen, ein îlen ein ros, ein rose in man, ein man ein burc, der ltriten kan* (c.1230, Freidank *Bescheidenheit*). Benjamin Franklin, the political and philosophical giant of his day, had a variation, the last two lines of which are pretty familiar: 'For the want of a battle the kingdom was lost,/And all for the want of a horseshoe nail' (B. Franklin, *Poor Richard's Almanack*, June 1758). As a point of interest, during the entire American War of Independence, Benjamin Franklin never heard a shot fired in anger or visited a field of battle during or after the conflict. He is proof that not all wars are won on land or at sea but rather as often in clandestine meeting rooms and in social halls. So it was, following the surrender of Major General John Burgoyne on 17 October 1777 to Benedict Arnold at Saratoga, Franklin secured a treaty by which France agreed to help with money, ships and men. The French of course were eager to revenge their previous defeats by the British, but their aid was an invaluable element in the American success. This surrender of Burgoyne was the real turning-point of the war, and four years and two days after his men laid down their arms, Lieutenant General Charles Cornwallis surrendered his army. The French army and navy made possible the final victory at Yorktown.

26. SHA *Sev. Alex.* 52.3.

27. *P Col.* 7.188.15–19.

28. Amm. Marc. 29.4.5, *P Oxy.* 2230, 2760.

29. *C Th.* VII.4.5, dating to 359.

30. Derived from the Latin term *buccella*, 'morsel, mouthful'.

31. Sour wine (*acetum*), as opposed to ordinary wine (*vinum*), was the drink of the ordinary soldier as proffered in an act of mercy to Christ on the cross (John 19:29), and could be mixed with water to make the time-honoured tipple of the proletariat, *posca* (Plautus *Miles Gloriosus* 837, *Truculentus* 610). Refreshing but less nutritious and palatable than wine, in some cases flavouring herbs, honey or eggs were also mixed in. Popular with travellers too, *posca* (from *potor*, 'to drink') was a thirst-quenching drink on the road. Like soldiers, they carried the sour wine in a flask, ready to dilute when they found water. As for *vinum*, the ancients mixed their wine with two or even three parts water for normal beverage use, which became universal as soon as they recognized the use of the alcohol content as ensuring a safe liquid to drink as opposed to questionable water sources. The Italian polymath Girolamo Cardano, in his *Neronis encomium* of 1562, attributed the superiority of the Roman armies to three factors: manpower, training and *posca*. Wine had an alcoholic content up to about 10 per cent, at which point the alcohol level kills off the fermenting agents. All ancient wine was thus, in our terms, relatively weak, and would remain so until factory distillation was developed in Europe in the eighteenth century.

32. *C Th.* VII.4.11, dating to 360, cf. Amm. Marc. 16.2.8, 17.8.2, 9.2. The *Codex Theodosianus* (VII.4.25) refers to a complaint received from the city council of Epiphaneia, who stated that it had become too expensive to supply the soldiers with aged wine. It was therefore agreed from November 398 that the soldiers should be supplied with new

wine from the latest batch. This latter regulation was still in force during the reign of Iustinianus (*C Ius.* XII.37.10).

33. Veg. 3.3.

34. Source: The National Archives, London State Papers, SP 41/27, *Food for Soldiers*. Likewise, the Peninsular War soldier subsisted on no delicately balanced diet. The Duke of Wellington issued the following order for his army heading to Portugal in 1809: 'There shall be six women to every hundred men and these shall be drawn by lot before embarkation. All men shall have one pound of biscuit and one pound of meat every day, with wine if the meat is salt. The women shall be on half-rations and no wine, however salt the meat.' The wine issued was one pint, or alternatively this part of the daily ration could be one half-pint of spirits, rum or gin usually. For his daily ration a soldier was docked 3s 6d per week. *Vide* S.G.P. Ward, *Wellington's Headquarters: A Study of the Administrative Problems in the Peninsula 1809–1814* (Oxford, 1957), p.79.

35. On the plus side, if you can call it such, the British soldier did have his tobacco. This was relished as a bulwark against hunger and loneliness.

36. Plin. 23.27.

37. Polyb. 2.15.3.

38. Plin. 8.77.

39. Amm. Marc. 25.2.2. The Hannibalic war veteran Marcus Porcius Cato (234–149 BC), a grouchy senator known by many epithets (the Censor, the Wise or the Elder), provides a simple recipe for *puls*: 'Make porridge in this way. Pour a half-pound of clean wheat into a clean bowl, wash well, remove the husk thoroughly, and clean well. Pour into a pot with pure water and boil. When done, add milk slowly until it makes a thick cream' (*De agri cultura* 86). For soldiers in the field, as Cato himself knew, having campaigned in Hispania, their porridge probably lacked the milk.

40. Iul. *Misop.* 340B.

41. Marcus Aurelius *Meditations* 1:6 (τὸ σκίμποδος καὶ δορᾶς).

42. Xen. *Hell.* 7.2.22.

43. Herod. 4.7.5. This reminds us of that oft-quoted elegiac couplet from Archilochos in his striking self-portrait: 'In my spear is my daily bread,/In my spear my Ismaric wine,/ On my spear I lean and drink' (fr. 2). The daily bread of our soldier poet was of course μᾶζα, barley bread. Ismaros was a Greek *polis* on the Thracian coast not far from the island of Thasos. Its highly esteemed wines are mentioned by Athenaios (1.30) and Ovid (*Metamorphoses* 9.641). Homer says it is a heady 'sweet wine' from Ismaros that the quick-witted Odysseus gives to the Cyclops Polyphemos to make him drunk, which enables him to put out his one eye and effect his escape (*Od.* 9.196–8, 205 Lattimore); there is a common Chinese saying: 'wine can accomplish a deed but it can also bring about a downfall.' Anyway, according to Odysseus, Ismaric is so divinely potent that to one cup of it are mixed 'twenty measures of water' (ibid. 9.209 Lattimore). No *vin ordinaire* then, for though the ancient Greeks habitually drank their wine diluted with water, the usual proportions of water to wine were 3:1, 5:3 or 3:2. The precise taste of ancient wines is hard to imagine or reproduce. Two characteristics would have stood out. Firstly they would on average have been a lot sweeter than present-day wines, and secondly, given that they were normally diluted with water, they would have been drunk at a lower alcoholic strength than present-day wines (three to eight degrees).

44. Xen. *Kyr.* 6.2.31.

45. Plin. 18.27.105, cf. Cato *De agri cultura* 74.
46. SHA *Aurel.* 9.6.
47. Xen. *Kyr.* 6.2.18. A gentle browse through Xenophon's *Anabasis* will reveal that the Ten Thousand dined a great deal of the time on barley meal (ἄλφιτα, e.g. *Anab.* 4.5.26, 5.3.9, 6.1.15, 2.3, 5.1, 7.1.37, cf. Thuc. 8.100.2): barley meal was barley grain that had been roasted and milled.
48. Technically bread, as opposed to hardtack, can be made without salt but the result is not so pleasing…take my word for it.
49. Mentioned in *C Ius.* XI.43.6.
50. Prokop. *Wars* 3.13.15.
51. Anonymous *Peri Stratēgikes* 2.4.
52. Another hazard facing soldiers was tooth decay. For instance, analysis of loaves found in Egyptian burial chambers has revealed that Egyptian bread contained substantial traces of abrasive minerals (sand, feldspar, mica, sandstone), introduced either into the flour as it was laboriously ground on an arrangement of stones known as a saddle quern, a hand-mill shaped as its name indicates like a saddle, or by wind-blown sand and dust. Over a period of time this grit wore down the enamel of teeth, causing at best some discomfort and pain, and at worst, serious abscesses and infections, which could prove fatal.
53. The Greeks were quite right to call them ἀρτοφάγοι/*artophágoi* ('bread-eaters') for the main staple for most ancient Egyptians had been bread, and a number of varieties were made from both barley (*Hordeum vulgare*) and emmer wheat (*Triticum dicoccum*), the latter being the domesticated form of the wild emmer grass. Indeed, the poorest people in ancient Egypt seem to have subsisted on bread, beer and a few vegetables, notably radishes and onions. According to Herodotos (2.124), a noted visitor to Egypt in about 450 BC, it was with these very commodities that the builders of the Great Pyramids were paid, while the *Tale of the Eloquent Peasant*, a Middle Kingdom wisdom text as well as a folk-tale, says a worker's basic wage (paid in kind) was reckoned at 'ten loaves of bread, and two jars of beer daily' (Papyrus Berlin 10499, 3023, 3025 B1 116). Similarly the prayer asking for offerings to be brought to the deceased, known as the offering formula and inscribed in Egyptian tombs from the Old Kingdom onwards, usually included a request for 'a thousand of bread, a thousand of beer', or just simply 'bread and beer'.
54. Plin. 18.149.
55. Athenaios 7.304b, cf. Aischylos *Agamemnon* 1041. The Greek rhetorician and grammarian Athenaios of Naukratis was writing around the turn of the third century and produced a voluminous and curious book, the super-stuffy *Deipnosophistae*, 'The Philologists' Banquet', in which twenty-four named doctoral types come together to discuss literature and learned literary matters. It is the source of many of our quotations from lost Greek writers.
56. Spelt closely resembles the more refined wheat we know today, but is not easily husked. The Latin word for spelt is *far*, hence *farina*, meaning flour, wholemeal of course. Incidentally, the Latin word for the traditional wedding took its name from spelt, *confarreatio*, because the bride and groom shared a coarse spelt loaf, *farreum*, on their wedding night.

57. Revelations 6:6 NKJV with amendments. A *choinix* is roughly equivalent to one imperial quart or 1.14 litres, and equalled a daily ration of grain for a soldier. A *choinix* of barley meal is equivalent to 567g/20oz of sifted flour. This, when cooked (bread/cake/porridge) and digested will provide 1,897 usable calories plus 63g of protein (c.57g in the case of porridge). A 120lb-individual engaged in carrying a moderate load for eight hours in addition to other normal activities requires 3,402 calories. In comparison, when I was soldiering the US Army reckoned that 3,600 calories per day would sustain a soldier in combat conditions ($\equiv$ 1.08kg/38oz of barley meal). This daily calorie intake should include at least 70g/2.77oz of protein in order to avoid malnutrition, and at least 2.25 litres of water to prevent dehydration (cf. the US forces during the First Gulf War required at least 10 litres per day). Even with such supplements as cheese, onions, garlic and olives, as was the case with the Ten Thousand (*vide* Xen. *An.* 7.1.37 in which Xenophon specifically mentions barley meal, wine, olives, garlic and onions as part of the soldier's daily diet), the US combat soldier would have found daily survival on the ancient soldier's basic diet somewhat taxing. *Vide*: (i) weights & measures – *Mrs Beaton's All About Cookery*, Pan Books (London, 1963) pp.50–2; (ii) calorific values of cereals and usable calories – Lin Foxhall and Hamish A. Forbes 'Σιτομετρεία: the role of grain as a staple food in classical antiquity', in *Chiron 12* (1982) pp.41, 90; (iii) calorific requirements – Colin Clark and Margaret Haswell, *The Economy of Subsistence Agriculture* (London, 1970), pp.11–13; (iv) US Army's statistics – US Army Reserve Officers Training Corps Quartermasters, University of Texas, quoted in Engels 1980: 123.
58. Suet. *Aug.* 24.2, Frontin. 4.1.25, 37, Plut. *Ant.* 39.7, Veg. 1.13, cf. Polyb. 6.38.3.
59. Caes. *B civ.* 3.47.
60. Clausewitz *Vom Kriege*, bk. 5, ch. 14, p.396. Howard & Paret, cf. Honoré de Balzac, *Maxims et pensées de Napoléon* (Paris, 1838), maxim n° 108: 'The foremost quality of a soldier is his capacity for withstanding fatigue; courage comes only the second to this.' Ibid maxim n° 110: 'Hardship and misery are the soldier's true teachers.' Persian nobles, according to the on-the-spot eyewitness Xenophon (*Kyr.* 1.2.11), were quite prepared to count one day's rations as two in order to harden themselves against possible shortages of food during a campaign.
61. Amm. Marc. 21.12.15, 29.4.5, Zos. 5.7.2–3 (in friendly territory), Amm. Marc. 16.11.11–12, 17.1.11, 9.2–3, 27.10.7, Zos. 3.14.2, 23.1–2, 27.3, Lib. *Or.* 18.52 (in enemy territory). 'To know... how to draw supplies of all kinds from the country you occupy', Napoléon wrote to his brother Joseph, 'makes up a large part of the art of war' (*Correspondance de Napoléon Ier* [Paris, 1857–70], vol. XII, no. 9944, to Joseph Bonaparte, 8 March 1806). This 'logistical system' was inherited by the Revolution and Napoléon from the practice of the standing armies introduced after the Thirty Years' War.
62. Amm. Marc. 21.7.2.
63. Iul. *Ep. ad Ath.* 286B.
64. Lib. *Or.* 18.83.
65. *Vide* Engels 1980: 123–30.
66. G.W.F. Hegel, *Grundlinien der Philosophie des Rechts* (Berlin, 1820), preface.
67. Amm. Marc. 22.4.6–7A.
68. *AE* 1981, 777 = *SEG* 1116.
69. De Blois 1976: 26.

70. Zos. 1.40.1.
71. SHA *Sev. Alex.* 61.8, *Maximini Duo* 11.1, 11.7, Herod. 7.2.1–2, cf. 8.1.3, Zos. 1.15.1, Zon. 1.26.7.
72. Southern-Dixon 2000: 12.
73. Kedren. p.454.
74. Tomlin 1989: 223.
75. De Blois 1976: 28.
76. Ferrill 1986: 32.
77. Southern-Dixon 2000: 13.
78. *ILS* 569.
79. Southern-Dixon 2000: 14.
80. Claudius came to power in a typical *putsch* as the candidate of a *junta* of army commanders. As he was later alleged to be the ancestor of the house of Constantinus, it was dressed up by the sources, including Aurelius Victor: 'The soldiers eagerly approved and praised the accession of Claudius, being compelled by the desperate state of affairs, almost against their natural inclinations, to make the right decisions' (34.1).
81. Zos. 1.40.2, 43.2, SHA *Gallieni Duo* 14.4, 9.
82. SHA *Aurel.* 18.1.
83. Ibid. 6.2.
84. Zos. 1.45, SHA *Claud.* 11.3–9.
85. Zos. 1.50.3–51.1, 52.3–4. Zosimos does not actually say where the battle took place, but Eutropius (9.13.2), Jordanes (*Rom.* §291) and Synkellos (I 721.10–11) place it at the town of Immae, some 68km east of Antioch.
86. Kedren. p.455.2.
87. Zos. 1.62.2–3, Zon. 12.27, Aur. Vict. *Caes.* 35.8, 36.2, J Ant. fr. 156, Eutr. 9.15.2, SHA *Aurel.* 36.5–6.
88. Zos. 2.17.
89. Hoffman 1969: 281.
90. *ND occ.* IX.4–8, *or.* XI.4–10. The earliest evidence for the *scholae* is Constantinian in date, though Jones (1964: 54) traces them back to the Tetrarchy.
91. Jones 1964: 649–52.
92. *Vide* Parker 1935: 272–3, Jones 1964: 54–5, Southern-Dixon 2000: 15–17 (Diocletianus), Nischer 1923: 10–12, Williams 2000: 93 (Constantinus).
93. *P Oxy.* 1.43 col. 2.24–8.
94. *CIL* III.6196 = *ILS* 2781.
95. *CIL* III.5565 = *ILS* 664. *Vide* Hoffman 1969: 257–8.
96. *FIRA²* I, no. 93. This bronze tablet records Licinianus' grant of tax privileges to his soldiers and veterans.
97. *ND occ.* XXXIII.55.
98. *C Th.* VII.20.4.
99. Parker 1933: 189.
100. *ND or.* XV.16.
101. *Legio* V *Macedonica* was originally levied as *legio* V *Urbana* in 43 BC by Caius Vibius Pansa Caetronianus as part of his consular series for the defence of Rome during the war against Marcus Antonius (App. *B civ.* 3.93). Inscriptional evidence for *Quinta Macedonica* exists from 635 at Memphis in Aegyptus, that is seven years prior to the Arabs, inspired by Islam, taking Alexandria.

102. Jones 1964: 682.
103. Amm. Marc. 24.2.3, 24.3.10, cf. Veg. 1.9, Prokop. *Wars* 4.13.32–3.
104. Retrospectively, we can see the Arch of Constantine was prophetic: the *Cornuti* (as well as other Germanic *auxilia*) are in Constantinus' victorious army, not in Maxentius' defeated one.
105. Ammianus Marcellinus' figures are 13,000 Roman troops against an alliance of 35,000 Alamanni, of which 6,000 were left on the field while in their retreat to the Rhenus many more were drowned (16.12.2, 26, 63, cf. Lib. *Or.* 18.60 says 8,000). For the battle, Iul. *Ep. ad Ath.* 279B, Amm. Marc. 16.12, Lib. *Or.* 18.52–67.
106. Amm. Marc. 16.12.43, cf. 21.13.15, 26.7.17, 31.7.11, Tac. *Germ.* 3.1, Veg. 3.18.9–10, SHA *Sev. Alex.* 53.8–9. The *barritus* was an undulating war cry that began from silence and started with a low murmuring that gradually crescendoed to a loud roaring, the warriors 'putting their shields to their mouths, so that, by reverberation, it may swell into a fuller and deeper sound' (Tac. *Germ.* 3.2). It was probably first used among Principate-era *auxilia* from east of the Rhenus, particularly by the Batavi. Unsurprisingly, later battle cries increasingly took the form of Christian invocations, notably *Deus nobiscum*, 'God [is/be] with us' (Maur. 2.18, cf. Veg. 3.5.3–4), and, perhaps also *Alleluia* (*Vita San Germani* 3.18). Towards the end of the period, *Adiuta Deus*, 'God help us', was officially sanctioned (Maur. 12.B.16.42–3, 24.15–16). For the *Cornuti* and *Brachiati* paired, *vide* Amm. Marc. 15.3.30.
107. Amm. Marc. 26.5.1–4.
108. *C Th.* VIII.1.10, dating to 365.
109. One of the standard-bearers of the *Petulantes*, a certain Maurus, placed the crown (in fact a golden torc) on Iulianus' head proclaiming him *Augustus* (Amm. Marc. 20.4.18, cf. Iul. *Ep. ad Ath.* 284A-285C).
110. Amm. Marc. 20.4.2, 21.3.2, 22.12.6, 31.10.4. For the *Celtae* and *Petulantes* paired, *vide* also ibid. 20.4.20, 5.9.
111. Zos. 3.12.5–13.1, though the text is ambiguous and could also be interpreted as 65,000. Whatever its true size, Iulianus' assembly of his forces in Syria prior to his invasion of Persia precipitated a famine in Antioch requiring the import of grain from Aegyptus to alleviate it. Not only that, Libanius (*Or.* 47.4–5, 13–14), admittedly a hostile source, complains bitterly of soldiers' behaviour in Antioch, accusing them of brawling and armed extortion, going on to note that their camp followers were no better. Even so, the eyewitness Ammianus Marcellinus (21.5.8, 22.12.6) says that his fellow soldiers' behaviour in Antioch was appalling. Then again, as Napoléon rightly pointed out, 'you need only a few men per company to corrupt a whole regiment' (*Correspondance de Napoléon Ier* [Paris, 1857–70], vol. XXII, no. 17672, p.126, to Minister of War Clarke, Saint-Cloud, 30 April 1811). Most people of Antioch found the emperor's method of solving the problem of food shortage inadequate, and when on 5 March 363, Iulianus departed from the city on the Orontes to start his Persian campaign, nothing was left of the initial enthusiasm for the young emperor. The Antiochenes disliked Iulianus as an antiquarian prig. They mocked his beard, and made fun of his obvious dislike of public entertainments. Iulianus himself felt deeply aggrieved. He replied in kind. His satire entitled *Misopogon* ('Beard-hater') shows the streak of irresponsibility and levity that was his weakness. To the few Antiochenes who saw him off on 5 March 363 he gave to understand that he would never set foot in their wretched city again, and that

on his way back from Persia he would go directly to Tarsus. Prophetic words: shortly after Iulianus had died in Mesopotamia his mortal remains were buried in a suburb of Tarsus (Amm. 23.2.5, 25.9.12–13, 10.5).

112. Amm. Marc. 16.12.2.

113. By the sixth century, cavalry had undoubtedly become an increasingly important element in the Roman army, but the balance had not tipped decisively in favour of this arm. A striking feature of a number of battles is in the way in which cavalry dismounted and fought on foot alongside infantry, as happened at Taginae and Mons Lactarius in Italy, Mammes in North Africa and the River Hippis in Lazica (Prokop. *Wars* 8.31.5, 35.19, 4.11.50, 8.8.30–1).

114. Anonymous *Peri Stratēgikes* 15–16, 18–25, Maur. 12B.

115. *ND occ.* V, cf. VII.156.

116. *C Th.* VIII.1.10. According to Ammianus Marcellinus (25.7.9), five provinces east of the Tigris were surrendered to the Persians (cf. Zos. 3.31.1 only four), along with fifteen fortresses besides Nisibis, Singara and Castra Maurorum. The anger is still hot in Ammianus Marcellinus when he tells the story of the loss of Nisibis and of Iovianus' triumph, a ceremony 'never before celebrated by Rome for anything that had been lost' (25.9.9). The recovery of Nisibis was still on the imperial agenda two centuries later, but the agreement of 363 ushered in the most prolonged period of peace the Roman eastern frontier had ever experienced; a crucial fact in the survival of the East during the fifth century.

117. Situated below the Tigris gorges, Bezabde was where the road from Antioch via Edessa reached the Tigris; it was here that Xenophon and the Ten Thousand had turned aside into the rocky Kurdish hills (Xen. *Anab.* 4.1.5). The ruins of the fortress city lie at Eski Hendek, the meeting-place of three frontiers: Türkiye, Syria and Iraq.

118. Amm. Marc. 20.7.1, *ND or.* VII.49, 50, Malal. 13.332.

119. Zos. 2.34.

120. Whitaker 1994: 206–7.

121. *C Ius.* XII.35.15.

122. *ILS* 2781.

123. Eunap. fr. 82, Zos. 5.21.9, J Ant. fr. 190, Theod. *Hist. eccl.* 5.32, Philostorg. 11.8, Sok. 6.6, Soz. 8.4.

124. Zos. 4.57.2, 58.2, J Ant. frs. 187, 190.

125. Claud. *In Ruf. II* 410, Philostorg. 11.3, Zos. 5.7.4, Jer. *Ep.* 60.16, Sok. 6.1, Soz. 8.1.

126. Eunap. fr. 75, Zos. 5.13.1–2, 17.4, Soz. 8.4.

127. Zos. 5.15–18.

128. Sok. 6.6, Soz. 8.4, Theod. *Hist. eccl.* 5.32.

129. Zos. 5.18.8–9.

130. Eunap. fr. 79, Philostorg. 11.8, Sok. 6.5–6, Soz. 8.4, Theod. *Hist. eccl.* 5.30, Zos. 5.18.9–10. Contrary to Zosimos and the ecclesiastical historians, Gaïnas had no intention of destroying Constantinopolis or the empire or of assuming power himself (Syn. *Prov.* 1.15–18).

131. Syn. *Prov.* 2.1–2.

132. Zosimos describes Fravitta 'by birth a barbarian, but otherwise a Hellene [viz. pagan] not only in habits, but also in character and religion' (5.20.3).

133. Eunap. frs. 81–2, Philostorg. 11.8, Zos. 5.19.6–21.4, J Ant. fr. 190, Sok. 6.6, Soz. 8.4. Fravitta himself would eventually fall foul of the court in Constantinopolis; he was

accused by Aelia Eudoxia's favourite Hierax of some crime and executed (Eunap. frs. 85–7).

134. Zos. 5.21.9–22.2, J Ant. fr. 190, Soz. 8.4.

135. His name is given variously: Uldin (Oros. 7.37.12), Uldes (Zos. 5.22.3), Uldis (Soz. 9.5), Huldin (Jord. *Rom.* §321).

136. Zos. 5.22.3. For a summary of Gaïnas' career, *vide* Wolfram 1988: 148–50. After the revolt, Arcadius erected the Column of Arcadius, on which a spiralling frieze of reliefs depicted *his* triumph over Gaïnas and the Gothic *foederati* rebels. Destroyed by an earthquake in 1719, only its massive masonry base survives.

137. Amm. Marc. 39.3.7.

138. *ND occ.* XXVIII.23, XXXVI.7.

139. Ibid. VII. The first recorded *comes Britanniarum* was Gratianus Funarius, the father of Valentinianus I, who started his military career right at the bottom as a *pedes*. Famed for his great physical strength and skill at wrestling in the soldiers' fashion – he was, as Ammianus Marcellinus aptly puts it, 'a second Milo of Croton' (30.7.3) – the elder Gratianus had risen from the ranks to become successively *protector*, *tribunus* and *comes Africae*; accused of peculation, he remained under a cloud, only to later be given the command in Britannia.

140. Amm. Marc. 23.3.5. In 358, as *dux Aegypti*, Sebastianus expelled bishop Athanasios I (r. 328–339, 346–373) from Alexandria (Athan. *Hist. Ar.* 59–70, Soz. 4.10–11).

141. Amm. Marc. 23.3.5, 24.7.8, 25.8.7, 16, 26.6.2, Zos. 3.12.5, Lib. *Or.* 18.214.

142. Amm. Marc. 27.10.6, 10, 15.

143. Ibid. 30.5.13.

144. Ibid. 30.10.3.

145. Ibid. 31.11.1, Zos. 4.22.4, 23.1, Eunap. fr. 47.

146. Amm. Marc. 31.13.18, Lib. *Or.* 24.3. For the career and titles of Sebastianus see *PLRE* I, p.813. Ammianus Marcellinus, who knew him personally, describes Sebastianus as 'a quiet and peace-loving man' and 'a commander of well-known vigilance' (30.10.3, 31.11.1), but does also admit that Sebastianus exaggerated his exploits (31.12.1). At Adrianopolis Sebastianus was the principal officer who advised Valens not to wait until the forces of Gratianus arrived before bringing the Goths to battle (ibid. 12.6). In retrospect, of course, it was the wrong counsel.

147. *AE* 1934, 193.

148. E.g. *C Th.* XV.1.13.

149. E.g. ibid. VII.1.9.

150. Ibid. 22.5.

151. Ibid. VI.23.1, 24.11.

152. Their full title, *protector lateris divini Augusti nostri*, appears in an inscription in Ephemeris Epigraphica, v. 121 (no. 4).

153. Jones 1964: 53–4, de Blois 1976: 85.

154. Amm. Marc. 14.7.9, 16.5.3.

155. Ibid. 18.3.5.

156. Ibid. 15.5.22.

157. Veg. 2.7.

158. Amm. Marc. 14.7.18, 15.5.9.

159. Ibid. 14.10.8, 30.5.19.

160. Veg. 2.9.

161. Ibid. 4.32.
162. Evagr. 2.1. According to Jordanes, when Marcianus became emperor in 450 he saved 'the realm that his dainty predecessors, ruling turn by turn for almost sixty years, had made small' (*Regnum quod delicati decessores prodecessoresque eius per annos fere sexaginta vicissim imperantes minuerant...reparavit*, Rom. §332), that is, from Arcadius and Honorius, through Theodosius II to Valentinianus III.
163. At the time of writing, while the military is among the most trusted public institutions in many European countries, this does not mean that a career in the military is considered particularly appealing or prestigious. And so far, the Russia-Ukraine war has led to a recruitment slump, rather than a rise, among European militaries, despite government campaigns.
164. *C Th.* VII.23.1.
165. Ibid.1.5, dating to 364. On sons following father see also *ILS* 2777, 2787, 2805, Amm. Marc. 14.10.2.
166. *C Th.* VII.22.1.
167. Sulp. Sev. *V Mart.* 2.2–5.
168. Ibid. 4.1. It is known that at the age of 18 (around 354) Martin was stationed at Samarobiva Ambianorum (Amiens, France), which happened to be the birthplace of the usurper Magnus Magnentius.
169. *C Th.* VII.1.8, 22.9.
170. Ibid. 22.8, dating to 372.
171. Amm. Marc. 31.4.4.
172. Ibid. 14.11.7.
173. *C Th.* VII.13.7.
174. Ibid. 22.2.
175. Ibid. 13.1, see also Jones 1964: 616.
176. *C Th.* VII.13.3, cf. Veg. 1.5. From the third century onwards, the Roman foot measured 294.2mm as opposed to the imperial foot of 304.8mm.
177. *C Th.* VII.22.8.
178. Ibid. 18.9.1, dating to 396.
179. *Vita Pachomius* §4.
180. *C Th.* VII.18.4.3.
181. Ibid. 18.2.
182. Ibid. 18.4, 13.
183. Ibid. 18.4.
184. *Dig.* XXXIX.1.42.
185. *C Th.* X.22.4.
186. *Vide* Suet. *Calig.* 27.3 (*stigmatum notis*), *C Th.* IX.4.20 (*scribatur*).
187. Veg. 1.8, 2.5. *Vide* Jones 1987, who rightly argues that later Roman soldiers were tattooed (viz. *stigmata* are tattoos and not brand-marks).
188. Cassius Dion was the grandson or great-grandson of his namesake the historian, whose family originated in Bithynia. He was *consul posterior* (291), *pro consule* of Africa (294–295) and *praefectus urbis Romae* (296–297).
189. That is, not quite 5ft 8in or 1.72m.
190. *Acta Maximiliani* 1.2–5, apud H.A. Musurillo (ed. & trans.), *The Acts of the Christian Martyrs* (Oxford, 2000/1972), chap. 17, pp.244–9. However, Musurillo translates *signetur* as 'the military seal'.

191. Ibid. 1.1.
192. Ibid. 2.5.
193. Ibid. 2.1.
194. *Dig.* XLIX.16.4.10.
195. *Acta Maximiliani* 3.1.
196. Brock 1994: 199–200.
197. *Acta Maximiliani* 2.3.
198. Ibid. 3.4. Cyprianus had preached a gospel of non-violence, though he had employed a military vocabulary that sometimes jarred with his peaceable message. On the one hand he denounced war and its horrors. On the other his attitude to the question of military service was ambiguous. He too was sentenced to die by the sword.
199. Maximilianus' feast day is observed on 12 March. Around six decades or so later, Martin, according to his hagiographer Sulpicius Severus, having thus far served the emperor (viz. Constantius II) in his army and wishing hereafter to serve God and lead an ascetic life, had declared before the eve of battle (viz. under Caesar Iulianus) '*Christus ego miles sum; pugnare mihi non licet*' (*V Mart.* 4.3). When taxed with cowardice, Martin volunteered to stand in front of the battleline armed only with a cross. But then, according to legend, the enemy surrendered immediately.
200. Jones 1987: 149. The *signaculum* was presented to the recruit (*tiro*) at the moment of enrolment; it was inscribed with his name and the name of the *legio* of which he was a member. It was stamped on the reverse to authenticate it. The first 'dog tags' we know of in history belonged to the Spartans. They wrote their names on split sticks tied to their left wrist; the left arm of course bore the *aspís*.
201. Aetius 8.12, apud A. Olivieri (ed.), *Corpus Medicorum Graecorum* VIII 2 (Berlin, 1950), pp.417–18.
202. Veg. 1.8 (*Signatis itaque tironibus*).
203. *C Th.* VII.22.8.
204. Ibid. 22.2.
205. Ibid. 13.4, dating to 367. The practice is attested, but as a rarity, in the reigns of Augustus (Suet. *Aug.* 24.1) and Traianus (*Dig.* XLIX.16.4.12).
206. *C Th.* VII.13.5, dating to 368.
207. Ibid. 13.10.
208. Amm. Marc. 15.12.3.
209. *C Th.* VII.13.16, issued 17 April 406.
210. Ibid. 13.8, 11.
211. Ibid. 13.17, issued 19 April 406.
212. Jones 1964: 244.
213. *ILS* 2788.
214. Ibid. 2805, dating to 327.
215. *C Th.* VII.22.2.
216. *CIL* III.14406A, V.8740, 8758, J. Lyd. *De mag.* 1.48, 3.2.7, 21.
217. Veg. 2.8.
218. *CIL* V.8760, VIII.17414.
219. *C Th.* VI.24.7, 8, 9. *C Ius.* I.27.2, XII.29.2.
220. The name of the city is linked to the memory of Iulius Caesar and of Octavianus and celebrates the entente in 42 BC between the *triumviri*.

221. *CIL* V.8737, 8739–40, 8743–44, 8750–3, 8759, 8761, 8767, 8776. They are housed in the Museo Nazionale Concordiese di Portogruaro, Veneto. *Vide* Hoffman 1963, Lettich 1983.

222. *CIL* V.8773. Found in June 2018, a grave-marker bearing a Latin inscription highlighted in red (the original paint survives) from a later Roman cemetery in Ljubljana (Emona) mentions Harietonis, a *campidoctor* in the *numerus invictorum seniores*. Dated to the last quarter of the fourth century or the early part of the fifth century, the slab is housed in the Mestini Muzej. Ammianus Marcellinus (15.3.10) knew of a former *campidoctor* who was now serving as a *tribunus*. The *Batavi* were found in the *auxilia palatina* (*ND occ.* V.163, 186), *vexillationes palatinae* (ibid. VI.147, 51), as *cohortes* in Raetia (ibid. XXXV.24) and Britannia (ibid. XL.39) and as *laeti* (ibid. XLII.34, 40, 41).

223. Aurelius Victor (*Caes.* 39.15) notes that when Diocletianus gained the epithet *Iovius* for his worship of the god, and likewise Maximianus *Herculius*, two *legiones*, which stood out in the army, also gained these two honorary titles.

Chapter Four

1. The exact number of porphyry blocks is disputed, but common figures range from seven up to as many as eleven. Pierre Gilles (*De topographia Constantinopoleos*, 3.3), for example, opts for eight blocks, while Edward Gibbon (*D&F* vol. 1, ch. 17, p.441) plumps for ten.

2. Like many of his recent soldierly predecessors Lucius Domitius Aurelianus, to give him his full and proper name, was of humble provincial origins. He was born in Illyria of peasant stock (9 September 214 or 215), although his mother was said to have been a priestess of Sol Invictus. This story was undoubtedly put out much later when Sol Invictus became the most important deity for Aurelianus, to the divine assistance of whom he had attributed his remarkable run of victories, especially in the east. Consequently, the emperor elevated the sun god to one of the premier divinities of the empire and erected a new temple for Sol in Rome, which was dedicated on 25 December 274; that is, on the feast of the winter solstice, thereafter known as *dies Invicti Natalis*. Thus the *Chronographus Anni CCCLIIII* of Furius Dionysius Filocalus gives the festival of NATALIS INVICTI on 25 December (Part 6). The same calendar also mentions the birth of Jesus Christ, stating that the 'Lord Jesus Christ was born eight days before the kalends of January on the day of Venus Moon 15' (Part 8); that is, on 25 December. See also, Iul. *Or.* 4.156B-C. The identity of Aurelianus' sun god remains highly controversial. For this, *vide* Watson 2004: 193–6.

3. Zon. 13.3, cf. Anna Komnene *Alexiad* 12.4.5.

4. Kedren. 1.564–5.

5. Virgil *Aeneid* 2.166.

6. On the Forum of Constantinus and the column, *vide* Janin 1964: 62–4, 79.

7. *C Ius.* III.12.2. Note the Jewish Sabbath (Friday sunset to Saturday sunset) was a day of freedom for all people, regardless of occupation. This extends to farmers too, 'even during the ploughing season and harvest' (Exodus 34:21 NIV). Note Augustus granted the Jewish people freedom to keep the Sabbath from Friday 15.00 hours until Sabbath ended; apparently Claudius did the same (Joseph. *AJ* 16.6.2, 19.5.3). A law (*C Th.* XVI.8.20) enacted in the early fifth century mentions that earlier emperors had granted protection to the Jewish people for the Sabbath. It is assumed that Constantinus was among them.

8. On 3 July 321 Constantinus issued his second Sunday law, granting people (again in the cities) freedom from most kinds of legal business on the day. However, proceedings to free slaves were allowed (*C Th.* II.8.1).

9. *Vide* Ignatius, bishop of Antioch, writing in 110, advocates the idea that Christians should observe the Lord's Day every Sunday rather than the Jewish Sabbath on Saturdays: 'If, therefore, those who were brought up in the ancient order of things have come to the possession of a new hope, no longer observing the Sabbath, but living in the observance of the Lord's Day, on which also our life has sprung up again by Him and by His death...' (*Epistle to the Magnesians* 9).

10. Euseb. *V Const.* 4.18.1, 2.

11. E.g. Soz. 1.8. Note also the Council of Laodikeia (363–364), a regional Christian synod of some thirty clerics from Asia Minor, outlawed the keeping of the Sabbath and encouraged rest on Sunday: 'But if any shall be found to be judaisers, let them be anathema from Christ' (Canon 29). Yet many Christians in the East still observed the Sabbath: 'There are many among us now, who fast on the same day as the Jews, and keep the Sabbaths in the same manner' (Chrys. *Galat.* 1.7, cf. Aug. *Ep.* 82.14, Soz. 7.19, Sok. 5.22, 6.8).

12. In Greek the dominant meaning of παγανός/*paganós* meant 'civilian' as opposed to 'military', there being no need for a new term for pagan as the word 'Greek' – Ἕλλην/ *Hellēn* – had for some time been the normal Christian expression. In the Latin-speaking West, however, Christians referred to those 'outside' their community, viz. non-Christians, as *pagani*. Purists might object to the use of the term 'pagan', but there is no workable alternative. Besides, 'pagan' is by far the simplest, most familiar and most apposite term. *Vide* Cameron 2013: 14–25.

13. Euseb. *Tric.* 16.4.

14. Ibid. *V Const.* 1.21.

15. *Anon. Vales.* 2 §4, Euseb. *Hist. eccl.* 8.13, Iul. *Or.* 1.13, Zos. 2.9, Sok. 1.2.1, cf. Lact. *De mort. pers.* 24.8.

16. SHA *Carus, Carinus et Numerianus* 18.4.

17. [Aur. Vict.] *Epit.* 49–50.

18. Lact. *De mort. pers.* 25.

19. Euseb. *V Const.* 2.28, 2.24–42 for the complete letter, cf. Soz. 1. 8 for an epitome.

20. Euseb. *V Const.* 4.9.

21. Originally built in 109 BC, the Pons Mulvius, or Ponte Milvio as it is now known, still stands, though it has been many times rebuilt and restored, most recently by Pope Pius IX in 1850 after Garibaldi (1807–82) had blown it up in the year before. In February 1849, some nineteen centuries after its demise, the Roman Republic was revived. In France the ambitious new president of the Second Republic, Louis-Napoléon Bonaparte (before long Napoléon III, *l'empereur des Français*), dispatched an army to restore the pope and 'liberate' Rome from the handful of dangerous radicals who, as he saw it, had forced themselves upon the unwilling citizens. On 27 April Garibaldi led his followers into Rome through streets packed with people shouting his name. He entered the city riding a white horse and wearing a black slouch hat and a swirling white poncho, which was flung back to show his celebrated red shirt. Behind him clattered his 'brigand-band' of red-shirted followers, the Garibaldini (this idiosyncratic shirt had evolved, six years earlier, out of a requisitioned stock of bright red overalls destined for slaughterhouse

workers). The Roman commander was General Giuseppe Avezzana (1797–1879), an Italian businessman and soldier who had fought in the revolutionary wars of Europe and the Americas, and of the almost 20,000 men under his command, the Garibaldini constituted only a small fraction, but Giuseppe Garibaldi is remembered as the defender of the brief Roman Republic.

22. Eutr. 10. 2, Zos. 2. 9, Sok. 1.2.

23. In 2012, with a hotchpotch of civic pride, football populism and political conviction, the then mayor of Rome (2008–13), Gianni Alemanno, a politician with a neo-fascist background, organized the celebrations for the 1700th anniversary of the battle of the Pons Mulvius. 'That battle,' stressed Alemanno, 'represents an epochal transition not only for Rome, but for the whole of Christianity, regarded as the bedrock of European civilization and identity' (*Ponte Milvio, celebrazioni per i 1700 anni della battaglia*, http:// terpag.blogspot.it/2012/10/ponte-milvio-celebrazioni-per-i-1700.htm). According to the mayor, 'such an important event in the history of humanity' had to be remembered not in an 'oversimplified way' but 'with uprightness, seriousness and sobriety' (*Anno 312, Costantino vince a Ponte Milvio il Campidoglio celebra l'anniversario, La Repubblica*, 25 Octobre 2012, http://roma.repubblica.it/cronaca/2012/10/25/news/alemanno - 45300935.htm).

24. Euseb. *V Const.* 1.28–9.

25. Most scholars agree that Eusebius is describing the *labarum* as it appeared after 326, based on the description that he gives at *Vita Constantini* 1.30–1; specifically the mention of the head-and-shoulders portrait of Constantinus and his sons in some relation to the tapestry hanging from the transverse bar.

26. Jer. *Chron.* s.a. 318 (230e), *vir. ill.* 80.

27. Lact. *De mort. pers.* 44.5.

28. *Pan. Lat.* 12 (9) passim.

29. *Pan. Lat.* 12 (9).2.4, 5, 4.1, 2, 5, 13.2, 16.2, 22.1, 26.1.

30. Ibid. 3.3.

31. Euseb. *Hist. eccl.* 9.9.2.

32. *Pan. Lat.* 12 (9).17.2.

33. Euseb. *Hist. eccl.* 9.9.5–6.

34. According to Lactantius, no friend of the pagan Maxentius, he was tempted by a dubious Sibylline prophecy: 'On the same day the enemy of the Romans would perish' (*De mort. pers.* 44.8), which thus prompted Maxentius to quit Rome and meet Constantinus in pitched battle.

35. Ibid. 44.9.

36. Euseb. *Hist. eccl.* 9.9.17 passim.

37. [Aur. Vict.] *Epit.* 40.6.

38. Euseb. *Hist. eccl.* 9.9.5, Aur. Vict. *Caes.* 40.23, Zos. 2.16.2–4.

39. Lact. *De mort. pers.* 44.9 ('The hand of God was over the battleline'), Euseb. *Hist. eccl.* 9.9.

40. *Pan. Lat.* 12 (9).16 passim.

41. Euseb. *V Const.* 1.28.

42. Iul. *Or.* 2.37B.

43. Lact. *De mort. pers.* 45.1, Aur. Vict. *Caes.* 41.2, [Aur. Vict.] *Epit.* 41.4, Euseb. *Hist. eccl.* 10.8.2, *V Const.* 1.49–50, Zos. 2.45.1, Soz. 1.6, Zon. 12.34. Flavia Iulia Constantia, one of the six children of Constantius I Chlorus and Flavia Maximiana Theodora

(Eutr. 9.22.1) and half-sister to Constantinus I (his mother was Helena). Constantia had been betrothed to Licinianus in the winter of 311/312 (Lact. *De mort. pers.* 43.2, Zos. 2.17.2). Being an Arian, Constantia tried to have her bishops refuse assent to the decrees of the Nicaea council, 325 (Philostorg. 1.9). Gaza was renamed after her (Euseb. *V Const.* 4.38).

44. Euseb. *Hist. eccl.* 10.5.2, 4–5, 8, Lact. *De mort. pers.* 48, [Aur. Vict.] *Epit.* 39.7, 41.4.

45. According to the eyewitness testimony of Lactantius (*De mort. pers.* 48), the decree refers to 'the Christians' and 'now any one of these who wishes to observe Christian religion, may do so freely and openly, without molestation', and though it refers to God and 'the Deity', it is written as if referring to an all-encompassing spiritual figure.

46. Euseb. *V Const.* 1.58–9, Aur. Vict. *Caes.* 41, Zos. 2.17.

47. Zos. 2.25–6.

48. Lact. *De mort. pers.* 47–50.

49. *Anon. Vales.* 5 §29, Eutr. 10.5 [Aur. Vic.] *Epit.* 41.7, Zos. 2.28.2, Zon. 13.1, cf. Euseb. *V Const.* 2.58–9.

50. Licinianus Iunior had been adopted (*C Th.* IV.6.2).

51. Eutr. 10.6.

52. Soz. 2.3, Zos. 2.30.1, cf. Zon. 13.3. The reason why it was abandoned, albeit after the erection of part of the walls, is obvious: by then, the great bay that had been the *raison d'être* for Troy's existence for more than three millennia had silted up and ceased to exist. Troy no longer guarded and controlled the entrance to 'the hard-running passage of Helle' (Hom. *Il.* 12.30 Lattimore).

53. Philostorg. 2.9. Was Constantinus consciously imitating Alexander the Great, for legend has it that Alexander himself, accompanied by his engineers and architects, traced out the outlines of his new city of Alexander-by-Egypt?

54. *Anon. Vales.* 6 §30.

55. The names Istanbul and Stamboul are corruptions of the Greek εις την πόλιν, *eis tin pólin*, meaning 'into the city' or 'to the city', a phrase that is still used today by Greeks when referring to the Christian imperial capital once known as Κωνσταντινούπολις.

56. In his earlier, hedonistic days Augustine had offered up the famous prayer 'Grant me chastity and continence – but not yet' (*Conf.* 8.7 §17).

57. Euseb. *V Const.* 4.61.2–62.4, Jer. *Chron.* s.a. 337 (234a).

58. Kedren. p.476.5–15. Whether his mother Helena was Constantius' legal first wife or merely a concubine is in doubt. Some have asserted that Helena was a woman 'indifferent honest' (Zos. 2. 8), and the birth of Constantinus illegitimate, others that she was legally his wife (Eutr. 10.2, Euseb. *Hist. eccl.* 8.13). It is, however, undisputed that Helena was of very humble origins, and that Constantinus' father Constantius later married Flavia Maximiana Theodora, daughter of the emperor Maximianus. Far better known than her partner, Helena famously went on pilgrimage to Jerusalem aged 80, where Christian tradition has it that she discovered the True Cross. Eusebius, bishop of Caesarea Palestinae, did not refer to the True Cross in his *Vita Constantini*, and it was Ambrose, bishop of Mediolanum (r. 374–397), who was responsible for linking the legend of its discovery to Helena. His Latin account, which is a funeral oration for Theodosius I (25 February 395), is the earliest version and thought to be the most original rendering of this celebrated but unhistorical divine event. According to Ambrose, Helena found the *titulus*, the wooden plaque bearing the inscription

IESUS NAZARENUS REX IDUDAEORUM, which Pontius Pilate had ordered to be attached to Jesus' cross (John 19:19, cf. Matthew 27:37), along with 'three crosses in disarray'. Helena also found the nails of the Crucifixion, which she sent to Constantinopolis (Ambr. *Obit. Theod.* §§40–9, cf. Sok. 1.7). Writing two years after Ambrose, Rufinus of Aquileia (10.7–8) adds that a piece of the cross itself was sent to Constantinus in Constantinopolis. According to bishop Theodoretos of Kyrrhos, 'She [Helena] had part of the cross of our Saviour conveyed to the palace. The rest was enclosed in a covering of silver, and committed to the care of the bishop of the city, whom she exhorted to preserve it carefully, in order that it might be transmitted uninjured to posterity' (*Hist. eccl.* 17). Helena was born probably at Drépanon, Bithynia, afterwards renamed Helenopolis in her honour by Constantinus (Prokop. *De aedif.* 5.2). In a conceit dating to Geoffrey of Monmouth (c. 1095–1155) Helena is made to be the daughter of Coel of Camulodunum (Colchester, England), a Roman client king and the legendary 'Old King Coel' of the popular nursery rhyme.

59. [Aur. Vict.] *Epit.* 41.14, 16.
60. Sue. *Caes.* 45.3.
61. Euseb. *L Const.* 5.6.
62. Jacob Burckhardt, *Die Zeit Constantins des Großen* (rev. ed. Leipzig, 1880).
63. Otto Seeck, *Geschicte des Untergangs der antiken Welt*, 6 Bände (Stuttgart, 1895–1920).
64. Constantinus died on 22 May 337, on Pentecost, after becoming seriously ill two months earlier, just before Easter (Euseb. *V Const.* 4.64). On his deathbed he explained to a gathering of bishops that he had always wanted to be baptized in the Jordan but that in view of his illness it was too late for that now. The honour of baptizing the first Christian emperor fell to Eusebius, bishop of Nicomedia (not to be confused with Eusebius the bishop writer from Caesarea). Not everybody was happy with this choice as there were stories that Eusebius was a follower of the 'heresies' of Arius. As for infant baptism, it was Augustine who promoted this doctrine (*vide* ch. 7 of *Confessiones*), which cancelled, *ex opere operato*, birth sin and hereditary guilt, that is to say, while infants have no sins of their own, they inherit original sin. This is the sin entered into the world by Adam, as Paul of Tarsus explains: 'Therefore, just as sin entered the world through one man, and death came to all men, because all sinned' (Romans 5:12 NIV, cf. Aug. *Conf.* 10.20 §29). Following the custom of the time in the Church, Augustine was not baptized as a child, although he had been enrolled among the catechumens. Jerome too, likewise born a Christian, was not baptized until his mid-20s or possibly even his early 30s, while Synesios was simultaneously baptized and ordained as a bishop (Syn. *Ep.* 105).
65. The bulk of Tertullian's thoughts and beliefs are contained in his homily *De baptismo*.
66. Thompson 2014: 14.
67. *Pan. Lat.* 6 (7).21.3–7, 22.1.
68. Constantinus frequently used the legend SOL INVICTO COMITI, claiming the 'Unconquered Sun' as his companion. The last inscription (*CIL* VI.1778) referring to Sol Invictus dates to 387, and there were enough devotees in the following century that Augustine (*Sermones* 12) found it necessary to fulminate against.
69. Euseb. *V Const.* 1.28–32.
70. Acts 26:13 NIV.

71. The story of the vision of Paul occurs three times in Acts of the Apostles, at 9:1–19, 22:1–21 and 26:9–21, and although the experience is not told in exactly the same way each time, all three versions have strong continuities.

72. Van Dam 2007: 11. IMPERATOR • CAESAR • AUGUSTUS • CONSUL • PRO CONSULE • PONTIFEX MAXIMVS • MAGNVS • MAXIMVS • PIVS • FELIX • FIEDELIS • MANSVETVS • BENIFICVS • CLEMENTISSIMVS • VICTOR • INVICTVS • TRIUMPHATOR • SALVS REI PVBLICAE • BETICVS • ALMANNICVS • GOTHICVS • SARMATICUS • GERMANICVS • BRITANNICVS • HUNNICVS • GALLICANVS is a portion of his title, as gathered from coins, inscriptions and various documents.

73. Voltaire, *Dictionnaire philosophique* (London, 2004), p.48, sv Arius. Apparently, according to Lactantius, Diocletianus once referred to Constantinus as 'that dancing, carousing drunkard who turns night into day and day into night' (*De mort. pers.* 18).

74. Iul. *Caes.* 335–6.

75. Soz. 2.3, cf. Iul. *Or.* 1.8.

76. In 320 Constantinus ruled that the clergy and their families did not have to pay taxes (*C Th.* XVI.2.10).

77. Amm. Marc. 21.16.18.

78. Jer. *Ep.* 22.28.

79. Jer. *Vita Malchi* praef. apud *PL* 23.55.

80. E.g. Anna Komnene (*Alexiad* 14.8) would confidently call Constantinus the Thirteenth Apostle, and likens him to her father, the emperor Alexios I Komnenos (r. 1081–1118).

81. At some point, 21 May became the day when the Orthodox Church remembered the emperor and his mother as οἱ ἅγιοι Κωνσταντίνος καὶ Ἑλένη οἱ Ἰσαπόστολοι. In the modern Orthodox liturgy, the *tropárion*, the short verse chanted towards the close of vespers to set the theme for the services of the coming day, includes the following: 'He saw the image of the Cross in the heavens,/and, like Paul, he did not receive his call from men, O Lord./Your apostle among rulers, the emperor Constantinus,/was appointed by Your hand as ruler over the imperial City/that he preserved in peace for many years,/through the prayers of the Theotokos, O only lover of mankind.' The Theotokos (Gk. Θεοτόκος) is the Blessed Virgin Mary as the 'God-bearer'. The title explains the nature of Christ as both divine (*theo-*) and human (*-tolkos*, 'born').

82. This was probably a morganatic marriage or concubinage ([Aur. Vic.] *Epit.* 41, Zos. 2.20; Zon. 13.2). The improbability that Constantinus should have marked out an illegitimate son as his successor as the only argument against this is reduced to a minimum in view of Constantinus' law for the legitimization of natural children by rescript (*C Ius.* V.27).

83. Aur. Vict. *Caes.* 41.11.

84. Jer. *Chron.* s.a. 328 (232a).

85. *C Ius.* V.26, issued 14 June 326.

86. Philostorg. 2.4.

87. Zos. 2.29.1.

88. Ibid. 2.29.2, Zon. 13.2.5D.

89. Soz. 1.5. Sopateros had been a disciple of Iamblichos (Eunap. *VS* 462), and as a close confidant of Constantinus had assisted in the foundation of Constantinopolis (J Lyd. *De mens.* 4.2) and had been connected with his conversion to Christianity (Soz. 1.5). However, when the Egyptian grain ships did not reach the capital, the people blamed

Sopateros and, at the urging of Flavius Ablabios (cos. 331), the current *vicarius Asianae* (324–326), Constantinus had him put to death (Zos. 2.40.3, Eunap. *VS* 462).

90. *CIL* II.4107, III.7172, V.8021, 8030, 9.6386, *ILS* 708, 710.

91. Zos. 2.20.2, Aur. Vict. *Caes.* 41.6, [Aur. Vict.] *Epit.* 41.4. Note Crispus was 'already a young man' when made *Caesar* (Zos. 2.30).

92. *Pan. Lat.* 4 (10).17, 36.

93. Euseb. *Hist. eccl.* 10.9.4, 6, Zos. 2.22–3, Zon. 13.2, Iul. *Or.* 1.9D.

94. Sid. Apoll. *Ep.* 5.8.2.

95. [Aur. Vict.] *Epit.* 41.20, cf. Zos. 2.39.1, who claims the three sons were bastards.

96. Genesis 4:16. The Hebrew *nōd* best translates as 'wandering' (*vide* Genesis 4:12, 14, Psalm 56:8). Augustine describes unconverted Jews as dwellers in the land of Nod, which he defines as 'the land of commotion, that is, of carnal disquietude' (*contra Faustum* 12.13).

97. Livy 1.7.3.

Chapter Five

1. Charles-Maurice de Talleyrand-Périgord, *Correspondance inédite du Prince du Talleyrand et du Roi Louis XVIII* (1881), p.22. At the Congress of Vienna Talleyrand replied to the criticism of Tsar Alexander I of Russia of those who 'betrayed the cause of Europe'; often quoted as 'treason is a matter of dates'.

2. Amm. Marc. 30.6, Sok. 4.3.6, Soz. 6.36.

3. Amm. Marc. 30.5.13, 17, Zos. 4.17.1. Merobaudes had served as an officer with Iulianus and was one of those who escorted his body back to Tarsus where he was buried near that of the Tetrarch Maximinus Daia (Philostorg. 8.1), another passionate pagan who lost out in Constantinus' rapid rise to the top. It was perhaps Iovianus who ordered the following epitaph: 'By the silvery Kydnos, coming from the streams of the Euphrates/ and the land of Persia, after launching his army/on a task it did not complete, Iulianus found this tomb./He was a good emperor and a brave warrior' (Zon. 13.13.24, Kedren. p.539, 6–9, cf. Zos. 3.34.3).

4. [Aur. Vict.] *Epit.* 45.10, Rufin. 2.12, Sok. 4.31, Soz. 6.36.

5. Amm. Marc. 30.10.2–3, Zos. 4.19.1.

6. Amm. Marc. 27.6.1–3.

7. With Merobaudes there begins a line of commanders who rivalled and often surpassed the emperor in power. It is a formidable line, and their existence complicates any simplistic image of the western half of the empire as a basket case. It begins with Arbogastes, followed by Stilicho, who practically governed the western empire (394–408), followed by Constantius (411–421), whose victories enabled the empire to recover from the Alaric crisis, and who married Galla Placidia, the daughter of Theodosius, and during the last months of his life held the rank of *Augustus*. Beyond our period of study there was Flavius Aëtius (435–454) whose victories postponed the collapse of the imperial organization in Gaul. He was followed by the *magister militum* Flavius Ricimer (456–472), the son of a Suevic father and Visigothic mother, who took a decisive part in the deposition of the emperor Avitus (r. 455–456) – he had been installed by the Visigothic king Theodoric II (r. 453–466) following the Vandal sack of Rome – and subsequently played a leading part first in the appointment and then in the deposition and murder of the emperors Maiorianus (r. 457–461), Libius Severus

(r. 461–465) and Anthemius (r. 467–472), whose daughter Alypia Ricimer married. As an Arian and a '*barbarus*' Ricimer could not aspire to the throne, but puppet emperors would serve his purposes well enough. In 472 Ricimer, the *patricius* (a title he had held since 457) who no emperor could satisfy in the long run, brought about the fall and assassination of his father-in-law. A few weeks later Ricimer himself would be dead, possibly of tuberculosis, and before the end of the year the emperor he had set up, the accommodating senator Olybrius, was also no more. Next up was the *magister militum* Orestes (475–476), a Roman from Pannonia who boasted of having been the personal secretary of Attila, and then finally the Scirian Odovacer (r. 476–493) who deposed Romulus Augustulus (r. 475–476, †511), the son of Orestes and last emperor of the West, who reigned as the first 'barbarian' king of Italy for the rest of his life. The year 476 was not the end of the Roman Empire, of course, but it was a definite turning-point because the emperors of the West exited the world stage and were replaced by the kings of Germanic kingdoms. In this sense, therefore, the West can be declared to be past tense.

8. *PLRE* I, pp.598–9.
9. Merobaudes seems to have transferred his allegiance to Magnus Maximus (he was *cons. desig.* 388), and his subsequent suicide was probably connected to this change of loyalty (Pac. 28.4).
10. Sok. 5.25.1.
11. Zos. 4.54.1, J Ant. fr. 187.
12. Soz. 4.54.1, Philostorg. 11.2. Vienne was called *Vienna* by the Romans – not to be confused with today's Vienna (German *Wien*), then known as *Vindobona* in Pannonia Prima. Vienne-*Vienna* is of course famous for the tradition that Pontius Pilate was buried there.
13. His actual Germanic name, *Arbogastiz*, is also otherwise attested; it is derived from the elements *arbo-* 'heir, inheritance' and *-gastiz*, 'guest, spirit'.
14. *Contra* Cameron 2013: 85–7, who invites us to consider the notion that Arbogastes was possibly a Christian.
15. Zos. 4.54.1, J Ant. fr. 187.
16. Amm. Marc. 31.7.4–5.
17. Ibid. 31.12.15–17.
18. Symm. *Ep.* 3.58, Themist. 16.201, *C Th.* VII.1.13.
19. Lib. *Or.* 1.219.
20. *C Th.* VII.1.13.
21. Philostorg. 10.8.
22. Zos. 4.55.2–3, J Ant. fr. 187.
23. The Alani, having migrated westward from Central Asia, are mentioned in the Vologases inscription, which informs us that Vologases (*Walagaš*) I of Parthia (r. 51–78) battled Kuluk, king of the Alani, in the eleventh year of his reign. The inscription is supplemented by Josephus, who reports the Alani crossed the Gates of Alexander (L *Caspia claustra*: Pass of Derbent, Russia, or Darial Gorge, Georgia-Russia border) seeking plunder and defeated the armies of Pakoros (*Pakur*) of Media Atropatene and Tiridates (*Tiridāt*) I of Armenia (r. 52–58, 62–88), two brothers of Vologases I: 'So the Alani...laid waste the country, and drove a great multitude of the men, and a great

quantity of the other booty from both kingdoms, along with them, and then retreated back to their own country' (Joseph. *B Iud.* 7.8.4), that is, north-east of the Caspian Sea. 'In their plundering and hunting expeditions', as Ammianus Marcellinus says of the Alani of his day, 'they roam here and there as far as the Maeotic Sea [Sea of Azov] and the Cimmerian Bosporus [Kerch Strait], and also to Armenia and Media' (31.2.21). Of course, in the history of the Alani the invasion of Media Atropatene and Armenia was an episode, albeit an important one. Two things can be learned from it. First, it shows what great distances the Alani were able to cover in one campaign. Second, the Alani carried away many men into captivity.

24. Ammianus Marcellinus (31.8.4) mentions in passing, among the horsemen that came to the dramatic rescue of the Goths penned in among the steep defiles of Mount Haemos in Thracia by a Roman army, a band of Huns (autumn 377). Now it is not reported that this band had left the Goths before Adrianopolis (summer 378). Immediately after the battle, when the Goths had a made a vain attempt to surprise Adrianopolis itself, we hear of these same Huns again. Ammianus says that the chief Gothic leader, Fritigern, 'had shrewdly won them to his side by the prospect of wonderful rewards' (31.16.3). In other words, this band of Huns joined the Goths as mercenaries. There could have been no more than a few hundred, probably operating as outriders for the main Gothic force, but they were the first Huns to reach Roman Europe.

25. Themist. 16.206d.

26. Amm. Marc. 31.13.19.

27. Ambr. *De fide* prologue.

28. *Romanae legiones usque ad internicionem caesae sunt a Gothis*, Jer. *Chron.* s.a. 379 (249c).

29. Rufin. 2.13.

30. The battle has itself been the subject of considerable reinterpretation. Burns (1973) describes it as an infantry battle, but others still persist in the myth of Gothic horsemen ushering in the mediaeval epoch and the dominance of heavy cavalry. It all began with Sir Charles Oman when he made the following bold statement: 'The military importance of Adrianople was unmistakable; it was a victory of cavalry over infantry' (*A History of the Art of War in the Middle Ages, AD 378–1485* [London, 1924], vol. 1, p.13). Bury (1957: 41–2) accepts the 'obvious' success of Gothic horsemen without question, as does Maenchen-Helfen when he states that 'Adrianople, one of the decisive battles of history, was won by *equitatus Gothorum*' (1973: 29). Wolfram, on the other hand, gives a more reasoned view: 'Above all, it is not true that Gothic horsemen were from this time invincible, and it is equally inaccurate to infer from the disaster of Adrianople a fundamental superiority of cavalry over infantry' (1988: 127). See also Williams-Friell: 1998: 152–6.

31. Dù Mù commentating on Sun Tzu *Art of War* 8.18 ('If reckless, he can be killed'). Dù Mù (803–52) was a Chinese calligrapher, poet and politician who wrote a commentary on *Art of War*.

32. Maurice de Saxe, *Mes Rêveries* (Edinburgh, 1759), bk. 2, ch. 12, p.221. The work is not just one of military theory, but also a treatise on military life, which de Saxe lived to the full.

33. At the battle of Fontenoy (11 May 1745), Maurice de Saxe, in spite of his illness (oedema caused by congestive heart failure), showed incredible courage not just in the face of shot and disaster, but in the face of his monarch too: Louis XV had come out

from his court at Versailles to watch the contest. Interestingly, de Saxe had an exotic escort of African bodyguards, like the Mamlük personal guard of Napoléon fifty-five years later.

34. Many of the powdered courtiers of Louis XV despised Maurice de Saxe as an upstart Lutheran foreigner (Hermann Moritz von Sachsen was Saxon, after all, one of the many illegitimate children of Augustus II the Strong, King of Poland and Elector of Saxony); they were jealous of his favour with their young king and his (to them) undeserved promotion to *maréchal de France* ('carpet generals' as de Saxe disparaged them, more useful at court ceremonial than fighting).

35. Before serving France, Maurice de Saxe had fought under Prince Eugene of Savoy (sieges of Tournai and Mons, and the battle of Malplaquet), Peter the Great (against the Swedes), and Emperor Charles VI (against the Ottomans), as well as under his father (siege of Stralsund and the battle of Gadebusch). During the War of the Polish Succession (1733–35), he fought for France against Saxony, plus Russia and Austria, an indication of the loose national ties that bound members of the European aristocracy of that time. Generally, officers were all noble-born, or at least 'gentlemen', and the French army became so strict that a man could rarely secure even the lowest commission unless his ancestors had been nobles for several generations.

36. Heather 2007: 181.

37. Believed to be immediately south of the Turkish village of Muratçali, 16km north of the centre of Edirne (MacDowall 2001: 68, cf. Runkel 1903).

38. Amm. Marc. 31.12.3.

39. Elton 1997: 15–88.

40. Liebeschuetz 1991: 48–85, 1992. As a healthy antidote to trusting war record totals, see especially H. Delbrück, *Numbers in History* (London, 1913).

41. See especially Heather 1991: 122–56, 193–226.

42. Amm. Marc. 31.12.11.

43. Claud. *In Ruf. II* 127–9, cf. *IV Cons.* 466, *Cons. Stil. I* 94–5, *B Goth.* 83, 604. Vegetius tells us that the barbarians (viz. Goths, Alani, Huns) of his day 'spend nights from attack behind their wagons linked together in a circle like a military camp' (3.10).

44. Amm. Marc. 31.12.17.

45. In his detailed analysis of the *Notitia Dignitatum*, Hoffman (1969: 452) concluded that many infantry units were shattered at Adrianopolis and never re-established.

46. Greg. Naz. *Or.* 22.2.

47. According to Ambrose (*Obit. Theod.* §53), following the arrest and execution at Carthage (now a suburb of Tunis, Tunisia) in early 376 of the elder Theodosius, at the time holding the rank of *magister militum*, the life of the younger Theodosius was threatened by his father's enemies. Nothing is known of the reasons for this killing, but successful *magistri militum* could be a serious threat to a new emperor. It does appear that on his elevation Gratianus proceeded to rid himself of his father's associates.

48. Pac. 10.3–4, Theod. *Hist. eccl.* 5.5, Them. *Or.* 14, [Aur. Vict.] *Epit.* 47.3, 48.8, Soz. 7.2, 4, Zon. 13.17, cf. Zos. 4.24.4, who telescope summons by Gratianus and proclamation as emperor. *Vide* Jones 1964: 156.

49. *Pan. Lat.* 2 (12).32.2. Ten emperors/usurpers were born in or near Sirmium: Traianus Decius (r. 249–251), Herennius Etruscus (r. 251), Hostilianus (r. 251), Claudius II Gothicus (r. 268–270), Quintilus (r. 270), Aurelianus (r. 270–275), Probus (r. 276–282),

Maximianus (r. 286–305, 306–310), Constantius II (r. 337–361) and Gratianus (r. 367–383).

50. E.g. Veg. 2 praef. 'the conqueror of all barbarian races' (*domitori omnium gentium barbarorum*).

51. Before his father's death, Theodosius had commanded a frontier army as *dux* of Moesia Prima (374), where he had some success against the Sauromatae. Prior to this independent command, he had accompanied his father (and Magnus Maximus) to Britannia (368–369) to suppress the *barbarica conspiratio* that had capitalized on a depleted military force brought about by Magnentius' huge losses on the broad plains of Mursa (351) during his unsuccessful bid for the purple: Constantius' victory would be remembered for its appalling losses; 30,000 dead, it was alleged, from an army of 80,000. The elder Theodosius held the post of *comes rei militaris* and for the job was given by Valentinianus I four first-class disciplined units, the *auxilia palatina* pair of *Batavi seniores* and *Heruli seniores*, along with the *auxilia palatina* pair of *Iovii seniores* and *Victores seniores* (Amm. Marc. 27.8.1, 7, cf. 25.6.2–3, 26.7.13, 31.13.9). As for the *barbarica conspiratio*, Valentinianus was on the road to Augusta Treverorum (Trier, Germany) from Augustodunum (Autun, France) when news was brought to him of the utter chaos in Britannia. The various barbarian peoples that had been harassing both Britannia and the north-western seaboard of Gaul had suddenly combined to organize a concerted attack with the Picti, which are described by Ammianus Marcellinus as 'divided into two peoples, Dicalydonae and Verturiones' (27.8.5); cf. Ptolemaios (*Geographia* 2.3.8–12), the Attacotti and the Scotti assaulting Britannia, and the Franks and Saxones ravaging the coasts of Gaul. Such a *barbarica conspiratio* was extremely rare. In fact, if our reading of Ammianus is correct, this major incursion into the empire came by sea as well as by land. One threat was from the Scotti of 'ice-bound Hibernia', and perhaps also from the Attacotti, an otherwise little-known people. Another was from the Picti from Caledonia. A third was from those sea-raiders the Roman sources call *Saxones* but who appear to have included contingents from several peoples along what is now called the North Sea littoral from Frisia, Saxony and the Jutland peninsula. It is interesting to note that Zosimos (4.35.5), when he mentions the events of the previous year, speaks of small raiding parties attacking Britannia.

52. The names that are conventionally used to distinguish the Goths – 'Visigoths' and 'Ostrogoths' – are anachronistic. In the literary sources of the sixth and seventh centuries these Germanic peoples are just referred to as Goths. More significantly, quite different names for them were used before the fifth century. In literary sources of the mid-fourth century, two tribes were identified as dominating the region north of the Danuvius and the Euxine prior to the rise of the Hun hegemony, and these were known as the *Teruingi* and the *Greuthungi* (Amm. Marc. 31.3.1–13.19, 4.1–5).

53. Claud. *III Cons.* 66 (*barbarus exul*), *IV Cons.* 74 (*Germanus exul*).

54. *RE* Suppl. XII, 608–10, *magister militum*.

55. Zos. 4.33.1–2, 53.1, Eunap. fr. 53, Ambr. *Ep.* 24.8. There is no corroborative evidence for the claim of Ioannnes Antiochensis, perhaps on the basis of their shared Frankish heritage and his succession of Bauto as *magister militum*, that Arbogastes was 'the son of Bauto' (Βαύδωνος υἱος, fr. 187). Bauto, however, did have a daughter, Aelia Eudoxia. She was so thoroughly educated as a Roman that she later became wife of Arcadius and *Augusta* of the East (Zos. 5.3.2), and despite her Frankish paternity was closely associated with the anti-German reaction in Constantinopolis (Philostorg. 11.6).

Eudoxia married Arcadius on 27 April 395, bore him Flaccilla (27 June 397), Pulcheria (19 January 399), Arcadia (3 April 400), the future emperor Theodosius II (10 April 401) and Marina (10 February 403). Much like her father before her, Eudoxia was deeply involved in court politics. She was instrumental in the overthrow of the eunuch courtier Eutropius, the chief advisor to Arcadius (Philostorg. 11.6, Soz. 8.7), appointed *Augusta* (9 January 400), and henceforth was the main power in the East. Notorious for bribery (Zos. 5.25.4, Zon. 13.20), influenced by eunuchs and women (Zos. 5.24.2), suspected of adultery (ibid. 5.18.8). She supported the Nicene faith (Sok. 6.8, Soz. 8.8), and incited Arcadius against both pagans and Arians (op. cit.). Her history is mostly connected with Ioannes Chrysostomos, with whom she was at first friendly (Sok. 6.8, Soz. 8.4) until he attacked her rapacity, but they both supported the Egyptian monks against Theophilos of Alexandria (Soz. 8.13), until Ioannes thought her dealings with his enemy, Epiphanios of Salamis, offensive and denounced her again (Sok. 6.15, Soz. 8.16, Zos. 5.23.2). Eudoxia sought reconciliation when he was exiled in July 403 (Soz. 8.18). On his return, he denounced Eudoxia's statue erected near Hagia Sophia, and she threatened to influence against him the synod called to exonerate him of the charges that had resulted in his exile (Sok. 6.18, Soz. 8.20, Zos. 5.24.3). Eudoxia died of a miscarriage on 6 October 404 (Sok. 6.19, Soz. 8.27) and was buried in the Church of the Holy Apostles.

56. Zos. 4.33.1, Philostorg. 11.6, J Ant. fr. 187.

57. *Wledig, gwledig*, 'ruler, prince', he is remembered as the ancestor of several British princely dynasties. Precisely what significance this may have is not clear, but it is possible that Magnus Maximus established reliable local subordinates for defensive purposes. 'The Dream of Macsen Wledig', in which Maximus is immortalized as a folk hero with a British wife, is one of the eleven prose tales in *The Mabinogion*. Magnus Maximus is also a character in Rudyard Kipling's 'A Centurion of the Thirteenth', one of the short stories in his historical fantasy book *Puck of Pook's Hill* (1906).

58. *PLRE* I, p.588. According to Gregory of Tours (1.43), Magnus Maximus was *comes Britanniarum*.

59. *Pan. Lat.* 2 (12).23.3, 38.2, [Aur. Vict.] *Epit.* 47.7, Rufin. 1.14, Oros. 7.34.9, Sulp. Sev. *Chron.* 2.49.5, Sok. 5.11, Soz. 7.13. Was he responsible (Zos. 4.35.4–5), or was he forced by his troops (Sulp. Sev. *V. Mart.* 20.3)?

60. The proclamation of Iulianus is only the best documented example of a victorious commander being proclaimed *Augustus* by his own officers and soldiers (Amm. Marc. 20.4.1–5.10).

61. Lib. *Or.* 59.137, Amm. Marc. 20.1.1.

62. According to Sozomenos (9.11.2), the army in Britannia elevated all three of their pretenders, one after the other, during the winter of 406/407 (viz. Marcus, Gratianus and Constantinus) in order to gain the West. Marcus was very shortly murdered by mutinous troops, while Gratianus, who was possibly a local magistrate, was unseated and slain after a perfunctory reign of four months (Olympiod. fr. 12 Müller, Soz. 9.11.1). This series of three short-lived usurpations in Britannia, culminating in that of Constantinus, apparently a devout Christian and a common soldier, was a response to an invasion of Asding and Siling Vandals, Alani and Suevi from across the Rhenus and into Gaul (Zos. 6.3.1, Oros. 7.40.4), soon to be followed by Alamanni and Burgundi. Apparently, he was elevated only because of his name (Oros. op. cit.,

Soz. 9.11); note the propaganda value of his sons' (new?) names (Constans, Iulianus). Like his predecessor Magnus Maximus, Constantinus III – as he is known to history – stripped Britannia of its troops and crossed to Bononia, winning over the prefecture of Gallia (Olympiod. fr. 12 Müller, Zos. 5.31.4, 6.2.2, Soz. 9.11, Oros. 7.40.4). Stilicho sent an army under Sarus against him, but it was forced to retreat after initial successes. Constantinus won victories over the invading Germani (Zos. 6.3.2, Oros. 7.40.4). Honorius planned to send Alaric against Constantinus and the army was assembled at Ticinum (Zos. 5.31.5), but Stilicho's fall left the emperor with a vacuum in his military command, which led to a switch in his policy and accommodation with the usurper. He was recognized as a colleague (Olymp. fr. 12 Müller, Zos. 5.43, Soz. 9.11, Prokop. *Wars* 3.2.31) and apparently shared the western consulship with Honorius in 409. In the same year, Gerontius, one of Constantinus' generals, betrayed him and Hispania was lost to the invading Germani. Following the failure of Constantinus' expedition into Italy in early 410 (Olympiod. fr. 16 Müller), a new usurper, Iovinus, was set up in Gaul (Greg. Tur. 2.9). Constantinus thereupon laid down his power and took refuge in a church, but his army surrendered him and Iulianus to Honorius who put them to death (Olympiod. fr. 16 Müller, Soz. 9.15, Oros. 7.42.3); Constans, the eldest son, having already been murdered by Gerontius (Olympiod. fr. 16 Müller, Soz. 9.12–13, Oros. 7.42.4). As a reminder to others, Constantinus' head was displayed in public. In 411 Gerontius committed suicide when his army went over to Honorius; by 413 Iovinus had been captured and executed.

63. Jer. *Ep.* 133.9 (*Britannia fertilis provincia tyrannorum*). Zosimos also describes the army of Britannia dominated by 'insolence and irascibility' (αὐθαδείᾳ καὶ θυμῷ, 4.35.3). In truth, the Diocese Britanniae, to give it its proper title, was under military pressure in the last decades of the fourth century, and looked to the elevation of its 'own' *Augustus* of the West to solve the continuing problem.

64. Prosper Tiro *Epitoma Chronicon* s.a. 384.

65. Zos. 4.53.2–6 = Eunap. fr. 51.

66. Amm. Marc. 31.10.18.

67. On Valentinianus' military abilities, *vide* Zos. 4.12.1, Amm. Marc. 30.7.6–11, 30.9.4, 31.14.2–4.

68. *Pan. Lat.* 2 (12).23.4, 24.1, [Aur. Vict.] *Epit.* 47.7, Ambr. *Ep.* 24.10, Jer. *Ep.* 60.15, Rufin. 1.14.

69. Sok. 5.11, Soz. 7.13. For some reason, Zosimos (4.36.6) has Gratianus done away with in Singidunum (Belgrade, Serbia), Illyricum. Jordanes (*Rom.* §145), on the other hand, makes the crass blunder of connecting Eugenius with the murder of Gratianus. Perhaps Jordanes has confused the two usurper Magnus Maximus and Eugenius.

70. Ambr. *Expo. in Ps.* 61.26, *Ep.* 24.10.

71. [Aur. Vict.] *Epit.* 47.7 (*tyrannidem arripuisset*). The Latin term *tyranny* should not be confused with the modern equivalent; here it means usurpers of the imperial dignity.

72. The prime treatise on Maximus' unimpeachable orthodoxy is his letter *Contra Arianos*, quoted by Rufinus (11.16). The Greek noun αἵρεσις/*haíresis*, 'choosing/choice', had originally been entirely neutral, simply meaning a set of beliefs or practices, and a 'heretic' is one who makes a choice. Now, however, 'heresies', deviant beliefs, were catalogued and demonologized, as the Church took on an increasing authoritarian role in defining what was to be regarded as correct.

73. Oros. 7.34.9.

74. Sulp. Sev. *V. Mart.* 20.3. Sulpicius Severus, a wealthy senator from south-west Gaul, knew Martin personally and wrote the *Vita Martini*, which was the first account of the saint's life, while Martin was still living; he died in 397 (Greg. Tur. 1.48, 10.31). This skilful hagiography was designed to show that the West could produce a saint superior to any ascetic in the Egyptian wastes. Martin was praised for dividing his military cloak, for his miracles (casting out demons, raising the paralytic and the dead), and for blessing Turones with his presence. Still, if the real Martin resembled the figure portrayed by his hagiographer, he was a notably eccentric miracle-worker. Georgius Florentius Gregorius, better known as Gregory of Tours, was the master propagandist for Martin, even going so far as to champion the saint's divine role at the crucial battle of Vouillé, where the Frankish Clovis trounced and killed the Visigothic Alaric II (*vide* Greg. Tur. 2.37–8). This spelled the end of Gaul's Visigothic future – the Gallic domination of the Visigoths of Tolosa was reduced to Narbo and its hinterland (Septimania) – and the birth of Francia...but not quite yet. Saint Martin, the leading confessor of Gaul, whose tomb witnessed frequent miracles, is a national saint of France and the patron saint of soldiers, vintners, innkeepers and tailors. The Feast of Saint Martin is 11 November. The life of bishop Gregory bears little resemblance to that of his cherished predecessor, the Pannonian soldier turned monk.

75. On withdrawing the *comitatenses* from Britannia, Honorius, in his famous rescript of 410, advises the *civitates* (Gk. πόλεις) to organize themselves in a programme of self-help (Zos. 6.10.2, cf. Prokop. 3.2.38). The emperor's advice to the Romano-Britons meant they had a choice: either to hire mercenaries from the barbarians or to defend themselves. They took the second choice and did indeed organize, in an admirable way, in sharp contrast to the response in Gaul, which was subjugated within seventy or so years by the Franks. Resistance to the Saxones was so stubborn at the turn of the early sixth century that many migrants returned to their homeland or settled in north-west Gaul. By the middle of the century the advance of the Saxones began again, this time into south-western Britain with its rich, rolling farmlands. This advance was the final phase of the permanent Germanizing of a large part of the British lowlands. Archaeology bears out the view that Britannia, or Britain as we should now call it, became detached from the empire in the early fifth century, whatever sentiments lingered among some Romano-Britons. For instance, the import of fresh imperial coinage into Britain appears to have ceased after the reign of Constantinus III (407–411) – first as *tyrannus* but then recognized in desperation by Honorius (Soz. 9.11, Prokop. *Wars* 3.2.31) – implying both a disconnection from the imperial payment of troops and the imperial taxation system.

76. Bede 1.9.

77. Rufin. 11.17, Sok. 5.11, 13, Soz. 7.13–14, Theod. *Hist. eccl.* 5.15.

78. Oros. 7.35.2 (*sola fide maior*).

79. Pac. 12.24.1, 31.1.

80. Zos. 4.35.3.

81. Jer. *Ep.* 3.5.2, written sometime in 374.

82. This was the infamous trial of the Hispano-Roman Priscillianus who had attracted a substantial spiritual following in Hispania and Gaul teaching the following oddities: lay people must renounce marriage; fasting on Sundays; ascetic retreats for the laity during Lent; bringing the Eucharist home; using the title 'doctor', which is the Latin

for 'teacher'; studying not only the Bible but also apocryphal books. Although he was elected bishop of Avela (Ávila, Spain), his extreme ascetic contempt for humankind's sordid physical existence caused the hierarchy to suspect he was a Manichaean. In 384, with the approval of Magnus Maximus, Priscillianus was condemned by a church synod at Burdigala (Bordeaux, France), and in the following year, after being judged by a secular court at Augusta Treverorum and found guilty not of heresy but of the civil crime of sorcery (a capital offence) and immorality, he was executed along with five of his companions. Other Priscillianists were banished to the remote Isles of Scilly (*Scillonia insula*, Sulp. Sev. *Chron.* 2.51.4). Some (though not all) of his writings were condemned as heretical and were burned.

83. Before leaving the emperor's presence, Martin had obtained a promise from Maximus that he would not sentence the defendants to death, declaring that church and state should each be content to occupy themselves with their own affairs (Sulp. Sev. *Chron.* 2.50.6–7). When Martin departed Augusta Treverorum, the emperor ordered Priscillian and his followers to be beheaded in 385. Incidentally, Ambrose, who generally favoured rough treatment of heretics and schismatics, agreed with Martin. Aghast, he and the new pope, Siricius (r. 384–399), excommunicated those who had brought the fatal charges, two gluttonous and foul-mouthed Hispanic bishops. Despite the fact that Siricius disapproved of Priscillianism, the pope had the wit to appreciate the destructive polarization of stances that the politicization of liturgical differences could cause.

84. *D&F*, vol. 2, chap. 27, p.70.

85. Ambr. *Ep.* 24, Rufin. 1.15, Sok. 5.11, Soz. 7.13. See also *ILS* 787 from Africa, which has the names of Theodosius, Valentinianus, Maximus and Honorius.

86. Zon. 13.8.17. Apparently, Constantius' incredibly bloody victory had been foretold by the appearance of a cross in the sky at Jerusalem on 7 May 351 (Iul. *Orat.* 1.36, 2.59, Sok. 2.28.22, Soz. 4.5, Zon. 13.8.17). According to Philostorgius the cross was also visible on the day of the battle, inspiring the men of Constantius with invincible bravery, while terrifying those of Magnentius 'inasmuch as they were utterly given over to the worship of demons' (3.26). The second occurrence of this rare atmospheric optical occurrence (viz. a solar halo phenomenon called a parhelion or sun dog) sounds very much like a double of the first. Saint Birgitta of Sweden (†1373) probably experienced a similar marvel when she was at Bethlehem: 'I saw a star, but not the kind that shines in the sky; I saw a light, but not the kind that shines in this world' (*The Revelations of Saint Birgitta of Sweden*, bk. 1, ch. 10).

87. Jer. *Chron.* s.a. 351 (238d).

88. Iul. *Or.* 1.48B-C, Amm. Marc. 15.5.33.

89. Ibid. 1.36–8, 48, 2.57–60, Amm. Marc. 15.5.33, Eutr. 10.12.1, [Aur. Vict.] *Epit.* 42.4, Zos. 2.50.4–51, J Ant. fr. 174.

90. Theoph. 44.15.

91. [Aur. Vict.] *Epit.* 42.5.6, Iul. *Or.* 1.38C-40B, 2.71C-74, Eutr. 10.12.23, Zon. 13.8–9, Sok. 2.32, Lib. *Or.* 18.33–4, Jer. *Chron.* s.a. 353 (238h).

92. Amm. Marc. 14.1.1, Iul. *Or.* 1.38C-40B, Aur. Vict. *Caes.* 42.8, Eutr. 10.12.23, Oros. 7.29.13, Zos. 2.53.2–54.2, Zon. 13.9, Sok. 2.32, Soz. 4.7, Jer. *Chron.* s.a. 353 (238h).

93. Aug. *Civ.* 3.29.

94. Zos. 4.37.3.

95. *ILS* 787, from Africa, has names of Theodosius, Valentinianus, Maximus and Honorius.

96. Thucydides 5.89.1.
97. Zos. 4.45.4, 47.2.
98. Ambr. *Ep.* 24.7.
99. *PLRE* I, p.159. According to Ambrose (*Ep.* 24.8), Magnus Maximus accused Bauto of deploying barbarian troops against him.
100. Pac. 12.35.
101. Ibid. 38.4–42.
102. *Pan. Lat.* 2 (12).45, Ambr. *Ep.* 40.25.
103. Zos. 4.47.1, [Aur. Vict.] *Epit.* 48.6, Oros. 7.35.10. Flavius Victor had been given the title *Augustus* after Gratianus' murder (*ILS* 788).
104. Pac. 16.5, 45.3.
105. Ambr. *Ep.* 24.4.
106. Ibid. 24.6–8.
107. Bauto died at some point before 388 (Zos. 4.53.1).
108. Zos. 4.53.1, J Ant. fr. 187.
109. Philostorg. 10.8.
110. Flavius Rumoridus (*cos.* 403) was of Germanic origin and was a pagan. Ambrose describes him in a letter to Eugenius as maintaining 'the religious practice (*cultus*) of the gentile nations' (*Ep.* 57.3).
111. Nubel, a petty king (L *regulus*) among the Mauri (Amm. Marc. 29.5.2), was a member of an outstandingly powerful clan, and in his time had been a Roman officer. His son Firmus in 373 led a large-scale revolt against the Roman government, whereby he allowed himself to be proclaimed emperor (Amm. Marc. 29.5.2–3, 20, Zos. 4.16.3). He took the title *Augustus* (*CIL* VIII.5338), apparently coined money, and secured Moorish and Donatist support (Amm. Marc. 29.5.28, 30.7.10, Aug. *Ep.* 87.10). Nubel's brother Gildo, a Donatist, aided the elder Theodosius to defeat Firmus; the usurper committed suicide (Oros. 7.33.5, Claud. *B Gild.* 330–1, [Aur. Vic.] *Epit.* 45.7, Symm. *Ep.* 10.1, *Or.* 6.4). As a reward Gildo was given the command of the Roman forces in Africa. His daughter married Nebridius, a nephew of the empress Flaccilla (Jer. *Ep.* 79). In 397 he too rebelled, only to be defeated by a Roman expeditionary force commanded by his brother Mascezel, whose children had been murdered by their uncle when Mascezel had taken refuge in Mediolanum. Gildo was not only the *magister utriusque militiae per Africam* but a hereditary tribal leader too and so a very great landowner: his property was confiscated and a separate financial department created to administer it (*ND occ.* XII.5). In a very real sense, these unruly Mauri nobles acted as local warlords along the desert fringe of North Africa.
112. Sulpicius Alexander, apud Greg. Tur. 2.9.
113. Oros. 7.35.11.
114. Zos. 4.53.1, Paulin. §30, Sulpicius Alexander, apud Greg. Tur. 2.9.
115. J Ant. fr. 187.

Chapter Six
1. Zos. 4.53.2–4.
2. Sulpicius Alexander, apud Greg. Tur. 2.9.
3. J Ant. fr. 187, Philostorg. 11.1, Sok. 5.11, Oros. 7.35.10.
4. Claud. *IV cons.* 75, 93, Sid. Apoll. *Ep.* 5.355.

5. Sok. 5.11.

6. Soz. 7.22, Rufin. 2.31, Aug. *Civ.* 5.26.

7. Rufin. 2.31.

8. Aug. *Civ.* 5.26.

9. *D&F*, vol. 2, ch. 27, p.90, n. 1.

10. Oros. 7.35.10.

11. Zos. 4.54.3.

12. Zon. 13.18.2, also Kedren. p.568.10.

13. Ambrose first talks of it as sudden death – '*de celeritate mortis non de genere loquor*' (*Obit. Val.* §33) – and then most significantly three years later, in 395, he (*Obit. Theod.* §§39–40) omits any mention of the murder and avenging of Valentinianus alongside that of Gratianus.

14. *Vide* Croke 1976.

15. *C Th.* II.8.20, III.17.3, IV.4.2, VI.27.6, 11.38, XIV.7.9, 17.10, XV.1.25, *ILS* 821, Zos. 4.45.1–2. On the fall of father and son Zos. 52.1–4 = Eunap. fr. 59. The *praefectus urbis Romae* held significant judicial powers and was responsible for overseeing the major guilds and corporations, administering the city's all-important grain supply, and managing the drainage of the Tiber and the sewage and water systems. Likewise, the *praefectus urbis Constantinopoleos* (or *eparchos*) was no small fry either. He was effectively the governor of Constantinopolis, his duties including the maintenance of law and order, superintendence of the circus factions, control of the guilds and above all the supply of grain. In the absence of the emperor, he presided over the imperial supreme court.

16. Ironically, in the Hippodrome there are two epigrams carved on the stylobate of the plinth of the Obelisk of Theodosius, one in Latin (east face) and one in Greek (west face), which reminds us of the bilingual character of the capital at this date. Both inscriptions claim that the obelisk was erected in a mere thirty-two days from start to finish, under the supervision of Proklos in 388: the occasion was Theodosius' victory over the western usurper Magnus Maximus. On the Obelisk *vide* Fields 2017: 106.

17. *PLRE* I, p.293.

18. Sulpicius Alexander, apud Greg. Tur. 2.9.

19. Paulin. §30, *ILS* 790 (Köln). In December 355, following a lengthy siege, the fortress had been lost to the Franks because it was not relieved by a Roman force (Amm. Marc. 15.8.19).

20. Galla was the youngest daughter of Valentinianus I and Iustina (Sok. 4.31, Philostorg. 9.16, J Ant. fr. 187). Having fled east with her mother and brother, she married Theodosius at Thessaloniki in the autumn of 387 (Zos. 4.43–4, Philostorg. 10.7). She died in 394 of a miscarriage (Zos. 4.57.3, J Ant. fr. 187).

21. Zos. 4.44.3–4.

22. Galla had three children with Theodosius, but Aelia Galla Placidia (388–450) was the only one to survive to adulthood. When Theodosius fell ill she was summoned to Mediolanum at the same time as Honorius, and so was present at her father's death. After his death she was raised in the household of Stilicho and Serena so as to protect her from her jealous half-brother Arcadius. She later became *Augusta* in her own right.

23. Zos. 4.19.1, 43.1, J Ant. fr. 187. Her father Iustus, *consularis Piceni*, was executed for dealings with Magnus Magnentius (Sok. 4.31, J Ant. fr. 187).

24. Zos. 2.54.1, cf. Iul. *Or.* 1.34D, who observes that Franks and Saxones from beyond the Rhenus had followed Magnus Magnentius most eagerly because they were his people, tied by race. As a *laetus*, Magnentius was a Roman citizen. At the time of his usurpation he held the rank of *comes* and commanded two crack units of the *comitatus*, the *Ioviani* and the *Herculiani* (Zos. 2.42.2, Zon. 13.6.1).

25. Them. *Or.* 2.36.

26. Another of his imperial victims that year was Nepotianus, who ruled the city of Rome for twenty-eight days before being liquidated by Magnentius' *magister officiorum* Marcellinus. Nepotianus was the son of Eutropia, the half-sister of Constantinus I, and Virius Nepotianus (*cos.* 336): on his mother's side he was the grandson of Constantius I Chlorus and Flavia Maximiana Theodora (Eutr. 9.22). After the revolt of Magnentius, Nepotianus proclaimed himself emperor and entered Rome with a band of gladiators on 3 June 350. Despatched by Magnentius, Marcellinus fought his way into Rome and Nepotianus was hurried away to his death in the resulting struggle on 30 June; according to Eutropius (10.11) and Jerome (*Chron.* s.a. 350 [238b]) the head of the short-lived pretender was put on a spear and borne around the city. In the following days, his mother Eutropia was hunted down and killed along with supporters of Nepotianus (Iul. *Or.* 2.58D, Aur. Vict. *Caes.* 42.6, [Aur. Vic.] *Epit.* 42.6, Zos. 2.59, Zos. 2.43.2–4). Eutropia's murder was mentioned by Athanasios I, bishop of Alexandria (r. 328–339, 346–373), in a letter to Constantius II: '... butchered those who so kindly entertained me in Rome; for instance, your departed Aunt Eutropia, whose disposition answered to her name' (*Apologia ad Constantium* 6). The polite cleric (one of the fiercest opponents of Arius and his followers, he was at loggerheads with the Arian emperor) is obviously referring to the literal meaning of Eutropia's name, 'of good manners'.

27. Zos. 2.42.1, 47.3, Aur. Vict. *Caes.* 41.24.

28. Amm. Marc. 15.5.16, [Aur. Vict.] *Epit.* 41.23, Eutr. *Hist. eccl.* 10.9.4, Jer. *Chron.* s.a. 350 (237c), Zos. 2.42.5, J Ant. fr. 172, Theoph. 43.32.

29. [Ioannes Damascenus] *Artemii passio* 10, p.49.23–5. Flavius Artemius held the position of *dux Aegypti* in the final years of the reign of Constantinus II, and supported the Arian bishop of Alexandria, Georgios the Kappadokian, in his campaign against pagans and Nicene Christians (Iul. *Ep.* 60.379A-B, Amm. Marc. 22.11.2, Theod. *Hist. eccl.* 3.18.1, *P Oxy.* 7.1103). This included the sack of the temple of Serapis as well as the hounding of the Nicene bishop of Alexandria, Athanasios I (*Ep.* A 360), an indefatigable opponent of absolutely everyone who rejected the doctrine of the Holy Trinity that had been accepted at the Nicene Council of 325, who had been expelled two years previously, in 358, by the former *dux Aegypti* Sebastianus. Ammianus Marcellinus (22.11.3) says Artemius, no longer *dux Aegypti*, was executed in 362, probably in Antioch, for his crimes against the people of Alexandria. According to Christian hagiography, however, Artemius was tortured and beheaded on the orders of the emperor Iulianus (e.g. Kedren. p.537.4–8), and was therefore considered a martyr and a saint in the Catholic, Orthodox and Maronite churches despite his adherence to Arianism during his life (as a saint he possessed healing powers, being especially good at curing diseases of the spine and the genitals). This is a good example of what the French scholar Albert Dufourcq (*Étude sur les Gesta martyrum romains* [Paris, 1900], p.242) has dubbed '*Julianisation*', the tendency of Christian authors to ascribe to Iulianus Apostata all sorts of heinous deeds, whether he committed them or not.

As for the Arian bishop Georgios, he would himself suffer a terrible fate. When the news of Constantius' decease and Iulianus' sole emperorship had reached the city, the Alexandrian populace – traditionally a turbulent lot – directed its fury against the hated Georgios – his arrogant and headstrong behaviour had incurred the hatred of many Alexandrians – and other protégés of Constantius. The bishop was put in chains and imprisoned, supposedly in anticipation of a trial, but it did not come to that. After a few weeks, on 24 December 361, Georgios was dragged from his prison by a furious mob and severely beaten up. Subsequently he was hogtied to a camel. Having been carried through the city he was killed and burned. His ashes were scattered at sea; the camel and some of Constantius' officials met with the same fate (Iul. *Ep.* 60, Amm. Marc. 22.11.8–10, Sok. 3.2.1–3, Soz. 5.7.7, Philostorg. 7.2). Following the lynching of Georgios, Athanasios seized the bishop's see of Alexandria; Athanasios had exceeded his authority, according to Iulianus, and had to be cut down to size. Consequently, the bishop who had been banished before by the Arians was now exiled by the pagan Iulianus (Iul. *Ep.* 110, 111, 112, Athan. *Fest. Ind.* s.a. 363). Athanasios would secretly return to Alexandria on his own initiative as soon as he learned of Iulianus' death.

30. *Vide* Williams-Friell 1998: 42–3.
31. Called Placidia in Greek sources. Aelia Flavia Flaccilla married Theodosius before his accession and bore him Arcadius (377), Aelia Pulcheria (before 379) and Honorius (384). She was renowned for her piety and meekness (Theod. *Hist. eccl.* 5.19, Greg. Nyss. *Fun. Pulch.* 881, 884, Ambr. *Obit. Theod.* §40) and was a strong opponent of the Arians (Greg. Nyss. *Fun. Pulch.* 892). She was alive in early 386 (Claud. *IV Cons.* 158), but died soon after in Thracia (Greg. Nyss. *Fun. Pulch.* 884, Lib. *Or.* 20.4, 22.8, Philostorg. 10.7). The empress is commemorated as a saint in the Eastern Orthodox Church; her feast day is observed on 14 September.
32. Claud. *IV Cons.* 72–7.
33. *PLRE* I, pp.14–15.
34. Zos. 4.57.1, J Ant. fr. 187.
35. Zos. 4.55.2.

Chapter Seven
1. Written by the American science fiction and fantasy writer R.A. Lafferty (1914–2002), his quirky non-fiction book *The Fall of Rome* (1971) was republished as *Alaric: the Day the World Ended* (1993).
2. Iul. *Or.* 1.34C-D, 2.56B-D (Magnentius), Lib. *Or.* 12.62, Amm. Marc. 20.8.1 (Constantius).
3. Ambr. *Ep.* 24.4.
4. Philostorg. 11.2.
5. Zos. 4.39.5.
6. Ambr. *Ep.* 40.22.
7. Amm. Marc. 25.6.13, 31.10.18, Claud. *B Goth.* 241–5, Philostorg. 10.8, Zos. 4.45.3, Pac. 12.32.3–4, 33.4–5, Sok. 5.25, 7.10. Pacatus says Theodosius 'accepted the barbarian peoples who vowed to lend him their help as fellow combatants' (12.32.2). Thus, according to Eunapios, 'many Huns from Thracia serving under their native leaders' (apud J Ant. fr. 187) served Theodosius. His youngest son Honorius, as emperor of the West, would maintain at least 300 Huns as part of his *scholae palatinae* at Ravenna (Zos.

5.45.6), and in 409 he would employ 10,000 Huns against Alaric (Olympiod. apud Zos. 5.50.1), or so it seems, for they appeared to have done nothing to stop the Gothic warlord from investing Rome. Of course, it would not be quite correct to suggest that the Huns had a radical effect on the Roman world. However, we would not be amiss in saying that the Huns were often excellent auxiliaries who could provide reliable bodyguards for emperors and local magnates, as well as for the big militarists, those *generalissimos* like Stilicho and later Aëtius and Aspar. Personally recruited and paid for out of his own pocket, these private retainers, known as *bucellarii*, could be relied upon to follow their Roman commander wherever he went and, due to the need for range and mobility, they were exclusively horse warriors. The court poet Claudian (*In Ruf.* 2.76–7, cf. 270–1) tells us that Arcadius' *praefectus praetorio* Rufinus maintained an armed retinue of barbarians (he does not specify what race), and we learn from another authority (*Chron. min.* I 650.34) that this large personal following was composed exclusively of Huns. Rufinus' great rival Stilicho also sought to ensure his own safety by hiring a private army of Huns, and before his enemies could set about murdering him they had to deal with these tough, no-nonsense retainers first (Zos. 5.34.1). *Vide* Maenchen-Helfen 1973: 30–7, Wolfram 1988: 132 n. 92 on Theodosius employing Huns settled in the diocese of Pannonia Secunda, Goths settled in the *provinciae* of Pannonia and Phrygia and the Alani settled in the diocese of Pannonia Valeria.

8. Pac. 12.32.
9. Zos. 4.57.2–3 = Eunap. fr. 60, J Ant. fr. 187, Sok. 7.10. Saul was an Alani commanding the Goths, Huns and Alani of Pannonia. He would later assist Stilicho against Alaric at Pollentia in 402 (Oros. 7.37.2), where he would fall in battle. Bacurios, who had survived Adrianopolis, is recorded as being Armenian (Zos. 4.57.3), but is more likely to have been a Caucasian Iberian (Amm. Marc. 31.13.16, *PLRE* I, p.144). He was *tribunus sagittariorum* at Adrianopolis (Amm. Marc. 31.13.16), *dux Palestinae* for the years 378–394, where he became friendly with the historian Rufinus of Aquileia (1.10–11, Sok. 1.20) and devoted to the sophist Libanius (*Ep.* 1043–4). At the Frigidus he served as *comes domesticorum* (Rufin. 1.10), where he showed great bravery (Zos. 4.58.3, Sok. 5.25), and did not fall there according to Rufinus (2.33, *contra* Zos. op. cit.). The Goths Gaïnas and Alaric (Sok. 7.10, Zos. 5.5.4) commanded the Gothic contingent from Thracia, although the former was given a higher command than the latter.
10. Oros. 7.35.11.
11. Sulp. Sev. fr. 2.
12. Zos. 4.35.2, Ambr. *Expositio evangelii secundum Lucam* 10.10, Amm. Marc. 31.3.1. Arbogastes' army almost certainly included those two crack *legiones palatinae*, the *Ioviani seniores* and the *Herculiani seniores*. According to the *Notitia Dignitatum* (*ND occ.* VII.3–4), this pair of units was part of the command of the *comes Italiae*, and it is known that they participated in the punitive expedition against Gildo, the rebel *magister utriusque militiae per Africam*, in 397. Orosius (7.36.6) gives a total of 5,000 Gallo-Roman veterans for the campaign against Gildo, while Claudianus (*B Gild.* 418–23) lists these men unit by unit, which included the *Ioviani* and the *Herculiani*, the units that often are mentioned in the same breath together and the most senior pair of *legiones palatinae*. *Vide* Woods 1995: 65.

13. From 297 onwards the *laeti* are attested in the surviving sources (Jones 1964: 620). These were farmers of mainly Germanic origin who after their defeat had been allowed to settle in homogeneous settlements, *terrae laeticae* (*C Th.* 13.11.10, dating to 399), which were under the control of the military administration. The object was to restore the productivity and prosperity of districts whose agriculture had been abandoned (*agri deserti*) during the troubles of the second half of the third century. In times of war these *laeti* served under *praefecti laetorum* (*ND occ.* XLII.33–44), officers appointed specifically for that task. The *laeti* are found only in the prefectures of Gallia and Italia.

14. We use this term to describe all the foreign enemies of the Roman Empire, east and west (the Sāsānian Persians being the exception, of course), even though many of them had reached a considerable advance in what the Romans recognized as civilization.

15. Zos. 4.53.2, 54.4.

16. Jones 1964: 1076–7, 1417–50.

17. Jones (ibid. 1449) breaks down the western *comitatus* into 5,000 *vexillationes palatinae*, 17,000 *vexillationes comitatenses*, 12,000 *legiones palatinae*, 33,000 *legiones comitatenses*, 32,000 *auxilia palatina* and 14,000 *pseudocomitatenses*.

18. Ibid. 1450.

19. The African forces of the *comes Tingitaniae*, *dux Mauretaniae* and *dux Tripolitania* (*ND occ.* XXV, XXX, XXXI) were most likely to follow Gildo's lead and remain loyal to Theodosius.

20. *ND occ.* VII, XXXII-XXXV, *or.* IX.

21. Jones (1964: 1449) breaks down the eastern *comitatus* into 7,000 *vexillationes palatinae*, 14,500 *vexillationes comitatenses*, 13,000 *legiones palatinae*, 38,000 *legiones comitatenses*, 21,500 *auxilia palatina* and 10,000 *pseudocomitatenses*.

22. Ibid. 1450.

23. Theodoret speaks vaguely of 'many barbarian auxiliaries from beyond the Ister [viz. Danuvius]' (5.24.3), while both Sokrates Scholastikos (5.25) and Sozomenos (7.24) simply declare that the Roman auxiliaries were from the banks of the Danuvius and beyond.

24. Oros. 7.35.19. There again, Orosius is noted for his fondness for magnifying the number of the battlefield dead. A classic example of what some scholars would call his barefaced inventions is his account of two battles Caius Marius fought against the combined forces of Iugurtha of Numidia and Bocchus of Mauretania (winter 106/105 BC). In the first battle the enemy had 60,000 horsemen; in the second, a total force of 90,000. Both armies were wiped out (Oros. 5.15.10–18).

25. Jord. *Get.* §145, cf. Sok. 5.25 ('a large number').

26. Zos. 4.57.2.

27. J Ant. fr. 187.

28. Claud. *B Gild.* 243–5, *III Cons.* 68–72, *Cons. Stil. I* 54–8.

29. Štekar 2014: 7, *contra* Crawford, who says 'that both armies could have had a regular Roman nucleus of at least 40,000' (2012: 42).

30. Maur. 3.8, 10.

Chapter Eight

1. Zos. 4.58.1.

2. Rufin. 11.33.

3. Ambr. *Ep.* 62.4.

4. Gaspard Gourgaud, *Mémoires pour servir l'histoire de France, sous Napoléon* (Paris, 1823–25), vol. II, p.191.

5. Veg. 3.9.

6. App. *Illyr.* 4.22–4.

7. Fest. 7.6.

8. Tacitus, in his account of the mutiny of the Pannonian legions after the death of Augustus in the year AD 14, writes the following: 'Meanwhile the maniples (*manipuli*) which previous to the mutiny had been sent to Nauportus to make roads and bridges (*itenera et pontes*) and for other purposes, when they heard the tumult in the camp, tore up the standards and having plundered the neighbouring villages and Nauportus itself, which was like a town, assailed the centurions who restrained them with jeers and insults, last of all, with blows' (*Ann.* 1.20).

9. Strabo (7.5.2) calls the river Korkóras, now the River Ljubljanica. According to the elder Pliny (3.128), this was where the Argonauts, on their return journey following their quest for the fleece of the golden ram, landed and founded the town. This was probably on account of the false etymology of the name *navis* (Gk. ναῦς/*naüs*), 'ship', and *portare*, 'to carry'. Much later, when Nauportus ceased to be an important settlement, as it had been during the Augustan period, Emona (Ljubljana) became associated with the band of heroes known as the Argonauts and Iason was regarded as its founder (Zos. 5.29.1–3, Soz. 1.6.5).

10. It is perhaps wise to recall that before the advent of mechanical transport in war, such as the railways of the American Civil War, no army could move faster than its feet would carry it. Roman soldiers were trained to march, both at the standard rate of 20 Roman miles (30km) and at the full pace of 24 miles (36km) in five hours, as well as in running and jumping (Veg. 1.9). However, on campaign a day's march obviously varied: Prokop. *Wars* 4.13.32–3, 9.7km per day for seven days; Amm. Marc. 24.2.3, 37km in two days; ibid. 10, 23km in one day. A Roman mile, consisting of 1,000 Roman paces or 5,000 Roman feet, is comparable to 1,478.5m.

11. *Vide* Kos 2014, Ciglenečki 2016.

12. This was captured by capturing through treachery Constantius' commander Actus who was defending the *claustra Alpium Iuliarum* (Amm. Marc. 31.11.3).

13. Zos. 2.48.4, Claud. *III Cons.* 89–92.

14. Oros. 7.35.13.

15. Soz. 7.24.

16. Clausewitz, *Vom Kriege*, bk. 1, ch. 1, p.83, Howard & Paret.

17. Hervé Coutau-Bégarie, *Traité de stratégie* (Paris, 2011).

18. Clausewitz, *Vom Kriege*, bk. 1, ch. 3, p.117, Howard & Paret.

19. *D&F*, vol. 2, ch. 27, p.92.

20. Clausewitz, *Vom Kriege*, bk. 6, ch. 1, pp.427, 429, Howard & Paret.

21. Zos. 4.58.2.

22. Oros. 7.35.19.

23. Zos. 5.5.4.

24. Oros. 7.35.19.

25. Zos. 4.58.3.

26. Sun Tzu *Art of War* 6.1–2 Griffith.

27. Theod. *Hist. eccl.* 5.24.5–7. In earlier Roman times the riders were usually Castor and Pollux, the Heavenly Twins (revered in Greece as sons of Zeus and brothers of Helen of Sparta, she who caught the eye of foppish Paris). Livy (2.19.3–20.13), describing the battle of Lake Regillus (499 BC), enlivens his stirring narrative with hints of the divine presence of those inseparable heroes Castor and Pollux. Rufinus of Aquileia (11.32) mentions that Theodosius had sought blessing from a holy hermit named Ioannes before setting out on his westward march, and the religious motif of the campaign is continued by this story.

28. Zos. 4.58.4.

29. Oros. 7.35.16.

30. Lafferty 1971: 117.

Chapter Nine

1. Aug. *Civ.* 5.26, Theod. *Hist. eccl.* 5.24.4, 17. It has been argued by David Woods (1995: 63–5) that these claims of Augustine and Theodoret are not to be taken literally, suggesting they have intentionally misrepresented the presence of two crack *legiones palatinae*, *Ioviani seniores* and *Herculiani seniores*, with their customary military standards in Arbogastes' army. As their titles suggest, they were of course a Diocletianic creation, and according to Vegetius (1.7) the emperor preferred them above all other units, and they were noted for their skill and dexterity with the five *plumbatae* they carried in the concavity of their shields. Regarding the military standards, the *Passio Sanctorum Bonosi et Maximiliani*, a Christian tale of two standard-bearers serving in these two units during the reign of Iulianus, imparts that they were executed for refusing to remove the Christian elements of their standards and restore the former pagan ones. Indeed, it would appear that the *Herculiani seniores* bore a likeness of Hercules bearing a club and a lion skin as a standard until the reign of Constantinus, that it reverted to this form under Iulianus and apparently was still so under Eugenius.

2. *PG* 63.491, English translation Cameron 2013: 108.

3. Claud. *III Cons.* 93–6. Note the poetical account of Cannae by Silius Italicus (*Punica* 9.491–507) where he has Iuno ordering Aeolus to release a wind (Vulturnus, god of the East Wind) to blow in the face of the Romans, blinding them with dust and causing their spears (*lancae*) to fall uselessly behind them. It has been suggested that Claudianus used Silius, the sudden wind that turned-the-tide-of-battle motif, but reversed the wind so as to give victory and not defeat (Cameron 2013: 116).

4. Oros. 7.35.21 (*pagunus pervicacissimus*).

5. E.g. Hom. *Od.* 10.2.

6. Claud. *III Cons.* 97.

7. Aug. *Civ.* 5.26.

8. Oros. 7.35.21.

9. Zos. 4.58.5, Sok. 5.25, Philostorg. 11.2, J Ant. fr. 187. The chronicler Ioannes Malalas (13.341), a contemporary of Jordanes and Prokopios, has Eugenius proclaimed emperor by the Senate on the death of Valentinianus I, only to perish twenty-two days later!

10. Zos. 4.58.6, Oros. 7.35.19. The reference by Claudianus (*III Cons.* 102–3) to two swords bearing Arbogastes' blood may suggest that his suicide was assisted by an attendant. Having lost his army on Mount Gilboa, Saul fled, hotly pursued by the Philistines, who manage to severely wound him with their arrows. Giving up all hope of surviving

and dreading the thought of falling into the hands of his 'uncircumcised' foes, he called upon his armour-bearer to run him through with his sword, but the armour-bearer was afraid and refused to obey. Saul therefore 'took his own sword and fell on it' (1 Samuel 31:3–4 NIV). Saul, the first anointed king of the Israelites, forfeited the Lord's pleasure and was beyond forgiveness. On the other hand, Arbogastes' situation was not exactly like that of Saul; Saul's sin had been an act of mercy, not sedition.

11. Zos. 4.58.6. Zosimos on Theodosius' clemency is confirmed by *C Th.* XV.14.11, Claud. *IV Cons.* 111–7, Symm. *Ep.* 4.51.2, Ambr. *Ep.* 61.7, 62.3, *Obit. Theod.* §4, Aug. *Civ.* 5.26.

12. *Pan. Lat.* 2 (12).47.3, Sok. 5.14.

13. Theod. *Hist. eccl.* 5.23.8.

14. *CIL* VI.1738 = *ILS* 2948.

15. J Ant. fr. 187.

16. Zos. 5.38.

17. For discussions on this topic, *vide* Ensslin 1953: 500–07 (for); Cameron 1968: 247–8 (against).

18. Robert Graves, 'The Persian Version': 'Truth-loving Persians do not dwell upon/The trivial skirmish fought near Marathon.'

19. RA 11.33.

20. Op. cit. (*qui aderant duces*). Observe Augustine, who claims to have his account of the miraculous wind from '*milites…qui aderant*' (soldiers who were present, *Civ.* 5.26).

21. Oros. 7.35.13–19.

22. Paulin. §31.2. *Vide* Cameron 2013: 84, who sets out to challenge the veracity of this threat.

23. Ambr. *Ep.* 61.3.

24. Ibid. 62.4.

25. Joshua 6:20, 10:11–14.

26. Cf. Joseph performs the burial rites for his father Jacob after forty days (Genesis 50:2–3).

27. Ambr. *Obit. Theod.* §7.

28. A rather fitting biblical parallel is when aged Moses climbs to the top of a hill and raises his hands in prayer so that Joshua and the Israelites might defeat the Amalekites (Exodus 17:9–12).

29. 2 Kings 6:18, where the prophet prays to the Lord that the Arameans, who have *surrounded* the Israelites, be blinded. Blindness is sometimes taken as a divine punishment on unbelieving peoples (*gōy*, Genesis 19:11).

30. Ambr. *Obit. Theod.* §10.

31. Psalm 36:1, 12 NIV.

32. Ambr. *Explan. psalm.* 36.25.2–4, Cameron 2013: 114, Drake 2017: 27–31.

33. *Vide* Salzman 2010: 195, 222–3, *contra* Cameron (2013: 124–6, 128–30), who sees Rufinus of Aquileia (his *Historia ecclesiastica* is dated to 402 or 403 and is a continuation of Eusebius' *Historia ecclesiastica*, covering events between 324 and 395) as the principal source for disseminating versions of these events.

34. Abraham Lincoln, 'Meditation on the Divine Will' (2 September 1862), apud Roy P. Basier (ed.), *The Collected Works of Abraham Lincoln*, 8 vols (New Brunswick, NJ, 1953).

35. Soz. 7.22.4.

36. Ambr. *Ep.* 61.1 (*barbari latronis…usurpatoris indigni*). Buttoned-up academic purists may well object to the collective use of 'barbarian' to denote non-Romans, but then again they have plenty to complain about. The Greeks and Romans called all and any people living beyond the bounds of their Mediterranean civilization a 'barbarian'. The frontier of the empire could be seen as a moral barrier. Inside were the arts, discipline and humanity (*humanitas*). Outside were wildness, irrationality, savagery and barbarity (*barbaritas*). 'You know well,' writes Libanios to the Caesar Iulianus in 358, 'that if anyone extinguishes our literature, we are put on a level with the barbarians' (*Ep.* 369.9). This pejorative term has also found its way into modern usage implying, as it did in classical antiquity, someone who is uncouth, uneducated and uncivilized. Unmistakably, in the eyes of our good learned bishop, Arbogastes, being a Frank, is a barbarian. In a way, little has changed, for we still view the Mediterranean as the great lake around which European civilization grew; books have been written about it.

37. *Pan. Lat.* 12 (9).17.2, 4 (10).6.2, 7.1.

38. Cameron 2013: 95.

39. Tomlin 1998: 21–51.

40. Ambr. *Obit. Theod.* §8 ('Theodosius' faith was turned into a victory').

41. Among Anglophone historians, the best-known Enlightenment *philosophes* is Edward Gibbon (1737–94), who left us an eighteenth-century version of a Tweet when he summed up the fall of Rome as 'the triumph of barbarism and religion' (*D&F*, vol. 3, ch. 71, p.803).

42. Eutr. 9.14.1, Zon. 12.30.

43. SHA *Carus, Carinus et Numerianus* 8, Aur. Vic. *Caes.* 38, Eutr. 9.18.

44. Erasmus, 'The soldier and the Carthusian', *Colloquies* [1518] vol. 1, §§5383–5.

45. Cf. Archil. fr. 24 Edmonds ('And I shall be called a soldier-of-fortune [ἐπίκουρος] like a Carian'). Naturally, there is no conclusive evidence that Archilochos operated as a mercenary, but equally there is no proof that he did not act in such a capacity for some part of his soldiering career. Some translators interpret ἐπίκουρος as 'allied fighter' (fr. 216 Swift) or 'auxiliary' (fr. 216 West). For a discussion on the term ἐπίκουρος, *vide* Fields 1994.

46. Archil. fr. 302 West.

47. Hor. *Carm.* 2.7.9–14, cf. Archil. frs. 5, 115a Swift. In 43 BC Horace (65–8 BC) had left Athens, where he was studying, to become a *tribunus militum* in the army of Marcus Brutus (Hor. *Ep.* 2.2.46–50, *Sat.* 1.6.45–8). Brutus (and Cassius) met with a crushing defeat at the double engagement of Philippi (Philíppoi, Greece) on the Via Egnatia (3 & 23 October 42 BC), and committed suicide. Quintus Horatius Flaccus, an auctioneer's son from Venusia, Apulia, was an unwarlike young man with protruding ears and poetic ambitions who would be famous as the great Augustan lyric poet and satirist Horace. This literary lion confesses, or so he would have the reader believe, that he 'knew defeat and speedy flight/at Philippi, my little shield abandoned' (*Carm.* 2.7.9–10 Kaimowitz). He knows intuitively the meaning of our English rhyme 'He who fights and runs away/Lives to fight another day.' Once we have crossed that line, it becomes clear that this is the better way for us in the short life we have allotted to us, and life is a more precious commodity than anything else we possess. Horace is likely best known today as the author of the phrase *carpe diem*, 'seize [or, more literally, "pluck"] the day' (*Carm.* 1.11.8), which has become a part of the small change of culture. Even

people without any knowledge of Latin (beyond *etcetera*, *status quo*, *ipso facto* and *vice versa*) know those two words.

48. Polyb. 12.25g.1.

49. 'Run, old hare! If I was an old hare, I'd run, too.' As recounted by Shelby Dade Foote Jr. (1916–2005) in Ken Burns' 1990 PBS documentary *The Civil War* (episode 5, 'The Universe of Battle').

50. On 1, 2 and 3 July 1863 in the gentle farmland of south Pennsylvania there was fought the greatest single battle of the American Civil War: Gettysburg, a terrible and spectacular drama which, properly or not, is usually looked upon as the great moment of decision. The climactic moment came at about 1400 hours (or 1500 hours, depending on which source you read) on 3 July, when approximately 12,500 men under Major General George E. Pickett made that gallant but doomed assault on the Union centre arrayed along Cemetery Ridge. Following Pickett's charge, the Confederate army was all but exhausted, but the Union troops had no stomach or energy to mount a counterattack. The overall casualties were enormous, with between 46,000 and 51,000 killed, wounded, missing or captured (Union casualties were 3,155 killed, 14,531 wounded and 5,369 captured or missing, while Confederate casualties are more difficult to estimate).

51. Ardent du Picq 1947: 118.

52. Archil. fr. 128 Swift, cf. Hom. *Od.* 20.18–21.

53. Polyb. 4.8.9.

54. Ibid. 4.8.5. Aratos' memoirs, no longer extant, were an important source for Polybios' *Historíai*.

55. Plut. *Arat.* 29.5–6. Naval tradition has it that Admiral Lord Howe once turned to an officer serving on his flagship and asked: 'Pray tell me Mr– how fear feels. I can see very well how it looks.'

56. Cf. Wilfred Owen, *Letter to His Brother*, 14 May 1917: 'The sensations of going over the top are about as exhilarating as those dreams of falling over a precipice, when you see the rocks at the bottom surging up to you. I woke up without being squashed. Some didn't. Then we were caught in a tornado of shells. The various *waves* were broken up, and we carried on like a crowd moving off a cricket-field. When I looked back and saw the ground all crawling and wormy with wounded bodies, I felt no horror at all, but only an immense exultation at having got through the barrage.'

57. Eileen Hathaway (ed.), *A Dorset Rifleman: The Recollections of Benjamin Harris* (Swanage, 1996/2001), p.41.

58. Edward Gibbon was not far off the mark when he wrote 'the violence of the storm was magnified by the superstitious terrors of the Gaul [viz. Gallo-Roman]; and they yielded without shame to the invisible powers of heaven, who seemed to militate on the side of the pious emperor' (*D&F*, vol. 2, ch. 27, p.93). This reminds us of the prelude to the battle of Mortimer's Cross, fought on a bitter cold Tuesday, Saint Blaise's Day, 3 February 1461 near Kingsland in Herefordshire, which is supposed to have involved the appearance of a halo display with three 'suns', a meteorological phenomenon known as a parhelion or sun dog, which is caused by atmospheric ice crystals and is only seen in very cold weather. The quick-witted Yorkist commander, a month away from becoming Edward IV of England (r. 1461–70, 1471–83), convinced his initially frightened followers that 'thys ys a good sygne, for these iij sonys betoken the Fader, the Sone, and the Holy Gost, and therefore late vs haue good harte, and in the name

of Almyghtye God go we agayns oure enemyes' (*An English Chronicle*, p.110 Davies). The Yorkist army went on to win a crushing victory over their Lancastrian opponents; an event immortalized by the Shakespearean line 'Three glorious suns, each one a perfect sun' (*3 Henry VI* 2.1.26). Having cut his teeth in this battle and turn around his fortunes that day – his father, Richard Plantagenet, Duke of York and his brother Edmund were recently slain at the battle of Wakefield (30 December 1460) – as the first Yorkist king, Edward IV adopted the 'sun in splendour' as his badge.

59. 2 Samuel 22:7–18.

60. Joshua 10:11.

61. Hor. *Carm.* 3.2.13.

62. Eileen Hathaway (ed.), *A Dorset Rifleman: The Recollections of Benjamin Harris* (Swanage, 1996/2001), pp.172–73.

63. It is worthy of note that the later militant pagan Zosimos (via Eunapios, his main source for the period) only mentions an (unhistorical?) eclipse of the sun on the *first* day, 'which made it seem like night instead of day for most of the time' (4.58.3). Solar eclipses are calculated for 20.11.393 and 6.4.395, with partial eclipses on 21.4.395 and 14.10.395.

64. There is a street in the Cittavecchia, old town of Trieste named after the Bora, the *Via della Bora*: rumour has it that it is impossible to walk through this street when the Bora blows. Trieste's particular geographic configuration and location between a relatively warm sea and an elevated, cold backdrop of mountain passes, produces a large difference in temperature and atmospheric pressure, thus it is known as *la citta del vento*. The French consul at Trieste, Marie-Henri Beyle (1783–1842), better known by his *nom de plume* Stendhal, posted here in 1830 – then part of Austro-Hungary, Metternich refused his *exequatur* on account of Stendhal's advanced and outspoken political liberalism and anticlericalism – explains poignantly the difference between a strong wind and the Bora. He says a strong wind is when one has to constantly hold on to his hat, but it is a Bora when one is afraid of breaking an arm. In 2004 Trieste inaugurated the Museo della Bora.

65. Note Vegetius (4.38), in his discussion on the twelve-point wind scale, has Boréās (L *Aquilo*) blow from the north-north-east. Boréās was the son of Eos, goddess of daybreak, and the Titan Astræos. He resided in Thrace, north of the Aegean Sea. Boréās was the opposite of the mild Zephyros (L *Subvespertinus*), the West Wind, and was notorious for his terrible storms. In Greek iconography he is usually depicted with two faces and enormous wings.

66. Jan Morris, *Trieste and the Meaning of Nowhere* (New York, NY, 2001), p.82.

67. Cameron 2013: 114.

68. Appianus *Keltika* fr. 13.

69. Iulius Obsequens *Book of Prodigies* §38. Note Augustine pokes fun at prodigies: 'I say nothing of manifestations which were more remarkable than harmful; talking oxen, unborn infants shouting words while still in the womb, flying serpents, women turning into men, hens into cocks and so on' (*Civ.* 3.31).

70. Aitken-Burt reckons that the deity depicted on An the Column of Marcus Aurelius 'is simply an artistic allegory to represent "Rain" borrowing the bearded and winged elements of traditional water and wind deities' (2016: 31). She also refers to the words of Marcus Aurelius himself: 'pray to Zeus, the chief god, for rain' (*Meditations* 5:7).

71. Column of Marcus Aurelius, scene XVI, cf. XI ('Lightning Miracle'). Cassius Dio states that as a result of the miracle 'He (Marcus) was now saluted *imperator* by the soldiers, for the seventh time' (71(72).10.4), and IMP. VII can be dated by coins and inscriptions to summer 174 (*BMC* 604–21). Note, however, Aitken-Burt (2016: 28–9) dates the 'Rain Miracle' to the beginning of the war in 171. The column remains in situ in the ancient Campus Martius, today's Piazza Colonna. Scene XVI is low down on the third spiral, making it easy to identify, which would of course also have been intensified by details being picked out in paint.

72. Dio 71(72).8–10.

73. Tertullian *Apologeticum* 5.25, cf. *Ad Scapulam* §4 ('…by the prayers [Marcus Aurelius'] Christian soldiers offered to God').

74. Euseb. *Hist. eccl.* 5.5.1–7.

75. *CIL* VI.3492. This was the same legion that had lost its *Aquila* under Caius Cestius Gallus, *legatus* of Syria, in AD 66 during the revolt in Iudaea (Suet. *Vesp.* 4.5). Rome had taken over Iudaea and turned it into a province under the direction of a procurator in AD 6 after fierce nationalistic resistance led by Iudas of Gamala. With the customary ruthlessness of military occupiers, Rome squashed the revolt, but Iudaea remained an unhappy place.

76. Ibid. III.504, 507, 509, 6097, 7261, V.2520, IX.435, X.7351. Probably in origin this was *legio* XII raised from scratch (along with *legio* XI) by Iulius Caesar in 58 BC for the campaign against the Helvetii (Caes. *B Gall.* 1.10.3). The Caesarian origin is confirmed by the fact that Marcus Cassius Scaeva, promoted to *primus pilus* of the legion for his epic courage, is in all probability Caesar's old centurion (Caes. *B civ.* 3.53.3–4, 5). He is mentioned by Cicero in a letter written in April 44 BC (*Att.* 14.10.2), and was still serving as the *primus pilus* of *legio* XII in 41/40 BC (*CIL* XI.06721.28).

77. Dio 71(72).8. The god invoked by Harnouphis was probably Thoth-Shu, the Egyptian god of air and wind. In the Ptolemaic period he became associated with Hermes.

78. M-C Budischovsky, *La diffusion des cultes isiaques autour de la Mer Adriatique* (Leyde, 1977), pp.124–5 (no. 25). Note the Scriptores Historia Augustae credits Marcus Aurelius as the agent of the 'Rain miracle': 'By his prayers he summoned a thunderbolt from heaven against a war-engine of the enemy and successfully brought rain for his men when they were suffering from thirst' (SHA *Marcus Aurelius* 24.4). In fact, this is a distortion and conflation of *two* events depicted on the Column of Marcus Aurelius, namely the 'Rain Miracle' and the 'Lightning Miracle'.

79. Tertullian *Apologeticum* 5.6.

80. Ibid. *De corona* §1.

81. Ibid. §11.

82. *Jomsvíkinga-saga* 21 Hollander.

83. Op cit. Such storms with a sudden drop in temperature, hail and lightning are very rare on the west coast of Norway.

Chapter Ten

1. Claud. *In Ruf. I* 137, *C Th.* X.22.3, Lib. *Ep.* 865, Theod. 5.18, Eunap. fr. 59, Zos. 4.52, 5.2, Amb. *Ep.* 52, J Lyd. *De mag.* 2.10, 3.23.

2. *C Th.* VII.4.18, 9.3. At this time Stilicho was still an eastern commander; he was one of the five *magistri utriusque militiae* in the eastern half of the empire.

3. Zos. 4.57.2. J Ant. fr. 187.

4. For the early career of Stilicho and his titles see *PLRE* I, pp.853–58.

5. *C Th.* XV.14.14. A purely honorary title, *patricius* was open only to those who had held the positions of *praefectus praetorio, praefectus urbi, magister equitum, magister peditum* or *consul ordinaries.*

6. Theodosius had thoroughly reorganized the eastern armies in the autumn of 387 or soon after in the spring of 388 when he was staying in Thessaloniki. Timasios, for instance, was still *magister equitum* in 386 (*C Th.* IV.17.5), but *magister equitum et peditum* by 388 (Ambr. *Ep.* 1.42.27). Under the new system, five equally ranked commanders held the title of *magister utriusque militiae* (Zos. 4.27.1–2, though he wrongly dates the reform to 380); two of them commanded *palatinae* troops and were styled *magistri utriusque militiae praesentalis*, while the other three, styled *magister peditum et equitum per Thracias, per Illyricum* and *per Orientem*, commanded the field armies of Thracia, of Illyricum and of the East respectively (*ND or.* I.6–8, VII-IX). We know of the five *magistri utriusque militiae* in 393: Richomeres, Timasios, Stilicho, Abundantius and Addaeus. Not only did this five-fold arrangement reduce the chances of any one individual having too much military power at his disposal, it also diverted the energies of *magistri* into rivalry with one another (Jones 1964: 609–10). In the West, following the earlier Constantinian system, the two *magistri praesentalis* were still sometimes styled *magister peditum* and *magister equitum*, and their spheres of activity covered the entire West and overlapped completely.

7. In 386 Flavius Timasios held the rank of *comes et magister equitum* (*C Th.* IV.17.5), in 388 *magister equitum et peditum* in the war against Magnus Maximus (Ambr. *Ep.* 1.42.27, Philostorg. 10.8), was *consul* in 389, and in 393, along with Stilicho, *magister utriusque militiae*, and held this rank in the campaign against Eugenius the following year (Zos. 4.49, 57.2).

8. Returning East, Timasios retained his rank under Arcadius, but was accused of treason by Eutropius and banished to Oasis in Egypt (Zos. 5.8–9, Soz. 8.7, cf. *C Th.* IX.32.1 Olympiod. fr. 33 Müller), where he either died of thirst (Soz. 8.7) or was rescued by his son (Zos. 5.9.7). According to Eunapios (fr. 70), he was ambitious, avaricious and a hard drinker.

9. O'Flynn 1983: x-xi.

10. E.g. '...but by the crime of a half-barbarian traitor who with our money has armed our foes against us', Jer. *Ep.* 123.17, though admittedly writing after Stilicho's downfall in 408.

11. Philostorg. 11.2, Sok. 5.26.

12. Zos. 5.4.3, Olympiod. fr. 2.

13. Ambr. *Obit. Theod.* §5.

14. *Ut ventum ad sedes, cunctos discedere tectis/dux iubet et generum compellat talibus ultro,* Claud. *III Cons.* 142–3.

15. *Illumque diem sub corde referres,/quo tibi confusa dubiis formidine rebus/infantem genitor moriens commisit alendum,* Claud. *IV Cons.* 11.581–3.

16. Zos. 5.4.2, cf. 7.3–4.

17. Claud. *B Gild.* 153–5, cf. 253–517, Gildo had shown disloyalty in the past and Theodosius had planned to deal with him personally before being prevented by his own death.

18. Eunap. fr. 62.

19. According to Edward Gibbon (*D&F*, vol. 2, chap. 32, p.223, n. 2), before he had gained the top of the Constantinopolis greasy pole, Eutropius had a rather colourful if somewhat sordid career, serving as a *catamite* to a groom or trooper in the imperial stables, a pimp for an aging general and finally as a body servant to the daughter of the aforesaid general. Of course our noble historian has presented us the more sordid details of the powerful eunuch's life. Eutropius was born as a slave in Assyria (Claud. *In Eutr.* 1.58, Philostorg. 11.4), given to the *magister peditum* Arinthaeus (Claud. *In Eutr.* 40, 61, 478). Freed as an old man, he entered palace service under Theodosius and was promoted by the *magister militum* Abundantius (Claud. *In Eutr.* 143, 154), a Scythian who had served under Gratianus prior to serving Theodosius and had reached the consulship of 393 (*P Oxy.* 1712, Sok. 5.25). Eutropius conspired with Stilicho against Flavius Rufinus, taking over on his post as Arcadius' chief advisor following his death in November 395 (Zos. 5.8). He was the Grand Chamberlain, *praepositus sacri cubicula* (*C Th.* IX.40.17, Zos. 5.9.2, Philostorg. 11.4, Sok. 6.5), on the accession of Arcadius at the very latest, perhaps as early as 393, a position in which he dominated Arcadius during the period 396–399 (Eunap. frs. 66, 69, 74, Zos. 5.8, 5.11.1, 5.12.1, 5.14.1, Claud. *In Eutr.* 1.170–1). He resumed the persecution of pagans and heretics (*C Th.* XV.1.36, XVI.5.31–4, 7.6, 10, 14, 16, Philostorg. 11.5, Soz. 8.1). He compelled Theophilos of Alexandria to accept Ioannes Chrysostomos as bishop in 398 (Sok. 6.2, Soz. 8.2). Much legislation he passed was for personal reasons: restriction of religious asylum (*C Th.* IX.40.16, 45.3, XI.30.57, Sok. 6.5, Soz. 8.7, Chrys. *Eutr.* 3), exceptions to prohibition on bribery (*C Th.* X.10.21), freeing of freedmen of all restrictions (*C Th.* VIII.17.1), and strict penalties for conspiracy (*C Th.* IX.14.3). He relied on a system of spies (Eunap. fr. 67, Zos. 5.10.4) and became very rich (Chrys. *Eutr.* 1.3) through confiscations (Zos. 5.8.2, 12.2, 13.1, Claud. *In Eutr.* 1.167–8) and sale of office (Claud. *In Eutr.* 1.190–1, J Ant. fr. 189); provinces were even divided to increase this income (Claud. *In Eutr.* 2.586) and the Jews won privileges through bribery (*C Th.* II.1.10, XVI.8.10–13). He curbed the powers of the *praefectus praetorio per Orientis* and saw to it that those military men such as Abundantius – who had risen through his patronage – and Timasios were removed (J Lyd. *De mag.* 2.10, 3.23, 3.40–1). He summoned Stilicho to confront Alaric in Greece (Claud. *In Eutr.* 2.544–5), but when he was unsuccessful, Alaric was appointed *magister militum per Illyricum*. Eutropius played a leading part in Gildo's revolt. He was given the title *patricius* (Zos. 5.17.4, *C Th.* IX.40.17, Claud. *In Eutr.* 1.109, 2.68, 561, Soz. 8.7, Philostorg. 11.4) and the same powers of appeal as a *praefectus* (Claud. *In Eutr.* 1.105, 286, *C Th.* IX.40.16, XI.30.57). He then held a military command against the Huns in 398 (Claud. *In Eutr.* 1.236–7, *C Th.* IX.40.17), for which success he was nominated *consul* for 399 – not recognized in the West (Claud. *In Eutr.* 2.126) – the first eunuch to hold that office. When Tribigild revolted, Gaïnas demanded Eutropius' surrender (Eunap. frs. 75–6, Zos. 5.17.2–5). Arcadius wept (Chrys. *Eutr.* 4), but was overborne by Aelia Eudoxia, anxious to increase her own influence (Philostorg. 11.6, Soz. 8.7). Fearing for his life, Eutropius fled to the church (Zos. 5.18.1, Sok. 6.5, Soz. 8.7) where Ioannes Chrysostomos delivered a sermon over him. When riot threatened, Eutropius left the church and was arrested; his property was confiscated, his *acta* annulled and he was exiled to Cyprus (*C Th.* IX.40.17). He was later recalled, tried and beheaded (Zos. 5.18.2, Philostorg. 11.6, Sok. 6.5, Soz. 8.7).

20. Syn. *De reg.* 14.3 [1089]. One sixth-century source claimed that Theodosius had explicitly ruled that his sons were not to engage in campaigning (J Lyd. *De mag.* 2.11, 3.41), but this seems more likely to reflect a desire on the part of emperors and/or courtiers to offer an *apologia* and counter the kind of criticisms Synesios had voiced.

21. Olympiod. fr. 2 Müller.

22. Flavius Rufinus had been left in control of the eastern half of the empire, nominally under the authority of Arcadius, when Theodosius set out against Arbogastes and Eugenius. He had been advanced rapidly by Theodosius, and was clearly a favoured civilian official (Zos. 4.57.4 = Eunap. frs. 62–3, J Ant. frs. 188, 190, Oros. 7.37.1). He intended his daughter to marry Arcadius, but was outwitted by his rival Eutropius, a master of palace intrigue (Zos. 5.1.4, 5.3, J Ant. fr. 190); Eutropius' success in hoodwinking Rufinus over Arcadius' marriage is probably explained by the latter's absence at Antioch (Zos. 5.2.3). Rufinus was a zealous Nicene Christian (Theod. *Hist. eccl.* 5.18, Soz. 8.17).

23. Oros. 7.38.5, Zos. 5.32.1, Rutil. 2.41–60. However, in the law of 22 November 408 (*C Th.* IX.42.22) by which Honorius intended to justify the killing of Stilicho, the charge is that of stirring up the barbarians, with no mention of *affectation regni*. It was alleged that the father of Theodosius II was not Arcadius, but one of the councillors of Aelia Eudoxia called Ioannes: there were rumours of the empress's sexual improprieties with said courtier.

24. Claud. *Cons. Stil. I* 35–9.

25. The only judgemental writers regarding his origin were Jerome, who refers to Stilicho as a *'semibarbarus proditor'* (*Ep.* 123.16) and Orosius (7.38). Augustine (*Ep.* 97.2–3) and Rutilius Namatianus (2.41–60) are both hostile, but make no mention of his origin.

26. Jones 1964: 326–8.

27. One of the names of God, it is used 235 times in the Bible. 'Host', of course, could refer either to an army or a great number or multitude. The first time it appears in the Bible is right at the beginning, in the creation account: 'Thus the heavens and the earth, and all the host of them, were finished' (Genesis 2:1 NKJV).

28. *Acta Marcelli* 2–3, 4 (his rank).

29. *Acta Maximilianus* 2.8.

30. Soz. 1.8, Theod. *Ep.* 2, cf. Maur. 2.18.13–23.

31. Sulp. Sev. *V Mart.* 2.2.

32. *C Th.* VII.20.12.2.

33. Aug. *contra Faustum* 22.75.

34. Jord. *Get.* §146, cf. 42. *Vide* Wolfram 1988: 32–3, 94–6 and Heather 1991: 10–12, 28–32 for an opposing view.

35. Jer. *Ep.* 123.16, Oros. 7.38.1.

36. Formed by Constantinus I, their predecessors were the *protectores divini lateris*, 'protectors of the sacred rank', (re)formed by Gallienus and attached to the imperial retinue (Jones 1964: 53–4). Obviously this unit consisted solely of men loyal to Gallienus and acknowledged so by its special title.

37. *CIL* VI.1730 = *ILS* 1277.

38. *CIL* VI.1730, 1731 = *ILS* 1277, 1278. Claudianus says (*Laus Ser.* 190–3) that the appointment to take charge of the horses in the imperial stables was Stilicho's *primus*

honor after his marriage to Serena. It is possible that Stilicho held both these positions at the same time, e.g. *CIL* VI.1731, where he is called *comes domesticorum et stabuli sacri.*

39. Claud. *Cons. Stil. I* 69–70, *Laus Ser.* 179f, Olympiod. fr. 2 Müller.

40. Claud. *Laus Ser.* 104 (adoption), *Cons. Stil. I* 71–3, *Fesc.* 3.8 (son-in-law), cf. *Cons. Stil. II* 176–81, Serena described as the 'royal mother' of Eucherius and Theodosius as his 'imperial grandsire' who dandles his 'grandson' on his knee. On the other hand, Zosimos only refers to Serena as the daughter of Honorius, the brother of Theodosius (4.57.2, 5.4.1), and he describes Stilicho as 'married to the niece (ἀδελφιδῆς)' of Theodosius (5.34.6). It appears that Theodosius adopted Serena in fact, but not legally, after her father's death ([Aur. Vict.] *Epit.* 48.18). On the face of it, Serena played the role of mother, aunt, cousin and sister to the three children of Theodosius, a thankless task as it happened: she was to be murdered on the secret orders of the third, then 21 years old, with the active connivance of the second and with the tacit consent of the first. For the persuasive argument that Serena was *not* formally adopted by Theodosius, *vide* Cameron 2016.

41. Claud. *Cons. Stil. I* 69–94, *Laus Ser.* 177–85, Zos. 4.57.2, 5.4.1, Olympiod. fr. 2 Müller.

42. Claud. *Nupt.* 41, *VI Cons.* 92–3.

43. Zos. 5.12.1. Claudianus' words are an eloquent expression of Stilicho's hopes: 'May Maria's womb grow big and a little Honorius (*parvus Honoriades*), born to the purple, rest on his grandsire's lap' (*Nupt.* 335–41).

44. Olympiod. fr. 3 Müller, Philostorg. 12.2, Jord. *Rom.* §332, *Get.* §154, Zos. 5.28.1, Zon. 13.21. The marriage was repudiated after her father's death (Zos. 5.35.3).

45. After the Frigidus, according to Sokrates Scholastikos (7.10), Alaric was made *comes rei militaris.* He soon gained the title of *magister militum per Illyricum* (Claud. *In Eutr.* 214–20, *B Goth.* 535–9) from Arcadius, an office in which he was confirmed a few years later by Honorius out of short-term motives as well.

46. Out of 181 units of the western *comitatenses*, 76 had perished between the eve of the Frigidus, the wars against the Gothic chieftains Alaric and Radagaisus, and the countless civil wars against usurpers. The drastic loss in manpower could only be compensated in makeshift ways by transferring garrison troops into mobile field armies; from ninety-seven newly-raised units, sixty-two had been frontier troops upgraded 'on paper' (Jones 1964: 355). What we see here is the long shadow cast by the horrendous defeat of the western army at the Frigidus: in the decade that followed western forces were constantly required to juggle one challenge after another without adequate time to rebuild themselves to full strength.

47. Claud. *In Ruf. II* 410, Philostorg. 11.3, Zos. 5.7.5–6, Jer. *Ep.* 60.16, Sok. 6.1, Soz. 8.1.

48. *ND occ.* IX.15–19. *Vide* Jones 1964: 183.

49. Claud. *B. Goth.* 536–7.

50. Sid. Apoll. *Ep.* 5.480. Of course, in Sidonius' day, Gaul was divided among at least three governments less able to safeguard the free movement of persons than, for instance, the occasionally quarrelling Frankish kings of the time of Gregory, bishop of Tours, a century later.

Chapter Eleven

1. *ILS* 9465.

2. Ambr. *Ep.* 57, Soz. 7.22.

3. Ambr. *Ep.* 17.10, Symm. *Rel.* 3.1. Against the assumption apropos the influence of Ambrose, Cameron 2013: 34–7.

4. Her temple on the Palatine only dates back to 294 BC.

5. Dio 51.22, cf. Suet. *Aug.* 35.

6. Plin. 3.5.39.

7. Tac. *Ger.* 33.1.

8. Hor. *Carm.* 3.6.5–8.

9. Cic *Phil.* 1.14 (*oderint dum metuant*).

10. Ambr. *Ep.* 72.9.

11. Amm. Marc. 16.10.4–12, Symm. *Rel.* 3.7. By the reign of Gratianus it had been well over a century since an emperor had resided in Rome. Besides Constantius' one, Constantinus paid three brief visits (312, 315, 326), Theodosius definitely one (389) and possibly a second (394), while Gratianus himself not even one.

12. However lukewarm his devotion to this Christian offshoot may have been, Constantius was still a meddling heretic; one Christian writer, Hilary de Poitiérs (*In Constantium* 11) went so far as to call him the Antichrist.

13. *C Th.* XVI.10.2, 10.4–5, 10.6, cf. Lib. *Or.* 17.7, 18.23. Despite the ban, sacrifice itself did not stop (Amm. Marc. 19.12.12, Lib. *Or.* 1.27, cf. *Ep.* 1351.3), and a law promulgated by Theodosius, Arcadius and Honorius was still attempting to forbid it in 392 (*C Th.* XVI.10.12).

14. *P Meyer* 15.

15. Amm. Marc. 30.9.5.

16. Soz. 6.6.2.

17. Amm. Marc. 18.2.19, Eunap. fr. 13, Zos. 3.4.4–7.

18. Gallus' original name was Flavius Claudius Gallus (*ILS* 737, *CIL* VIII.8475, XII.5560); the name Constantius was taken only on his elevation by Constantius II (Aur. Vict. *Caes.* 42.9, Sok. 2.28). He escaped murder in 337 because he was thought to be too ill to survive (Sok. 3.1) and retiring to the east (Sok. 2.28, Amm. Marc. 15.2.7, Soz. 5.2). From here he was summoned by Constantius to be *Caesar* (Iul. *Ep. ad Ath.* 272A, Aur. Vict. *Caes.* 42.9, Eutr. 10.12.2) and to ensure his loyalty found himself married to Constantius' older sister Constantia ([Aur. Vict.] *Epit.* 42.1, Zon. 13.8) ; she had been married for a couple of years to Gallus' uncle, who had been a victim of the fratricide of 337. Although she is represented as a saint in Christian hagiography, according to Ammianus Marcellinus she was 'a human Fury, constantly fuelling her husband's rage and as insatiable as he for human blood' (14.1.2). This political marriage was because Constantius was currently caught up in the war with Magnentius and needed a commander against the continuing Persian harassments (Amm. Marc. 21.13.11, Zon. 13.8, cf. Zos. 2.45.1). Gallus won minor victories; although the Persians were fairly quiet (Amm. Marc. 14.13.1, 16.9.3, Iul. *Or.* 1.28D, 2.66D, Zon. 13.7), the anonymous author of the *Artemii passio* (12–13, pp.53.19–55.16) has Constantinus jealous of Gallus's success against Šāpūr II. Magnentius attempted to have him murdered, but the plot was discovered (Zon. 13.8, Amm. Marc. 14.7.4). Gallus's tyrannical nature (Iul. *Ep. ad Ath.* 271D, Amm. Marc. 14.11.3, Aur. Vict. *Caes.* 42.11, J Ant. fr. 174, Eutr. 10.13, Zon. 13.8, Sok. 2.33) was now excited, and his wife spurred him on (Amm. Marc. 14.1.2, 8, 9, Zon. 13.9, Philostorg. 3.28). This was revealed in bloody games (Amm. Marc. 14.7.3, 1.2, 4, Iul. *Misop.* 340A), executions and exiles without trial (Amm.

Marc. 14.1.3, 5, 14.9, 3, 6), and his attempt to execute the entire council of Antioch (Amm. Marc. 14.7.2, Lib. *Or.* 1.96). To history, Gallus was an old-school bloodthirsty despot, a mini-Nero. He was, however, a devout Christian (Soz. 3.15, 4.19), and an Arian (Philostorg. 3.27). Under constant pressure from Constantius – apparently, he was enticed by the news that Constantius planned to raise him to the rank of *Augustus* and to enlist his aid in some future campaign – he finally returned to Poetovio where he was arrested and in October 354 handed over for public execution in Pola, Histria (Amm. Marc. 14.7.9–21, 11.6–23, Lib. *Or.* 18.24, Philostrog. 3.28, 4.1, Zos. 2.55.3, Sok. 2.24, Zon. 13.9) just like his cousin Crispus. Iulianus' epitaph for his brother was fitting: 'He deserved to live, even if he was unfit to rule' (*Ep. ad Ath.* 272A).

19. *Anon. Vales.* 1 §2, Philostrog. 2.16, *Pan. Lat.* 10 (2).11.4. Some sources, however, refer to Flavia Theodora as the stepdaughter of Maximianus, which suggests she was born from an earlier marriage between Eutropia, wife of Maximianus, and Afranius Hannibalianus ([Aur. Vic.] *Epit.* 39.25, Eutr. 9.22). This man was *consul* in 292 and *praefectus praetorio* under Diocletianus.

20. Philostorg. 2.16, Zon. 13.4. Iulianus' parents, Iulius Constantius (*PLRE* I, p.226) and Basilina (*PLRE* I, p.148), married sometime after the death of Constantius' former wife and the mother of Iulianus' half-brother Gallus, Galla (*PLRE* I, p.382), an event for which Gallus's birth in 325/326 provides a *terminus post quem*, and a date of about nine months before Iulianus' birth in May or June of 332, a *terminus ante quem*. Basilina died shortly after Iulianus' birth.

21. The brothers evidently met in Pannonia in the early autumn and, by the date of their formal acclamation as *Augusti* on 9 September, had worked out among themselves a division of the empire and some order of precedence that seems to have recognized Constantinus' pre-eminence in the college of rulers. Moreover, there is little doubt that the massacre was, if not engineered by Constantius II, Constantinus' favourite son and soon-to-be emperor of the East, then not stopped by him. Iulianus certainly laid the blame at his door, and was later to write of Constantius: 'Our fathers were brothers, sons of the same father. And close relations as we were how this most humane emperor treated us. He put to death six of our cousins, my father [Iulius Constantius] who was his uncle, another of our uncles on my father's side and my eldest brother [Gallus, in 354], without trial' (*Ep. ad Ath.* 270C). The official line, according to Zosimos, was that 'the will of the soldiers was used to justify the murder of other relatives with potential claims' (2.40.3, cf. Euseb. *V Const.* 4.68.2). Iulianus was not taken in by Constantius' continued protestations of innocence. As he wrote with some scorn several years later: 'They kept telling us [viz. he and his brother Gallus] and tried to convince us that Constantinus had acted in this way partly because he was deceived and partly because he gave into the violence and tumult of an undisciplined and mutinous army' (*Ep. ad Ath.* 271B).

22. Jer. *Chron.* s.a. 340 (235a), Theoph. 35.30.

23. A reference to John's comment that 'a prophet does not come of Galilee' (John 7:52 NIV).

24. The Romans celebrated the Saturnalia at the time when Helios was residing in Capricornus, the *domus* of Kronos (Saturn), and the momentary freedom enjoyed by slaves during the festival's fooleries was a form of rebirth.

25. Its date of composition is disputed: some scholars opt for the winter of 361/362 at Constantinopolis; others for the winter of 362/363 at Antioch. Antioch at that time

was one of the principal cities of the empire, '*orientis apex pulcher*' in the proud words of its native son Ammianus Marcellinus (22.19.14).

26. Iul. *Caes.* 336A-B. Here Iulianus has parodied a passage from Matthew, 'Come to me, all you who are weary and burdened, and I will give you rest' (11:28 NIV), and is ridiculing the sacrament of baptism (Constantinus had deliberately postponed his baptism to the very last day of his life).

27. Voltaire, *Dictionnaire philosophique* (London, 2004), p.60, sv *Baptême*: Baptism.

28. Iul. *Ep.* 36, cf. *C Th.* XII.3.5, issued 17 June 362.

29. Otto von Bismarck interview (11 August 1867) with Friedrich Meyer von Waldeck of the *St. Petersburgische Zeitung*, apud Heinrich Ritter von Poschinger, *Fürst Bismarck: neue Tischgespräche und Interviews* (Stuttgart, 1895), vol. 1, p.248.

30. Greg. Naz. *Or.* 4.101. It is notable that Iulianus, who knew Gregory during his studies in Athens (in July 355 he had been allowed to go to Athens), but one can look in vain for his name in the writings of Iulianus; it appears that the emperor did not think the bishop was even worth mentioning. Gregory Nazianzen has left us more poetry than any other Greek writer from antiquity: Christians, he insists, should have literature that is as good as pagan literature. The pagans do not have all the best tunes. Incidentally, it was Gregory (*Or.* 4.1, 18.32) who was the first to call Iulianus 'Apostate' (Gk. ἀποστάτης/ *apostátēs*). His brother Caesarius, a famous doctor, served for a while at Iulianus' court.

31. Amm. Marc. 22.10.7, cf. 25.4.20. The soldier historian made Iulianus the central figure in Books 15–25 of his *Res Gestae* and more than once expresses his admiration for him without glossing over his shortcomings. He himself saw in Iulianus the personification of the four cardinal virtues (prudence, justice, temperance and courage), though it must be said that the historical integrity of Ammianus Marcellinus does present the darker side of Iulianus' character, a certain annoying flippancy that probably came from an insecure desire to be praised: 'a degenerate Greek from Asia and a liar and a fool who pretended to be wise... Babbling mole, ape in purple, Greek dilettante' (ibid. 17.9.3, 11.1), such was the clamour of detractors at court or on the Rhenus where he was serving. An even less flattering portrait was drawn by Gregory Nazianzen when they both were students in Athens: 'The loosely jointed neck, the shoulders continually shrugging...the eye...with that insane glitter...his proud disdainful snorting...the violent guffaws of laughter...the disorderly unintelligent questions pouring out in an incoherent stream....' (*Or.* 5.23); Gregory's unflattering description is longer than this paraphrase and was clearly crafted to make anyone immediately recognize Iulianus for what he was: an unstable fiend.

32. Theod. *Hist. eccl.* 3.4, citing Aristophanes (*Aves* 808), who in turn was citing Aischylos (*Myrmidons* fr. 139). Iulianus (fr. 7) himself was to wield the same quotation writing against the Christians. There again, many Christians of our period of study (Ambrose, Jerome, Augustine, Sulpicius Severus, Paulinus of Nola, Prudentius) were at least as well-read as pagans like Praetextatus and Symmachus.

33. Theod. *Hist. eccl.* 3.21, cf. Rufin. 10.37.

34. Amm. Marc. 22.5.4.

35. Ammianus Marcellinus (25.6.6) does not know who struck the emperor, but rules out a Roman. Most other contemporary sources did not know either (Eutr. 10.16, Fest. 28.3), but Libanius (*Or.* 18.274–5, 24 *passim*) charged the Christians. Although later ecclesiastical historians took this up, Sozomenos (6.1–2) even going so far as to praise

the man who threw the spear and calling him a brave tyrannicide, the silence of Gregory Nazianzen is crucial (*Or.* 5.13, either a Persian, a Saracen or a disgruntled Roman).

36. As he bled, the dying emperor groaned, 'You have conquered, Galilean!' (Gk. νείκηκας Γαλιλαῖε), while collecting the blood that gushed out of his wound and throwing it heavenward, or at least that is what later Christian reports claimed. Theodoret (3.20) is believed to be the origin of these last words, and early rumours suggested that a Christian soldier from the Roman ranks had assassinated Iulianus. No mention of such a declaration by Iulianus occurs in the accounts of earlier writers, even those most hostile to the emperor, and such nonsense should be relegated to the realm of fables.

37. Amm. Marc. 25.5.3.

38. See *ILS* 1255 for the early career of Saturninius Secundus Salutius. He had been despatched by Constantius II to Gaul to watch over Iulianus (Iul. *Ep. ad Ath.* 281D), but got on well with him. Constantius suspected he was helping Iulianus and recalled him (ibid. 281D, 8.242A, Zos. 3.5.3–4, Lib. *Or.* 12.58, 18.85). He was appointed *praefectus praetorio per Orientis* by Iulianus (Amm. Marc. 22.3.1, Zos. 3.29.3, *C Th.* I.16.5), and served as the chief judge of Constantius' creatures (Amm. Marc. 22.3.1, Eunap. fr. 17, Lib. *Or.* 18.182), cautiously opposing Iulianus' paganism at Antioch (Iul. *Ep. ad Ath.* 277–8, Amm. Marc. 16.1.5, 16.5, 17.9.6, 20.5.4, 22.3.7, Lib. *Or.* 18.42, Sok. 3.19, Soz. 5.10, 20). He took part in the ill-fated Persian expedition, being responsible for its organization (Lib. *Or.* 18.214, Amm. Marc. 23.5.6), although very ill (Amm. Marc. 25.3.21, 25.5.3), and risked his life in battle (ibid. 25.3.14, Zos. 3.29.3). Secundus Salutius was highly educated (Iul. *Ep. ad Ath.* 8.252), and a pagan (Iulianus' *Oratio* IV is dedicated to him).

39. Amm. Marc. 25.7.14, Zos. 3.33.1.

40. For the political machinations behind Iovianus' elevation, *vide* Amm Marc. 25.5.1–4, [Aur; Vict.] *Epit.* 44.1, Eutr. 10.17.1, Zon. 13.14, Sok. 3.22, Soz. 6.3, cf. Zos. 3.30.1.

41. Amm Marc. 25.5.4.

42. Soz. 5.15.

43. Ambr. *Ep.* 57.

44. *Uno itinere non potest perveniri ad tam grande secretum*, Symm. *Rel.* 3.10.

45. The removal of the *ara Victoriae* would provoke, over a period of three years, a series of oratorical duels between Symmachus and Ambrose. Bauto, Gratianus' *magister militum*, although a pagan himself (cf. Cameron 2013: 85), seems to have supported Ambrose's rejection of the request by Symmachus for restoration of the *ara Victoriae* (Ambr. *Ep.* 57.3, cf. *Ep.* 17.18). Nevertheless, Bauto enjoyed the friendship of traditionally-minded senator Symmachus (Symm. *Ep.* 4.15, 16).

46. Many educated Christian writers, including Jerome, who always felt tortured guilt about his love of Cicero ('You follow Cicero, not Christ – your heart lies where your treasure is', Jer. *Ep.* 22.30), felt uncomfortably conscious about the 'simplicity' of Christian literature, which had supposedly developed from what they called *sermo piscatorius*, 'the language of fishermen'. Part of the problem was the Bible; not only what it said but the way in which it said it. The gospels of the old Latin Bible were written in a distinctly demotic style, rich in grammatical solecisms and the sort of words that grated on educated ears. As Jerome laments, the style of sections of the Bible is 'rude and repellent' (op. cit.). Still, as he explains further on in the same letter, his conversion had

been from one sort of literature to another: 'Since then, I have read the divine books with more care than I formerly applied to reading mortal ones' (op. cit.).
47. Symm. *Mem.* 3.10.
48. For Ambrose's high opinion of Symmachus, *vide* Ambr. *Ep.* 57.2.

Chapter Twelve

1. Lib. *Or.* 17.2. With its dark undertones of civilization under attack by barbarism (viz. Christianity), Libanius has artfully adapted a passage from Herodotos: 'As far as I can see it, gentlemen [the Spartan ephors], if the Athenians desert us and make an alliance with Persia, then, however strongly the Isthmus is fortified, the postern gates are wide open for the Persian invasion of the Peloponnese' (9.9).
2. Greg. Naz. *Or.* 4.1.
3. *Historia Acephala* §12.
4. Zos. 2.29.2.
5. The Synod of Nicene issued a creed that confessed the consubstantiality of the Father and the Son, and stated in no uncertain terms: 'We believe in one God, the Father Almighty, Maker of all things visible and invisible. And in one Lord Jesus Christ, the Son of God, begotten of the Father the only-begotten; that is, of the essence of the Father, God of God, Light of Light, very God of very God, begotten, not made, being of one substance (ὁμοούσιον) with the Father; by whom all things were made both in heaven and on earth; who for us men, and for our salvation, came down and was incarnate and was made man; he suffered, and the third day he rose again, ascended into heaven; from thence he shall come to judge the quick and the dead. And in the Holy Spirit. But those who say: "There was a time when he was not"; and "He was not before he was made"; and "He was made out of nothing", or "He is of another substance" or "essence", or "The Son of God is created", or "changeable", or "alterable"; they are condemned by the holy catholic and apostolic Church' (Decree of the First Œcumenical Synod, Nicaea). This and other Ecumenical Councils are considered as formulating binding definitions of the faith, which cannot be changed since they were inspired by the Holy Spirit.
6. It is interesting to note that the third-century Alexandrian theologian Origen of Caesarea reports the following: 'It is easy to count the Christians who died for their religion, because few died, and only from time to time, and at intervals' (*contra Celsus* §3).
7. *Vide* Fields 2017: 59–62, 77–83.
8. Greg. Nyss. *PG* 46.557. In Greek: Ἐὰν περὶ τῶν ὀβολῶν ἐρωτήσῃς, ὁ δέ σοι περὶ γεννητοῦ καὶ ἀγεννήτου ἐφιλοσόφησε·κἂν περὶ τιμήματος ἄρτου πύθοιο, Μείζων ὁ Πατὴρ, ἀποκρίνεται, καὶ ὁ Υἱὸς ὑποχείριος. Εἰ δὲ, τὸ λουτρὸν ἐπιτήδειόν ἐστιν, εἴποις, ὁ δὲ ἐξ οὐκ ὄντων τὸν Υἱὸν εἶναι διωρίσατο (trans. A.H.M. Jones).
9. The Roman Catholic Church is the Chalcedonian Church of the West, which recognizes the supreme authority of the pope of Rome as the Vicar (viz. representative) of Christ. On the other hand, the Orthodox Church, which still uses the title the Catholic Orthodox Church, is the group of Christian communities belonging to the Eastern Orthodox or Chalcedonian Church of the Byzantine Empire: it rejects the supremacy of the 'patriarch' of Rome, still adhering to the system of the five patriarchates that by 451 (Fourth Ecumenical Council, Chalcedon) consisted of – in order of honour, *not* supremacy – Rome, Constantinopolis, Antioch, Alexandria and Jerusalem.

10. Nestorianism, proselytizing India and China in its brief and fertile race, was to have seven metropolitan provinces and more than eighty bishoprics at the time of the Islamic invasion, and Nisibis as its chief centre after Seleukeia-on-Tigris. Its almost miraculously swift spread had been aided by the caravan routes that crossed all frontiers.

11. Napoléon Bonaparte, Archive nationales, Paris, 390 Archives privées 25, MS of September 1816 (10 Septembre), pp.4–5. As he said elsewhere, 'Muhammad's superiority consisted in having founded a religion without a hell' (Honoré de Balzac, *Maxims et pensées de Napoléon* [Paris, 1838], maxim no. 70).

12. Literally, 'chained upon this rock'.

13. As Napoléon said, not without a large dose of melancholy, of his final fate: 'A new Prometheus, I am attached to a rock where a vulture is gnawing at me. I had stolen the fire of heaven to endow France with it, the fire has come back to its source, and here I am' (Honoré de Balzac, *Maxims et pensées de Napoléon* [Paris, 1838], maxim no. 525). It was, of course, an eagle of loud-thundering Zeus that appeared every two days to peck out a piece of Prometheus' liver, which renewed itself as fast as it was eaten. Perhaps Napoléon's gnawing vulture represented 'perfidious Albion'.

14. M. le Chevalier de Beauterne, *Sentiment de Napoléon sur le Christianisme: conversations religieuses, recueillies à Sainte-Hélène par M. le général comte de Montholon* (3e éd., Paris, 1843), part II, chap. 2.

15. '*D'inestingubil odio/E d'indomato amor.*' So wrote Alessandro Manzoni (1785–1873), the Milanese novelist and poet-prophet of Italian unity, in his seminal poem *Il cinque maggio* (vv. 59–60). On 16 July 1821, Manzoni read of the death of Napoléon and the following day he began to feverishly scribble 108 verses of poetry about him. On 19 July – only three days later – Manzoni titled his poem *Il cinque maggio* ('The Fifth of May'), and put down his pen. Because the Austrian censors thought Manzoni was one of Napoléon's former officers and anything Napoleonic was taboo to the Habsburg overlords, the poem did not appear in print in Italy until 1822. That it finally did so was thanks to the elderly Goethe, who correctly believed Manzoni was a genius and published the poem in a German magazine. *Il cinque maggio* became one of the most popular lyrics in the Italian language. In a letter to his good friend, the historian and poet Cesare Cantù (1807–95), Manzoni described the deceased French emperor and former King of Italy as 'a man who one had to admire without being able to love; the greatest tactician, the most indefatigable conqueror, in possession of the greatest quality befitting of a politician: the ability to know when to wait and when to act. His death shook me. It was as if the world were missing some essential element.'

16. One of the aphorisms of the Duke of Wellington (1769–1852) says of Napoléon that he was 'unquestionably the greatest military genius that ever existed'. Privately, however, he wrote long memoranda lambasting Napoléon's campaigning techniques. Napoléon, on the other hand, was publicly scathing about Wellington's abilities, seemingly referring to him as a mere '*général de Cipayes*', that is to say, one fit for nothing better than fighting in India. 'I should pronounce him to be *un homme de peu d'esprit, sans générosité et sans grandeur d'âme*' (Barry E. O'Meara, *Napoleon in Exile* [Philadelphia, PN, 1822], vol. 2, p.147). In private, however, he praised his ruthlessness. By way of comparison, Napoléon had won sixty of his seventy battles; Wellington had fought far fewer but won them all; a string that included inflicting bitter defeats on six of the emperor's own *mareschals* among the arid hills of Portugal and Spain. For both of

them, Waterloo was to be their last battle. The phrase *général de Cipayes* first appears in the *Gazette nationale ou le Moniteur universel*, 9 October 1809, p.2. Though obviously referring to Wellington who was then campaigning in Portugal, there is no direct link to Napoléon at that date.

17. Moved by the alleged conversion to Christianity of Napoléon before his death, a conversion that happened to coincide with his own, Manzoni decided to view Napoléon in a more spiritual light and leave the historical judgement of the man to posterity. In fact there is a couplet in the ode which has become a popular expression in Italy: *'Fu vera gloria? Ai posteri/l'aruda sentenza'* ('Is this true fame? Posterity/The arduous verdict will declare', *Il cinque maggio*, vv. 31–2).

18. One of Napoléon's first acts as consul was to bring back religion to France after the atheistic years of the revolution. Thus the concordat with the Catholic Church on 15 July 1801 reaffirmed the Roman Catholic Church as the majority church of France and reinstated most of its civil status. Still, on 10 June 1809 he was excommunicated by Pius VII though the bull *Quum memoranda*, but it was a rather timid excommunication. While the bull excommunicated all those who 'usurp, encourage, advise or perform' violation of the temporal sovereignty of the Holy See – papal territories had been seized and added to 'my kingdom in Italy', which was soon followed by Rome being added to *le Premier Empire* – Napoléon, the usurper, encourager and advisor, was not explicitly named. There were to be serious repercussions. On the night of 5/6 July 1809 Pius VII was kidnapped when a French raiding party led by *Général* Radet broke into the Vatican. Though furious when he heard about it, Napoléon kept the Holy Roman Pontiff under house arrest for the next five years, first in Savona (1809–12) and then in Fontainebleau (1812–14). On 24 May 1814, Pius VII was rescued by *Husaren-Regiment, Graf Radetsky Nr. 5*. The Hungarian hussars then escorted the pope over the Alps back to Rome where he was restored to the throne of Saint Peter. Napoléon reconciled with Pius VII and the Roman Catholic Church during his exile on Saint Helena.

19. Hilaire Belloc, *The Great Heresies* (Manassas, 1987), ch. 3, p.29. Of course, it must not be forgotten that the destruction of images of holy things, or iconoclasm, had marked the early days of Calvinism in Switzerland.

20. Iul. *Ep.* 90.

21. The major controversy was theological, and was focused upon the relationship of Christ the Son to God the Father. Arius, a priest of the congregation at Baucalis, near Alexandria's harbour, had maintained that Christ had been born in time, was a mutable creature that did not fully share in the divine essence and thus should be seen as subordinate to the Father. Alexander, his bishop, had opposed this teaching, asserting that Christ was the eternal Word of God, the Logos, shared fully in the divine essence, and therefore should be worshipped as equal to the Father. The bishop convened a council of bishops of Egypt and Libya, which condemned Arius' position and excommunicated those who maintained it.

22. This polytheistic view actually goes back to one of the most prolific writers in the early Church: Ioannes Chrysostomos, bishop of Constantinopolis (r. 397–403, †407), who represents pagans as pointing the finger and crying: 'Who is this Father? Who is this Son? Who is this Holy Spirit?' (Chrys. *Hom.* 17.4). Popular with the common folk, he was to fall foul of the empress Aelia Eudoxia over his denunciations of imperial (and clerical) excess. This was his famous denunciation of women, especially those at court

and the allusion to the empress as Jezebel (the sermon is no longer extant, but *vide* Sok. 6.15, cf. Soz. 8.20–2). The conflict was to lead to his banishment by Arcadius (20 June 404). As well as Iulianus, the future emperor, the sophist Libanios (b. 314) had also taught Ioannes Chrysostomos as his favourite pupil: 'the two ships had sailed out of the same harbour for separate ports' (Stark 2012: 318).

23. Amm. Marc. 20.4.17–18, Lib. *Or.* 13.34, Eutr. 10.15.1.
24. Amm. Marc. 22.3–4.
25. Sok. 3.21.6–7, Iul. *Or.* 6, Amm. Marc. 21.8.3, cf. 24.4.27 (*Alexandrum imitates*).

Chapter Thirteen

1. Ambr. *Obit. Theod.* §12.
2. Sok. 5.7, Soz. 7.5, Philostorg. 9.19.
3. *C Th.* XVI.5.6, issued 10 January 381.
4. In the winter of 379 Theodosius had fallen gravely ill, to the point where in February 380 he seemed to be dying. Like his father he received the solemn sacrament of baptism (Theodosius' father had been baptized before his execution), which would purge him of all sin. However, Theodosius made a full recovery by the spring, which he quite naturally attributed to the divine grace of baptism and the countless prayers and masses said on his behalf. Soon afterwards he was to throw his full imperial authority behind the Nicene bishops, and unify the doctrine and worship of the Orthodox Church by the force of law.
5. *C Th.* XVI.10.10 (February 391, from Aquileia), 10.11 (June 391, from Mediolanum), 10.12 (November 392, from Constantinopolis). Nonetheless, whether or not these anti-pagan edicts of Theodosius I were effective is questionable: the *Codex Theodosianus* includes no fewer than twenty-five laws drawn up by Theodosius II and his predecessors, directed against paganism in all its forms. Likewise, the prohibition of sacrifice and the destruction or conversion of pagan places of devotion had to be reiterated throughout the fifth century (*C Ius.* I.11.7, 8 dating to 451 and 472 respectively).
6. Ambr. *Obit. Theod.* §4. This is a reference to Jacob's wife Rachel stealing the household gods of her father Laban. She then returned to Jacob's tent 'and put them inside her camel's saddle and was sitting on them', claiming she could not stand when her father entered because, as she says, 'I'm having my period' (Genesis 31:34, 35 NIV). In other words, such idols were unclean.
7. *D&F*, vol. 2, ch. 28, pp.112–16.
8. Sulp. Sev. *V Mart.* 11.
9. Jer. *Ep.* 107.1.
10. Aug. *Civ.* 5.26.48 (*simulacra gentilium ubique evertanda praecepit*).
11. Aug. *Sermones* 279.4.
12. Theod. *Hist. eccl.* 5.21.
13. Lib. *Or.* 30.8. A law (*C Th.* XV.1.36) addressed to the *comes Orientis* in 397, whose headquarters was in Antioch, ordered the use of stone from destroyed pagan temples for public works.
14. Known as the *Decretum Gelasianum*, it consists of five parts, the last of which provides a list of apocryphal works that were deemed to be heretical. The Catholic Church's *Index Liborum Prohibitorum*, 'List of Prohibited Books', has existed from the time of the Council of Trent (1545–63) all the way through till 14 June 1966. Over time, the

works of such literary luminaries as John Milton, Jean-Jacques Rousseau, David Hume, René Descartes and Edward Gibbon, to name but a few, have been blacklisted.

15. *C Th.* IX.16.2.

16. Sok. 1.9, cf. 3.23, where the author asserts that Porphyrios was once a Christian. Jerome describes Porphyrios as an 'impious man...who wrote against us [viz. the Christians] and vomited out his madness in many books' (*On the beginning of Mark*). However, from what survives of his writings, Porphyrios knew his Bible better than many Christians today.

17. Gelasius of Caesarea *Historia ecclesiastica* 2.36.

18. *C Th.* XVI.10.15, 17–18.

19. Ibid. 10.19, 5.41.

20. Rutil. 2.51–6. These books were actually copies of the original prophetic scrolls kept on the Capitoline, which had been destroyed by fire in 83 BC. Augustus had these copies moved to the temple of Palatine Apollo.

21. Amm. Marc. 22.16.15. Of particular interest here is the sole surviving tapestry of the series of nine commissioned by Henry VIII of England depicting the life of Saint Paul at a time when his kingdom was in the grip of religious turmoil. Rediscovered in 2018, the tapestry depicts an episode of the burning of pagan books. It was woven in Brussels around 1535 following a design by Belgian master Pieter Coecke van Aelst (1502–50), who created tapestry designs for the major courts of Europe using wool, silk and gold and silver threads (the cost of a gold-embroidered tapestry was almost equal to a fully-armed warship).

22. From the Greek *hairesis*, 'choice', 'sect'. The fourth- and fifth-century controversies were mainly Christological in character; that is, they centred on the exact nature of Christ in relation to God on the one hand and mankind on the other.

23. Aug. *Expo. in Ps.* 94.

24. E.g. Psalm 96:5 NKJV, 'For *all* the gods of the peoples *are* idols,/but the LORD made the heavens.' Idols, of course, were considered connected to demons.

25. Tertullian *De praescriptione haereticorum* §7.

26. Ambr. *Expo. in Ps.* 118.22.

27. Euseb. *V Const.* 2.60. Constantinus did issue an edict following the Ecumenical Council of Nicaea, which banned a number of heresies, confiscating their churches and forbidding private meetings (op.cit. 3.64–5). No formal acts of the Ecumenical Council Nicaea survive.

28. Euseb. *Hist. eccl.* 10.5.

29. The emperor brothers Valentinianus and Valens were Pannonians by origin and consequently Valens was viewed as a 'base Pannonian' (Amm. Marc. 26.7.16) and once abused as a '*sabaia*-swiller (*Sabaiarius*)', Pannonia being well-known for *sabaia*, 'a wretched drink made in Illyricum out of barley or some other grain' (ibid. 26.8.2, cf. Lib. *Or.* 19.16, 20.14).

30. Ambr. *De fide* 2.16. Ambrose tells his reader that he wrote the first two books of *De fide* 'hastily and summarily, and in rough rather than exact form' (ibid. 2.129). A treatise written for Gratianus on the Divinity of Christ, he composed them after learning of the 'heretic' Valens' death, which obviously did not grieve the bishop, although the deceased was Gratianus' uncle. He hailed the young orthodox emperor as 'the ruler of the whole world' who would conquer the Goths (ibid. 1.3, 2.136–42); this was either

wishful thinking or sheer flattery on Ambrose's part. He subsequently added three more books in 379 or 380. Valens, by the way, suffered divine punishment at Adrianopolis for infecting the Goths with Arian error, or so says Jordanes (*Get.* §§131–2, §138), while for Gregory of Tours Valens earns death 'for the blood of the saintly men which he had shed' (1.41).

31. Eunap. fr. 44.
32. Lib. *Or.* 1.179.
33. Amm. Marc. 31.13.18, cf. Zos. 4.24.2 ('the battle was almost a total massacre').
34. Genesis 18:16–33.
35. Rutil. 2.51–6. Still, this burning of the Sibylline oracles by Stilicho is not mentioned elsewhere. These oracles were in Greek verse, and dated back to the last king of Rome, Tarquinius (Lact. *Div. Inst. VII* 1.6). They were consulted by the Senate during times of danger or disaster. From the reign of Augustus onwards, only emperors were authorized to order consultation; he had them placed in the temple of Palatine Apollo, where they remained until their destruction. Apparently Augustus himself, in his capacity as *pontifex maximus*, consigned thousands of lines of the Sibylline oracles deemed defeatist to the flames (Suet. *Aug.* 31.1). The last known occasions when they were consulted concerned warfare. The first was when Maxentius supposedly did so prior to the battle of the Pons Mulvius in 312: he was told (with Delphic ambiguity) on that day that the enemy of the Romans would perish, mentioned by Lactantius (*De mort. pers.* 44.8) and Zosimos (2.16.1), though it is notable that Zosimos mentions only this pagan prophecy, although fatal to Maxentius, and naturally ignores any 'vision' of Constantinus. The second was when Iulianus ordered them consulted in preparation for marching against Persia in 363, and then disregarded the warning not to leave his frontiers that year (Amm. Marc. 23.1.7). If anything, it appears that the oracles were hostile to pagan emperors.
36. Rutil. 1.115–38. One question that has long engaged scholars is whether Rutilius Namatianus should be considered strongly anti-Christian, a member of what has been called the pagan resistance. *Vide* Cameron 2013: 207–08, 217–18.
37. Books 1–3 appeared in 412, 4–5 in 414/415 and 6–11 in 416.
38. Nixey 2017: 32.
39. Ibid. 26.
40. The motto *écrasez l'infâme* ('crush the infamy') was strongly identified with Voltaire – real name François-Marie Arouet – and this was a reference to crushing superstition.
41. John Wesley, *Journals* (1739–89), no. 20, 26 August 1784, no. 19, 6 July 1781.
42. Wesley's *A Short Roman History* (Bristol, 1773), like Gibbon's *Decline and Fall*, covered two millennia. However, the similarities between the two end there. In the Enlightenment's most celebrated and 'notorious' work of history, Gibbon's often harsh treatment of the conduct of the early Christians, his scepticism of miracles and hostility to institutional Christianity caused notoriety and marked him as an enemy of the Christian religion. Blending religion and politics, Gibbon was the past master of deliberate elusiveness and artful insinuation.
43. Philostorg. 10.8.
44. Jord. *Get.* §145, Oros. 7.35.11–12, Sok. 5.25, Zos. 4.58.2, J Ant. fr. 187.
45. E.g. MacMullen 1988: 176–7, Liebeschuetz 1991: 7–10. For an alternative unorthodox view, *vide* Elton 1997: 136–52.

46. Syn. *De reg.* 14.4–15.1 [1089B-93B]. However, in this oration to Arcadius on how to be the ideal emperor, Synesios is mostly referring to the emperor's *scholae palatinae*.

47. Zos. 4.31.1, 33.2, 40.2, 6, 56.1.

48. *C Th.* VII.13.8–11.

49. *Vide* Amm. Marc. 31.16.8, commenting on numbers of barbarians but not passing judgement.

50. The *Epitoma* was written and dedicated to an unnamed emperor at a much-disputed point between 383 and 450, with a date in the reign of Theodosius I (379–395) preferred here.

51. Veg. 3.26, cf. 1.1.

52. Take, for example, the Spartiate Aristodemos, who was posthumously censored for having left the ranks and sacrificed his life in heroic deeds (Hdt. 9.71). Again, take Isidas, son of Phoebidas, who was first honoured for his individual heroism and then promptly fined by the *ephors* of Sparta for daring to risk his life in combat without his armour (Plut. *Ages.* 34.8). In a modern army a bad soldier is not only a liability to his unit, he is also, in action, a positive menace and a danger to his comrades. A high percentage of casualties on active service, more in action, are caused by accidents that can be attributed to a low standard of training.

53. On cases of treachery involving barbarians, *vide* Amm. Marc. 14.10.7–8, 29.4.7, Sid. Apoll. *Carm.* 2.280–306, Jord. *Get.* §§194–5, Zos. 4.45.3, 48.1. For suggestion of treachery, *vide* Syn. *De reg.* 14.5 [1091].

54. *PLRE* I, pp.840–1.

55. Amm. Marc. 15.5.33.

56. J Ant. fr. 174, cf. Iul. *Or.* 2.48C, where Iulianus writes that Silvanus' soldiers 'set on him as though he was a wolf and tore him limb from limb'.

57. Amm. Marc. 15.5.16.

58. Ibid. 32.

59. We note that the red-haired Frank in Jerome's *Vita Hilarionis* spoke his native Frankish and fluent Latin and, speaking in tongues, answered Hilarion in 'pure Syriac' (22).

60. *CIL* XIII.3576 = *ILS* 2814. The inscription is currently housed in the Magyar Nemzeti Múzeum, Budapest.

61. Pac. 12.32.3–4, cf. Jord. *Get.* §145, who points out that the Goths served Rome faithfully.

62. Today, more than thirty nation states include outsiders in their armed forces. They populate the militaries of democracies and autocracies alike, from Australia, India, the United Kingdom and the United States to Chad, Iran, Russia and Saudi Arabia. In democratic western states units of outsiders such as the French *Légion Étrangère* (Foreign Legion) or the Gurkhas in the British army are elements of unquestionable loyalty and quality, with the Nepalese Gurkhas demonstrating how a particular external group can forge a close community of interest with the employing state. However, it should be remembered that these outsiders are under the command of French and British officers respectively. This was certainly not the case with the Gothic *foederati*.

63. Prokop. *Wars* 3.11.3–4.

64. E.g. Zosimos (4.30, 4.33.2, 4.40.2, 4.40.6, 4.56.1) goes out of his way to detail the unfortunate consequences of Theodosius' friendly reception of the Goths into the empire, without specifically mentioning the treaty of 382. Likewise, the writings of

Ambrose show a distinct awareness of the threat posed by the settlement of the Goths in Roman territory.

65. E.g. Jones 1964: 156–7.

66. Amm. Marc. 32.2.1–2.

67. Pac. 12.33. *Vide* Heather (1991: 162), who explains that although the Gothic leaders were left in charge of their own men, these leaders were ultimately under the overall command of Roman officers.

68. The military crisis also produced severe conscription (*C Th.* VII.13.8–11).

69. Themist. 16.121c, d.

70. Ibid. 16.212a.

71. Pac. 12.32.5.

72. Jord. *Get.* §146.

73. Syn. *De reg.* 15.13 [1099]. Of course what special talents Sparta held in a small way – warfare – Rome had possessed in a larger way and Sparta had been made obsolete. Yet back in Sparta's all-conquering heyday, the terrible fate of the conquered Messenians meant they were now helots (literally, 'captives in war') whose reduced status was very much akin to the mediaeval serf, as he and his family were the property of the Spartan state because they were tied to the land. The first reference to helots is to be found in two fragments of Tyrtaios' poetry, a Spartan poet who flourished in the mid-seventh century BC. In the first of these fragments the poet talks of the Messenians being 'like donkeys suffering under heavy loads,/by painful force compelled to bring their masters half/of all the produce that the soil brought forth' (fr. 6 West). In the second we read of the helots 'making a wailing funeral chorus, they and their wives/when one of their masters met his destiny' (fr. 7 West). The main responsibility of the helots was to provide their individual Spartan masters with a fixed quota of natural produce. From that tribute the Spartiate paid over to his *phidition*, military mess, the amount required to maintain his citizen status. So by law helots were property of the Spartan community rather than individual Spartiates and, unlike chattel slaves, were allowed to reproduce themselves through family relations. Actual figures for helots are unavailable. Herodotos (9.10, 29) implies an unacceptably high 7:1 ratio, and Xenophon (*Hell.* 3.3.4–11) confirms they outnumbered their masters by some way. Nonetheless, helots held a very low position in the order of things, if they held a place at all.

74. The present course of the Byzantine ramparts was adopted when Theodosius was based in the city. The length of the circuit was some 8km, about half of which survives with upwards of forty towers, almost all square, spaced very irregularly. The construction is largely of rubble with courses of brick, though in places it is entirely of brick, sometimes with rows of brick arches to provide additional strength.

75. *PLRE* I, p.166, where his name is Latinized as *Buthericus*.

76. Soz. 7.25.1–7. *Vide* Williams-Friell 1998: 55.

77. E.g. King 1960: 68. The mistake arises from the standard English translation of Sozomenos, which contains the following garbled sentence regarding the rape: 'When Buthericus [*sic*] was general of the troops in Illyria, a charioteer saw him shamefully exposed at a tavern, and attempted an outrage; he was apprehended and put in custody' (7.25.3).

78. Leviticus 18:22 NIV.

79. *C Th.* IX.7.6, dating to May 390.

80. Aug. *De mendacio* 7.10.

81. Soz. 7.25.1–7, cf. Zon. 13.18.86, who raised the number of dead to 'almost 15,000'.

82. Theod. *Hist. eccl.* 5.17.

83. During the Nika riots in Constantinopolis in 532, the number of people crowded and cut down in the Hippodrome allegedly exceeded 30,000 as the sun set over the Bosporus on the final day (Prokop. *Wars* 1.24.37). Belisarius, long considered one of history's finest tacticians, played a leading role in quashing this dissent, and according to the early seventh-century *Chronicon Paschale*, 'the *patricius* Belisarius, the *magister militum*, came out [from the palace] with a multitude of Goths and cut down many [rioters] until evening' (s.a. 621). Loyal to Belisarius, most of these troops were in fact Goths and Thracians with no allegiance to either of the circus factions. One should not forget, however, that Belisarius, supremely gifted general or not, was also a paid sword, first and foremost loyal to his patron and emperor. As such, he was not averse to engaging in state-sanctioned acts of extreme brutality. While we are on the subject, the Nika riots were so named because the united factions adopted as their joint battle cry the pregnant watchword νίκα, 'conquer'. To fulfil their stated purpose, Hypatius, a nephew of the previous emperor but one, Anastasius I (r. 491–518), was promptly elevated to the purple against his will and carried by the jubilant mob to the Hippodrome. In an era without plastic bullets, flash-bangs or tear gas, the hysteria of a street rabble braying for vengeance inspired immediate terror. It must be said, however, that the sixth-century Constantinopolis was far from a hotbed of anarchy. It was one of the most sophisticated cities in the world, with a social order underpinned by a vast legal code. The catalyst for the Nika riots was Iustinianus' refusal to pardon two convicts (one Green and one Blue) who escaped the hangman's noose on the night of 10 January 532, a plea offered by the chariot-racing fans. A crowd of 100,000 people cried out for the release of the two convicts at the Hippodrome the following Tuesday. When the emperor refused to respond, the people simply took matters into their own hands. The emperor of a day was to meet a martyr's death. For chariot-racing in Constantinopolis, *vide* Fields 2017: ch. 13.

84. This image had been cultivated especially by Themistios, who had served several emperors in this public relations role. One of the key words used by Themistios was *philanthrōpia*, 'love of mankind' (e.g. *Orationes* 34).

85. Ambr. *Ep.* 51, cf. *Obit. Theod.* §34, where Ambrose speaks of the 'deceit of others', which caused the emperor's guilt. Ambrose went on to treat King David in a separate work, the *Apology of David*, much of which is an invitation to penitence.

86. Kedren. 558.17–559.17.

87. Ambr. *Obit. Theod.* §34, cf. Paulin. §24, who sees fit to have Ambrose humiliating a *defiant* emperor.

88. Serapis, a god generally believed to have been the creation of Ptolemaios I Soter (r. 305–282 BC), the first king of Hellenistic Egypt who aimed to gather Greeks and Egyptians together around a single deity. The very name of the god seems to result from a contraction of Osiris (associated with death, resurrection and fertility) and Aspis (the sacred bull of Memphis). He was represented as a Greek god, bearded and majestic. Rapidly spreading throughout the Mediterranean world, his mystery cult was not confined to Hellenes, though the phenomenon of cultural syncretism was essentially a feature of urban centres. Osiris was frequently associated with Isis (the

archetypal wife and mother and sister-wife to Osiris). The Serapeion of Alexandria was built by Ptolemaios III Euergetes (r. 246–222 BC), the grandson of Ptolemaios I.

89. Amm. Marc. 22.16.12, cf. Rufin. 2.23, Sok. 5.16.
90. Soz. 7.15.

Chapter Fourteen

1. *Vide* Fields 1991.
2. Alī al-Masʿūdī, *Murūj al-dhahab wa maʿādin al-jawhar* ('The Meadows of Gold and Mines of Gems').
3. Politically, Sumer was divided into several petty, warring temple states, consisting of a capital city ringed by outlying towns and villages and surrounded by rich, irrigated, agricultural land and uncultivated pasturage. As these states nestled between the southern reaches of the Tigris and the Euphrates, endemic squabbles over watercourses and hinterland were the norm. The turning-point came with the rise of Sargon of Akkad (r. c.2334–2279 BC middle chronology), the foremost figure of his age and prototype of all those world conquerors who came after. One-time cupbearer of Ur-Zababa, priest king of Kish and governor of Agade, Sargon survived his master's overthrow by his rival, the priest king of Uruk and overlord of all southern Sumer, Lugal-zage-si, and eventually (c.2316 BC) liberated Kish and went on to bring the whole of Sumer solely under his rule. In order to suppress the fiercely independent traditions of the conquered temple states, Sargon replaced their rulers with his own governors, invariably Akkadians and members of his own clan, but his imperialistic designs did not terminate at Sumer's frontiers. Following Sumer's conquest, he campaigned in what is now Iran against a confederation of four kings headed by the ruler of Awan, which was a powerful state centred on the southern Zagros mountains, and established his own governors in the subjugated territories. Campaigns to the north-west resulted in the crushing of the Syrian states of Mari, Iarmuti, Ibla and Tutul and, more importantly, the control of the cedar forests and silver mines of what is now Lebanon (Nippon Inscription of Sargon). Akkad became an empire that recognized no boundaries of language, religion or geography, for Sargon's writ ran, according to one inscription, from 'the Upper Sea [the Mediterranean] and the Lower Sea [the Gulf]' (Inscription of Sargon E.2.1.1.1). Sargon's physical instrument for controlling this polyglot empire was a sizeable standing army. In one inscription he boasts that no fewer than '5,400 warriors ate bread daily before him' (Nippon Inscription of Sargon), and these household retainers undoubtedly formed the professional core of his royal army. This was the time of big armies that combined troops from many temple states, outlying kingdoms and foreign mercenaries. The Sumerian war machine even included a clunky forerunner to the war chariot, a four-wheeled 'battlewagon' drawn by four onagers. Formidable instruments of intimidation, they are depicted on The Standard of Ur (London, British Museum, inv. WA121201), a double-sided panel from an Early Dynastic IIIA tomb (PG779) in the royal cemetery at Ur. The battle scene shows four-wheeled 'battlewagons' equipped with quivers containing javelins and short spears and containing two occupants: a driver and a warrior. Their primary function was to charge, frighten the enemy and engage him at medium range with javelins, and then close in with the spear, but it is the nature of empires to rise and fall and Akkad was no exception. The far-flung empire created

by Sargon jolted through a multitude of internal revolts, finally to collapse with the sacking of Kish (c.2154 BC).

4. Invented in 1861 by Richard Jordan Gatling (1818–1903), the hand-cranked multi-barrelled Gatling gun is an early machine gun and a forerunner of the modern electric-motor-driven rotary cannon (e.g. M-134 Minigun, M-61A1 Vulcan). The cluster of brass barrels, generally six or ten in number, revolve in order to fire. As the barrels were rotated, each in succession came level with the magazine (drum or vertical clip), where a cartridge was fed by gravity into its loading tray. The cartridge was then forced into the chamber by a rammer, was fired and had its spent case extracted as the barrels turned.

5. Honoré de Balzac, *Maxims et pensées de Napoléon* (Paris, 1838), maxim no. 392.

6. It should be noted that foreign mercenaries at one point made up more than one-third of the army of Friedrich II der Große (r. 1740–86).

7. This was the meaning of the lines in *La Marseillaise*: 'If they fall, our young heroes,/ Will be produced anew from the ground,/Ready to fight against you!' (*S'ils tombent, nos jeunes héros,/La terre en produit de nouveaux,/Contre vous tout prêts se batte!*, v. 4, ll. 6–8).

8. It was Helmuth von Moltke der Ältere who famously remarked, or so it is said, that he saw no point in studying the American Civil War because it had been fought by 'two armed mobs' running around the countryside and beating each other up, and in a way – but only in a way – he was quite right: you only have to review the unspeakable slaughter at the two-day battle of Shiloh (6–7 April 1862), where most of the troops, Union and Confederate alike, had never tasted battle before. That is not all. These American armies, North and South, very indifferently clad as they were, simply did not follow the 'hallowed' military traditions of European armies. One of the most important features of the Civil War, from a historian's point of view, is the degree of literacy displayed by the rank and file, as is evident from the wealth of extant letters, diaries, etc.

9. For better or worse, the map is back. Repeatedly over the past century, the demise of history, the decline of violence – especially wars between nation states – and the triumph of liberal internationalism appeared poised to render maps obsolete. Conflict, it turns out, is eminently mappable. Peace and prosperity, less so. The map itself serves as a stinging rebuke to those who imagined humanity would overcome its atavistic divisions under the umbrella of a deregulated neoliberal economy in a fully-formed world.

10. Michael Doukas, *Historia Turco-byzantia* col. 307. One span is a unit of measurement equal to the distance across a man's outstretched hand between the point of the thumb and that of the little finger ($\equiv$ 223mm). Because of the hairline fractures in the impure metal, the intense heat of the explosions caused the Basilika to eventually crack and split into many pieces, killing and wounding some of its numerous crew. Strengthened with iron hoops and pressed back into service, it soon cracked again. The Basilika simply exceeded the tolerances of contemporary metallurgy.

11. At the time it was commanded by Marcus Ulpius Traianus, the father of the future emperor. According to Theodor Mommsen – and there is no reason to doubt him on this – the legion received its nickname *Fretensis* ('of the sea straits') because it guarded the *Fretum Siculum*, today's Straits of Messina, and was active during the naval battles of Mylae and Naulochus in 36 BC during Octavianus' war with the last Pompeian, Sextus Pompeius.

12. Joseph. *B Iud.* 5.6.3. By the time of Ammianus Marcellinus and Vegetius, however, the Romans were employing the one-armed *onager* (literally, 'wild ass') as their torsion stone-throwing machine (Amm. Marc. 19.2.7, 7.6–7, 20.7.10, 23.4.4–7, 24.4.13, 4.16, 4.28, 31.15.12, Veg. 2.10, 3.3, 14, 4.8, 9, 22, 28, 44), while the term *ballista* now referred to a twin-armed torsion bolt-firing machine (Amm. Marc. 19.1.7, 5.1, 5.6, 7.2, 7.5–7, 20.7.2, 7.10, 23.4.1, 4.3, 24.2.13, 4.16). Hence Prokopios (5.21.14, 18), during Belisarius' defence of Rome (2 March 537–12 March 538), says that bolt-firing *ballistae* were installed in the towers and that stone-throwing *onagri* were mounted on the curtains. Ammianus says 'the bolt, driven by the power within, flies from the *ballista* out of sight' (23.4.3), which suggests that the effective range of these bolt-firing machines was around 400m.

13. A play on the Hebrew terms *hab-bēn* and *ha eben*, 'the son' and 'the stone'.

14. Joseph. *B Iud.* 5.6.3.

15. E.g. Veg. 1.20, 4.22.

16. Each machine was tailored to a missile of particular size, and for the Macedonians the popular bolt-firing machine (*katapéltēs óxybelēs*) was the one that could take a 1.5-cubit (1 cubit = 24 dactyls = 46.24cm) bolt that could be fired some 400m. The preferred material for the vertical torsion springs into which the bow arm was inserted was twisted sinew or human hair, horse hair being considered inferior. The bowstring was drawn back by lever power and was held in place by a ratchet. When the bowstring was released, the torsion springs released their tension and the bow arm whipped forward, launching a stone ball or bronze-tipped bolt. Bolts had a three-finned bronze head and were usually flighted.

17. Joseph. *B Iud.* 3.7.23. It should be noted that Josephus uses the Greek term ὀξυβελης/ *óxybelēs*. Flavius Josephus, former Jewish military leader and Romano-Jewish historian, wrote in Aramaic and Greek on the recent Jewish revolt (*Bellum Iudaicum*) and, at greater length, on Jewish history (*Antiquitates Iudaicae*) with a view to making his fellow Jews better known and more acceptable to the Graeco-Roman public. Josephus meant his massive *Antiquitates Iudaicae* to be a counterpart to the monumental *Roman Antiquities* of Dionysios of Halikarnassos. Unintentionally, he provided the Christians of the third and later centuries with some of their most cherished reading.

18. Prokop. *Wars* 5.23.9–11.

19. In 1776 *Lieutenant Général* Jean-Baptiste Vaquette de Gribeauval (1715–89) was appointed France's inspector of artillery. He pushed through a new method of barrel manufacture, casting guns as a single block and then drilling out the bore. The result was an improved fit between bore and ball – making guns more powerful – and thinner, therefore lighter, brass barrels (10 parts copper to 1 part tin) of equal strength to the heavier barrels of the past. He also created a new system of standardized calibres, *le systéme Gribeauval*, with an emphasis on lighter battlefield pieces. During the Napoleonic Wars the French artillery service also benefited from the fact that Napoléon was originally a gunner, of course. 'Great battles are won by artillery', wrote Napoléon to Prince Eugène (*Correspondance de Napoléon Ier* [Paris, 1857–70], vol. XXVI, no. 20929, p.458), and he spared no pains to see that his armies possessed a sufficiency of cannon.

20. Known calibres for the *katapéltēs lithobólos* are based on the 353 beautifully finished stone balls discovered outside the ancient circuit walls of Rhodes. These Rhodian shot of blue crystalline limestone were carefully inscribed with Greek letters indicating their

weight, most of which still show traces of red paint applied to the incisions to make the weight-marks readily visible. Calibration of shot was generally one of a graduated series, which rose by differences of 5 or 10 *minae* up to a common maximum of 60 *minae* (= 1 *tálanton* = 26.2kg/57.76lb) by the mid-third century BC (Philon *Poliorkētiká* 1.29, 70–3). A 30-*minae* shot could be launched most effectively over ranges below 400m and, according to the Greek engineer Philon of Byzantium (*fl.* 250 BC), 30-*minae* engines 'have the most appropriate dimensions and are most forceful in their blows' (*Poliorkētiká* 96.10). For instance, on the basis of the shot found, the most popular calibres at Rhodes appear to have been those of 25 *minae* (85-shot) and 30 *minae* (83-shot). Rhodes was besieged by Demetrios of Macedon, which gained him the title *Poliorketēs*, 'the Besieger', in 305–304 BC (Diod. 20.85–8, 91–9). For the Rhodian shot, *vide* L. Laurenzi '*Projettili dell'artiglieria antica scoperti a Rodi*' (Roma, 1938), pp.33–6.

21. During the Punic wars of the third century BC, the Romans became acquainted with Hellenistic torsion-powered artillery. Roman engineers took these designs and in typical Roman fashion reworked them, and in so doing created weapons that prefigured gunpowder artillery.

22. The most enduring of any firearm issued to British forces, the actual origins of the affectionate nickname 'Brown Bess', which first appeared in official print in 1771 (there is an earlier reference in a letter written by John Grose of the East India Company dated 17 October 1763), has been lost to time. It has been postulated by some scholars that the name came from a combination of the musket's browned iron parts – to prevent reflections and inhibit rusting – and polished, oiled walnut stock. However, all the parts of the Brown Bess were originally polished bright, and while some early musket stocks had been stained black, the natural brown walnut look was no novelty by the mid-eighteenth century. Others suggest it could have been a tribute to some tavern maid or lady of the night, or simply an alliterative term of endearment that the common soldier often gives to a trusted sidearm. As one veteran corporal said to his mess mate on the eve of Waterloo: 'You can pray to Jesus all you like, but the only religion I need is my Brown Bess and my bayonet.' In any event, by the Napoleonic Wars it was in common enough usage to merit an entry in Captain Francis Grose's *1811 Dictionary of the Vulgar Tongue*: 'BROWN BESS. Soldier's firelock. To hug Brown Bess; to carry a firelock, or serve as a private soldier.' The 1771 reference appeared in the American *Connecticut Courant* newspaper issue of 2 April 1771, which was actually reprinted from British papers of earlier that year. This reported the remarks made by Hannah Snell (1723–92), famous for having successfully posed as a man and served as a soldier, Marine and sailor in the service of the British Crown under the pseudonym James Gray, the name of her brother-in-law. She said: '...but if you are afraid of the sea, take Brown Bess on your shoulders and march through Germany as I have done.' Snell pursued an adventurous military career from 1745 to 1750, and her taste for warfare included a stint in Colonel Fraser's Regiment of Marines at the siege of Pondicherry. She was wounded in the legs eleven times and also received one shot in the groin.

23. Source: Von H.F. Rumpf, *Allemeine Real-encylopädie der gesammten Kriegskunst* (Berlin, 1827).

24. While the calibre of the Brown Bess was .75, the calibre of the roughly 1oz spherical lead ball was .71: the difference, called 'windage', allowed ease of loading, especially when the barrel became fouled. However, the ball's loose fit in the barrel meant that

much of the energy of the exploding gunpowder charge in the barrel escaped round the ball rather than propelling it forward with maximum force.

25. Colonel George Hanger, *A Letter to the Right Hon. Lord Castlereagh, Secretary of State, etc., etc., etc., from Colonel George Hanger* (London, 1808), p.78, written on 10 May 1808. 'In this distinguished Service, you will carry a Rifle no heavier than a Fowling-Piece. You will knock down your Enemy at Five Hundred Yards, instead of missing him at Fifty', as it proudly proclaims on the 95th (Rifle) Regiment of Foot recruitment poster of 1808, now on display in The Royal Green Jackets (Rifles) Museum, Winchester. The aforementioned rifle was of course the now legendary Baker rifle designed by the London gunsmith Ezekiel Baker, and adopted for service in 1800. With a calibre of 0.625 (15.9mm), the 30.375in (762mm) barrel was rifled with seven grooves. Overall length was 45.75in (1.162m), considerably shorter than the Brown Bess at 58.5in (1.49m), and therefore much more suited to nimble skirmishing work from behind cover. More importantly, as opposed to the ordinary infantryman who loaded his musket standing up and standing still, the Baker rifle allowed the rifleman to load while running or lying down.

26. The rifle-armed *Jäger* (literally 'hunter') battalions exclusively recruited trained huntsmen as these stealthy men were particularly suited to service as sharpshooters (sg. *schützen*).

27. Having left a five-year trail of death and terror across the battlegrounds of the Thirteen Colonies with his green-coated Loyalist cavalrymen, 'Bloody' Tarleton emerged from the war with a reputation as brilliant in England as it was infamous in America, but his later years were disappointing to those who had hoped from better things from him. Having shot his bolt young, he became a hanger-on of London high society in which eccentricity was the chief note of distinction.

28. Friedrich II der Große: quoted in Jay Luvaas, *Frederick the Great on the Art of War* (New York, NY, 1998), p.146.

29. Kelly 2004: 141.

30. Though produced at a number of French arsenals, the *Fusil Charleville* was named after the arsenal in Charleville on the River Meuse.

31. In 1810 the Prussian army under Gerhard von Scharnhorst (1755–1813), a Hanoverian who had transferred to Prussian service nine years earlier, conducted some field firing experiments with various European muskets, including its own new musket, the *Infanteriegewehr Modell 1809* or the *Neupreußisches Infanteriegewehr*. After setting up a large canvas target the approximate size of an infantry company, the different muskets were fired at 320 yards and 160 yards. Out of 200 rounds, the following number of hits was recorded: *Infanteriegewehr Modell 1782*, 42 and 64; *Infanteriegewehr Modell 1809*, 42 and 113; British India Pattern, 55 and 116; *Fusil Charleville Modèle 1777*, 55 and 99. A field experiment carried out by Garry James in 2010 using an original India Pattern Brown Bess – probably the most commonly encountered of all the British flintlock muskets – manufactured post-1809 produced the following results when five shots each were fired at 2x4ft target boards with central bull's eyes placed at distances of 100, 50 and 25 yards: at 100 yards only three balls struck the board at the bottom with a spread of 11.5in; at 50 yards all five balls hit with a grouping of 20 in; at 25 yards an 8in spread of all five balls. As James points out, 'up to 50 yards, if someone were firing at you with a Brown Bess it looks like you were pretty much toast' (https://www.rifleshootermag.com/editorial/featured_rifles_bess_092407/83445). The average

British ball weighed about 1oz (c.28.35g), and at close range could smash bones and cause massive bleeding. Even slight musket-ball wounds carried the deadly potential of infection as the projectile would take with it small pieces of uniform as well as dirt. If bone had been struck then the resulting splinters added to the bacterial danger and there was always just the risk of bleeding to death. Soldiers carried around sixty cartridges that were already made up with an appropriate amount of gunpowder and a ball wrapped in a cylinder of tough greased paper in a flapped leather pouch with a slotted wooden interior.

32. Bishop-Coulston 1993: 48.

33. Junkelmann 1991: 188.

34. Amm. Marc. 16.12.21–54.

35. Veg. 1.17.

36. E.g. Plut. *Ant.* 45.3.

37. 1 Samuel 16:11, 19, 20, 28, 17:34.

38. Onasandros *Stratēgikós* 17.

39. For slingers *vide* Amm. Marc. 19.5.1, 31.15.13, Iul. *Or.* 2.57D, Veg. 1.16, 2.13, 3.14.

40. Onasandros *Stratēgikós* 19.3.

41. Celsus *De medicina* 5.26, 7.55.

42. 1 Samuel 17:40–9.

43. Veg. 1.16.

44. The actual range and performance of the composite bow is open to debate, and a number of varied figures have been suggested. Vegetius (2.23) recommends a practice range of 600 Roman feet (c.177m), while later Islamic works expect an archer to display consistent accuracy at 69m. With the admirable study of the Graeco-Roman sources by Wallace McLeod (1962: 13–19, 1965: 8), the range of ancient composite bows has been reasonably established: bowmen were quite accurate up to 50–60m, their effective range extended at least 160–175m, but not as far as 350–450m. A replica of an Egyptian angular composite bow, made by the anthropologist Saxton Pope, cast an arrow a distance of 230–260m on several occasions (McLeod 1970: 37).

45. A needle-gun was a rifle that was fired by driving a long needle-like firing pin through a paper cartridge to strike the detonator, placed in the middle of the propellant charge to ensure even combustion. Early versions were muzzle-loading, but the most famous was the breech-loading Dreyse *Zündnadelgewehr*, first adopted by the Prussian army in 1841.

46. With the Dreyse needle-gun the detonation was inside the gun for the first time. This gun was a boon to the infantryman. He could at last load his weapon easily while in the prone position instead of having to stand erect. A startling display of its tactical prowess was first demonstrated on the field of Königgrätz (3 July 1866), when its sheer rapidity of fire cut swathes through the Austrian infantry and their Saxon allies (44,000 Austrians and Saxons lost compared to just 9,000 Prussians), so terminating the brief Bohemian campaign that was to assert Prussia's right to the leadership of a united Germany, minus Austria. The Austro-Prussian War (also called the Seven Weeks' War) also shows the Prussian General Staff, under the leadership of Helmuth von Moltke der Ältere (1800–91), first triumph as the brains and nervous system of the army. Although Moltke had been Chief of the General Staff (*Chefs des Generalstabs*) since 1857, he was relatively unknown in the Prussian army. At Königgrätz one divisional

general commented that the written instructions he received 'were entirely in order, but who is this General von Moltke?' After the battle the question would not be asked again. French public opinion resented the Prussian victory and demanded '*Revanche pour Sadova*', 'Revenge for Sadova' (Sadová/Sadowa being the alternative name for the battle), which formed part of the background to the Franco-Prussian War of 1870. Helmuth von Moltke was of course the older of the two notable generals von Moltke and who made his fame in the Franco-Prussian War.

47. Polybios says (3.84.7) some 15,000 Romans and Latin-Italians perished in that misty basin by Lake Trasimene, but this was probably the total of all who were killed, as Livy (22.7.1), citing the contemporary account of Fabius Pictor, makes clear, while Polybios' total of more than 15,000 prisoners (3.85.2) is probably highly pessimistic too. Livy says (22.7.2, cf. App. *Hannib.* 2.10) that 10,000 escaped, but since he makes no mention of prisoners, this figure perhaps included all those who survived the day and were taken prisoner, though no doubt some individuals did manage to slip away. As for Cannae, Livy says that 45,000 infantry and 2,700 cavalry were killed (22.49.15), and that altogether 19,300 prisoners were taken: 4,500 on the field (22.49.18), 2,000 who had fled to Cannae (22.49.12) and 12,800 in the two Roman camps.

48. Humphrey Carpenter, *J.R.R. Tolkien: A Biography* (Boston, 2000/1977), p.86, quoting Second Lieutenant J.R.R. Tolkien, B/11 Lancaster Fusiliers, experiencing battle for the first time on 14 July 1916 during the Somme offensive.

49. Major L.F. Ellis, *Victory in the West Volume I: The Battle of Normandy* (London, 1974/1962), p.493. These figures are for the 21st Army Group, which included Canadian and Polish troops.

50. It should be noted that since at least 1917 it has been extremely hard to break through properly supplied defences that are disposed in depth, supported by operational reserves and prepared with forward positions that are covered and concealed. Indeed, this combination enforced the trench stalemate on the Western Front in the First World War. Even during the mid- and late-war offensives of the Second World War against properly prepared defences commonly produced results looked less like blitzkrieg (e.g. France 1940, Russia 1941, Sinai 1967 and Kuwait 1991) and more like the slow, costly, grinding advance of the Hundred Days offensives of 1918. Concentrated armour-heavy attacks at the Mareth Line in 1943, Kursk in 1943, Operations EPSOM, GOODWOOD or MARKET GARDEN in 1944, the Siegfried Line in 1944 or the Gothic Line in 1944–45 all failed to produce quick breakthroughs and devolved into slow, methodical slogs at best, or armoured divisions riding to death and immortality at worst. More recently, the Israeli invasion of Lebanon in 2006 and Georgia's invasion of South Ossetia in 2008 all showed a similar pattern wherein mechanized offensives made painfully slow progress when they encountered deep, prepared defences.

51. Duke of Wellington: quoted in Philip Henry Stanhope, *Notes of Conversations with the Duke of Wellington* (London, 1888), entry for 4 November 1831. The last straw was the immediate aftermath of Vitoria in 1813. A total victory had been achieved and Wellington ordered a pursuit. Accordingly the cavalry went hotfoot in the chase and the infantry pressed on as best they could. The pursuers came across a massive French baggage train blocking the road, and here the soldiers began looting, stripping bare in the process a French treasure convoy upon which Wellington was relying for the means to pay his campaign expenses. Furious, Wellington wrote sourly in a letter dated

29 July to the Secretary of State for War, Lord Bathurst: 'We have in the service the scum of the earth as common soldiers.' Harsh but true. Like most European armies of the time, the British army had a long tradition of recruiting primarily among the poorest and most desperate of society, drawn to the colours either by the pay or their own poverty depending on how you want to look at it; a tradition that was still hale and hearty when I saw service. Even if the army was a refuge from drudgery for most, obviously not all Britain's soldiers were rogues, cutthroats and thieves, but certainly a good percentage of the ranks were less than model citizens who occasionally could not resist the temptation of debauchery. It has been said that one in every seven or eight men of Wellington's army was a drunkard, a malingerer or a thief. Naturally, an army reflects to some extent the customs of its time, and so we must remember that in Wellington's day, drinking among all social classes was very heavy, and in a soldier's situation he could drink himself stupid: continual drunkenness may well lead to petty or even serious crime. In what was almost inevitably a misogynistic environment, men were judged on their mettle and tenacity, not on their morals or truthfulness. Yet, if the truth be told, for many soldiers it was a matter of what the French call *égoïsme sacré*, a healthy drive to survive. To escape hunger and avoid disease were their main concerns, and this is what frequently transformed them into daredevil, good-for-nothing brutes.

52. Honoré de Balzac, *Maxims et pensées de Napoléon* (Paris, 1838), maxim no. 148.

53. A maxim more often than not attributed to Napoléon.

54. How much security is enough security? When I served in the infantry during the Cold War in what was then West Germany, the question was rather straightforward. NATO, which has been around longer than I have, had one adversary – the Soviet Union – which it would need to deter and, if necessary, defeat. Defending Western Europe from the Soviet threat was its sole purpose, its *raison d'être*. When NATO leaders gathered in Lisbon in 1952 three years after its creation, the alliance hoped to have fifty combat divisions deployed to deter this apparent Soviet threat. By the end of the Cold War, which should have been its extinction point, it had more than 100. At the end of June 2022, with the war full tilt in Ukraine, NATO leaders gathered in Madrid to discuss the war on their doorstep having just eight forward-deployed (in Bulgaria, Estonia, Hungry, Latvia, Lithuania, Poland, Romania and Slovakia) multinational battlegroups (approximate total of 9,641 troops) at their disposal, the smallest numbering 643 troops (in Slovakia) and the largest numbering 1,887 troops (in Latvia). Despite the strategy of tank-heavy manoeuvre formations and large numbers of lumbering artillery systems, Cold War infantry soldiers were still the 'queen of battle'. Although the western alliance has shrunk to a fraction of its Cold War strength by almost every measure – in vessels, aircraft personnel and tanks (the tank is not completely obsolete just yet) – infantry soldiers are still proving their worth as the 'queen of battle' on the post-Cold War battlefields of today.

55. Plut. *Mar.* 7.2, 3.

56. Archil. fr. 114 Swift.

57. Ibid. fr. 236 Swift.

58. Of course there were and are exceptions. Take, for instance, Napoléon's brother-in-law, Prince Joachim Murat. The swaggering, dashing cavalry commander was as noted for his gorgeous red boots and extravagant plumes and epaulettes as he was for his fearlessness in a cavalry charge.

59. Plautus *Miles Gloriosus* 1.1.54 (*At peditastelli quia errant*). Cf. Edmond Rostand, *L'Aiglon*, acte II, scène 9: 'And us, the men, the mean, the rank and file?/Us, tramping broken, wounded, muddy, dying,/Having no hope of duchies and endowments,/Marching along and never getting further,/Too simple and too ignorant to covet/The famous marshal's baton in our knapsacks?' (*'Et nous, les petits, les obscures, les sans-grades,/Nous qui marchions fourbus, blesses, crottés malades,/Sans espoir de duchés ni de dotations;/Nous qui marchions toujours et jamais n'avancions;/Trop simples et trop gueux pour que l'espoir nous berne/De ce fameux bâton du'on a dans sa giberne.'*) English translation by L.N. Parker (New York, NY, 1900).

Chapter Fifteen

1. Naomi Feigelson Chase, *The Journals of Empress Galla Placidia From Her Faithful Servant Lepida: A Novel in Verse* (Cincinnati, OH, 2016), p.18.
2. Jord. *Get.* §121.
3. The migration from Scandinavia has no attestation outside Jordanes. The Goths pose no problem as inhabitants of Scythia; Isidore of Seville (*Historia de regibus Gothorum, Vandalorum et Suevorum* 1), their later historian, would have them come only from there.
4. Gordianus III was the grandson of Gordianus I by his daughter (Herod. 7.10.7). Gordianus III departed Rome for the eastern front in 242 and campaigned successfully against Persia through 243 until his death in battle sometime in the spring of 244.
5. The battle site, known locally as *Poleto* (the Field), has been located in the valley of the River Beli Lom to the south of the village of Dryanovets. Here were a large number of Roman coins (including *aurei* minted during the reign of Traianus Decius) and military equipment including *spatha*-type swords, spearheads, shield bosses, *lorica squamata* armour and greaves, along with military paraphernalia such as tent pegs, all of which suggests the last Roman camp prior to the battle. *Vide* Aleksander Bursche, 'The battle of Arbittus, the imperial treasury and *aurei* in Barbaricum', *Numismatic Chronicle* 173 (2013): 151–70.
6. [Aur. Vict.] *Epit.* 29.3–4, cf. Zos. 1.23, Zon. 12.20. Jordanes claims that Herennius Etruscus was killed by an arrow during a skirmish prior to the battle. His father, addressing his soldiers, allegedly said: 'Let no one mourn. The death of one soldier is not a great loss to the Republic' (Jord. *Get.* §103).
7. Lact. *De mort. pers.* 4.
8. The Huns, as we well know, would be regarded by the Romans as the stuff of nightmares: it is Jerome who neatly summarizes this when he says 'the soldiers of Rome...tremble and shrink in fear at the sight of them' (*Ep.* 60.17). It sounds as if the Huns simply terrified their way into victory. Be that as it may, the seeds of their movement westward out of the harsh steppe lands may lay in desperation. The nomadic tribes lived a predatory existence, keeping to their ancestral grasslands while the going was good, but prepared to invade the grazing lands of others and repel invasions of their own lands as severe weather conditions drove the nomads and their herds here and there over the central Asian steppe. So it may have been a series of particularly devastating droughts – a regular hazard on the semi-arid steppes – that broke the usual grazing cycles of nomads around the Aral and Caspian seas and spurred them on to new pastures, hence clashing with the Alani and the Goths. Yet climate alone is not a sufficient explanation, for to a lesser tribe drought would have proved fatal. It seems

likely, therefore, that the Huns were a confederation of Turkic tribes that moved westward. The nomadic way of life and the common hardships that such a lifestyle presented resulted in a degree of cultural unity among all the steppe-dwellers of central Asia. With the right mixture of need, self-interest and leadership, these ethnic nomad groupings could come together to forge alliances and then would fall apart to fight among themselves with great speed. The nomadic peoples had a legend in which a mother figure rebuked her quarrelling sons by telling them each to take an arrow and break it; something they could do easily. Then she told them to put together as many arrows as there were sons and break them; something none of them could do (Selby 2003: 260). Then again this Hun movement may have been the result of a pressure of population. As it so happened, the fourth and early fifth centuries in northern China were tumultuous, a time between the great days of Han and Tang referred to as the Period of Disunion. The chaos lessened somewhat when a Turkic group, the Toba (T'o-pa in Wade-Giles), established north of the Yangtze a sinicized dynasty known as the Northern Wei in 386. Yet the emergence and collapse of dynasties may have sent shock waves of refugees westward. The rulers of northern China at this time, being of nomadic stock, certainly shared a cultural archery heritage with the Huns. They brought to China improved techniques in horse-breeding, together with advances in saddlery and stirrups, which allowed further developments in mounted archery skills (Selby 2003: 187). The Huns themselves would eventually cross the Danuvius into the fertile lands of the Roman Empire.

9. The Arabian and Syrian deserts provided a convenient buffer zone between the two empires, but from the upper Euphrates to the Euxine there was no natural boundary. Instead there lay a wedge of disputed territory 200–300km broad centred on the kingdom of Armenia. Towards the northern apex of the desert divide were two cities: Palmyra on the western limit of the Roman province of Syria and Doura Europos 200km to the east, guarding a crossing-point on the Euphrates.

10. Zos. 4.20.6, cf. Eunap. fr. 42 (jealousy of the western emperors), Amm. Marc. 31.4.4 (for recruits).

11. Eunap. fr. 42.

12. Amm. Marc. 31.4.6.

13. Ibid. 4.11.

14. The story is that, at the signing of the Declaration of Independence in Philadelphia at the Second Continental Congress on 4 July 1776, Benjamin Franklin warned his fellow patriots that 'we must, indeed, all hang together, or assuredly we shall all hang separately.' Unlike many of Franklin's other pithy quotations, there is no solid evidence that he said it at all at the signing of the Declaration of Independence and Franklin (its oldest signer) did not get attached to this quote until 1840, when it appeared in a ten-volume compendium of his writings by Jared Sparks. As is often the case, Sparks gave no source citation for this particular quote. The 'hang together or hang alone' saying has been traced in print to John Dryden's 1717 book *The Spanish Fryar*, where it is referred to as a Flemish proverb (Benjamin Franklin was 11 years old in 1717), and given that it is listed as a proverb, it probably predates 1717.

15. Jord. *Get.* §130, cf. §82, §98.

16. Wolfram 1988: 26.

17. Amm. Marc. 31.4.1–5.

18. In 418 or 419 Theodoric I (r. 418–451) made a treaty with the Romans, which granted his people Aquitania Secunda in return for a military alliance with the western empire; that is, to serve as *foederati*. Under the alliance the Visigoths (as the confederation is now known) helped subdue the Vandals and Alani, which gave them territory in Hispania and allowed expansion in southern Gaul. The Visigothic kingdom lasted in southern Gaul until 507, when the Frankish king Clovis (r. 481–511), a Nicene Christian (though his baptism date – though conversion and baptism can be two very different issues – ranges from 496 to 508), defeated the Visigothic king Alaric II (r. 484–507), an Arian Christian, at Vouillé (variously called *Voglada*, *Boglada*, *Boglodoreta* or the *Campus Vogladensis*), 10.6 Roman miles (15.7km) north-west of Pictavium, Poitiers as it is now known (*vide* Greg. Tur. 2.37: 'on *campo Vogladensi* at the tenth milestone from the city of Pictavium'). Thereafter Gaul was soon to be Francia, while the Visigoths were confined to Septimania and the Iberian Peninsula until 711 when their kingdom fell to the Arabs of North Africa.
19. *Vide* Collins 2004: 22–4.
20. For dependents *vide* Zos. 4.25.3, 39.4.
21. Claud. *VI Cons.* 442–4, *Chron. min.* I 229.
22. Claud. *B Goth.* 623–8.
23. Alaric lost his camp and baggage to the Roman cavalry under the leadership of the Alan Saul, who was under some suspicion of treachery, but proved his loyalty to the Roman cause by dying in battle for it (Oros. 7.37.2–3, Claud. *B Goth.* 580–97, cf. Zos. 4.58.2–3, who has Saul escape in headlong flight). Unsurprisingly, Claudianus claims Stilicho's victory as further proof of his patron's superiority and masculinity. On the other hand, Orosius states the result was inconclusive because the two commanders, both Christians, were being punished for fighting on a holy day. For some strange reason Jordanes (*Get.* §§154–6, §159) has Alaric capturing Rome directly after the battle of Pollentia instead of being separated, as in reality, by eight years, and is soon followed by a second sacking, this time at the hands of Ataulf, Alaric's successor.
24. Claud. *VI Cons.* 123–6.
25. *D&F*, vol. 2, ch. 30, p.145.
26. Claud. *VI Cons.* 251–2.
27. Zos. 5.26.3. The number is certainly an exaggeration, but it was clearly a large enough group to make a strong impression, cf. Oros. 7.37.4, more than 200,000 Goths. All in all, Zosimus' account of this invasion is a mixture of good information and plain nonsense.
28. Oros. 7.37.12–16, Jord. *Rom.* §321. Uldin, the first Hunnic leader to impinge on Roman history, and his horsemen were to raid deep into Thracia in 408; once defeated they were dispersed as *coloni* rather than enrolled as *foederati*. When the Romans had tried to buy him off, Uldin rejected their offer by merely pointing towards the rising sun and said that, if he so wished, he would find it easy to subdue all the lands on which the sun shone. He demanded an impossible sum as the price of peace, but the envoy was not at a loss. He protracted the negotiations with Uldin and at the same time entered into secret talks with his senior officers. His propositions (and payoffs) were agreeable. Many of Uldin's followers deserted, and he himself only escaped with difficulty. Many of those who decided to stay with him on his desperate dash to the Danuvius were captured and carted off to Constantinopolis in chains (*C Th.* V.6.2,

3 [issued 23 March 409], Soz. 9.5.2–7). The rise and fall of Uldin reflects the fragile position of Hunnic leaders.

29. Oros. 7.37.12, Jord. *Rom.* §321. Sarus was a Gothic chieftain renowned for his strength and valour in battle (Olympiod. fr. 3 Müller, Zos. 5.34.1, 36.2, Soz. 9.9), brother and enemy of Sigeric and cousin of Alaric. After aiding Stilicho against Radagaisus, he was sent against Constantinus in Gaul in early 408. There he killed Iustinianus and besieged Constantinus in Valentia, but was forced to return to Italy (Zos. 6.2). Instigated by Stilicho to mutiny at Ravenna in 408 (ibid. 5.30.3), he killed Stilicho's private horse army, *buccellarii*, who were Huns when Stilicho did not revenge those who fell at Ticinum (ibid. 5.34.1); this was an indication of the Goths' wrath with Stilicho's apparent weakness. In response to this, Stilicho urged the Italian cities to keep the barbarians' families as hostages. Sarus was not employed by Honorius against Alaric (ibid. 5.36.2–3). He is next found wandering around the Italian peninsula with 200–300 men (Olympiod. fr. 3 Müller, Zos. 6.13.2, Soz. 9.9), but fled to Honorius when confronted by Ataulf. Sarus was taken into service against Alaric, but provoked him to march on Rome (Olympiod. fr. 3 Müller, Soz. 9.9, Philostorg. 12.3). When Honorius would not punish the murderer of Belleridus, Sarus' *domesticus* in 412, he went to serve Iovinus in Gaul, but was captured by Ataulf, with whom he had a blood feud, and died in captivity (Olympiod. fr. 17 Müller, Soz. 9.15). Such was the convoluted life of Sarus.

30. Paulin. §50, Oros. 7.37.13.

31. Oros. 7.37.15.

32. Oros. 7.37.16, Zos. 5.22.3, 26.3–5, Aug. *Civ.* 5.23, *ILS* 798–9, *Chron. min.* I 652.54. Olympiodorus (fr. 9 Müller) claims 12,000 *optimates* ('best men') were enrolled in the army, though this may have been an exceptional case seeing that Alaric was threatening Italy. On other occasions smaller numbers are known to have been enrolled (Amm. Marc. 17.2.3, Zos. 4.39.5).

33. The final, tragic scene of Stilicho's life is related in Zos. 5.32–4.

34. Ibid. 34.4, 5.

35. Zos. 6.7.5–6, 8.3, 9.1–2, Soz. 9.8, Oros. 7.42.10.

36. Zos. 6.11, Soz. 9.8. Heracleianus would invade Italy in 413 (Oros. 7.42.12–13), only to be defeated and condemned to death by Honorius (ibid. 42.14, *C Th.* XV.14.13), but he fled to Carthage where he was murdered (Oros. 7.42.14, Philostorg. 12.6, Olympiod. fr. 23 Müller).

37. Zos. 5.34.5, 35.5.

38. Olympiod. fr. 6 Müller, Zos. 5.37.4, Philostorg. 12.3, *C Th.* IX.42.22.

39. According to Zosimos (5.28.2) when Honorius married Maria (398), who was still underage, Serena is reputed to have procured his impotence. On the other hand, Philostorgius (12.2) reckons it was Stilicho's doing and not his wife's, cf. Claud. *Cons. Stil. II* 339–61 describes Stilicho's hoped-for grandson by Honorius and Maria as a 'grandson born to rule' ('*recturo...nepoti*').

40. Claud. *Cons. Stil. II.* 354–9, *IV Cons.* 552. Galla Placidia was biologically the second cousin of Eucherius, but by adoption was his aunt.

41. Zos. 5.34.7.

42. On Stilicho's possible (and not unreasonable) ambitions for Eucherius, *vide* Oost 1968: 71–4, 81.

43. Zos. 5.35.6, cf. 5.42.3, 40,000.

44. *Vide* Liebeschuetz 1992.

45. Apparently, it was Serena who influenced Honorius to move to Ravenna in 408 (Zos. 5.30.2).

46. Zos. 5.41.1.

47. Olympiod. fr. 4 Müller, Soz. 9.6–7, Philostorg. 12.3, Oros. 7.38–40.

48. Olympiod. fr. 5 Müller. One Roman pound = 0.7219lb avp or 327.45g. Forty *centenaria* of gold was 4,000 pounds, which was equivalent to 300,000 *solidi* (the gold *solidus* – 72 to the Roman pound or *libra* – was introduced by Constantinus, and unlike the silver *denarius* of earlier days, it was never debased). In 400 the orator Symmachus, a senator of seemingly moderate wealth descended from generations of consuls, expended 2,000 pounds of gold for his son's praetorian games (Symm. *Ep.* 6.62, 64). Symmachus owned three houses in Rome and at least thirteen more in various parts of Italy, as well as others dotted around Sicilia and Africa. His other sources of revenue, much like his fellow senators, derived from grain and wine and other forms of produce.

49. Olympiod. fr. 5 Müller (*Non est ista pax, sed pactio servitutis*), repeated verbatim in Zos. 5.29.7.

50. Zos. 5.30.1.

51. Oros. 7.38.2–4.

52. Philostorg. 12.3, Sok. 7.10, Soz. 9.8.

53. Zos. 6.1.2.

54. Ibid. 5.50.1, Soz. 9.5.

55. Olympiod. fr. 3 Müller, Zos. 5.46.1. Priscus Attalus was the son of Ampelius, *proconsulares Achaiae* in 359 and *praefectus urbis Romae* during the years 370–72. Attalus was born in Antioch (Soz. 9.9, Philostorg. 12.3). He was the friend of leading pagans such as Symmachus (Symm. *Ep.* 7.15–25). A *vir spectabilis* by 394 (ibid. 2.82), envoy to Honorius from the Senate over recruitment for 398 (ibid. 6.58, 7.21, 54, 113–4), was appointed *comes sine loco et praefectus urbis Romae* in 409 (Zos. 5.46.1) when he was set up as a puppet emperor at Rome by Alaric.

56. Zos. 6.7.2, Soz. 9.8.2. In 414 Priscus Attalus would be called upon again for the role by Alaric's successor Ataulf. On both occasions Attalus was removed from his position with very little ceremony when his Gothic masters no longer found him useful (Olympiod. fr. 13 Müller). Captured in 416, Attalus graced a Roman triumph the following June and, still later, 'when he approached the neighbourhood of Ravenna, he had two fingers of his right hand cut off and was banished from the country to the island of Lipara' (op. cit., cf. Philostorg. 12.4–5, Oros. 7.42.9).

57. Zos. 5.38.1–2, 39.1, Olympiod. fr. 6 Müller.

58. Soz. 9.9.

59. Orosius (7.39.1–14) praises the Goths for not looting ecclesiastical vessels and for not harming those of the citizens who had taken refuge in churches in the course of their sack.

60. Jord. *Get.* §157. Alaric was around 40 years of age when he died.

61. Drake 2017: 200. The fallout from this failure to keep the empire safe was dealt with brilliantly in a work of theology that became the cornerstone of western Christianity, Augustine's *De civitate Dei contra paganos*, rendered as 'City of God' though *civitate* rather means a gathering of *cives*, citizens, what we would call 'community'. He

challenges the claims of his opponents that the empire had an exceptional god-given destiny – Iuppiter in Virgil's *Aeneid* famously promised the Romans 'empire without end' (1.278–9, cf. 6.781–2, Ov. *Fast.* 2.688) – writing in Latin (a marker of a classical education) and deploying the classical Latin authorities (as opposed to Iudaeo-Christian scripture) to make his case.

62. For centuries, writers had played with the notion that the city of Rome, the *Urbs Romana*, encompassed or was synonymous with the world (*orbis*): as Ovid, with a clever play on words, once put it: 'Earth has given other peoples fixed boundaries,/the extent of the city of Rome (*Urbis*) and the world (*orbis*) is the same' (*Fast.* 2.683–4). The idea that the Romans had conquered the whole world was not confined only to Augustan poetry. The Alexandrian philosopher Philo (*Legum allegoriae* 8, cf. Plin. 3.5) described the Romans ruling over all the earth and sea.

63. Pall. 54.7.

64. *Or. Sib.* 8.165–73.

65. Lact. *Div. Inst. VII* 25.7.

66. Jer. *Ep.* 127.12 (*Capitur urbs quae totum cepit orbem*). Much earlier, when he was living in Rome, Jerome had declared the metropolis the great harlot arrayed in purple and scarlet that had appeared in the vision of John the Revelator at Patmos (Revelations 17:1–6). There again Jerome was a singularly arid and self-centred man, all guilt and escape from a world where 'those that are in the flesh cannot be pleasing to Christ' (*Epit.* 27.3).

67. Letter of Pelagius apud Brown 2000: 287.

68. *Carmen de Providentia Dei* 903–09. The poem is generally attributed to Prosper of Aquitaine, who was a Gaulish monk and theologian who lived in the first half of the fifth century and, among many other works, wrote a chronicle of his own times that he revised several times in the course of a long life.

69. Prokop. *Wars* 3.2.25–6.

70. Ibid. 7.22.9.

71. Olympiod. fr. 10 Müller, Oros. 7.43.2.

72. Oros. 7.43.4–7.

73. Note Jordanes (*Get.* §§159–63) promotes the notion that by association with Galla Placidia, Ataulf visibly changes from a despoiler of Rome into an auxiliary of the empire.

74. Whether or not it was Sigeric's doing he was Ataulf's enemy and rival, rumour had it that it was done at the instigation of Placidia's half-brother, Honorius.

75. Granddaughter, daughter, sister, wife and mother of emperors, Galla Placidia was captured by Alaric (Olympiod. fr. 3 Müller, Jord. *Rom.* §323, *Get.* §159). She went with the Gothic king Ataulf to Gaul, where she was to be handed over in return for supplies, but Honorius did not keep the bargain (Olympiod. frs. 19–21). Ataulf then sought her hand, which she reluctantly gave, the marriage being held at Narbo (Narbonne, France) in January 414 (Olympiod. frs. 22, 24 Müller, Oros. 7.40.2). Their son Theodosius died soon after birth (Olympiod. fr. 27 Müller). After the death of Ataulf (assassinated either while he bathed or was attending to his horse), she married Flavius Constantius (417–421), who had the extremely rare honour of holding three consulships (414, 417, 420) and would reign for seven months in 421 as Constantius III. The sudden death of her second husband came as no surprise, but it had aroused a sense of scandal in court circles, particularly regarding Galla Placidia, who had

never wanted to marry her half-brother's gauche and shifty *generalissimo* in the first place. 'So great had grown the affection of Honorius for his own sister,' rumoured one contemporaneous palace pen-pusher, 'that their immoderate passion and their continuous kissing on the mouth brought them under a shameful suspicion in the eyes of many people' (Olympiod. fr. 40 Müller). Having spent some five or six years among the Goths – she had been captured by Alaric before the sack of Rome, probably during the blockade of 409 (Zos. 6.12.3, cf. Olympiod. fr. 3 Müller, carried off during the sack of 410) – Galla Placidia came to admire them and trusted her protection to a personal retinue composed of Goths (Olympiod. fr. 40 Müller), a bodyguard known as *buccellarii*, 'biscuit men' – as the contemporary Olympiodoros says, 'The name *bucellarius* in the days of Honorius was applied not only to Roman soldiers but also to certain Goths' (fr. 7.4 Müller). Once again, Ravenna was doubtless scandalized. Nonetheless, what was in effect a private army gave her not only power but independence too; a *buccellarius* probably entered a patron/client bond with his employer and so he normally was more loyal to his employer than the emperor. With the death of the childless Honorius, the redoubtable Galla Placidia became the tutor and advisor of her son Valentinianus III (b. 2 July 419). Her varied life, which had seen so many dramatic ups and downs, is a most extraordinary story worthy of the Hollywood treatment, and she deserves more than the hurried mention she is receiving in this endnote. *Vide* Oost 1968, Hagith 2011, Salisbury 2015.

76. Vallia died soon after leading his people to their new abode, and Theodoric I reigned in his stead. The Goths received remarkably favourable terms, as the Roman landowners had to surrender two-thirds of their property to them.

77. Generally speaking, Gothic horsemen were shock troops, fighting in close formation with the primary function of defeating the enemy in a mêlée. Ostrogothic horsemen were mostly unarmoured except chieftains and their companions and close personal followers. By the time the Ostrogoths had settled in Italy, however, a majority of their horsemen had acquired good body armour and helmets. Horsemen were armed with stout spears and heavy slashing swords derived from those of the Sauromatae. On quality, *vide* Veg. 1.20, Oros. 7.34.5.

78. Veg. 1.20.

79. Amm. Marc. 31.7.12.

80. Weapon burials are not found among the Vandals, are rare among the continental Saxones, and comparatively rare among the Goths and the Franks. Nevertheless, there is evidence that the deceased was often buried grasping his spear, while other weapons (if any) were laid round him. The Goths appear to have had spearheads adorned with runic inscriptions, dating back to the early third century, such as the one from Suszycnzo, Ukraine, which is inscribed ᛏᛁᛚᚨᚱᛁᛞᛊ (*tilarids*, 'sure-hitter'). Another example, from Dahmsdorf-Müncheberg, Germany, bears the inscription ᚱᚨᚾᛃᚨ (*renja*, 'router'). With the conversion of the Goths to Christianity (Arianism), the Gothic alphabet had replaced runes by the mid-fourth century.

81. Amm. Marc. 31.6.3.

82. The magnificent *Codex Argenteus*, 'Silver Book/Codex', is a sixth-century illuminated manuscript originally containing part of the fourth-century translation of the Bible into the Gothic language. It was probably written for the Ostrogothic king Theodoric the Amal (r. 493–526), either at his royal seat in Ravenna or at Brixia (Brescia, Italy). It

was written with gold and silver ink on high-quality thin vellum stained a regal purple. A part of it is on permanent display at the Carolina Rediviva building in Uppsala, Sweden. Theodoric (*cos.* 484), then *magister militum praesentalis*, had been sent west in 488 by the eastern emperor Zeno (r. 474–475, 476–491), to dispatch the usurper Odovacer, which he did in a typically tribal way. In the course of finalizing a treaty with Odovacer at a banquet – both parties had agreed to rule over Italy – Theodoric knifed him to death. However, once he looked at the West, especially the desperate conditions of things, the Ostrogothic *magister militum praesentalis* refused to hand over Italy to the current emperor sitting in Constantinopolis, but 'chose rather to seek a livelihood by exertion after the usual manner of his people' (Jord. *Get.* §290): in 497 Anastasius I (r. 491–518) recognized him as ruler of Italy. Now lord of the land, Theodoric set about restoring the damage wrought by more than a century of neglect, civil war, invasion and destruction. He set about repairing roads and aqueducts, and under his rule Italy witnessed a mini-renaissance, its last breath of culture for much of the remaining millennium. Educated in Constantinopolis – in 461/462 he had been sent to the metropolis as a hostage where he was to remain for ten years – but remaining illiterate all his life, Theodoric was that perplexing paradox of both perfidy and perceptivity.

83. The earliest written records for individual languages are spaced out over many centuries: Mycenaean Greek from 1200 BC, Sanskrit from 1000 BC, Latin from 300 BC, Celtic and Germanic only from the first centuries AD. The earliest literary tradition for a Germanic language is in fact Gothic, while the other members of the Germanic group, such as Old English and Old High German, began only in the eighth century.

84. Sok. 4.33, Philostorg. 2.5. Ulfilas was born about 311, the grandchild of a Kappadokian captive taken in one of the great Gothic raids before 270. He was therefore born a Goth, and would later be bishop to his people north of the Danuvius and a tribal leader.

85. *Vide* Gothic Bible, Romans 13:12, Ephesians 6:11, 13 (*sarwa*); John 18:3, Corinthians II 6:7, 10:4 (*wēpn*); Ephesians 6:14, Thessalonians I 5:8 (*brunjō*); Ephesians 6:17, Thessalonians I 5:8 (*hilms*); Ephesians 6:16 (*skildus*); Ephesians 6:17 (*mēki*); John 18:11 (*fōdr*); Luke 2:13, 8:30 (*harjis*); John 18:3, 18:12, Luke 6:17, Mark 15:16 (*hansa*).

86. Philostorg. 2.5.

Principal Literary Sources

1. Philostratos *Vita Apollonii* 42.
2. Irenaeus, *Adversus haereses*, bk. 1, praef. 3.
3. The teachings of Arius (250–336), a priest of Alexandria, were fairly widely accepted in the early part of the fourth century. Like Unitarians in recent times, Arius and his followers believed that Jesus was a man created by God the Father. He was from God, but Jesus and the Father were not the same being and Jesus was therefore of distinctly subordinate status, belonging to the created order. This was vigorously opposed by Alexander, Arius' bishop, as tending towards two divinities (Ditheism). In 325 Constantinus called, for the first time, an ecumenical council of some 300 bishops from all over the empire at Nicaea in Bithynia, one of Constantinus' imperial residences. By a large majority it condemned Arius' denial of the divine nature of the Son as heresy, and he was then banished by the emperor. Constantinus' son and successor Constantius was pro-Arian and did much to undermine the Nicene party. Supported by the Arian

bishop Eusebios of Nicomedia, he manipulated special councils at Arles, Mursa and Constantinopolis, and finally had the Arian formula of *homoioúsios* (Gk. ὁμοιούσιος), 'of similar essence', declared orthodoxy. Summoned by Theodosius in 381, at a second ecumenical council at Constantinopolis the Arian doctrine that the Son and the Father were similar but not the same was finally declared heretical. The Nicene Creed – Father, Son and Spirit are exactly equal, or *homöousios* (Gk. ὁμοούσιος), 'one-in-essence' (L *consubstantialis*) – became the only acceptable interpretation of Christianity and the matter of the extra iota (*ı*) was finally settled. Or was it?

4. Lib. *Ep.* 983.

5. Amm. Marc. 29.3.5.

6. Ibid. 21.12.24, 27.3.3, 9.8.

7. *D&F* vol. 2, ch. 26, p.48.

8. Amm. Marc. 26.5.14.

9. Ibid. 22.16.12.

10. Ibid. 27.11.1, 29.6.15.

11. As Augustine himself admits, 'I came to Carthage, where a cauldron of unholy loves was seething and bubbling all around me' (*Veni Karthaginem, et circumstrepebat me undique sartago flagitiosorum amorum, Conf.* 3.1 §1). Is it not a truism that history tells us the facts, while poetry tells us how it feels? As T.S. Eliot recalls in the third section of *The Waste Land*, 'The Fire Sermon', 'To Carthage then I came/Burning burning burning burning/O Lord Thou pluckest me out/O Lord Thou pluckest/burning' (307–11). First appearing in October 1922 in the inaugural issue of Eliot's own critical monthly (later quarterly) literary journal *The Criterion*, this radical, knotty 434-line poem shows Eliot grappling to find a form of Christianity, culminating in his conversion to the highest of Anglican modes, Anglo-Catholicism, in 1927 (Virginia Woolf, his friend and fellow Modernist, did not think he was serious; he absolutely was and remained so until his death in 1965). Eliot's family were Bostonian Unitarians with its distant roots in Calvinism, but that austere theology had been so watered down over the centuries that its key doctrines – belief in original sin, election to eternal redemption and damnation, the Trinity, the sacraments of baptism and communion, the idea of Jesus as the incarnate Son of God, his miracles and resurrection and so on – had been jettisoned. Instantly notorious, the poem mixed fragments of languages, religions, references from ancient poems, books, plays, opera and music hall, passages of eloquent speech and scraps of everyday conversations. In the poem various narrators and characters take the reader through shifting landscapes and scenes: shimmering deserts, boundless plains, bubbling rivers of oil and tar, ornate rooms, noisy bars, the busy bridges and streets of an unreal city. A densely allusive work that draws upon Ovid, Dante, Shakespeare, Jacobean tragedy, tarot and the Upanishads to create a dazzling portrait of both the ruin of post-war Europe and the inner alienation of modernity. Today, Eliot can seem an effete, politically unattractive character (any fan of Eliot's poetry must navigate the many instances of misogyny, racism and anti-Semitism in his work). Nonetheless, what better shorthand for today's political shiftiness than the repeated refrain from *Macavity: The Mystery Cat* that runs, when you reach the scene of crime, 'Macavity's not there!'

12. Manichaeism was founded by the prophet Māni (216–274). Born in Parthia, Māni was raised as a member of the Jewish-Christian sect of the Elkesaites, but at the ages of 12 and 24 had visionary experiences of a 'heavenly twin' calling him to leave his father's sect and preach the true message of Jesus in a new religion. Manichaeism was based

on a rigid dualism of good and evil or light and darkness locked in eternal struggle. Manichaeans viewed Christianity as a flawed and incomplete religion. Māni died a martyr: he was incarcerated by the fourth Sāsānian king, Bahrām I (r. 271–274), a devotee of the intolerant Zoroastrian reformer Kardēr and persecutor of Manichaeans, and died in prison within a month. The followers of Māni depicted his death as a crucifixion. Augustine became a follower in 373, accepting Manichaean teaching as a higher form of Christianity than the old wives' tales on which he had been brought up. Ten years later he had moved towards Scepticism, subsequently breaking away and turning to Neo-Platonism. Falling under the influence of Ambrose in Mediolanum, he was eventually baptized on 25 April 387 at Easter. Nonetheless, the Manichaean doctrine of good and evil shines through when Augustine, for instance, accepts that there are good nations and evil nations, just as there are good and evil individuals. Thus, when the moral elements are removed from the life of the state, 'what are states but great robberies?' (*'quid sunt regna nisi magna latrocinia?'*, Aug. *Civ.* 4.4).

13. Aug. *Civ.* 5.26, Oros. 7.35.21.

14. Jord. *Get.* §38, §107, §143, §168, §§289–90.

15. Only one authentic fragment of it survives, quoted by its author in a letter dated to 536 (*'exemplum quod in historia nostra magna intentione retulimus'*, Cassiodorus *Variae* 12.20.4). Cassiodorus, an Italo-Roman and senator, worked in Ravenna at a Gothic court that was Arian in religion. Himself a Nicene Christian, he took pains not to offend the religious susceptibilities of his patrons. Potentially, he had access to excellent sources of information about the Gothic past, including oral traditions. Theodoric the Amal himself sponsored the history (ibid. 9.25.4–6).

16. Jord. *Get.* §266, §316.

17. Jord. *Rom.* §363, §366, §375, §§386–7, *Get.* §§171–2, §303, §313, §315.

18. Arnaldo Dante Momigliano, *Studies in Historiography* (London, 1966), p.196.

19. Maenchen-Helfen 1973: 17, cf. 17 n. 101.

20. *Vide* O'Flynn 1983: 20.

21. On 15 August 423 Honorius died. After two years of the usurper Ioannes, the boy Flavius Placidus Valentinianus came to the throne as Valentinianus III. For the first dozen years of his reign his mother Aelia Galla Placidia acted as regent. She died quietly in her sleep in Rome in 450 at the age of 58. He was hacked to pieces on 15 March 455 by Hunnic followers of Flavius Aëtius who the emperor had murdered the previous year (J Ant. fr. 201.2, 4–5). With him died the Theodosian house. As they say, dynasties never last. Over the next two decades the West begins to fade away in a miserable succession of brief reigns.

22. J Lyd. *De mag.* 3.42, 68.

23. Jerome's improved versions of the Gospels led to howls of protest. He responded by describing his critics as 'two-legged asses' who preferred to lap up muddy rivulets when they could have drunk, as he did, from the pellucid fountain of the Gospels' original Greek. Obviously, this was an attack on their mastery of Latin as well as Greek.

24. Jer. *contra Rufinum* 1.1.

25. It is clear from the many back references in the surviving books of Ammianus Marcellinus that he was well informed about the third century. There is little doubt, therefore, that he must have provided a more accurate and sober account of this century than the Scriptores Historiae Augustae.

26. Sid. Apoll. *Ep.* 4.22, 8.15.
27. The hallmark of the Antiochene School was a more literal and historical approach as against the allegory and symbolism deployed by its traditional rival of Alexandria.
28. The death-knell of intellectual paganism was Iustinianus' ban on pagans holding university chairs in 529 (Agathias *Historiae* 2.30).
29. Zos. 5.50.2, for the theme of degeneration and Theodosius' mixed character.
30. Ibid. 5.27.1.
31. E.g. the neglect of pagan rites and stress on oracles (Eunap. *VS* 6.9.17, 7.3.5), neglect of pagan statues (Olympiod. fr. 15 Müller).
32. *Vide* Walter Goffart, 'Zosimus, the first historian of Rome's fall' in *American Historical Review* 76/2 (Oxford, 1971), pp.412–41.

Bibliography

Aitken-Burt, L., 'Rain from God(s)? How can the reliefs depicting the "Rain Miracle" from the Column of Marcus Aurelius in Rome illuminate the conflicting Christian and pagan textual accounts of the event?' *Rosetta*, 18: 16–47 (2016)

Alföldi, A., *The Conversion of Constantine and Pagan Rome* (Oxford: Oxford University Press, 1948)

Ando, C., *Imperial Rome AD 193 to 284: the Critical Century* (Edinburgh: Edinburgh University Press, 2012)

Ayers, L., *Nicaea and Its Legacy: an Approach to Fourth-Century Trinitarian Theology* (Oxford: Oxford University Press, 2004)

Baker, G.P., *Constantine the Great and the Christian Revolution* (New York, NY: Cooper Square Press, 1992)

Barlow, J., 'Identity and fourth-century Franks', *Historia* , 45/2: 223–39 (1996)

de la Bédoyère, G., *Defying Rome: the Rebels of Roman Britain* (Stroud: Tempus Publishing, 2003)

Bird, H.W., 'Diocletian and the deaths of Carus, Numerian and Carinus', *Latomus*, 35: 123–32 (1976)

Bishop, M.C. and Coulston, J.C.N., *Roman Military Equipment from the Punic Wars to the Fall of Rome* (London: Batsford, 1993)

de Blois, L., *The Policy of the Emperor Gallienus* (Leiden: E.J. Brill, 1976)

Braudel, F. (trans. S. Reynolds, 2001), *The Mediterranean in the Ancient World* (London: Penguin, 1998)

Brock, P., 'Why did St. Maximilian refuse to serve in the Roman army?', *Journal of Ecclesiastical History*, 45/2: 195–209 (1994)

Brock, P., *The Riddle of St. Maximilian of Tebessa* (Toronto: University of Toronto, 2000)

Brown, P., *Augustine of Hippo: A Biography* (Berkeley/Los Angeles, CA: University California Press, 2000/1967 (second edition))

Burns, T.S., 'The Battle of Adrianople: a reconsideration', *Historia*, 22: 336–45 (1973)

Burns, T.S., *Barbarians within the Gates of Rome: A Study of Roman Military Policy and the Barbarians, ca. 375–425 AD* (Bloomington, IN, 1994)

Bury, J.B., *History of the Later Roman Empire*, 2 vols. (London: Macmillan, 1923 (second edition))

Bury, J.B., *The Invasion of Europe by the Barbarians* (London: Macmillan, 1928)

Cameron, A., 'Theodosius the Great and the regency of Stilicho', *Harvard Studies in Classical Philology*, 73: 247–80 (1968)

Cameron, A., *Claudian: Poetry and Propaganda at the Court of Honorius* (Oxford: Oxford University Press, 1970)

Cameron, A., *The Last Pagans of Rome* (Oxford: Oxford University Press, 2013/2011)

Cameron, A., 'The status of Serena and the Stilicho diptych', *Journal of Roman Archaeology*, 29: 509–16 (2016)

Cameron, A. and Long, J., *Barbarian and Politics at the Court of Arcadius* (Berkeley/Los Angeles, CA: University California Press, 1993)

Cameron, A.M., *The Later Roman Empire* (London: Fontana Press, 1993)

Christiansen, P.G. and Christiansen, D., 'Claudian: the last great pagan poet', *L'Antiquité Classique*, 78: 133–44 (2009)

Ciglenečki, S. (trans. A. Maver), '*Claustra Alpium Iuliarum, tractus Italiae circa Alpes* and the defence of Italy in the final part of the late Roman period', *Arheološki vestnik*, 67: 409–24 (2016)

Collins, R., *Visigothic Spain, 409–711* (Oxford: Blackwell Publishing, 2004)

Crawford, P.T., 'The Battle of Frigidus River', *Ancient World* 43: 33–52 (2012)

Croke, B., 'Arbogast and the death of Valentinian II', *Historia* 25/2: 235–44 (1976)

Cromwell, R.S., *The Rise and Decline of the Late Roman Field Army* (Shippensburg, PA: White Mane Publishing, 1998)

van Dam, R., *The Roman Revolution of Constantine* (Cambridge: Cambridge University Press, 2007)

Drake, H.A., *Constantine and the Bishops: the Politics of Intolerance* (Baltimore, MD: John Hopkins University Press, 2000)

Drake, H.A., *A Century of Miracle: Christians, Pagans, Jews and the Supernatural, 312–410* (Oxford: Oxford University Press, 2017)

Drinkwater, J.F., *The Gallic Empire: Separatism and Continuity in the North-Western Provinces of the Roman Empire, AD 260–274* (Stuttgart: Steiner, 1987)

Elton, H., *Warfare in Roman Europe AD 350–425* (Oxford: Clarendon Press, 1997/1996)

Elton, H., *The Roman Empire in Late Antiquity: A Political and Military History* (Cambridge: Cambridge University Press, 2018)

Engels, D.W., *Alexander the Great and the Logistics of the Macedonian Army* (Berkeley/Los Angeles, CA: University California Press, 1980/1978)

Ensslin, W., 'War Kaiser Theodosius I zweimal in Rom?', *Hermes*, 81: 500–07 (1953)

Erdkamp, P. (ed.), *A Companion to the Roman Army* (Oxford: Blackwell Publishing, 2007)

Ferrill, A.L., *The Fall of the Roman Empire: the Military Explanation* (London: Thames and Hudson, 1986)

Fields, N., 'The first military empires' in R. Cross (ed.), *The Guinness Encyclopedia of Warfare* (London: Quarto Publishing 1991) 8–13.

Fields, N., 'Apollo: god of war, protector of mercenaries' in K.A. Sheedy (ed.), *Archaeology of the Peloponnese: New Excavations and Research* (Oxford: Oxbow Books (Oxbow Monograph 48), 1994), 95–113.

Fields, N., *Rome's Saxon Shore: Coastal Defences of Roman Britain AD 250–500* (Oxford: Osprey Publishing (Fortress 56), 2006A)

Fields, N., *The Hun: Scourge of God AD 375–565* (Oxford: Osprey Publishing (Warrior 111), 2006B)

Fields, N., *The Walls of Rome* (Oxford: Osprey Publishing (Fortress 71), 2008)

Fields, N., *God's City: Byzantine Constantinople* (Barnsley: Pen & Sword Military, 2017)

Fox, R.L., *Pagans and Christians* (London: Penguin Books, 1989)

Frend, W.H.C., *The Early Church* (Philadelphia, PN: J.B. Lippincott, 1966)

Grant, M., *The Fall of the Roman Empire* (New York, NY: Collier Books, 1990 (rev. edn))

Gutherie, P., 'The execution of Crispus', *Phoenix* 20/4 (1966), 325–31.

Hagith, S., *Galla Placidia: the Last Roman Empress* (Oxford: Oxford University Press, 2011)

Harries, J. and Wood, I.N. (eds), *The Theodosian Code* (Ithaca, NY: Cornell University Press, 1993)

Heather, P.J., *Goths and Romans, 332–489* (Oxford: Clarendon Press, 1991)

Heather, P.J., *The Goths* (Oxford: Blackwell Publishing, 1996)

Heather, P.J., *The Fall of the Roman Empire: A New History of Rome and the Barbarians* (Oxford: Oxford University Press, 2007)

Hodgkin, T., *Italy and her Invaders* (Oxford: Clarendon Press, 1892 (second edition))

Hoffman, D., 'Die spätrömische Soldatengrabschriften von Concordia', *Museum Helveticum* (1963), 20: 22–37.

Hoffman, D., *Die spätrömische Bewegungsheer und die Notitia Dignitatum*, 2 vols (Düsseldorf: Rheinland Verlag (Epigraphische Studien 7), 1969–70)

Hoffman, R.J., *Porphyry's against the Christians: the Literary Remains* (New York, NY: Prometheus Books, 1994)

Holum, K., *Theodosian Empresses: Women and Imperial Dominion in Late Antiquity* (Berkeley/ Los Angeles: University of California Press, 1982)

Hughes, I., *Stilicho: the Vandal who Saved Rome* (Barnsley: Pen & Sword Military, 2010)

James, B., *Flags of Our Fathers: Heroes of Iwo Jima* (New York, NY: Delacourt Press, 2001)

James, S., 'The *fabricae*: state arms factories of the later Roman empire' in J.C.N. Coulston (ed.), *Military Equipment and the Identity of Roman Soldiers* (Oxford: Proceeding of the Fourth Roman Military Equipment Conference, 257–332 [BAR S394], 1988)

Janin, R., *Constantinople byzantine: developpement urbain et repertoire topographique* (Paris: Institut Français d'Études Byzantines (2ᵉ éd.), 1964)

Jones, A.H.M., *The Later Roman Empire, 284–602: A Social, Economic and Administrative Survey* (Oxford: Blackwell, 1964)

Jones, C.P., '*Stigma*: tattooing and branding in Graeco-Roman antiquity', *JRS* 77: 139–55 (1987)

Junkelmann, M., *Die Legionen des Augustus: Der romische Soldat im archaologischen Experiment* (Mainz-am-Rhein: Philipp von Zabern, 1991)

Lafferty, R.A., *The Fall of Rome* (Garden City, NY: Doubleday, 1971)

Laing, J., *Warriors of the Dark Age* (Stroud: Sutton, 2000)

Kelly, J., *Gunpowder: A History of the Explosion that Changed the World* (London: Atlantic Books, 2004)

King, N.Q., *The Emperor Theodosius and the Establishment of Christianity* (Philadelphia, PA: The Westminster Press, 1960)

Kos, P., *Ad Pirum (Hrušica) in claustra Alpium Iuliarum* (Ljubljana: Zavod za varstvo kulturne dediščine Slovenije, Vestnik 26/1 [in Slovenian], 2014)

Kovač, M., 'Bora or summer storm: meteorological aspect of the battle at Frigidus' in R. Bratoz (ed.), *Westillyricum und Nordostitalien in der Spätromischen Zeit* (Ljubljana: Narodni muzej, 1996), 109–19.

Kovács, P., *Marcus Aurelius' Rain Miracle and the Marcomannic Wars* (Leiden: E.J. Brill, 2006)

Kulikowski, M., 'Barbarians in Gaul. Usurpers in Britain', *Britannia* (2000), 31: 325–45.

Lettich, G., *Iscrizioni spepoicrali tardoantiche di Concordia* (Trieste: Centro studi storico-religiosi Friuli-Venezia Guilia, 1983)

Liebeschuetz, J.H.W.G., *From Diocletian to the Arab Conquest: Change in the Late Roman Empire* (Aldershot, 1990)

Liebeschuetz, J.H.W.G., *Barbarians and Bishops* (Oxford: Clarendon Press, 1991/1989)

Liebeschuetz, J.H.W.G., 'Alaric's Goths: nation or army?' in J. Drinkwater and H. Elton (eds) *Fifth-Century Gaul: A Crisis of Identity* (Cambridge: Cambridge University Press, 1992), 75–83.

MacDowall, S., *Adrianople AD 378: the Goths Crush Rome's Legions* (Oxford: Osprey Publishing (Campaign 84), 2001)

MacGeorge, P., *Late Roman Warlords* (Oxford: Oxford University Press, 2002)

MacMullen, R., *Corruption and the Decline of Rome* (New Haven, CN: Yale University Press, 1988)

Maenchen-Helfen, O.J., *The World of the Huns: Studies in their History and Culture* (Berkeley/Los Angeles, CA: University California Press, 1973)

Mann, J.C., 'A note on the *legion* IV *Italica*', *Zeitschrift für Papyrologie und Epigraphik* (1999), 126: 228.

Matthews, J.F., *Western Aristocracies and the Imperial Court* (Oxford: Oxford University Press, 1975)

Matthews, J.F., *The Roman Empire of Ammianus Marcellinus* (London, 1988)

McDonald Jr., K., *Constantine and the Sabbath* (Seven Points, WI: The Biblical Sabbath Association, 2022)

McEvoy, M.A., 2013. *Child Emperor Rule in the Late Roman West, AD 367–455.* Oxford: Oxford University Press

McLeod, W.E., 'Egyptian composite bows in New York', *AJA* (1962), 66: 13–19.

McLeod, W.E., 'The range of the ancient bow', *Phoenix* (1965), 19: 1–14.

McLeod, W.E., *Composite Bows from the Tomb of Tutankhamun* (Oxford: Griffith Institute, 1970)

Murdoch, A., *The Last Pagan: Julian the Apostate and the Death of the Ancient World* (Stroud: Sutton Publishing, 2003)

Nischer, E.C., 'Army reforms of Diocletian and Constantine and their modifications up to the time of the *Notitia Dignitatum*', *JRS* (1923), 13: 16–55.

Nixey, C., *The Darkening Age: the Christian Destruction of the Classical World* (London: Macmillan Publishers, 2017)

Nixon, C.E.V. (ed. & trans.), *Pacatus: Panegyric to the Emperor Theodosius* (Liverpool: Liverpool University Press (*Translated Texts for Historians*, Latin Series II), 1987)

Nixon, C.E.V. and Rodgers, B., *In Praise of Later Roman Emperors* (Berkeley/Los Angeles, CA: University California Press, 1994)

Odahl, C.M., 'Constantine and God: imperial theocracy for the Christian divinity in the first Christian emperor's beliefs and policies', *The Ancient World* (2015), 46/1: 25–64.

O'Flynn, J.M., *Generalissimos of the Western Roman Empire* (Edmonton: University of Alberta Press, 1983)

Oost, S.I., *Galla Placidia Augusta. A Biographical Essay* (Chicago, IL: University of Chicago Press, 1968)

Osier, J., 'The emergence of the third-century equestrian military commanders', *Latomus* (1977), 36: 674–87.

Osmuk, N., 'Ajdovščina – Castra. Stanje arheoloških raziskav (1994)', *Arh. vest.* (1997), 48: 119–30 (in Slovenian)

Pack, R., 'Notes on the *Caesars* of Julian', *Transactions of the American Philosophical Association*, (1946), 77: 151–7.

Parker, H.M.D., 'The legions of Diocletian and Constantine', *JRS* (1933), 23: 175–89.

Parker, H.M.D., *History of the Roman World AD 138–337* (London: Methuen, 1935)

Pickard, J., *Behind the Myths: the Foundations of Judaism, Christianity and Islam* (Bloomington, IN: AuthorHouse, 2013)

Pohlsander, H., 'Crispus: brilliant career and tragic end', *Historiae* (1984), 33: 76–106.

Potter, D.S., *The Roman Empire at Bay, AD 187–395* (Routledge: London, 2004)

Runkel, F., *Die schlacht bei Adrianopel* (Rostock: C. Boldt'sche hofbuchdruckerei, 1903)

Sabin, P., Van Wees, H. and Whitby, M., *The Cambridge History of Greek and Roman Warfare*, Vol. II: *Rome from the late Republic to the late Empire* (Cambridge: University of Cambridge Press, 2007)

Salisbury, J.E., *Rome's Christian Empress: Galla Placidia Rules at the Twilight of the Empire* (Baltimore, MD: Johns Hopkins University Press, 2015)

Salzman, M.R., 'Ambrose and the usurpation of Arbogastes and Eugenius: reflections on pagan-Christian conflict narratives', *Journal of Early Christian Studies* (2010), 18/2: 191–223.

Seeck, O. (ed.), *Notitia Dignitatum* (Berlin: Weidmann, 1876 (repr. 1962, Frankfurt am Main))

Seeck, O. und Veith, G., 'Die Schlacht am Frigidus', *Klio* (1913), 13/1: 451–67.

Selby, S., *Chinese Archery* (Hong Kong: Hong Kong University Press, 2003/2000)

Sheridan, J.J., 'The Altar of Victory – paganism's last battle', *L'Antiquité Classique* (1966), 35/1: 186–206.

Southern, P., *The Roman Empire from Severus to Constantine* (London: Routledge, 2001)

Southern, P. and Dixon, K.R., *The Late Roman Army* (London: Routledge, 2000/1996)

Stark, F., *Rome on the Euphrates: the Story of a Frontier* (London: Tauris Parke Paperbacks, 2012/1962)

Štekar, A., 'Poskus lociranja bitke pri Frigidu leta 394 na območju med Sanaborjem in Colom' ('An attempt to locate the battle of the Frigidus river in 394 in the area between Sanabor and Col'), *Annales: anali za istrske in mediteranske študije* (in Slovenian, English and Italian) (2013), 23/1: 1–14.

Štekar, A., 'Nekaj novih dognanj o lociranju bitke pri Frigidu' ('Some new findings about the location of the battle of the Frigidus river'), *Vipaski Glas* (2014), 29: 1–14 (in Slovenian and English)

Teitler, H.C., *The Last Pagan Emperor: Julian the Apostate and the War against Christianity* (Oxford: Oxford University Press, 2017)

Thompson, E. A., *The Visigoths in the Time of Ulfila* (Oxford: Oxford University Press, 1966)

Thompson, G.L., 'From sinner to saint? Seeking a consistent Constantine' in Smither, E.L. (ed.), *Rethinking Constantine: History, Theology and Legacy* (Eugene, OR: Pickwick Publishing, 2014), 5–25.

Todd, M., *The Early Germans* (Oxford: Blackwell Publishing, 2004, second edition)

Tomlin, R.S.O., 'The late Roman Empire' in General Sir John Hackett (ed.), *Warfare in the Ancient World* (London: Guild Publishing, 1989), 222–49.

Tomlin, R.S.O., 'Christianity and the Roman army' in S.N.C. Lieu and D. Montserrat (eds), *Constantine: History, Hagiography and Legend* (London: Routledge, 1998), 21–51.

Toom, T., 'Constantine's *summus dues* and the Nicene *unus dues*: imperial agenda and ecclesiastical conviction', *Vox Patrum* (2014), 34 t. 61: 103–22.

Watson, A., *Aurelian and the Third Century* (London: Routledge, 2004/1999)

Whitby, M., *Rome at War AD 293–696* (Oxford: Osprey Publishing [Essential Histories 21], 2002)

White, C., *The Emergence of Christianity: Classical Traditions in Contemporary Perspective* (Minneapolis, MN: Fortress Press, 2010/2007)

Williams, S., *Diocletian and the Roman Recovery* (London: Routledge, 2000/1985)

Williams, S. and Friell, G., *Theodosius: the Empire at Bay* (London: Routledge, 1998/1994)

Wolfram, H. (trans. T.J. Dunlap), *History of the Goths* (Berkeley/Los Angeles, CA: University California Press, 1988)

Wolfram, H. (trans. T.J. Dunlap), *The Roman Empire and its Germanic Peoples* (Berkeley/Los Angeles: University of California Press, 1997)

Woods, D., 'Julian, Arbogastes and the *signa* of the *Ioviani* and the *Herculiani*', *Journal of Roman Military Equipment Studies* (1995), 6: 61–8.

Woods, D., 'On the death of the empress Fausta', *Greece & Rome* (1998), 45/1: 70–86.

Woods, D., 'Constantine, cookery and sacrifice', *Journal of Theological Studies* (2018), 69/2: 577–87.

Zuiddam, B.A., 'Battle for the Bible in the early church', *Journal of Creation* (2015), 29/1: 64–71.

Index

Abritus, battle of (June 251) 183, 277 n.5
Achilles xxvi, xxvii, 124
Adrianopolis
    battle of (30 April 313) 57
    battle of (24 July 324) 58
    battle of (9 August 378) 23, 42, 48,
        69–70, 71–3, 221 n.146, 232 n.24,
        232 n.30
        consequences of 129, 156–7, 161–2,
            184, 185, 192, 213 n.23, 233 n.45
Adriatic Sea x, 59, 96, 116, 163
Aeneas xxvi, xxvii, 51, 211 n.1
Aëtius, Flavius (†454), *patricius et magister
    militum* 230 n.7, 243 n.7, 286 n.21
Aëtius of Amida, Greek physician 48
Aion, Valerius, *centurio* 25
Alamanni 8, 9, 10, 33, 35, 38–9, 53, 65, 89,
    133, 235 n.62
    see also Argentorate (357)
Alani 69, 75, 89, 161, 186, 231–2 n.23, 233
    n.43, 235 n.62, 243 n.7, 277 n.8, 279
    n.18
    at Frigidus 88, 90, 243 n.9
Alaric, leader of Goths (†410) 128, 129,
    157, 158, 182, 187–8, 191, 236 n.62, 255
    n.46, 281 n.60, 282–3 n.75
    at Frigidus 88, 96–7, 101, 243 n.9
    magister militum per Illyricum 130, 253
        n.19, 255 n.45
    magister utriusque militiae 186
    at Pollentia (5 April 402) 185–6, 243
        n.9, 279 n.23
    sacks Rome (August 410) 188–90, 280
        n.29
Alaric II, king of Visigoths (r. 484–507)
    237 n.74, 279 n.18
Alexander (the Great) III of Macedon
    (r. 336–323 bc) 60, 146, 148, 163, 173,
    227 n.53

Alexandria (in Egypt) 143, 166, 218 n.101,
    241–2 n.29, 260 n.9, 262 n.21, 287 n.27
    pogrom of 391 166, 196
Allectus, usurper (r. 293–296) 75
Alpes Iuliani (Julian Alps) 92–3, 94, 96,
    101, 105
    claustra Alpium Iuliarum 93, 94, 245
        n.12
Ambrose (Saint), theologian and Nicene
    bishop of Mediolanum
    (r. 374–397) *passim*
    on Adrianopolis (9 August 378) 70
    and Eugenius 105
    on Frigidus 105–8
    and Nicene orthodoxy 109, 133, 150–1,
        155, 158, 194, 238 n.83, 264–5 n.30
    and Symmachus 131, 140–1, 259 n.45,
        260 n.48
    and Theodosius I 92, 124, 144, 165–6,
        227 n.58, 268 n.85, 268 n.87
    and Valentinianus II 80, 82–3, 240
        n.13
American Civil War (1861–5) 171, 245
    n.10, 270 n.8
    Gettysburg, battle of (1–3 July 1863)
        249 n.50
        Pickett's charge 249 n.50
    Shiloh, battle of (6–7 April 1862) 270
        n.8
American War of Independence (1775–83)
    174, 214 n.25, 272 n.22
Ammianus Marcellinus, soldier and
    historian *passim*
    on Adrianopolis (9 August 378) 70,
        71–2, 192, 232 n.24
    on Argentorate (357) 176, 219 n.105
    on 'barbarization' 159
    on Christians 63, 138, 153
    on Gratianus 75

on Iulianus 26–7, 138, 198, 258 n.31,
    258 n.35
  on *scholae palatinae* 32
  on Serapeion 166
  Res Gestae 195–6, 286 n.25
Anastasius I, Romano-Byzantine emperor
    (r. 491–518) 268 n.83, 284 n.82
Angles 210 n.57
Anna Komneni (1083–1153), Byzantine
    princess and chronicler 229 n.80
Anthemius, western emperor (r. 467–472)
    231 n.7
Antioch 7, 195, 197, 198, 204, 207 n.9, 220
    n.117, 241 n.29, 254 n.22, 257 n.18, 260
    n.9, 263 n.13, 281 n.51
  see also Iulianus
Apollo, Palatine 264 n.20, 265 n.35
  as Sol Invictus 50, 61, 224 n.2, 228 n.68
Apollonius of Tyana 194
Aquileia 3, 7, 80, 96, 119, 134, 201, 208
    n.14, 263 n.5
Aquincum (Budapest) 68, 161
Aquitania Secunda 279 n.18
ara Victoriae (Altar of Victory) 131–3, 140,
    153, 259 n.45
Arabia 7
  desert of 278 n.9
Arbogastes, Flavius (Frank), *magister
    militum in praesenti* 69, 73–4, 105, 108,
    123, 187, 198, 211 n.4, 231 n.14, 234
    n.55, 248 n.36, 254 n.22
  at Frigidus 89–91, 92–3, 95–9, 101–3,
    121, 243 n.12, 246 n.1, 246–7 n.10
  power behind throne 80–1, 84–7, 127,
    230 n.7
  and death of Valentinianus II 82–4
Arcadius, western emperor (r. 395–408)
    41–2, 48–9, 86, 87, 122, 123–4, 125–6,
    130, 141, 204, 221 n.136, 222 n.162,
    234–5 n.55, 240 n.22, 242 n.31, 243 n.7,
    252 n.8, 253 n.19, 254 n.22, 254 n.23,
    255 n.45, 256 n.13, 263 n.22, 266 n.46
Archilochos, Greek soldier poet 111, 113,
    181, 215 n.43, 248 n.45
Arelate (Arles) 18
Argentorate, battle of (357) 23, 30–1, 39,
    133, 176, 219 n.105
Argonauts 245 n.9
Arian(s)/Arianism 42, 59, 78, 109, 132,
    133, 139, 144, 147, 148, 150, 155, 194,
    227 n.43, 235 n.55, 283 n.80, 286 n.15
  homoioúsios 200, 285 n.3
  see also Arius
Aristotle, post-Sokratic philosopher 155,
    194, 204
Arius, presbyter of Alexandria (†336) 200,
    228 n.64, 241 n.26, 241 n.29, 262 n.21,
    284 n.3
  see also Arian(s)/Arianism
army, later Roman *passim*
  'barbarisation' of 159–61, 205
  barritus (war cry) 38, 219 n.106
  conscription 19, 45 –9, 88, 159, 161, 267
    n.68
    deserters 44, 46
      tattooing 46–7, 48, 222 n.187
    sacramentum 46, 120
  diet
    acetum 25–6, 29, 214 n.31
    bread 25, 26, 27, 29, 216 n.48, 216
      n.52, 216 n.53, 217 n.57
      unleavened 27–8, 29, 180, 215 n.43
    buccellatum (hardtack) 25, 26, 28–9,
      216 n.48
    puls 26–7, 215 n.39
    vinum 25, 207–8 n.13, 214 n.31,
      214–15 n.32
  foederati 73, 75, 109, 125, 159–60, 161,
    182, 184, 186, 187, 191, 221 n.136,
    266 n.49, 266 n.62, 279 n.18, 279
    n.28, 280 n.32
    at Frigidus 88, 92, 96–8, 101
  numbers 21–2, 39, 89, 90–1, 244 n.17,
    244 n.21
  organisation
    ala(*e*) 32, 34, 35, 37, 40, 44
      Parthorum 11
    auxilia 21, 22, 24, 36, 39, 219 n.104,
      243 n.7, 244 n.23
    Brachiati 38, 219 n.106
    Celtae 39, 219 n.110
    Cornuti 38, 219 n.106
    Petulantes 39, 219 n.110

cohors(*tes*) 22, 32, 37, 39, 40, 44, 244 n.222
   equitata(*e*) 34
legio(*nes*), 24, 32–3, 36, 37, 38–9, 40, 44, 49, 223 n.200
   I–II Armeniaca 40
   II Herculia 122
   Herculiani 224 n.223, 241 n.24
   Ioviani 39, 49, 224 n.223, 241 n.24
   V Macedonia 38, 218 n.101
   IIII Martia 22, 213 n.13
numerus(*i*) 44, 224 n.222
palatina(*e*) 252 n.6
   auxilia
      Batavi 49, 224 n.222, 234 n.51
      Brachiati 49
      Heruli 49, 234 n.51
      Iovii 234 n.51
      Mattiaci 49
      Victores 234 n.51
   legiones
      Herculiani 224 n.223, 243 n.12, 246 n.1
      Ioviani 224 n.223, 243 n.12, 246 n.1
      scholae 32, 36–7, 44, 45, 49, 128, 218 n.90, 242–3 n.7, 266 n.46
      vexillationes 22, 224 n.222, 244 n.17, 244 n.21
   vexillatio(*nes*) 20–1, 32–3, 35, 37, 38, 43, 44, 49, 244 n.17, 244 n.21
ranks
   biarchus 49
   campidoctor 49, 224 n.222
   centenarius 49
   centurio 11, 25, 44, 127, 210 n.66
   circitor 48, 49
   decurio 11
   ducenarius 49
   lanciarius 33, 37, 41
   optio 33
   pedes 41, 221 n.139
   primicerius 44, 49
   semissalis 49
   senator 49
  see also cavalry, infantry, slingers
armour, later Roman
   iron/ring mail (*lorica hamata*) 22, 213 n.14
   scale (*lorica squamata*) 22, 213 n.14, 277 n.5
   segmented (*lorica segmentata*) 22
artillery
   Macedonian 272 n.21
      katapéltēs lithobólos 271–2 n.20
      katapéltēs óxybelēs 271 n.16
   Roman
      ballista(*e*) 172, 173
      onager(*ri*) 271 n.12
      scorpio(*nes*) 172–3
Artemius, Flavius, *dux Aegypti*, 241 n.29
Ataulf, leader of Goths 191, 279 n.23, 280 n.29, 281 n.56, 282 n.73, 282 n.74, 282 n.75
Athanasios I (Saint), Nicene bishop of Alexandria (r. 328–339, 346–373) 139, 140, 221 n.140, 241 n.26, 241–2 n.29
Athena 31
   Palladium of 51
Attacotti 234 n.51
Attalus Priscus, puppet emperor (r. 409, 414) 186, 189, 281 n.55, 281 n.56
Attila, king of the Huns (r. 434–453) 202, 231 n.7
Augusta Treverorum (Trier) 18, 68, 75, 77, 80, 194, 234 n.51, 238 n.82, 238 n.83
Augustodunum (Autun) 9, 85, 234 n.51
Augustine, bishop of Canterbury 210 n.57
Augustine (Saint, †430), bishop of Hippo Regius 69, 157, 164, 196, 227 n.56, 228 n.64, 230 n.96, 254 n.25, 258 n.32
   De Civitate Dei 158, 281–2 n.61
   Eliot, T.S., *The Waste Land* 285 n.11
   on Frigidus 102, 246 n.1, 247 n.20
   and Manichaeism 196, 286 n.12
   and Neo-Platonism 286 n.12
   on pagans/paganism 151, 153–4, 228 n.68, 250 n.69
   on death of Valentinianus II 83
   on war 78, 127–8
Augustus, emperor (r. 27 BC–AD 14) 13, 19, 21, 22, 94, 119, 122, 131, 154, 205, 223 n.205, 223 n.220, 224 n.7, 312 n.11, 245 n.8, 264 n.20, 265 n.35

Aurelianus, Lucius Domitius, emperor
(r. 270–275) 7–8, 9–10, 11, 12, 50, 183,
209 n.42, 209 n.54, 224 n.2, 234 n.49
assassination of 10, 36
horse army of 35–6
restitutor orbis 10, 210 n.61
triumph of 8
see also Palmyra
Aurelius, Marcus, emperor (r. 161–180) 4,
14, 27, 212–13 n.7
'Rain Miracle' 118–19, 250 n.70, 251
n.78, 251 n.71, 251 n.78
Meditations 118
Aurelius Victor, Sextus, *praefectus urbis
Romae* and historian, 12, 56, 210 n.68,
218 n.80, 224 n.223
Aureolus, cavalry commander 5
revolt of 6, 34
Austro-Prussian War (1866) 171, 274 n.46
Königgrätz, battle of (3 July 1866)
274–5 n.46
Avitus, western emperor (r. 455–456) 203,
230 n.7

Bacurios (Caucasian Iberian), *dux
Palestinae* (or *magister militum*) 88, 98,
243 n.9
Bahrām I, king of Persia (r. 271–274) 286
n.12
Bahrām II, king of Persia (r. 274–293)
110
Baker rifle 273 n.75
Balbinus and Pupienus, co-emperors (238)
1, 3
Basilika (Ottoman bombard) 172, 270
n.10
Batavi (people) 208 n.22, 219 n.106
Bauto, Flavius (Frank), *magister militum*
74, 79, 80, 127, 211 n.4, 234 n.55, 239
n.99, 239 n.107, 259 n.45
Bede (†735), Anglian monk and scholar
76, 210 n.57
Belisarius (†565), Romano-Byzantine
patricius et magister militum 191, 201,
271 n.12
and Nika riots (532) 268 n.83

Belloc, Joseph Hilaire Pierre René
(1870–1953), Franco-English Catholic
apologist 147
Beowulf xxvi, xxvii
Bismarck, Otto von, Chancellor of
Germany (r. 1871–90) 137, 258 n.29
Black Sea (Euxine) 41, 182, 183, 234 n.52,
278 n.9
book banning/burning 152, 153, 263–4
n.14, 264 n.21
Bosporus 11, 57, 58, 268 n.83
bow(s) 176, 177–8, 192
composite 178, 274 n.44
Brigetio (Szőny) 68
Tablet 37
Britannia 5, 15, 16, 26, 30, 53, 66, 78, 86,
210 n.57, 211 n.5, 234 n.51
barbarica conspiratio (367) 234 n.51
garrison of 20, 33, 38, 43, 74, 75–6, 159,
224 n.222, 235–6 n.62, 236 n.63
withdrawn (410) 237 n.75
Brown Bess (Land Pattern Musket) 173–4,
175, 178, 272 n.22, 272 n.24, 273 n.25,
273 n.31
Snell, Hannah (1723–92) 272 n.22
see also Fusil Charleville Modèle 1777
bucellarius(ii) 243 n.7, 283 n.75
Burckhardt, Jacob 60
Burgundi 89, 235 n.62
Butheric (Goth), *magister militum*
163–4, 267 n.75, 267 n.77
see also Thessaloniki
Byzantium 36, 57, 58–9, 209 n.54
see also Constantinopolis

Cain (and Abel) 59, 66
Caracalla, emperor (r. 211–217) 20, 27, 66,
210 n.61
Carbo, Cnaeus Papirius (consul 113 bc)
117–18
Carinus, co-emperor (r. 283–285) 13, 110,
202, 211 n.3
Carnuntum, conference of (11 November
308) 18
Carus, emperor (r. 282–283) 110
Carausius, Marcus Aurelius Mausaeus,
usurper (r. 286–293) 75

Castra Maurorum 220 n.116
Catholic and Apostolic Church (Early Church) 144–5, 260 n.5
Catholic Orthodox Church (Eastern Orthodox Church) 64, 229 n.81, 242 n.31, 260 n.9,
Catholic Orthodox Church (Roman Catholic Church) 64, 145, 147, 150, 170, 196, 260 n.9, 263 n.4, 263–4 n.14
cataphractus(ii), Palmyrene 5, 7, 36, 209 n.30
Cato (the Elder), Marcus Porcius (234–149 BC) 215 n.39
cavalry, later Roman 6, 7, 21, 22, 23, 24, 33–4, 37, 38, 39, 40, 43, 48, 49, 72, 78, 220 n.113
    equites 35, 40
        legionis 33
        promoti 25, 49
    equites Dalmatae 6, 34, 35–6
        Cecropius (or Heracleianus) 6, 209 n.37
    equites Mauri 34, 35–6
    horse army 33–6
cereal(s) 26, 27, 28, 217 n.57
    barley 27, 29–30, 215 n.43, 216 n.47, 216 n.53, 317 n.57, 264 n.29
    oats 29
    rye 29
    wheat (spelt) 29–30, 215 n.39, 216 n.53, 216 n.56
chariot racing/charioteer(s) 163–4, 267 n.77, 268 n.83
    see also Thessaloniki
China xxvii, 31, 261 n.10, 278 n.8,
Chrysopolis, battle of (18 September 324) 58
clades Variana (AD 9) 70, 212 n.7
Claudianus, Claudius (†404), court poet 71–2, 86, 124, 129, 185, 196–7, 243 n.7, 254–5 n.38, 255 n.43, 279 n.23
    on Frigidus 90, 102, 243 n.12, 246 n.3, 246 n.10
Claudius II Gothicus, emperor (r. 268–270) 5, 7, 34, 35–6, 59, 183, 218 n.80, 233–4 n.49
    death of 7, 209 n.42

von Clausewitz, Carl Maria (1780–1831), Prussian general and military theorist xxviii, 30, 95, 96
clibanarus(ii), Sāsānian 208–9 n.30
Clovis, Frankish king (r. 481–511) 184, 237 n.74, 279 n.18
Codex Theodosianus 197, 214–15 n.32, 263 n.5
Cohortes praetoriae (Praetorian Guard) 33, 36, 54
Colonia Claudia Ara Agrippinensium (Köln) 84, 89, 160
Cold War 276 n.54
comes 43, 69, 99, 122, 199, 205, 241 n.24, 252 n.7, 281 n.55
    Africae 186, 221 n.139
    Britanniarum 43, 74, 221 n.139, 235 n.58
    domesticorum 69, 128, 243 n.9, 255 n.38
    Italiae 243 n.12
    Mauretaniae Tingitanae 49, 244 n.19
    Orientis 263 n.13
    rei militaris 41, 43, 68, 74, 88, 234 n.51, 255 n.45
    stabuli sacri 128, 255 n.38
comitatus/comitatenses 20, 22, 31, 34–40, 41, 42, 43, 44, 46, 48, 66, 73–4, 90, 109, 124, 129, 159, 184, 199, 237 n.75, 241 n.24, 244 n.17, 244 n.21 ,255 n.46
    praesentalis(ae) 37, 38, 39
    see also army
Constans I, emperor (r. 337–350) 66, 134, 212 n.21
    overthrown and killed 85–6, 134
    visits Britannia (343) 75
Constantia, Flavia Iulia, half-sister of Constantinus I and wife of Licinius 56, 226–7 n.43
    Arian policy of 227 n.43
    pleas for husband's life 58
Constantia, sister of Constantius II, 256 n.18
Constantinopolis *passim*
    Column of Constantinus 50–1
    Hippodrome 84, 268 n.83
        Obelisk of Theodosius 240 n.16

Holy Apostles, church of 101, 124, 235
n.55
Constantinus I, Flavius Valerius
(Constantine the Great), emperor
(r. 306–337) *passim*
and army 14, 21–2, 34, 36–8, 39, 40–2,
44, 48, 254 n.36
his baptism 59–62, 64, 135, 143–4, 228
n.64, 258 n.26
his celestial vision xxiv, 54–5, 56, 61,
154, 229 n.81, 265 n.35
and *Dies Solis* 51–2, 224 n.7, 225 n.8,
225 n.9, 225 n.11
and Edict of Toleration (313) 56–7,
155–6
foundation of Constantinopolis 50,
58–9, 62, 227 n.53
law on adultery 65
letter to Šāpūr II (324) 53
at Pons Mulvius (28 October 312) 54,
56, 219 n.104, 226 n.34
his rise to power 18, 52–8, 75
visits Rome (312, 315, 326) 256 n.11
and Sol Invictus 50, 61, 228 n.68
as sole emperor (324–337) 58, 62, 65
Thirteenth Apostle 229 n.80
Constantinus II, emperor (r. 337–340) 66,
134, 212 n.21, 241 n.29
Constantinus III, co-emperor (r. 407–411)
75, 235–6 n.62, 237 n.75, 280 n.29
Constantius I Chlorus, Flavius, *Caesar*
(r. 293–305), *Augustus* (r. 305–306) 16,
17, 18, 38, 52, 59, 134, 226 n.43, 227
n.58, 241 n.26
Constantius, Iulius, father of Iulianus 134,
257 n.20
Constantius II, emperor (r. 337–361) 45,
66, 134, 138, 212 n.21, 223 n.199, 234
n.49, 241 n.26, 257 n.21, 259 n.38
removes *ara Victoriae* 132
Arian policy of 63, 132, 241–2 n.29, 256
n.12, 284–5 n.3
and civil wars
against Iulianus 30, 147–8
against Magnus Magnentius 77–8, 88,
94, 134, 160, 234 n.51, 238 n.86
makes Gallus *Caesar* 256–7 n.18

and logistics 25–6
visits Rome (357) 132, 256 n.11
as sole emperor 86
Constantius III, Flavius, *magister peditum*,
co-emperor (r. 421) 126, 191, 230 n.7,
282 n.75
marries Galla Placidia (417) 191, 230
n.7, 282–3 n.75
Crispus, Flavius Iulius, *Caesar* and son of
Constantinus I (†326) 55, 65, 143, 230
n.91
executed 62, 64–5, 257 n.18
Ctesiphon 6, 110
Cyprianus, bishop of Carthage
(r. 248–258) 48, 223 n.198

Danuvius (Danube) 4, 7, 8, 10, 20, 33,
37, 42, 58, 59, 71, 75, 78, 89, 119, 129,
182–5, 186, 188, 192, 213 n.7
army on 43, 68, 90, 214 n.24
see also Alani, Goths, Huns
David (and Goliath) xxvii–xxviii, 176, 177,
206 n.8
De rebus bellicis, anonymous military
treatise 23
Diocletianus, *Augustus* (r. 284–305 †311) 3,
12, 13, 18, 197, 211 n.2, 211 n.12
abdication and death of 17, 211 n.15
administrative reforms of 13–17, 52–4,
58, 211 n.7
army reforms of 21–2, 32, 36, 37–8, 39,
40–1, 44–5, 48, 49
diocese(s) 15, 211 n.5
Britanniae 15, 75, 159, 236 n.63
Dacia 73, 193
Illyricum 211 n.5
Macedonia 73
Pannonia 193
Secunda 243 n.7
Valeria 243 n.7
Thracia 73
'dog tags' 223 n.200
Donatists 62
Doura Europos 43, 278 n.9
Dreyse needle-gun 178, 274 n.45, 274 n.46
dux 14, 43–4, 88, 161, 199
Aegypti 7, 43, 221 n.140, 241 n.29

Arabiae 213 n.14
Britanniarum 74
Libyarum 16
Mauretaniae 244 n.19
Moesia Prima 234 n.51
Palestinae 243 n.9
Raetiae 43
ripae Mesopotamiae 43
Tripolitania 244 n.19
Valeriae 43

Eboracum (York) 20, 52, 53
Edict of Toleration (313) 56–7, 132
Edward IV of England (r. 1461–70,
    1471–83) 249–50 n.58
Emesa, battle of (272) 7
Emona (Ljubljana) 224 n.222, 245 n.9
Erocus, *rex* of Alamanni 53
Eudokia, Aelia (†404), *Augusta* and wife
    of Arcadius 125, 221 n.133, 234–5 n.55,
    253 n.19, 254 n.23, 262–3 n.22
Eugenius, Flavius, usurper (r. 392–394)
    xxiii, 83, 86–7, 88, 92, 211 n.4, 236 n.69
    elevation of 83–5, 246 n.9
    at Frigidus 91, 99, 101–3, 121, 159, 199
    his religious policy/toleration 69, 105,
        108–9, 131, 140, 148, 155, 239 n.110,
        246 n.1
Euphrates 5, 8, 33, 90, 278 n.9
    army on 43, 58, 59
Eunapios of Sardis (b. 346), Greek anti-
    church historian 125, 157, 184, 193, 205,
    242 n.7, 250 n.63, 252 n.8
Eusebius of Caesarea Palestinae (†339),
    hagiographer 65, 154, 202, 207, 227
    n.58, 247 n.33
    on Constantinus I 51–2, 59–60,
    on Constantinus' vision 54, 55–6, 61
    on the *labarum* 54, 226 n.25
    on 'Rain Miracle' 119
Eusebius, Arian bishop of Nicomedia
    (†342) 59, 228 n.64
Eutropius (†399), *patricius et praepositus
    sacri cubiculi* 125, 130, 235 n.55, 252 n.8,
    254 n.22
    career of 253 n.19
    execution of 41, 130

Eutropius (*fl.* 368–387), epitomist 208
    n.28, 218 n.85, 241 n.26
Euxine *see* Black Sea

fabricae 24, 44, 46, 130, 213 n.14, 214 n.24
Faesulae, battle of (8 August 406) 186
Falklands/Malvinas War (April-June
    1982) 116
Fausta, Flavia Maxima (†326), daughter of
    Maximianus and wife of Constantinus I
    18, 212 n.21
    murdered 62, 64–5, 143
Firmus, usurper (373) 239 n.111
Flaccilla Augusta, Aelia Flavia (†386), first
    wife of Theodosius I 86, 239 n.111, 242
    n.31
Flavianus, Virius Nicomachus, *praefectus
    praetorio per Italiae* 84, 86, 87, 105, 108,
    140
Flavianus, Nicomachus the Younger,
    praefectus urbis Romae 86
Fontenoy, battle of (11 May 1745) 232–3
    n.13
Franco-Prussian War (1870) 112, 178, 275
    n.46
Franklin, Benjamin (1706–90), American
    diplomat 184, 214 n.25, 278 n.14
Franks 8, 18, 65, 84, 234 n.51, 237 n.75,
    240 n.19, 283 n.80
    at Frigidus 92, 96
    recruited 39, 80, 88, 89, 161, 241 n.24
Fravitta (Goth) 42, 220n.132, 220–1 n.133
Friedrich II der Große, king of Prussia
    (r. 1740–86) 174–5, 270 n.6, 273 n.28
    Chotusitz, battle of (17 May 1742) 175
    Mollwitz, battle of (10 April 1741)
        174–5
French Revolutionary Wars (1792–1802)
    170
    levée en masse 170–1
    La Marseillaise 270 n.7
Frigidus, battle of (5–6 September 394)
    passim
    'miraculous' wind 101–3, 104–7, 114,
        117, 121, 203, 247 n.20
        Bora/Boréās 116–17, 121, 250 n.64,
            250 n.65

Aeolus, Keeper of the Winds 102,
    246 n.3
  size of forces 89, 90–1, 97–8
  topography of
    Castra ad Fluvium Frigidum
      (Ajdovščina) 93–4, 117
    Hrušica Plateau 93, 95
      Ad Pirum (Hrušica) 93–4, 185
    Postojna Gate 95–6, 98, 99
    Vipava, river/valley xxiii, 117
Fritigern, leader of Goths 72, 74, 157, 232
  n.24
Fusil Charleville Modèle 1777 146, 175, 273
  n.30, 273 n.31

Gaïnas (Goth), *magister utriusque militae*
  41–2, 129, 253 n.19
  at Frigidus 88, 96–7, 243 n.9
  revolt of (400) 42, 220 n.130, 221 n.136
Gaiseric, king of Vandals (r. 428–477) 202
Galerius, Valerius Maximus, *Caesar*
  (r.293–305), *Augustus* (r. 305–311) 16,
  17–18, 41, 52–3, 57, 59
Galla (†394), daughter of Valentinianus I
  and second wife of Theodosius I 85, 240
  n.20, 240 n.22
Gallic empire (260–274) 9, 33, 35, 208
  n.28
Gallienus, emperor (r. 253–268) 3, 4–6, 9,
  11, 14, 43, 44, 254 n.36
  assassination of 6, 7, 208 n.18, 209 n.37
  horse army of 20, 33–6
Gallus, Flavius Claudius (Constantius),
  Caesar 134, 257 n.20, 257 n.21
  career of 256–7 n.18
  execution of (354) 257 n.18
Garibaldi, Giuseppe (1807–82), Italian
  revolutionary 225–6 n.21
Gatling gun 169, 270 n.4
Georgios of Kappadokia, Arian bishop of
  Alexandria 241–2 n.29
Gildo (Mauretanian), *magister utriusque
  militiae per Africam* 80, 90, 244 n.19
  rebellion of 125, 197, 239 n.111, 243
  n.12, 252 n.17
Gibbon, Edward (1737–94), English
  politician and historian 158–9, 186, 208

n.23, 224 n.1, 248 n.41, 253 n.19, 263–4
  n.14, 265 n.42
  on Ammianus Marcellinus 195
  on Frigidus 249 n.58
Gordianus I, emperor (r.238) 277 n.4
Gordianus III, emperor (r. 238–244) 183,
  277 n.4
Gothic alphabet 192, 283 n.80
  Gothic Bible (*Codex Argenteus*) 192,
    283–4 n.82, 284 n.85
Goths *passim*
  fighting style 71–2, 182, 192
  at Frigidus 41, 88–9, 96–8, 128, 243
    n.9
  as *foederati* 42, 73–4, 89, 101, 161–3,
    184, 243 n.7, 266 n.61, 266–7 n.64,
    283 n.76
  Greuthungi and *Teruingi* 185, 188, 234
    n.52
  see also Adrianopolis (9 August 378),
    Alaric, Visigoths
Gratianus, Flavius, emperor (r. 367–383)
  45, 46, 48, 68, 69, 71, 73–4, 79, 85, 86,
  89, 213 n.14, 221 n.146, 233 n.47, 233
  n.48, 233–4 n.49, 253 n.19, 256 n.11,
  264–5 n.30
  and *ara Victoriae* 131
  fall and murder of 75–7, 82, 236 n.69,
    240 n.13
Gratianus Funarius, *comes Britanniarum*
  221 n.139
Greek authors/language 76, 108, 153, 176,
  193–4, 197–8, 200–1, 204–5, 216 n.55,
  258 n.30, 286 n.23
  see also Latin language
Gregory Nazianzen (Saint), bishop of
  Constantinopolis (r. 378–381) 72–3,
  150
  on Iulianus 137, 142, 258 n.30, 258
    n.31, 259 n.35
Gregory (†395), bishop of Nyssa 145
Gregory I, pope (r. 590–604) 210 n.57
Gregory of Tours (†594), Gallo-Roman
  historian 207 n.1, 235 n.58, 237 n.74,
  255 n.50, 265 n.30
de Gribeauval, Jean-Baptiste Vaquette
  (1715–89) 271 n.19

Hanger, Lieutenant Colonel George
(1751–1824), 4th Baron Coleraine 174,
273 n.75
   on Brown Bess 174
   see also Brown Bess (Land Pattern
   Musket)
Hannibalic War (218–202 BC) 178
   Cannae, battle of (216 BC) 70, 157, 178,
   246 n.3, 275 n.47
   Lake Trasimene, battle of (217 BC) 178,
   275 n.47
Harris, Benjamin, Rifleman 113–14, 115
Helena (Saint, †328), mother of
   Constantinus I 58, 65, 227 n.43, 227–8
   n.58
   discovers True Cross 227–8 n.58
Hellespont 42
   battle of (324) 65
helmet(s) 130, 173, 177, 192, 213 n.14, 283
   n.77
   Intercisa 24
   Kammhelm 24
   Spangenhelm 24
   Weisenau-Niedermörmter 24
Herodian of Syria, historian 1, 2, 3, 11,
   197–8
Herodotos, Greek historian 137, 201, 216
   n.53, 260 n.1, 267 n.73
Heruli (people) 183
Hilarius (Hilary de Poitiérs), bishop of
   Pictavium 45, 256 n.12
Hjörungavágr, battle of (986) 120
Homer, Greek bard 124, 136–7, 194, 215
   n.43
Honorius, western emperor (r. 395–423)
Horace, Augustan poet 111, 115, 131–2,
   140, 248–9 n.47
Huns 42, 69, 183, 184–5, 186, 188–9,
   202–3, 232 n.24, 233 n.43, 242–3 n.7,
   243 n.9, 253 n.19, 280 n.29
   at Frigidus (?) 88, 89, 90, 161, 242 n.7
   origins of 277–8 n.8

Illyricum
   diocese of 211 n.5
   province of 4, 16

prefecture of 15, 38, 39, 66, 73, 74, 78,
   81, 87, 90, 92, 130, 163, 188, 264
   n.29
   see also Pannonia
Immae, battle of (272) 7, 36, 218 n.85
infantry, later Roman 21–4, 34, 37–8,
   39–40, 42–3, 97, 213 n.14, 220 n.113,
   at Adrianopolis (9 August 378) 69,
   71–2, 232 n.30, 233 n.45
Ingenuus, usurper (r. 260) 4
Ioannis Chrysostomos, bishop of
   Constantinopolis (r. 397–403, †407) 235
   n.55, 253 n.19, 262–3 n.22
   on Frigidus 101–2, 106
Iovianus, Flavius, emperor (r. 363–364)
   133, 139, 230 n.3, 259 n.40
   treaty with Persia 40, 139–40, 220
   n.116
Iudaea 7, 251 n.75
Iulianus, Flavius Claudius (Julian the
   Apostate), *Caesar* (r. 355–360), emperor
   (r. 361–363) *passim*
   in Antioch 27, 135, 219–20 n.111,
   257–8 n.25, 259 n.38
   Caesares 135–6, 258 n.26
   Misopogon 219 n.111
   death of (26 June 363) 139, 142–3, 230
   n.3, 259 n.36
   on classical education 137–8, 258 n.32
   in Gaul and Germania (357–359) 26–7,
   30–1, 38, 131
   his pagan policy 131, 133–7, 138–9, 141,
   147
   Persian campaign (363) 19, 39, 40, 43,
   148, 219–20 n.111, 265 n.35
Iustina, mother of Valentinianus II 68, 79,
   82, 85, 240 n.20
Iustinianus I (Justinian the Great),
   Romano-Byzantine emperor
   (r. 527–565) 8, 38, 191, 198, 200, 201,
   214–15 n.32, 287 n.28
   and Nika riots 268 n.83
Iuthungi 7
   see also Alamanni
Iwo Jima, battle for (19 February–26
   March 1945) xxv–xxvii

Jeanne d'Arc (Saint, †1431) xxvi, xxvii
Jerome (Saint, †420) 64, 75, 151, 193, 228
    n.64, 241 n.26, 254 n.25, 258 n.32, 264
    n.16, 266 n.59, 277 n.8, 286 n.23
    on Adrianopolis (9 August 378) 70
    disowns Cicero 259–60 n.46
    on clergy 63–4
    on Mursa (28 September 351) 78
    and Origen 201–2
    on sack of Rome 122, 189, 282 n.66
John of Antioch (Ioannes Antiochensis),
    Byzantine chronicler 90, 103, 198
John the Kappadokian, *praefectus praetorio
    urbis Constantinopoleos* 28–9
John the Lydian (Ioannes Lydos),
    Romano-Byzantine historian 21, 200
Jordanes (†583), Romano-Byzantine-
    Gothic historian 128, 162, 184, 198–9,
    207 n.4, 218 n.85, 222 n.162, 236 n.69,
    265 n.30, 277 n.6, 279 n.23, 282 n.73
    on 'Balthi' 128
    on Frigidus 90
    on origins of Goths 182, 277 n.3
Josephus, Flavius, Jewish military leader
    and Romano-Jewish historian 172, 208
    n.29, 231 n.23, 271 n.17

Kappadokia 6, 136, 145, 200, 213 n.7
Kedrenos, Georgios, Byzantine chronicler,
    7, 34, 165
Kniva, leader of Goths 183

labarum 54, 226 n.25
Lactantius, Latin rhetor and Christian
    polemicist 17, 65, 183, 189, 208 n.19,
    211 n.2
    on Edict of Toleration 227 n.45
    on tetrarchs 21, 211 n.7, 211 n.15, 226
        n.34, 229 n.73
    on Pons Mulvius (28 October 312)
        55–6, 265 n.35
Lafferty, R.A. (1914–2002), American
    science fiction and fantasy writer 88,
    100, 242 n.1
Laodikeia, Council of (363–364) 225 n.11
laeti 39, 43, 89, 224 n.222, 244 n.13

Lagertha, shield maiden xxvi, xxvii
Latin authors/language 21, 37, 52, 54, 131,
    140, 158, 159, 193–4, 195, 196–7, 198–9,
    200, 201, 210 n.57, 225 n.12, 227 n.58,
    259–60 n.46, 282 n.61, 284 n.83, 286
    n.23
    see also Greek authors/language
legio antiqua 4, 11, 21–2, 212–13 n.7, 245
    n.8
    number of 212 n.7
    V *Alaudae* 212 n.7
    II *Augusta* 40
    III *Augusta* 43
    XI *Claudia* 37, 41
    XXII *Deiotariana* 213 n.7
    IIII *Flavia* 11
    X *Fretensis* 172, 270 n.11
    XII *Fulminata* 119, 251 n.75
    VIII *Hispana* 212–13 n.7
    II–III *Italica* 213 n.7
    IIII (*Italica?*) 21, 212 n.7
    V *Macedonica* 218 n.101
    I *Parthica* 11
    II *Parthica* 3, 11, 33, 43, 208 n.14
    III *Parthica* 11
    XXI *Rapax* 212 n.7
    II *Traiana* 212 n.7
    XXX *Ulpia* 212 n.7
Libanius of Antioch, pagan sophist 193,
    219 n.111, 243 n.9, 260 n.1
    on death of Iulianus 142, 258 n.35
Libius Severus, western emperor
    (r. 461–465) 230–1 n.7
Licinius, Valerius Licinianus, *Augustus*
    (r. 308–324 †325) 52, 55, 56–8, 62, 65,
    155, 160
Licinius Iunior (†326) 58, 62, 65
limitanei 22, 37, 40–1, 44, 46, 48, 90
    see also army, *pseudo-comitatenses*
Lugdunum (Lyon) 76, 78, 194, 202, 203
Lutetia (Paris) 75–6, 148

Macrianus and Quietus (r. 260), usurpers 4
magister/magistri 42, 88
    equitum 42, 252 n.5, 252 n.6, 252 n.7
        per Gallias 44

equitum et peditum 42, 252 n.6, 252 n.7
   per Illyricum 252 n.6
   per Orientem 252 n.6
   per Thracias 252 n.6
memoriae 5, 94
militum 42, 44, 73, 74, 76, 79, 80–1, 88,
   95, 186, 201, 230–1 n.7, 253 n.47, 234
   n.55, 253 n.19, 259 n.45, 268 n.83
   per Illyricum 130, 163, 253 n.19, 255
    n.45
   per Orientem 38, 40, 69
   in praesenti/praesentalis 69, 86, 199,
    284 n.82
   per Thracias 122
officiorum 122, 241 n.26
peditum 42, 43, 252 n.5, 252 n.6, 253
   n.19
   per Gallias 68, 160
   praesentalis 42–3
scrinii 69
utriusque militum/militiae 41, 42–3, 69,
   122, 189, 251 n.2, 252 n.6, 252 n.7
   per Africam 90, 239 n.111, 243 n.12
   praesentalis 122, 252 n.6
Magnus Magnentius, Flavius, usurper
   (r. 350–353) 77–8, 85–6, 88, 94, 134,
   160, 222 n.168, 234 n.51, 238 n.86, 240
   n.23, 241 n.24, 241 n.26, 256 n.18
Maiorianus, western emperor (r. 457–461)
   130, 203, 230–1 n.7
Mamaea, Iulia Avita, mother of Severus
   Alexander 2, 207 n.7, 207 n.8, 207 n.9
Māni (216–274), prophet 285–6 n.12
Manzoni, Alessandro (1785–1873),
   Milanese novelist and poet 261 n.15,
   262 n.17
Marcianus, western emperor (r. 450–457)
   45, 222 n.162
Marco Polo xxvi, xxvii
Margus, battle of (285) 13
Maria (†408), first wife of Honorius 129,
   255 n.43, 280 n.39
Martin of Turones (Saint, †397) 45, 76,
   127, 151, 222 n.168, 223 n.199, 237
   n.74, 238 n.83
Mary, Blessed Virgin (Theotokos) 221
   n.81

Mary Magdalene 51
Marius, Caius (consul 107 BC, 104–100 BC,
   86 BC) 180–1, 244 n.24
Massilia (Marseille) 18
al-Masʿūdī, Baghdadi Alī (†957), Arab
   historian and geographer 167
Maurikios, Romano-Byzantine emperor
   (r. 582–602) 23, 91, 213 n.23
Maxentius, usurper (r. 306–312) 17–18, 52,
   57, 108, 211 n.17
   at Pons Mulvius (28 October 312) 21,
    54, 55–6, 219 n.104, 226 n.34, 265
    n.35
Maximianus, *Augustus* (r. 286–305),
   usurper (r. 306–310) 16, 17–18, 38, 52,
   62, 134, 211 n.12, 212 n.21, 212 n.23,
   224 n.223, 227 n.58, 234 n.49, 257
   n.19
Maximilianus, Christian martyr 47–8, 223
   n.199
Maximinus Daia, usurper (r. 313) 17–18,
   52, 57, 212 n.23, 230 n.3
Maximinus Thrax, Caius Iulius Verus,
   emperor (r. 235–238) 1–3, 21, 34, 207
   n.13
   early career of 1, 207 n.4
Maximus, Magnus, usurper (r. 383–388)
   68, 69, 74, 75–7, 78–80, 82, 84, 85–6, 87,
   88, 89, 92, 94, 123, 141, 159, 162, 194,
   231 n.9, 234 n.51, 235 n.58, 236 n.69,
   238 n.82, 238 n.83, 239 n.99, 240 n.16
   execution of (28 August 388) 80, 102
   Contra Arianos 236 n.72
   in Welsh mythology 74, 235 n.57
Mediolanum (Milan) 6, 33, 35, 56–7, 59,
   69, 79, 83, 92, 102, 103, 105, 106, 123,
   124, 132, 164, 196–7, 239 n.111, 240
   n.22, 263 n.5
   see also Ambrose (Saint)
Memorius, Flavius, veteran 49
Merobaudes, Flavius (Frank), *magister*
   peditum per Gallias 68, 230 n.3, 230 n.7,
   231 n.9
Mesopotamia 39, 43, 136, 139, 148, 167,
   168, 220 n.111
   province of 5–6, 34

Moesia
 diocese of 192, 234 n.51
 province of 1, 13, 212 n.7
  Inferior 183, 210 n.65
Mogontiacum (Mainz) 2, 5
von Moltke der Ältere, Helmuth
 (1800–91) 270 n.8, 274–5 n.46
Mortimer's Cross, battle of (3 February
 1461) 249–50 n.58
Murat, Prince Joachim (1767–1815) 276
 n.58
Mursa, battle of (28 September 351) 77–8,
 134, 160, 234 n.51,

NATO 276 n.54
Naissus (Niš) 39
Napoléon Bonaparte (1769–1821) 19, 30,
 93, 146–7, 180, 217 n.61, 233 n.33, 261
 n.13, 261–2 n.16, 271 n.19, 276 n.53
 on Bible 146
 and Roman Catholic Church 147, 170,
  262 n.17, 262 n.18, 262 n.18
 on soldiers 217 n.60, 219 n.11
 on Qur'an/Islam 145, 261 n.11
Napoléon III, *l'empereur des Français* 225
 n.21
Napoleonic Wars (1803–15) 170–1
 canon de 8 Gribeauval 173
 la Grande Armée 171
Narses (†573), Romano-Byzantine
 patricius et magister militum 191
Nauportus (Vrhnika) 94, 245 n.8, 245 n.9
Neo-Platonism 4, 152, 286 n.12
Nepotianus, usurper (r. 350) 134, 241 n.26
Nicomedia 13, 58, 59
Nisibis 6, 220 n.16, 261 n.10
Normandy, campaign of (6 June–31
 August 1944) 179, 275 n.49
Notitia Dignitatum 21–2, 37, 38–40, 42–3,
 89–90, 129, 199, 213 n.14, 214 n.24, 233
 n.45, 243 n.12
Numerianus, co-emperor (r. 283–284) 110,
 death of 13, 211 n.1

Odaenathus, Septimius (†267) 5–6
Odovacer (Scirian), king of Italy
 (r. 476–493) 231 n.7, 284 n.82

Odysseus xxvi, xxvii, 215 n.43
Œcumenical synods
 First (Nicaea I 325) 144–5, 147, 203,
  227 n.43, 260 n.5, 264 n.27, 284–5
  n.3
  Nicene Creed 144, 150, 156
   homöousios 200, 260 n.5, 285 n.3
 Second (Constantinople I 381) 285 n.3
 Fourth (Chalcedon 451) 204, 260 n.9
Olybrius, western emperor (r. 472) 231 n.7
Orestes, *magister militum* and father of
 Romulus Augustulus 231 n.7
Origen of Caesarea, ante-Nicene
 theologian 201, 207 n.9, 260 n.6
Orosius, Paulus, historian 76, 89, 186, 191,
 199–200, 207 n.9, 243 n.12, 254 n.25,
 279 n.23, 281 n.59
 on Frigidus 90, 97, 99, 102, 104, 197,
  244 n.24
 on death of Valentinianus II 83

Palmyra 5–6
 razed (274) 8, 208–9 n.30, 209 n.44, 278
  n.9
 see also cataphractus(*ii*), Odaenathus,
  Zenobia
Pannonia
 dioceses of 33, 43, 92, 96, 134, 193, 211
  n.5, 212 n.7, 231 n.7, 243 n.9, 257
  n.21, 264 n.29
  Prima 18, 79–80, 231 n.12
  Secunda 73, 78, 161, 210 n.68, 243
   n.7
  Valeria 68, 243 n.7
 province of 4, 245 n.8
 renamed Illyricum 211 n.5, 236 n.69,
  252 n.6
Paul of Tarsus (Saint) 157, 228 n.64, 264
 n.21
 his conversion 61, 229 n.71, 229 n.81
Paulinus Mediolanensis, secretary to
 Ambrose 92, 109
Pelagius (†420), Romano-Briton
 theologian 190
Peninsular War (1808–14) 178, 215 n.34
 Roliça, battle of (17 August 1808) 113

Persian(s)
  Achaemenid 104, 169, 171, 217 n.60,
    247 n.18, 260 n.1
  Sāsānian 4, 5–6, 17, 20, 24, 36, 40, 110,
    138, 139, 148, 183, 213 n.23, 220
    n.116, 244 n.14, 256 n.18
Philippi, battle of (3 & 23 October 42 BC)
  248 n.47
Philon of Byzantium (*fl.* 250 BC), Greek
  engineer 272 n.20
Photinos, Arian bishop of Sirmium 147
du Picq, Ardent (1821–70), French army
  officer and military theorist 112–13
Picti 234 n.51
pilum(a) 21, 22, 24, 174
  range and penetration 175–6
Placidia, Aelia Galla (388–450), daughter
  of Theodosius I 182, 187, 189, 280 n.40,
  282 n.74
  career 282–3 n.75
  marriages 191, 230 n.7, 282 n.73
  as regent for Valentinianus III 240 n.22,
    283 n.75, 286 n.21
Plato, post-Sokratic philosopher 133, 152,
  194
Plotinus, Neo-Platonist philosopher 4
Pollentia, battle of (5 April 402) 185, 243
  n.9, 279 n.23
plumbata(ae)/martiobarbus(i) 22–3, 175–6,
  213 n.15, 246 n.1
Poetovio (Ptuj) 79, 257 n.18
Pons Mulvius, battle of (28 October 312)
  xxiv, 21, 54–6, 61, 139, 155, 225 n.21,
  226 n.23, 265 n.35
Pontius Pilate, *praefectus* of Iudaea 19
Porphyrios of Tyre, Neo-Platonist
  philosopher (†305) 152, 264 n.16
  Adversus Christianos 152, 153
Postumus, Marcus Cassianius Latinius,
  usurper (r. 260–269) 5, 6, 9–10, 33, 74,
  208 n.21, 208 n.23, 208 n.28
praefectus(i) 11, 21, 42, 253 n.19, 257 n.19
  alae 44
  annonae 86
  laetorum 244 n.13
  legionis 11, 15, 44

praetorio 13, 123, 211 n.5, 252 n.5
  per Gallias 203
  per Orientis 15, 41, 84, 122, 125, 139,
    253 n.19, 259 n.38
  per Italiae 15, 84, 86, 140
numeri 44
urbis Constantinopoleos 15, 28–9, 84, 201,
  240 n.15, 243 n.7, 252 n.5
urbis Romae 15, 86, 103, 189, 204, 210
  n.68, 222 n.188, 240 n.15, 252 n.5
Priscillianus (†385), bishop of Avela 237–8
  n.82, 238 n.83, 281 n.55
Probus, emperor (r. 276–282) 10, 196, 234
  n.49
Proculus (or Proklos), *praefectus urbis
  Constantinopoleos* 84, 240 n.16
Prokopios of Caesarea Palestinae, legal
  secretary to Belisarius and historian 29,
  159, 161, 172–3, 190, 200–1, 271 n.12
protectores (et domestici) 11, 41, 44, 69, 128,
  195, 221 n.139, 221 n.152, 254 n.36
pseudocomitatenses 37, 40, 244 n.17, 244
  n.21
  see also army, *limitanei*

Qín Shĭ Huáng, emperor of China
  (r. 221–210 BC) 152
Quadi 68, 119
Quintillus, emperor (r. 270) 7, 209 n.42

Radagaisus, leader of Goths 48, 186, 255
  n.46, 280 n.29
von Ranke, Leopold (1795–1886), German
  historian xxvi
Ravenna 59, 128, 187, 188, 190, 197,
  242–3 n.7, 280 n.29, 281 n.45, 283 n.75,
  283 n.82, 286 n.15
Regalianus, usurper (r. 260) 4
Rhenus (Rhine) 8, 10, 18, 35, 38–9, 58, 59,
  61, 70, 75, 77, 84, 89, 129, 133, 160, 219
  n.105, 219 n.106, 235 n.62, 241 n.24
  army on 5, 20, 21, 30, 33–4, 68, 89, 90,
    199, 212 n.7, 214 n.24
  see also Franks, Saxones
Richomeres, Flavius (Frank, †394),
  magister militum per Orientem 69, 88,
  109, 211 n.4, 259 n.6

Ricimer (Suevic-Visigoth, †472), *patricius et magister militum* 230–1 n.7
ripenses/riparienses 37
   see also army, *limitanei*
Rome *passim*
   Arch of Constantinus 38, 56, 61, 219 n.104
   Aurelian Walls 10, 36, 190, 211 n.17
   sacked by Alaric (August 410) 156, 157, 158, 188–90, 280 n.29
Romulus (and Remus) 66
Romulus Augustulus, western emperor (r. 475–476, †511) 203, 231 n.7
Rufinus of Aquileia (†412), theologian 70, 83, 201–2, 228 n.58, 236 n.72, 243 n.9
   on Frigidus 104, 108, 246 n.27, 247 n.33
Rufinus, Flavius (Gaul, †395), *praefectus praetorio per Orientis* 41, 122, 125, 126, 129–30, 211 n.4, 243 n.7, 253 n.19, 254 n.22
Rutilius Namatianus, pagan poet, 157–8, 254 n.25, 265 n.36

Samarobiva Ambianorum (Amiens) 222 n.168
Šāpūr I, king of Persia (r. 241–272) 5
Šāpūr II, king of Persia (r. 310–381) 53, 66, 256 n.18
Serapeion 166, 196, 268–9 n.88
Sarmatian(s) 24, 68, 182
Sarus (Alan), *magister militum* 186, 236 n.62
Sarus, leader of Goths 280 n.29
Saul, king of Israelites 103, 177, 246–7 n.10
Saul (Alan) 243 n.9, 279 n.23
de Saxe, Maurice (1696–1750), *maréchal de France* 70, 232 n.32, 232–3 n.33, 233 n.34, 233 n.35
Saxones 8, 210 n.57, 234 n.51, 237 n.75, 283 n.80
   recruited 88, 241 n.24
Scotti 234 n.51
Sebastianus (Bithynian), *comes rei militaris* 43, 68, 221 n.140, 221 n.146, 241 n.29
Secundus Salutius, Saturninius, *praefectus praetorio per Orientis* 139, 259 n.38
Seeck, Otto 60

Septimius Severus, Lucius, emperor (r. 193–211) 10, 11, 19, 20, 25, 34, 207 n.4, 208 n.14
Serdica (Sofia) 65, 210 n.61
Serena (†409), niece of Theodosius I and wife of Stilicho 128–9, 187, 240 n.222, 255 n.40, 280 n.39, 281 n.45
   execution of 189
Severus Alexander, Marcus Aurelius, emperor (r. 222–235) 21, 34, 207 n.7
   assassination of 1–2, 32
Severus II, Flavius Valerius, *Augustus* (r. 306–307) 17–18
shield(s) 23, 25, 55, 72, 98, 104, 107, 111, 148, 173, 176, 178, 192, 213 n.14, 219 n.106, 246 n.1, 248 n.47
   boss(es) of 277 n.5
   scutum(a) 21, 22
Sibylline Books 153, 157, 264 n.20
Sidonius Apollinaris (†488), bishop of Arverna 130, 202–3, 255 n.50
Silvanus (Frank), *magister peditum per Gallias* 160–1, 266 n.56
   at Mursa (28 September 351) 78
Singara 220 n.116
Singidunum (Belgrade) 163, 236 n.69
Siricius, pope (r. 384–399) 238 n.83
Sirmium (Sremska Mitrovica) 7, 73, 233–4 n.49
slingers, later Roman 176–7, 274 n.39
   see also army
Sol Invictus *see* Apollo
Somme, first day (1 July 1916) 178–9
Sozomenos, Salamenes Hermias (†450), theologian 108, 203–4, 235 n.62, 244 n.23, 258–9 n.35, 267 n.77
Spalatum (Split) 17
spear(s) 22, 25, 72, 98, 130, 246 n.3, 283 n.77
   contus 209 n.30
   at Frigidus 101–2, 107, 117
   in Germanic burials 192, 283 n.80
   kills Iulianus 139, 148, 258–9 n.35
Stilicho, Flavius, *patricius et magister utriusque militum praesentalis passim*
   early career of 128–30, 252 n.4, 254–5 n.38

'*demibarbarus*' origins 15, 123, 126, 197,
    254 n.25
  fall and execution of (13 August 408)
      186–7, 188, 236 n.62, 252 n.10, 254
      n.23, 280 n.33
  at Frigidus 88, 122–3, 252 n.7
  guardian of Theodosius' sons 123–4, 126
Suevi 8, 89, 191, 235 n.62
Sulpicius Severus (†420), hagiographer
    151, 223 n.199, 237 n.74, 258 n.32
Sumer, Early Dynastic 168, 269–70 n.3
Sun Tzu, Chinese general and military
    theorist xxvii, xxviii, 98, 232 n.31
Symmachus, Quintus Aurelius, senator
    and pagan 69, 193, 204, 258 n.32, 281
    n.48, 281 n.55
  and *ara Victoriae* 131, 140–1, 259 n.45,
      260 n.48
Symmachi 141
Synesios, Neo-Platonist bishop of
    Ptolemais 16, 64, 125–6, 159, 162, 228
    n.64, 254 n.20, 266 n.46
Syria 66, 151, 204, 219 n.111
  province of 5, 7, 16, 57, 212 n.7, 278 n.9
  desert of 278 n.9
sword(s) 25, 32, 47, 72, 130, 162, 186, 223
    n.198
  in burials 192
  gladius(*ii*) 21, 22, 24
  spatha(*e*) 24, 277n.5, 283 n.77

Tacitus, historian 3–4, 131, 195, 208 n.22,
    212 n.7, 245 n.8
Talleyrand (Charles-Maurice de
    Talleyrand-Périgord), 68, 230 n.1
Tarleton, Lieutenant Colonel Banastre
    (1754–1833) 174, 273 n.27
Tatianus, Flavius Eutolmius, *praefectus
    praetorio per Orientis* 84
Tertullian of Carthage (155–220), ante-
    Nicene theologian 154
  on baptism 60, 228 n.65
  on 'Rain Miracle' 119–20
Tetricus, usurper (271–274) 9–10
Themistios (†388), court orator 69–70,
    162, 204, 268 n.84

Theodora, Flavia Maximiana, daughter
    of Maximianus and second wife of
    Constantius I Chlorus 134, 266–7 n.43,
    227 n.58, 241 n.26, 257 n.19
Theodoret (†466), theologian and bishop
    of Kyrrhos 138, 204, 228 n.58, 259 n.36
  on Frigidus 98, 108, 244 n.23, 246 n.1
  on Thessaloniki massacre 164
Theodoric I, king of Visigoths (r. 418–451)
    279 n.18, 283 n.76
Theodoric II, king of Visigoths
    (r. 453–466) 230 n.7
Theodoric II the Amal, king of Ostrogoths
    (r. 493–526) 283–4 n.82, 286 n.15
Theodosius I (the Great), emperor
    (r. 379–395) *passim*
  and Ambrose 124, 109, 144, 227 n.58,
      268 n.87
    compares to biblical David 92, 105,
        107, 115, 165, 268 n.85
    excommunicates 164–6
  anti-pagan edicts of 144, 148, 150–1,
      256 n.13, 263 n.5
  death of (17 January 395) 106, 122–3
  elevation of 73, 75
  at Frigidus xxiii, 88–91, 92–100, 101–3,
      104, 106, 114, 246 n.27
  and Nicene orthodoxy 57, 76, 77, 107–8,
      121, 141, 144–5, 149–50, 155, 248
      n.40, 263 n.4
  visits Rome 103, 256 n.11
  and treaty (3 October 382) 73, 74, 89,
      161–2, 184, 266–7 n.64
Theodosius II, eastern emperor
    (r. 408–450) 126, 152, 153, 197, 204, 222
    n.162, 235 n.55, 254 n.23, 263 n.5
Theodosius (the Elder), Flavius, *magister
    militum* 233 n.47, 234 n.51, 239 n.111
Theophilos, Nicene bishop of Alexandria
    (r. 385–412) 166, 235 n.55, 253 n.19
Thermantia, second wife of Honorius 129,
    186
Thessaloniki (Thessalonica) 78, 163, 240
    n.20, 252 n.6
  defences of 9, 267 n.74
  massacre (April 390) 163–5
Theveste (Tébessa) 47

Tiber 54, 55, 56, 240 n.15

Tigris 43, 110, 220 n.116, 220 n.117, 269 n.3

Tolkien, J.R.R. 275 n.48

Tolosa (Toulouse) 237 n.74

Tolstoy, Leo, Russian author and *peacenik* 146

Traianus Decius, emperor (r. 249–251) 3, 132, 183, 233 n.49, 277 n.5
  see also Abritus (June 251)

tribunus(i) 44, 78, 127, 128, 221 n.139, 224 n.222, 243 n.9

Troy xxvi, xxvii, 51, 58, 227 n.52

Uldin, leader of Huns 42, 186, 221 n.135, 279–80 n.28

Ulfilas, Arian bishop among Goths 192, 284 n.84

US Marine Corps/US Marines xxiv–xxvi, xxvii, 206 n.4, 206 n.5, 206 n.6

Valens, co-emperor (r. 364–378) 23, 43, 45, 68, 184, 269 n.29
  accession of 39
  at Adrianopolis (9 August 378) 69, 71–2, 156–7, 184, 221 n.146
  and Arianism 150, 156, 264–5 n.30

Valentinianus I, emperor (r. 364–375) 23, 42, 43, 44, 48, 75, 77, 156, 195, 234 n.51, 236 n.67, 240 n.20, 264 n.29
  sudden death of 68, 157
  division of army and empire 39
  religious policy of 133

Valentinianus II, emperor (r. 375–392) xxiii, 45, 46, 48, 77–81, 86, 141, 187
  death of 82–4, 86–7, 240 n.13
  elevation of 68

Valentinianus III, Flavius Placidus, western emperor (r. 426–454) 153, 199, 203, 222 n.162, 283 n.75, 286 n.21

Valerianus, emperor (r. 253–260) 3, 5, 9, 11
  capture of 5, 10, 208 n.19
  division of empire 4, 14

Vallia, leader of Goths 191, 283 n.76

Vandals 89, 191, 279 n.18, 283 n.80
  Asding 7, 235 n.62
  sack Rome (450) 203
  Siling 235 n.62

Vegetius, Publius (or Flavius) Renatus, *vir illustris et comes* 23, 25, 93, 159, 192, 213 n.14, 233 n.43, 271 n.12, 274 n.44
  on Boréās 250 n.65
  on *plumbatae* 176, 213 n.15, 246 n.1
  on slingshot 177
  on tattooing 46, 48
  Epitoma rei militaris 159–60, 266 n.50

Verona 9
  battle of (June 402) 185–6

Verus, Lucius, co-emperor (r. 161–169) 14

Via Aemilia 188

Via Annia 49

Via Egnatia 163, 248 n.47

Via Flaminia 54, 56, 188

Via Gemina 93, 94

Via Salaria 188

vicarius(ii) 15, 44
  Asianae 230 n.89

Victor, Fabius, veteran and father of Maximilianus 47–8

Victor, Flavius, son of Magnus Maximus 80, 239 n.103

Victorinus, usurper (r. 269–271) 208 n.28

Vienna (Vienne) 69, 82–3, 231 n.12

Visigoths 184–5, 191, 234 n.52, 237 n.74, 279 n.18
  see also Goths

Voltaire (François-Marie Arouet), French polymath 62, 135, 143, 149, 159, 265 n.40

Wakefield, battle of (30 December 1460) 250 n.58

Wesley, John (1703–91), English cleric and theologian 158–9, 265 n.42

Wellesley, Arthur (1769–1852), 1st Duke of Wellington xxiii, 178, 180, 215 n.34, 261–2 n.16, 275–6 n.51

Xenophon, Greek mercenary and historian 27, 216 n.47, 217 n.57, 217 n.60, 220 n.117, 267 n.73

Zabdas, Septimius, Syro-Palmyrene general 7

Zelenskiy, Volodymyr Oleksandrovych, 6th President of Ukraine (2019–) 147

Zeno I, Romano-Byzantine emperor
    (r. 474–475, 476–491) 284 n.82
Zenobia, Septimia, queen of Palmyra 5,
    6–8, 10, 209 n.54
Zonaras, Ioannes, Byzantine epitomist
    64–5, 78, 83, 204–5

Zosimos, Romano-Byzantine anti-church
    historian 205, 209 n.54, 218 n.85, 220
    n.130, 220 n.132